D0151639

An Expanding World
Volume 15

Slave Trades, 1500–1800: Globalization of Forced Labour

AN EXPANDING WORLD
The European Impact on World History, 1450–1800

General Editor: A.J.R. Russell-Wood

An Expanding World
The European Impact on World History 1450–1800

Volume 15

Slave Trades, 1500–1800: Globalization of Forced Labour

edited by
Patrick Manning

VARIORUM
1996

This edition copyright © 1996 by Variorum, Ashgate Publishing Limited, and Introduction Patrick Manning. For copyright of individual articles refer to the Acknowledgements.

Published by VARIORUM
          Ashgate Publishing Limited
          Gower House, Croft Road
          Aldershot, Hampshire GU11 3HR
          Great Britain

          Ashgate Publishing Company
          Old Post Road
          Brookfield, Vermont 05036
          USA

ISBN 0–86078–512–2

British Library CIP data
      Slave Trades, 1500–1800: Globalization of Forced Labour.
      (An Expanding World: The European Impact on World History,
      1450–1800: Vol. 15).
      1. Slave trade–History. 2. Slavery–History.
      I. Manning, Patrick.
      380 .1' 44' 0903

US Library of Congress CIP data
      Slave Trades, 1500–1800: Globalization of Forced Labour / edited
      by Patrick Manning.
      p. cm. – (An Expanding World: Vol. 15).
      Includes bibliographical references and index (cloth: alk. paper).
      1. Slave trade–History.
      I. Manning, Patrick, 1941–   . III. Series.
      HT985. S54 1996   96–3760
      382' .44' 09–dc20

This book is printed on acid free paper.

Printed and bound in Great Britain by Biddles Limited,
Guildford and King's Lynn.

AN EXPANDING WORLD 15

Contents

Acknowledgements

The chapters in this volume are taken from the sources listed below, for which the editor and publishers wish to thank their authors, original publishers or other copyright holders for their permission to use their material as follows:

Chapter 1: Ralph A. Austen, 'The Mediterranean Islamic Slave Trade out of Africa: A Tentative Census', *Slavery and Abolition* XIII (1992), pp. 214–248. Copyright © 1982 by Frank Cass & Co. Ltd.

Chapter 2: Paul E. Lovejoy, 'The Volume of the Atlantic Slave Trade: A Synthesis', *Journal of African History* XXIII (1982), pp. 473–501. Copyright © 1982 by Cambridge University Press.

Chapter 3: Patrick Manning, 'Migrations of Africans to the Americas: The Impact on Africans, Africa, and the New World', *The History Teacher* XXVI (1993), pp. 279–296. Copyright © 1993 by the Society for the History of Education, California State University.

Chapter 4: Luiz Felipe de Alencastro, 'The Apprenticeship of Colonization', in ed. Barbara L. Solow, *Slavery and the Rise of the Atlantic System* (Cambridge, 1991), pp. 151–176. Copyright © 1991 by Cambridge University Press.

Chapter 5: John M. Monteiro, 'From Indian to Slave: Forced Native Labour and Colonial Society in São Paulo During the Seventeenth Century', *Slavery and Abolition* IX (1988), pp. 105–127. Copyright © 1988 by Frank Cass & Co. Ltd.

Chapter 6: John Thornton, 'Sexual Demography: The Impact of the Slave Trade on Family Structure', in eds. Claire C. Robertson and Martin A. Klein, *Women and Slavery in Africa* (Madison, 1983), pp. 39–48. Copyright © 1983 by The Board of Regents of the University of Wisconsin System. Reprinted by permission of The University of Wisconsin Press.

Chapter 7: Ann M. Pescatello, 'The African Presence in Portuguese India', *Journal of Asian History* XI (1977), pp. 26–48. Copyright © 1977 by Otto Harassowitz. Reprinted by permission of the editor, Denis Sinor.

Chapter 8: Ronald C. Jennings, 'Black Slaves and Free Blacks in Ottoman Cyprus, 1590–1640', *Journal of the Economic and Social History of the Orient* XXX (1987), pp. 286–302. Copyright © 1987 by E.J. Brill.

Chapter 9: Richard Rathbone, 'Resistance to Enslavement in West Africa', in ed. Serge Daget, *De la Traite à l'esclavage: Actes du Colloque international sur la traite des Noirs (Nantes 1985)* I: Ve–XVIIIe siècles (Nantes, 1988), pp. 173–184. Copyright © 1988 by the Société française d'histoire d'outre-mer.

Chapter 10: Steven Deyle, '"By Farr the Most Profitable Trade": Slave Trading in British Colonial North America', *Slavery and Abolition* X (1989), pp.107–125. Copyright © 1989 by Frank Cass & Co. Ltd.

Chapter 11: Joseph C. Miller, 'A Marginal Institution on the Margin of the Atlantic System: The Portuguese Southern Atlantic Slave Trade in the Eighteenth Century', in ed. Barbara L. Solow, *Slavery and the Rise of the Atlantic System* (Cambridge, 1991), pp. 120–150. Copyright © 1991 by Cambridge University Press.

Chapter 12: Jean-Michel Filliot, 'La traite vers l'Ile de France', in eds. U. Bissoondoyal and S.B.C. Servansing, *Slavery in the South West Indian Ocean* (Moka, Mauritius, 1989), pp. 84–95. Copyright © 1989 by the Mahatma Gandhi Institute.

Chapter 13: David Geggus, 'Sex, Ratio, Age and Ethnicity in the Atlantic Slave Trade: Data from French Shipping and Plantation Records', *Journal of African History* XXX (1989), pp. 23–44. Copyright © 1989 by Cambridge University Press.

Chapter 14: Thomas M. Ricks, 'Slaves and Slave Traders in the Persian Gulf, 18th and 19th Centuries: An Assessment', *Slavery and Abolition* IX (1988), pp. 60–70. Copyright © 1988 by Frank Cass & Co. Ltd.

Chapter 15: Barbara Bush, 'Survival and Resistance: Slave Women and Coercive Labour Regimes in the British Caribbean, 1750 to 1838', in ed. Serge Daget, *De la Traite à l'esclavage: Actes du Colloque international sur la traite des Noirs (Nantes 1985)* II: XVIIIe–XIXe siècles (Nantes, 1988), pp. 193–204. Copyright © 1988 by the Société française d'histoire d'outre-mer.

Chapter 16: David Richardson, 'The Slave Trade, Sugar, and British Economic Growth, 1748–1776', *The Journal of Interdisciplinary History* XVII, no. 4 (1987), pp. 739–769. Copyright © 1987 by The Massachusetts Institute of Technology and the editors of *The Journal of Interdisciplinary History*.

Chapter 17: Seymour Drescher, 'The Slaving Capital of the World: Liverpool and National Opinion in the Age of Abolition', *Slavery and Abolition* IX (1988), pp. 128–143. Copyright © 1988 by Frank Cass & Co. Ltd.

Every effort has been made to trace all the copyright holders, but if any have been inadvertently overlooked the publishers will be pleased to make the necessary arrangement at the first opportunity.

General Editor's Preface

A.J.R. Russell-Wood

An Expanding World: The European Impact on World History, 1450–1800 is designed to meet two objectives: first, each volume covers a specific aspect of the European initiative and reaction across time and space; second, the series represents a superb overview and compendium of knowledge and is an invaluable reference source on the European presence beyond Europe in the early modern period, interaction with non-Europeans, and experiences of peoples of other continents, religions, and races in relation to Europe and Europeans. The series reflects revisionist interpretations and new approaches to what has been called 'the expansion of Europe' and whose historiography traditionally bore the hallmarks of a narrowly Eurocentric perspective, focus on the achievements of individual nations, and characterization of the European presence as one of dominance, conquest, and control. Fragmentation characterized much of this literature: fragmentation by national groups, by geography, and by chronology.

The volumes of *An Expanding World* seek to transcend nationalist histories and to examine on the global stage rather than in discrete regions important selected facets of the European presence overseas. One result has been to bring to the fore the multicontinental, multi-oceanic and multinational dimension of the European activities. A further outcome is compensatory in the emphasis placed on the cross-cultural context of European activities and on how collaboration and cooperation between peoples transcended real or perceived boundaries of religion, nationality, race, and language and were no less important aspects of the European experience in Africa, Asia, the Americas, and Australia than the highly publicized confrontational, bellicose, and exploitative dimensions. Recent scholarship has not only led to greater understanding of peoples, cultures, and institutions of Africa, Asia, the Americas, and Australasia with whom Europeans interacted and the complexity of such interactions and transactions, but also of relations between Europeans of different nationalities and religious persuasions.

The initial five volumes reflect the changing historiography and set the stage for volumes encompassing the broad themes of technology and science, trade and commerce, exploitation as reflected in agriculture and the extractive industries and through systems of forced and coerced labour, government of empire, and society and culture in European colonies and settlements overseas. Final volumes examine the image of Europe and Europeans as 'the other' and the impact of the wider world on European *mentalités* and mores.

An international team of editors was selected to reflect a diversity of educational backgrounds, nationalities, and scholars at different stages of their professional careers. Few would claim to be 'world historians', but each is a recognized authority in his or her field and has the demonstrated capacity to ask the significant questions and provide a conceptual framework for the selection of articles which combine analysis with interpretation. Editors were exhorted to place their specific subjects within a global context and over the *longue durée*. I have been delighted by the enthusiasm with which they took up this intellectual challenge, their courage in venturing beyond their immediate research fields to look over the fences into the gardens of their academic neighbours, and the collegiality which has led to a generous informal exchange of information. Editors were posed the daunting task of surveying a rich historical literature and selecting those essays which they regarded as significant contributions to an understanding of the specific field or representative of the historiography. They were asked to give priority to articles in scholarly journals; essays from conference volumes and *Festschriften* were acceptable; excluded (with some few exceptions) were excerpts from recent monographs or paperback volumes. After much discussion and agonizing, the decision was taken to incorporate essays only in English, French, and Spanish. This has led to the exclusion of the extensive scholarly literature in Danish, Dutch, German and Portuguese. The ramifications of these decisions and how these have had an impact on the representative quality of selections of articles have varied, depending on the theme, and have been addressed by editors in their introductions.

The introduction to each volume enables readers to assess the importance of the topic *per se* and place this in the broader context of European activities overseas. It acquaints readers with broad trends in the historiography and alerts them to controversies and conflicting interpretations. Editors clarify the conceptual framework for each volume and explain the rationale for the selection of articles and how they relate to each other. Introductions permit volume editors to assess the impact on their treatments of discrete topics of constraints of language, format, and chronology, assess the completeness of the journal literature, and address *lacunae*. A further charge to editors was to describe and evaluate the importance of change over time, explain differences attributable to differing geographical, cultural, institutional, and economic circumstances and suggest the potential for cross-cultural, comparative, and interdisciplinary approaches. The addition of notes and bibliographies enhances the scholarly value of the introductions and suggests avenues for further enquiry.

I should like to express my thanks to the volume editors for their willing participation, enthusiasm, sage counsel, invaluable suggestions, and good judgment. Evidence of the timeliness and importance of the series was illustrated by the decision, based on extensive consultation with the scholarly community, to expand a series, which had originally been projected not to exceed eight volumes, to more than thirty volumes. It was John Smedley's initiative which gave rise to discussions as to the viability and need for such a series and he has overseen the publishing, publicity, and marketing of *An Expanding World*. As

General Editor, my task was greatly facilitated by the tireless assistance of Dr Mark Steele who was initially responsible for the 'operations' component of the series as it got under way, latterly this assistance has been provided by staff at Variorum.

The Department of History,
The Johns Hopkins University

Introduction

Patrick Manning

Slavery caused the slave trade; just as relentlessly, the slave trade brought new slavery. The exploitation of persons as property maintained an indissoluble link to the recruitment of new slaves and the exchange of those already in slavery. The question of whether slavery did more to create the slave trade, or whether the slave trade did more to create slavery, seems likely to remain a conundrum of social history. This volume is intended not to resolve that conundrum, but to illustrate one side of it: the rise and transformation of the slave trades in the early-modern world, 1500–1800. In seventeen chapters, the authors characterize a range of interconnected slave trades, show their magnitude and changing character, their links to changing systems of slavery, and their place in the more general transformation of human society.

Trade in slaves formed a painful yet central element of early-modern world history. Traffic in humans, predicated on social and economic inequalities, served to reinforce those inequalities and create new divisions; yet this same traffic linked distant regions into global systems, thereby engendering new commonalities and new equalities in societies. The slave trade served at once to create and destroy wealth. From the moral perspective of the twentieth century, the slave trade is easily seen as having been costly, brutal and unnecessary. But given the early-modern evolution of demand for slave labour, and the eventual assemblage of huge slave labour forces populating every continent – developments themselves arising out of a complex contingency – large-scale and systematic slave trade was virtually necessary and inevitable.

The 'exploitation' of slaves – the institution of slavery, along with the life and work of slaves – did much to influence the early-modern world. But that is another story. The focus of this volume is the 'procurement' of slaves. The direct and indirect effects of slave trafficking gave shape to the physical and social realities of the early-modern era and to the conceptions through which men and women viewed their world.

The direct effects of the slave trade brought the capture and transport of millions of persons from their societies of origin, and into the hands of owners in distant societies who forced them to labour and serve on command. The costs were immense. That grim ledger, beginning with the pain brought by oppression and degradation of the survivors – including the cruelty of their subjugation, training and renaming – must also account for the losses through premature death of the many who expired in the course of capture, transportation and seasoning. Those left behind had to bear a different loss: adjusting to the absence of the parents, children, brothers and sisters who were carried away into slavery. Yet the slave trade continued because of the benefits it brought. The benefits – distributed most unevenly – stemmed in the long-run from domination of the large numbers of persons delivered in bondage to new regions, where they would perform productive and reproductive work as slaves, and in the short-run from the use of force, guile, law and wealth to sell stolen persons for profit.

The indirect effects of the slave trade ramified in every direction. Population was lost to the sending areas, and increased (to a lesser extent) in the receiving areas. Impoverishment was the lot of the majority in sending areas (excepting those who profited by sale of their neighbours), while revenues flowed to those who sustained the flow of slaves by selling food and clothing, by acting as guards, or by building and operating slave ships. The uneven age and sex composition developed in sending areas meant that new divisions of labour had to spring up; similarly, new family and sexual relations developed. For instance, the export of so many young adult West African males as slaves left a relative surplus of young females, many of them in slavery, so that the expansion of female concubinage was reinforced steadily in Africa. The patterns of slave trade led further to classification of slaves and slave merchants by each other, according to their roles in the trade. Slaves became known by ethnic or national categories and by racial categories that were in large part arbitrary labels ('ladino', 'Congo', 'English', 'mulatto', 'creole'); much the same can be said for slave merchants and owners. The high death rates of slaves in many receiving areas, and the high rates of emancipation in others, left a perpetual 'shortage' of slaves which sustained a demand for new captives.

The indirect effects of the slave trade worked their way into a wide range of ideas and actions. The contrast of slavery and freedom came to be reinforced in the minds of people in every corner of this global system. Resistance against capture continued, and the notion of human rights grew to be specified in contrast to the status of slavery. Religion served to comfort the slave, assuring him or her of ultimate salvation; religion served also to protect owners from revenge by the slaves. On the other hand, religion asserted the equality of all in the eyes of God. As time passed, first Christianity and then Islam came to argue that if all were equal in the eyes of God, then man had no right to enslave another.

Slavery and slave trade: links and distinctions

Although this volume focuses on the slave trade rather than on slavery, it will not be possible to make a neat separation of the two phenomena, for they overlapped in almost every particular. Instead, we may use some terminological distinctions to help locate the boundaries between slavery and the slave trade, and to delineate some distinct aspects of the slave trade. For instance, it is helpful to distinguish between 'captives', persons being transported and exchanged in slave trade, and 'slaves', those being exploited in slavery. The distinction is not absolute, as the slave trade also included the sale of persons long enslaved or born into slavery; for instance, the sale of New England slaves to southern states in the late-eighteenth century, as the New England states moved to abolish slavery. Still, the difference between new captives and seasoned slaves showed up in the significantly higher prices of the latter.

In the trade of slaves, one may distinguish 'interregional trade' (e.g., the sale of Africans to the Americas or to the Persian Gulf), 'regional trade' (e.g., the sale of Indians in the Americas or of Africans in Africa), and 'local trade', in which slaves traveled small distances. Thus, while the Middle Passage across the Atlantic – though which millions of Africans suffered in bondage, cramped and humiliated – remains the central image of the slave trade in general, the full scope of even the interregional slave trade went far beyond the image and reality of this voyage. Slaves were traded across the Sahara desert and the Red Sea from Africa to the Muslim Mediterranean, in continuation of a trade that reached back into medieval times. North and east of the Mediterranean, a trade in Slavic-speaking and Caucasian peoples sent captives to the Ottoman Empire. Captives from East Africa and Madagascar went to Asia, to Indian Ocean islands, to the Americas and to the African mainland. The Slave trades of the Indian subcontinent and the islands and peninsulas of Southeast Asia sent captives to near and distant shores of the Indian Ocean, including to South Africa, where their descendants came to be known as Malays.

The slave trades 'within' major world regions, in turn, have provided a significant dimension to the overall movement of captives, and these regional trades have risen and fallen in interaction with the swings in interregional trade. In the Americas, few captives were sent overseas. Many Native Americans, however, were captured and held in slavery on the continent of their birth. Spain abolished trade in Indian captives and emancipated Indian slaves in the sixteenth century, following the celebrated defense of their case by Bartolomé de las Casas, but Portuguese and, to a lesser extent, French and English colonies permitted enslavement of Indians. Slave trade within the Americas moved both African and Indian slaves to Minas Gerais in Brazil with the gold boom at the turn of the eighteenth century, and moved slaves from English and Dutch importers through the Caribbean and into the hands of Spanish and other purchasers. In Africa, the export slave trade led to greatly expanded African use of slaves and thus to a large regional slave trade. The expansion of slavery in sixteenth-century Russia occasioned enslavement and movement of large numbers of Russians. In South and Southeast Asia, slaves from one part of the region were settled to work in other parts of the region. This trade led to expansion of plantations on Java and Ceylon in the seventeenth and eighteenth century, and in the Philippines later on.

Local slave trades, finally, centered on the exchange of persons already enslaved among various owners. The trade at any marketplace – such as the great markets at Cairo, Cartagena, and later at Kano and New Orleans – lumped together transactions in interregional, regional, and local trade in slaves. For the totality of these transactions, and especially in the eighteenth century, one may say that there existed a world market for slave labour, in which changing levels of demand and supply in slaves led to price fluctuations and to diversions in the flow of slaves in adjustment to market conditions. Through the capture and sale of slaves, labour – a factor of production normally difficult to move – was rendered mobile.

The abolition of the slave trade, in modern times, began in the late-eighteenth century. Much of the writing on the slave trade in that era and subsequently, has stemmed from the long campaign to abolish it. In the terms that have grown up in the literature, one speaks not of the 'abolition' of the slave trade, but of the 'emancipation' of slaves. In slave-owing societies, it was generally the case that support for ending the transportation or importing of slaves rose to a higher level at an earlier time than did support for freeing the slaves.

These distinctions have been of great importance from time to time: the British abolished the transatlantic slave trade in 1808, but allowed sale of slaves already held in British colonies until declaring emancipation of all slaves in 1838. In later times, British conquerors in Africa suppressed 'slave raiding' wherever possible, but allowed 'slave dealing', the sale of those previously enslaved, into the 1930s. For the United States, abolition took place in 1808, and emancipation in 1865. France legislated both abolition and emancipation in 1794, rescinded both in 1802, and then emancipated slaves again in 1848.

Slave trade in world history

The history of the slave trade provides a counterweight to whiggish interpretations of early-modern world history. The opening of global maritime contact did bring technical, intellectual and perhaps social advances, creating a global order. But the study of the slave trades reminds us of the violence, oppression and inequality that expanded along with the technical and social changes. The study of the slave trade is thus more than a footnote to world history, more than a side trip through the seamy side of our common past: it provides insight into the fundamental complexity of modern world history, and draws attention to the pain and loss that seem necessarily to have accompanied the triumphs of globalization. Thus the abolitionist movement of the eighteenth and nineteenth centuries appears, through one optic, as a breakthrough in humanitarian thinking and action, setting patterns for later reform movements. Seen from another angle, however, its innovations were not so much a smooth progress of the intellect as a set of bold moves to counter the unprecedented level of organized oppression posed by expanding slavery and slave trade.

The history of the slave trade emphasizes links among regions of the early-modern world. The influence of the slave trade in world affairs began before 1500, and it continued well after 1800. But in the early-modern period there developed a particular nexus in which the slave trade played the role of carrying labourers to areas of economic expansion at the profitable margins of the growing world economy. The institution of slavery brought the exploitation and the reconstruction of much of the world: the Americas, Africa, the contiguous regions from the Mediterranean to the South China Sea, and into the Russian steppes. The trade in slaves brought these regions and Europe into repeated contact, and set the terms of the hierarchy among them.

The theme of the slave trade gives particular emphasis to social and demographic dimensions of world history. This emphasis provides an important counterweight to the usual topics of world-historical analysis. That is, much of world history, as presently written, centers on great-power relationships, on military history, on commercial history, and on technological transfer. World-historical interpretations tend to rely on a diffusionist approach, one emphasizing the flow of power and innovations from certain central places – usually in Europe – to other regions of the world. The history of the slave trade, in contrast, focuses on numbers of people, on their age and sex distribution, their life and death, and their movements to numerous places. Where studies of the exploitation of slaves tend to focus on one region at a time, or on comparison of slavery in two regions, studies on the procurement of slaves tend to explore complex links among the various regions brought into contact by slave trade.[1] Analyses of the slave trade and slavery focus on the questions of class, race, and work which are otherwise underemphasized in studies of world history. The study of the slave trade is thus not simply a distinct topic to be studied in isolation, but yields an approach to world history with particular strengths and insights, whose benefits can perhaps be extended to other areas of world-historical investigation.

A rapid narrative of the history of the slave trade – its rise, spread, transformation, restriction, and suppression – may thus give an indication of broader pulsations in global interaction over the centuries. In one sense there is a single history of the slave trade, stretching from its origin in ancient times until its extinction in the early-twentieth century. In another sense, however, one may identify several distinct cycles of the slave trade, each centered on recruitment of labourers for a specific set of purchasers, based in a social and economic system specific to a given time and place. For each of these, one may discern an era of expansion and an era of decline, with the processes of abolition and emancipation in the latter stages of decline.

---

[1] Comparative studies of slavery in different regions of the Americas include Frank Tannenbaum, *Slave and Citizen: The Negro in the Americas* (New York, 1946); Herbert S. Klein, *Slavery in the Americas: A Comparative Study of Virginia and Cuba* (Chicago, 1967); and Gwendolyn M. Hall, *Social Control in Slave Plantation Societies: A Comparison of St. Dominque and Cuba* (Baltimore, 1971). An early but insightful study taking an interactive approach to the culture of the African diaspora is Janheinz Jahn, *Muntu, the New African Culture* (New York, 1961).

We may begin with the cycle of the slave trade in late-medieval times. Centered on the Mediterranean basin, it brought slaves to the regimes of the Mamluks in Egypt and the Ottomans in Anatolia, and included slaves forced to produce sugar on Mediterranean islands. While some of these slaves came across the Sahara, most of them came from areas adjoining the Black Sea, whence they were carried by Venetian and Genoese merchants. The latter trade died down as Ottoman influence expanded in the sixteenth century.[2]

The cycle of maritime expansion in the slave trade arose with the sixteenth-century Portuguese and Spanish seizure of lands in the Americas and at the fringes of the Atlantic and Indian oceans. African slaves, predominantly from Senegambia, Upper Guinea, and Angola, went first to the islands of the Atlantic and the Caribbean, and then to north-east Brazil and the highlands of Mexico and the Andes. In smaller numbers, the Portuguese carried slaves to their Indian and other Asian territories. In the same era, Ottoman and Russian societies expanded their slave holdings, the Ottomans drawing slaves from the fringes of their lands, and the Russians enslaving unfortunates within their own society. This cycle of slave trade peaked in the seventeenth century, and declined in the eighteenth century. Enslavement of native populations in Brazil declined in the eighteenth century, as did the delivery of African slaves to Mexico, Peru, and Colombia.

A third and larger cycle of slave trade developed with the expansion of commercial capitalism during the seventeenth and eighteenth centuries, under leadership of Dutch, English, French and Brazilian slave traders. This cycle focused heavily on western Africa: slaves came in largest numbers from the Bight of Benin, Angola, the Bight of Biafra and the Congo coast, with smaller but significant numbers coming from Gold Coast, Upper Guinea and Senegambia. In the Americas, slaves were delivered primarily to the British and French Caribbean, but also to Bahia and Minas Gerais in Brazil and to British North America. The results in Africa led to a significant disruption and decline in population, to a relative shortage of adult males and, it appears, to enslavement of many of the women who remained in western Africa. The smaller slave trades across the Sahara and the Red sea may have declined somewhat during this cycle. The Indian Ocean slave trade, led by Dutch and French merchants, expanded somewhat: the French drew slaves from Madagascar and Mozambique to send to the Mascarene Islands, while the Dutch collected slaves there, in Malaya and India to settle in Java and South Africa.

The sharp decline in this cycle of slave trade, at the turn of the nineteenth century, resulted from the democratic revolutions, the Napoleonic wars, and

---

[2] Charles Verlinden, *L'Esclavage dans l'Europe médiévale*, 2 vols. (Bruges, Ghent, 1955, 1977); Daniel Evans, 'Slave Coast of Europe', *Slavery and Abolition* (1985), 41–58.

humanitarian abolitionism. Not only did the demand for slaves decline because of changing economic and demographic conditions, but a formal campaign against enslavement arose out of Enlightenment philosophy and social mores. Denmark was the first nation to abolish the slave trade, in 1792. There were even instances of emancipation in this period, first by political leaders in the northern United States, and then by slaves themselves in French Saint-Domingue.

A fourth and final cycle of the slave trade expanded along with industrial capitalism. (Since most of the events in this cycle took place after 1800, they lie beyond the scope of this volume, but we may review them briefly.) As slavery declined in some areas, it expanded in others. Great quantities of captives were brought in the nineteenth century to Cuba and southern Brazil; through internal migration, many slaves moved from the Old South to new areas of the United States. Most of those carried across the Atlantic came from Angola, Congo, and the Bights of Benin and Biafra. As compared with earlier times, these captives included larger proportions of captives from Africa's far interior (these almost entirely male) and larger proportions of children.[3] In the same period, demand for slaves expanded sharply in the Indian Ocean and in the Muslim Mediterranean, apparently in response to expanded opportunities in global commerce. Captives went from the Nile Valley and the Central Sudan to Saharan oases, to Egypt, the Ottoman heartland, and the Arabian peninsula. Captives from the Horn of Africa, particularly women, went to the Arabian peninsula.[4] Captives from the areas of modern Tanzania, Mozambique and Madagascar went to Indian Ocean islands and to the Persian Gulf.[5] Linked to this expanded export of slaves was a great expansion of the slave trade and slavery on the African continent. A similar expansion of the slave trade, in a context of expanding commerce, took place in areas of Southeast Asia.[6]

The humanitarian campaign for abolition of the slave trade, in one sense continuing from the previous cycle, now took more pointed forms. It included the British naval and diplomatic campaign for suppression of the slave trade, the Civil War of the United States, the Ten Years' War in Cuba, the end of the empire

---

[3] David Eltis, *Economic Growth and the Ending of the Transatlantic Slave Trade* (New York, 1987).

[4] Janet Ewald, *Soldiers, Traders, and Slaves: State Formation and Economic Transformation in the Greater Nile Valley, 1700–1885* (Madison, 1990); Timothy Fernyhough, 'Slavery and the Slave Trade in Southern Ethiopia in the Nineteenth Century', *Slavery and Abolition* (1988), 103–30.

[5] Abdul Sheriff, *Slaves, Spices and Ivory in Zanzibar* (London, 1987); Frederick Cooper, *Plantation Slavery on the East African Coast* (New Haven, 1977); Thomas M. Ricks, See above chapter 14.

[6] James F. Warren, 'Slave Markets and Exchange in the Malay World: The Sulu Sultanate, 1770–1878', *Journal of Southeast Asian Studies* (1977), 162–75.

in Brazil, and the European conquests of Africa and the Middle East. The debates on slavery in this era became more complex, as humanitarian anti-slavery had to contend with rising doctrines of racial discrimination.

Development of debate and research on slave trade

The contemporary and historical literatures on the slave trade have retained a world-historical focus from early days. Eighteenth-century writers such as Jean-Baptiste Labat traced the routes of slaves across the Atlantic in the course of presenting a view of the world. Abolitionist writers Thomas Clarkson and Thomas Fowell Buxton, while centered very deeply in their British national tradition, nonetheless showed a global sweep in their presentation of the devastation brought by the slave trade.[7] The writings of David Livingstone and other missionary critics of the slave trade in its latter days may seem rather parochial by contrast, but by their time the reality of slavery and the slave trade was largely restricted to Africa and the Middle East.[8]

The era of imperial conquest and expansion, in the late-nineteenth and early-twentieth centuries, brought a number of major scholarly studies of slavery and the slave trade. These alternated in approach between those sharply critical of slavery and those rationalizing it. W.E.B. DuBois's historical study traced the long campaign for suppression of the Atlantic slave trade to North America. The Dutch scholar H.J. Nieboer, in an encyclopedic anthropological investigation, chose to treat slavery as the independent invention of each society around the world, and ignored slave trade as a modern global system.[9] Ulrich B. Phillips for the American South (in 1918) and Gilberto Freyre for Brazil (in 1933) published studies which analyzed slavery meticulously, but which had the effect of rationalizing the need for slavery in the development of the regional or national culture of each. In Britain, Reginald Coupland published a biography of William Wilberforce in 1922 and a celebration of the British anti-slavery movement in 1933. In the United States, Lowell Ragatz wrote a critique of the planter class in the British Caribbean, and Elizabeth Donnan produced a massive collection of documents on the history of the slave trade, which has been mined with profit

---

[7] Jean-Baptiste Labat, *Nouveau voyage aux isles de l'Amérique* (Paris, 1722); Labat, *Voyage du chevalier Des Marchais en Guinée*, 4 vols. (Paris, 1730); Thomas Clarkson, *The Cries of Africa to the Inhabitants of Europe* (London, 1822); Thomas Fowell Buxton, *The African Slave-Trade and its Remedy* (London, 1839).

[8] David Livingstone, in ed. Horace Waller *The Last Journals of David Livingstone in Central Africa*, 2 vols. (London, 1974); François Renault, *Lavigerie, l'esclavage africain et l'Europe, 1868–1892*, 2 vols. (Paris, 1971).

[9] W.E.B. DuBois, *The Suppression of the African Slave-Trade to the United States of America, 1638–1870* (New York, 1969; first published 1896); H.J. Nieboer, *Slavery as an Industrial System: Ethnological Researches* (The Hague, 1900).

by scholars ever since. In France, Gaston Martin published studies on the slave trade of Nantes.[10]

Of the studies appearing during and just after World War II, the most prominent has remained *Capitalism and Slavery*, by the Trinidadian historian Eric Williams. He argued that the profits of slavery and the slave trade in the British Caribbean contributed significantly to Britain's industrial revolution, but that the expansion of the wage-labour system caused British industrial leaders to press for abolition of the competing trade in slaves; debate on this thesis continues to this day. Other major studies of the period resulted from the work of Christopher Lloyd on the British naval suppression of slave trade, Mauricio Goulart on slave trade and slavery in Brazil, and Noel Deerr on the history of sugar.[11]

The era of decolonization (in Africa and the Caribbean) and of civil rights struggles (in the United States) brought a new level of attention to the study of slave trade. As a harbinger of the coming scholarly focus, Daniel Mannix and Malcolm Cowley published a general survey of the Atlantic slave trade, *Black Cargoes*, in 1962. The detailed studies began in earnest with the 1969 publication of Philip D. Curtin's *The Atlantic Slave Trade: A Census*.[12] Drawing on available published material, Curtin constructed a global estimate of the volume of the Atlantic slave trade, broken down by time period, by African region of origin, by the nation of the slave carriers, and by American region in which slaves were landed. That book and the scholarly response to it have determined both the outlines and the controversies of the discussion ever since. It focused an immense amount of scholarly energy on collecting data on the slave trade, and brought forth waves of interpretive summaries.

The main initial debate centered on the volume of Atlantic slave trade, because Curtin's estimates (totalling just under ten million slaves delivered to the Americas) were smaller than those which had been cited before. Another topic

---

[10] Ulrich B. Phillips, *American Negro Slavery* (New York, 1918); Gilberto Freyre, *Casa-grande e Senzala* (Rio de Janeiro, 1933); Reginald Coupland, *Wilberforce* (Oxford, 1923); Coupland, *The British Anti-Slavery Movement* (London, 1933); Lowell J. Ragatz, *The Fall of the Planter Class in the British Caribbean, 1763–1833* (New York, 1928); Elizabeth Donnan, *Documents Illustrative of the History of the Slave Trade to America*, 4 vols. (Washington, 1930–35); Gaston Martin, *Nantes au XVIIIe siècle : l'ère des négriers (1714–1774)* (Paris, 1931).

[11] Eric Williams, *Capitalism and Slavery* (Chapel Hill, 1944); Christopher Lloyd, *The Navy and the Slave Trade* (London, 1949); Mauricio Goulart, *Escravidão africana no Brasil* (São Paulo, 1950); Noel Deerr, *The History of Sugar*, 2 vols. (London, 1949–50). In 1946, Frank Tannenbaum published *Slave and Citizen*, a concise but influential comparison of slavery in Catholic and Protestant regions of the Americas.

[12] Daniel P. Mannix and Malcolm Cowley, *Black Cargoes: A History of the Atlantic Slave Trade, 1518–1862* (New York, 1962); Philip D. Curtin, *The Atlantic Slave Trade: A Census* (Madison, 1969). Curtin, 'Epidemiology and the Slave Trade', *Political Science Quarterly* LXXXIII (1968), 190–216.

of early debate was the distribution of slaves in the Americas: Curtin's figures suggested that slaves delivered to the United States had totalled only five percent of all deliveries. This figure contrasted with the large African-descended population of the United States, which totaled perhaps 30% of the African-descended population of the Americas.[13]

Indeed, in the first decade after appearance of the *Census*, scholars tended to use the new data to counter the prevailing 'conventional wisdom' and minimize the impact of the slave trade on world history. Among economic historians, Evsey Domar had already taken up Nieboer's approach to explaining the presence or absence of slavery in terms of land-labour ratios, thus abstracting them from the practical realities of the slave trade. Stanley Engerman and Roger Anstey independently launched critiques of Eric Williams' thesis, arguing that the profits of the slave trade and of Caribbean slavery were too small to have had much impact on British industrialization. John Fage compared Curtin's figures on slave exports to estimates of West-African population, and concluded that the slave trade had done no more than to 'cream-off surplus population' in West Africa.[14] These minimalist interpretations of the 1970s did show that simple, causal assertions of global transformation through the slave trade could be challenged with the newly available data.

Collection and publication of additional data has provided the most basic contribution to the development of research on the slave trade. For the Atlantic slave trade, the most important collections of data have been the work of Jean Mettas and Serge Daget on the French trade (based on shipping records), the work of David Eltis on the nineteenth-century Atlantic slave trade (based on British naval and consular records), the work of Johannes Postma on the Dutch trade, of Joseph Miller on the Portuguese trade, and of David Richardson on the English trade.[15] The slave trade from sub-Saharan Africa to the north and east, across the Sahara, the Red Sea and the Indian Ocean, is much more difficult to

---

[13] See the chapter by Lovejoy in this volume.

[14] Evsey Domar, 'The Causes of Slavery or Serfdom: A Hypothesis', *Journal of Economic History* (1970), 18–32; Stanley L. Engerman, 'The Slave Trade and British Capital Formation in the Eighteenth Century: A Comment on the Williams Thesis', *Business History Review* (1972), 430–43; John D. Fage, 'Slavery and the Slave Trade in the Context of West African History', *Journal of African History* (1969), 393–404.

Ronald W. Bailey argues that the sum of scholarship into the 1960s represented a 'conventional wisdom' that slavery and the slave trade had brought major changes to European and American societies. He takes Engerman's 1972 article as a key turn away from this earlier consensus. Bailey, 'Africa, the Slave Trade, and the Rise of Industrial Capitalism in Europe and the United States: A Historiographic Review', *American History* (1986), 1–91.

[15] See Bibliography, section 1, for these and other recent contributions of new data. Recently a data bank on transatlantic slave voyages has been established at the W.E.B. DuBois Institute of Harvard University, under the direction of David Eltis.

document, especially for early times. Ralph Austen developed a system of cataloguing the many scattered references to the volume and composition of these trades, and has drawn up estimates of their total volume.[16] On the prices of slaves in the Atlantic trade, Richard Bean constructed an important set of early estimates; David Galenson and David Richardson have collected additional and more precise prices.[17] More recently, Richardson and Paul Lovejoy have begun systematic collection of slave prices on the African continent.[18] Beyond the Atlantic, the largest body of new data on early modern slavery is presented in the work of Richard Hellie on Russia.[19]

A series of conferences during the 1970s and 1980s led to the publication of a remarkable collection of edited volumes containing studies on slavery and the slave trade in many parts of the world, but especially in the Atlantic world.[20] Following closely upon the edited collections of studies appeared a large number of monographic studies of slavery and the slave trade, including both new evidence and new analysis.[21] General surveys of slave trade have appeared regularly, mostly focusing on the Americas and Africa, but including surveys of the Indian Ocean and the Middle East.[22]

In some cases, particular themes on the slave trade came to prominence. Curtin's *Census* and the initial responses spoke in terms of slaves in general, without much attention to their distribution by age and sex. With time, however, scholars began to focus more on demographic details, and the demographic history of the slave trade became a significant subfield of slave trade studies.[23] In pursuing the economic linkages of the slave trade, Jan Hogendorn and Marion Johnson produced an excellent analysis of the cowrie trade.[24]

---

[16] Ralph A. Austen, 'The Islamic Red Sea Slave Trade: An Effort at Quantification', *Proceedings of the Fifth International Conference on Ethiopian Studies* (Chicago, 1979); see also Austen's chapter in this volume.

[17] Richard Bean, *The British Trans-Atlantic Slave Trade, 1650–1775* (New York, 1975). E. Phillip LeVeen conducted an analysis of slave prices after 1770, but relied on scanty data. See LeVeen, *British Slave Trade Suppression Policies, 1821–1865* (New York, 1977). Joseph C. Miller, 'Slave Prices in the Portuguese Southern Atlantic', in ed. Paul E. Lovejoy *Africans in Bondage* (Madison, 1986), 43–77.

[18] Richardson and Lovejoy, forthcoming.

[19] Richard Hellie, *Slavery in Russia, 1450–1725* (Chicago, 1982). The documents are on the lives of slaves, rather than on their purchase and sale.

[20] See Bibliography, section 2.

[21] See Bibliography, section 3.

[22] See Bibliography, section 4.

[23] See Bibliography, section 5.

[24] Hogendorn, Jan S., and Marion Johnson, *The Shell Money of the Slave Trade* (Cambridge, 1986). For a general economic historical analysis of African slave trade, see the forthcoming monograph of Stefano Fenoaltea.

As research proceeded, the minimalist interpretations of the 1970s came under challenge in the 1980s and early 1990s. The counter-challenge, mounted by scholars who could be called interactionist in their approach, focused on reaffirming a nexus of the slave trade and world history. Thus the new data, in the hands of the minimalists, had initially brought renunciation of the rather one-dimensionally causal linkages of capitalism and slavery in the 'conventional wisdom'. Now the same data, when explored through sufficiently nuanced analytical models, could support interactive statements linking the slave trade to global transformation.[25] The slave trade seems now to be reconfirmed as a significant ingredient in early-modern world history.

The concentration of the slave trade literature on Africa and Africans should be evident to the reader. Specialists on Africa have done most of the work on the slave trade in the past three decades.[26] The detailed work done in tracing exports of slaves from African regions has not met with equivalent work on tracing slave imports by specialists on the Americas, the Middle East and North Africa, and the Indian Ocean basin. Particularly for Asian regions, slavery was a less prominent and less controversial institution than in the Americas: historians have chosen to focus on other issues. But slavery and the slave trade did exist in many parts of the Asian mainland and islands, and the documents for its analysis exist in considerable quantity, so that slavery, the slave trade and their influence can be elucidated for Asia as well as Africa and the Americas. Richard Hellie's study of slavery in early modern Russia is exemplary in this regard.

Finally, years of systematic work by Joseph C. Miller have resulted in an extraordinarily comprehensive bibliography on slavery and the slave trade, organized efficiently by time period, by region, and by topic. These citations appear each year as a bibliographical supplement to the main journal in the field, *Slavery and Abolition*, and have twice been collected into separate volumes, edited by Miller.[27]

---

[25] Eltis, *Transatlantic Slave Trade*; Joseph Inikori, 'Slavery and the Development of Industrial Capitalism', *Journal of Interdisciplinary History* (1987), 771–95; Joseph C. Miller, *Way of Death: Merchant Capitalism and the Angolan Slave Trade, 1730–1830* (Madison, 1989); Patrick Manning, *Slavery and African Life* (Cambridge, 1990); John Thornton, *Africa and Africans in the Formation of the Modern World, 1600–1800* (Cambridge, 1992); Gwendolyn M. Hall, *Africans in Colonial Louisiana: The Development of Afro-Creole Culture* (Baton Rouge, 1992); and the chapter by David Richardson in this volume. Of these authors, Eltis and Miller, while showing extensive ramifications of slave trade, argue that its negative effect on African population was limited.

[26] For all the work on African slave trade, we still lack major empirical studies of slave trade within Africa before the nineteenth century. This results partly from the shortage of data, but also from the decision of historians to focus on export slave trade. For examples of studies of African slave trade in the nineteenth century, see Michael Mason, 'Captive and client labour and the economy of the Bida Emirate, 1857–1901', *Journal of African History* (1973), 453–71; and Dennis D. Cordell, *Dar al-Kuti and the Last Years of the Trans-Saharan Slave Trade* (Madison, 1985).

[27] See Bibliography, section 6.

Articles in this volume

The articles selected for republication in this volume stand out in that, individually and collectively, they present major recent contributions to the literature by addressing the key issues in analyses of the slave trade, and the main flows of slaves. While the literature is large and diverse, so that many other articles were strong candidates for inclusion, these seventeen were selected for individual strength and topical balance.

The opening section offers three overviews of slave trade. Ralph Austen's article (see Chapter 1 below) presents his revised estimate of the volume of the trans-Saharan trade, showing its character, its longevity, its ups and downs. Paul Lovejoy (see chapter 2 below) gives an analogous estimate of the Atlantic slave trade, published thirteen years after Curtin's *Census*. The article summarizes not just numerical totals, but also the directions of the slave trade and the main carriers of slaves. His results show the great accumulation of detail in the years following Curtin's study, and the modest increase in the estimated volume of the slave trade. Patrick Manning (see chapter 3 below) offers a discussion of the impact of Atlantic trade on the Americas, on Africa, and on those who travelled. The article gives emphasis to the resulting development of the slave trade and slavery within Africa, and also notes the concentration of arrivals from Africa in the Caribbean and Brazil.

Five articles then detail the slave trade from the fifteenth through seventeenth centuries. Luiz Felipe de Alencastro (see chapter 4 below) explores Portuguese imperial policy during that time, and its impact on the movement of slaves. John Monteiro's study of Brazil (see chapter 5 below) emphasizes that the Portuguese took many Indian slaves in Brazil: it documents the capture and settlement of Indian slaves during the seventeenth century, and their interactions with African slaves. John Thornton's concise study (see chapter 6 below) of Upper Guinea in Portuguese times notes that mostly men were taken as slaves, and mostly women were left behind. The resulting changes in social structure and economic roles suggest that life in Africa began to change, under the influence of the slave trade, as early as the sixteenth century. For the same period in India, Ann Pescatello (see chapter 7 below) argues that the Portuguese expanded slavery in areas of the subcontinent under their influence. Slave labour, though small in volume compared to peasant labour, became economically and socially significant, especially in urban settings. In this 1972 article, Pescatello proposed a research agenda on slavery in India which has not, unfortunately, been pursued with energy.[28] The patterns of slave trade to the eastern Mediterranean are reflected in Ronald Jennings' tracing of the lives of several dozen slaves who crossed the

---

[28] For a new study, see R.R. Singh Chauhen, *Africans in India: From Slavery to Royalty.*

Sahara to be settled in Cyprus, where many of them were placed in service as domestics (see chapter 8 below).

Six studies of the slave trade in the eighteenth century document the slave trade at its peak. Richard Rathbone (see chapter 9 below) emphasizes that resistance and escape by captives was as much a factor in Africa and on board ship as it was among slaves in the Americas. His insights on this point have been followed by later scholars. Stephen Deyle (see chapter 10 below) presents an overview of recent work showing the details of the slave trade to British North America. In particular, his work provides a reminder that slaves were sent to the northern as well as the southern colonies. Joseph Miller's analysis of the Portuguese slave trade (see chapter 11 below) emphasizes that it grew to a very large volume in the eighteenth century, and that it ran on quite different principles than the better-known British and French trades. He characterizes this trade as marginal, yet conveys at the same time a sense of its centrality. For the Indian Ocean, Jean-Michel Filliot (see chapter 12 below) shows that the French trade from Madagascar and East Africa to the Mascarenes replaced the Portuguese trade to India, and that this slave trade resembled the Atlantic trade in many particulars. David Geggus (see chapter 13 below) draws on records of French slavery and slave trade to reveal patterns of age, sex, and ethnicity among eighteenth-century slaves. His results show the sharp variations in the composition of slave cargoes taken from different parts of the African coast. Thomas Ricks (see chapter 14 below) summarizes the expansion of the slave trade from East Africa to the Persian Gulf in the late-eighteenth century, as part of a regional commercial expansion linked to increased English trade in the Gulf.

The concluding section of the volume includes three articles on the effects of slave trade. Barbara Bush (see chapter 15 below) reviews the role of women in Caribbean slavery, showing how the heavy usage of slaves led to a need for their replacement with new arrivals. David Richardson (see chapter 16 below) presents a new analysis of the effects of the slave trade on eighteenth-century English economic growth. This revised analysis notes the significance of slave trade at certain key points in English industrial development, and also notes the question of the impact of slave trade on economic growth in the Americas and in Africa. Finally, Seymour Drescher (see chapter 17 below) provides us with a tour of Liverpool, the greatest slave-trading port, at the moment when the abolitionist movement gained the upper hand there.

Conclusion

The slave trade linked diverse regions of the world, but in antagonism rather than in unity. The slave trade represented no peaceful expansion of European influence. It brought violent confrontation of wealth with need, of momentary power with momentary weakness. It was primitive accumulation: the rank redistribution of wealth and power. Demand for slaves emanated from areas short of population, or short of particular types of workers. Supply focused on areas populous but vulnerable; on workers skilled but available at a price. Mortality and disruption in the supplying areas became part of the price.

If the institution of slavery entailed as a counterpoint, over time, the establishment of certain reciprocal, familial and affectionate relations between master and slave, such was not the case in the slave trade. Relations linking captive and owner could rarely have developed beyond physical coupling.

Periodically, the economic advantage of such cruel exploitation subsided. If it coincided with a broadening of definitions of rights – by nation, race, religion – then slavery and enslavement were abolished or at least limited. Otherwise it could rebound. Out of the slave trade grew some of the most invidious of distinctions among men – discrimination by race, by 'civilization', by status of slavery. Enslavement permitted and enhanced sexual discrimination on all the continents.

The ironies of the slave trade underscore the importance of utilizing a global framework to evaluate the slave trade. Thus, Africa was monetized, increasingly, through the impact of the slave trade. But increased monetary flow coincided with the degradation of the African commercial order, not its enrichment or elevation.

Only those few who traveled the full circuit – from the lands of the enslaved, to the lands of slavery, to the lands profiting from slavery – could appreciate the magnitude, the irony, the cruelty, the waste of the system. Some of these were European travellers like Jean-Baptiste Labat and Mungo Park. Many more were slaves. A few of the slaves were able to record their views.[29] The most sweeping and comprehensive view, presented in epic terms, is the narrative of Olaudah Equiano. Equiano, whose travels throughout the North Atlantic formed the basis of his 1792 book, became a devout Christian yet retained pride in the Ibo society of his birth. He condemned the slave trade in language linking Calvinism to Enlightenment humanism, and tying individual emotions to global interactions.[30]

> I remember in the vessel in which I was brought over, in the man's apartment, there were several brothers, who, in the sale, were sold in different lots; and it was very moving on this occasion to see their distress and hear their cries in parting. O, ye nominal Christians! might not an African ask you, 'learned you this from your God, who says unto you, Do unto all men as you would men should do unto you?... Surely this is a new refinement in cruelty, which, while it has no advantage to atone for it, thus aggravates distress, and adds fresh horrors even to the wretchedness of slavery'....
>
> But is not the slave trade entirely a war with the heart of man? And surely that which is begun by breaking down the barriers of virtue, involves in its continuance destruction to every principle, and buries all sentiments in ruin!

---

[29] Philip D. Curtin, ed., *Africa Remembered* (Madison, 1962).

[30] Olaudah Equiano, *The Interesting Narrative of the Life of Olaudah Equiano or Gustavus Vassa, the African* (Revised edn, Leeds, 1814), reprinted in Henry Louis Gates, Jr., ed., *The Classic Slave Narratives* (New York, 1987), 38, 79.

Bibliography

1. Major sources of new quantitative data on slave trade

Anstey, Roger, *The Atlantic Slave Trade and British Abolition, 1760–1810* (Cambridge, 1975).

Curtin, Philip D., *The Atlantic Slave Trade: A Census* (Madison, 1969).

Daget, Serge, *Répertoire des expéditions négrières françaises à la traite illégale (1814–1850)* (Nantes, 1988).

Eltis, David, *Economic Growth and the Ending of the Transatlantic Slave Trade* (Oxford, 1987).

Inikori, Joseph, 'The Import of Firearms into West Africa, 1750–1897: A Quantitative Analysis', *Journal of African History* XVIII (1977), 339–68.

Mettas, Jean, in ed. Serge Daget, *Répertoire des expéditions négrières françaises au XVIIIe siècle*, 2 vols (Paris, 1978–84).

Miller, Joseph C., *Way of Death: Merchant Capitalism and the Angolan Slave Trade, 1730–1830* (Madison, 1989).

Postma, Johannes, *The Dutch in the Atlantic Slave Trade, 1600–1814* (Cambridge, 1990).

Richardson, David, 'Slave Exports from West and West-Central Africa, 1700–1810: New Estimates of Volume and Distribution', *Journal of African History* XXX (1989), 1–22.

2. Collective works including chapters on slave trade

Additional collective volumes focusing on individual countries, especially the United States, are not listed.

Clarence-Smith, William Gervase, ed., *The Economics of the Indian Ocean Slave Trade* (London, 1989).

Craton, Michael, ed., *Roots and Branches: Current Directions in Slave Studies* (Toronto, 1979).

Daget, Serge, ed., *De la traite à l'esclavage: Actes du colloque international sur la traite des Noirs, Nantes 1985*, 2 vols. (Nantes, 1988).

Eltis, David, and James Walvin, eds., *The Abolition of the Atlantic Slave Trade* (Madison, 1981).

Engerman, Stanley L., and Eugene D. Genovese, eds., *Race and Slavery in the Western Hemisphere: Quantitative Studies* (Princeton, 1975).

Gemery, Henry A., and Jan S. Hogendorn, eds., *The Uncommon Market: Essays in the Economic History of the Atlantic Slave Trade* (New York, 1979).

Inikori, J.E., ed., *Forced Migration*, (London, 1982).

Inikori, J.E., and Stanley L. Engerman, eds., *The Atlantic Slave Trade* (Durham, 1992).

Lovejoy, Paul E., ed., *The Ideology of Slavery in Africa*. (Beverly Hills, 1981).

—, ed., *Africans in Bondage: Studies in Slavery and the Slave Trade*, (Madison, 1986).

Meillassoux, Claude, ed., *L'Esclavage en Afrique précoloniale* (Paris, 1975).

Miers, Suzanne, and Igor Kopytoff, eds., *Slavery in Africa: Historical and Anthropological Perspectives* (Madison, 1977).

Miers, Suzanne, and Richard Roberts eds., *The End of Slavery in Africa* (Madison, 1988).

Robertson, Claire C., and Martin Klein, eds., *Women and Slavery in Africa* (Madison, 1983).

Société Française d'Histoire d'Outre-Mer, *La Traite des noirs par l'Atlantique, nouvelles approches* (Paris, 1976).

Solow, Barbara, ed., *Slavery and the Rise of the Atlantic System* (Cambridge, 1991).

Solow, Barbara, and Stanley L. Engerman, eds., *British Capitalism and Caribbean Slavery: The Legacy of Eric Williams* (Cambridge, 1987).

Toplin, Robert Brent, ed., *Slavery and Race Relations in Latin America* (Westport, 1974).

Watson, James L., ed., *Asian and African Systems of slavery* (Berkeley, 1980).

Willis, John Ralph, ed., *Slaves and Slavery in Muslim Africa*, 2 vols. (London, 1985).

3.   Monographic studies including emphasis on slave trade

Alpers, Edward A., *Ivory and Slaves in East Central Africa: Changing Patterns of International Trade to the Later Nineteenth Century* (Berkeley, 1975).

Anstey, Roger, *The Atlantic Slave Trade and British Abolition 1760–1810* (Cambridge, 1975).

Bowser, Frederick, *The African Slave in Colonial Peru, 1524–1650* (Stanford, 1973).

Conrad, Robert, *The Destruction of Brazilian Slavery* (Berkeley 1972).

Cooper, Frederick, *Plantation Slavery on the East Coast of Africa* (New Haven, 1977).

—, *From Slaves to Squatters: Plantation Labor and Agriculture in Zanzibar and Coastal Kenya, 1890–1925* (New Haven, 1980).

Hall, Gwendolyn Midlo, *Africans in Colonial Louisiana: The Development of Afro-Creole Culture* (Baton Rouge, 1992).

Curtin, Philip D., *Economic Change in Precolonial Africa: Senegambia in the Era of the Slave Trade*, 2 vols. (Madison, 1975).

Debien, Gabriel, *Les Esclaves aux Antilles françaises, XVIIe–XVIIIe siècles* (Basse-Terre and Fort-de-France, 1979).

Eltis, David *Economic Growth and the Ending of the Transatlantic Slave Trade* (Oxford, 1987).

Filliot, Jean-Michel, *La Traite des esclaves vers les Mascareignes au XVIIIème siècle* (Paris, 1974).

Harms, Robert, *River of Wealth, River of Sorrow* (New Haven, 1981).

Hellie, Richard, *Slavery in Russia, 1430–1725* (Chicago, 1982).

Higman, B.W. *Slave Population and Economy in Jamaica, 1807–1834* (Cambridge, 1976).

Hogendorn, Jan S., and Marion Johnson, *The Shell Money of the Slave Trade* (Cambridge, 1986).

Isaacman, Allen, *Mozambique: The Africanization of a European Institution: The Zambezi Prazos, 1750–1902* (Madison, 1972).

Klein, Herbert S., *The Middle Passage: Comparative Studies in the Atlantic Slave Trade* (Princeton, 1978).

Knight, Franklin W., *Slave Society in Cuba during the Nineteenth Century* (Madison, 1970).

Lobo Cabrera, Manuel, *La Esclavitud en las Canarias Orientales en el Siglo XVI* (Gran Canaria, 1982).

Manning, Patrick, *Slavery, Colonialism and Economic Growth in Dahomey, 1640–1960* (Cambridge, 1982).

Martin, Phyllis M., *The External Trade of the Loango Coast* (Oxford, 1972).

Meillassoux, Claude, *Anthropologie de l'esclavage: le ventre de fer et d'argent* (Paris, 1986).

Miller, Joseph C., *Way of Death: Merchant Capitalism and the Angolan Slave Trade, 1730–1830* (Madison, 1989).

Northrup, David, *Trade Without Rulers: Pre-Colonial Economic Development in South-Eastern Nigeria* (Oxford, 1978).

Palmer, Colin W., *Slaves of the White God: Blacks in Mexico, 1570–1650* (Cambridge, Mass., 1976).

—, *Human Cargoes, the British Slave Trade to Spanish America, 1700–1730* (Urbana, 1981).

Peukert, Werner, *Der Atlantische Sklavenhandel von Dahomey, 1740–1797* (Wiesbaden, 1978).

Roberts, Richard, *Warriors, Merchants, and Slaves: The State and the Economy in the Middle Niger Valley, 1700–1914* (Stanford, 1987).

Saunders, A.C. de C.M., *A Social History of Black Slaves and Freedmen in Portugal, 1441–1555* (Cambridge, 1982).

Sheriff, Abdul, *Slaves, Spices and Ivory in Zanzibar* (London, 1987).

4. Surveys of slave trade and slavery

Beachey, R.W., *The Slave Trade of Eastern Africa* (London, 1976).

Blackburn, Robin, *The Overthrow of Colonial Slavery, 1776–1848* (London, 1988).

Deschamps, Hubert, *Histoire de la traite des Noirs de l'antiquité à nos jours* (Paris, 1971).

Fisher, Allan G.B., and Humphrey J. Fisher, *Slavery and Muslim Society in Africa* (London, 1970).

Harris, Joseph H., *The African Presence in Asia: Consequences of the East African Slave Trade* (Evanston, 1971).

Klein, Herbert S., *African Slavery in Latin America and the Caribbean* (New York, 1986).

Lewis, Bernard, *Race and Slavery in the Middle East: An Historical Enquiry* (New York, 1990).

Lovejoy, Paul E., *Transformations in Slavery. A History of Slavery in Africa* (Cambridge, 1983).

Manning, Patrick, *Slavery and African Life: Occidental, Oriental and African Slave Trades* (Cambridge, 1990).

Mannix, Daniel, and Malcolm Cowley, *Black Cargoes* (1962).

Mellafe, Rolando, *La esclavitud en Hispanoamérica* (Buenos Aires, 1964).

Rawley, James, *The Transatlantic Slave Trade: A History* (New York, 1981).

Renault, François, and Serge Daget, *Les Traites négrières en Afrique* (Paris, 1985).

Reynolds, Edward, *Stand the Storm: A History of the Atlantic Slave Trade* (London, 1985).

5. Demographic studies of slave trade

Fage, John D., 'Slavery and the Slave Trade in the Context of West African History', *Journal of African History* X (1969), 393–404.

—, 'The effect of the Export Slave Trade on African Populations', in eds., R.P. Ross and R.J.A. Rathbone, *The Population Factor in African Studies* (London, 1975), 15–23.

—, 'Slaves and Society in Western Africa, c. 1445–c.1700', *Journal of African History* XXI (1980), 289–310.

Geggus, David, 'Sex Ratio, Age, and Ethnicity in the Atlantic Slave Trade: Data from French Shipping and Plantation Records', *Journal of African History* XXX (1989), 23–44.

Manning, Patrick, 'The Enslavement of Africans: A Demographic Model', *Canadian Journal of African Studies* XV (1981), 499–526.

—, 'The Impact of Slave Trade Exports on the Population of the Western Coast of Africa, 1700–1850', in ed. Serge Daget, *De la traite à l'esclavage* (Nantes, 1988), vol. 2, 111–34.

—, 'Slave Trade: The Formal Demography of a Global System', *Social Science History* XIV (1990), 225–79.

—, and William S. Griffiths, 'Divining the Unprovable: Simulating and

Demography of African Slavery', *Journal of Interdisciplinary History* XIX (1988), 177–201.

Thornton, John, 'An Eighteenth-Century Baptismal Register and the Demographic History of Manguenzo', in eds. C. Fyfe and D. McMaster, *African Historical Demography* I (1977), 405–15.

—, 'Demography and History in the Kingdom of Kongo, 1550–1750', *Journal of African History* XVIII (1977), 507–30.

—, 'The Slave Trade in Eighteenth Century Angola: Effects of Demographic Structures', *Canadian Journal of African Studies* XIV (1981), 417–27.

—, 'The Demographic Effect of the Slave Trade on Western Africa, 1500–1850', in eds. C. Fyfe and D. McMaster, *African Historical Demography* II (1981), 691–720.

6. *Bibliographies of slave trade*

Hogg, Peter C., *The African Slave Trade and its Suppression* (London, 1973).

Miller, Joseph C., *Slavery, A Comparative Teaching Bibliography* (Honolulu, 1977).

—, *Slavery: A Worldwide Bibliography, 1900–1982* (White Plains, NY, 1985).

—, *Slavery and Slaving in World History: A Bibliography, 1900–1991* (Millwood, NY, 1993).

1

The Mediterranean Islamic Spice Trade out of Africa: A Tentative Census

Ralph A. Austen

Efforts to tabulate the number of slaves taken from Africa by Muslims have always been a subject of political polemics and academic controversy both because of their ideological implications (were Arabs 'worse' for Africa than Europeans?) and their methodological dimensions (how can one count the uncountable and what does one accomplish by such efforts anyway?). However, the calculation of the slave trade across the Sahara Desert and down the Nile Valley has aroused far less controversy than similar efforts for the Indian Ocean Islamic slave trade.[1] Muslim merchants and shippers in Egypt and the Maghrib did not enter into as much direct conflict with European abolitionists as their East African brethren and the issue of slave trading is less central to colonial penetration of northern Africa. Thus, disputes among students of this commerce have few ideological overtones and major disparities among seriously documented estimates are mainly the result of differing definitions of the zones in question.[2]

The present paper follows the methodology of the author's previous work in this area. All significant observations of both slave trading and the presence of African slaves and/or ex-slaves in receiving Mediterranean areas are presented in tabular form (see Tables 1 to 5).[3] The number of observations is greatly increased by those published in 1979, and the analysis of their quantitative meaning is more developed. Nevertheless, the results are far from precise; indeed, greater sophistication has, as will be seen, often led to greater scepticism about clear conclusions.

The evidence used falls into two broad categories: literary accounts and serial data. The former, by far the most abundant, consists of statements by observers at greater or lesser distance from the trade and its aftermath (this distance is indicated in the annotations of 'original source' in the tables). Apart from the various distortions due to the ignorance or bias of the observers, such evidence usually describes the slave trade itself in the form of 'capacity estimates', that is, statements about what could be expected under maximal conditions (almost always just previous to the period actually being observed) rather than calculations of what occurred statistically over normally varying conditions.[4]

The serial data consists mainly of customs records from Cairo and Tripoli (Libya).[5] These have the advantage of relative disinterestedness, in that they were not constructed for purposes of making arguments about the scale of slave trading. However, they remain seriously incomplete in two senses. First, none of the records reveals the full scale of the trade, since much slave traffic in both places went on outside the scrutiny and particularly the fiscal capacity of relatively weak local bureaucracies. Secondly, the customs information is always given at second hand and only covers selected years. In addition to customs data, there are also some rudimentary demographic surveys and military muster rolls in Tables 3–5; these are useful but suffer from obvious limitations.

The definition of 'out of Africa' in this study includes the Mediterranean portions of the continent (Egypt, Maghrib and northern Sahara) but not the northern Nilotic Sudan. The latter was a major consumer of slaves among masters who considered themselves Arabs, but I have omitted it both because slave imports here are difficult to calculate and because, on the analogy of the East African Swahili coast, the northern Sudan is normally considered part of sub-Saharan Africa. Slave trade to such zones should be considered (as with much of West Africa) as an issue of forced internal migration and the impact of servile institutions upon indigenous African development rather than one of net demographic transfer to societies which functioned under the control of an alien Mediterranean world.

The definition of Mediterranean used here is mainly Islamic. However, it includes Europe in the cases (of limited statistical significance) where Europeans imported black slaves via Egypt or the Maghrib.

THE EGYPTIAN SLAVE TRADE

Egypt was, from the earliest Islamic period, one of the major centres of trade in black slaves. Not only did large quantities of Africans pass through here to the rest of the Mediterranean but also, because of Egypt's wealth and dense urban population (as well as occasional agricultural manpower needs), it absorbed many imported slaves into its own society. Egypt's location in the lower end of the Nile Valley and on the main African route to the Red Sea gave it access to major sources of slaves both originating in or passing through various portions of the Nilotic Sudan as well as those accompanying pilgrimage caravans (Table 1/A/6,9).

For the first ten centuries of Islam in Egypt, there is no serious direct statistical evidence of the scale of the slave trade, although plenty of indication that such commerce existed at a significant level. The information on the *baqt* (Table 1/A/1,3) and the tax/tribute data (Table 1/A/7,8,11)

TABLE 1
SLAVE TRADE: EGYPT AND THE NILOTIC SUDAN

	Date	Quantity	Comments	Original Source	Reference
A. Egypt					
1.	650–1373	420	baqt slave tribute, Christian Nubia to Egypt; problematic data	various Arab, Coptic chronicles	Renault, 1989, pp. 10ff.
3.	831–50		baqt at 1,400 slaves; not paid for 14 years; renegotiated at 400 every 3 years	Coptic Church chronicles	Meinardus, 1966, pp. 147–8
6.	1416	1,700	Takrūr (W. Sudan) pilgrim caravan brings slaves to Cairo	Maqrīzī, d. 1442	Cuoq, 1975, p. 392
7.	1419	300	slaves seized as tax from upper Egypt bedouins	Maqrīzī, b. Hajar	Garcin, 1976, p. 479
8.	1420	1,800	slaves seized as tax from upper Egypt for Cairo	'Ayni, 1361–1451	Garcin, 1976, p. 431
9.	1439		Takrūr (W. Sudan) pilgrim caravans sells 'numerous slaves' in Cairo	Maqrīzī	Cuoq, 1975, p. 392
10.	1483		'great number' of black and white slaves in Cairo market	Fabri, Swiss traveller	Fabri, 1975, p. 436
11.	1560		black slaves in annual Egyptian tribute caravan to Istanbul via Palestine	Ottoman records	Heyd, 1960
12.	1570s	c. 5,000	'many thousands' of blacks on sale in Cairo on market days	Pinon, French traveller	Raymond and Wiet, 1979, p. 225
13.	1581		more than 400 slaves at a time in Cairo market; majority are black	Palerne, French traveller	Palerne, 1971
14.	1583	670	Cairo market; 70 men 600 women	Radzivill, Polish traveller	Radzivill, 1614, p. 170
15.	1587		'great number of black Moors' brought by annual Ethiopia caravan to Cairo	Lichtenstein, German traveller	Lichtenstein, 1972, pp. 13–14

No.	Date	Number	Description	Observer	Reference
16.	1588		annual caravan brings many black slaves to Cairo for rest of Ottoman empire	Keichel, German traveller	Keichel, 1972, p.126
17.	1589–90		'an infinity of slave men and women' on Cairo market	Villamont, French traveller	Villamont, 1971, p.18
18.	1598		'great quantity' in Cairo market, majority are blacks	Harant, Bohemian traveller	Harant, 1972, p.202
19.	1608	600	slave cargo of 9 ships, Egypt-Istanbul, taken by Tuscan fleet	Tuscan records	Galuzzi, 1781, III, pp.252–3
20.	1631	750	seen together Cairo slave market 'almost all black'; 2 annual 'Libya' caravans	Stochove, Flemish traveller	Stochove, 1975, p.50
21.	1652		great numbers of black slaves in Cairo market	Thevenot, French traveller	Thevenot, 1689, III, p.452
22.	1665–66*	3,500	sometimes 3–4,000 imported into Egypt p.a.; 800–1,000 seen in Cairo market 1 day	Gonzales, Spanish/ Belgian traveller	Gonzales, 1977, I, pp.37, 110
23.	1666	30	'little black eunuchs' shipped to Sultan in Istanbul	Gonzales	Gonzales, 1977, I, p.264
24.	1692–1708	2,500	annual Sinnâr caravan, 2–3,000 slaves	Maillet, French consul, scholar	Maillet, 1735, II, p.197
25.	1700s*	1,200	annual Cairo slave imports	Antoine Bonnefons, French traveller	Wiet, 1943, p.79
26.	1712–14		Nubians bring 'a quantity of black slaves' for sale in the rest of Egypt	Sicard, Jesuit missionary, scholar	Sicard, 1717, II, p.118
27.	1714–17		3 caravans p.a. Borno and Zanfaras to Manfalant	Lucas, French traveller	Lucas, 1724, p.32
28.	early 1750s		black and white slaves in Cairo; 'blacks cheaper: multitudes ... from Ethiopia'	Van Egmont, Dutch traveller	Van Egmont, 1759, II, p.269
29.	1768–98*	3,500	3–4,500 = peak annual Egyptian imports	Cairo slave market overseers, clerks	Frank, 1807, p.ccxi

TABLE 1 (continued)

A. Egypt

No.	Date	Value	Description	Source	Reference
30.	1777–80*	1,750	twice annual Nubia caravans bring 1,500–2,000 slaves to Cairo market	Sonnini de Mononcour, French naval engineer	Sonnini, VII/1799, II, p.381
31.	1783–85	1,100	1,000–1,200 annual Sinnâr caravan	Volney, French traveller	Volney, 1788, I, p.207
32.	c. 1788*	4,000	Dâr Fûr exports to Cairo	Venture de Paradis, French consul	Lalande, 1794, III, p.305
33.	1788*	7,500	total Egyptian imports for 2 to 4-year period = 20,000	Rosetti, Venetian consul	Hallet, 1964, p.60
34.	1789*	4,500	imports do not exceed 5,000 p.a.	Baldwin, British merchant, Alexandria	Baldwin, 1790, p.128
35.	1790–92	1,260	Cairo customs records for 3 years =	Girard, French traveller 3,780 slaves	Girard, 1824, p.383
36.	1798–1800*	1,200	average of 3-year period; 3–4 vs.	Frank, French traveller normal 7–8 caravans	Frank, 1807, p.ccxi
37.	1798–1800	350	annual average of Sinnâr caravans	Lapanouse, French traveller	Lapanouse, 1801, p.98
38.	1799*	5,500	5–6,000 in Dâr Fûr caravan at Asyut	Girard, French traveller	Girard, 1824, p.582
39.	1799	150	Sinnâr caravan at arrival	Girard, French traveller	Girard, 1824, p.93
40.	1805	2,000	population of caravan said to have perished in Libyan desert	Minutoli, German traveller, 1820–21	Minutoli, 1824, pp.201–02
41.	1810		Dâr Fûr caravans small over last few years; diverted to Red Sea	Drovetti, French consul, Cairo	LaRue, n.d.
42.	1813		Dâr Fûr slave caravan seen at Asyut	Buckingham, British traveller	Buckingham, 1855, II, pp.138–9
43.	1817*	3,000	6,000 slaves in biannual Dâr Fûr caravan	Trecourt, French vice-consul, Damietta	LaRue, n.d.
44.	1817	c. 3,000	'several thousand slaves' in great Dâr Fûr caravan, interrupted several years	Roussel, French consul, Alexandria	Driault, 1927, p.64
50.	1830s	1,000	10–12,000 = total Egyptian imports	Bowring, British scholar, emissary	PP 1840, XXI, 'Report on Egypt', p.85

B. Sudan

No.	Date	Number	Description	Source	Reference
2.	1699		Sinnār slaves cheap; 'Egyptian merchants buy a great number every year'	Poncet, French traveller	Foster, 1949, p.105
3.	1796	5,000	Dār Fūr caravan at departure	Browne, British traveller	Browne, 1799, p.298
4.	1800–60	15,000	Exports from Ethiopia to Sudan	various	Pankhurst, 1964, pp.226–7
5.	1814	5,000	Shendy (Sinnār) market 1,500 slaves to Egypt; 3,500 going elsewhere	Burckhardt, Swiss traveller	Burckhardt, 1822, p.290
6.	1822	c. 5,500	slaves seized in single raid by Egyptian army	Muḥammad 'Alī correspondance, 19/7, 7/8/22	Prunier, 1988, p.526

Egypt: Totals, 1400–1900

	per annum	sub-total
1400–1820	3,000	1,260,000
1820–39	5,000	50,000
1830–39	10,000	100,000
1840–49	5,000	50,000
1850–59	3,500	35,000
1860–69	10,000	100,000
1870–77	2,000	16,000
1878–1900	500	11,000
total:		1,622,000

suggests that slaves were an established regional commodity. Major evidence on the scale of this trade will come from military data discussed below.

We begin to obtain more information on trade with accounts left by the many European travellers to Egypt (and some in the Nilotic Sudan) from the late fifteenth through the early nineteenth centuries.[6] This span is treated as a single period since the recorded observations suggest a fairly consistent range of slave imports and because Muḥammad ʿAlī's conquest of the Sudan in 1820 marks an obvious break in this pattern (Table 1).

Between 1483 and 1820 there are thirty-nine accounts of various aspects of the Egyptian slave trade (Table 1/A/9–44, B/2,3,5), but only ten of these (see dates marked with asterisk) give anything resembling general statistics for Egypt in that they discuss total imports or the Dār Fūr caravan, which seems to have been the main slave supplier through much of this period.[7] If these are simply tabulated they yield an annual average of about 3,565. However several of the figures in this series seem inordinately high (Table 1/A/33,38); the second of these may refer to the number of slaves who left Dār Fūr as opposed to those who survived the notorious *dār al-arbaʿīn* (forty-day route). Three of the other observations are explicitly presented as capacity estimates (A/22,29,34); however, one observation (A/36) specifically takes into account the low points in the trade cycles, and several others (A/25,30,35) do so implicitly. Thus, if we make a second calculation omitting the two highest figures, the average shifts to a little under three thousand (2,831), and if this is raised slightly to account for the Sinnār imports, omitted in several accounts but still of some significance (see A/24,31,37), we arrive at a working estimate of three thousand.

This last figure is also consistent with the one set of customs figures available from the Cairo slave market in the latter eighteenth century (A/35). These data were clearly understood not to represent more than a portion of the total annual imports, since a certain percentage of the slaves entering the country remained in Upper Egypt (see Table 4/1), were sold directly in the Delta, or were purchased or requisitioned by Cairene elites without passing through the marketplace.[8]

Given the general consistency of conditions in Egypt between 1400 and 1820 and the evidence in the various European travel accounts and the fewer Islamic documents of a generally high level of slave trading activity, we can tentatively project the 1665–66 estimates backwards at least to the beginning of the fifteenth century. This projection will have to be reconsidered when a wider variety of conditioning factors in the areas of slave supply and demand are taken more fully into account than is possible in this essay.

For the nineteenth century, we have a great deal of information about slave trading both in Egypt itself and in the main source region, the Nilotic Sudan. Clearly, the invasion of the Sudan during this period and especially the penetration of Egyptian troops and armed private merchants into the ultimate source of slaves, the southern Sudan, vastly increased the supply to Egypt at the same time as a number of political and economic factors increased Egyptian demand for black African manpower. However, the quantitative information available to us for this later period is far less susceptible to even the rudimentary statistical methods used previously.

First of all, we cannot use observations made over several decades to establish any kind of average tendency, since the evidence clearly indicates that the scale of the slave trade changed radically from one decade to the next; also, available sources for the same decades often disagree with one another. Moreover, while the Nilotic Sudan data provides some general check against estimates of Egyptian imports, it is only useful in a very general way; a large portion of the slaves captured and even brought to markets in the Sudan did not go to Egypt but rather stayed in the Sudan itself or were passed eastward into the comparably expanding Red Sea trade (Table 1/B/5). Especially problematic are the large numbers of Sudanese captured in army raiding expeditions (Table 1/B/6). During the early 1820s a major portion of the male captives from these *razzias* (*ghazwa*) were recruited into the Egyptian army (see Table 5/B); but after 1822, the majority joined the military forces in the Sudan itself, just as many thousands of other enslaved men and women were put to work in local agriculture.[9] However, an unspecified proportion of the military captives were sold to merchants who made their greatest profits by export sales, especially to Egypt. The same problems arise with regard to information about Ethiopian slaves exported into the Sudan (Table 1/B/4). Finally, the ease of communications between Egypt and the Sudan in this period and the great quantities of slaves transported by a variety of means (including river boats and barges) meant that it was no longer possible to calculate the levels of the trade by observations of one or more key annual caravans.[10]

The Sudan data at least makes it possible to take seriously some of the higher estimates for Egyptian imports during this period. The years 1820–50 and 1860–70 represent peaks, spurred by the effects of the initial invasion, military recruitment, and agricultural-demographic factors to be discussed below (see Table 4). The 1850s apparently experienced a slowing down of the slave traffic, probably because early trade in the southern Sudan concentrated on ivory, and Egyptian military and agricultural demands were stabilized. The large numbers reported for the 1860s can be explained by the establishment of militarized *zarā'ibs* (fortified camps) by slave-traders in the Baḥr al-Ghazāl as well as the consumer and labour demands of the simultaneous Egyptian cotton boom.[11]

Declining Egyptian demand and some effective measures of prohibition explain the lower figures of the 1870s. These same factors, combined with the Mahdist revolt in the Sudan, brought about a virtual termination of slave imports into Egypt between the end of the decade and the early 1880s.

THE MAGHRIB TRANS-SAHARAN TRADE

Table 2 provides the rather extensive data which have been found for the trade which brought African peoples across the Sahara to Morocco, Algeria, Tunisia and (especially) Libya. The sources of this trade were the populations living at or (mainly) south of the Sudanic regions stretching from the Atlantic Coast of Africa as far east as present-day Chad. The western part of this zone overlapped with the Atlantic slave trade, which is only cited once (Table 2/A/8). A more complicated issue is the role of the easternmost entrepôts, Murzūq in the Fazzān and Wadai in Chad. Both of these areas supplied slaves to the Maghrib region as a whole, although not all of these desert imports are reflected in the figures for Libyan exports. Some of the differences result from the lateral movement of slaves into Egypt, which is treated here as an essentially separate slave-receiving and exporting zone. The adjustments which have been made in the total import data are not entirely satisfactory and may be improved upon in future calculations.

The period from the Islamic conquest of North Africa (667) through the second half of the sixteenth century remains too thinly documented for any direct calculation of its scale. An estimate for this period will await the examination of indirect evidence on at least military deployment and also projections from the relationship between general trends in this era with those of better documented centuries.

For those periods in which we have richer documentation – the late sixteenth century onward, it is clear that Libya was the major slave outlet. In fact, while the few pre-seventeenth-century quantitative observations which cite areas are almost entirely limited to the western Maghrib and adjacent Saharan zones, we know from extensive non-quantitative evidence[12] that even in medieval times the Fazzān was the principal Saharan entrepôt for Sudanic slaves, many of whom must thus have exited Africa via Tripoli, the closest Mediterranean port. Probably it was just this concentration on human exports, which did not attract the same commercial and geographical interest as gold, that made the eastern Maghrib (and its adjoining Sudanic partner state, Kanem-Borno) less visible to foreign observers

TABLE 2

SLAVE TRADE: 'MAGHRIB' AND SAHARA

	Date	Quantity	Comments	Original Source	Reference
A. General Medieval					
8.	1455	900	800–1,000 in Sahara diverted by Portuguese from Maghrib to Arguīn	Ca da Mosto, Venetian merchant	Ca da Mosto, 1966, pp. 26–7
B. Libya					
1.	c.1480	201	188 'negri … some black girls' from Tripoli to Egypt by Venetians	Venetian merchant archives	Ashtor, 1974, p.29
3.	1585	300	slave cargo of 1 ship, Tripoli to Levant, taken by Knights of Malta	Pozzo, Maltese chronicler	Pignon, 1964, p.106, n.195
6.	1634	650	slave cargo (includes Berbers), 4 Tripoli ships, taken by Knights of Malta	Pozzo, Maltese chronicler	Pignon, 1964, p.106, n.195
7.	1638	200	Borno tribute to Tripoli of 100 young girls, 100 young men	anon. French slave, Tripoli	Fresnel, 1849, p.254
8.	1653	125	Borno letter to Tripoli announces gift of 100 slaves + dwarfs, eunuchs	anon. French slave, Tripoli	Fresnel, 1849, p.254
9.	1686	550	estimate of Libyan exports in war-disrupted year	Lemaire, French consul	Renault, 1982, p.168
10.	1696	7,000	Mai Idris of Borno through Fazzān with slaves for Mecca pilgrimage	Petit la Croix, French traveller	Petit la Croix, 1697, fol.311
13.	1722	1,750	slaves on 10 French ships	French consular records	Renault, 1982, p.169
14.	1724	200	slaves on single French vessel from Tripoli	Martin, French consul	Renault, 1982, p.167
15.	1725	250	slaves on single French vessel from Tripoli	Martin, French consul	Renault, 1982, p.167

TABLE 2 (continued)

B. Libya

No.	Date	Number	Description	Source	Reference
16.	c.1728	200	slaves on single French vessel from Tripoli	unknown	Feraud, 1927, p. 235
18.	1753–56	1,918	average Libyan imports over three 'seasons'	Caullet, detailed report	Dyer, 1987, pp. 122–4
19.	1753–56	1,514	average Libyan imports over 4 calendar years	Caullet, detailed report	Dyer, 1987, pp. 122–4
21.	1763–74	1,000	estimate of p.a. exports from Libya via French ships	French consular records	Renault, 1982, p. 166
28.	1777–93	320	estimate of p.a. exports from Libya via Venetian ships	Venetian consular records	Renault, 1982, p. 167
31.	1780	3,000	Libyan slave exports	d'André, French consul	Dyer, 1987, p. 125
33.	1783–87	1,000	estimate of p.a. exports from Libya via French ships	French consular records	Renault, 1982, p. 166
34.	1786	200	slaves on single Ragusian vessel	Bellatio, Venetian consul	Renault, 1982, p. 168
35.	1786	50	slaves on single French ship with Mecca pilgrims	Vallière, French consul	Renault, 1982, p. 168
40.	1788 +	750	Fazzān exports 7–800 slaves p.a. plus tribute to Tripoli	anon. French ms.	Renault, 1982, p. 172
49.	1839*	2,250	2,000–2,500 exported p.a.; during periods of disorder diverted to Egypt, Tunisia	McCanley, US Consul, Tripoli	USNA, T40, Roll 7, Tripoli-US, 3 Oct. 1839
75.	1850	2,400	slaves transported Wadai to Benghazi 2.5–3,000 lost *en route*	Sardinian consul, Tripoli	Rossi, 1968, p. 316
76.	1850	1,200	Wadai-Benghazi caravan, only 770 arrive (30% loss)	Herman, British vice-consul, Benghazi	FO 84/815 27/5/50

C. Morocco

No.	Year	Number	Description	Source	Reference
5.	1693		Moroccans import 'great number' of blacks for military and other uses	Pidou de St. Olon, French envoy	St. Olon, 1695
6.	1697		Sultan's Guinea trade brings 'blacks with which his kingdoms are filled'	Estelle, French consul	Abitbol, 1979, p. 199
7.	1701		Emperor Mulāy Ismaʻīl imports slaves from Guinea	Neant, French redemptionist priest	Cosee Brissac, 1960, VI, p. 688
8.	1708–28		Sultan regular tribute expedition gathers slaves from Sudan in 2–4 year stay	de Leon, Spanish resident	La Veronne, 1974, p. 63
11.	1789	3,500	Timbuktu to Morocco and Algeria	Matra, British consul	Hallet, 1964, pp. 80–1
12.	1790–91	4,000	Timbuktu to Morocco and rest of Maghrib	Lemprière, British traveller	Lemprière, 1814, p. 78
23.	1850	200	slaves in Timbuktu-Goulmine caravan	Panet, Afro-French traveller	Panet, 1850, pp. 176–7
25.	1864	750	500–1,000 Timbuktu to Tuāt (Morocco)	Rohlfs, German traveller	Rohlfs, 1868a, pp. 119–20
30.	1876–78	4,000	annual imports, projected from Marrakesh market sales	Marrakesh market tax records	Schroeter, 1992
33.	1887	520	main Timbuktu caravan at Tindouf	Douls	Douls, 1888, p. 450
34.	1888–94	6,500	annual imports, projected from Marrakesh market sales	Marrakesh market tax records	Schroeter, 1992

D. Algeria

No.	Year	Number	Description	Source	Reference
7.	late 1840	3,300	enter Algeria via Oran	not given	Julien, 1964, p. 348
11.	1858	700	enter Algeria via Ghāt; enrolled in French army	Reade, British consul administrator	PP 1859,2 XXXIV, p. 517, pp. 31–33

E. Tunisia

No.	Year	Number	Description	Source	Reference
4.	1724–25		2 annual caravans, Fazzān-Tunis bring slaves	Peysonnel, French envoy, 1724–25	Peysonnel, 1838, p. 79

TABLE 2 (continued)

E. Tunisia

No.	Date	Number	Description	Source	Reference
5.	1752		'fairly large revenue' from biannual Ghadāmis gold, slave caravan	Poiron, French traveller	Poiron, 1925, p. 19
6.	1788		few slaves, Ghadāmis to Tunis	Nyssen, Dutch consul	Monchicort, 1929, pp. 23–4
7.	c. 1788		3 caravans p.a. from Ghadāmis bring slaves; exports unmeasurable	Venture de Paradis, French consul	Venture de Paradis, 1788, Tunis, fol. 59–60
8.	1789	1,000	Ghadāmis to Tunis; plus 2–300 sold at Ghadāmis	Traill, British consul	Hallet, 1964, p. 83
9.	c. 1810	1,100	1,000–1,200 Ghadāmis to Tunis annual Ghadāmis-Tunis caravan brings slaves	Frank, French physician	Frank, 1856, p. 115
10.	1812			French consulate, Tunis	Abitbol, 1979, p. 209
11.	1814	400	3 annual Ghadāmis-Tunis caravans 'some bring to the number of 200 slaves	Macgill, British merchant	Macgill, 1811, p. 148
13.	1896		slave trade via Ghadāmis continues	al-Hashaishi, Tunisian scholar	El-Hachaichi, 1912, p. 217

F. Sahara

No.	Date	Number	Description	Source	Reference
2.	1701–2	2,500	Fazzān-Egypt caravan lost; first in 12–15 years	French consular report	Raymond, 1973, p. 163
10.	1843*	2,200	Murzūq imports	Gagliuffi, British consul	Richardson, 1848, II, p. 323
20.	1847*	1,281	slaves arriving Murzūq; huge deaths en route from smallpox	Gagliuffi, British vice-consul, Murzūq	FO 84/737 28/2/48
22.	1849	1,600	1,600 slaves die of thirst in Borno caravan	Gagliuffi, British vice-consul, Murzūq	FO 84/774 9/8/49
23.	1849*	2,384	slaves arriving Murzūq; 834 more (34% of total) die en route	Gagliuffi, British vice-consul, Murzūq	FO 84/815 20/1/50
40.	1891	2,000	2,000 slaves from Wadai at Jale Oasis, 1/2 for Sanūsi Maqrīzi	Ricard, French vice-consul, Benghazi	MAE, Turquie: Tripoli, 27, pp. 200–201
44.	1896		Ghāt still major slave market for Sudan and Tuāt	al-Hashaishi	El-Hachaichi, 1912, p. 176

Maghrib: Totals

Libya, 1400–1900

	per annum	sub-total
1550–1699	1,500	225,000
1700–1799	2,700	270,000
1800–1856	3,100	176,700
1857–1913	2,000	113,000
total rounded		784,700 / 785,000

Algeria, 1700–1900

	per annum	sub-total
1700–1839	500	70,000
1840–1879	700	21,000
1880–1900	500	10,000
total rounded		101,000 / 100,000

Tunisia, 1700–1900

	per annum	sub-total
1700–1799	800	80,000
1800–1850	700	35,000
1851–1900	200	10,000
total		125,000

Morocco, 1700–1890

	per annum	sub-total
1700–1810	2,000	220,000
1811–1840	3,000	90,000
1841–1875	2,000	70,000
1876–1895	5,000	100,000
total		480,000

Adjustment for Death Rates

	arrival total	death rate[1]	adjusted total
Libya	785,000	20%	942,000
Morocco	480,000	6%[2]	509,900
Algeria	100,000	10%[3]	110,000
Tunisia	125,000	15%[4]	144,000

1. All percentages based upon Gagliuffi in F10 with adjustments as indicated.
2. Based on the western Sudanic rate given by Gagliuffi but using it's lower range on the assumption that the Moroccan desert entrepôts were easier to reach than Murziq.
3. Assuming a majority coming via Morocco.
4. Assuming Libya as main source, but mixture of Sudan and Borno without Wadai-Benghazi.

than the western Sahara and the neighbouring Ghana, Mali, and Songhai empires. For the post-medieval period, I have tried to distinguish the estimates of Libyan exports (equated here with arrivals on the coast) from arrivals in the Fazzān, for reasons explained in the discussion of the Sahara below.

The figure of 1,000 for Libya from the end of the sixteenth through the end of the seventeenth century is not based directly upon the observations available, since none (except for the unrealistically high 1696 pilgrimage account, Table 2/B/10) add up to this amount. However these records (except for the 1686 French estimate, Table 2/B/9) also describe only part of the trade, mainly the slaves collected in tribute from the Fazzān and Borno. However, just as with the Egyptian *baqṭ*, such evidence indicates that slaves were a major regional commodity who must have moved through market as well as prestational channels.

In periods of political disorder, the tribute and markets must both have declined, leading to reduced totals such as that given by Lemaire for 1686, but in normal periods the total should have been a significantly higher than the tribute amounts. The absence of regular European representation before the 1680s may indicate a lower level of trade in general, including slaves, than in the subsequent century, although this provisional estimate will have to be reconsidered when indirect factors are taken into account.

The calculations for the Libyan trade from 1700 to 1800 are largely based on Renault's very valuable 1982 article.[13] I have raised the quantity slightly, from 1,500 per annum to 1,700 because: (a) I have somewhat more confidence in the shipping data (Table 2/B/13–16,21,28, 33–35) than Renault does, especially when comparing it with the three additional accounts from the late fifteenth and sixteenth and early seventeenth centuries (Table 2/B/1–3,6); (b) Dyer's additions to this set of data all indicate a slightly higher average.[14]

During the first half of the nineteenth century, the Libyan slave trade reached its historical peak. The cut-off date of 1856 is chosen because in 1857 the Ottoman government formally prohibited slave trading within its realms (which included Libya). The suppression was not initially anywhere near complete, but it had a very direct effect on Libyan exports[15] as opposed to imports into the Fazzān and the interior of Cyrenaica, as indicated below.

There are enough estimates of annual export figures for the 1800–56 period (see items marked with an asterisk in original tables) to do an actual calculation. The result (2,075 rounded up to 2,100) is hardly precise, since it includes reports for only 28 per cent of the years covered and comprises estimates of very varying reliability. There is some balance, however, between the likely exaggerations of some of the larger appraisals (particularly

Table 2/B/40, 1819 by Ritchie who was not actually on the coast) and the probable underestimates in the United States consular accounts and all later figures based only on exports reported to local customs officials. The results significantly reduce the previous estimates of Boahen, myself and Lovejoy because those accounts all tended to treat the highest export years as normal, thus producing classical capacity estimates.[16]

After 1856, we have less information on Libyan slave exports, since the Ottoman anti-slavery firman suppressed the official record-keeping far more effectively than it affected the substance of the trade. However, those estimates which are available suggest an average level of about 1,000 per annum. Again, this is lower than previous accounts but here the Saharan figures will provide a major counterweight.

Because none of the other three Maghribian countries ever served as a major conduit for slave exports, their imports of human chattel across the Sahara are far less precisely recorded than those of Libya. However, all of them imported more black Africans for domestic deployment than did Libya, being more densely populated, more agriculturally developed, and the centres of states which relied on black slave troops at various times. Thus, we are left with a major portion of the trans-Saharan slave trade which remains difficult to tabulate.

Existing records at least indicate that for the period from the fifteenth century onward, when Egyptian and Libyan slave imports can be estimated with some degree of reliability, Tunisia and Algeria did not play a very significant role in this commerce. Morocco, on the other hand, always maintained a major independent caravan link with the Sudan and even exercised some degree of political control over Timbuktu and its environs from the late sixteenth through the mid-eighteenth century. Beginning in the late seventeenth century, the Moroccan rulers also maintained a large black army, although its relationship to the slave trade is not clear[17] and will have to be taken up in the general discussion of African slave troops in the Islamic world.

The first quantitative statements which provide anything resembling a statistical account of the Moroccan slave trade occur near the end of the eighteenth century (Table 2/C/11,12). Even these estimates (as well as almost all that follow) are based on reports from north-western coastal cities of caravans entering the Saharan entrepôts of south-eastern Morocco, where (unlike Murzūq and Ghadāmis in the Fazzān) there was never a long-term European presence. Occasional reports of the 'Akbar' or major annual Timbuktu caravan suggest much lower figures (Table 2/C/12, 23,25,33); however, given the close ties between Morocco and the Western Sudan (much like Egypt and the Nilotic Sudan after 1820), it is difficult to calculate total slave imports from this source.[18]

In consideration of these flaws in the data, I am now inclined to scale down the reported global figures, assuming again that they are capacity estimates rather than serious attempts to calculate the average rate of an inevitably fluctuating trade. Moreover, if we are to assess a separate Algerian slave trade, it is important not to double-count the Moroccan imports. The figures for the end of the eighteenth century probably represent an average annual import of about 2,000. This most likely increased after 1810 as did most slave trades, but it is still difficult to accept Miège's figures. He assumes that the recorded estimates are too *low* and himself exaggerates the demand — to be examined below — for slaves in the desert regions themselves. Even the carefully considered projections by Graeberg probably overestimate the average, as the same observer's calculations did for Libya.

There is a consensus in the sources of a drop after 1840 but strong evidence from internal Moroccan market data (Table 2/C/30, 34) that imports rose in the last decades of the century. The explanation for this rise, which goes against the trends for the rest of the Islamic slave trade in both the Sahara and the Red Sea/Indian Ocean region, is probably the greatly increased supply of slaves generated by the wars against the French in the western Sudan, as described in the accompanying chapters of this volume by Martin Klein and Ann McDougall plus the absence of any abolitionist measures in Morocco. Despite the resulting great increase in estimates for the last period, the total figure for Morocco constitutes a slight decline from my 1979 calculations.

Algeria clearly has the smallest slave trade of any North African country. Here, there is only one capacity estimate (Table 2/D/7) to deflate but one needs to consider whether the reported imports through the traditional Algerian entrepôts of the Mzāb are independent of the trade figures for Morocco and the Fazzān. It is significant that despite the French colonial presence (or because of it according to some sources, Table 2/D/11) the trade estimates for Algeria increase towards the end of nineteenth century, as do those of Morocco. Again, Sudanic supply rather than Mediterranean demand may be the key factor here.[19] On whatever basis they are measured, the Algerian imports cannot ever have been very large. However, the present estimate (influenced by population data, see below) represents a slight increase over my previous count.

Tunisia is again a small importer, feeding mainly off the Ghadāmis market (see below) linked to the Sudan. We can assume that the estimates of Frank and Traill (Table 2/B/7,8) are slightly above the average while Macgill (Table 2/B/10) may be too low by a greater amount. In any case, the increasing trade of the early nineteenth century seems to have fallen off quite abruptly here with the prohibition by the local government in

1850. Possibly the deteriorating Tunisian economic conditions during this latter period[20] had as much to do with the decline of the local slave trade as the government's decrees.

After these figures for the exports and coastal deployment of slaves in the Maghrib it is necessary to give special attention to the slaves entering the Saharan portions of the region and remaining there. As already indicated, there is no significant direct evidence of slave-trading in the Saharan portions of the western Maghrib beyond the information used to estimate general imports. However, after the indirect demographic evidence is examined, some attempt will be made to add a percentage to the existing figures for slaves imported into southern Morocco, Algeria and Tunisia.

The Fazzān region of present-day Libya and the neighbouring desert portions of Tripolitania and Cyrenaica represent a special case. Not only is this zone the largest single avenue for slave traffic into the entire Maghrib (with some portion also going to Egypt) but it also, at least during the nineteenth century, absorbed a much larger (and more visible) proportion of these forced immigrants than did the more western desert regions. Furthermore, the valuable data from this region (as well as some of the Benghazi accounts of individual caravans) gives us some idea of the mortality rates of slaves taken across the Sahara, a critical factor in determining the overall demographic impact of the Islamic trade.

Renault's figure of 2,700 slaves entering Murzūq and Ghadāmis during the eighteenth century is not as carefully calculated as his Tripoli export statistics, since we have almost no data on trade in this area before 1800. It must also be remembered that (as Table 2/F/2 indicates) a certain portion of these slaves (particularly during periods of disorder – see Table 2/B/49) were sent to Egypt. A more regular portion went from the Fazzān to Tunisia, but mainly via Ghadāmis (Table 2/E/4–11,13). Moreover, there is no evidence of a particularly high demand for slaves within the southern regions of Libya at this point. Nonetheless, the slave populations of Murzūq and Ghadāmis, estimated by Hornemann and Dickson at about 8,000 (see Table 3) were still considerable and would require a significant slave trade to maintain their levels, given the accompanying reports of high resident death rates. Moreover, even in the urban sectors of coastal Libya there would be some demand for the replacement of domestic slaves. Thus Renault is justified in adding something over 1,000 to the export figures in establishing a total Libyan import level. I have added a lesser figure of 500 for the fifteenth and sixteenth centuries on the assumption (to be re-examined carefully when indirect evidence is taken more fully into account) that all aspects of the Libyan slave trade were at a lower level during this period.

We have very good records for Murzūq (and sometimes the alternative

TABLE 3

RECEIVING AREA: GENERAL SLAVE/BLACK POPULATION

Date	Quantity	Comments	Original Source	Reference
A. General Mediterranean				
1. general		consistently higher death rates for blacks from plagues	various chronicles	Dols, 1977, pp. 178–85f.
B. Egypt				
1. general		consistently higher death rates for blacks from various epidemics	various chronicles	Dols, 1977, pp. 178–85f.
2. 1400s		slave trade manual says Abysinnians do not live long outside country	Abū Sati, 1407–96 Egyptian author	Mueller, 1980, p. 135
5. 1701–1879		'astonishingly low' birth rate among Cairo black female slaves	court probate records	Walz, 1985, pp. 149–52
6. 1798	12,000	Egyptian black population: includes some non-slave-descended Nubians	Jomard, French scholar, traveller	Jomard, 1829, pp. 363ff.
7. 1821	14,000	slave plague deaths 'within a few years'; total deaths are 70,000	Scholz, German traveller	Scholz, 1922, p. 48
8. 1822	40,000	Black slaves throughout Egypt	Gailliaud, French traveller	Gailliaud, 1826, III, p. 117
9. 1830	18,000	Blacks throughout Egypt	Cadalvene, French traveller	Cadalvene, 1836, p. 104
10. 1834		Alexandria plague death rate exceptionally high for 'Negroes and Berbers'	various French local physicians	Sticker, 1908, pp. 311–12
11. 1834	4,000	'Negroes and Berbers' in total Alexandria population of 42,000	various French local physicians	Sticker, 1908, p. 312
12. 1840	14,000	slaves in Cairo	Bowring, British official study	Bowring, 1840, p. 10

13.	1840	24,000	Blacks throughout Egypt	Clot Bey, French physician, Egypt	Clot Bey, 1840, I, p.168
14.	c.1840	25,000	Blacks in Egypt (total population 3 mil.) based on house count estimate	Census by Muhammad 'Ali	Marcel, 1877, p.103
15.	1840	22,000	estimate of total slave population of Egypt	Campbell, British diplomat	Fredriksen, 1977, p.52
16.	1850–55	11,500	Blacks in Cairo; aftermath of high cholera deaths among blacks	Colucci, Italian Egyptian official	Colucci, 1862, pp.604–6
18.	1868	16,442	free black population of Egypt	official census	Walz, 1985, p.152
19.	1873	40,000	'Nubians and Soudanis (mostly slaves)' in total Egyptian pop. of 5.5 mil.	estimates from official census	McCoan, 1877, p.23
20.	1877–8	23,000	slaves manumitted via official procedures	records of Khedevial manumission offices	PP 1883, LXXXIII, PP 1889, LXXXVII
C. Algeria					
3.	c.1835	1,800	slaves in Algiers, 2/3 are women	Baude, French officer	Baude, 1838, p.927
4.	1838	3,382	black population, Algiers; various occupational niches, low reproduction rate	French government census	Lespes, 1930, pp.182, 513,
5.	1839–40	400	Negro 'corporation' in Algiers; membership 390–408 individuals	Baude, French official	Baude, 1841, p.328
6.	1843	2,872	black pop., areas under Fr. administration (1,595 free, 1,277 slaves)	French census	Corelle, 1850, p.109
7.	1844	8,000	Black slaves throughout Algeria	Projection from limited military census	Carette and Roget, 1856, pp.158–9
8.	1844	12,000	4,000 black slaves; 8,000 blacks	military census plus other documents	Emerit, 1949, pp.30–1
9.	1847	1,380	black population of Algiers (total 24,996)	French census	Corelle, 1850, p.41
10.	1848	18,329	slave population of Algeria	abolition indeminity commission	Julien, 1964, p.348

TABLE 3 (continued)

C. Algeria				
11.	1848	20,000	total black pop. of Algeria	French official estimates	Corelle, 1850, p.109
12.	1882	1,228	327 slaves, 901 free blacks in Mzāb at French conquest; total Mzāb pop. = 30,000	Robin, 1884 book	Briggs, 1958, p.74
13.	c. 1900		Algerian Black African cults; numerous w. ref. to specific Sudanic areas	Andrews, French traveller	Andrews, 1903
14.	1940s	125,000	Blacks in southern region of Algeria (possibly not all slave-descended)	Capot-Rey, French geographer	Capot-Rey, 1953, pp.163–75
D. Libya				
1.	1631–73		black servants in many urban homes, frequent manumission	Girard, French resident surgeon	Girard, ms., 72–3
2.	1891	6,000	black slaves throughout Libya	British consul, Benghazi	PP 1893/94, LXXXV, p.245
E. Tunisia				
2.	1700s		Sidi Sa'ad, black marabout, becomes object of saint cult	al-Wazīr al-Sarrāj, fl. 1724–28	Cherif, 1984, pp.585–6
4.	1800		pagan cults of local blacks denounced to Bey as threatening Islam	letter of Aḥmad Baba al-Timbuktui	Limam, 1981, pp.351–4
5.	early 1800s		high mortality in early childhood for blacks; c. 200 manumissions p.a.	Frank, French resident physician	Frank, 1850, pp.115–19
F. Sahara				
4.	1883	2,000	Slaves at main Sanūsi centre, Cyrenaica, Libya	Duveyrier, French traveller	Duveyrier, 1884, pp.21–2

entrepôt of Ghăt) slave imports up through the 1860s. Until the late l850s
the level of this trade corresponds roughly to Libyan exports, with the
residual slaves who remained in the country corresponding to the situation
in the eighteenth century. The continuation of this trade at such a high
rate after exports from Libya had dropped can be accounted for by the
increased demands in Egypt during the late l850s but particularly the
1860s (see Table 1 and discussion above). After the late 1870s, when
Egyptian demand also fell, the Fazzăn slave trade seems to have gone
into an irreversible decline.

However, during this same period the Sanūsī order had established a
set of lodges in southern Cyrenaica, providing not only a basis of support
for the newly developed (and until then very hazardous) Wadai-Benghazi
trade route,[21] but also a terminal market for slaves coming along this
route. It is clear from accounts of Central African slave exports (Table
2/F/40,44) that the slave trade from this area remained high in the last
quarter of the nineteenth century as well as the early twentieth century.
After the decline of the Egyptian market for black labour the 2,000 or so
slaves coming through Wadai each year must have stayed in eastern Libya
as part of the growing Sanūsī oasis population. These slaves have been
added to the data on Tripoli and Benghazi exports in estimating the total
Libyan import figures at the end of Table 2.

Finally, the Saharan trade reports of the nineteenth century give some
indications of slave mortality in the desert caravans. The various accounts
by Gagliuffi in the 1840s (Table 2/F/10,20, 22,23) indicate very high
death rates on the Borno-Murzūq route although much smaller ones on
caravans coming from the Niger Bend. Possibly the lower unit value of
slaves acquired in the wars of the central Sudan and raids into the relatively
populated but vulnerable equatorial regions account for this brutal treatment of slaves. In any case, it (and the equally high figures for the
Wadai-Benghazi route in Table 2/B/75,76) suggest that estimates of the
slaves who actually arrived in northern Africa must be supplemented by
varying, sometimes quite large, factors, as indicated in the very tentative
adjusted figures at the end of the table.

I have deliberately avoided drawing up grand totals for either the
Egyptian-Sudan or the Maghrib-Sahara slave trades at the end of Tables 1
and 2. The figures for partial periods are really the significant portion
of the present findings and will later have to be combined with indirect
evidence to provide an estimate for longer time periods (in any case, the
time periods for the various regions counted here do not match). In comparison with my 1979 publication, the figures for the nineteenth century
here are somewhat reduced and those for the eighteenth raised. This will
probably result in a lowering of the totals for the Mediterranean Islamic

slave trade, since the estimates for the pre-eighteenth century periods are constructed from projections based upon the 1800s, the period with the highest directly calculated rate. As this base is reduced, so will be the projections. However, much of this procedure also depends upon the examination of indirect evidence from the slave-receiving areas.

INDIRECT EVIDENCE: RECEIVING AREAS

Because direct evidence on the Islamic slave trade is insufficient to estab-lish reliable calculations, it must be used together with documentation of African slaves in the countries where they were eventually settled. This indirect evidence is necessary not only to check upon the relatively precise eighteenth and nineteenth century figures presented in Tables 1 and 2 but also to provide indicators for making projections about the scale of the slave trade in periods for which there is insufficient quantitative data to make direct calculations.[22]

General and Urban Populations

In discussing the various conditions and occupations of black slaves and their descendants in Islamic Mediterranean countries, the emphasis here will be on quantities of demand rather than such social issues as upward mobility and the role of eunuchs. It is assumed that the majority of slaves entered urban households where they played various domestic roles and also moved out into related artisanal and extra-mural service occupations. Evidence on these factors is all included in the general demographic material of Table 3. The only occupations to which specific attention has been given are those of agriculture and mining (see Table 4) and military/ political service (Table 5).

   None of the observations contained in Table 3 constitutes reliable counts of even the general population of the areas in question, let alone their slave and components. We can get some idea of the range of blacks and their ratio to other groups from the various eighteenth and nineteenth-century Egyptian demographic estimates (Table 3/B/6,8,9,11−16,18−20) as well as French figures for Algeria (Table 3/C/3−12,14) and other statements on Libya, Tunisia and the Sahara. The bases upon which these tabulations were made are at best intelligent projections (for example, the house count in Table 2/B/14) and usually do not even pretend to cover either the entire territory in question or the combined population of enslaved and manumitted blacks. Given the number of slaves reported leaving Egypt and especially Libya for the eastern Mediterranean, it would be useful to have more information on their presence in such areas as Istanbul, but this seems difficult to obtain. The ratios of slaves to general urban populations given for Egypt and Algeria (about 4 to 5 per cent) might be used for projections where no specific count of slaves exist, but no such effort is made here.

What we can conclude is that blacks did form a significant proportion of urban society throughout Egypt and North Africa, numbering in the region of tens of thousands for each separate territory. For the Maghrib, this impression is reinforced by the prominence of African religious cults in Algeria and Tunisia (Table 3/C/13,14;E/2,4).

Equally relevant for calculating the slave trade is the consistent evidence that such black populations failed to reproduce themselves. High African susceptibility to Mediterranean diseases is reported from medieval times onward (Table 3/A/1) and through all the northern African regions (Table 3/B/1,3,7,10,16; E/5). Walz's analysis of court records (Table 3/B/5) adds hard evidence to the general impression (Table 3/D/4) that black women also had few children after being brought north. Given the fact that the majority of such slaves were women, and that such children as they had could, in cases where the father was free, be absorbed into general society, it is obvious that any black slave population in the Mediterranean would require a considerable rate of immigration to keep it up.[23]

It is impossible to translate any of this very broad demographic information into a mathematical equation, but it is obvious that the maintenance of a slave population within the range indicated here would have required a slave trade on the scale suggested for the eighteenth and nineteenth centuries in the previous section.

Rural Labour

It is a fixed convention, in contrasting Islamic with European New World slavery, to point out that the former system lacked intensive labour demands comparable to the Atlantic plantation economy. Broadly speaking this is true, and by far the most common occupations of black slaves in the Muslim world were the household and other urban roles cited in Table 3. However, in given times and places agricultural and other non-urban enterprises drew heavily upon African slaves. The most important examples of such servile labour demand were found in the Persian Gulf and Red Sea where slaves played a major role in date and coffee planting as well as pearl fishing; however, these workers came almost entirely from East African sources and thus did not influence the scale of the Mediterranean slave trade. The Mediterranean Islamic rural regions using slave labour are more restricted than those of the Indian Ocean but in Egypt (including for present purposes the extreme northern Sudan), the Maghrib and the Sahara, we do find a number of significant sectors.

TABLE 4
RECEIVING AREA: SLAVES IN AGRICULTURE AND MINING

Date	Quantity	Comments	Original Source	Reference
A. Egypt				
1. 889/90		slaves in gold mines, Wadi Allaqi, south of Aswān	Ya'qūbī, d. 897	Yacoubi, 1937, p.190
2. 940s–950s		'numerous black slaves' at Shabūr in Delta	ibn Hawqal, Arab traveller, geographer	ibn Hauqal, 1964, p.138
4. 1830s		despite low prices, use of slave cultivators proves too costly vs. peasants	Bowring, British scholar, emissary	PP 1840, XXI, pp.88–9
5. 1,750		slaves sold at Tanta, mainly bought by peasants for farm labour	Reade, British consular agent	Mowafi, 1981, p.24
B. Algeria				
1. 750+		West African, presumedly slave, cultivators in Jabal Nafūsa	Ibadite chronicle, 12th century	Lewicki, 1985, pp.94–6
2. 1862		black slaves, freedmen of Mzāb do irrigation work; much disease	Colombien, French traveller	Colombien, 1862, p.192
C. Tunisia				
1. 825	1,000	black oasis labourers recruited by rebel against Aghlabids	b.'Idhari	Dyer, 1979, p.13
D. Sahara				
1. c.1270		black slaves employed in Taghaza salt mines under Masūfa Berbers	al-Janahānī, merchant; al-Qazwīnī, 1275	Hopkins/Levtzion, 1981, p.178
2. 1352		black slaves employed in Taghaza salt mines under Masūfa Berbers	b. Baṭṭūṭa, Arab traveller	Hopkins/Levtzion, p.282
3. 1356		slaves of both sexes work copper mines, Takādda	b. Baṭṭūṭa, Arab traveller	Cuoq, 1975, p.318

TABLE 5

RECEIVING AREA: BLACK SERVILE MILITARY/POLITICAL DEPLOYMENT

	Date	Quantity	Comments	Original Source	Reference
Egypt					
9.	990–1160		replacement rate, Fatimid army: 10% active troops plus 6 year training period	various	Hamblin, 1985, pp. 66–82
11.	1046	40,000	recalculation of Naṣiri-Khusrow observations	Naṣiri-Khusrow	Hamblin, 1985, pp. 305–8
19.	1177	18,000	Saladin Qaraghulam in battle against Crusaders	William, Archbishop and observer	William, 1943, p. 431
20.	1881	1,153	Saladin Qaraghulam after troop reductions	Maqrizi (based on diary of witness)	Gibb, 1951, p. 310
21.	1497–98	500	Egyptian Mamluks create black arquebus corps, quickly suppress it	various chronicles	Ayalon, 1956, pp. 68–71

In addition to the Egyptian section, there are entries for Iraq (9), Tunisia-Libya (12), Morocco (26), Spain (3) and Algeria (1).

Egypt generally represents the antithesis of an agricultural system likely to make extensive use of slaves. Instead of the classic land abundance and labour scarcity, this is a country whose native population has always been crowded into a narrow strip of irrigated soil and sufficiently controlled by political authorities so that little income was left over to purchase outside workers (Table 4/A/4). There is very little evidence of slavery in pre-Islamic Egyptian agriculture[24] or for most of the Islamic period. During medieval times, the only reports of extensive rural labour come from the gold mines in northern Nubia and one agricultural region of the Delta (Table 4/A/1,2) but these practices do not seem to have continued on the same scale after the tenth century AD. The use of slave cultivators by Arab tribes in upper Egypt (Table 4/A/2) is probably more continuous but not statically very significant unless we assimilate it to the Saharan regions further west which, however, deserve a separate discussion.

In the middle of the nineteenth century, Egypt briefly experienced conditions which encouraged fairly extensive agricultural slavery. On the one hand, commercialized sugar and especially cotton cultivation provided incentives for major investments in rural production. At the same time the indigenous population, struck by various epidemics cited in Table 2/B, had not yet undergone that massive growth which would characterize Egypt from the latter nineteenth century onwards. Thus, both elites (Table 4/A/4) and even peasants (Table 4/A/5) found it possible and profitable to purchase large numbers of African slaves to work their lands. As noted some time ago by Gabriel Baer (1969, 186–7), indigenous demographic change in the last quarter of the century, which reduced the value of rural slave labour, played an important part in Egyptian accession to western abolitionist pressures.

In the Maghrib, the great period and place of servile employment in agriculture appears to have been ninth century Tunisia under the Aghlabids, but the source of labour here was apparently Sicily rather than the Sudan.[25] After that period (and for blacks, even during it; see Table 4/C/1), Maghribi rural servile populations appear to be heavily concentrated in the south, which is to say the Sahara, where it is difficult to distinguish between descendants of Sudani slaves and a presumably indigenous black population referred to as ḥarāṭīn. In any case, the data in Table 4/C,D (as well as the indications of black Saharan populations in Table 2) indicate a heavy use of slave labour in North African oasis cultivation. However, except for the rapid growth of Sanūsī settlements in the Cyrenaica desert in the late nineteenth century (Table 3/F/4), the total numbers of population involved in this sector would account for only a small, if steady, proportion of the ongoing desert slave trade. Similarly, the Saharan copper-mining economies reported in the Sahara in the thirteenth and fourteenth centuries (Table 4/D/1–3) may have demanded significant slave imports but the salt mines of later periods were generally located farther to the south and also were not very intensively worked,[26] so that they cannot really be calculated into trans-Saharan slave trade estimates. Likewise, the evidence for a major sugar industry in Morocco during the sixteenth century seems too imprecise to indicate a large-scale demand for slaves.[27]

BLACK MILITARY AND PALACE SLAVES

For the most part, the data on general population and rural labour concentrate on the same modern era for which we have the greatest direct slave-trade evidence. The indirect evidence thus confirms what we can already surmise and also provides some indication of the correlations between given levels of supply and forms of demand. Information on the use of black slaves in Islamic military forces, however, is both more plentiful than other forms of indirect evidence and distributed broadly over all the Islamic centuries. Therefore, it tells us about Muslim demand for black slaves during periods in which there are virtually no quantitative observations of the trade itself.

The precise quantification of the military evidence remains problematic. Even those numbers which are given must usually be treated as more metaphorical − equivalents of 'very many' − rather than the result of real counts. This is particularly true of battle descriptions where even a self-proclaimed 'careful count' by a scholarly cleric such as William of Tyre (Table 5/B/19) can be far out of line with other observations of the same forces (Table 5/B/20,21). However, tabulations of troops displayed at parades are more reliable and can also be adjusted (Table 5/B/11) so as to provide reasonable estimates.[28]

Even if we can take the numbers of troops seriously, the relationship of a given military formation to the slave trade remains difficult to calculate. Hamblin (Table 5/B/9) has provided some idea of a replacement rate, assuming of course that the force is maintained at the level described in the available observations over a considerable period of time. However, even in cases where a military group is given a name meaning 'black slaves' (qaraghulam, 'abīd) we cannot be sure that the troops are really black or, if so, the recruitment base is an ongoing slave trade.[29]

For the present, no attempt has been made to calculate rigorously from this data either the size of Muslim black armies and palace corps or the level of slave-trade demand that each size would generate. It is, however, reasonable to assume that there were extended periods during which several thousands of slaves per annum (and sometimes tens of thousands in a few years) would have been required to meet this need. Military demand will thus provide (as did more limited data in my 1979 essay) a major component of the coefficients for slave-trade demand in various historical periods.

CONCLUSIONS

This essay is tentative in two senses. First of all, because it represents only a stage in bringing together data for a comprehensive account of the Islamic African slave trade; second, because it indicates how limited a basis we can ever attain for determining the scale of this traffic. The publication of such an intermediate set of findings and their accompanying doubts is intended both to provide students with the considerable new material which has come to light on this subject and also to invite them to join in the effort to produce as definitive an account as possible of this major confrontation between Africa and the outside world.

NOTES

1. On the latter, see William Gervase Clarence-Smith (ed.), *The Economics of the Indian Ocean Slave Trade in the Nineteenth Century*, London: Frank Cass, 1989, 21–44, also published as a special number of *Slavery and Abolition*, Vol. 9 (1988); and especially my own contribution to this collection, 'The 19th Century Islamic Slave Trade from East Africa (Swahili and Red Sea Coasts): A Tentative Census'.

2. For a discussion of earlier estimates see Ralph A. Austen, 'The Trans-Saharan Slave Trade: A Tentative Census', in H. Gemery and J. Hogendorn, *The Uncommon Market: Essays in the Economic History of the Atlantic Slave Trade*, New York: Academic, 1979, 23–76; there is a general criticism of this effort in David Henige, 'Measuring the Unmeasurable: the Atlantic Slave Trace, West African Population and the Pyrronic Critic', *Journal of African History* [hereafter *JAH*], 27,2 (1986), 269–93; smaller disputes with my findings have been produced by Renault, 1982 and Lovejoy, 1984; both argue that I underestimated the Libyan data, a point which I accept in Renault's case (I have incorporated the data into the present revision) but do not, for reasons, to be discussed below, for Lovejoy.

3. (Editor's note: because of limitations of length, it was necessary to abbreviate both tables and bibliography to those entries specifically cited in the text. The numbers have been kept to indicate the original length. The author plans to publish the tables in their entirety until which time further details may be had by writing to R. Austen at the Committee on African and African-American Studies, University of Chicago.)

4. I am beholden for this, as for many other insights into the study of the slave trade, to Philip Curtin.

5. On Marrakesh market data, see the accompanying essay in this volume by Daniel Schroeter, 185–213.

6. The Institut Français d'Archéologie Orientale du Caire has to be thanked for its publication of various studies of Egyptian economic history as well as its series of carefully edited and indexed French-language publications of pre-1700 travel accounts which would otherwise be almost impossible to find and, in any case, very difficult to use for a project of this kind.

7. Renault reports (personal communication) that the archives of European consular representatives in pre-nineteenth-century Egypt yield no data which add significantly to this evidence.

8. Walz, 1978, 202–6.

9. Jay Spaulding, 'Slavery, Land Tenure and Social Class in the Northern Turkish Sudan,' *International Journal of African Historical Studies* [hereafter *IJAHS*] 15,1 (1982), 1–20.

10. This point is made by perhaps the most energetic and careful of the nineteenth-century observers of the trade who nevertheless produces one of the highest figures (Bowring in Table 1/A/50).

11. On Sudan chronology, Gray (1963) and Prunier (1988); on Egyptian agriculture as well as the role of developments in autonomous African sectors such as Dār Fūr, Wadai, etc., see later sections of this paper.

12. Michael Brett, 'Ifriqiya as a Market for Saharan Trade from the tenth of the twelfth century A.D.', *JAH*, 10,3 (1969), 347–64.

13. Dyer, 1987, adds additional data to this record (Table 2/B/18,19,31) but his dissertation takes no cognizance of Renault's work.

14. I come out with a slightly *lower* number than both Dyer and Renault for the critical Caullet observations (Table 2/B/18,19) by running them over the longer period of available calendar years; the restriction to winter 'seasons' in the earlier accounts makes sense for studying caravan operations but has no value in calculating statistical averages.

15. Ehud Toledano, *The Ottoman Slave Trade and its Suppression, 1840–1890*, Princeton: Princeton University, 1982, 192–202.

16. Austen, 'Trans-Saharan Slave Trade'; Adu Boahen, *Britain, the Sahara, and the Western Sudan*, 1788–1861, Oxford: Clarendon, 1964; Lovejoy, 1984. My estimates in this earlier essay were largely based on Boahen; Lovejoy's work is an upward revision of my own results. An excellent model of calculations based upon the inevitable fluctuations downward from peak trade years is Renault's article on eighteenth-century Libya.

17. Allen E. Meyers, 'Slave Soldiers and State Politics in Early 'Alawi Morocco, 1655–1727', *IJAHS*, 16,1 (1983), 39–48; this article argues that the connection was negligible, but see Table 2/C5–8.

18. This point is more fully discussed in the accompanying chapter by Daniel Schroeter as are the statistical observations in Fig. 3, 199, attributed to Schroeter.

19. For a 'supply-side' analysis of the entire African (as well as medieval European) slave trade, see the forthcoming study by Stefano Fenoaltea, 'Europe in the African Mirror: the Slave Trade and the Rise of Feudalism'.

20. Lucette Valensi, *Tunisian Peasants in the Eighteenth and Nineteenth Centuries*, Princeton: Princeton University, 1977, 183ff.

21. Dennis D. Cordell, 'Eastern Libya, Wadai and the Sanusiya: a tariqa and a Trade Route', *JAH*, 18,3 (1977), 28–9.

22. For examfples of such projections, see Austen, 1979. No such effort has yet been made for the revised data presented here.

23. In my 1979 paper I calculated this at 15 per cent on the assumption that the average service life (time between arrival and death or manumission) was seven years. I could use guidance on probable rates of manumission (I assumed an average of ten years after enslavement) and the substitutability of non-slave (especially freedmen) for slaves in various urban occupations.

24. Liza Beizunstra-Malowist, 'Le travail servile dans l'agriculture de l'Egypte romaine', *V Congrès International d'Histoire Economique*, Leningrad, 1970.

25. Mohamed Talbi, 'Droit et économie en Ifriqiya au IIᵉ/IXᵉ siècle', in A. Udovitch (ed.), *The Islamic Middle East, 700–1900: Studies in Economic and Social History*, Princeton: Darwin Press, 1981, 215f.

26. Ann McDougall, 'The Sahara Reconsidered: Pastoralism, Politics and Salt in the Eighth through the Twelfth Centuries', *African Economic History*, 12 (1983), 263–86.

244   THE HUMAN COMMODITY

27. Paul Berthier, *Les anciens sucreries du Maroc et leurs réseaux hydrologiques*, Rabat: Ministère d'Education Nationale, 1966.
28. *Pace* Henige, 1986, 302, 304–5, who rejects all military statistics as 'of no value whatever' apparently because 'War is, after all, the ultimate polemic'.
29. Gibb, 1951, 309 argues that in latter twelfth-century Egyptian military parlance, *Qaraghulam* had taken on a technical meaning (lower order mamluk cavalry) rather than a literal one (servile blacks); he is probably right not only because William of Tyre describes the *Qaraghulam* as *gregoriorum* (common gentlemen) rather than as racially distinct, but also because in earlier Egyptian military systems using many black Africans the latter almost always served in the infantry. On the connection between the seventeenth and nineteenth century Moroccan *'Abīd al-Buhārī* and the slave trade, see Meyers, n. 15 above; as evidence in Table 5/D/24,26 suggests, by the nineteenth century, the *'abīd* had certainly become a self-reproducing Makhzan (state-allied) tribe rather than the product of continuing slave imports.

BIBLIOGRAPHY

Abbreviations: *IFAOC*   Institut Français d'Archéologie Orientale du Caire (numbered items are volumes in the 'Collection des voyageurs occidentaux en Égypte')
IJMES   International Journal of Middle East Studies
JAH   Journal of African History
MAE   Ministère des Affaires Étrangères (France), archival files
PP   Parliamentary Papers (Great Britain)
PUF   Presse Universitaire de France
SRGE   Société Royale de Géographie d'Égypte
BSG   *Bulletin de la Société Géographique*

Abitbol, Michel. *Tombouctou et les Arma*. Paris: Maisonneuve, 1979.
Andrews, J. B. *Les fontaines de Génies (Seba Aiun): croyances soudanaises à Alger*. Algiers: A. Jourdan.
Ashtor, Eliyahu. 'The Venetian Supremacy in Levantine Trade: Monopoly or Pre-Colonialism', *Journal of European Economic History*, 3, (1974), 5–53.
Ayalon, David. *Gunpowder and Firearms in the Mamluk Kingdom*. London: Vallentine, Mitchell, 1956.
Bachrach, Jere L. 'The Use of Black Troops in Medieval Egypt and Iraq'. Unpublished paper, American Historical Association, 1975.
Bachrach, Jere L. 'African Military Slaves in the Medieval Middle East: the Cases of Iraq (869–955) and Egypt (868–1171)', *IJMES*, 13, (1975), 471–95.
Baer, Gabriel. *Studies in the Social History of Modern Egypt*. Chicago: University of Chicago, 1969.
Baldwin, George. 'Memorial Relating to the Trade in Slaves in Egypt,' *European Magazine and London Review*, 17, (1790), 127–9.
Baude, Baron. *L'Algérie*. Paris: Arthur Bertrand, 1841.
Ben Joshua, Joseph. *Divre ha-yamin le-malkhe Tsarefat*. Jerusalem, 1967.
Bianquis, Thierry. 'La prise de pouvoir par les Fatimides en Égypte (357–363/968–974)', *Annales Islamologiques*, XI (1972), 49–108.
Bowring, J. *Report on Egypt and Candia*. London: printed by W. Clowes for Her Majesty's Stationery Office, 1840.
Browne, W. G. *Travels in Africa, Egypt, and Syria*. London: printed for T. Cadell Jr. and W. Davies, etc., 1799.
Buckingham, James Silk. *Autobiography*. London: Longman *et al.*, 1855.
Burckhardt, John Lewis. *Travels in Nubia*. London: published by the Association for promoting the discovery of the interior parts of Africa, 2nd edn., J. Murray, 1822.

Ca da Mosto, Alvise. *Le Navigazioni Atlantiche*. (Tullia Gasparrini Leporace, ed.), Rome: Instituto poligrafico dello Stato, Libreria dello Stato, 1966.

Cadalvene, Edmond de and J. de Breuvery. *L'Égypte et la Turquie de 1829 à 1836*. Paris: A. Bertrand, 1836.

Caille, Jacques. *La Mission du Capitaine Burel au Maroc en 1808*. Paris-Rabat: Arts et Métiers graphiques, 1953.

Cailliaud, Frederic. *Voyage à Meroe ... 1819 ... 1822*. Paris: Par autorisation du Roi, à l'Imprimerie Royale, 1826.

Capot-Rey, Robert. *Le Sahara français*. Paris: Presses universitaires de France, 1953.

Cattaui, René. *Le Règne de Mohammed Aly d'après les archives russes en Égypte*. Cairo: *SRGE*, 1935.

Cherif, M.-H. 'Hommes de religion et pouvoir dans la Tunisie de l'époque moderne', *Annales ESC*, 35 (1985), 580–97.

Clot-Bey, Alphonse B. *Aperçu général sur l'Égypte*. Paris: Fortin, Masson, 1840.

Colombiem, V. 'Voyage dans le Sahara algérien', *Tour du Monde*, VIII, 1862.

Colucci, M. J. 'Quelques notes sur le cholera', *Mémoires ou travaux originaux présentes et lus à l'Institut Égyptien*, 1 (1862), 601–7.

Corelle, M. 'Algérie', in *Univers Pittoresques: l'Afrique*. Paris: Firmin Didot, 1850.

Cuoq, Joseph M. *Recueil des sources arabes concernant l'Afrique Occidentale du VIIIe au XVIe siècle*. Paris: Centre National des Recherches Scientifiques, 1975.

Dickson, C. H. 'Account of Ghadamis', *Journal of the Royal Geographical Society*, 30 (1860), 255–60.

Dols, Michael. *The Black Death in the Middle East*. Princeton: Princeton University, 1977.

Douin, Georges. *L'Égypte de 1828 à 1830*. Rome: *SRGE*, 1935.

Douin, Georges and E. C. Fawtier-Jones. *L'Angleterre et l'Égypte: la politique mamelouke (1801–1803)*. Cairo: IFAOC, 1929.

Douls, Camille. 'À travers le Sahara occidental et le Sud Marocain', *BSG*, 7e série, 9,3, (1888), 437–79.

Driault, Edouard. *La formation de l'empire de Mohamed Ali (1814–1823)*. Cairo: *SRGE*, 1927.

Duveyrier, Henri. *La Confrèrie musulmane de Sidi Mohammed Ben Ali Es Senousi*. Paris: Société de Géographie, 1884.

Dyer, Mark. *Central Saharan Slave Trade in the Early Islamic Centuries*. Boston: Boston University African Studies Center, 1979.

Dyer, Mark. 'The Foreign Trade of Western Libya, 1750–1830'. Ph.D. diss., Boston University, 1987.

El-Hachaichi, Mohammed ben Otsmane. *Voyage au pays des Senoussia*. V. Serres (trans.), Lasram. Paris: Augustin Callamel, 1912.

Fabri, Brother Felix. *Evagitorium*. *IFAOC*, 14 (1975), R. P. Jacques Masson (trans.).

Farhi, David. 'Nizam-i Cedid- Military Reform in Egypt under Mehmed 'Ali', *Asian and African Studies*, 8 (1973), 151–83.

Feraud, Laurent Charles, *Annales tripolitaines*. Tunis: Librairie Tournie.

Fitūrī, Aḥmad Saʿīd. 'Tripolitania, Cyrenaica and Bilad-as-Sudan: Trade Relations during the Second Half of the Nineteenth Century'. Ph.D. diss., University of Michigan, 1982.

FO 84. Great Britain, Public Records Office, Foreign Office files, Slave Trade series.

Foster, William (ed.). *The Red Sea and Adjacent Countries at the Close of the Seventeenth Century*. London: Hakluyt Society, 1949.

Frank, Louis. 'Tunis', L'*Univers pittoresque: l'Afrique*. Paris: Firmin Didot, 1850.

Frank, Louis. *La Tunisie*. Paris: Firmin-Didot frères, 1856.

Frank, Louis. 'Mémoire sur le commerce des Nègres au Caire ...' appendix to Denon, Vicanto *Voyage dans le Busse et le Haut Égypte*. London, 1807.

Fredriksen, Broge. 'Slavery and it Abolition in Egypt'. Doctoral diss., University of Bergen (Norway), 1977.

Fresnel, Fulgence. 'Chronologie de rois de Borno de 1512 à 1677 par un français esclave à Tripoli ... *BSG*, 3e série (1849), 252–9.

246   THE HUMAN COMMODITY

Galuzzi, Riguccio. *Istoria de Granducato di Toscana setto il governo della casa Medici.* Florence: Gaetano Cambiagi, 1781.
Garcin, Jean Claude. *Un centre musulman de la Haute-Égypte médiévale: Qus.* Cairo: *IFAOC*, 1976.
Gibb, Hamilton A. R. 'The Armies of Saladin', *Cahiers d'Histoire Égyptienne*, II, 4 (1951), 304–20.
Girard, P. S. 'Mémoire sur l'agriculture, l'industrie et le commerce de l'Égypte', *Déscription de l'Égypte*, Vol. 17 (1824), Paris, 1–420.
Gonzales, Fr. Antonius. Hierusalemsche Reyse ... *IFAOC*, 19 (1977), Charles Libois (trans.).
Graeberg de Hemsoe, Jacob. 'Prospetto del Commercio di Tripoli d'Africa ...', *Antologia*, Florence, 1827, 1828, 81, 79–99; 88, 1–29.
Gray, Richard. *A History of the Southern Sudan, 1839–1889.* London: OUP, 1961.
Hallett, Robin. *Records of the African Association.* London: T. Nelson, 1964.
Hamblin, William James. 'The Fatimid Army during the Early Crusades', Ph.D. diss., University of Michigan, 1985.
Harant, Christophe. Voyage ... [original Czech title not given]. *IFAOC*, 5, (1972), Anne Brejnik (trans.).
Hasan, Yusuf Fadl. *The Arabs in the Sudan.* Edinburgh: Edinburgh University Press, 1967.
Heyd, Uriel. *Ottoman Documents on Palestine.* Oxford: OUP, 1960.
Hopkins, J. F. P. and Nehemiah Levtzion. *Corpus of Early Islamic Sources for West African History.* Cambridge: CUP, 1981.
ibn Hauqal. *Configuration de la terre.* J. H. Kramers, G. Wiet (trans.). Beirut: Commission Internationale pour la Traduction des Chefs-d'Oeuvre, 1964.
Idris, Roger Hady. *La Berberie Orientale sous les Zirides.* 2 vols., Paris, Librairie d'Amerique, et d'Orient Adrien-Maisonneuve, 1962.
Jomard, E. 'Description de la ville et la citadelle du Kaire', *Description de l'Égypte.* Vol. 18, Part 2, 113–538, 1829.
Julien, Charles André. *Histoire de l'Algérie Contemporaine.* Paris: PUF, 1964.
Keichel, Samuel. 1972. *Die Reisen des ...* Ursuala Castel (trans.). Cairo: *IFAOC*, 6 (1972).
La Veronne, Chantal de (ed., trans.). *La Vie de Moulay Ismail ... d'après Joseph de Leon (1708–1728).* Paris: J. Geuthner, 1974.
Lalande, Jerome. *Mémoire sur l'intérieur de l'Afrique.* Paris: Imprimerie des Administrations Nationales, 1794.
Lapanouse, Joseph Mercure. 'Sur les caravanes venant du royaume de Sennaar', *Mémoires sur l'Égypte.* Paris: Vol. 4, 89–124, [1801] an XI.
LaRue, G.M. 'The Export Trade of DarFur, c. 1785 to 1875'. unpublished ms. n.d. [1984].
Legh, Thomas, *Narrative of a Journey in Egypt.* London: J. Murray, 1817.
Lemprière, William. 'A Tour from Gibraltar to ... Morocco', in çol. 15, 681–801 of John Pinkerton (ed.), *A General Collection of the Best and Most Interesting Voyages*, 1814.
Lenz, Oskar. *Timbuktu: Reise durch Marokko, die Sahara und den Sudan.* Leipzig: Brockhaus, 1884.
Lespes, René. *Alger.* Algiers: Bastide-Jourdon.
Lewicki, Tadeusz. *Étude ibāḍites Nord-Africaines.* Warsaw: Panstwowe Wydawnictwo Naukowe, 1985.
Lichtenstein, Hans Ludwig von. *Grosse Reisen und Begebenheiten ...* Ursula Castel (trans.). Cairo: *IFAOC*, 6. 1972.
Limam, Rashed. 'Some documents concerning slavery in Tunisia at the end of the 18th century', *Révue d'Histoire Maghrebine*, 23/24 (1972), 349–57.
Lovejoy, Paul. 'Commercial Sectors in the Economy of the Nineteenth-Century Central Sudan: the Trans-Saharan Trade and the Salt Trade', *African Economic History*, 13 (1984), 85–116.
Lucas, Paul. *Voyage fait en ... Haut et Basse Égypte*, etc. Paris, 1724.
Macgill, Thomas. *An Account of Tunis.* London: Longman *et al.*, 1811.
Madden, R. R. *Travels in Turkey, Egypt, Nubia and Palestine.* London: H. Colburn, 1829.
MAE, Correspondance Politique, Turquie: Consulats: Égypte.

MAE, Correspondance Consulaire, Tripoli de Barbarie.

MAE, Correspondance Politique, Turquie: Consulats: Tripoli de Barbarie.

MAE, Correspondance Politique, Turquie: Consulats: Tunis.

Maillet, Benoit de. *Description de l'Égypte* ... Paris: Genneau & Rollin, 1735.

Marcel, M. J. *L'Égypte depuis la conquête arabe jusqu'à la domination française*. Paris: Firmin-Didot, 1877.

McCoan, James Carlisle. *Egypt as it Is*. New York: Holt, 1877.

Meinardus, Otto F.A. 'The Christian Kingdom of Nubia', *Cahiers d'Histoire Égyptienne*, 10 (1966), 133–64.

Mengin, Felix. *Histoire de l'Égypte sous le gouvernment de Mohammed Aly*. Paris: A. Bertrand, 1823.

Miège, Jean Louis. *Le Maroc et l'Europe (1830–1894)*. 4 vols. Paris: PUF, 1961.

Minutoli, Heinrich. *Reise zum Tempel des Jupiter Ammon ... 1820 und 1821*. Berlin: Ruecher, 1824.

Monchicourt, Charles. *Relations inédites de Nyssen, Fillippi, et Calligaris*. Paris: Société d'éditions géographiques, maritimes et coloniales, 1929.

Mowafi, Reda. *Slavery, Slave Trade and Abolition Attempts in Egypt and the Sudan, 1820–1882*. Lund: Scandinavian University Books, 1981.

Mueller, Hans. *Die Kunst des Sklavenhandels nach arabischen, persischen und tuerkischen Ratgebern vom zehnten bis zum achtzenhten Jahrhundert*. Freiburg: Klaus Schwarz, 1980.

Nasir-i-Khusraw. *Sefer Nameh*. C. Schefer (trans.). Paris: E.Leroux, 1881.

Palerne, Jean. *Pérégrinations. IFAOC*, 2. 1971.

Panet, Leopold. 'Relation d'un voyage du Sénégal à Soueira (Mogador)'. *Révue Coloniale*, (1850), 31–190.

Petit la Croix. 'Suite des remarques de Tripoli de Barbarie', (1697), n.a. fr. 7488, Bibliothèque Nationale, Paris.

Peysonnel, Jean André. *Relation d'un voyage sur les côtes de Barbarie fait par ordre du roi en 1724 et 1725*. Paris: Librarie de Gide, 1838.

Pignon, Jean. *Un document inédit sur la Tunisie au XVII* siècle*. Paris: PUF, 1964.

Poiron, M. *Mémoire concernant l'état présent du Royaume de Tunis*. Paris: Institut des Hautes Études Marocaines, 1925.

PP 1788, Minutes of Evidence ... respecting the Transportation of the Natives of Africa, VI, 'Trade in the Interior Part'.

PP 1870, LXI, C141, Correspondance ... Slave Trade (B) East Coast of Africa.

PP 1883, LXXXIII, Further Correspondance ... Egypt (C. 3529).

PP 1889, LXXXVII, Further Correspondance ... Egypt (C. 5178).

Prunier, Gérard. 'La traite soudanaise (1820–1885): structures et périodisation'. In Serge Daget (ed.), *De la traite à l'esclavage*, Tome II XVIIIe-IXe siècles. 521–35. Nantes: Centre de Récherche sur l'Histoire du Monde Atlantique: colloque sur la traite des Noirs, 1988.

Quatremère, Etienne. *Histoire des sultans Mamlouks de l'Égypte*. Paris: The Oriental Translation Fund of Great Britain and Ireland, 1837–45.

Radzivill, Mikolaj Krzystof. *Ieroslymitana perigrinatio*. Antwerp: I Moreti, 1614.

Raymond, André. *Artisans et commercants au Caire au XVIIIe siècle*. Damascus: Institut Français de Damas, 1973.

Raymond, André and Gaston Wiet. *Les Marches du Caire*. Cairo: IFAOC, 1979.

Renault, François. 'La Traite des esclaves noirs en Libye au XVIIIe siècle', *JAH*, 23, 2 (1982), 163–82.

Renault, François. *La traite des Noirs au Proche-Orient médiéval, VIIe-XIVe siècles*. Paris: Geunther, 1989.

Richardson, James. *Travels in the Great Desert of the Sahara*. 2 vols. London: R. Bentley, 1848.

Rohlfs, Gerhard. *Reise durch Marokko*. Bremen: J. Kuhtmann, 1868a.

Rossi, Ettore. *Storia di Tripoli e della Tripolitania*. Rome: Instituto per l'oriente, 1968.

Rotter, Gernot. 'Die Stellung des negers in der Islamisch-Arabischen Gesellschaft bis zum XVIe Jahrhundert', doctoral diss., Bonn, 1967.

Sayous, Andre-Emile. *La commerce des Européens à Tunis depuis le XIIe jusqu'à la fin du XVIe siècle.* Paris: Société d'éditions géographiques, maritimes et coloniales, 1929.

Scholz, John Martin Augustus. *Travels in the Countries between Alexandria and Paraetonium, The Libyan Desert, Siwa, Egypt, Palestine and Syria in 1821.* London: Richard Phillips (*New Voyages and Travels*, No. 15, Vol. 8, 1823).

Schroeter, Daniel. 'Slave Markets and Slavery in Moroccan Urban Society', 185–213 in this volume.

Sicard, Claude. *Nouveaux mémoires des missions de la Compagnie de Jésus dans le Levant.* Paris: Nicholas le Clerc, 1717.

Sonnini de Mononcour, C. N. Sigisbert, VII (1799). *Voyage en Haut et Basse Égypte ...* Paris: F. Buisson.

St. Olon, [Pidou de]. *The Present State of the the Empire of Morocco. London, 1695.*

Sticker, Georg. Abhandlungen aus der Seuchenlehre ... Geschichte. Geissen: A. Toepelmann, 1908.

Stochove, Vincent. *Voyage ... IFAOC*, 15 (1975).

Talbi, Mohamed. *L'Emirat Aghlabide.* Paris: Librairie d'Amérique et d'Orient, 1966.

Thevenot, Jean. *Rélation de Voyage fait au Levant.* Paris: Ch. Augot, 1689.

USNA (United States National Archives), State Department Correspondence, Microfilm T40 (Tripoli).

Valensi, Lucette. 'Esclaves chrétiens et esclaves noirs à Tunis au XVIIIe siècle', *Annales ESC*, 22 (6) (1967), 1267–88.

Van Egmont, J. Aegidius and John Heyman. *Travels.* London: Davis and Reymers, 1759.

Venture de Paradis, 'Mémoire sur le Tunis', Raynal Papers, ms. fr. 6429, Bibliothèque Nationale, Paris.

Villamont, Seigneur de. *Voyage ... IFAOC*, 3, 1971.

Volney, Constantin Francois Chasseboeuf. *Travels through Syria and Egypt, 1783–1785.* London: G.G.J. and J. Robinson, 1788.

Walz, Terence. *Trade between Egypt and the Bilad As-Sudan, 1700–1820.* Cairo: IFAOC, 1978.

Walz, Terence. 1985, 'Black Slavery in Egypt during the Nineteenth Century as Refelcted in the Makhama Archives of Cairo', in Willis, II.

Wiet, Gaston (ed.), J.-B. Trecourt, *Mémoires sur l'Égypte année 1791.* Cairo: Société Royale de Géographie, 1942.

Wiet, Gaston. [*Mudhakhirat Niqula Turc*] *Nicholas Turc: Chronique d'Égypte, 1798–1804.* Cairo: IFAOC, 1950.

William, Archbishop of Tyre. *A History of Deeds Done Beyond the Sea.* E. A. Babcock, A. C. Krey (trans.). New York: Columbia University, 1943.

Willis, John Ralph (ed.), *Slaves and Slavery in Muslim Africa.* 2 vols. London: Frank Cass, 1985.

Yacoubi. *Les Pays* G. Wiet (trans.). Cairo: IFAOC, 1937.

2

The Volume of the Atlantic Slave Trade: A Synthesis

Paul E. Lovejoy

SINCE its publication in 1969, Philip D. Curtin's *The Atlantic Slave Trade: A Census* has been the subject of a lively debate. On the basis of published material, Curtin estimated that 9,566,100 slaves were imported into the Americas and other parts of the Atlantic basin from 1451 to 1870.[2] Curtin intended his study as a 'point of departure that will be modified in time as new research produces new data, and harder data worthy of more sophisticated forms of calculation. It will have served its purpose if it challenges others to correct and complete its findings.'[3] Scholars responded quickly to Curtin's challenge. Individuals working on specific sectors of the trade have used new data, gleaned from archives the world over, to modify Curtin's estimates for various portions of the trade. These revisions have even led one scholar – J. E. Inikori – to reject the validity of Curtin's entire census. Indeed Inikori states categorically that 'there is now some consensus among specialists that Curtin underestimated the volume of Atlantic exports'.[4] Are Curtin's 'global figures . . . much too low', as Inikori claims?[5] This article is an attempt to synthesize the various revisions into a new global estimate. As such it provides both a review of the literature since 1969 and presents a revised set of tables on the volume and direction of the slave trade across the Atlantic. On the basis of these revisions, it is clear that Inikori is premature in claiming the emergence of a consensus. Curtin's initial projection of total imports appears to have been remarkably accurate, despite numerous modifications in his partial figures.

The significance of these efforts to quantify the slave trade hardly needs to be mentioned. Ever since J. D. Fage first used Curtin's 1969 figures in his seminal article on the impact of the slave trade on West Africa,[6] scholars have

[1] An earlier version of this article was presented at the African Studies Association annual meeting, Bloomington, Indiana, 1981. I wish to thank David Eltis, Stanley Engerman, Joseph C. Miller, Henry Gemery, P. C. Emmer, Patrick Manning, Robert Stein, Philip D. Curtin, and Russell Chace for their comments and assistance at various stages of this synthesis. While I am solely responsible for any remaining errors, their efforts were crucial in catching more than a few mistakes. I do not wish to hold them responsible for my conclusions, but in more ways than is usually the case, this synthesis was a group effort.

[2] Philip D. Curtin, *The Atlantic Slave Trade: A Census* (Madison, Wisconsin, 1969), 268. [3] Curtin, *Census*, xviii.

[4] J. E. Inikori, 'Introduction', in *Forced Migration: The Impact of the Export Slave Trade on African Societies* (London, 1981), 20. Also see Inikori, 'Measuring the Atlantic slave trade: an assessment of Curtin and Anstey', *Journal of African History*, XVII, ii (1976), 197–223; Inikori, 'Measuring the Atlantic slave trade: a rejoinder', *Journal of African History*, XVII, iv (1976), 607–27; and Inikori, 'The origin of the Diaspora: the slave trade from Africa', *Tarikh*, v, iv (1978), 8.

[5] Inikori, 'Introduction', 19.

[6] J. D. Fage, 'Slavery and the slave trade in the context of West African history', *Journal of African History*, x, iii (1969), 393–407.

attempted to correspond export figures with political and economic developments in Africa. This literature in turn has spawned its own controversies.[7] Curtin's *Census* lowered the estimate for the scale of the slave trade – which some scholars have taken to mean that the impact on Africa was less than previously thought. For example, Fage has argued that demographically, at least, the trade had a minimal impact, although politically and economically the trade had profound repercussions.[8] Other scholars – notably Manning and Thornton – have shown that the demographic effects were significant, no matter what the absolute totals. Manning has postulated a demographic model which distinguishes between slave-depleted areas, slave-importing areas, and slave-trading areas,[9] while Thornton has uncovered census data for late eighteenth-century Angola that confirm the sexual imbalance in local societies which matches the sex ratios in the trans-Atlantic trade.[10] Finally, Inikori – using figures considerably higher than Curtin's *Census* – has argued that the demographic impact of slave exports had a retardative impact on African development.[11] Hence the debate over the slave trade is far from a quibble over numbers; the debate ultimately relates to a major theme in the history of the Atlantic coastal basin and, also, southeastern Africa.[12]

A number of Curtin's 1969 estimates have been revised upwards, some partial figures by substantial amounts, and consequently it is easy to see why Curtin's global estimate for the total volume of the trans-Atlantic trade has been challenged. Robert Stein, for example, has presented a figure for the eighteenth-century French trade which is 21·4 per cent higher than Curtin's figure.[13] Roger Anstey reached a total for the British trade from 1761 to 1807 which was 10·3 per cent above Curtin's figure; subsequent revisions of Anstey's calculations increased the total still further – to a level 18·3 per cent

[7] See, for example, Inikori, *Forced Migration*, which contains an excellent sample of articles and sections of books relating to the debate; Roger Anstey, *The Atlantic Slave Trade and British Abolition, 1760–1810* (London, 1975), 58–88; and my own study: *Transformations in Slavery: A History of Slavery in Africa* (Cambridge, forthcoming).

[8] J. D. Fage, *A History of Africa* (London, 1978), 244–88.

[9] Patrick Manning, 'The enslavement of Africans: a demographic model', *Canadian Journal of African Studies*, xv, iii (1981), 499–526; and *Slavery, Colonialism and Economic Growth in Dahomey, 1640–1960* (Cambridge, 1982). It should be noted that Manning is working on a book which will examine the demographic impact of the slave trade on Africa; see his preliminary paper, 'The political economy of African slavery', presented at the Johns Hopkins University, 1 December 1981.

[10] John Thornton, 'The slave trade in eighteenth century Angola: effects on demographic structures', *Canadian Journal of African Studies*, xiv, iii (1980), 417–27.

[11] Inikori, 'Introduction', 20–59.

[12] For example, Anstey (*Atlantic Slave Trade*, 79–88) argues that there was no net population loss in the interior of the Bight of Biafra. David Northrup. *Trade without Rulers: Pre-Colonial Economic Development in South-Eastern Nigeria* (Oxford, 1978), 81–2, argues that the region only sustained the loss of population because of higher natural growth rates than Anstey allows.

[13] Robert Stein, 'Measuring the French slave trade, 1713–1792/3', *Journal of African History*, xix, iv (1978), 515–21. Also see Stein, *The French Slave Trade in the Eighteenth Century: An Old Regime Business* (Madison, 1979). Stein notes that 'It must be recognized that the estimates advanced by Curtin for French slave exports were too low . . . due to the quality of the available published data'. ('Measuring', 520.)

higher than in the 1969 census.[14] Enriqueta Vila Vilar took Curtin to task for his treatment of the early trade to Spanish America; new data showed that the figure Curtin used was wrong by 135,000 slaves in a forty-five-year period.[15] David Eltis examined the nineteenth-century trade with a similar result: Curtin's data were 30 per cent too low for the period from 1821–43.[16] In all fairness to these and other scholars who could be cited, these same individuals praised Curtin's efforts and accorded him the honour of providing the scholarly community with sets of figures which could be tested. They responded to Curtin's original challenge and generally adopted the same statistical methodology as Curtin in attempting to arrive at more accurate figures. Despite the upward revisions of different portions of the trade, however, none of these scholars attempted a reassessment of Curtin's global figure for the slave trade. The impression which gradually emerged was that Curtin must be wrong on that score too; after all, if the partial totals required upward revision, so must the global figure.

Leslie B. Rout Jr. was one of the first scholars to suggest that errors in the calculation of partial totals might indicate that Curtin's entire census was suspect. In 1973 he questioned 'the credibility of Curtin's computations' for the volume of the slave trade to Spanish America before 1810. Rout considered Curtin's projection of 925,000 slave imports off by 62 per cent; instead he estimated a figure of 1·5–1·6 million slaves, although he did not add any new data of his own.[17] Rout's claims are reminiscent of the projections of those scholars whom Curtin criticized in his discussion of the historiography of the slave trade.[18] Rout favoured an educated guess to the detailed efforts at quantification represented in Curtin's study. His figure is also important because Inikori – Curtin's most serious critic – relies on it.

[14] Roger Anstey, 'The volume and profitability of the British slave trade, 1761–1807', in Stanley Engerman and Eugene Genovese, eds., *Race and Slavery in the Western Hemisphere: Quantitative Studies* (Princeton, 1975), 12. Anstey's estimate is 'based on material not known to Curtin's authorities and therefore supersedes his results'.

[15] Enriqueta Vila Vilar, 'The large-scale introduction of Africans into Veracruz and Cartagena', in Vera Rubin and Arthur Tuden, eds., *Comparative Perspectives on Slavery in New World Plantation Societies* (New York, 1977), 267–80; and *Hispanoamerica y el comercio de esclavos: Los Asientos Portugueses* (Seville, 1977).

[16] David Eltis, 'The export of slaves from Africa, 1821–1843', *Journal of Economic History*, XXXVII (1977), 410–15; and 'The direction and fluctuation of the Transatlantic slave trade, 1821–1843: a revision of the 1845 Parliamentary Paper', in Henry Gemery and Jan Hogendorn, eds., *The Uncommon Market: Essays in the Economic History of the Atlantic Slave Trade* (New York, 1979), 273–301; see especially page 291. It should be noted that D. R. Murray was one of the first to question the accuracy of Curtin's estimates ('Statistics of the slave trade to Cuba, 1790–1867', *Journal of Latin American Studies*, III, ii, 1971, 131–49). Murray demonstrated that imports into Cuba were greater than Curtin allowed. In my calculations, Murray's comments are not relevant for two reasons. Firstly, I base my estimates on the volume of slaves carried by the ships of different countries and not by import area for 1790–1810. Secondly, I rely on Eltis's research for the period after 1820, which supersedes Murray's work. It should be noted also that the totals in Murray's article have been corrected in his book: *Odious Commerce: Britain, Spain and the Abolition of the Cuban Slave Trade* (Cambridge, 1980), 18, 80, 111, 112, 244.

[17] Leslie B. Rout, Jr., *The African Experience in Spanish America: 1502 to the Present Day* (Cambridge, 1973), 65.   [18] Curtin, *Census*, 3–13.

Inikori's challenge came at a conference in 1975; the revised paper was subsequently published in the *Journal of African History* in 1976 and resulted in a series of exchanges involving Inikori, Curtin, Anstey and Seymour Drescher.[19] Inikori used a straightforward (but dubious) method of adjusting Curtin's global figure upwards by 4,400,000, obtaining a figure of 15,400,000 slaves exported from Africa and 13,392,000 slaves imported into the Americas. The method is dubious because Inikori transformed Curtin's estimate for imports into the Americas into an export figure – which Curtin did not do – using a percentage of approximately 13 per cent to allow for losses in transit. Inikori thereby arrived at an estimate for exports from Africa of 11,000,000 slaves, which he effectively attributes to Curtin. Inikori then added his own projection for the eighteenth-century British trade (49·2 per cent higher than Curtin's estimate for British exports), with Eltis's revision for the period of 1821–43 (34·4 per cent higher than Curtin's estimate), and Robert Stein's reassessment of the eighteenth-century French trade (21·4 per cent higher than Curtin's figure). These modifications accounted for an additional 1,800,000 slaves, or so Inikori claimed. He also accepted Rout's 'correction' of the Spanish-American import figure, even though Rout's figure was only a 'guesstimate'. Presumably, Inikori also converted Rout's import estimate into an export figure by allowing for losses in transit of 13 per cent, thereby accounting for approximately 660,000 more slaves. Finally, Inikori allowed a correction of almost 2,000,000 for other slaves which he claimed were exported to the Americas in the sixteenth and seventeenth centuries or otherwise were unrecorded in Curtin's estimates for the Portuguese trade.[20] As will be demonstrated below, this kind of manipulation of statistics cannot be accepted. Inikori makes a basic mistake in mixing different sets of data without accounting for the duplication resulting from such a mixture.

James Rawley, following a different procedure, makes the same mistake of mixing data which overlap. His computation of a global figure for the slave trade is also considerably higher than Curtin's estimate for imports into the Americas (11,345,000 compared to Curtin's figure of 9,566,100).[21] Rawley's method is more reliable than Inikori's, if the errors are corrected, and the results can be used as an alternative to the method employed in this article in reaching a global estimate. Rawley basically employs the same procedure as Curtin did in 1969 – he estimates total slave imports into the Americas,

[19] Inikori, 'Assessment of Curtin and Anstey', 197–223; 'Rejoinder', 607–27: 'Introduction,' 19–21, 277–8 fn; Philip D. Curtin, 'Measuring the Atlantic slave trade once again', *Journal of African History*, XVII, iv, (1976), 595–605; Roger Anstey, 'The British slave trade 1751–1807: a comment', *Journal of African History*, XVII, iv (1976), 606–7; and Seymour Drescher, *Econocide: British Slavery in the Era of Abolition* (Pittsburgh, 1977), 205–13.

[20] Inikori, 'Introduction', 20–1.

[21] James A. Rawley, *The Transatlantic Slave Trade: A History* (New York, 1981), 428, for a summary of Rawley's calculations. In an earlier article, Rawley demonstrated that the London share of the eighteenth-century British trade was much greater than previously known and indicated that upward revision in the British trade was necessary to allow for his reassessment. He did not present alternative figures at the time, however. See 'The port of London and the eighteenth century slave trade: historians, sources and a reappraisal', *African Economic History*, IX (1980), 85–100. The revision suggested is an additional 75,000 slaves (*Slave Trade*, 428).

attempting to bypass shipping data. Unfortunately, he did not remain true to this procedure in estimating the volume of imports into the British Caribbean, and he made a serious mathematical error in computing the Brazilian sector.[22] These errors alone account for an excess of 1,110,000 slaves, so that an adjustment for these sectors alone reduces Rawley's global estimate to 10,235,000, which is well within range of Curtin's original projection. Rawley also makes allowance for 122,000 slaves shipped to other parts of the Atlantic basin, other than the Americas after 1600, which Curtin did not record.[23] An adjustment in Curtin's global figure for this trade would bring Rawley's and Curtin's estimates even more into line.

The procedure I have followed differs from the methods employed by Curtin, Inikori and Rawley, although there is invariably some overlap between all approaches. I have essentially used Curtin's findings – with minor adjustments – before 1700 and have used the partial totals of a variety of scholars for the eighteenth and nineteenth centuries. For 1701–1810, these partial totals are based on the different sectors of the carrying trade, rather than on estimates for imports into different colonies. For most of the nineteenth century, my estimates are based on shipping data as analysed by David Eltis. The details of my calculations are discussed below, but it should be pointed out that when the revisions of the scholars who have worked on the various sectors of the trade are analysed, it becomes clear that the claims of Inikori, Rout and Rawley are indeed extreme. The volume of the Atlantic slave trade is here estimated at 11,698,000 slaves exported from Africa between 1450 and 1900 (Table 1). This total estimate for the export trade is then used to derive a figure for the number of slaves imported into the Americas and other parts of the Atlantic basin between 1450 and 1867 (excluding the offshore islands after 1600), which I calculate as 9,778,500

---

[22] Rawley refers to table 7.1 (*Slave Trade*, 165) for British exports, 1690–1807, and adds 75,000 slaves to compensate for what he claims is an allowance for the previously underestimated London trade. These calculations produce an estimate for the volume of British slave exports from Africa, not the number of slaves imported into the British Caribbean. Furthermore, Rawley accepts Curtin's calculations for imports into the British Caribbean (pp. 164–7 and table 7.3), although table 7.3 does not record all the slaves tabulated by Curtin for the British Caribbean (see *Census*, 140). Rawley provides no explanation for the discrepancy. Rawley also makes the mistake of adding an estimate for slaves carried on British ships after 1807, basing this revision on the estimated 80,000 slaves calculated by David Eltis ('The British contribution to the nineteenth-century Transatlantic slave trade', *Economic History Review*, XXXII, ii, 1979, 226). Rawley again mixes exports by national carrier with imports by receiving area. British-transported slaves and slaves imported into British territory are simply not the same. For imports into Brazil before 1600, Rawley has counted all Portuguese slave imports as Brazilian imports, which produces an error for Brazil of 224,900 slaves, since these imports are also included in his totals for the Old World and Spanish America (see table 2.1, p. 25, which is derived from Curtin, *Census*, 116, for the period 1451–1600). There is another error in the nineteenth-century calculation: Rawley refers to Eltis ('Transatlantic slave trade, 1821–1843', 273–301) in modifying Curtin's figure, but Eltis raises Curtin's total for 1821–43 by 192,100 (p. 289), not 300,000 as Rawley has it. The combined error is 332,800 for Brazil and 778,000 for imports into the British Caribbean. It also should be noted that Rawley refers to Table 14.1 as a source for his estimate for imports into British North America, but since there is no such table it is not possible to examine his calculations.

[23] Rawley relies on T. Bentley Duncan, *Atlantic Islands; Madeira, the Azores, and the Cape Verdes in Seventeenth Century Commerce and Navigation* (Chicago, 1972), 210.

Table 1. *Slave exports from Africa: the Atlantic trade*

Period	Volume	Per cent
1450–1600	367,000	3·1
1601–1700	1,868,000	16·0
1701–1800	6,133,000	52·4
1801–1900	3,330,000	28·5
Total	11,698,000	100·0

Source: Tables 2–4, 6, 7.

slaves (Table 8). My import figure is then compared with the import estimates of Curtin, Inikori, Rawley and other scholars, and it is shown that my estimate is remarkably close to Curtin's original global estimate of 9,566,100.

THE VOLUME OF THE EXPORT TRADE

There have been only a few revisions of Curtin's figures for the period before 1700, although both Inikori and Rout claim that more extensive revision is called for. Neither presents convincing proof that Curtin's figures are wrong, especially once the relatively minor changes are made. Hence an estimate for exports from Africa in this period depends largely on Curtin's import calculations, which are primarily based on estimates of the slave population in the Americas and the islands of the Atlantic basin. The volume of exports in the period before 1700 (Tables 2 and 3) has been reached by allowing for losses at sea on the order of 15, 20 and 25 per cent – the preferred series is based on 20 per cent losses.[24] Exports from 1450 to 1700 are calculated at 2,235,000 slaves, which amounted to an estimated 19·1 per cent of total Atlantic shipments during the whole period of the slave trade.

The modifications in Curtin's total for this period require an upward revision of 172,900 in total imports, which translates into 216,100 exports. The revisions come from two studies. Vila Vilar examined import data for Spanish America from 1595 to 1640 and calculated that Aguirre Beltrán's figure was too low by 135,600 slaves.[25] Robert Fogel and Stanley Engerman

[24] The Royal African Company recorded losses in transit of 23·5 per cent between 1680 and 1688 (K. G. Davies, *The Royal African Company* [New York, 1970], 292); Dutch exports suffered to the extent of 17·9 per cent losses in transit between 1637 and 1645 (sample of 27,477 slaves) (Ernst van den Boogaart and Pieter C. Emmer, 'The Dutch participation in the Atlantic slave trade, 1596–1650', in Gemery and Hogendorn, *Uncommon Market*, 367). Also see Curtin, *Census*, 276–7.

[25] In her initial tabulation, Vila Vilar estimated that 220,800 slaves were imported through Cartagena and Vera Cruz alone between 1595 and 1640 ('Veracruz and Cartagena', 275), but she later revised these figures as follows: Cartagena, 135,000; Vera Cruz, 69,560; Rio de la Plata, 44,000; and the Caribbean islands, 19,664 (*Comercio de esclavos*, 206–9). Her total is 268,664, but I have added these figures as 268,200, rounding off to the nearest hundred. Vila Vilar's figures replace the earlier estimates of Gonzalo Aguirre Beltrán, *La población negra de México, 1519–1810* (Mexico, 1946), 220, whose

added another 20,500 slaves on the basis that Curtin had underestimated imports into North America.[26] Otherwise, there has been no substantial evidence presented which would require a further upward revision for the period before 1700.

Because Rout has claimed – and Inikori has accepted the claim – that the volume of imports into Spanish America should be adjusted upwards substantially, it is necessary to examine the basis of Rout's arguments. Rout published before the work of Vila Vilar appeared, but Vila Vilar's revisions are hardly on the order of Rout's 'guesstimate'. Nonetheless, she accounts for the period from 1595 to 1640, so that it is only necessary to consider the last sixty years of the seventeenth century. For the whole period, including the decades before 1640 when his estimates are now shown to be too low, Curtin used the figures for the various *asientos* – the legal contracts issued by the Spanish government to different countries – as a guide to the volume of imports into Spanish America, and as a result, Curtin may well be too high – rather than too low – in his estimate for the last sixty years of the seventeenth century, and indeed for the first seventy years of the eighteenth century. Curtin was well aware that the *asiento*, as the legal trade, did not include contraband traffic and private licences, nor did it allow for the system of calculating the trade on the basis of *piezas* – an idealized standard less than the actual number of slaves imported. He used the *asiento* as a capacity figure which represented the estimated labour requirements of the Spanish regime. *Asiento* contracts were rarely filled and often fell well short of the number of slaves specified; hence his decision to disregard the *pieza*, illegal trade and licenses was an attempt to adjust for the inevitable overestimation of the *asiento* figures.[27]

Although it is not possible at present to substitute new data for Curtin's figures for Spanish imports between 1641 and 1700 – as Vila Vilar did for the period 1595–1640 – it is possible to use the data assembled by Jorge

figure of 132,600 was used by Curtin in calculating the imports into Spanish America in this period (*Census*, 23). It should be noted, however, that my figures for the whole period from 1575 to 1650 are calculated as follows: I used Curtin's average for each quarter century to account for the years not covered by Vila Vilar. Inikori does not refer to Vila Vilar's work.

For the period before 1595, Colin A. Palmer has challenged Curtin's estimate for Spanish American imports, raising Curtin's figure (51,300) (*Census*, 25) to 73,000; see *Slaves of the White God: Blacks in Mexico, 1570–1650* (Cambridge, Mass., 1976), 26–8, but because my recalculation of the totals based on Vila Vilar, Fogel and Engerman, and Curtin is higher than a simple addition of the revisions to Curtin's original figure, I have not adjusted for Palmer's suggestion. It should be noted, moreover, that Palmer's estimate is not based on as strong evidence as the other two revisions. He relies on two population estimates for the number of slaves in Spanish America, as well as scattered information on various contracts to deliver slaves. The first population estimate, for 1553, indicates a slave population of 20,000, which seems too high. The second, for 1570, indicates a similar level, which seems more likely (p. 28).

[26] Robert Fogel and Stanley Engerman, *Time on the Cross: Evidence and Methods* (Boston, 1974), 30. Fogel and Engerman calculated the following time pattern: 1620–50, 1432 slaves; 1650–70, 1946 slaves; 1670–80, 1443 slaves; 1680–1700, 15,659 slaves; total, 20,480 slaves. (Personal communication, S. Engerman.) I have rounded off the figures to the nearest hundred and divided the estimates into quarter centuries.

[27] Curtin, *Census*, 21–5. Curtin estimated that 516,100 slaves were imported into Spanish America between 1641 and 1773, for an average of 3,880 slaves per year.

PAUL E. LOVEJOY

Table 2. *Growth of the Atlantic slave trade, 1451–1600*

Period	Imports	Annual Average	Exports (15% loss in transit)	Exports (20% loss in transit)	Exports (25% loss in transit)	Annual Average (20% loss in transit)
1451–1475	15,000	600	17,600	18,800	20,000	750
1476–1500	18,500	700	21,800	23,100	24,700	900
1501–1525	42,500	1,700	50,000	53,100	56,700	2,100
1526–1550	43,800	1,800	51,500	54,800	58,400	2,200
1551–1575	61,000	2,500	72,100	76,600	81,700	3,100
1576–1600	112,300	4,500	132,100	140,400	149,700	5,600
Total	293,400	—	345,100	366,800	391,200	—

Source: Philip D. Curtin, *The Atlantic Slave Trade: A Census* (Madison, 1969), 116; and Enriqueta Vila Vilar, *Hispanoamerica y el comercio de esclavos: Los Asientos Portugueses* (Seville, 1977), 206–9.

VOLUME OF THE ATLANTIC SLAVE TRADE 481

Table 3. *Atlantic Slave Trade, 1601–1700*

	Imports	Exports (15% loss in transit)	Exports (20% loss in transit)	Exports (25% loss in transit)	Annual Average (20% loss in transit)
1601–1625	261,800	308,000	327,300	349,100	13,100
1626–1650	242,600	285,400	303,300	323,500	12,100
1651–1675	371,200	436,700	464,000	494,900	18,600
1676–1700	618,900	728,100	773,600	825,200	30,900
Total	1,494,500	1,758,200	1,868,200	1,992,700	

Source: Philip D. Curtin, *The Atlantic Slave Trade: A Census* (Madison, 1969), 119; Enriqueta Vila Vilar, *Hispanoamerica y el comercio de esclavos: Los Asientos Portugueses* (Seville, 1977), 206–9; and R. Fogel and S. L. Engerman, *Time on the Cross: Evidence and Methods* (Boston, 1974), 30. The mortality figure of 20 per cent is based on the following: K. G. Davies (*The Royal African Company*, London, 1957, 292) reports that the Royal African Company experienced losses at sea on the order of 23·5 per cent between 1680 and 1688. Ernst van den Boogaart and Pieter C. Emmer ('The Dutch participation in the Atlantic slave trade, 1596–1650', in H. Gemery and J. S. Hogendorn, eds., *The Uncommon Market: Essays in the Economic History of the Atlantic Slave Trade*, New York, 1979, 367) calculate an average loss of 17·9 per cent on Dutch ships between 1637 and 1645 (sample of 27,477 slaves). The loss in the trade to Brazil was on the order of 15–20 per cent in the sixteenth and seventeenth centuries (see M. Goulart, *Escravidão africana no Brasil* (São Paulo, 1950), 278, as discussed in Curtin, *Census*, 277).

Palacios Preciado to check the validity of Curtin's work.[28] Preciado's information on imports into Cartagena and other parts of Spanish America, indeed, supports Curtin's belief that even when allowance is made for the contraband traffic and the other factors the *asiento* figures are still too high. Data for 1663–74, for example, show that 17,853 *piezas* (perhaps 22,000 slaves) were legally imported into Spanish America, an average of 1,840 slaves per year,[29] a time when Curtin estimated that annual imports were on the order of 3,880.[30] Licenses and contraband traffic could have accounted for an additional 2,000 slaves per year, but hardly the volume necessary to support the claims of Rout and Inikori. Cartagena was the major port for Spanish America during much of the seventeenth and eighteenth centuries; yet for 1676–9, legal imports were only 150–200 slaves per year, despite the fact that the *asiento* allowed for an import of 1,500 per year.[31] For 1685–6, only 490 slaves were legally imported.[32] Again, the illegal traffic, while important, could not have accounted for the levels necessary to sustain the claims of Rout and Inikori. For the period from 1650 to 1697, Preciado estimates that legal imports into Cartagena probably did not exceed 400 slaves per year.[33] In the last years of the seventeenth century, the volume of legal imports into Cartagena increased dramatically, but the range of imports was still on the order of Curtin's estimate. Under the Portuguese *asiento*, imports totalled 2,886 in 1698, 2,699 in 1699, 2,600 in 1700 and 1,668 in 1701.[34] If illegal imports and the legal imports into other Spanish American ports were known, it is likely that total imports were greater than Curtin's average for these years, but for the period 1640–1700 as a whole, the average was probably less than Curtin estimated.[35]

The eighteenth century trade, which amounted to 6,133,000 slaves or 52·4 per cent of total trans-Atlantic shipments in all periods, has been calculated on the basis of numerous revisions. These are incorporated into Tables 4 and 5 and include material directly based on the volume of slave exports from Africa. The scholars who have presented partial revisions include Johannes Postma,[36] who has calculated the Dutch trade from archival sources; Stein, who has done similar archival work on the French trade;[37] Drescher, Inikori

---

[28] Jorge Palacios Preciado, *La Trata de Negros por Cartagena de Indias* (Tunja, 1973).

[29] Preciado, *Trata de Negros*, 29, 39 fn.

[30] Curtin, *Census*, 25.

[31] Preciado, *Trata de Negros*, 30–1.

[32] *Ibid.*, 31.

[33] *Ibid.*, 32.

[34] *Ibid.*, 99.

[35] Certainly the imports into Buenos Aires, which was only a minor centre of the trade in this period, were small; see Russell Chace, 'The African impact on colonial Argentina (Ph.D. thesis, unpublished, University of California, Santa Barbara, 1969), 36–41. Chace notes that the volume of imports probably was on the order of 500–600 slaves per year in the 1640s, but in the second half of the century, when the Spanish colonies suffered an economic recession, trade was unstable at best.

[36] Johannes Postma, 'The origin of African slaves: the Dutch activities on the Guinea Coast, 1675–1795', in Engerman and Genovese, *Race and Slavery*, 49; and Postma 'The Dutch slave trade: a quantitative assessment', *Revue française d'histoire d'outre-mer*, LXII (1975), 237. Postma bases his study on the records of the Dutch West India Company.

[37] Stein, 'French slave trade', 519; and Stein, *French Slave Trade*, 11,207. Stein bases his study on the records of the Amirauté which kept detailed accounts of ships and cargoes.

VOLUME OF THE ATLANTIC SLAVE TRADE 483

Table 4. *Atlantic slave trade, 1701–1800*

Carrier	Total
English	2,532,300
Portuguese	1,796,300
French	1,180,300
Dutch	350,900
North American	194,200
Danish	73,900
Other (Swedish, Brandenburger)	5,000
Total	6,132,900

Sources: English trade: for 1701–50, Curtin, *Census*, 151; for 1751–1800, Roger Anstey, 'The British slave trade 1751–1807: a comment', *Journal of African History*, XVII, iv (1976), 607. I have adjusted for Anstey's total by allowing a figure of 245,000 for 1801–7; see Seymour Drescher, *Econocide: British Slavery in the Era of Abolition* (Pittsburgh, 1977), 28. Also see Anstey, 'The volume and profitability of the British slave trade, 1761–1807', in Stanley L. Engerman and Eugene D. Genovese, eds., *Race and Slavery in the Western Hemisphere: Quantitative Studies* (Princeton, 1975), 13.
Portuguese trade: Herbert S. Klein, *The Middle Passage: Comparative Studies in the Atlantic Slave Trade* (Princeton, 1978), 27, for Angola, 1701–60; Curtin, *Atlantic Slave Trade*, 207, for West Africa, 1701–60; Roger Anstey, 'The slave trade of the continental powers, 1760–1810', *The Economic History Review*, XXX, ii (1977), 261, for 1761–1800;
French trade: Curtin, *Census*, 211, for 1701–10; and Robert Stein, 'Measuring the French slave trade, 1713–1792/4, *Journal of African History*, XIX, iv (1978), 519. I have also added 10,000 to the total for the French trade in order to allow for unrecorded vessels between 1713 and 1728 (Stein, personal communication).
Dutch trade: Johannes Postma, 'The origin of African slaves: the Dutch activities on the Guinea Coast, 1675–1795', in Engerman and Genovese, *Race and Slavery*, 49. I have preferred this estimate to the one in Johannes Postma, 'The Dutch slave trade: a quantitative assessment', *Revue française d'histoire d'outre-mer*, LXII (1975), 237. North American trade: Roger Anstey, 'The volume of the North American slave-carrying trade from Africa, 1761–1810', *Revue française d'histoire d'outre-mer*, LXII (1975), 201, for 1733–60, and Anstey, 'Continental powers', 267, for 1761–1800. Danish trade: for 1733–60, Svend Erik Green-Pedersen, 'The history of the Danish Negro slave trade, 1733–1807', *Revue française d'histoire d'outre-mer*, LXII (1975), 201; for 1761–1800, Anstey 'Continental Powers', 267.

and Anstey, whose combined archival work on the British trade covers the years 1751–1800;[38] Herbert Klein, who has done comparable archival work on the Portuguese trade from west-central Africa from 1710 to 1800;[39] and

[38] Drescher, *Econocide*, 28; Anstey, 'British slave trade', 13; and Inikori, 'Assessment of Curtin and Anstey', 213–4. Drescher and Inikori used Customs series 3 and 17 in the Public Record Office for 1777–1807, while Anstey used clearance lists for British ships for 1761–1807.
[39] Herbert Klein, *The Middle Passage: Comparative Studies in the Atlantic Trade* (Princeton, 1978), 27. Klein used shipping records from Rio de Janeiro and Angola for the Portuguese trade.

Svend Erik Green-Pedersen, who has calculated the relatively small Danish trade from primary sources.[40] Anstey has also revised the figures for the North American and various European carriers from 1761 to 1800.[41] I am also making an allowance of 5,000 slaves for other minor carriers in the eighteenth century. Only in the years before 1761 are any of Curtin's original projections used: these include the British trade from 1701 to 1750, the Portuguese trade from West Africa, 1701–10, and the French trade for 1701–10.

The two tables on the eighteenth-century trade analyse the volume of exports according to carrier and export region. It should be noted that 619,600 slaves are not accounted for in Table 5, exports by coastal region. Some of these slaves came from South-east Africa and Madagascar, but the coastal origin of the vast majority is simply not known. While it is possible to assign these slaves to the different regions according to the known distribution, this has not been done here. For purposes of calculating total exports for the century, therefore, the summation of the revisions of the different carriers is clearly superior to the summation of exports by coastal origin, or by area of import in the Americas, which was Curtin's method for reaching a total for the century.

Stein's 1978 calculations raise Curtin's 1969 estimate for eighteenth-century French exports by 184,760 slaves. Since Stein's work is based on shipping data previously not used, this revision is an important one. There is one problem, however. Except for 33 ships in the years before 1713, Stein has no data for the early years of the eighteenth century, when Europe was at war and French participation in the trade is difficult to assess. The French were supposed to deliver 4,000 slaves per year to Spanish America but were not able to achieve this figure.[42] Elena F. Scheuss de Studer has recorded 3,474 slaves imported into Buenos Aires under the French *asiento*, of which 2,574 were imported between 1703 and 1710.[43] Preciado accounts for another 13,734 slaves imported into the other parts of Spanish America by the

---

[40] Svend Erik Green-Pedersen, 'The history of the Danish Negro slave trade, 1733–1807', *Revue française d'histoire d'outre-mer*, LXII (1975), 201. Green-Pedersen relies primarily on the records of the Great Negro Trade Commission of Denmark.

[41] For Anstey's synthesis of the continental trade, see 'The slave trade of the continental powers, 1760–1810', *The Economic History Review*, xxx, ii, (1977), 261. In his reconstruction, Anstey relies on the work of Herbert Klein, Postma, Green-Pedersen and Curtin. For the North American trade, see Anstey, 'The volume of the North American slave-carrying trade from Africa, 1761–1810', *Revue française d'histoire d'outre-mer*, LXII (1975), 65. Anstey uses widely scattered data in his synthesis of the North American trade, especially the material in Elizabeth Donnan, ed., *Documents Relating to the Slave Trade* (Washington, 1930–5), which includes some archival material (e.g. Charleston Customs records, 1803–7). Fogel and Engerman have provided some verification of Anstey's revision: they calculate that Curtin's estimate for total imports into the United States was 148,000 too low for the period 1760–1810 (*Time on the Cross: Evidence and Methods*, 30–1).

[42] Stein, *French Slave Trade*, 11,207. Ships carried an average of 306 slaves; hence the 33 documented ships may have had as many as 10,000 slaves on board. Stein does not state when these ships sailed, and some, if not most, may have traded in 1711 or 1712. For my purposes, however, I am assuming that these 33 ships contributed to the portion of the total French trade assigned to 1701–10.

[43] Elena F. Scheuss de Studer, *La trata de negros en el Río de la Plata durante el siglo XVIII* (Buenos Aires, 1958), 126. For a fuller discussion of the Argentine trade, see Chace, 'African Impact on Argentina', 47–51.

VOLUME OF THE ATLANTIC SLAVE TRADE 485

Table 5. *Regional origins of slaves in the eighteenth-century Atlantic trade (000's) (Dutch, British, French and Portuguese)*

Region	1701–10	1711–20	1721–30	1731–40	1741–50	1751–60	1761–70	1771–80	1781–90	1791–1800	Totals
Senegambia	18·4	30·9	22·5	26·2	25·0	22·5	14·4	12·4	22·1	7·0	201·3
Sierra Leone	17·4	20·6	22·5	33·3	49·4	45·2	108·1	82·2	47·2	58·0	483·9
Gold Coast	25·0	46·6	72·7	85·6	91·4	66·3	63·4	56·0	93·7	76·7	677·4
Bight of Benin	161·3	169·3	160·3	154·8	109·9	98·7	102·7	90·7	159·8	71·1	1,278·6
Bight of Biafra	10·0	10·0	4·5	45·1	71·3	100·7	126·3	127·3	133·8	185·4	814·4
West-central Africa	80·1	72·0	115·5	177·3	189·2	195·6	220·2	211·4	431·1	365·3	2,057·7
Totals	312·2	349·4	398·0	522·3	536·2	529·0	635·0	580·0	887·7	763·5	5,513·3

Source: for all figures in the period 1711–1800 for West African regions; see Philip D. Curtin, 'Measuring the Atlantic slave trade', in S. L. Engerman and E. D. Genovese, eds., *Race and Slavery in the Western Hemisphere: Quantitative Studies* (Princeton, 1975), 112; for Central African figures, 1711–1800: Herbert S. Klein, *The Middle Passage: Comparative Studies in the Atlantic Slave Trade* (Princeton, 1978), 27; a regional breakdown for the decade 1701–10 is not available but has been reconstructed on the basis of the following sources: Johannes Postma, 'The origin of African slaves: the Dutch activities on the Guinea Coast, 1675–1795', in Engerman and Genovese, *Race and Slavery*, 42, 49; Philip D. Curtin, *The Atlantic Slave Trade: A Census* (Madison, 1969), 207; Kwame Yeboa Daaku, *Trade and Politics on the Gold Coast, 1600–1720* (Oxford, 1970), 46; Patrick Manning, 'The slave trade in the Bight of Benin, 1640–1890', in Henry Gemery and Jan S. Hogendorn, eds., *The Uncommon Market: Essays in the Economic History of the Atlantic Slave Trade* (New York, 1979), 117; and K. G. Davies, *The Royal African Company* (London, 1957), 226. A figure of 10·0 has also been assigned to the Bight of Biafra, on the assumption that the trade was on the order of 1,000 slaves per year in this decade. Curtin has no estimate for this period, and it is likely that his estimate for the 1720's is low; see David Northrup, *Trade Without Rulers, Pre-colonial Economic Development in South-Eastern Nigeria* (Oxford, 1978), 54, although the figures used here are considerably more conservative than those suggested by Northrup. Following the analysis of Adam Jones and Marion Johnson, 'Slaves from the Windward Coast', *Journal of African History*, xxi, i (1980), 17–34, the slaves previously attributed to the Windward Coast have been reassigned to the Sierra Leone and Guinea coasts for British exports and to the Slave Coast for French exports. There is room for considerable error in this assessment, since some slaves did come from the Western Ivory Coast and Liberia, in the case of the British, and some of the French trade probably included purchases on the Gold Coast and in the Bight of Biafra. Nonetheless, the majority of slaves in both cases almost certainly came from the areas to which they have been assigned. Hopefully the forthcoming work of Jones and Johnson will help clarify this matter. Curtin's figures for 1761–80 ('Measuring', 112) include the revisions of Roger Anstey, 'The volume and profitability of the British slave trade, 1761–1807', in Engerman and Genovese, *Race and Slavery*, 13; and Postma, 'Origin of African Slaves', 42–9. I have also used Anstey, 'The slave trade of the Continental powers', *Economic History Review*, xxx, ii (1977), 261. For 1781–90 I have accepted J. E. Inikori's tabulation of the number of British ships involved in the slave trade but have employed a slave/ship ratio from Anstey and assigned these slaves to different regions following Curtin's formula, as discussed in the text. For the 1790s I have substituted the total for the British trade derived by Seymour Drescher, *Econocide: British Slavery in the Era of Abolition* (Pittsburgh, 1977), 28, following Anstey's distributional formula.

French.[44] Hence the French delivered at least 17,208 slaves; exports were probably on the order of 21,000 slaves. It seems likely that at least another 9,000 were exported to French colonial possessions. Stein's figures are also too low for 1713–28, perhaps by another 10,000 slaves, because data are missing for some French ports for some years.[45] Hence my total for the French trade is 40,000 higher than Stein's figure for 1713–92/3.

Although the volume of the eighteenth-century trade is calculated here on the basis of national carrier and not importing region, it is necessary to return to the problem of imports into Spanish America in order to continue the assessment of Rout's and Inikori's criticism of Curtin on this point. As the information on the French *asiento* between 1703 and 1713 makes clear, legal imports were still on an order compatible with Curtin's estimate: 1,564 slaves per year, which would allow the possibility of 2,300 slaves imported illegally. At Cartagena, the scattered returns for the next several decades do not suggest a higher level of imports. Before 1720, imports averaged 286 per year; in the 1720s, imports increased to 789 per year.[46] Between 1730 and 1736, another 4,986 slaves are recorded, which averages 712 per year,[47] and the level of legal imports was scarcely any higher in the middle decade of the century, at least not for those years when data are available. Between 1747 and 1753, for example, average annual imports into Cartagena were 263 slaves.[48] It would have taken a considerable number of illegal imports both at Cartagena and elsewhere to produce a volume on the order claimed by Curtin's critics. Certainly, a more detailed study of the trade to Spanish America is warranted, but until one is done, the speculations of Rout and Inikori cannot be taken as a contribution to sound historical reconstruction.[49]

Anstey, Drescher and Inikori have used new data for the British trade in the last decades of the British trade, and by combining their studies it is possible to revise Curtin's figure for the British trade in the period from 1751 to 1807. Anstey presented an initial revision in 1975,[50] but the real break-

[44] Preciado, *Trata de Negros*, 165. It should be noted that Preciado's data on imports into Buenos Aires differs from Scheuss de Studer's figure. Preciado accounts for 3,057 slaves.

[45] Stein would allow for one or two ships per year (personal communication). This estimate for the unrecorded vessels is partially confirmed by John C. Clark (*La Rochelle and the Atlantic Economy during the Eighteenth Century* [Baltimore, 1981], 29), who records eight ships leaving for Africa between 1710 and 1719 and eleven ships between 1720 and 1729, although the size of the ships and the number of slaves purchased are not known. Stein appears to have included a few of these ships – for the years 1728 and 1729 – but not the others. I wish to thank Professor Stein for discussing this problem with me. I have not attempted to compare Stein's material with the data on the French trade collected by Jean Mettas (*Répertoire des expeditions negrières françaises au XVIIIᵉ siècle*, ed. Serge Daget, Nantes, 1978). A second volume of material collected by Mettas is forthcoming.

[46] Preciado, *Trata de Negros*, 312.

[47] *Op. cit.* 338.

[48] *Op. cit.* 32–3, 40 fn.

[49] Chace, 'African impact', 53–64. Colin A. Palmer, *Human Cargoes: The British Slave Trade to Spanish America* (Chicago, 1981), 110–11, shows British imports into Spanish America, 1715–39, as 74,760, with illicit trade another one-third to one-half – 3,000–15,000 higher that Curtin's figures for these years. But as Curtin used an annual average (3,880) for the period 1641–1773, his estimate is not altered significantly, if at all.

[50] Anstey, 'British slave trade', 3–31; see especially p. 13.

through in the study of these decades was the discovery of Customs records, series 3 and 17, at the Public Record Office; Inikori and Drescher, working independently, examined these documents.[51] Their tabulation of the raw data was slightly different, but far more significantly, Inikori and Drescher came to far different conclusions in their interpretation of these data. Anstey joined the debate in defence of his own calculation, and he reassessed the data himself, incorporating Inikori's findings on the number of ships involved in the British trade.[52] Since Inikori and Drescher counted the actual ships involved in the slave trade, the problems of interpretation centre on the number of slaves per ship. Drescher and Anstey used similar ratios, and hence their totals are approximately the same. Inikori used a much greater ratio, thereby resulting in a greater estimated volume. In this case, I defer to Anstey and Drescher, who reached similar results working independently, although Drescher did not attempt an estimate for the period before 1777.

The revised figure for the British trade from 1751 to 1807 accepted here is 1,913,380 slaves, which is 18·4 per cent higher than Curtin's original estimate for British exports in this period. Inikori calculated the British trade variously, ranging from 2,307,986 to 2,476,959.[53] For the period in which both Inikori and Drescher used the same archival material – 1777–1807 – Inikori was also considerably higher in his calculation. Drescher reached a total of 1,099,300, while Inikori's figure was 1,481,500.[54] In order to reach a figure for 1701–1807 I have accepted Anstey's figure for 1751–1807, and I have used Curtin's estimate for the first half of the century (863,900); for a total of 2,777,300 slaves.[55] It should be noted that Inikori's estimate for the British trade from 1701 to 1807 (3,699,572) is 922,300 greater than the Curtin–Anstey figure used here. It is possible that Curtin's figure for the first half of the century is low, but Inikori has not accounted for his difference with Curtin (418,800) on the basis of new statistical evidence.[56] His argument is based on an assessment of commercial patterns and an allowance for error in existing figures. It should be noted, however, that even if Inikori's calculations on the British trade are accepted – (a) for the period before 1750, (b) for the period after 1750, (c) for both – my global estimate for exports would be affected as follows: (a) an increase of 418,800; (b) an increase ranging from 394,600 to 563,600; or (c) an increase of 922,300.

The other problem with the eighteenth century relates to an assessment of the minor slaving countries. Curtin made a rough estimate for North American, Dutch and Danish ships, and now there are better results,

---

[51] Inikori, 'Assessment of Curtin and Anstey', 214; and Drescher, *Econocide*, 28.

[52] Anstey, 'Comment', 605–6.

[53] Inikori, 'Assessment of Curtin and Anstey', 214 for estimates of 2,365,014, making allowance for non-slave carrying vessels, and 2,476,959, assuming unrecorded ships more than made up for non-slave carriers. Inikori, 'Rejoinder', 624, presents different estimates: 2,307,986, taking no account of unrecorded trade, and 2,416,910, taking into account unrecorded trade. Inikori does not indicate how he arrived at these conflicting figures.

[54] Drescher, *Econocide*, 28. Drescher's calculation is 10·4 per cent higher than Curtin's original estimate, while Inikori's figure is 48·8 per cent higher.

[55] Anstey's revision for 1751–1807 is 1,913,380 slaves ('Comment', 607), while Curtin's figure for 1701–50 is 863,900 (*Census*, 142). Drescher's estimate of 245,000 slaves for 1801–1807 is in *Econocide*, 28.

[56] Inikori, 'Rejoinder', 624.

although the total for all minor carriers is not significantly different from Curtin's initial estimate.[57] Postma used archival material to reach a figure of 116,416 slaves for the Dutch trade from 1761 to 1794.[58] Curtin had allowed 173,600 as a figure for Dutch exports in this period.[59] Postma also accounts for 234,472 slaves handled by the Dutch from 1701 to 1760, again basing his calculations on archival data.[60] The Danish trade has now been estimated at 72,000, while the North American trade after 1761 was 194,170,[61] and the Swedish, Brandenburger and others probably took only a few thousand slaves in the course of the whole century – here estimated at 5,000. Since all these carriers only transported about 10 per cent of total slave exports in the eighteenth century, adjustments in the partial figures of these carriers, while important for an analysis of individual countries, hardly affect the overall total for the slave trade.

David Eltis has led the way in a reassessment of the nineteenth-century trade, which is here estimated at 3,330,000 slaves, or 28·5 per cent of the total slave trade (see Tables 6 and 7). Eltis's major contribution is his study of the period from 1821 to 1867, although I have also relied on some of his estimates for the decade, 1811–20.[62] A discussion of the nineteenth century, therefore, primarily involves the first two decades and the period after 1867.

The calculation for the first decade of the nineteenth century is based on the revisions of Anstey, Drescher, Miller and Green-Pedersen for most of the export volume.[63] Drescher accounts for 245,000 slaves carried by British ships; Anstey has estimated that U.S. ships handled another 100,470 slaves; Green-Pedersen allows 2,000 slaves for the Danish trade; and Anstey estimates that a few slaves – 110 – were on French ships. The Portuguese trade is based on Miller's data for Angola; Curtin's original estimates for the rest of the Portuguese trade largely stand.[64] Miller shows that west-central

[57] Curtin, Census, 210–20.

[58] Postma, 'Origin of African slaves', 49.

[59] Curtin, Census, 212.

[60] Postma, 'Origin of African slaves', 49.

[61] Green-Pedersen, 'Danish Negro slave trade', 201; Anstey, 'Continental powers', 267; and Anstey, 'North American slave-carrying trade', 65.

[62] Eltis, 'Transatlantic slave trade, 1821–1843', 273–301; and Eltis, 'The direction and fluctuation of the transatlantic trade, 1844–1867', unpublished paper presented at the African Studies Association annual meeting, Bloomington, Indiana, 1981. It should be noted that Eltis's revision of 1844–67 supersedes the calculations of David R. Murray, Odious Commerce: Britain, Spain and the Abolition of the Cuban Slave Trade (Cambridge, 1980). I have not seen Serge Daget's thesis on the nineteenth century French trade, but a preliminary discussion is provided in 'British repression of the illegal French slave trade: some considerations', in Gemery and Hogendorn, Uncommon Market, 419–42. Daget accounts for approximately 118,000 slaves exported on French ships before 1845. Eltis has allowed for the illegal French trade, although his calculations may be low; see 'Transatlantic slave trade, 1821–1843', 287–8, 299–301.

[63] Anstey, 'Slave trade of the continental powers', 261; Anstey, 'North American slave-carrying trade', 65; Drescher, Econocide, 28; Joseph C. Miller, 'Legal Portuguese slaving from Angola. Some preliminary indications of volume and direction', Revue française d'histoire d'outre-mer, LXII (1975), 161; Green-Pedersen, 'Danish Negro slave Trade', 201.

[64] Curtin, Census, 211; and Anstey, 'Slave trade of the continental powers', 261. I have now allowed for the thirteen French ships which sailed for Africa between 1804–6 from Nantes; see Robert Stein, 'The Nantes slave traders, 1783–1815' (Ph.D. thesis, York

Africa exported 188,400 slaves, exclusive of Cabinda, and I have substituted this figure for the one used by Anstey. Otherwise, Anstey's summary of the 1801–10 Portuguese trade is used.[65] The 15,100 slaves he lists as unrecorded is an allowance for Cabinda and southeastern Africa. Curtin had estimated exports from southeastern Africa at 5,800, but I have adjusted this upward to 10,000 as a result of scattered data for Mozambique for 1802, 1803 and 1809. E. A. Alpers has reported information on one Brazil-bound ship in 1802 with 620 slaves; in 1803 Portuguese exports from Mozambique Island alone were 5,239 slaves, although most of these went to the Mascarenes and not Brazil. In 1809, 1500 to 2,000 slaves were sent to Brazil.[66] While these figures barely affect the figure for total Portuguese exports to the Americas, they do suggest that the volume of exports from southeastern Africa was significant and very likely spilled over into the Atlantic, perhaps to a level even greater than 10,000 for the decade. I have assigned 5,000 of Anstey's 15,100 unrecorded slaves to Cabinda, i.e. west-central Africa, and 4,300 to southeastern Africa, which combined with 5,700 slaves previously assigned to southeastern Africa brings its total to 10,000. The difference is 6,800 which I have left unassigned.

The calculation of the trade in the second decade of the nineteenth century has been divided into Portuguese and non-Portuguese sectors. For the Portuguese sector I estimate a total of 385,600 slaves. Miller has shown that west-central Africa exported 246,600 slaves, although again there is a gap in the data for the region north of the Zaire River and for imports into Pernambuco.[67] I have allowed 10,000 slaves for these sectors. Furthermore, Miller has accounted for 22,500 exports from southeastern Africa,[68] but other data suggest that this figure should be higher still; the allowance here is 60,000 although a figure of 75,000 may not be too high. Custom records for Mozambique Island show that 8,164 slaves were exported in 1818, 7,920 in 1819, and 12,272 in 1821, and it is likely that several thousand slaves per year were being sent in the early years of the second decade. Custom records for Quelimane, the other major port in southeastern Africa, show that 17,241 slaves were exported from 1814 to 1820. I have allowed 9,000 slaves for Mozambique Island in 1820, and 5,000 per year for 1816 and 1817.[69] The

University, 1975), 271–3. Stein suspects that there were at least as many more ships from other French ports in these years, which could have involved the transfer of a total of 5,000 slaves (personal communication).

[65] Anstey, 'Slave trade of the continental powers', 261; and Miller, 'Portuguese slaving from Angola', 161.

[66] E. A. Alpers, *Ivory and Slaves in East Central Africa* (London, 1975), 187–9.

[67] Miller, 'Portuguese slaving from Angola', 161. Miller's data on the Portuguese trade in the decade 1811–20 are based on British consular reports from Brazil which were not included in the 1845 Parliamentary Paper. For the years 1811–14 and 1819, the reports show both the number of slaves embarked in Africa and the number delivered in Brazil, while in 1815 and 1816 only slaves delivered are recorded. For 1817, and 1818 and 1820 there are no returns.

[68] Miller, 'Portuguese slaving from Angola', 161. Also see Joseph C. Miller, 'Sources and knowledge of the slave trade in the Southern Atlantic', unpublished paper read to the Pacific Coast Branch of the American Historical Association, 1976.

[69] Alpers, *Ivory and Slaves*, 213, 216; and Allen Isaacman, *Mozambique: The Africanization of a European Institution: The Zambezi Prazos, 1750–1902* (Madison, 1972), 92; Leroy Vail and Landeg White, *Capitalism and Colonialism in Mozambique – A Study of Quelimane District* (London, 1980), 6–50.

Table 6. *Trans-Atlantic slave trade, 1801–67*

Region	1801–10	Per Cent	1811–20	Per Cent	1821–43	Per Cent	1844–67	Per Cent	Total	Per Cent
Western Africa (Senegambia to Gold Coast)	66,000	12·8	52,000	9·7	161,000	10·8	47,000	7·5	326,000	10·3
Bight of Benin	82,800	16·1	99,300	18·5	268,000	18·0	102,400	16·3	552,500	17·5
Bight of Biafra	100,100	19·5	68,200	12·7	227,000	15·3	12,200	1·9	407,500	12·9
West-Central Africa	255,500	49·7	256,600	47·9	624,000	42·0	381,200	60·8	1,517,300	48·0
Southeast Africa	10,000	1·9	60,000	11·2	206,000	13·9	84,300	13·4	360,300	11·4
Total	514,400	100·0	536,100	100·0	1,486,000	100·0	627,100	99·9	3,163,600	100·1
Adjusted Total	617,200						634,700		3,274,000	

Sources: Philip D. Curtin, 'Measuring the Atlantic slave trade,' in S. L. Engerman and E. D. Genovese, eds., *Race and Slavery in the Western Hemisphere: Quantitative Studies* (Princeton, 1975), 112; Curtin, *The Atlantic Slave Trade: A Census* (Madison, 1969), 234, 261; David Eltis, 'The export of slaves from Africa, 1821–1843', *Journal of Economic History*, XXXVII, ii (1977), 429; Joseph C. Miller, 'Legal Portuguese slaving from Angola. Some Preliminary Indications of Volume and Direction,' *Revue française d'histoire d'outre-mer*, LXII (1975), 161; Patrick Manning, 'The slave trade in the Bight of Benin, 1640–1890', in H. A. Gemery and J. S. Hogendorn, eds., *The Uncommon Market: Essays in the Economic History of the Atlantic Slave Trade* (New York, 1979), 117; Roger Anstey, 'The slave trade of the Continental powers, 1760–1810', *The Economic History Review*, XXX, ii (1977), 261, 165; Anstey, 'The volume of the North American slave-carrying trade from Africa, 1761–1807', *Revue française d'histoire d'outre-mer*, LXII (1975), 65, which accounts for 100,470 slaves in the adjusted total for 1801–10. The adjusted total also includes 6,800 slaves carried on Portuguese ships and 110 slaves on French ships (Anstey, 'Continental powers', 261, 265), and the figure allows for 2,000 slaves on Danish ships for 1801–02 (S. E. Green-Pedersen, 'The history of the Danish Negro slave trade, 1733–1807,' *Revue française d'histoire d'outre-mer*, LXII, 1975, 201). The calculations on the trade from Southeast Africa between 1801 and 1820 are examined below in the text. It should be noted that figures for 1811–20 are otherwise derived from the calculations of David Eltis, who kindly shared his findings with me. For the period 1844–67, see David Eltis, 'The direction and fluctuation of the Transatlantic trade 1844–1867', unpublished paper presented at the African Studies Association annual meeting, Bloomington, 1981. The adjusted total for these years includes 7,600 slaves of unknown origin. Eltis's figures have been rounded off to the nearest hundred. P. C. Emmer also provided information on 2,000 slaves exported from the Gold Coast between 1858 and 1862 (personal communication).

total, using these estimators, is 52,325, and it seems reasonable to allow another 8,000 for the early years of the decade. Exports to Bahia from the Bight of Benin account for another 59,000 slaves, and another 10,000 slaves probably went to Brazil from the far western shores of Africa.[70]

The non-Portuguese sector is estimated on the basis of Curtin's import-based data for the American receiving areas other than Brazil. Imports totalled about 127,700: 86,300 into the Spanish Caribbean, 31,400 into the French Caribbean, and 10,000 into the United States.[71] A reasonable mortality rate for the middle passage would be 15 per cent, so that exports probably were 150,200. The distribution of these slaves presents a problem, but I have adopted Eltis's distributional breakdown for 1821-25, i.e. Western Guinea 27·9 per cent, Bight of Benin 26·8 per cent, Bight of Biafra 45·4 per cent. Eltis believes that this distribution is more appropriate than the breakdown for the 1820s as a whole because the rush to buy slaves for the Brazilian market before abolition took effect influenced the pattern in the late 1820s.[72] It should be noted that assignment of slaves according to Eltis's model results in a much smaller total for the Bight of Biafra (68,200) than David Northrup's speculative revision of 150,000 slaves.[73] Possibly Biafran exports were higher than 68,200; the Bights of Benin and Biafra are often confused in the sources, so that the total for the Bight of Benin (99,300) may be too high. The combined figure for the Bights (167,500) is probably close to the mark, and additional research may lead to a reassessment. Even so, it is doubtful that an upward revision for the Bight of Biafra would attain the level Northrup has proposed.

Eltis's work on the period from 1821 to 1867 is so thorough that there

---

[70] Patrick Manning, 'The slave trade in the Bight of Benin, 1640-1890', in Gemery and Hogendorn, *Uncommon Market*, 117, 137-8. Manning derives his estimate from the shipping data presented in Pierre Verger, *Flux et reflux de la traite des nègres entre le golfe de Bénin et Bahia de Todos os Santos du 17ᵉ et 18ᵉ siècles* (The Hague, 1968), 655, 667.

[71] Curtin, *Census*, 234, for the volume of imports. These estimates can be checked against exports in the case of the French trade, although the volume of the French trade in the decade 1811-20 presents a problem. Curtin's 1969 estimate was 31,400 slaves imported into the French Caribbean (234); since then Serge Daget has located data on 193 slaving voyages between 1814 and 1820, most of which would have been to French possessions. These voyages may have carried some 61,000 slaves. Curtin's estimate may be too low by half, therefore, if it is assumed that these ships carried an average of 310 slaves per ship and that virtually the whole of French imports was confined to French ships (Eltis, 'Transatlantic slave trade 1821-1843', 287; and Daget, 'Illegal French slave trade', 427, 429). The size of slave cargoes has been determined from the calculations of Eltis for the French trade from 1821-33, when he estimates 338 ships carried 105,000 slaves to the French Caribbean (p. 288). It may be, however, that only half of the French ships stopped at the French islands between 1814 and 1820, if the pattern identified by Eltis for 1821-33 also applied to this earlier period. It is hoped that Daget's work will resolve some of these problems.

[72] Eltis, 'Export of slaves from Africa', 423.

[73] David Northrup, 'The compatibility of the slave and palm oil trades in the Bight of Biafra', *Journal of African History*, XVII, iii (1976), 358. It should be noted, however, that there appears to have been no serious economic depression in the Bight of Biafra in the decade after 1810. If Eltis is correct that the trade was much smaller than Northrup claims, then there should have been an economic set back. It may well be, therefore, that Northrup is correct. If he is, then the distributional sample used by Eltis contains a serious error which must be explained.

PAUL E. LOVEJOY

Table 7. *The traffic in Libertos, 1876–1900*

Year	Volume	Year	Volume
1876–84	10,535	1893	2,130
1885	2,066	1894	2,223
1886	1,468	1895	2,173
1887	1,681	1896	2,691
1888	1,664	1897	3,786
1889	1,425	1898	3,131
1890	8,066	1899	3,510
1891	3,191	1900	4,740
1892	1,409	—	—
		Total	55,889

Source: James Duffy, *A Question of Slavery* (Cambridge, Mass., 1967), 98. It should be noted that this trade was primarily to islands off the African coast.

is little to be said in the way of comment. He compiled a data set of over 5,000 records, including the 2313 voyages contained in the 1845 British Parliamentary Paper on the trans-Atlantic slave trade, which in turn was a compilation of information gathered by the British Foreign Office, especially its Slave Trade Department.[74] While it is possible that Serge Daget's work on the French trade may result in some upward revision of the totals for the 1820s and 1830s, Eltis has already accounted for most of this trade. The only other modification is an allowance for Dutch exports from the Gold Coast between 1836 and 1842 and again from 1858 to 1862. The modification is miniscule, however: the total is about 2,500 slaves who were purchased as recruits for the Dutch colonial army, principally in the East Indies.[75] The final modification is in the period after 1867, when some slaves were still purchased for use on São Thomé and Principe. James Duffy tabulated the trade between 1876 and 1900 (Table 7), when 56,000 slaves, who were called *libertos* as a ploy, were exported.[76] There were probably more before 1876, and the French were involved in a similar subterfuge – they called the slaves *engagés à temps*. Eltis accounted for the *engagés*, but since he stopped in 1867, he did not include *libertos*. Curtin noted the *libertos* in his 1969 *Census*, but he did not include them in his total for the Atlantic slave trade.[77] Nor did

[74] Eltis, 'Export of slaves from Africa', 410–5; Eltis, 'Transatlantic slave trade, 1821–1843', 273–301; and Eltis, 'Direction and fluctuation of the transatlantic trade, 1844–1867'.

[75] For the Dutch trade in some of these years, see Joseph R. La Torre, 'Wealth surpasses everything: An economic history of Asante, 1750–1874' (Ph.D. thesis, unpublished, University of California, Berkeley, 1978), 415. La Torre records 1,170 slaves, but I am basing the figures used here on the information gathered from the archives of the Dutch recruitment agency in Kumasi (P. C. Emmer has kindly shared this information with me).

[76] James Duffy, *A Question of Slavery* (Cambridge, Mass., 1967), 98.

[77] Curtin, *Census*, 251.

he estimate the volume of trade to the other Atlantic islands in the period after 1600, or for São Thomé after 1700. I have also excluded this trade from my analysis.

There are some specific problems relating to the distribution of slaves to different parts of the African coast. These problems do not affect the estimate for the total volume of the slave trade, but they do affect efforts to gauge the impact of the slave trade on Africa. Shipping data are often confused and incomplete with respect to African destination, so that all estimates of coastal origin contain the possibility of considerable error. Hence the suggested distribution presented here should be taken as a challenge to scholars to undertake more detailed work on each decade and coastal region. Even then, it may not be possible to arrive at more satisfactory estimates.

The Bights of Benin and Biafra represent one kind of problem in delimiting the origins of slaves, as reference to the decade of the 1780s makes clear. In Anstey's revision of Curtin's estimate for the British trade, Anstey estimated that only 18,630 slaves came from the Bight of Benin, in contrast to 140,764 from the Bight of Biafra.[78] While Curtin subsequently accepted Anstey's revisions for the other decades between 1761 and 1810, he still relied on the contemporary account of Norris in devising a formula for the distribution of British purchases during the 1780s.[79] I have also followed Curtin's formula – applying the percentage breakdown for the British trade devised in 1969 – but I have used Inikori's tabulation for the total number of British ships involved in the trade and Anstey's slave/ship ratio, as proposed in Anstey's revision of his own calculations.[80] I have also taken Anstey's formula for the 1790s and applied it to the revised volume of the British trade for that decade. In this way, I have adjusted for the upward revision in the British trade for the 1780s and 1790s, but I have not been able to do so for the 1750s, 1760s and 1770s, and for those decades I have relied on Anstey's first estimates of the distributional origins of British slave purchases.

Another modification in the regional origin of slaves relates to the elimination of the Windward Coast as a category. Adam Jones and Marion Johnson have argued that the Windward Coast, which was used in Curtin's 1969 *Census* and employed by virtually every scholar since 1969, is an elusive term which meant different things to the British and French; Jones and Johnson contend that the British really meant Sierra Leone and the upper Guinea coast, while the French were referring to the area to the east, especially the Bight of Benin.[81] Accordingly, I have disaggregated the figures for the Windward Coast and reassigned the French and British portions to the Bight of Benin and Sierra Leone, respectively, except for a few thousand slaves whom the French probably obtained on the Gold Coast and the eastern Ivory Coast. Undoubtedly a few slaves did come from the area of Liberia and western Ivory Coast previously designated the Windward Coast; hence there is likely to be considerable error in my calculations, but until Jones and Johnson publish more detailed material, the size of the error is unknown. The

[78] Anstey, 'British slave trade', 13.

[79] Curtin, 'Measuring', 110–11.

[80] See Anstey, 'Comment', 606–7. I wish to thank Professor Curtin for his advice on this matter.

[81] Adam Jones and Marion Johnson, 'Slaves from the Windward Coast', *Journal of African History*, XXI, i (1980), 17–34.

number of slaves reassigned to the Bight of Benin is 163,400, although some of these may have come from the Bight of Biafra.[82]

Finally, exports from Madagascar represent a problem; slaves from Madagascar are not included as a category, although J. T. Hardyman has estimated that about 12,000 slaves were shipped to the Americas in the seventeenth and eighteenth centuries, the majority between 1675 and 1725.[83] At least 6,000, and perhaps as many as 20,000 slaves were imported into the Dutch settlement at Cape Town, most of them from Madagascar.[84] By far the greatest number of slaves from Madagascar went to the Mascarene islands in the Indian Ocean, however, and since these islands were developed as European plantation colonies not unlike the American colonies, the slave trade to the Mascarenes should perhaps be included in a discussion of the total European trade, even though the trade was not across the Atlantic. On the order of 135,000 slaves were imported from Africa before 1810; assuming losses at sea of 10 per cent, the export trade probably totalled 150,000, of which 52 per cent came from Madagascar and 46 per cent came from East Africa; the rest came from West Africa. This trade continued after 1810, although there has been no attempt to estimate its total volume, other than for the *engagé* trade.[85] Total volume for the nineteenth century may well have been on the order of 100,000 slaves.

THE VOLUME OF SLAVE IMPORTS INTO THE AMERICAS AND ATLANTIC BASIN

The impression that Curtin's census has been steadily revised upwards is based on a serious misunderstanding of the debate which has arisen since 1969. As I have demonstrated, many of the partial totals that Curtin developed

---

[82] Curtin, *Census*, 150, 170. The reassignment of slaves from the Windward Coast to the Bight of Benin accounts for the difference between my estimates and those of Manning ('Bight of Benin', 117).

[83] J. T. Hardyman, 'The Madagascar slave-trade to the Americas (1632–1830)', in *Océan Indien et Méditerranée: Travaux du Sixième Colloque International d'Histoire Maritime et du Deuxième Congrès de l'Association Historique Internationale de l'Océan Indien* (Lisbon, 1963), 516. Also see Gwyn Campbell, 'Madagascar and the slave trade, 1810–1895', *Journal of African History*, XXII, ii, 1981, 203–27, although Campbell does not make any projections for total exports.

[84] James C. Armstrong, 'The slaves, 1652–1795', in Richard Elphick and Hermann Giliomee, eds., *The Shaping of South African Society, 1652–1820* (London, 1979), 77–84. Armstrong accounts for 4,300 slaves imported on ships of the Dutch East India Company, 66 per cent of whom came from Madagascar, between 1652 and 1795. Other slaves were brought in by private merchants, officials trading on their own account, ships returning from the East Indies, and slavers on their way to the Americas. While Armstrong does not hazard an estimate for total imports, it is clear that the number must have been considerably larger than the volume of company imports in order to account for the size of the slave population by the 1790s – estimated at 25,000.

[85] J. M. Filliot, *La Traite des esclaves vers les Mascareignes au XVIIIᵉ siècle* (Paris, 1974), 54, 69; M. D. D. Newitt, *The Portuguese Settlement on the Zambezi* (London, 1973), 221, where it is estimated that 7,000 slaves per year were exported to the Mascarenes between 1815 and 1830; Alpers, *Ivory and Slaves*, 214, where it is noted that the trade between Mozambique and the Mascarenes continued in the 1810s and 1820s; and François Renault, *Libération d'esclaves et nouvelle servitude* (Paris, 1976), 158, where the *engagé* trade is estimated at 45,000 between 1848 and the end of the century.

VOLUME OF THE ATLANTIC SLAVE TRADE 495

have been revised, indeed some of them upwards by substantial amounts, but such increases in single components of the trade do not necessarily modify Curtin's original estimate of the total number of slaves imported into the Americas. Although his figure of 9,566,100 is often used for convenience, Curtin states that the total was 'about ten million', with an allowance for error of several hundred thousand. He claimed that 'it is extremely unlikely that the ultimate total will turn out to be less than 8,000,000 or more than 10,500,000'.[86] My synthesis of the partial totals supports Curtin's total estimate for imports into the Americas and the islands of the Atlantic basin.

The misunderstanding has arisen from a failure to distinguish between Curtin's various estimates for different portions of the export trade from Africa, on the one hand, and his overall projection for total imports into the Americas, on the other hand. Curtin did not attempt to reach a figure for total exports from Africa based on export data because of gaps in his material,[87] although, as is evident from the preceding section of this article, it is now possible to calculate a figure which is based largely on export data. Revisions of Curtin's census have concentrated on partial totals, and the unwary scholar may well have been fooled by these revisions. After all, there is a logical connexion between the export trade and the level of imports – the difference being losses in transit. Nonetheless, upward revisions of the partial figures for slave exports do not necessarily affect Curtin's total estimate for slave imports, since revisions can cancel each other or fill in gaps in the export data.

As Curtin demonstrated in his analysis of the historiography of earlier estimates of slave imports into the Americas, Noel Deerr is the only modern scholar to advance a serious figure before 1969, and Deerr's figure of 11,970,000 slaves was virtually ignored by other scholars.[88] The fashionable estimate was 15 million – usually considered a conservative estimate – and some guesses ranged as high as 50 million and more. Except for Deerr, most scholars relied – knowingly or not – on an American publicist for the Mexican government, one Edward E. Dunbar, who in 1861 estimated the number of imports at 13,877,500, or Robert Dale Owen, who in 1864 calculated the volume of imports at 15,520,000 (Table 8). Inikori's figure of 13,392,000 and Rawley's figure of 11,345,000 are the only other estimates since 1969 – before my own.

In order to compare the various estimates of Deerr, Curtin, Inikori, Rawley and others, I have adjusted their import totals – incorporating a percentage for losses at sea – to arrive at export figures, and I have estimated the volume of slave imports into the Americas for my export figure (Table 8). My calculation for total imports (9,778,500) does not include the 56,000 *libertos*

---

[86] Curtin, *Census*, 86–93, 269.

[87] Curtin considered the problem of estimating the volume of the trade by comparing data on slave exports with data on slave imports (*Census*, 217–220). For the period 1761–1810 his calculations for exports – based on shipping data for the non-Portuguese carriers – was 8 per cent lower than his calculations for imports into the Americas (other than Brazil, whose imports were equated with the Portuguese trade). Curtin thought that this discrepancy was more likely to be a result of double counting in the import series than in an underestimation of the volume of exports from Africa, but he warned that a clear solution was not possible on the evidence available in 1969. It is now clear that Curtin was right in suspecting the import data, although he was also low on the export data.

[88] Noel Deerr, *The History of Sugar* (London, 1950), II, 284; and Curtin, *Census*, 3–13.

PAUL E. LOVEJOY

Table 8. *Estimates of the Atlantic slave trade, 1450–1867*

Source	Imports	Exports (10% loss at sea)	Exports (15% loss at sea)	Exports (20% loss at sea)
Owen	15,520,000	17,244,000	18,259,000	19,400,000
Dunbar	13,887,500	15,431,000	16,338,000	17,359,000
Kuczynski	14,650,000	16,278,000	17,235,000	18,313,000
Deerr	11,970,000	13,300,000	14,082,000	14,963,000
Curtin	9,566,100	10,629,000	11,254,000	11,957,600
Inikori	13,392,000	15,400,000		
Rawley	11,345,000	12,606,000	13,348,000	14,181,000
Lovejoy	9,778,500	11,642,000		

Sources: Robert Dale Owen, *The Wrong of Slavery: The Right of Emancipation and the Future of the African Race in the United States* (Philadelphia, 1864), 38; Edward E. Dunbar, 'History of the rise and decline of commercial slavery in America, with reference to the future of Mexico', *The Mexican Papers*, 1 (1861), 269–70; Robert R. Kuczynski, *Population Movements* (Oxford, 1936), 12; Noel Deerr, *The History of Sugar* (London, 1950), II, 284; Philip D. Curtin, *The Atlantic Slave Trade: A Census* (Madison, 1969), 268; J. E. Inikori, 'The origin of the Diaspora: The slave from Africa', *Tarikh*, v, iv (1978), 8; James A. Rawley, *The Transatlantic Slave Trade: A History* (New York, 1981), 428. For a discussion of the estimates by Dunbar, Kuczynski, Deer and others, see Curtin, *Census*, 3–13. My own estimates are from Tables 1 and 9, although the figure for total exports does not include the transport of *libertos* after 1870 and hence is 56,000 lower than the global total of Table 1.

taken to São Thomé after 1876, because the other estimates have also disregarded these slaves. The closeness of my results to Curtin's is not completely surprising, since there is an overlap in the data used. In particular, my figures are largely the same as Curtin's for the period before 1700, except for the addition of Vila Vilar and Fogel and Engerman. As explained above, Vila Vilar added 135,600 slaves to Curtin's estimate for imports into Spanish America, and Fogel and Engerman increased Curtin's figure for North American imports by 20,500. Other revisions – particularly Postma's work on the Dutch trade – do not affect the estimate for this period, since his estimate is based on shipping data and mine is based on population data in the Americas. For the eighteenth and nineteenth centuries, however, the partial figures of Anstey, Klein, Stein, Postma, Drescher, Miller, Eltis and others largely replace the earlier calculations of Curtin, except for some parts of the trade in the first half of the eighteenth century and the second decade of the nineteenth century. Consequently, my synthesis of the partial estimates – which relies on Curtin only to fill gaps in the different series – confirms Curtin's original projection of total imports, even though there are important modifications.

A comparison of Curtin's *Census* and the figures derived from the revisions suggests that Curtin's overall estimate was probably too high for the eighteenth century and too low for the nineteenth century, but the differences

Table 9. *Slaves imported into the Americas and Atlantic Basin*

Period	Curtin's 1969 census	Revision	Difference
1451–1600	274,900	293,400	+ 18,500
1601–1700	1,341,100	1,494,500	+153,400
1701–1810	6,051,700	5,737,600	−314,100
1811–1867	1,898,400	2,253,000	+354,600
Total	9,566,100	9,778,500	+212,400

Sources; Curtin, *Census*, 268. For the revisions, see Table 2 for 1451–1600, Table 3 for 1601–1700, Table 4 for 1701–1800 and Table 6 for 1801–10 (allowance is made for losses at sea on the order of 15 per cent), see text for 1811–67. Curtin did not include the 56,000 *libertos* transported to São Thomé between 1876 and 1900 in his estimate of the slave trade. Hence I have subtracted these slaves in my calculation.

almost cancel each other. The difference for the whole trade is 212,000 slaves (Table 9), and given the quality of the data, this difference is not very significant. Because the gross figures for slave imports are based on a combination of estimated slave populations in the Americas and shipping data, the difference between Curtin's 1969 *Census* and later revisions cannot be compared in a simple, straightforward way. Stein, Drescher, Anstey and Inikori appear to increase Curtin's estimate for 1701–1810 by several hundred thousand slaves, but Curtin's import-based estimates appear to have been too high by almost that amount. In order to estimate imports between 1701 and 1810, I have taken my figure for total exports and allowed for losses at sea on the order of 15 per cent.[89] At the height of the British trade in the last three decades of the eighteenth century, losses were considerably less; hence a figure of 12 or 13 per cent may be more accurate. If 13 per cent is used, then the number of imports would have been 5,872,500 slaves, which would be closer to Curtin's original estimate for the volume of imports in this period. The difference between Curtin's original estimate and my revision would be 179,200 instead of 314,100 slaves. This change would mean

[89] Average losses at sea between 1680 and 1749, based on a sample of 182 Dutch ships, was 20·5 per cent, while average losses between 1740 and 1795, based on a sample of 130 ships, was 17·4 per cent (Johannes Postma, 'Mortality in the Dutch slave trade, 1675–1795', in Gemery and Hogendorn, *Uncommon Market*, 255). The losses at sea for French vessels in the eighteenth century were 12·2 per cent for ships from the upper Guinea coast (based on a sample of 175 ships), 15·6 per cent for ships from the Gold Coast (based on a sample of 156 ships) and 11·0 per cent from ships from Angola (based on a sample of 101 ships), (Herbert S. Klein and Stanley L. Engerman, 'A note on mortality in the French slave trade in the eighteenth century', in Gemery and Hogendorn, *Uncommon Market*, 269). Klein and Engerman demonstrate that average losses varied with the length of voyage, but for purposes here these variations are not significant. The average losses for 441 ships, including 9 whose coastal origin is unknown (12·9 per cent losses), was 13·1 per cent. Other figures are cited in Curtin, *Census*, 277–9: T. F. Buxton recorded losses in the British trade at 8·75 per cent for 1791 (15,754 slaves) and 17 per cent for 1792 (31,554 slaves). In the Nantes trade from 1748 to 1792, losses averaged 15·2 per cent, and losses were slightly higher in the period before 1748, averaging 16·2 per cent from 1715 to 1775.

that my estimate for imports would be 347,300 slaves greater than Curtin's figure – a global estimate of 9,913,000. Other changes in the estimates for losses at sea would affect the global figure, too; for this reason all that I am claiming is that the revisions made since 1969 do not significantly alter Curtin's original global estimate. The changes do require adjustments in the distribution of exports over time, however.

Revisions for the nineteenth century, for example, balance Curtin's overestimation for the eighteenth century. In reaching a total for the period after 1810, I have estimated imports for three distinct periods: firstly, 1811–20; secondly, 1821–43, and thirdly, 1844–67. In the first period 441,000 slaves were imported. This figure is derived as follows. Curtin estimated 127,700 slaves imported into Spanish America, the French Caribbean and the United States. Another 45,000 slaves came from Mozambique, primarily to Brazil (allowance is made for 25 per cent losses at sea). Another 218,000 slaves came from West-Central Africa, while 50,000 slaves were imported into Brazil from the Bight of Benin on Portuguese ships. In the 1821–43 period, following the work of Eltis, 1,300,000 slaves were imported, which allows for losses at sea of 10 per cent, and accounts for slaves who were liberated before reaching the Americas.[90] Finally, 512,300 slaves were imported between 1844 and 1867. The period after 1820 is particularly well documented, and while Eltis has shown that Curtin's estimates need to be raised for the years 1821–43, the estimate for the last twenty-four years of the trade requires virtually no adjustment. As Eltis has noted for these years:

> the aggregate picture, for...African exports, is uncannily close to that drawn by Curtin. The latter estimated total imports in this period at 510,000 compared to estimates here of 511,750. But then the present researcher is not alone in having toiled through the archives only to finish up with data which largely confirm the broad estimates contained in the *Census*.[91]

I have added another few hundred to account for Dutch exports from the Gold Coast, but such a minor adjustment only serves to confirm Eltis's sense of the uncanny.

Another way to estimate the total volume of imports is to adjust Curtin's original projection by incorporating the revisions of those scholars who have presented alternative figures for imports into the different receiving areas in the Americas. Rawley attempted to follow this procedure, but he confused the import totals for different colonies with the carrying trade of the various European countries. Nonetheless, if the figures for North America, Spanish America and Brazil are adjusted according to the findings of Fogel and Engerman, Vila Vilar and Eltis, a more accurate revision of Curtin's census can be obtained. At present, however, this revision must be considered tentative, for I have not attempted to assess the volume of imports into the majority of receiving areas. Inikori criticized Curtin's estimates for French

[90] Average losses at sea between 1821 and 1843 varied with the coastal origin and destination, the major determinant being distance of the voyage. Losses from Senegambia averaged 15·5 per cent (based on a sample of 28 ships); from the Bights of Benin and Biafra, 10·2 per cent (based on a sample of 83 ships); from western-central Africa, 6·7 per cent (based on a sample of 509 ships); and from southeastern Africa, 16·7 per cent (based on a sample of 167 ships). The average for all ships, including 18 from unspecified origins (18 per cent losses), was 10·1 per cent (sample of 805 ships) Eltis, 'Transatlantic slave trade, 1821–1843', 292).

[91] Eltis, 'Direction and fluctuation of the Transatlantic trade, 1844–1867'.

VOLUME OF THE ATLANTIC SLAVE TRADE   499

Saint-Domingue, and it may well be that a thorough investigation of imports into the French Caribbean will result in an upward revision of Curtin's estimate.[92] On the other hand, a review of Spanish America from 1640 to 1773 may require a downward revision of Curtin's estimate, despite Rout's claim to the contrary.

Present revisions of the estimates for slave imports into different receiving areas suggest that Curtin's figure should be raised by 600,000 slaves. Vila Vilar has accounted for an additional 135,600 slaves imported into Spanish America between 1595 and 1640.[93] Fogel and Engerman have established that North American imports were probably 168,000 higher than Curtin allowed.[94] Finally, Eltis has suggested that Curtin's import data for 1821–43 is too low, although it is difficult to establish a figure, since Curtin and Eltis made estimates for different periods.[95] Eltis has estimated 511,750 slaves imported from 1844–67 and just under 1·3 million slaves from 1821–43, for a total of over 1·8 million for 1821–67. Curtin estimated 1,898,400 slaves imported from 1811 to 1870.[96] As discussed above, I have estimated that 441,000 slaves were imported in the second decade of the nineteenth century; hence the difference between the revisions of Eltis and Curtin's original calculation is about 340,000 additional slaves.

As a rough guide, therefore, an estimate for the slave trade derived from import-based data is approximately 10,210,000 slaves, which is very close to the estimate suggested in Rawley's calculation, once his tables are corrected for errors. This rough estimate is, of course, still within the range of Curtin's original projection, and it provides some confirmation that my global total is of the right order of magnitude. Until additional research is done on the volume of imports into the different receiving areas, however, my global estimate for imports (9·8–9·9 million slaves) is preferred. Further revisions could well require the addition of another hundred thousand slaves or so in order to allow for the trade of the minor ports in France, Britain and elsewhere in the eighteenth century and the trade to the offshore islands (Madeira, Cape Verde, etc.) after 1600. Again it must be stressed, therefore, that my synthesis is only the next stage in the continuing effort to calculate the volume of the Atlantic slave trade.

CONCLUSION

There is no question that the Atlantic slave trade had a tremendous impact on Africa. Despite the probable error in the regional breakdown of slave shipments, this impact can be quantified in broad outline for virtually the whole of the trade. Western central Africa (the Angolan coast north to Cabinda) was drawn into the trade on a significant scale in the sixteenth century and remained a major exporting region until the end of the trade in the nineteenth century. The Bight of Benin became a second major source

---

[92] Inikori, 'Assessment of Curtin and Anstey', 202–4; and Inikori, 'Rejoinder', 617–22.

[93] Vila Vilar, *Comercio de esclavos*, 206–9.

[94] Fogel and Engerman, *Time on the Cross. Evidence and Methods*, 30–1.

[95] Eltis, 'Transatlantic slave trade, 1821–1843', 291, where Eltis estimates that his total for 1821–43 is 30 per cent higher than Curtin's figure, but my calculation suggests that Eltis is about 19 per cent higher.

[96] Curtin, *Census*, 268.

of slaves in the second half of the seventeenth century, and from there the trade spread westward to the Gold Coast by 1700 and eastward to the Bight of Biafra by the 1740s. The Sierra Leone coast, including the rivers to the north, was another focal point of the export trade, although the expansion of slave exports there grew relatively slowly until the middle of the eighteenth century, when for two decades exports were very large. Senegambia entered the trade early and retained a relatively fixed, but small, place in total exports until the nineteenth century. Southeast Africa, by contrast, was drawn in relatively late; only after the movement to end the slave trade began to have an impact was it advantageous to seek slaves so far from the Americas. The decline of slave exports occurred in parallel stages to the rise of the trade. The Gold Coast ceased to supply large numbers of slaves by the first decade of the nineteenth century, while the supplies from the Bight of Biafra fell off in the 1830s. The Bight of Benin and western-central Africa remained important sources of slaves until the 1850s, and southeastern Africa also continued to supply exports until the end.

While these broad patterns have been understood for some time, is is now possible to analyse internal African developments much more fully, now that Curtin's export figures have been revised and tested. Scholars are likely to modify these estimates further. For the time being, however, it can be expected that detailed studies of political, economic and social changes will attempt to correlate the volume of exports with local developments. Because slaves were a peculiar commodity, representing labour power lost to local societies as well as a commodity whose value could be exchanged on the international market, the export trade distorted the historical process in an equally peculiar way. Various scholars have attempted to analyse the nature of this distortion: Walter Rodney talked about the process in terms of under-development;[97] Fage has emphasized the political impact while attempting to minimize the demographic consequences;[98] Inikori has argued that the trade retarded economic development, particularly because of severe demographic losses.[99] I have argued that the growth of the export trade was related to the consolidation of a mode of production based on slavery.[100] These examples are but a few of the many studies which take the 'numbers game' seriously.[101] Slaves were more than commodities and numbers, of course, which is a major reason why the study of slavery retains its significance.

[97] Walter Rodney, How Europe Underdeveloped Africa (London, 1972).

[98] Fage, History of Africa, 244–88.

[99] Inikori, 'Introduction', 13–60.

[100] Lovejoy, Transformations in Slavery.

[101] Edward Reynolds, Stand the Storm: A History of the Atlantic Slave Trade (New York, 1982), does not attempt a new estimate for the volume of the trade, and instead relies on Curtin's study. Nonetheless, his analysis of the impact of the slave trade on Africa is an important aspect of his study.

3

Migrations of Africans to the Americas: The Impact on Africans, Africa, and the New World

Patrick Manning

THE MOVEMENT OF AFRICANS to the Americas from the seventeenth to the nineteenth centuries may be accounted as mankind's second-largest transoceanic migration. This migration, along with the concurrent African migration to the Middle East and North Africa, was distinct from other major modern migrations in its involuntary nature, and in the high rates of mortality and social dislocation caused by the methods of capture and transportation. A related migratory pattern, the capture and settling of millions of slaves within Africa, grew up in eighteenth- and nineteenth-century Africa as a consequence of the two patterns of overseas slave trade.

These three dimensions to the enslavement of Africans—which I have elsewhere labelled as the Occidental, Oriental, and African slave trades—were interrelated, so that there are advantages to treating them as an ensemble.[1] At the same time, my purpose here is to focus on migration to the Americas, where Africans interacted with native American inhabitants and with European settlers. This paper is therefore divided into three sections, considering the migration of Africans to the Americas first in an American perspective, then in an African perspective, and finally in a global perspective including the Americas, Africa, and the Atlantic.

To simplify the presentation, I have restricted the quantitative data to the period from 1600 to 1800. The earlier slave trade, before 1600, was quantitatively small but socially significant. The later slave trade, after 1800, was large and significant, bringing nearly three million slaves (roughly one fourth of the total) to the Americas; African captives reached the shores of Cuba and Brazil into the late 1860s.[2] Still, the patterns I describe below for the period 1600-1800 apply, in large measure, to the entire period of the Atlantic slave trade.

The American Perspective

David Eltis posed, in a 1983 article, a striking contrast in the population history of the Americas.[3] By 1820, there had been about 8.4 million African immigrants to the Americas, and 2.4 million European immigrants. But by that date the Euro-American population of some 12 million exceeded the Afro-American population of about 11 million. The rates of survival and reproduction of African immigrants were, apparently, dramatically lower than those of European immigrants. Eltis's contrast drew attention to the range of demographic comparisons necessary to make sense of this puzzle: the rates of fertility and mortality, the timing and location of immigration, the sex ratios and the social identification of persons.

The table below shows estimated numbers of immigrants from Africa up to 1800, by the region to which they immigrated. These figures, despite their apparent precision, are very rough indeed: they involve a

African Immigrants, by Period and Place of Arrival (All figures in thousands of persons.)					
Region	to 1600	1600– 1640	1640– 1700	1700– 1760	1760– 1800
North America (Br, Fr, Sp)	–	1	20	171	177
Caribbean – non-Spanish	–	9	454	1623	1809
British Caribbean	–	8	255	900	1085
French Caribbean	–	1	155	474	573
Other Caribbean	–	–	44	249	151
Spanish America	75	269	186	271	235
Spanish Caribbean	7	20	14	27	140
Mexico & Central America	23	70	48	13	5
Venezuela-Colombia-Peru	45	135	93	160	60
La Plata-Bolivia	–	44	30	71	30
Brazil	50	160	400	960	726
Total	125	439	1060	3025	2947
Annual average, in thousands	1	11	18	50	70

number of assumptions, extrapolations and interpolations, including the inevitable confusion between numbers of slaves exported from Africa and imported to the Americas. As a result, all the figures, and particularly the smaller ones, must be seen as having margins of error of perhaps twenty percent. Nonetheless, they are worth presenting for the clear patterns they reveal. The table accounts for a total of about 7.6 million immigrant slaves up to 1800; nearly three million more slaves would arrive, principally to Brazil and Cuba, during the nineteenth century.[4]

To display some of the immigration data in schematic form, I have prepared FIGURE 1, which gives estimates, for various regions of the Americas, of the numbers of African immigrants in the 1620s (before North European entry into the trade), in the 1700s (once the Caribbean sugar trade had become fully established and the prices of African slaves had risen sharply), and in the 1780s (at the height of the Atlantic slave trade).

The figure, while it indicates the wide geographical distribution of African slaves throughout the Americas, also emphasizes their concentration in the English and French Caribbean. There, on the sugar plantations of the eighteenth century, over three million slaves were consigned to oblivion. The African-descended population of the Caribbean is today about twenty-five million, or less than a fifth of the more than one hundred and fifty million people of African descent in the Americas.

The migratory history of African slaves, once they landed in the Americas, sometimes continued for several further stages. The initial period of seasoning can be considered as migration through a change in status. Further, many slaves were physically transshipped, often over considerable distances. Slaves brought by the Dutch to Curaçao and by the English to Jamaica were transshipped to Cartagena, Portobelo, and on to various Spanish colonies. From Cartagena, some slaves were settled down in Colombia. A larger number of slaves went to Portobelo in Panama, walked overland, and then went by sea to Lima. Most remained there, but some went into the highlands. Slaves landed in the Rio de La Plata went overland for 900 kilometers to Tucuman and then on for another 600 kilometers to the silver mines at Potosi. In Brazil, with the gold rush in Minas Gerais at the turn of the eighteenth century, slaves were sent overland to the mining areas, 300 kilometers from Rio and a much longer distance overland from Bahia. Slaves entering the Chesapeake and South Carolina came, in significant proportion, after stopping in Barbados. A final stage in the migration of some slaves was their liberation—either by emancipation, by self-purchase, or by escape.

One reason for emphasizing the number of distinct stages in the migration of Africans is to draw attention to the distinct rates of mortal-

Patrick Manning

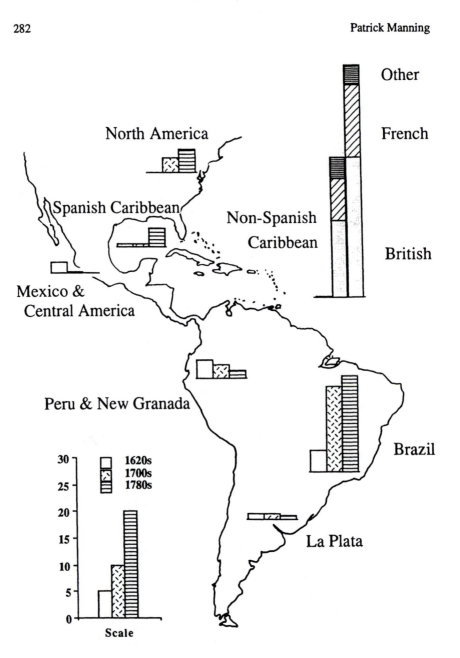

FIGURE 1.
Immigrants from Africa (1620s, 1700s, 1780s),
in thousands per decade.

ity and fertility at each stage. The mortality which is best known is that of the Atlantic crossing. (Crude mortality rates averaged about fifteen percent per voyage. While slave voyages averaged from two to three months in length, mortality is usually calculated on an annual basis. If slaves had encountered Middle Passage conditions for a full year, their motality rate might have come to over five hundred per thousand per year. We will return below to Middle Passage mortality.) The point here is that slaves who survived the crossing had then to undergo various other types of elevated mortality: that of further travel within the Americas, that of seasoning in the locale where they were settled, and that of daily existence in slave status, where mortality was generally higher than for equivalent persons of free status. To this list must be added the fact that most slaves were settled in low-lying tropical areas where the general level of mortality was greater than in higher, temperate regions.

Fertility rates were generally lower for populations of slave status than for free populations. Fertility rates for slaves in the course of transportation, while not recorded in any detail, were certainly at an exceptionally low level. Most studies on fertility of African-American populations have focused, as is traditional and simplest, on the fertility of women. But because of the large excess of men among immigrant Africans, and because they did have children not only with African women but also with Indian and European women, there is an argument for more systematic consideration of the fertility of male Africans and African-Americans than has been undertaken thus far.[5]

A thorough accounting of the migration of Africans to the Americas would include the regional African origins—even the ethnic origins, age and sex distribution—of those disembarking in each American region. Such an accounting could now be estimated, based on recently developed evidence, though I will not attempt such an estimate here. In this regard, it is perhaps of interest that in recent years, and especially for the eighteenth and nineteenth centuries, scholars have given more attention to regional breakdowns and global synthesis in migratory movements on the African side of the Atlantic than to the equivalent details of immigration to the Americas.[6]

To give but two of the many examples that could be given of the specificity and change in African origins of American populations: In Louisiana, the initial slave population settled by the French in the early eighteenth century drew heavily on Bambara men from the upper Niger valley. This male slave population maintained and passed on its traditions because the Bambara men married Native American women, also enslaved. After 1770, the larger number of slaves entering Louisiana under

Spanish rule was dominated by slaves from the Bight of Benin, including a large minority of women; these slaves brought the religion of vodoun to Louisiana. Second, while slaves from Congo and Angola were numerous among those imported to all regions of the Americas, they were virtually the only slaves imported to Rio de Janeiro from the seventeenth into the nineteenth century. The black populations of Rio, and to a lesser extent of Minas Gerais, had a degree of cultural homogeneity unusual for slaves in the Americas.[7]

The debates of the 1960s and 1970s focused on the total number of slaves crossing the Atlantic, and obscured questions of the distribution of African migrants over time, by age and by sex. The steady assemblage of slave trade data is permitting these issues to be addressed in increasing detail, and clear patterns have now come to light (FIGURE 2). With the passage of time from the seventeenth to the nineteenth centuries, the proportion of adult male slaves shipped increased slightly, the proportion of adult female slaves shipped decreased significantly, and the proportion of children shipped, both male and female, increased over time.[8]

For slave men, women, and children, the rate of labor force participation was generally high, as compared to free populations. Most of the work of slaves could be categorized into the occupations of mining, plantation work, artisanal work, transport, and domestic service. In Spanish America, slaves were concentrated most visibly in mining and artisanal work until the late eighteenth century, when sugar and tobacco plantation work began to dominate Cuba while slavery declined elsewhere. In Brazil, sugar plantation work dominated the sixteenth and seventeenth centuries, while mining work expanded greatly in the eighteenth century. The English and French Caribbean focused on sugar production, though coffee and livestock occupied significant numbers of slaves. Tobacco production occupied large numbers of slaves in Bahia and North America; cotton production expanded from the 1760s in Maranhão, and later in North America.

The rise to profitability of this succession of industries seems to have provided the main "pull" factor driving the movement of slaves to the Americas from Africa. The demand for sugar workers in sixteenth-century Brazil, the seventeenth-century Caribbean and nineteenth-century Cuba brought a supply response from Africa. Similarly, the demand for mine workers in eighteenth-century Minas Gerais and New Granada brought an African response. Overall, the African and African-descended population of the Americas grew steadily through the seventeenth and eighteenth centuries, though it went into decline for as much as several decades whenever and wherever the import of additional slaves came to a halt.

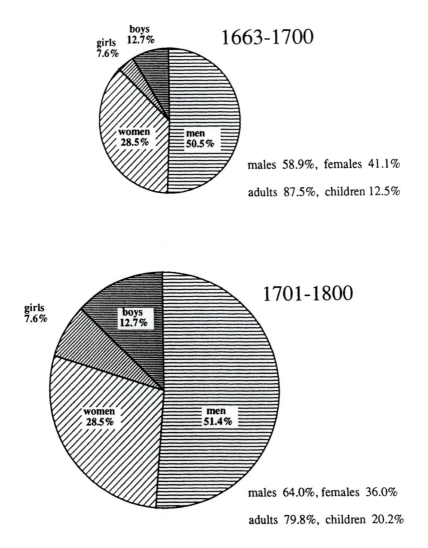

1663-1700

boys 12.7%
girls 7.6%
women 28.5%
men 50.5%

males 58.9%, females 41.1%

adults 87.5%, children 12.5%

1701-1800

girls 7.6%
boys 12.7%
women 28.5%
men 51.4%

males 64.0%, females 36.0%

adults 79.8%, children 20.2%

FIGURE 2.
African immigrants by age and sex,
seventeenth and eighteenth centuries (source: Eltis and Engerman).

The African Perspective

From the standpoint of the African continent, the slave trade to the Americas interacted with other migratory movements, including slave trading within Africa. Before the seventeenth century, sub-Saharan African societies lacked the powerful states and the lucrative trade routes necessary to support an extensive system of slavery, so that slavery in Africa was almost everywhere a marginal institution. The exceptions were the large states of the Saharan fringe, notably Songhai. The trade in slaves to Saharan oases, to North Africa and West Asia took an estimated ten thousand persons per year in the sixteenth century. The oceanic slave trade from Africa in the sixteenth century was dominated by the movement of slaves to Europe and to such Atlantic islands as the Canaries and São Thome.

By the mid-seventeenth century the migration of slaves to Europe and the Atlantic islands had declined sharply, and the trans-Atlantic trade had expanded to the point where it exceeded the volume of the Saharan trade. The expansion of the Occidental trade brought, as a by-product, the development of an African trade: growth in slave exports led to the creation of expanded networks of slave supply, and these permitted wealthy Africans to buy slaves in unprecedented numbers.

In the eighteenth century, the continued expansion of the Occidental trade brought a substantial growth in the African trade, particularly as female slaves were held within African societies. The effects of this slave trade were felt mostly in West Africa and West Central Africa. Then, late in the eighteenth century, the slave trade expanded to much of Eastern Africa. Occidental merchants began purchasing slaves from Mozambique. Growing Middle Eastern demand for slaves (occasioned by an apparent growth in Middle Eastern economies that is still not well explained) led to expansion of the slave trade in modern Sudan, the Horn, and the Indian Ocean coast of Africa. Expanded slave exports in turn stimulated the development of enslavement within Eastern Africa, a development which accelerated sharply during the nineteenth century.[9] These general movements provide the context for the examples of African emigration to the Americas given in FIGURE 3.

The movement of so many slaves to the African coast for export entailed large-scale capture and migration. Distances for the movement of slaves to the coast could be small (an average of less than 100 kilometers for the large number of slaves from the Bight of Benin in the early eighteenth century), or they could be immense (some 600 kilometers for the Bambara slaves from West Africa who formed the nucleus of the Louisiana slave population; similar distances for slaves of the Lunda who

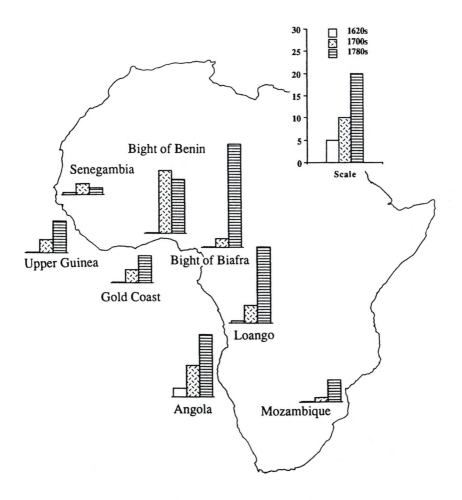

FIGURE 3.
African emigrants to the Americas (1620s, 1700s, 1780s),
in thousands per decade.

passed through Angola on their way to Rio.) These distances, travelled slowly and over long periods, brought elevated mortality with them.

Overall, then, the mortality of slaves within Africa was high, and their fertility was low. The considerations summarized above, with regard to the fertility and mortality of slaves in the Americas as they passed through transportation, seasoning, slave life and occasional liberation, apply in equivalent terms to the roughly equal numbers of persons in slave status at the same time in Africa. It must be emphasized that the high levels of mortality applied not only to the slaves delivered to the coast to be exported across the Atlantic, but to the nearly equal number of persons (most of them female) captured, transported to distant areas, and purchased as slaves within Africa.

This grim tale of slave mortality is not the whole of the story, of course, in that the purpose of the slave trade was to deliver live workers to the purchasers. We should therefore mention, at least, the economic network developed for supply of the trade in Africa. Considerable labor and investment were required to provide transport, finance, food, clothing, lodging, guards, and medicine for the slaves. These systems of slave delivery, though they differed from region to region, became a significant element in the African economic landscape.[10]

The slaves held within Africa, numerous though they were, did not become readily visible to outside observers until the nineteenth century. This was because, along the western coast of Africa, most eighteenth-century slaves were women: they were held within families, and their productivity was mainly aimed at expanding the family economy. However, the Scottish explorer Mungo Park, travelling in the Senegal and Niger valleys at the end of the eighteenth century, found large proportions of the population to be held in slavery.[11] He encountered a type of economic system that was to spread widely through the continent in the nineteenth century. Adult males as well as females were held in slavery in large numbers, and slave men and women now tended to live apart from their masters as a slave class; their productivity was focused on marketable commodities. These included such African exports as palm oil, peanuts and coffee, but were more focused on yams, grains and cotton for the domestic market.

The evidence of transformation in African economic life through the expansion of slavery gives some hint of the accompanying social and ideological changes. Classes of merchants and monarchs rose with the export trade, and classes of landowners rose with the nineteenth-century growth of market-oriented slavery. Values emphasizing hierarchy arose in the societies holding and trading in slaves; egalitarian values were reaffirmed in societies resisting enslavement.[12]

The most obvious "push" factors sending African slaves across the Atlantic were war and famine. The savanna areas of marginal rainfall—Angola and the grasslands extending from Senegambia east to Cameroon—underwent periodic drought and famine, and in these times desperate families sold both children and adults.[13] The relation between warfare and enslavement is in one sense obvious, but on the other hand there have been two centuries of debate over whether the African wars broke out for purely domestic reasons, or whether the European demand for slaves stimulated additional wars.

Overall, the export of slaves from Africa halted and then reversed growth of the continent's population. During the seventeenth century, such population decline took place in restricted areas of coastal Senegambia, Upper Guinea and Angola. After about 1730, the decline became general for the coast from Senegal to Angola, and continued to about 1850. The decline was slow rather than precipitous. Even though the number of slaves exported averaged little more than three per thousand of the African regional population, and even though the trade took more males than females, the combination of the mortality of capture and transportation with the concentration of captures on young adults meant that Africa lost enough young women to reverse an intrinsic growth rate of five per thousand. The same processes transformed the structure of the population, causing the adult sex ratio to decline to an average of 80 men per 100 women.[14]

A Global Perspective

Despite—indeed, because of—the immigration of Europeans and Africans, the total population of the Americas declined in the sixteenth and seventeenth centuries. While estimates of the pre-Columbian populations must remain speculative, the population of the Americas fell to perhaps as little as five million persons during the seventeenth century.[15]

The threatened void of population in the Americas encouraged the transformation of African slavery from a marginal institution to a central element in a global system of population and labor. The global market for slaves encompassed the Americas, Africa, the Indian Ocean and Western Asia in the eighteenth and nineteenth centuries; it interacted more broadly with the regimes of population and labor in the Americas, Europe and Western Asia. When slave prices rose sharply (as they did at the turn of the eighteenth century) or fell significantly (as they did in the eastern hemisphere in the early nineteenth century), slave laborers were moved in new directions in response to economic incentives. Free workers on every continent moved, similarly, in response to these changes in the value of labor.

Before 1600, African migration to the Americas, while it may have exceeded European migration, was small in magnitude. During the time when the Indian population was declining but still large, Africans in the Americas, while usually in slave status, were nonetheless often persons of relatively high value, serving in the military and in artisanal tasks. In Brazil, large-scale enslavement of Indians for work on sugar plantations characterized the late sixteenth century. African laborers, concentrated at first in the skilled occupations on the plantations, gradually displaced the disappearing Indians at all levels of work.

In the seventeenth century, the scarcity of Indian laborers made Africans appear, by comparison, more plentiful. Still, for much if not all of the century, the addition of African and European immigrants and their progeny was insufficient to offset the decline in Indian population.

By the eighteenth century, all the major population groups—those of Indian, European, African, and mestizo or mulatto ancestry—were growing, though from a very sparse base. However, in this period the large-scale removal of Africans from their homes to serve as slaves in the Americas, with all its attendant carnage, brought population decline for region after region in Africa, and finally for the western African coast as a whole. Consequently, the African addition to the population of the Americas (both by immigration and by natural reproduction) was insufficient to make up for the loss of population in Africa.

The centrality of African labor was costly to the slaves, and was costly in the longer run to their societies of origin. In the eighteenth and nineteenth centuries the populations of Europe, the Americas and Asia grew at unprecedented rates, apparently as a result of improved immunities, certain social changes, and perhaps improved public health conditions. In the nineteenth century these rapidly growing populations spun off millions of migrants, who searched near and far for the means to make a better living. For Africa, in contrast, the population remained stagnant or in decline, and labor migration mostly took place, even within the continent, by the forcible means which interfered with population growth.

If we link the American pull and African push factors noted above, we find that they do not yet cohere into a full theory for the migration. Three main factors have been advanced, by different groups of scholars, to explain the migration more generally. The first factor is epidemiology: the relative immunity of Africans to the diseases of the tropics enabled them to survive at a greater rate than Americans or Europeans. Hence they were more valuable and more sought after as plantation laborers. Second is relative productivity. Given the technical limits of African hoe agriculture in comparison to the more productive plow agriculture of Europeans, even a highly productive laborer in Africa could not produce as much food as an ordinary laborer in Europe. In these terms, the value or price of a European laborer was greater than that of an African. European merchants, therefore, were able to buy slaves by paying Africans more than the value of an average laborer in Africa, yet bring laborers to the Americas that were far cheaper than European laborers. The third factor is transportation costs. When Africans sought to buy goods on the world market, they had to offer local goods in exchange. Such export goods needed a high ratio of value to weight, or the high costs of transportation would consume all profits. Africa did export gold, but lacked minerals in many regions; African textiles and art work were not recognized as luxury goods overseas. Slaves were the next most valuable commodity, and so they came to dominate Africa's export trade. (In the nineteenth century, as transportation became more inexpensive, Africans turned steadily from the slave trade to exporting peanuts, palm oil and other agricultural commodities.)[16] The prices of slaves reflect the sum of these three factors, and perhaps others as well. Slave prices, however, have yet to be studied in a fully comparative and comprehensive fashion. We may hope that further studies will reveal more of the relative dominance and the interplay of these three factors — or, more simply, more of the reasons why the slave trade continued so long.

One way to signal the cost to Africa of this sort of participation in the world economy is to estimate the number of persons who died in the Middle Passage. Since the mortality schedule for the Middle Passage was somewhere between five and ten times higher than the normal mortality schedule, one is not far off by saying that all the deaths taking place on slave ships would not otherwise have taken place. Rough estimates of the cumulative total of deaths at sea come to a total of sixty thousand for the period before 1600, three hundred thousand for the seventeenth century, a million for the eighteenth century, and half a million for the nineteenth century. To get the total excess mortality brought about by the slave trade, aside from that of the condition of slavery itself, one would have to add the deaths in the course of African capture and transportation, and those in the course of resettlement and seasoning in the Americas.[17]

On the other hand, we may choose to emphasize life rather than death. As of the mid-eighteenth century, when the population of the Americas had rebounded to perhaps as much as ten million, that total included roughly two million black slaves and another million free persons of color, with the latter concentrated in the Portuguese and Spanish territories. Two million free whites and five million Indians rounded out the total. The regional distribution included a million inhabitants in the Caribbean, the most densely populated area. North America and Brazil each had populations of roughly one and one-half million, and the

Spanish mainland colonies had roughly five million inhabitants. The Americas grew rapidly in population during the eighteenth century, but trailed the Old World distantly. The population of sub-Saharan Africa totaled some fifty million persons, about twenty million of whom lived in the areas of the western coast of Africa from which slaves were dispatched across the Atlantic. Western Europe's population, far denser and in a smaller area, totaled roughly one hundred million.[18]

The European and African migrations to the Americas shared a number of characteristics in the seventeenth and eighteenth centuries. The migrants were dominantly male, and they suffered elevated levels of mortality. But several distinctions between European and African migration stand out. Africans had no pattern of return migration eastward across the Atlantic parallel to that of the Europeans, and Africans were not able to repatriate earnings to their home societies. Thus, while emigration strengthened the external trade of Africa, it did so with a weaker multiplier than that for Europe.[19] African migrants underwent an extra mortality cost in Africa and in the Middle Passage because of the violence of enslavement.

African rates of emigration were substantially higher than those of Europe. For the eighteenth century, the overall rate of emigration from the affected areas was three to four per thousand per year; this figure rose to as much as thirty per thousand per year for the Bight of Benin in the early eighteenth century. Since many more males than females left Africa, the sex ratio and marriage patterns on both sides of the Atlantic felt new pressures. In Africa, the relative surplus of adult women seems certain to have expanded the rate of polygynous marriage, and to have changed the sexual division of labor. In the Americas, very few men were able to have more than one wife, and many were unable to find a mate. This suggests a further contrast between African and European migrants: European males, because of their higher social status, had a wider range of choices of women among European, African and Indian populations, and were thus more likely to have offspring than African men.

To return to the puzzle posed by David Eltis, we can now recapitulate, though not yet in rank order, the factors responsible for the differential growth in American populations of European and African origin. Africans went in larger proportion to the high-mortality areas, the tropical lowlands. They arrived later than Europeans, on average, so that those populations which did become self-sustaining had less time to grow.[20] In addition, the condition of slavery increased the mortality and reduced the fertility of African immigrants. Finally, it may well be that the populations known as "white" and "mestizo" today include larger components of African and Indian ancestry than is now realized.

The transatlantic migration of slaves brought a rich African contribution to the culture of the Americas—in religion, cuisine, dress, language and philosophy. In language the African impact can be seen in two main ways. First is in the development of Creole languages, such as Haitian Creole, Jamaican Patois, Papiamento of the Dutch West Indies, and Gullah of South Carolina. In these languages the vocabulary is both European and African, and the grammar is mostly African. Haitian Kreyol is now a written official language of the country, and the similar Creole of the French Antilles is becoming the leading language of a new wave of multicultural music. Second is the impact of African speech on English, Spanish, French, and Portuguese as spoken in the Americas. The single biggest reason for the differences in these languages on the two sides of the Atlantic is the contribution of African expressions in the Americas.

These and other cultural patterns of the migration can be looked at in two ways. The first is in terms of survivals: that is, the continuity of West African religion in the vodoun of Haiti, or of West African cuisine in the gumbo or hot barbecue sauce of the American South. But we can also see African contributions to New World culture in patterns of change and innovation. Here the obvious example is in jazz music, which by definition is always in change, but where the rules for musical innovation can be traced back to Africa.

In addition to the heritage from Africa, the heritage of slavery created distinct patterns of community for Africans in the Americas. Other immigrants, arriving as free persons, had the opportunity to establish their own communities, in which people of similar linguistic and cultural background built up strong local units, usually maintaining some contact with the homeland—these ranged from Swiss farming towns in the American Midwest to Cantonese merchant communities to rural Japanese communities in Brazil. African communities in the Americas were largely prevented from recreating their home societies in this way because they were not free to move, and people of varying ethnic groups were often mixed purposely by their owners to reduce solidarity. As a result, inhabitants of African settlements in the Americas tended to refer back to Africa in general rather than to particular African regions, they thought of a romanticized African past rather than of the latest news because they were cut off from home, and they constructed a new, creolized culture out of the traditions available to them rather than maintain the traditions of a particular Old World region. Quite logically, therefore, the idea of the unity of Africa grew up in the Americas.

Most of the slaves died early and without progeny. In the Americas, much of their produce was exported, consumed and soon forgotten. Still, we can find ample remains of the investments of slaves in the construction of cities and the clearing of farms. I want to give particular emphasis to the value of the work done by African slaves—in the Americas, in Africa, and in the Orient—because the tradition of racist ideology in the last 150 years has done so much to deny their importance in constructing the world we live in, as well as to deny that the underdevelopment of Africa resulted in part from their forced migration. The very term, "Western Civilization," which we use to describe the continents of Europe, North and sometimes South America, reflects this denial of Africa's role in the modern world. The term carries with it the implication that the wealth and the achievement of these continents springs solely from the heritage of Europe. The migration I have discussed above is one of many ways to demonstrate that there is more to the modern world than the expansion of Europe.

Notes

1.   Patrick Manning, *Slavery and African Life: Occidental, Oriental, and African Slave Trades* (Cambridge, 1990).

2.   For two excellent studies of early slavery, see Frederick Bowser, *The African Slave in Colonial Peru, 1524-1650* (Stanford, 1971); and Colin Palmer, *Slaves of the White God: Blacks in Mexico, 1570-1650* (Cambridge, MA, 1976). The fullest quantitative study of nineteenth-century Atlantic slave trade is David Eltis, *Economic Growth and the Ending of the Transatlantic Slave Trade* (New York, 1987). For a survey of the abolition of the slave trade and slavery in the Americas and in Africa, see Manning, *Slavery*, 149-67. For an important review of recent literature contrasting the experiences of Atlantic Africa and Islamic Africa, see Janet J. Ewald, "Slavery in Africa and the Slave Trades from Africa," *American Historical Review*, 97 (1992), 465-85.

3.   David Eltis, "Free and Coerced Transatlantic Migrations: Some Comparisons," *American Historical Review*, 88 (1983), 278.

4.   The main sources for the table are Philip D. Curtin, *The Atlantic Slave Trade: A Census* (Madison, 1969); Paul E. Lovejoy, "The Volume of the Atlantic Slave Trade: A Synthesis," *Journal of African History*, 23 (1983), 473-501; and David Richardson, "Slave Exports from West and West-Central Africa, 1700-1810: New Estimates of Volume and Distribution," *Journal of African History*, 30 (1989), 1-22. On the distribution of slaves within Spanish America, I used Enriqueta Vila Vilar, *Hispanoamérica y el comercio de esclavos* (Seville, 1977); Herbert S. Klein, *African Slavery in Latin America and the Caribbean* (New York, 1986); Marisa Vega Franco, *El tráfico de esclavos con América (Asientos de Grillo y Lomelin, 1663-1674)* (Seville, 1984); and Colin Palmer, *Human Cargoes: The British Slave Trade to Spanish America, 1700-1739* (Urbana, 1981).

Despite the error margins, one may seek and may hope to find further detail: various scholars are coding up records ship by ship, which may give us immigration in decennial or even annual terms, showing African region of origin, the carrying nation, the age and sex composition of the slave cargo, and their rates of morbidity and mortality during the voyage.

5. The changing terms by which populations identify themselves provide writers with repeated challenges. In this presentation, I have used the term "Africans" to refer to those born in Africa, "African-Americans" to refer to persons of African descent born in the Americas, and "Indians" to refer to native American peoples of South and Central America, as I think the term "Native American" is used mainly by people of the U.S.

On fertility rates of slave and free persons, see Stanley L. Engerman and B. W. Higman, "The Demographic Structure of the Caribbean Slave Societies in the Eighteenth and Nineteenth Centuries," forthcoming in Franklin W. Knight, ed. *UNESCO General History of the Caribbean*, Vol. 3.

6. Richardson, "Slave Exports"; Manning, *Slavery and African Life*; Joseph C. Miller, *Way of Death: Merchant Capitalism and the Angolan Slave Trade, 1730-1830* (Madison, 1988); David Geggus, "Sex Ratio, Age and Ethnicity in the Atlantic Slave Trade: Data from French Shipping and Plantation Records," *Journal of African History*, 30 (1989), 23-44; Paul Lovejoy, "The Impact of the Atlantic Slave Trade on Africa: A Review of the Literature," *Journal of African History*, 30 (1989), 365-394. The exception, for the nineteenth century, is the work of David Eltis which has addressed both sides of the Atlantic. See his *Economic Growth and the Ending of the Transatlantic Slave Trade* (New York, 1987), and "The Nineteenth-Century Transatlantic Slave Trade: An Annual Time Series of Imports into the Americas Broken Down by Region," *Hispanic American Historical Review*, 67 (1987), 109-38.

7. Gwendolyn Hall, *Africans in Colonial Louisiana; The Development of Afro-Creole Culture in the Eighteenth Century* (Baton Rouge, 1992); Miller, *Way of Death*.

8. David Eltis and Stanley L. Engerman, "Was the Slave Trade Dominated by Men?" *Journal of Interdisciplinary History*, 23 (1992), 237-57. For early statements of the importance of age and sex distribution in the slave trade, see John Thornton, "The Slave Trade in Eighteenth Century Angola: Effects of Demographic Structures," *Canadian Journal of African Studies*, 14 (1980), 417-27; and Patrick Manning, "The Enslavement of Africans: A Demographic Model," *Canadian Journal of African Studies*, 15 (1981), 499-526.

9. Gervase Clarence-Mathew, ed., *The Economics of the Indian Ocean Slave Trade in the Nineteenth Century* (London, 1988).

10. Miller, *Way of Death*, pp. 173-283; David Northrup, *Trade Without Rulers: Precolonial Economic Development in South-Eastern Nigeria* (Oxford, 1978), pp. 69-76.

11. Mungo Park, *Travels*.

12. These generalizations are explored in Manning, *Slavery and African Life*, pp. 118-25, 131-41.

13. Joseph C. Miller, "The Significance of Drought, Disease and Famine in the Agriculturally Marginal Zone of West-Central Africa," *Journal of African History*, 22 (1982), 17-61; Charles Becker, "Notes sur les conditions écologiques en Sénégambie au 17e et 18e siècles," *African Economic History*, 14 (1985), 167-216.

14. Manning, *Slavery and African Life*, p. 72.

15. For a dependable review of the complex issues in estimating populations of early Spanish America, see Noble David Cook, *Demographic Collapse: Indian Peru, 1520-1620* (Cambridge, 1981).

16. Philip D. Curtin, "Epidemiology and the Slave Trade," *Political Science Quarterly*, 83 (1968), 190-216; Manning, *Slavery and African Life*, pp. 30-37; Stefano

296   Patrick Manning

Fenoaltea, *The Atlantic Slave Trade: An Economic Analysis*, forthcoming from Princeton University Press.

17.   Estimates of cumulative Middle Passage mortality are 15% of the export figures given in Lovejoy, "Volume of the Atlantic Slave Trade," 478. For an estimated mortality schedule for the Atlantic crossing, see Patrick Manning and William S. Griffiths, "Divining the Unprovable: Simulating the Demography of the Atlantic Slave Trade," *Journal of Interdisciplinary History*, 19 (1988).

One important disadvantage of cumulative demographic totals such as this—whether it be for those who reached the Americas or for those who died on the way—is that they do not have a dimension of time (except that of per century), and are thus difficult to compare to standard stocks and annual flows of population.

18.   On estimated mid-eighteenth-century population in the Americas, see Engerman and Higman, "Demographic Structure"; Angel Rosenblat, *La población indígena y el mestizaje en América* (Buenos Aires, 1950); Dauril Alder, "The Population of Brazil in the Late Eighteenth Century: A Preliminary Survey," *Hispanic American Historical Review*, 43 (1963), 191, 196; Klein, *African Slavery in Latin America*. On Africa, see Manning, *Slavery and African Life*.

19. In this regard, it would be of interest to compare the imports of Africa and of Europe in the seventeenth and eighteenth centuries, and to learn of their relative composition in luxury goods, general consumer goods, money, and goods useful in investment.

20.   From the vantage point of the twentieth century, this comparison is reversed. Because so many European immigrants arrived in the late nineteenth and twentieth centuries, it is now the case that the ancestors of the average European-American arrived in the New World more recently than the ancestors of the average African-American.

4

The Apprenticeship of Colonization

Luiz Felipe de Alencastro

In the sixteenth century, Iberian colonists went across three continents, dealt with exotic communities, and tried in several ways to ensure control over natives and exploit conquered territories. Sometimes, however, these practices were antagonistic either to the national mercantile network or to the metropolitan state apparatus. Before the Century of Discoveries came to an end, metropolitan powers resumed European expansion in order to colonize their own colonists.

"Among remote people they built the new kingdom they so much exalted," Camões wrote in the "Lusíadas." But how did the overseas "new kingdom" relate to the European "old kingdom?"

Although slavery and coerced labor allowed domination of conquered populations, they did not always entail successful colonial exploitation. These relations of production did not ensure the transformation of surplus labor wrested overseas into trade connected to metropolitan networks. Colonial surplus might be consumed by colonists or traded outside areas under the control of metropolitan powers. Therefore, the establishment of slavery and coerced labor was not a sufficient condition to implement dependent economies in overseas territories occupied by Portugal and Spain.

Moreover, even though the economic surplus of overseas territories was incorporated into the metropolitan network, Iberian expansion did not necessarily lead to the reinforcement of monarchic authority. New power relations emerged inside metropolitan states and conquered territories as mercantile zones expanded and merchants improved their political influence, complicating the ruling of European territorial monarchies.

152   *Luiz Felipe de Alencastro*

Three distinct problems combined, thus, to trouble the colonial order: (1) the consolidation of royal authority over the colonist; (2) the inclusion of production from conquered areas in Atlantic trades; and (3) the confrontation between authorities, colonists, and clergy over the control of natives. In Peru, Angola, Goa, Mozambique, and Brazil, as well as in other places, colonization went astray from the very start.

THE COLONISTS' OPTIONS

In Peru and most of Spanish America, conflicts pitting colonists against clergy and crown derived from the fight to control the natives. Between 1542 and 1543 Charles V proclaimed the "New Laws," acknowledging a certain sovereignty over the Amerindians. These laws abolished concessions of Indians granted to the conquerors and gradually turned all natives to dependence on the crown, to whom they would pay tribute. Such measures invalidated former concessions that had given colonists the opportunity to initiate, at their own cost, the first stages of the conquest.[1] Insurrections then broke out in Peru.

Searching for reasons for the mutiny led by Hernandéz Girón, the fiscal (attorney) of the Audiencia (High Court) in Lima summarized in 1550 the rebels' point of view: "They started saying that they realized your Majesty's wish was to have the whole of Peru to himself, and that being so, Peru could not forbear becoming sovereign and governing on its own, freely, as Venice did."[2] Yet troops loyal to the crown, mobilized and led by the clergy, triumphed over reluctant colonists. A compromise was reached by the two sides. The *conquistadores* kept the Indians but resigned themselves to the taxation imposed on the *encomiendas*. The crown precluded the emergence of hereditary fiefs and succeeded in establishing its authority over the conquered lands and peoples, as well as over future conquests.[3]

But the essential development occurred in rather different circumstances. By the mid-1540s, Peruvian silver mines began to send their metal into European markets, reorienting both intercolonial trade and colonial society.[4]

---

[1] Marcel Bataillon, *Etudes sur Bartolomé de Las Casas* (Paris, 1965).
[2] Alain Milhou, "*Sufficientia* – Les notions d'autosuffisance et de dépendance dans la pensée politique espagnole au XVIe s.: De la Castille des comuneros au Perou Colonial," in *Mélanges de la Casa de Velazquez*, (Paris, 1981), tome XVII pp. 106–45, 132.
[3] Bataillon, pp. 291–308; idem., "La rébellion pizarriste, enfantement de l'Amérique Espagnole," *Diogène*, Vol. 43 (1963), pp. 47–63.
[4] Huguette Chaunu and Pierre Chaunu, *Séville et l'Atlantique 1504–1650*, 12 vols. (Paris, 1955–9), 8 Vol. Vol. VIII, tome 2, part 1, pp. 255–352.

The apprenticeship of colonization 153

The situation in Angola bore some resemblance to the preceding case, except that there the crown also fought against the regular clergy, that is, the Jesuits. In 1571 that colony was given to Paulo Dias Novais grandson of Bartolomeu Dias, discoverer of Angola, in the form of a hereditary possession, according to the method already tried in the African island of São Tomé and in Brazil. Troubled with high expenses, Novais granted to the conquerors – some of his captains and the Jesuits – concessions of natives and lands.[5] These new feudatories, called *amos*, managed Angolan native chiefs (the *sobas*) and collected taxes from the Ambudu population. Most of the time these taxes were paid in the form of slaves, whom *amos* would soon export them to America.

Finding that Angola had no silver mines, as was initially supposed, and that the slave trade had turned out to be an important activity in the area, the crown resumed control over the colony: The hereditary possession was abolished, and a general-governor – an immediate entrustee of royal authority – was nominated by Lisbon.[6] Disappointed, the colonists and Jesuits revolted against Francisco de Almeida, who had been installed as general-governor in 1592 and, following royal orders, decreased the *amos'* power. Some months after his arrival at Luanda, Francisco de Almeida, excommunicated by the Jesuits and jailed by the colonists, was forced to sail to Brazil.[7] In 1605 the Jesuit Fernam Guerreiro justified the priests' attitudes in Angola: "There will be no better way of attracting and keeping them [the Ambudu] than by making them the priest's 'sobas'." However, he recognized that this opinion did not please the king, inasmuch as "some people at the Court were beginning to say that it was not convenient for the 'sobas' to acknowledge any other authority but that one of her Majesty; so that the 'sobas' should be put away from priests and captains."[8]

In 1607 the institution of the *amos* was abolished, and vassal native

---

[5] Carlos Couto, "Documentos para a história da sucessão de Paulo Dias Novais na doação da capitania de Angola," *Estudos Históricos*, Vol. 15 (1976), pp. 133–85; Pe. Antonio Brásio, *Monumenta Missionária Africana (MMA)*, Africa Occidental, first series, 15 vols. (Lisbon, 1953–88), Vol. III, pp. 36–51, Vol. IV, pp. 276–7; Ralph Delgado, *História de Angola*, 4 vols. (Banco de Angola, n.d.), Vol. I, pp. 258–62.

[6] Beatrix Heintze, "Die portugiesische Besiedlungs-und Wirtschaftspolitik in Angola 1570–1607," *Aufsätze zur portugiesischen Kulturgeschichte*, Vol. 17 (1981–2), pp. 200–19; idem., "Luso-African Feudalism in Angola? The Vassal Treaties of the 16th to the 18th Century," *Revista Portuguesa de História (RPH)*, Vol. XVIII, (1980), pp. 111–31.

[7] *MMA*, Vol. III, p. 476, und Vol. IV, pp. 53, 554; Delgado, Vol. I, pp. 372–7.

[8] Pe. Fernam Guerreiro, *Relação Anual das coisas que fizeram os Padres da Companhia de Jesus nas suas Missões*, 4 vols., 3 tomes (Evora, 1603–1611; Coimbra, 1930–42), tome I, p. 395; *MMA*, Vol. IV, pp. 442–52.

154   *Luiz Felipe de Alencastro*

chiefs were placed under the control of the crown.[9] Though quarrels still went on between governors and captains who intended to restore the *amos'* privileges, the action of the crown and of metropolitan merchants put Angola in the Atlantic trading system. In 1594 the first *asiento* gave the Portuguese a monopoly in providing Spanish America with slaves. Up to 1623, Portuguese merchants who owned the *asiento* were also contractors in Angola, managing the purchase of slaves in Luanda.[10] It is, indeed, the slave trade that connected Angola with the world market.

Unlike the events in Africa and America, Portuguese colonization produced a rather softened impact in the Indian Ocean. European conquerors tried to arrogate markets previously controlled by Arabs and Gujerati merchants. Lisbon intended to direct this trade toward the metropolitan network along the route of the Cape of Good Hope.[11] This policy created clashes between royal authority and Portuguese settled in India.

In Goa these colonists, called *casados* (married men) – as opposed to the group formed by Portuguese soldiers called *solteiros* (single men) – were wholesalers who carried out most of the important commercial business at seaports along trade routes to China and Japan. Represented by Goa's House Senate, the *casados* imposed the rule that no Jews, Indians, or Hindus converted to Catholicism were to be allowed to associate with Portuguese officials or military personnel trading at Asian seaports.[12]

The *casados* then get from Portugal's crown limitations on the activity of Lisbon's trade agents who had business with India. Facing also the *fidalgos* – the Portuguese military aristocracy holding the crown's authority in India – the *casados* tried to control the whole brokerage of European trade in Asia. Apparently the crown took no advantage in that situation, for in 1587 it gave the indigo monopoly – the main economic activity in Goa – to a group of Lisbon merchants.[13]

[9] "Regimento do governador Manuel Pereira Forjaz de 26 março 1607," *MMA*, Vol. V, pp. 264–79.
[10] Enriqueta Vila Vilar, *Hispano-America y El Comercio de Esclavos – Los Asientos Portugueses* (Seville, 1977), p. 27, n. 15.
[11] Ralph A. Austen, "From the Atlantic to the Indian Ocean: European Abolition, the African Slave Trade, and Asian Economic Structures," in D. Eltis and J. Walvin (eds.), *The Abolition of the Atlantic Slave Trade* (Madison, Wis., 1981), pp. 117–40, 118, 126; Vitorino Magalhães Godinho, *Os Descobrimentos e a Economia Mundial*, 4 vols. (Lisbon, 1981–3), Vol. I, pp. 183–208, and Vol. II, pp. 183–223.
[12] C. R. Boxer, *Portuguese Society in the Tropics – The Municipal Councils of Goa, Macao, Bahia and Luanda 1510–1800* (Madison, Wis., 1950), pp. 12–41.
[13] M. N. Pearson, "The People and Politics of Portuguese India during the Sixteenth

The apprenticeship of colonization 155

Revolts then broke out among the *casados* in Goa. Rebellions keep on disturbing the colony every time the crown increased tributes or tried to attract commerce involved in bilateral trade with Asia and the Persian Gulf, to the benefit of local traders – Portuguese, Persians, and Indians – but to the disadvantage of metropolitan merchants and Royal Treasure.[14] A study of those rebellions concludes: "Many of these incidents show a considerable lack of patriotism on the part of "casados" of Portuguese India; they usually place their trade above their loyalty to the Crown".[15]

It was in Goa that Diogo do Couto wrote, in 1593, his masterpiece *"O Soldado Prático"*, a key book of Lusitanian historical skepticism, pointing out frauds practiced by colonial officials who crossed cities and seas, plundering natives and robbing merchants. According to Diogo do Couto, "Nowhere else is the King [of Portugal] less obeyed than in India."[16] But as Magalhães Godinho explains: "Whatever were military and naval means gathered, and however righteous the official's honesty, the Portuguese could not afford substituting all Moors and Gentiles in interregional circuits. . . . Between the beginning and the middle the sixteenth century, Portuguese State of East Indies was set up; the Portuguese, very numerous, settled in many towns and thrust themselves into interregional trade circuits. From that time the Luso-oriental economic complex was opposed to the interests of Lisbon and of the route of the Cape."[17] That situation illustrated one of the colonial impasses mentioned earlier: The colonists' trade evaded the metropolitan networks.

In Mozambique the fragility of Lusitanian colonial intervention in the Indian Ocean was even more transparent. In its first stage, the Monomotapa pre-European empire was permeated by Portuguese conquerors who took over native feudatories' powers in domains (*prazos*) of the Zambezi valley. The first Europeans owning *prazos* (the *prazeiros*) were confirmed in their posts by the Monomotapa emperor himself.[18] *Prazeiros* got from their vassals – natives of the Tonga people

and Early Seventeenth Centuries," in D. Alden and W. Dean (eds.), *Essays Concerning the Socioeconomic History of Brazil and Portuguese India* (Gainesville, Fla., 1977), pp. 1–25, 16, 17; C. R. Boxer, *A India Portuguesa em meados de seculo XVII* (Lisbon, 1982), pp. 26–31.

[14] K. S. Mathew, "India Merchants and the Portuguese Trade on the Malabar Coast during the Sixteenth Century," in T. R. de Souza (ed.), *Indo-Portuguese History, Old Issues, New Question* (New Delhi, 1985), pp. 1–12; Guerreiro, tome 2, pp. 389, 390.

[15] Pearson, p. 23.

[16] Diogo do Couto, *O Soldado Prático* (1593) (Lisbon, 1954), pp. 30, 54.

[17] Magalhães Godinho, Vol. III, pp. 81–134, esp. pp. 133, 134; see also A. Farinha De Carvalho, *Diogo do Couto, o Soldado Prático e a India* (Lisbon, 1979), pp. 95–103.

[18] Thomas D. Boston, "On the Transition to Feudalism in Mozambique," *Journal of*

156   *Luiz Felipe de Alencastro*

– rent in ivory or maize or in labor (*mussôco*). The *prazeiros* themselves paid the Portuguese crown a tax in powdered gold. Where there was no Portuguese sovereignty, the colonists paid – only to the native authority – a tribute in cloths (*fatiota*). Those were the "lands in *fatiota*," located in the province of Tete.[19]

Gradually absorbed by the native society and institutions, the colonists tended to Africanize, or to "kaffirize," as a Portuguese author has pointed out.[20]

Leaving untouched native conditions of production, the Portuguese were unable to change the regional trade. The external exchanges remained directed toward the North and the East, with Omani Arabs controlling the slave trade to the Persian Gulf, the main market in the area.[21] The first Portuguese customs tariff to collect taxes on slaves was set in Mozambique in 1756, two and a half centuries after similar tariffs had come into operation in Portuguese West Africa. Except for some extra deliveries, Brazil would regularly receive East African slaves only from the second decade of the nineteenth century on. The emerging intercolonial division of labor had already designated the other side of Africa – mainly Angola – as the preferred market for the Luso-Brazilian slave ships.

In fact, the importance of Mozambique rested on its strategic situation between India and Europe. Portuguese fleets remained for several months at the Mozambican harbors waiting for the maritime monsoons to cease.[22] Having failed to achieve economic control over the area, Lisbon tightened its political authority over the Mozambique colonists.

African Studies (JAS), Vol. 8, No. 4 (1981–2), pp. 182–8; A. Lobato, _Colonização Senhorial da Zambézia e outros estudos_ (Lisbon, 1962), pp. 80, 81.

[19] Fritz Hoppe, _A Africa Oriental Portuguesa no tempo do Marques de Pombal_ (Lisbon, 1970), p. 40; A. Lobato, _Evolução Administrativa e Econômica de Mocambique 1752–1763_ (Lisbon, 1957), p. 231; M. D. D. Newitt, _Portuguese Settlement on the Zambezi: Exploration, Land Tenure, and Colonial Rule in East Africa_ (London and New York, 1973), pp. 181, 182; "Viagem que fez o Padre Ant. Gomes, da Companhia de Jesus, ao Imperio de Manomotapa; e assistencia que fez nas ditas terras de alguns anos (1648)," in _Studia_, No. 3 (Janeiro 1959), pp. 155–242, 239.

[20] Lobato, _Evolução_, p. 153; M. D. D. Newitt, "The Early History of the Marawi," _Journal of African History (JAH)_, Vol. 23 (1982), pp. 145–62.

[21] See Sebastião Xavier Botelho, _Memórias Estatísticas sobre os domínios portuguezes Africa Oriental_ (Lisbon, 1835); E. Alpers, _Ivory and Slaves in East Central Africa_ (London, 1975); Cyril A. Hromnik, "Canarins in the Rios de Cuama 1501–1576," _JAS_, Vol. 6, No. 1 (1979), pp. 27–37; Austen, pp. 117–26; Hubert Gerbeau, "La traite esclavagiste dans l'Océan Indien," in UNESCO, ed., _La traite négrière du XVe au XIXe siècle_ (Paris, 1979), pp. 194–217.

[22] W. G. L. Randles, _L'Empire du Monomotapa du XVe au XIXe siècle_, (Paris and La Haye, 1975), pp. 41–8; Justus Strandes, _The Portuguese Period in East Africa_, 3rd ed. (Nairobi, Dar es Salaam, and Kampala, 1968), p. 153.

The apprenticeship of colonization 157

From 1625 on, the domains of Zambezi were no longer hereditary possessions. Changed into *"prazos* of the crown," they were issued – under an emphyteusis contract – to petitioners for a period of three generations. The concession could either be renewed for the same family or granted to other petitioners. Concentration of *prazos* in the hands of one grantee alone was, however, very common, as the crown preferred to let the law lapse than leaving *prazos* uninhabited – "Not to break off the continuity of its control over the natives" – as Fritz Hopppe explains.[23]

The emphyteusis contract, linking the crown with the *prazeiro* marked the originality of Portuguese policy in the region.[24] Contrary to entire Lusitanian legislation – which excluded women from concessions' heritage as well as from estates bestowed by the crown – this contract determined that *prazos* were inherited in feminine lineage, when the heiress married a colonist born in Portugal – a *reinol* – or a *reinol's* son.[25] The *prazeiro* was therefore subjected to metropolitan sovereignty by a double temporary contract: the contract of three generations (the emphyteusis) established by the crown with his wife's family, and the contract of one generation, which he took over by marrying the legal proprietor of the crown's *prazo*. By forcing each heiress to marry a *reinol*, the crown hoped to restrain the colony's self-sufficiency and the overwhelming ascension of mulattos who took possession of the *prazos*.[26] This system gave birth to odd situations where by old women proprietors of *prazos* (the *donas*) were as much at strife as royal princesses: Many *donas* became successively widows and married suitors wishing to become proprietors.[27] In fact, *prazeiros'* powers rested more on compromises with natives than on the legal status acknowledged by Lisbon.

Among fifty-five *prazos* found in 1750 in the province of Tete, five

[23] Hoppe, p. 46.
[24] On *prazos* see M. D. D. Newitt, "The Portuguese on the Zambezi: an Historical Interpretation of the Prazo," *JAH*, Vol. X (1969), pp. 67–85; Allen F. Isaacman, *Mozambique, the Africanisation of a European Institution: The Zambezi Prazos 1705–1902* (Madison, Wis., 1972), esp. Appendix B, pp. 172ff; Botelho, pp. 264–271.
[25] See *Lei Mental* in Joel Serrão et al., *Dicionário de História a de Portugal*, 4 vols. *(DHP)* (Lisbon, 1963–71), Vol. III, pp. 29, 30; A. Lobato, *A Evolução*, pp. 216–18; Newitt, *Portuguese Settlement*, pp. 97–102.
[26] A. Lobato and G. Papagno gave a different explanation of the *prazos'* feminine inheritance. For Lobato, this law was created to help widows and orphans coming from Portugal (*Colonização*, p. 103 sq.); for Papagno the law was also made to stimulate migration from Portugal to Mozambique; see Giuseppe Papagno, *Colonialismo e feudalismo; la questione dei prazos da Coroa nel Mozambico fine del secolo XIX* (Torino, 1972), p. 39.
[27] Newitt, *"Portuguese Settlement,"* pp. 87, 88, 145.

158   *Luiz Felipe de Alencastro*

had a title of concession and twenty-five had no title at all. The other twenty-five *prazos* were either merely confirmed by local authorities or had doubtful property warrants.[28] Notwithstanding continuous raids launched against the natives, Portugal long delayed the imposition of sovereignty over the area. Following a practice previously adopted by Arab merchants, Portuguese governors and general-captains bestowed a gift on the Monomotapa – as a symbolical bond of vassalage – at the moment they took their posts in Mozambique. When this tribute – called *curva* and generally consisting of a certain amount of cloths – was not paid, trouble developed in the colony. In 1807, when three centuries of Portuguese presence would lead one to suppose that this custom was lost, the governor of one of Zambezi's provinces decided not to pay the *curva*, provoking a guerrilla revolt that ended only in 1826, when the Portuguese finally offered the tribute to the Monomotapa emperor.[29]

In 1752 Mozambique was separated from the State of India, on which it was administratively dependent, to become an autonomous colony in the Portuguese empire. Authorities tried to control the *prazos* in 1760, but the fragility of the links of these domains with metropolitan networks caused continuous rebellions among the *prazeiros*.[30] The *prazos* were disconnected from the pre-Portuguese social system in the first quarter of the nineteenth century when the Brazilian slave trade pulled Mozambique trade into the Atlantic stream.[31]

Colonial conquest, as we said at the outset, did not guarantee successful economic exploitation by the metropolis. The overseas surplus did not reach the metropolis when it was directly consumed by colonists, as happened in Mozambique, or when it was taken by trade running out of the Portuguese economic and fiscal networks, as was the case in Goa. The colonists' permanence in a territory did not guarantee the colonial exploitation of this territory. Political domination was not necessarily a synonym for colonial exploitation.

In Brazil, measures were taken accordingly in 1534 to consolidate the occupation and valorization of the territory, responding to French invasion at home as well as to the decline of Portuguese trade in Asia.

---

[28] Lobato, *Evolução*, pp. 228–33.
[29] "Viagem," *Studia, op. cit.*, p. 172, n. 31; Oliveira Boleo, "Vicissitudes históricas da politica de exploração mineira no Império de Monomotapa," *Studia*, No. 32 (June 1971), pp. 167–209, 207.
[30] J. J. Lopes De Lima and F. Bordalo, *Ensaios sobre a Statística das possessões portuguezas*, 5 vols. (Lisbon, 1844–62), Vol. IV, p. 245; Lobato, *Evolução*, pp. 219, 220.
[31] Papagno, pp. 141–74.

The apprenticeship of colonization   159

The colony was divided into fifteen hereditary captaincies yielded to twelve grantees. The crown offered several privileges to attract candidates to the position of donatary captain. Nevertheless, six of the first twelve donataries either never went to Brazil or came back at once to Portugal; two were killed; two others gave up their rights; and only two thrived: Duarte Coelho in Pernambuco and, somehow, as we will see later, Pero do Campo Tourinho in Porto Seguro. The *capitania* of São Vicente prospered for a certain time, though its donee had never visited it. In 1549 a general-government was established, impelling a movement of centralization designed to reduce donees' privileges.[32]

Circumstances peculiar to Pernambuco allowed local donataries to resist general-governors' attempts to assume their prerogatives.[33] In all other places, however, a central government authority was set up. In 1549 the economy based on Indian labor and exploitation of brazilwood started to change into an economy of agricultural production based on sugar mills and African slave labor. The colony's linkage with the Atlantic trade was deliberately emphasized by royal legislation restricting employment of Amerindian slave labor and stimulating African slave trade, as well as by measures restraining internal trade among Brazilian captaincies.[34]

This summary illustrates the antagonisms arising when the metropolis no longer confines itself to mere exercise of domination (*dominium*) but also asserts its rights over lands to be conquered and its guardianship of conquered peoples. The conflict between Iberian powers and their subjects had different effects on overseas territory. In Peru, the rise of the mining economy put an end to the colonists' move toward autonomy and stimulated integration of Spanish America markets into European trade. In Angola, maritime exchanges – triggered by the slave trade – gave Portugal additional means of control over the colony. In Mozambique, where Portuguese trade took its place in a pre-European mercantile network, colonists became kaffirized and fulfilled roles in the traditional trade network of the native society. Finally, in Goa, where exchanges with Arab and Indian merchants as well with the Far East provided profitable choices, trade

[32] J. Capistrano De Abreu, *O Descobrimento do Brasil*, 2nd ed. (Rio de Janeiro, 1976), pp. 75–8; Harold B. Johnson, "The Portuguese Settlement of Brazil 1500–1580," in Leslie Bethell (ed.), *The Cambridge History of Latin America (CHLA)*, 5 vols. (Cambridge, London, and New York, 1986), Vol. I, pp. 263–7.

[33] Francis A. Dutra, "Centralization vs. Donatorial Privilege: Pernambuco, 1602–1630," in D. Alden (ed.), *Colonial Roots of Modern Brazil* (London, 1973), pp. 19–60.

[34] "Regimento de Tomé de Souza (1548)," *Revista do Instituto Histórico e Geográfico Brasileiro*, Vol. LXI (1898), pp. 39–75.

160   *Luiz Felipe de Alencastro*

with the Portuguese gave way to more attractive opportunities outside metropolitan control.

THE METROPOLIS'S OPTIONS

It is well known that private investment in the first stages of Lusitanian colonization was not exclusively Portuguese. Except for some royal monopolies, Catholic foreigners, settled or not in Portugal, could get privileges similar to those of national Catholics for trade with Portuguese colonies. Moreover, if they employed a Portuguese crew, those foreigners were also allowed to use their own ships in this commerce.[35]

The *exclusivo colonial*, that is, the national trade monopoly over colonies, was imposed only after 1580. Through its association with the Spanish monarchy, the Portuguese crown became so involved in European conflicts that it ended by ruining its overseas domains.[36] Lisbon started, therefore, to restrain the activities of traders from other countries. After 1591, to avoid heresies – but also because it was "against all reason and good sense" that foreign merchants would be allowed to damage "the trade of the kingdom" – foreigners were forbidden to go to overseas territories. In 1605 a prohibition vetoed all foreign transactions in Portuguese domains. Aliens settled in Brazil had to go back to the kingdom within a year.[37]

Hence, a sharp move occurred in Portuguese colonial policy on the eve of the Century of Discoveries. Initially the crown granted powers both to its subjects owning capital and also to Catholic foreigners trading with its overseas markets. Some decades later, the monarchy moved back and impelled a movement of "metropolitan restoration" abroad, delimiting the autonomy of the main actors of colonial conquest. On the one hand, a national monopoly (the *exclusivo*) was established over colonial trade. On the other hand, new laws submitted colonists to general-governors entrusted with ample powers and charged to remind *urbi et orbi* the *purpose of colonization*, that is,

---

[35] Bailey W. Diffie, "The Legal Privileges of the Foreigners in Portugal and Sixteenth-Century Brazil," in H. H. Keith and S. F. Edwards (eds.), *Conflict and Continuity in Brazilian Society* (Columbia, S.C., 1969), pp. 1–19; Susan C. Schneider, "Commentary," ibid., pp. 20–3; Johnson, pp. 262–4; Magalhães Godinho, Vol. III, pp. 190–214.

[36] Stuart B. Schwartz, "Luso-Spanish Relations in Hapsburg Brazil, 1580–1640," *The Americas (TheA)*, Vol. XXV, No. 1 (1968), pp. 33–48, 45–8.

[37] *MMA*, Vol. I, p. 414; Vol. III, pp. 192–6; Vol. IV, pp. 62–6.

The apprenticeship of colonization   161

the colonial policy.[38] The crown had to learn how to make all colonial rivers flow toward the metropolitan sea. The colonists had to understand that the apprenticeship of colonization was mainly the apprenticeship of the market, which was, first and foremost, the metropolitan market. Only then could colonial domination and colonial exploitation coincide and correlate with each other.

Having decided to be the only bestower of lands and the only controller of natives to be conquered, the imperial power appeared also as the organizer of productive labor, the conveyor of social privileges, and the gendarme of religious orthodoxy.[39]

Like the Spanish monarchy, the Portuguese crown exerted direct control over secular clergy, thanks to the *jus patronatus* (the *padroado*), a set of privileges popes granted to Iberian monarchs between 1452 and 1514. According to these texts, the Iberian religious hierarchy could undertake its functions only after royal approval. The crown supported the secular clergy financially and could forbid the proclamation of pontifical edicts and briefs.[40] Framed by the *padroado*, the secular clergy and episcopate became chains of metropolitan power, especially in Brazil and Africa. In the context of migrations and cultural transfers, where accusations of heresy spread easily, exclusion from the ecclesiastic community brought harsh consequences. Hence excommunication became an efficient tool against colonists rebelling against metropolitan policy. Sometimes excommunication was pronounced *lato sensu*, that is, on a large scale, clearly to implement the royal monopoly. Responding to a request from the governor of Cape Verde Islands, the local bishop excommunicated in 1613 "all those who had robbed or defrauded any of Your Majesty's goods."[41] It is clear that religious orthodoxy had its share in the process of coloni

---

[38] See Caio Prado, Jr., *Formação do Brasil Contemporaneo* (São Paulo, 1971), pp. 19, 31; conceptual and historical implications of Prado's thesis on the "purpose of colonization" are discussed by Fernando A. Novais, "Caio Prado Jr. na historiografia brasileira," in R. Moraes et al. (eds.), *Inteligencia Brasileira* (São Paulo, 1986), pp. 68–9; idem., *Portugal e Brasil na Crise do Antigo Sistema Colonial 1777–1808* (São Paulo, 1979); see José Roberto de Amaral Lapa et al., *Modos de produção e Realidade Brasileira* (Petropolis, RJ, 1980).

[39] J. Lúcio de Azevedo, *História dos Cristãos Novos Portugueses*, 2nd ed. (Lisbon, 1975); Arnold Wiznitzer, *Os Judeus no Brasil Colonial* (São Paulo, 1966); Anita Novinsky, *Cristãos Novos na Bahia* (São Paulo, 1967); Maria Luiza Tucci Carneiro, *Preconceito Racial no Brasil Colonia – Os Cristãos Novos* (São Paulo, 1983).

[40] Bull of Sixto IV, "Clara devotionis," 21 August 1472 and bull of Alexandre VI, "Cum sicut nobis," 23 August 1499, in João Martins da Silva Marques, ed., *Descobrimentos Portugueses, Documentos para a sua historia (DP)*, 3 vols. (Lisbon, 1971), Vol. III (1461–1500), pp. 119, 120, 549, 550.

[41] *MMA*, Vol. IV, p. 502.

zation of colonists. The situation of Jesuits, Franciscans, Carmelites, and Benedictines – the regular clergy who engaged in missionary tasks in Brazil – must be examined in other perspectives. In their holistic strategy of evangelizing the Amerindians, the Jesuits came into conflict with the colonists and bishops but also set themselves against the crown. It is also necessary to point out the specific role of missions. As C. R. Boxer observes, since important military posts were nonexistent in the colonies before the second half of eighteenth century, it was mostly the clergy's task to keep the conquered populations loyal to the Iberian crown.[42]

The action of the Inquisition is more complex. In the metropolis, the Holy Office often appeared as a weapon of the aristocracy against the mercantile bourgeoisie. Also, when metropolitan merchants or the crown faced foreign competition, denunciations of Judaism abounded. Against all evidence, the captain of Santiago (Cape Verde) informed the court in 1544 that "Guinea [was] lost" to Portugal, since the land was already "crowded" with New Christians engaged in smuggling.[43] Accused of usury and heresy, important merchants were arrested in Brazil and put on trial by the Holy Office in Lisbon.[44] Between 1580 and 1640, when Portugal was associated with the Spanish crown, there was a new move of the inquisitorial power: The Holy Office's metropolitan agents decided to play the card of Madrid policies and attack Portuguese nationalistic movements. The same thing happened in Peru, where Spanish traders manipulated the Inquisition and decimated Portuguese merchants.[45] Unbelievers were permanently unsafe in the tropics, for the crown alternated repressive fury and usurpation with the desire to profit from the economic activity of the New Christians. Legislation concerning emigration reflected this contradictions. A law of 1587 forbade New Christians and their families to leave the kingdom. In 1601 this law was revoked, and they were allowed to move to the colonies. A warrant of 1612 abrogated the previous law, reestablishing the prohibitory order of 1587.[46] New

[42] Pe. Serafim Leite, *História da Companhia de Jesus no Brasil 1549–1760 (HCJB)*, 10 vols. (Lisbon and Rio de Janeiro, 1938–50), Vol. VI, p. 552; Boxer, *A Igreja, e a Expansão Ibérica* (Lisbon, 1978), pp. 98–100.

[43] See Armando Castro, *Doutrinas econômicas em Portugal, séculos XVI a XVIII* (Lisbon, 1978), pp. 79, 80; see also a more balanced analysis in Frederic Mauro, "La Bourgeoisie Portugaise au XVIIe siècle," in Foundation Gulbenkian, *Etudes Economiques sur l'Expansion Portugaise* (Paris, 1970), pp. 15–36; and David Grant Smith, "Old Christian Merchants and the Foundation of the Brazil Company, 1649," *HAHR*, Vol. 54 (1974), pp. 233–59.

[44] *MMA.*, Vol. II, p. 372.

[45] Wiznitzer, pp. 18, 19.

[46] Vitorino Magalhães Godinho, "Restauração," in J. Serrão et al., *DHP*, Vol. III,

The apprenticeship of colonization   163

liberations followed new prohibitions. Even though the number of executed individuals from Brazil stayed at around 20 and the number of convicts did not exceed 500 – a sum that current research may increase – the fear infused by the Inquisition struck many more men and women overseas.[47]

In Angola, the Inquisition interfered only after 1626. Permanent residence of New Christians was allowed if they were confined to the role of merchant.[48] However, missionaries' correspondence recorded several examples of indirect action of the inquisitorial hand.[49] Let us follow the priest Pero Tavares in his journey across the Angola back country in 1631. Arriving at a hamlet, he found an idol and was ready to destroy it. The local *soba* ran for help to an ally, a Portuguese colonist, asking him to save the idol that was "physician and remedy" for the natives. Entangled in a quarrel with the colonist amid a dangerous tumult arising in the hamlet, Tavares acted quickly:

I feared incidents and, thus, brought the matter to an end in a few words; I clearly told the man – for I knew he belonged to "the nation" [Jew, New Christian] – that he should no longer discuss such an affair, as I would inform the governor and the bishop of everything since these matters were to be undertaken by the Holy Office. Those were my last words . . . the poor Hebrew was almost struck dumb; then, self-composed, he said to me: Father of my soul, the one who said it is no longer here. Your Reverence may thus burn the idol.[50]

This apparently trivial incident shows the insidious efficacy of the pressures exerted by priests in Brazil and Angola, even though the fires of the Inquisition did not burn in those territories. A historical trait of Portuguese authoritarianism stands out here. Without thoroughly banishing the Jews, as Spain had done, or declaring open war on religious dissenters, as the French monarchy did against Protestants, Portugal punished, plundered, and usurped the rights of its crypto-Jewish mercantile bourgeoisie. The denial of civil rights to an economically powerful community was established as a political prin

pp. 609–28; José Veiga Torres, "Uma longa guerra social: Os ritmos da repressão inquisitorial em Portugal," *Revista de História Econômica e Social (RHES)* (Lisbon, 1978), Vol. 1, pp. 55–68; Harry E. Cross, "Commerce and Orthodoxy: A Spanish Response to Portuguese Commercial Penetration in the Viceroyalty of Peru, 1580–1640," *TheA.*, Vol. XXXV, No. 2 (1978), pp. 151–67.

[47] Novinsky, pp. 141–62; Tucci Carneiro, pp. 195–205; *MMA*, Vol. IV, pp. 15–17, 477–9; Tucci Carneiro, pp. 68–84.

[48] *MMA*, Vol. IV, p. 473; Delgado, Vol. II, pp. 129, 130.

[49] Lúcio De Azevedo, p. 232; *MMA*, Vol. VIII, p. 68.

[50] *MMA*, Vol. VIII, pp. 78, 79 passim.

ciple. This revenge of the aristocracy on the bourgeoisie dramatically marked the evolution of the Brazilian and Portuguese societies.

Through the indirect action of the Inquisition or the political zeal of the clergy, the church thus acted in a double way. On the one hand, it helped to consolidate the *dominium*, for in some regions it set up the occupation of the territory. On the other hand, it reinforced the *imperium* insofar as it led to a relation of submissiveness between the imperial people and the metropolis.

This brief view of the contrasting situations arising with the Discoveries makes clear the double drift that occurred some decades after the beginning of colonization.

Parallel to the political centralization carried on to the disadvantage of the colonists, a national trade monopoly was settled to restrain the activities of foreign Catholic merchants. At this time, the colonies' links with the Iberian metropolis depended more on knots tied by royal officials and clergy than on links provided by world-market exchanges. Only after the mining production in Spanish America and the connection of slave trade with Brazil would the dynamics of the Atlantic system come to involve Iberian possessions in Africa and America.

Spanish metropolitan control rested weakly on the colonial process of production and strongly on the commercialization of colonial goods. Spanish colonial goods – precious metals – were stocked and carried by a fleet system channeled through three American seaports and Seville, the only communication points allowed between Spain and America. Given the fact that the slave trade did not fit in with such restrictions, Madrid was compelled to establish *asientos*, subcontracting to Genoese and Portuguese the slave trade to Spanish America. In Portuguese America, the colonial process was rather different. The nature of tropical goods made it difficult to have, between Brazil and Portugal, a trade system similar to that of Spanish America. Rigid centralization, and long waits in buying, storing, and carrying goods, which characterized Spanish trade, were inadequate arrangements for the perishable quality and the price fluctuations of Brazilian agricultural products, as well as for the growing activity of Portugal's secondary ports.[51] In fact, the introduction of Africans and the prohibition of Indian enslavement allowed Portugal to control operations taking place upstream and downstream in Brazilian colonial production; colonists depended upon the metropolis to export their products but also to import their factors of production, that is, the African

[51] Schneider, pp. 21, 22.

The apprenticeship of colonization 165

slaves. Such phenomena fundamentally framed Portuguese colonization in South Atlantic.

Intermetropolitan wars in the second half of the seventeenth century led Lisbon to organize trade fleets between Brazil and Portugal
– a system that would be kept during the first half of the eighteenth
century to carry Brazilian gold to Lisbon. But that system was less
severe than the one in Spanish America. Discredited by colonists and
merchants, Brazil's organized fleets were extinguished in 1765.[52]

The slave trade, which formed the basis of colonial production, was
a decisive instrument in the achievement of the Portuguese colonial
system in the Atlantic. Gradually this trade transcended the economic
field and became integrated into the metropolitan political apparatus.
The two issues presented in the preceding pages thus gain their whole
meaning: The exercise of imperial power in overseas territories and
the set of exchanges between metropolis and colonies were equated
in the sphere of slave traffic.

Nevertheless, by allowing the colonization of colonists, that is, their
inclusion in the metropolitan network, the slave system's dynamics
contradictorily transformed the colonial system. After the seventeenth
and eighteenth centuries, this colonial pattern was breached as Luso-
Brazilian interests – distinct from metropolitan interests – stratified
on both sides of the Atlantic: in African slave trade ports as well as
in Brazilian slavery areas. Consequently, the notion of a "colonial
pact" loses, in the Brazilian case, part of the significance generally
attached to it. In fact, the slave trade was not just the traffic in slaves:
It involved more complex aspects than those derived from the single
operation of purchasing, selling, and transporting Africans from one
side of the Atlantic to the other.

THE AIMS OF THE PORTUGUESE SLAVE TRADE

Exploring the international essence of the mercantile capital already
accumulated in Europe, the Portuguese crown precociously laid the
bases of an imperial market area.[53] But Portugal had neither the means

---

[52] M. A. Soares De Azevedo, "Armadas do Brasil," *DHP*, Vol. 1, pp. 186–8; Arthur
Cézar Ferreira Reis, "O Comércio Colonial e as Companhias privilegiadas," in Sérgio
Buarque De Holanda, ed., *História Geral da Civilisação Brasileira*, tome I, Vol. 2 (São
Paulo, 1960), pp. 316–18; Virgílio Noya Pinto, *O Ouro brasileiro e o comércio anglo-
portugues* (São Paulo, 1979), pp. 133–84.

[53] Pe. Antonio Brasio, "Do último Cruzado ao Padroado Régio," *Studia* January (1959),
pp. 125–53; see also Antonio José Saraiva, "Le Père Antonio Vieira, S. J. et l'esclavage
des Noirs au XVIIe s.," *Annales E.C.S.*, Vol. 22 (1967), pp. 1289–1309; Magalhães
Godinho, *Os Descobrimentos*, Vol. I.

166   *Luiz Felipe de Alencastro*

nor the power to unify or keep this transcontinental space. Surpassed
by their European rivals, Portugal lost, mainly in Asia, control over
trade zones, peoples, and territories to nations better equipped for
this sort of imperial dominion. Nevertheless, the Portuguese crown
established in the South Atlantic a production economy that was more
efficiently exploited than the circulation economy of its former Asian
empire.[54] Facing the nonexistence of a regular surplus to be incorporated in maritime trade, the crown, supported by private capital,
stimulated in South America the production of export goods through
African slavery, thus giving rise to a more advanced system of colonial
exploitation. The superiority of the Portuguese colonial process soon
became evident: Benefitting from the Lusitanian example, other European maritime nations created in the seventeenth and eighteenth
centuries similar systems in the Caribbean and Africa.

In such a context, what were the initial aims of the Portuguese slave
trade? Papal edicts between 1455 and 1481 extinguished excommunication punishing Portuguese who bought slaves and gold from Muslims. The plea of an edict from 1481 justified this liberation by
explaining that the purpose of this trade was "to diminish the infidels'
power and not to increase it." In the political-military field, the treaty
of Alcaçovas, signed by Portugal and Spain in 1479, put an end to
the Succession War in Castile and transferred the Canary Islands to
Castilan sovereignty, but also recognized the Portuguese king as the
only lord of Madeira, the Azores, the Fez Kingdom (Morocco), and
the Cape Verde islands, as well as of the lands "discovered and . . .
the ones to be discovered" in Guinea, that is, in black Africa.[55] Insofar
as the legitimacy of Lusitanian conquest and trade in Africa was acknowledged by Spain and the pope, Lisbon was able to hold commercial and territorial guarantees that would make it play, for four
centuries, a decisive role in the great slave business.

In the first place, the slave traffic constituted a segment of the vast
commercial network connecting Portugal to Asia. In its relations with
Asia, Lisbon had to pay for its imports with shipments of gold (to
the Ottoman empire), silver (to the Far East), and copper (to India),

---

[54] In the 1550s, French smuggling had already provoked a fall in brazilwood prices at
Antwerp and a diminution of Portuguese profits in the Brazilian trade; see Johnson,
pp. 258, 259.

[55] Bulls of Sixte IV, "Aeterni Regis Clementia", 21 June 1481; Nicolau V, "Romanus
Pontifex," 8 January 1455; Calixto III, "Inter coetera," 13 March 1456; also articles
27 and 28 of the Alcáçovas Treaty, signed 4 September, 1479, in *DP*, Vol. III pp. 222–
38, 232; See also bull "Sedes Apostolica" of Julio II, 4 July 1505; idem., "Breve
Desideras," *MMA*, Vol. II, pp. 21–3, 27–8; *DP*, Vol. III, pp. 181–209, 206.

The apprenticeship of colonization   167

metals of which Portugal had little supply.[56] The first Portuguese expeditions in Africa searched for mines and native markets where those metals were traded. To get gold, the Portuguese, taking slaves farther in the East, at Benin, bartered and carried those slaves to the fort they built at São Jorge da Mina in 1482, as well as to other seaports of the Gold Coast, thus starting a maritime slave traffic in the area.[57] In a famous text, *Esmeraldo de situ orbis*, Duarte Pacheco Pereira described such operations in 1508. Slaves were sold to native merchants who brought gold to the fort, though they had no "asses or mules" to carry back inland the goods bartered with Europeans.[58]

In the second place, the slave trade constituted an income source to the royal treasury. Despite protests from the court of Lisbon and Portuguese slave owners, King Afonso V supported slave traders, refusing to forbid in 1472 the reselling abroad of slaves previously brought to Portugal.[59] In the Portuguese slave trade, the national demand for slaves – whether metropolitan or colonial – was only part of the total demand. Slaves from Portuguese Africa continued to be exported abroad. This strategy was consecrated by Luso-Spanish *asientos* between 1594 and 1640. After the Restoration of 1640 and the opening of hostilities between Portugal and Spain, the Portuguese crown made haste in separating war from trade, proclaiming the warrant of June 2, 1641, which allowed its vassals to sell Africans to Spaniards in America so long as one-third of the slaves were reserved for Brazilian markets. In 1647 that warrant was ratified, but the reserve of one-third of the slaves for Brazil was abolished. In 1651, the Ultramarine Council set up the official policy: Ships coming directly from Spanish America should have preference in Angola, because they brought silver for the purchase of slaves and paid high customs taxes. Those going directly from Spain to Angola should not be received, for they brought goods instead of gold, thus rivaling Portuguese commerce. In addition, "if all ships were admitted, slaves who

---

[56] Magalhães Godinho, *Os Descobrimentos*, Vol. I, pp. 219–73; Vol. II, pp. 36–49, 134–41.

[57] J. B. Ballong-Wen-Mewuda, "Le Commerce Portugais des esclaves entre la côte de l'actuel Nigéria et celle du Ghana Moderne aux XVeme et XVIeme siècles," in Université de Nantes, *Colloque International sur la Traite des Noirs (CITN)*, 3 vols. (Nantes, 1985); Ivor Wilks, "Waranga, Akan and the Portuguese in the Fifteenth and Sixteenth Centuries – I. The Matter of Bitu," *JAH*, Vol. 23, No. 3 (1982), pp. 333–49.

[58] Duarte Pacheco Pereira, *Esmeraldo de situ orbis* (1508) (Lisbon, 1975), pp. 115, 119.

[59] J. Lúcio De Azevedo, *Epocas de Portugal Econômico (1928)* (Porto, 1978), p. 74; A. C. de C. M. Saunders, *A Social History of Black Slaves and Freedmen in Portugal 1441–1555* (London and New York, 1982), p. 34.

are necessary to Brazilians' sugar mills might lack."[60] A certain priority was thus given to the Brazilian market, but it was not until 1751 that a new warrant stopped the export of Africans to foreign colonies, thus recognizing the exclusive Luso-Brazilian claim on the Luso-African supply of slaves.

In the third place, the slave trade constituted the productive vector of sugar plantations in the Atlantic Islands. There is a key text that allows us to understand the *moment* when the comparative advantages of the slave system over free labor in Atlantic sugar plantations were verified and turned into economic policy. This text is the royal law sent in 1562 to the farmers (*lavradores*) of Madeira:

Concerning the great expenses in sugar sales faced by owners at their farms and sugar plantations in the Island of Madeira, with laborers and men brought in salary and journal; and as some of those owners, afraid they may not cope [with] such expenses, many times give up cultivating the soil and end up by not getting as much sugar as they would *if they had their own slaves* constantly working to care and service of their farms; as it is thus necessary – so the mentioned farms can always be of good use and never damaged, and so they will not happen to decrease for need of the mentioned [slave] laborers, once such a fact makes the owners of those farms have heavy losses, and also because in my incomes too, there is waste on that account – as it is thus necessary, and as I do want to look after that . . . I am pleased to give them place and permission to equip a ship [yearly] in the mentioned island of Madeira . . . to go barter for slaves in the Rivers of Guinea . . . according to each owner's needs of slaves.[61] (Italics added)

This passage has a clear meaning: Given metropolitan experience with the slave system, it is possible to foresee in 1562 that royal income and plantations' productivity would increase as soon as the free laborers of Madeira were supplanted by slaves from Guinea. Thus proceeding, the king of Portugal permanently marked the horizon of the Atlantic economy.

Considering the international composition of mercantile capital accumulated in Europe, the slave and sugar businesses associated Genoese, Florentines, Germans, Spaniards, and Portuguese in rather itinerant activities. Indeed, Portuguese dealing with slaves and sugar

---

[60] Marcos Carneiro De Mendonça, *O Marquez de Pombal e o Brasil* (São Paulo, 1960), pp. 89–90; *MMA*, Vol. X, pp. 28, 29; Vol. XI, p. 67.

[61] "Alvarás" of 16 October 1562 and 30 October 1562; *MMA*, second series, Vol. II, pp. 491–8; see Virginia Rau, "The Madeiran Sugar Cane Plantations," in H. B. Johnson, Jr. (ed.), *From Reconquest to Empire: The Iberian Background to Latin American History* (New York, 1970), pp. 71–84.

The apprenticeship of colonization 169

exploited other American zones before definitely entering Brazil. At Hispaniola there were thirty sugar mills in 1550, set up and managed since 1535 by "more than two hundred Portuguese sugar technicians [*oficiais de açucares*]." Besides that, there were on the island many Portuguese tillers, masons, carpenters, and blacksmiths, generally from the Canary Islands. At the height of activity, in the years 1560–70, there were between 12,000 and 20,000 black slaves on the island, most of them provided by Portuguese slave ships. Thanks to Genoese capitalists and Portuguese craftsmen, slave traders, and sugar technicians, Hispaniola was then able to produce more sugar and possess more Africans than Brazil itself. However, that sugar industry stagnated when the fleets' itinerary and the pattern of Spanish economic geography were thoroughly reorganized under the impact of silver mines' activity on the continent.[62] In the last quarter of the sixteenth century, Brazil became an attractive market for slave traders. Around 1575, only 10,000 Africans had gone to Brazil, whereas Spanish America – where regular introductions of Africans had been going on since 1525 – had received around 37,500 slaves. The Atlantic islands had already imported 123,600 slaves. Up to 1600, Portuguese traded most of the 125,000 Africans deported to America, but Brazilian ports got just 40 percent of that amount.[63] Nevertheless, by 1580, Brazilian sugar achieved first place in the Portuguese empire. Brazilian sugar mills produced around 5,100 tons a year, whereas Madeira and São. Tomé, now declining, produced 590 and 300 tons, respectively.[64] Initially based on Indian slavery, the development of the Brazilian sugar culture became tributary to African labor and slave trade. That change occurred in response to a series of circumstances to be carefully examined.

THE SLAVE TRADE AS AN INSTRUMENT OF COLONIAL POLICY

The crown's action is clearly visible at the root of the productive process established in Brazil. The building of sugar mills, stimulated by fiscal measures assigned at a royal warrant (*alvará*) of July 23, 1554,

---

[62] Alain Milhou, "Los Intentos de Repoblacion de la Isla Espanola por Colonias de Labradores (1518–1603) – Razones de un Fracaso," in Université de Bordeaux, ed., *Actas del Quinto Congreso internacional de Hispanistas* (Bordeaux, 1977), Vol. II, pp. 643–54; Chanu and Chaunu, tome VI–2, Tables 240–7, pp. 496–502.

[63] J. D. Fage, *A History of West Africa* (Cambridge and New York, 1969), pp. 63–5.

[64] F. Mauro, *Le Portugal et l'Atlantique au XVIIe siécle 1570–1670* (Paris, 1960), pp. 183–200; idem., *Le XVIe s. européen – aspects économiques*, 3rd ed. (Paris, 1981), p. 155.

was completed by a warrant of March 29, 1559, allowing each mill owner to import 120 slaves from São Tomé (actually from the Congo, Angola, Gabon, and Nigeria), paying only one-third of the taxes.[65] Such measures attracted to Brazilian plantations a segment of the slave trade formerly directed to the Caribbean. Gradually, in successive stages – most of the time regular and generally expected – the slave trade with Brazil tied Portuguese enclaves in western Africa to the Atlantic trade. Far from being contradictory, the events occurring on the American and African coasts clarified each other through a series of reciprocal effects.

The introduction of Africans to American plantations progressively synchronized various stages of the colonial system. This consolidation of the structure historically determined by mercantile capitalism was activated at several levels:

1. The metropolis was invested with preeminent power, since control of the slave trade permitted it to control the reproduction of the slaves' productive cycle. For three centuries economic complementarity tied Africa to Brazil, making remote the possibility of diverging, and moreover competitive, development among Portuguese colonies on both sides of the South Atlantic.

Actually, the relevance of colonial exploitation in West and Central Africa to exploitation undertaken in South America was clearly perceived by Lisbon only in the seventeenth century. André Alvares de Almada, a mulatto from Cape Verde, finished his "Tratado Breve" (1594) by listing the advantages of Senegambia compared with Brazil: "Populated, it [Senegambia] would have a greater trade than Brazil, for in Brazil there is no more than sugar, brazilwood and cotton; in this land there is cotton and brazilwood, besides ivory, wax, gold, amber, malagueta pepper; many sugar mills can be built, and there is iron, lots of woods for the mills, and slaves to work at them."[66] In Angola colonists had land and slaves in rural properties similar to those in Brazil.[67] Also, the metropolis regularly sent instructions stating that sugar cane and cotton should be cultivated in Angolan lands. In 1655 the municipal chamber of Luanda made Lisbon authorities face the new colonial order, showing them that such a task ran up

---

[65] Instituto do Açucar e do Alcool, ed., *Documentos para a História do Açucar*, 3 vols. (Rio de Janeiro, 1954–63), Vol. I, pp. 11–113.

[66] André Alvares De Almada, "Tratado Breve dos Rios de Guiné do Cabo Verde" (1594), *MMA*, Vol. III, pp. 230–377, 376; see also "Carta de Bartolomeu Velho ao Rei" (1606), *MMA*, Vol. IV, pp. 114–25.

[67] *MMA*, Vol. IX, pp. 26ff; Beatrix Heintze, "Traite de 'Pièces' en Angola: ce que nos sources passent sous silence," *CITN*, Vol. II, pp. 1–21.

The apprenticeship of colonization 171

against problems concerning sugar (shortage of firewood and low quality of the sugar) and, mainly, the trade dominant in the Atlantic routes. Given the prevailing flows of trade, sugar and cotton culti- vated in Angola would go first to Brazil, and only afterward would be sent to Portugal. Burdened with freight costs, these Angolan prod- ucts could not compete with Brazilian tropical products.[68]

At this point, the cards to be played at the game in the South Atlantic were already on the table: Angola would not export sugar, and the sugar mills of São Tomé would gradually extinguish their furnaces.[69] Portuguese colonization in South Atlantic would be com- plementary, not competitive: Brazil would produce sugar, tobacco, cotton, and coffee, and Africa would provide slaves. The plan to create another Brazil in Angola would take shape again only in the second half of the nineteenth century, when Brazil escaped from Portuguese control and after the slave trade to America was extinguished.

2. Confrontation pitting the Jesuits against both the royal admin- istration and the colonists was provisionally avoided. Employment of African slaves made evangelization easier, relieving the Amerindians from coerced labor imposed by planters and authorities charged with providing public works.

The first serious clash between a donatory captain and the met- ropolitan apparatus happened in the captaincy of Porto Seguro and concerned the administration of Indian labor. After colliding with Vicar Bernardo de Aurejeac, Donatary Pero do Campo Tourinho was arrested and sent to the Inquisition Court in Lisbon. The interroga- tory, made in 1550, described the accusations against the defendant:

Asked whether he had said that in his captaincy no holiday was to be kept – nor lady-Day, the Apostles' Day or All Saints' Day – so much so that he had ordered his [Indian] servants to work on those days, he answered no, and said that he rather told them to keep and celebrate; and that he just sometimes reprimanded the French vicar [Aurejeac] for he wanted Saint William's, Saint Martin's, Saint George's and other Saints' Days to be kept as well, which were not ordered to be kept by Saint Mother Church and either by prelates in their constitutions, because the land was new and it was necessary to work to populate it. . . . [70]

This conflict between colonists' mercantile productivity and evan- gelization would be lessened by the slave trade. Two of the most

---

[68] Delgado, Vol. III, pp. 168–70; "Consulta do Conselho Ultramarino," 21 June 1655, *MMA*, Vol. XI, pp. 490, 491.
[69] Mauro, pp. 190–2.
[70] J. Capistrano De Abreu, "Atribulações de um Donatário," in *Caminhos Antigos e Povoamento do Brasil* (Rio de Janeiro, 1930), pp. 37–50.

important protectors of the Indians, the Dominican Bartolomé de Las Casas in the sixteenth century and the Jesuit Antonio Vieira in the seventeenth century, suggested to metropolitan authorities implementation of the African slave trade to free Indians from the servitude they were reduced to by the colonists.[71] Jesuits would quarrel with the colonists in areas where the slave trade had not penetrated and where Indian coerced labor prevailed. Insofar as their temporal power increased, the Jesuits would come into conflict with the authorities. That contest lasted until the crisis of the 1750s, when the Society of Jesus was driven from Portugal and the colonies. This conflict demonstrates the political nonviability of American colonial enclaves based on Indian coerced labor and placed outside metropolitan control.

3. The crown and the colonial administration found new income sources in the slave trade. This income came from export duties in African seaports, from entrance fees in Brazilian seaports, and from donations, subsidies, preferential duties, excise taxes, and other taxes included in the slaves' price. The civil administration was not the only one to benefit from such tributes: There was also the tax paid to the clergy for obligatory baptism of each slave in seaports. Around 1630 a slave went to Brazil burdened by tributes corresponding to 20 percent of his price and to Spanish America with taxes corresponding to 66 percent of his price in Angola.[72] After 1714, overland transportation of slaves to Brazilian mining regions was also taxed; and in 1809 a 5 percent tax was levied on the purchase and sale of slaves throughout the Brazilian territory. Portugal derived other advantages from its quasi-monopoly over the slave trade up to the first half of the seventeenth century. Thanks to this African trade, Portugal was able to enter Peru and the Caribbean, penetrating the Spanish silver monopoly, obtaining gold, and speculating on other American products such as the Venezuelan cocoa exported to Mexico.[73]

---

[71] Marcel Bataillon observes that when Las Casas proposed the African slave trade to Hispaniola (1516), the justice or injustice of that trade was not yet discussed in Europe; see Bataillon, pp. 91–4. In any case, this argument is inapplicable to Antonio Vieira, since his famous letter to Pará's municipal chamber recommending the employment of Angolan slaves in Pará and Maranhão was written in 1661, when abuses of African enslavement were widely known and discussed; see "Carta a Camara do Pará, 12 Feb. 1661," in J. L. de Azevedo, (ed.), *Cartas do Padre Antonio Vieira*, 3 vols. (Lisbon, 1925), Vol. I, p. 581.

[72] See De Azevedo, p. 71; D. de Abreu E. Brito, *Um Inquérito à vida administrativa e econômica de Angola e do Brasil 1591*, prefácio de A. de Albuquerque Felner (Coimbra, 1931), p. 30; *MMA*, first series, Vol. VIII, pp. 243, 394; B. Heintze, "The Angolan Vassal Tributes of the 17th Century," *RHES*, No. 6 (1980), pp. 57–78, p. 63 n. 14.

[73] Magalhães-Godinho, *Os Descobrimentos*, Vol. II, pp. 60–5, 98–9; Robert J. Ferry, "En-

The apprenticeship of colonization 173

4. Portuguese merchants in Brazil combined the advantages of oligopsony (in the purchase of sugar) with those of oligopoly (in the sale of slaves). Sustained by traders and royal officials living in Angola, the Gold Coast, and Senegambia, these merchants facilitated the sale of African slaves – by giving credit to planters – in order to control the commercialization of agricultural products.

Lack of money in the colony and intensification of Atlantic exchanges permitted the credit to take direct forms. In Brazil, sugar was exchanged for African slaves.[74] In Luanda and other African ports, barter goods were given to intermediaries on the condition of being exchanged for slaves. A Portuguese text from 1594 illustrates this: "The same way in Europe currency is gold and coined silver, and the same way in Brazil it is the sugar, in Angola and other neighborly courts the currency is the slave."[75] Of course, planters kept on exporting brazilwood during the low-sugar season.[76] And on the other side of the ocean, slave exports did not exclude trades of other African products. Up to the second half of the nineteenth century, Brazil would import African textiles from Senegambia and Niger.[77]

5. Exchanges between the metropolis and Brazil increased. The trade with Africa enlarged the demand and increased the permeability of the Brazilian colonial economy: The slave trade became a privileged instrument in showing the way to colonial complementarities of production. As the potential gains of properties served as a guarantee for the purchase of new factors of production (slaves), the economic surplus was productively invested. Soon the colonial system developed a mechanism able to stimulate regular development of production. At the same time, the transfer of income from the productive sector to the mercantile sector – a crucial factor of colonial exploitation – was assured.

Equipment for sugar mills and consumer goods was bought in the metropolis by colonists. Research has shown that luxury products were a minor item in foreign purchases of the colony's seigniorial class.[78] However, ostentatiously employed in households or in land

---

comienda, African Slavery, and Agriculture in Seventeenth-Century Caracas," *HAHR*, Vol. 61, No. 4 (1981), pp. 609–36.

[74] De Abreu E Brito, pp. 71, 72.

[75] Quoted by W. G. L. Randles, *L'Ancien royaume du Congo, des origines à la fin du XIXe s.* (Paris and La Haye, 1978), p. 176.

[76] Mauro, pp. 118ff.

[77] Robin Law, "Trade and Politics Behind the Slave Coast: The Lagoon Traffic and the Rise of Lagos 1500–1800," *JAH*, Vol. 24 (1983), pp. 321–48.

[78] Pe. Fernão Cardim, *Tratado da terra e qente do Brasil* (1585) (São Paulo, 1978), pp. 201, 202; on sugar mills' accounts see S. B. Schwartz, *Sugar Plantations in the Formation of*

174   *Luiz Felipe de Alencastro*

lords' social presentation, the slave also became a luxury product.
One of the main characteristics of Brazilian traditional society was the
habit of considering the number of domestic servants as a sign of
wealth. Obviously, the "qualification" of slaves did not change their
economic and juridical essence. Whatever his functions, his condition,
or his complexion, the slave went on being a factor of production and
a negotiable asset. Thus, he could also be "disqualified," reintegrated
in field labor, or sold, according to his master's convenience. Thus
the ostentatious attitudes of the dominant class also intensified the
demand for slaves. In 1845, when the free population in Rio de Janeiro
was already permeated by ways and customs spread by industrial
and bourgeois Europe, Martins Pena, a playwright, showed in one
of his plays a gift a gentleman brought, in a big basket, to his fiancée:
a slave, "around seven or eight years old, dressed in blue breeches
and a red cap," to be the girl's servant.[79]

6. Access to credit and the anticipated purchase of slaves favored
colonial planters as well. Considering the magnitude of the investment in the slave trade and the size of the African market, the supply
of African slaves became more regular and flexible than that of Amerindian slaves. In addition, the capture, the march toward the ports,
and the successive barters to which slaves were submitted in Africa,
as well as the crossing of the Atlantic, worked in a selective way. In
this sequence of exchanges and traumas, the unfit or physically weak
individuals were eliminated and the survivors underwent an intense
dissocialization. In his "Tratado da Terra do Brasil" (1570), Pero de
Magalhães Gandavo wrote: "One of the reasons that keeps Brazil
from growing even more are rebellions and daily escapes of [Indians]
slaves; if those Indians were not so fugitive and inconstant, Brazil's
wealth would be unique . . . there are also [in Brazil] many slaves from
Guinea, who are more constant than Indians and who never escape
[once] they have no place to go."[80] It was also known that, in contrast
to Indians, whose mortality was high due to their vulnerability to
microbial, bacterial, and viral shock that the discoveries brought to
America, Africans had already been victimized and partially immu-
nized by the same epidemic diseases that had hit the Europeans.[81]

Brazilian Society – Bahia 1550–1835 (Cambridge, London, and New York, 1985),
pp. 212–18.

[79] Martins Penna, "Os dois ou o ingles maquinista," in *Comédias* (Rio de Janeiro and
Paris, n.d.), cena 9, pp. 130, 131.

[80] Pero de Magalhães Gandavo, *Tratado da Terra do Brasil* (1570), introduction by Capistrano De Abreu (Rio de Janeiro, 1911), pp. 38, 39.

[81] Alfred W. Crosby, Jr., *The Columbian Exchange: Biological and Cultural Consequences of
1492* (Westport, Conn., 1972), pp. 3–34.

The apprenticeship of colonization 175

The introductions of Africans would soon provoke epidemic out-
breaks among American Indians, compelling planters to acquire
greater numbers of slaves from African populations already immu-
nized against contagious diseases, especially smallpox. Brandão, a
skilled merchant and eyewitness to the damage caused by smallpox
in Brazil between 1616 and 1617, stated that the epidemic made "lots
of rich men become poor." Following the time of Brandão, smallpox
was lethal among Indians, blacks from Senegambia, and whites and
mestizos born in Brazil, but affected few slaves from Allada and the
Congo. Such observations, recorded by Brandão, were surely known
to many Brazilian colonists. All those reasons combined to make the
exploitation of Africans in Brazil easier.

Nevertheless in the first quarter of the seventeenth century that resort
to non-American labor became irreversible in Brazil.[82] Since then, the
xenophagy of plantations – that is their appetite for incorporating
laborers from outside productive areas – appears to have been the
result of internal demand and of slave traders' pressures on the supply
level. From the beginning of the eighteenth century, colonial authorities also maintained the African slave trade's predominance in
order to prevent competition among different Brazilian productive
zones inside the territorial labor market.[83]

DEMAND FOR AND SUPPLY OF SLAVES: WHAT WAS THE "PRIMUM MOBILE"?

The introduction of Africans in Brazil is generally explained by the
insufficiency of the Indian population or by cultural and somatic factors making Indians unfit for slave labor. Historical tradition be-
queathed by the romantic writers of the nineteenth century imputed
the failure of Indian slavery to the rebelliousness of the Ameridians.
Thus, Africans and, more generally, blacks seemed more fit for slavery. Gilberto Freyre partially contested such a thesis, revaluing the
Africans and showing Indians as "backward" and "lazy."[84] Hence,
he did not question the idea that the transition from Indian slavery

---

[82] Goulart, pp. 99, 100. Stuart B. Schwartz, "Indian Labor and New World Plantations:
European Demands and Indian Response in the Northwestern Brazil," *American
Historical Review*, Vol. 83, No. 3, (1978), pp. 43–79; idem., *Sugar Plantations*, pp.
51–72.

[83] L. F. de Alencastro, "L'Empire du Bresil," in M. Duverger et al., eds., *Le Concept
d'empire* (Paris, 1980), pp. 301–9.

[84] Gilberto Freyre, *Casa Grande e Senzala*, 25th ed. (Rio de Janeiro, 1987), chaps. II
and V.

to African slavery was imposed by an Indian labor shortage. It is surely right that the colonists had been complaining since the seventeenth century of a "shortage of arms," but it is also true that they complained – more surprisingly – of a "shortage of lands."[85] Actually, we are dealing with an economy growing under the pressure of European demand. In such a context, land and labor are not independent factors but, rather, variables that are the result of forces ruling commercial capitalism. Insufficient recognition of this essential trait of colonization has given rise to confusion in Brazilian historiography. Whether intentional or not, the effects induced by the slave trade ensured accumulation peculiar to commercial capitalism, as well as to the Portuguese colonial system. More than any other, the slave trade was an administered trade. As has been suggested, metropolitan control over the reproduction of colonial production – or, better, the political establishment of the colonial economic system – had a fundamental importance in creating this process. It is also clear that trade in African slaves had already reached a large scale and had been strongly integrated with the Atlantic system *before* it was connected to Brazilian agriculture. Submitted for three centuries to the European power controlling a large part of the African slave market, Brazil became the colony receiving the majority of slaves carried to the New World. A lost link in Brazil's history, the African connection means that the slave trade is not a secondary effect of slavery but the reverse. This system led also to a differentiation between Brazilian slavery and its American counterparts; finally, it imposes an Atlantic interpretation on the formation of Brazilian nation.

[85] Ernesto Ennes, *Os Palmares – Subsídios para a sua historia* (Lisbon, 1938), p. 135.

5

From Indian to Slave: Forced Native Labour and Colonial Society in São Paulo During the Seventeenth Century

John M. Monteiro

I

Over the course of the seventeenth century, colonists from São Paulo and other nearby towns launched attacks on hundreds of Indian villages throughout the vast interior of Brazil, capturing thousands of Indians from diverse societies, and introducing them to colonial farms and plantations. These expeditions fed an emergent slave system in the São Paulo region, where a broad base of forced native labour made possible the production and transportation of agricultural surpluses from this comparatively poor and marginal colonial outpost.[1] But the dimensions and significance of Indian slavery in the region went far beyond this commercial nexus. In fact, virtually every aspect of the formation of São Paulo during its first two centuries was tied in some fundamental way to the expropriation, exploitation, and destruction of indigenous populations.

Yet, while the slaving expeditions of the Paulistas, or residents of São Paulo, occupy an important position in Brazilian historiography, very little is known about the structure and dynamics of the slave society they created. There are two reasons for this oversight. First, much of the historical literature focuses on the achievements of the intrepid *bandeirantes*, the backwoodsmen of São Paulo held responsible for the extension of Brazil's frontiers, for the discovery of precious metals in the interior, and, only secondarily, for the domination of numerous indigenous societies. Within this literature, slave hunting made up a distinct, early phase of *bandeirante* activities, in which the Paulistas supplied Indian labour to the coastal sugar plantations, supposedly suffering a crisis in the supply of African labour because of the Dutch invasion of northeastern Brazil and Angola.[2]

And second, the vast historiographical production on slavery in Brazil has attached little importance to the role of Indian labour in the formation of colonial society. Though important recent contributions have shed light on this neglected subject, the main trends in the literature continue to sustain a fundamentally biased and ingenuous view of the problem of

Indian slavery.[3] The notion of Indian slavery as a failed or incomplete institution remains strong in the literature. The Indian, within this perspective, proved incapable of adapting to the harsh conditions of plantation labour, primarily because of the burden of his backward, inflexible, 'neolithic' culture, soon giving way to the stronger and more productive African slave.[4]

The main problem with the prevailing literature, then, is that it denies a whole historical process of domination, one which involved the active participation of native peoples, who, for their part, faced the new situations of colonialism and enslavement with multiple, sometimes contradictory, responses. To be sure, the shock of conquest, aggravated by epidemic disease, debilitated and disarticulated indigenous social formations. But the Indians who survived the initial impact, and who came to be subjected to one of the several types of colonial domination, did not disappear. They were transformed from members of vigorous tribal societies to members of an indigent, exploited class.

This article examines the process of transformation from Indian to slave in the São Paulo region during the seventeenth century. The text is divided in five parts, each punctuating complementary aspects of this larger process. The first deals with the violent separation of Indians from their villages and their forced transfer to the sphere of Portuguese settlement. The second traces the ideological and institutional foundations of forced native labour, emphasizing the juridical redefinition of the Indian in the region. The third and fourth treat the social relations between masters and slaves, relations marked as much by the close ties that bound together these groups as by the autonomous activities of the latter, which often proved the source of contradiction and conflict. Finally, the fifth focuses on a particular aspect of these relations, namely slave flight, demonstrating the paradoxical relationship between accommodation and resistance in a well-articulated slave social formation. Taken together, these parts do not comprise an integrated whole, for an exhaustive description of the breadth and complexity of Indian slavery in the region would exceed greatly the space of an article; nonetheless, they do furnish substantial material for a critical revision of the history of Indian slavery in colonial Brazil.

II

At the beginning of the seventeenth century, the Portuguese colonists of the São Paulo region began to impose a greater distance − geographical and social − between the Indians they captured and the societies from which these slaves came. For much of the previous century, the Portuguese had attempted to appropriate the labour of the local inhabitants, though with only moderate success. Disease, indigenous resistance, and competition with the Jesuits, who sought to place the Indians in mission villages, all contributed to the depletion of Indian labour in the immediate region, and provoked the settlers to seek new sources among uncontacted indigenous groups. This reorganization of slaving activities gained significant pace once the expansion on to new lands and the introduction of commercial agriculture stimulated the large-scale transfer of captives from the remote interior to the European settlements.

The residents of São Paulo soon began to seek the Carijó, or Guarani, who inhabited villages spread throughout a vast territory located to the south and southwest of São Paulo. From the colonial point of view, the Guarani presented numerous advantages as potential captives. In the first place, Guarani villages represented the largest concentrations of population in southern Brazil, especially since the coastal Tupinambá had been practically exterminated by that point. Second, the Guarani enjoyed a reputation among the Europeans as great cultivators, which led to the assumption that they could be transformed into rural labourers without any great problems of adaptation. And, finally, several Guarani villages maintained bellicose relations with Tupi allies of the Portuguese, which facilitated their capture.

During the first decades of the seventeenth century, the Paulistas began to intensify their contacts with the Guarani in two regions, which came to be known respectively as the Sertão dos Patos and Sertão dos Carijós. The Sertão dos Patos, located in the interior of what is now the state of Santa Catarina, was inhabited almost exclusively by Guarani speakers, under diverse denominations such as Carijó, Araxá, and Patos. The Portuguese ordinarily reached this area by sea, disembarking at the site that later became the town of Laguna. Both settlers and Jesuits of São Paulo maintained contacts in the region dating from the mid-sixteenth century, and a modest coastal slave traffic already existed in the 1550s as a supplementary source of labour for the sugar mills of São Vicente.[5]

The Sertão dos Carijós included the vast stretches of territory beyond the Paranapanema River, to the southwest of São Paulo, inhabited primarily by Guarani, though also by diverse non-Guarani peoples. Most likely, this often vague reference specifically alluded to Guairá, an area circumscribed by the Piquiri, Paraná, Paranapanema, and Tibagi rivers. Beginning in the last quarter of the sixteenth century, this region became a field of intense competition between the Spanish settlers of Paraguay, the Portuguese colonists of São Paulo, and missionaries, particularly Jesuits, each seeking to gain control of its vast Guarani population.

Because of its relatively easy access, at a 40- to 60-day march from São Paulo, Guairá soon became the principal destination of the expeditions that set out from São Paulo. But this trek inevitably put the Paulistas in contact with other indigenous groups occupying the intermediate zone, particularly in the Paranapanema Valley. Two groups, the Tememinó and Tupinaé, appear in the documentation as the major victims of the expeditions carried out during the first decade of the seventeenth century. Little is known about the relations between the Portuguese and these groups besides the fact that large numbers of Tememinós, along with smaller numbers of Tupinaés, were introduced into São Paulo at two points: following the expedition of Nicolau Barreto of 1602–04, and in 1607, when Manuel Preto 'peacefully' persuaded a large group, which he encountered on his return from Spanish Guairá, to move their village to his plantation of Nossa Senhora d'Ó.[6]

Various other ethnic groups appear in early seventeenth-century inventories of probated estates. Over time, however, this diversity slackened, and by the 1610s almost all incoming captives were Carijó. This suggests that during the first decade of the new century the Paulistas occupied themselves with preparing the way for the large-scale assaults on the Guarani that characterized the period following until 1640. In addition to clearing the zones that served as buffers between São Paulo and the sources of Guarani labour, the Paulistas built up stocks of warriors who were to serve in the subsequent raids of Guairá. The Tememinó especially filled this purpose, for they were expert warriors and quite possibly traditional enemies of the Guarani. It is likely, then, that the Tupi warriors who made up the bulk of the Paulista armies that raided Guarani villages and Jesuit missions in Guairá were the Tememinó taken in these early manoeuvres. Manuel Preto, who became one of the principal raiders of the missions in the 1620s, boasted a legendary 999 archers, probably an inflated reference to the Tememinó warriors he had acquired in 1607.[7]

The mobilization of native warriors for the purpose of enslaving enemies was nothing new in Luso-Indian relations, but this practice began to assume clearly new characteristics and proportions in the case of seventeenth-century São Paulo. In the early years of their slaving activities, that is before they launched the large-scale, militarily-organized assaults against the missions, the Paulistas acquired slaves primarily through the use of Indian intermediaries. As in the sixteenth century, trade and alliance continued to play a prominent role in the relations between the Portuguese and independent Indian societies, and remained an important means to the European goal of labour acquisition. But these alliances, even when strengthened by occasional ties of kinship between colonists and Indians, proved fragile in the long run. The trajectory of Tupinikin – Portuguese relations in sixteenth-century São Paulo had set an important precedent, as these once-populous peoples passed from allies and relatives to slaves over a short period of time.

As in the case of the Tupinikin, the relations between Portuguese and Guarani of the Patos and Guairá regions soon degenerated, with barter giving way to outright violence practised directly by the Portuguese or executed by their indigenous subordinates. Pedro Rodrigues, a missionary familiar with the Patos region, related a specific case in which Portuguese traders arrived at Patos with the apparent intention of bartering with the local caciques, with whom they had already had some 'exchange and friendship'. Enticing the Indians to the port in order to trade, the Portuguese 'in bad faith took an Indian leader along with the others who accompanied him, about forty, placed them all in irons, and took them by force to the ship and soon arriving in São Vicente'.[8]

The artifice of exchange was not always employed as a preface to violence, though. A rare criminal investigation, inquiring into the death of Guarani chief Timacaúna, offers information on a common raid, the slaving method that began to substitute barter altogether over the course of the century. According to witnesses, Timacaúna had been in the process of moving his village voluntarily to the vicinity of São Paulo when the 'black *pombeiros*' of various Paulistas ambushed the group, murdering Timacaúna and enslaving his people, marching them to São Paulo and distributing them among the colonists.[9] It is interesting that the term *pombeiro* was employed here, being a word of African origin referring to the Africans or half-castes who were charged with acquiring slaves in the interior of that continent for the Portuguese traders of the coast. The 'black *pombeiros*' in this case were creolized Indian slaves specialized in the art of enslaving Indians from the independent villages of the interior. If this practice indeed was widespread, as it seems to have been, what appears then is a trend towards the internalization of the organizational aspects of labour acquisition, as the Paulistas came to depend less and less on independent intermediaries and to rely more and more on their own slaves. This represented a radical discontinuity in Indian – white relations, contributing significantly to the redefinition of captives as slaves.

This change in the organization of slave recruitment resulted in an immediate increase in Guarani captives transferred to São Paulo. This increased influx reached its greatest proportions between 1628 and 1632, when the Paulistas attacked the Jesuit missions of Guairá, destroying 13 of the 15 missions of that province, and forcing the relocation of the other two.[10] The returns of these expeditions, though not reaching the proportions declared by Spanish officials and by Jesuits, did lay a solid base of Guarani labourers in the São Paulo region, which was to influence the social composition of the Paulista population profoundly.[11]

While it remains difficult to assess the aggregate scale of the trade for this period accurately, somewhat clearer information on the composition and distribution of the captive population does exist for much of the seventeenth century. In 1615, for example, a detailed list was composed of 628 Guarani recently brought from Guairá and divided among the participants of the slaving expedition.[12] At first sight, the most prominent feature of the list was the top-heavy presence of women and children among the captives, representing about 70 per cent of the total. This apparent preference for Guarani women reflects to a certain degree the division of labour adopted in early settler agriculture, where women and possibly children executed the planting and harvesting functions, while the men served primarily in the transport of goods and in the reproduction of the labour force, through their indispensible participation in further slaving expeditions. At the same time, though, the recruitment of women and children represented a sharp break with precolonial patterns of captivity, where the vast majority of captives taken in battle were male warriors. In effect, then, this new pattern reinforced the strategy of the Portuguese in forging relations of domination with the Indians; while the sexual division of labour on the plantations presented a certain measure of continuity from pre-conquest times, the discontinuity represented by the redefinition of the status of captives weighed more heavily in the composition of the Paulista slave population.[13]

With the large-scale assaults of 1628–32 and of 1635–37, the enslavement of the Guarani reached its peak. At the end of the 1630s, however, a profound crisis in the recruitment of Indian labour began to set in, as Guarani and Jesuit resistance seriously challenged Paulista slaving activities in southern Brazil. One immediate result was the reorientation of Paulista expeditions, which had important repercussions in São Paulo. Initially, the Paulistas sought new sources of Tupi labour, which led the expeditions to distant lands in diverse directions. This preference for Tupi captives had both historical and practical roots, since the Portuguese had dealt primarily with Tupi and Guarani societies to that point, and because the movement of captives from one Tupi society to another provided a potential source of slaves. Furthermore, the adamant resistance of non-Tupi – particularly Gê – societies to enslavement, as well as the difficulties experienced in adapting them to the new work regime, caused the Portuguese to avoid these groups as far as possible. Gabriel Soares de Sousa, in describing the Gê-speaking Guaianá of the São Paulo region late in the sixteenth century, summarized the Portuguese attitude: 'Anyone who buys a Guaianá slave expects no service from him, because these people are lazy by nature and do not know how to work.'[14]

Nonetheless, the great distances between São Paulo and the Tupi groups eventually found by the Paulistas made the enslavement of these groups impractical and unprofitable. As an immediate solution, the colonists turned precisely to the Guaianá and Guarulhos, two Gê societies inhabiting areas close to São Paulo. The expeditions carried out against the Guaianá, Guarulhos, and various other societies resulted in the radical alteration of the ethnic composition of the slave population. The Guarani continued to make up the bulk of the Indian population because of the massive infusions of Carijó captives during the first half of the century, though they now shared the slave quarters with significant numbers of Guaianá and Guarulhos. As an example of this tendency, one slave owner, describing his vast holdings in his 1663 will, stated: 'I declare that I have in my service heathen of all nations.'[15]

One important development related to the change in ethnic composition was a shift in the sex ratio of the captive population. During the period of heaviest Guarani recruitment, women outnumbered men. But in the 1650s, precisely during the greatest influx of Guaianá, the number of men surpassed that of women for the first time. These general characteristics gain further meaning when the composition of the adult population by ethnic group is considered. Among the slave population identified as originally Guarani, the sex ratio remained around 80 males per 100 females, while among those identified as Guaianá, there were around 112 males per 100 females.[16]

This difference certainly owed much to the conditions of recruitment faced by the Paulistas. Since the demographic concentration of these peoples, who were primarily hunters and foragers, was far lower than that of the Guarani, the Paulistas rarely captured many at any one time. The absence of detailed descriptions of Guaianá villages suggests that the Paulistas did not frequent the 'lodgings' of these societies, encountering instead hunting or war parties removed from the domestic setting. In any case, whether due to the low population density or to the greater resistance to capture, the difficulties involved in Guaianá recruitment effectively elevated the costs of supplying labour to the European settlements. Several Paulistas recorded repeated losses of sons, slaves, and equipment in these uncertain ventures. Domingos de Góis, for example, reported that he sent his son to the wilderness three times, 'receiving more losses than profit because of the death of his Indians'.[17]

Those who were enslaved entailed further risk, as many succumbed to European diseases; and many who survived the immunological peril resisted the new work regime. For their part, the Paulistas, thoroughly accustomed to Guarani labour, faced serious obstacles in trying to understand the non-Tupi speakers, let alone in attempting to transform them into productive workers. Captain Antonio Raposo Barreto of Taubaté, for example, writing to a commercial correspondent in Rio de Janeiro in 1680, feared that he would lose the 40 slaves (probably Puri) his son had brought him from the Mantiqueira Range, since they were dying of a flu-like disease. 'And I do not know just how much they are suffering, because there is not an interpreter who can understand them,' he lamented.[18]

This new situation had serious implications for the reproduction and control of the local labour force. For example, the incidence of rebellion and running away increased markedly in this period, which was strongly correlated to the ethnic variable, since all the major revolts had mostly Guaianá and Guarulhos participants. But if the vicissitudes of recruitment influenced the formation of slave society in several respects, they still represented only the first step in the transformation of Indians into slaves.

III

'It is well known that a slave from the settlement is worth more than four brought fresh from the wilderness.'[19] Thus one colonist expressed the difference between slaves recently introduced and those born or acculturated in colonial society. To be sure, slave prices reflected this relationship throughout the seventeenth century. But the larger significance of this differentiated scale lay in the implicit process of acculturation through which the Indians passed.

The preference for 'creoles' over recently captured Indians had much to do with the expectations of the masters with respect to longevity, adaptability, and, most likely, productivity. From the perspective of the seventeenth-century colonist, Brazil had an inexhaustible supply of Indians, but access to Indians became increasingly difficult and costly as distances increased. In an effort to decrease dependency on this outside source for the physical reproduction of personal service, the Paulistas attempted to forge local structures that would afford a sound, local base for the survival of the system. Somewhat like the Jesuits, they wished to create a kind of Christian Indian — docile, disciplined, and socially inferior. The result was the development of fragile mechanisms that could not offset the strong trend of negative natural growth.

The ideological and institutional contours of Indian slavery acquired a well-defined shape over the course of the seventeenth century, especially once the introduction of thousands of Indians from distant lands created the need for an institutional structure capable of ordering the relations between masters and Indians. This process was far from simple, especially since Portuguese legislation expressly prohibited Indian slavery, save in a few exceptional cases, which ordinarily did not apply to the Paulista example. Even so, the colonists from São Paulo were able to circumvent the legal obstacles to Indian slavery, constructing an institutional arrangement that permitted the maintenance and reproduction of slave relations. Assuming the role of personal administrators of the Indians, who were judged incapable of administering themselves, the colonists appropriated the right to exercise full control over the person and property of the Indians they had introduced to 'settled' society, without characterizing this relationship formally as slavery.

The apparent contradiction between the explicit illegality of most Indian slavery and its widespread and persistent acceptance in São Paulo derived only in part from the inability of royal officials to enforce imperial law in remote areas of the empire. More specifically, it can be explained by the complementary existence and simultaneous observance of both written, positive law and customary practice. At the same time that the Crown codified an idealized and vague legislation for Brazil, royal officials and others who were delegated authority in the colony, including the Municipal

Councils, shaped a more practical current of legal procedures that reflected both the needs of the colonists and the conflicts generated by local conditions. While these procedures were based on Portuguese legal forms, they often contradicted the very letter of the law, as in the case of Indian slavery.

The settlers themselves recognized the paradox inherent in this system of forced 'free' labour. One settler voiced the opinion of many when he declared in his will that the ten Indians in his possession 'are free according to the laws of the Kingdom, and only by the practice and custom of the land are they forced servants'.[20] Another stated just as categorically in her will that 'the Indians whom we hold are free by the laws of Portugal, and therefore I cannot force them into servitude', but nonetheless that 'I have used their forced service like the other colonists'.[21]

The perceived right to forced labour found its justification in the argument that the colonists offered a great service to God, King, and the Indians themselves in transferring the natives from a barbarous to a civilized state. Over the course of the century, this perception became set firmly in the settlers' mentality as a traditional prerogative. According to one Jesuit, writing at the end of the century,

> the residents of this town remain so firm in their conviction that the Indians are slaves, that even if the Eternal Father descended from Heaven with Christ Crucified in his arms to tell them that the Indians were free, they would not believe it.[22]

Perhaps because of the uncertain condition of their Indian captives, Paulistas frequently reaffirmed their conception of the rights they held to the labour of the Indians they themselves had brought from the 'wilderness'. Domingos Jorge Velho, one of the most important Indian fighters and slavers of the second half of the century, explained this attitude in a letter to the Crown:

> If [after conquest] we use them in our fields, we do them no injustice for this is as much to support them and their children as to support ours. Far from enslaving them, we render them an unremunerated service by teaching them to till, plant, harvest, and work for their livelihood, something which until the Whites teach them they know not how to do.[23]

Slave owners frequently expressed these attitudes in their wills by referring to the Indians as their children, which by and large paralleled the posture adopted by the Jesuits in the missions and the stance implicit in Crown legislation. For example, Maria do Prado, nearing death, wrote:

> I declare that I do not own any captive slaves but I only possess ninety souls of the native heathen, as is the common practice, whom I have always treated as my children and in the same form I leave them to my heirs.[24]

The terminology employed in local legal documents also reveals the constant insecurity of the colonists in facing the juridical contradictions that this forced labour regime elicited. In referring to the freedom of the Indians, the colonists seldom used the term *livre* (free person), but almost always *forro* (freedman), thus implying that the natural condition of the Indian should be servile. The Indians were not slaves, then, only because of the intervention of royal legislation in the question, which, in a sense, set the Indians free.

In effect, the specific terminology employed by slave holders accompanied their permanent effort to redefine the Indian within the social context of the colony. Curiously, during the seventeenth century, the term '*indio*' referred specifically and exclusively to the residents of the mission villages of the region. At the same time, the terminology that referred to the population directly subordinate to the colonists sought to equate these Indians to slaves. For example, expressions such as '*peças do gentio de terra*' (native heathen pieces) or '*negros da terra*' (native blacks) paralleled the terms '*peças do gentio da Guiné*' (Guinea pieces) or '*negros da Guiné*' (Guinea blacks), which designated African slaves. With the increasing presence of Africans in the captive population, however, the distinction became more clear. By the end of the seventeenth century, colonists began to call their Indians '*gentio do cabelo corredio*' (straight-haired heathen), '*gente parda*' (dark-skinned people), or '*administrados*' (administered persons), while the Africans, when not called by the Tupi term *Tapanhunos* (black Tapuias), were clearly differentiated as legitimate captives.

Except in the case of recently introduced captives, the colonists avoided tribal denominations for their Indians. Curiously, though, by the end of the seventeenth century they opted for a tribal designation for the Indians subject to personal administration: Carijó. The adoption of this term explains much about the process of transformation faced by the native populations over the course of the century. Originally, Carijó referred to the Guarani in general; however, as mentioned above, relatively few Guarani were enslaved after 1640. This suggests that the introduction of thousands of Guarani during the first half of the century established a pattern defining the slave population.[25]

The language employed by colonists to define and defend the regime of personal service may have been paradoxical and even contradictory, but it reflected the colonists' persistent struggle to maintain and exploit Indian labour. To be sure, though repeatedly challenged by Jesuits and crown officials, the colonists' control over the Indians was never threatened seriously until the beginning of the eighteenth century. In any case, the hazy institutional context explains little beyond the rationale for forced native labour; its substance lies within the complex web of relations struck between masters and slaves.

IV

If the transformation of previously uncontacted Indians into the 'hands and feet' of the Paulistas required adjustments in attitude on the part of the masters, it also involved a process of acculturation on the part of the Indians, which worked unevenly over the course of the seventeenth century to develop the precarious structures that were to hold together the regime of personal service. To the slave owners, the ideal of conversion went far beyond the insistent justifications cited for Indian slavery; it was above all a means of putting a definitive distance between Indian servants and the tribal social organization and culture from which they had been abruptly separated. It is not entirely clear to what point the Paulistas inculcated Christianity in their slaves, nor what were the methods they had at their disposal. Clearly, though, the masters' religion reaffirmed relations of domination and ultimately served as a weapon to enforce authority. One example of this comes from a judicial inquest where an Indian informant, ironically named Inocêncio, was cautiously reminded by the interpreter who took his oath that 'he say the truth and not lie because he had sworn upon the evangelical saints and the Devil would take him should he not speak the truth'.[26]

Paulista slave holders introduced their Indians to the world of Catholicism primarily through the ritual of baptism and the assignment of Christian names. Parish registers reveal that many masters were content with baptizing Indians in collective rites shortly after bringing them from the interior. Others, however, evidently made a conscious effort to indoctrinate their Indians before baptism, suggested by the interval between the arrival of the Indians from their villages and their baptism. Many estate inventories included unbaptized Indians who were listed either without names or with their native appellations transcribed into an often undecipherable Portuguese. For example, Maria Moreira's inventory included 'Jacó and his wife with two children who being Tapuios and unbaptized do not have names', while Catarina Tavares' contained names so garbled by the imaginative scribe who penned them that their meanings remain lost for the modern researcher.[27] Those who did not yet have Christian names apparently went through some religious instruction before their baptism. When the infant Albana, daughter of Pantaleão and his 'pagan' wife, was christened, the vicar noted that Albana's mother 'now pagan, is to be called Luzia when she is baptized', which occurred more than a year later.[28]

In addition to bestowing Christian names on newborn and recently arrived Indians, the baptism ritual also introduced them to the practice of *compadrio*, or ritual coparentage, an important element of the Luso-Christian world. Though the data are somewhat unreliable, records of baptisms do suggest some patterns with useful explanatory value. There appears to have been a certain correlation between parentage and coparentage, which reflects the broader structure of slave society. At the lower end of a spectrum, Indians recently introduced to the settlement ordinarily received Indians as godparents. The best evidence of this comes from Sorocaba, where several collective baptisms of recently-enslaved Indians took place in the 1680s. Interestingly, almost all the Indians christened were children, registered as '*filhos de pagãos*' (children of pagans), which suggests that many of the adults brought on the expeditions were not immediately subjected to baptism. Early in 1685, João Leme de Silva had twelve Indians christened, of whom seven had Indian godparents, while the remaining five were christened by a white godfather and Indian godmother. At about the same time, André de Zuñega brought 53 captives to the font, of whom 46 had Indian godparents. And of the 31 Indians of Diogo Domingues de Faria who were baptized in a single ceremony, all had Indian godparents.[29] It would seem, then, that Indian godparents served as intermediaries in the acculturation process, at least in a symbolic sense.

Important exceptions to this pattern did exist, showing that other strategies of acculturation were considered. Martinho Garcia, for example, personally oversaw the baptism of 36 Indians he had brought on the Zuñega expedition, himself assuming the role of godfather to all the adults (seven) and seven children who received Christian names. His brother Miguel Garcia served as godfather to eleven children, while the remaining eleven, all girls, became the godchildren of the African slave Simão and the Indian Laura, both of the neighbouring plantation of Diogo Domingues de Faria.[30] Such proximity between masters and slaves' children was rare, though. In Sorocaba, masters appeared as godparents of their own slaves only in 25 cases out of nearly 700 baptisms.

The registers of child baptisms in Sorocaba reveal other interesting characteristics of ritual kinship in seventeenth-century São Paulo. Usually, children who were baptized fell into one of the following categories: children of Indian parents, where both parents were declared in the register; children of Indian mothers, whose fathers did not appear in the register; and children of Indian mothers with white fathers.[31] In the first category, 55 per cent of the children baptized had two Indians as godparents, while 30 per cent had a pair of white godparents, and 11 per cent had mixed godparents, being ordinarily a white godfather and Indian godmother. These percentages practically were inverted in the second category, as 57 per cent of children born to single mothers had two whites as godparents, 28 per cent had two

Indians, and 15 per cent had mixed godparents. And in the third category, all of the children baptized were presented by white godparents.

While the baptismal registers may suggest a differentiated pattern of socialization, they offer little evidence that suggests what importance Indians attached to Christian ritual kinship. The significance of *compadrio* to the Indians should not be overestimated, therefore, and any conclusions emerging from the data must be regarded with some suspicion. At times, the choice of godparents was no choice at all, as candidates were selected either by the masters or priests involved. In other cases, godparents assumed this role only because they were present at the time of the ceremony, which is suggested by the repeated appearance of certain godparents on the same date. Still, on other occasions, the responsibility fell upon the vicar's assistants, or even on the mother of the christened child herself. And when the choice was made, it sometimes followed a logic of its own. For example, when the twins Amaro and Sebastião were baptized, one had white godparents while the other was presented by two Indians.[32]

In any case, if coparentage did not have the same meaning for recently converted Indians as it did for the colonists of São Paulo, it did represent a significant step in the integration of Indians into Paulista society. For some it may have produced bonds of solidarity within the oppressed class; for others it strengthened the ties between masters and slaves. In most cases where Indians served as godparents, they were from the same rural estate as the child or adult who was baptized. This could be an indication that the master himself chose the godparents, or that, in the case of Indians recently brought from the interior, Indians already familiar with local practices were to play the role of introducing neophytes to the system. It appears as if some choice was involved at times, though, as in several instances godparents were selected from among the captives of other masters. If indeed a rational choice was involved, it makes some sense that Indians should choose white godparents for their children, rarely selecting their own masters to fulfil the duty. To have a white man as a *compadre* was in a sense a defiance of the rigid social hierarchy; at the same time, a white *compadre* could offer protection, and on more than one occasion slaves were known to seek refuge with either *compadres* or godfathers. It is significant, then, that masters appeared as godfathers to their own Indians only in cases where no father was declared, in adult baptisms, or where they themselves were the father of the child to be christened. That way they did not create bonds of equality with their male slaves, whereas the godfather – godchild relationship essentially reinforced the paternalistic ethos.

V

The development of a master – slave relationship in seventeenth-century São Paulo reflected the basic changes faced by the indigenous population of the region. In the sixteenth and early seventeenth centuries, the colonists were still in a position where they had to incorporate indigenous forms of organization in order to extract labour from the Indians. But even after slave relations of production had become dominant, Indians continued to maintain a certain measure of autonomy. Unable to reproduce preconquest organizational forms, however, they were forced to adjust to a new reality, where a somewhat separate existence was still possible, but which was defined and restricted by its position within Luso-Brazilian society.

The spatial organization of towns and rural estates introduced a first condition for this measure of autonomy. Indian living quarters figured prominently in both the urban and rural landscapes, and in both places were associated explicitly with the sphere of work. In the towns, Indians' quarters invariably were located in the depths of properties, usually alongside the kitchen, separated from the main house by a garden. In the countryside, the servants' quarters ordinarily were built around the *roça*, or subsistence plot.

The evolution of the servants' quarters reflected the general transformation of Luso-Indian relations in São Paulo. For much of the seventeenth century, the Indians on rural estates lived in single, large quarters. At the beginning of the century, these were straw-covered huts or lodges, probably similar to those found in Tupi societies, which the colonists called by the Guarani term *tijupar* (with variant spellings). Over time, however, these constructions began to assume the broad characteristics associated with the Paulista variety of colonial architecture. The quarters began to be covered by ceramic shingles instead of straw, and the basic layout revolved around single family units, much as the rural and urban homes of the dominant class. Though a few multiple living units appear, for the most part servant quarters were concentrated in single structures. The process apparently was complete by the beginning of the eighteenth century, when the term *senzala*, an African word for slave quarters, entered the Paulistas' vocabulary for the first time in reference to Indian housing.

In the rural sphere, Indians were expected to feed themselves with the produce that their own *roças*, or garden plots, yielded. While such autonomy could have afforded some continuity between pre- and post-conquest forms of organization of production, the demands of the colonial economy altered the division of labour so that Indian subsistence production no longer followed traditional patterns. Many women remained in agriculture, but the colonists seemed to prefer them as house servants, wet nurses, and concubines. For example, in the 1640 estate inventory of Antonia de Chaves, 11 of 15 female Indians were counted as house servants, while José Preto of Mogi das Cruzes listed 22 'black house servants', all women, among his 106 Indians.[33]

This division left some agricultural chores to men, which stood in marked contrast to indigenous forms of production. At the same time, the use of European tools exacerbated the rupture with tradition. Indian men were expected to, and did, assume a different work role. Jerônimo de Brito, a repentant slave owner at the time of his will, suggested this path for several of his Indians whom he freed, giving each a hoe, scythe, and axe 'so that each can make his *roça* to sustain himself'.[34] Further evidence that several Indians did set out on their own to establish independent production units surfaces in several land sale documents, which describe Indian farmers as neighbours.[35]

Other roles assigned to Indians in the local economy put further distance between themselves and an increasingly remote indigenous past. Almost all artisanal activities, including blacksmithing and goldsmithing, were executed by Indian craftsmen, who often worked as apprentices to European masters. For example, Isabel de Barcelos paid João Garcia over 200 pounds of cotton for teaching one of her Indians to be a weaver.[36] Many slave owners, particularly urban dwellers with few Indians, depended on their Indian artisans as an important source of income. Others concentrated larger numbers of Indian *oficiais* (master craftsmen) on their estates. José Ortiz de Camargo, for one, counted five cobblers, two blacksmiths, and two carpenters among his extensive slave corps, certainly adding to his earnings significantly. Captain Guilherme Pompeu de Almeida, who commanded hundreds of Indian and African slaves on his massive fazenda of Voturuna, dominated the crafts market of the town of Parnaíba at the end of the seventeenth century with his many craftsmen, a tradition carried on by his son, Father Guilherme.[37]

The modest market for goods and services that developed in the local towns provided opportunities for independent Indian artisans, producers, and vendors. By the 1650s, Indians began to compete seriously with Portuguese peddlers in the town of São Paulo, virtually controlling the exchange of local products, particularly foodstuffs and hides. Wills and inventories frequently attested to this activity, as many colonists owed Indians money for services or goods these had provided. Manuel Alves Pimentel, for example, owed an Indian named Pedro over 1 milreis for some sweets he had ordered; Antonio Vieira Tavares settled a debt with 'a black blacksmith named Salomão for a scythe he made', before he passed away.[38]

The Municipal Council of São Paulo tried to discourage the activities of this autonomous sector, repeatedly levying fines against colonists who purchased certain goods from Indian peddlers. The frequency with which such measures were passed suggests that local authorities were unable to suppress independent Indian commercial activities. The Municipal Council showed a persistent preoccupation for two important reasons. First, a black market of hides and meat developed, violating the monopoly privileges bestowed upon influential local merchants, whose purchase of the municipal meat contract gave them exclusive control of the cattle market. Second, much of the meat and hides sold in town by Indians was the product of plunder, which raised important questions concerning social control in the countryside. By the 1660s, the situation was practically out of hand. Several cases, mostly complaints about Indian plunder, were brought before local and Crown authorities. In her will, Grácia de Abreu mentioned that 'my people' had stolen two loads of wheat flour and killed some pigs belonging to Salvador Bicudo. It is likely that both of these items, with significant commercial value in the context of the local economy, found their way to the marketplace.[39] At about the same time, Francisco Cubas pressed a lawsuit against the heirs of José Ortiz de Camargo, claiming that Camargo's Indians repeatedly raided his cattle ranch in the Nossa Senhora do Ó neighbourhood, slaughtering cattle and looting crops.[40]

Above all, this wave of 'criminal' activity that swept the countryside reflected the patterns of adjustment to slave society experienced by Indians. In many ways, crimes perpetrated by Indians resembled those observed among African and creole slaves at other times and places.[41] Hog stealing, cattle rustling, and theft of valuables became common occurrences in the seventeenth century. Slave crime was far more than a visceral response to the disorienting changes that servitude imposed on its members, though in a few cases rebellions and cattle-killings represented primal rejections of slavery itself. Above all, crime was a form of accommodation promoted by the conditions present in slave societies and by the existence of radically opposite systems of values. It is highly unlikely that an Indian would consider the appropriation of a hog or cow from his own or another's master as stealing, especially if his own well-being depended on the consumption or marketing of that item. At the same time, masters condoned such activities, assuming the blame for any property stolen or destroyed by their Indians.[42]

It is instructive at this point to distinguish between the tribal hunter, who, at the margins of colonial society, attacked cattle either as game or as a reaction to the threat that cattle posed on his society, and the Indian slave who slaughtered cattle to sell meat and hides on the internal colonial market. Though both were described as criminals by colonial society, the hunter suffered immediate reprisals and often extermination, while the slave rarely faced punishment. In this sense, even though they challenged the stability of the slave regime, most 'crimes' perpetrated by Indian slaves above all reflected a determined level of acculturation, where the slave forged spaces of survival within his new social reality.

VI

The ambiguous process of accommodation also manifested itself through the widespread practices of flight and truancy among the captive population. While, within the context of slavery, running away constituted a well-characterized form of resistance, it expressed at the same time an advanced degree of acculturation among those who left the service of their masters. This assertion stands at odds with the prevailing historiography of colonial Brazil, which contends that Indians were much more likely to flee from slavery than their African counterparts, since they were native to Brazil and because their 'backward' culture stood in the way of their adaptation to the rigours of plantation agriculture. But an analysis of flight among Indians in São Paulo reveals a marked similarity between this and other slave societies.

A wide spectrum of reasons conceivably could have motivated slave flight. Bad treatment, the desire to be reunited to family members or to a mate living under another master, or simply the quest for freedom all were compelling motives for abandoning a particular household. Tetecola, for example, a Carijó, fled because she did not want to serve the heirs of her deceased master, Isabel Fernandes.[43] And Manuel Ruivo (Redhead), a mixed-blood who was one of the unsavoury group of henchmen commanded by the outlaw Bartolomeu Fernandes de Faria, explained to an interrogator how he arrived in Faria's service. After the death of his master Miguel da Costa, on whose estate he was born, he rejected the administration of Costa's heir Tomás Correia, running away to the plantation of Bartolomeu Fernandes de Faria.[44]

Most often, though, runaways were not fugitives at all but rather were coerced into serving someone else. It is difficult to distinguish between coercion and protection, however, as it is clear that some Indians sought refuge on rival estates, while others were obviously held against their will on the farms of different masters. In either case, the recuperation of runaways became a sticky legal issue, where the uncertain status of the Indian as property, and the relative immunity of private estates to local justice, lay in the balance. As an example, a suit pressed by Caterine do Prado in 1682 illustrates to a certain degree the ambiguity of fugitive status, and the role of the Indians themselves in these cases. Prado protested that eight years before, four 'native Blacks' belonging to Bartolomeu Bueno Cacunda invaded her estate and kidnapped Úrsula, an Indian in her work force. Úrsula, she argued, belonged to her because her husband, Estévão Ribeiro de Alvarenga, had brought her from her village another eight years before. After conflicting testimony was heard from different persons, the key witness, Úrsula, was summoned to 'inform' (slaves and Indians, by law, could not testify as witnesses, but only as informers). Through an interpreter, Úrsula, known as Bahehu 'in her land', told her side of the story. Asked, 'To whom do you belong?', the interpreter recorded her as answering:

> To Captain Bartolomeu Bueno Cacunda only, for having brought her from her land to his crops at Sapucaí where he left her, and when from the said crops she sought to make her living she was found by the said deceased Estévão Ribeiro de Alvarenga, who brought her to this settlement to his house with all her children who were in her company.

The investigator then asked: 'Why did it take you so long to return to your master's house?'

> She answered that she had not returned because they kept her imprisoned in chains, and as soon as she found herself unshackled she sought her master's house without being induced or counselled by anyone to do this but did it all on her own motivation.

The defendant, Bartolomeu Bueno, was absolved, and retained possession of Bahehu after 16 years of dispute.[45]

The incidence of slaves running off to the forest in search of freedom appears to have been fairly infrequent. A few reports of mass flight exist, but they had much to do with efforts to justify slaving missions, as in 1602 and again in 1628, when such allegations immediately preceded the large expeditions of Nicolau Barreto and Antonio Raposo Tavares. Slaves who did flee to the bush invariably were from local groups, mainly Guaianá and Guarulhos, and ordinarily had been brought to the Portuguese settlements only recently.[46] In general, it made little sense for Indian captives to flee to the wilderness, especially for those who came from distant homelands and who had seen much of the fabric of their tribal societies destroyed by the Paulistas. Unless whole groups succeeded in fleeing at once, as in the aftermath of the rebellion on Antonio Pedroso de Barros' estate, chances of survival were minimal for those who sought to recuperate the world that had been left behind.[47]

Usually, when masters reported that their Indians had run off to the *sertão,* or wilderness, they meant that the runaways had joined a slaving expedition. One slave owner declared that among her property there was 'one fugitive Black who some say has gone to the *sertão*'.[48] The term fugitive took on a particularly ambiguous meaning in these cases, since the truancy was not always a result of the slave's desire. In his will, Pedro Vaz de Barros noted that 'many of my slaves have run away, particularly with the people of Captain Fernão Dias Pais'.[49] Another distraught master claimed that the two Indians he had rented to Captain Braz Moreira Cabral as translators for a slaving expedition remained in the Vacaria region of Mato Grosso as Cabral's henchmen, only to be used 'against their master'.[50]

It was within the local economy that most fugitive slaves circulated. Frequently, references to fugitives included the location where they took refuge, as owners of fugitive Indians usually knew precisely where their truant labour was to be found. For example, Antonia Chaves recorded that one Indian, Isabel, had run away and 'it is certain that she is at the house of Antonio Ribeiro de Morais, resident of the town of São Paulo'.[51] Manuel Rodrigues de Góis declared: 'I own a young man of the Carijó nation who ran away and is at Salvador de Miranda's house'.[52] And upon the death of Estévão Furquim, his widow pressed a suit trying to recover a runaway who had been working for seven or eight years on the estate of Inés Rodrigues de Morais in distant Taubaté, 'in plain sight of everyone'. To consolidate her acquisition, Inés Rodrigues had married the runaway to one of her own servants, a stretegy to which more and more masters began to appeal as Indian labour became increasingly scarce.[53]

Many masters sheltered fugitives, though usually as a means of increasing their own labour force. Ana Machado de Lima revealingly noted in her will that of the ten Indians in her service, six belonged to other masters, 'as my husband well knows'.[54] João Missel Gigante, an important slave owner in Parnaíba, included among his last wishes that the Indians found on his estate who belonged to other colonists should be returned to their rightful owners, in order to rest with a clear conscience.[55] And Pedro Vidal declared: 'On my farm there are three Blacks and one old Black, fugitives of the Goianá nation, and it is not known who they belong to; should their owners appear, they are to be turned over to them.'[56]

Taking advantage of the institutional shortcomings of Indian slavery, then, owners effectively were able to integrate a form of Indian resistance into the system of forced labour. In the context of the local economy, Indian absenteeism resulted basically in the redistribution of labour. For the Indians, this allowed for a certain measure of mobility, restricted as it was. The sum advantage may well have been a lessening of tensions generated within the master – slave relationship. But, at the same time, this situation ultimately reinforced that relationship, favouring especially the wealthier and better-armed colonists, who were able to resist attempts by other slave owners to recuperate their fugitive or stolen property either through the uncertain wheels of justice or the risky use of force.

The case of the outlaw Bartolomeu Fernandes de Faria illustrates this clearly. When Faria was arrested in 1718, 98 Indians were confiscated by royal authorities from his plantations in Jacareí and Iguape. The list made of the captives revealed that nearly all were fugitives forced into the service of Faria. Most came from the rural chapel of Nossa Senhora da Penha, apparently left by Brigida Sobrinha in 1694, whose will also was found in the power of Faria. The list also included several *bastardas* (illegitimate mixed-bloods), considered free even by local standards, a few mission village residents, and even one white girl who had been a foundling, all 'snatched by the old man to serve him'.[57] Certainly not all settlers went to the extent that Faria did to ensure the availability of Indian labour in the midst of a supply crisis, but it became painfully clear to all that other strategies for acquiring – and maintaining – labour were necessary.

VII

The case of Captain Bartolomeu Fernandes de Faria, owner of over 200 Indian and African slaves, provides yet another example illustrating the process of transformation from Indian to slave. Among the free persons who had been subjected to slavery against their wills was Joana de Siqueira, who left an extensive testimony detailing the circumstances of her captivity. In 1718, a group of Faria's henchmen ambushed Joana along with two travel companions, including her lover, with whom they had a score to settle. Following the brutal murder of the two, Joana was taken to Faria's plantation, where she faced her new master for the first time:

> Bartolomeu Fernandes told her, the witness, 'come here, I want you to be my servant,' and ordered her to raise her skirt, placing a stick between her legs, and ordered her whipped by his son João Fernandes and by Antonio Fernandes, brother of João da Cunha, which they did until a quantity of blood ran from her, and Bartolomeu Fernandes de Faria said that he did this so that from then on she would recognize him as her master; and after she, the witness, saw herself cured in this town [of Iguape], the said Bartolomeu Fernandes took her to his farm and dressed her in a Tipoia and has used her until now as his captive.[58]

In short, violence and submission figured as crucial elements of the structure of domination that characterized Paulista society in the seventeenth century. Joana's humiliation played an important role in the affirmation of social relations, especially since she had been living as a free person, as Bartolomeu Fernandes sought to put her in what he considered to be her place. The donning of the tipoia, a sack-like dress originally worn in some Guarani societies, apparently had a particularly humbling significance, as it represented her identification as part of the Indian community. Its adoption among the slave community in São Paulo reinforced the formation of the Carijó archetype that came to define the Indian slave population.[59]

But violence and domination represented only one facet of the complex relationship between masters and slaves. Without it, to be sure, social control proved tenuous. Nonetheless, every master recognized the need to create other mechanisms to soften their inherently conflictual relationship with the oppressed class. These mechanisms ultimately were couched in the paternalistic discourse of the colonists, which always sought to justify their domination over the Indians. More than simple rhetoric, though, this posture also was manifest in practice, in the sense that masters took care to establish extra-economic bonds with their slaves, attempting to forge more stable ties within this inconstant system. Masters may have been interested primarily in the fruits of their servants' labour, but at the same time they adopted a protective attitude towards their social inferiors, which, far from being incompatible with economic exploitation, reinforced the relations of inequality that moved the system of production.

NOTES

1. On the relationship between Indian slavery and local production see my 'Celeiro do Brasil: Escravidão Indígena e a Agricultura Paulista no Século XVII', *História* (São Paulo), 7 (1988).

2. See, for example, Myriam Ellis, 'O Bandeirantismo na Expansão Geográfica do Brasil', in Sérgio Buarque de Hollanda, ed., *História Geral da Civilização Brasileira. Período Colonial*, 2 vols. (São Paulo, 1960), 1:283–96. A condensed version of Ellis' article, along with other useful texts, appears translated in Richard Morse, ed. *The Bandeirantes: Historical Role of the Brazilian Pathfinders* (New York, 1965). Carlos Davidoff, *Bandeirantismo, Verso e Reverso* (São Paulo, 1983), attempts a revision by criticizing the *bandeirantes* for their violent excesses, but in the end basically reinforces old arguments.

3. Among these contributions, two tendencies should be distinguished. The first approaches the Indian question from an institutional standpoint, emphasizing legislative aspects and the broader formation of colonial Indian policy, but consigning the Indian to the role of object or of passive victim. Included in this line are: Mathias Kieman, *The Indian Policy of Portugal in the Amazon Region, 1614–1693* (Washington, D.C., 1954), Georg Thomas, *Die portugiesische Indianerpolitik in Brasilien, 1500–1640* (Berlin, 1968), Urs Höner, *Die Versklavung der brasilienischen Indianer: der Arbeitsmarkt in portugiesische Amerika im XVI. Jahrhundert* (Zurich, 1980), and Heloísa Bellotto, 'Trabalho Indígena, Regalismo e Colonização no Estado do Maranhão nos Séculos XVII e XVIII', *Revista Brasileira de História* 4 (1982), 177–92. The second tendency includes important advances in the social and ethnohistory of the colony, insofar as they have sought to incorporate Indians and indigenous societies as historical actors in the colonial drama. For general approaches, see, especially, John Hemming, *Red Gold: The Conquest of the Brazilian Indians, 1500–1760* (Cambridge, Mass., 1978), and Berta Ribeiro, *O Índio na História do Brasil* (São Paulo, 1983). The more specialized literature includes Stuart Schwartz, 'Indian Labor and New World Plantations: European Demands and Indian Responses in Northeastern Brazil', *American Historical Review* 87 (1978), 43–79; David Sweet, 'A Rich Realm of Nature Destroyed: The Middle Amazon Valley, 1640–1750', Ph.D. Dissertation, University of Wisconsin, 1974; Dauril Alden, 'Indian versus Black Slavery in the State of Maranhão during the 17th and 18th Centuries', *Bibliotheca Americana* (Miami) 1, no. 3 (1983), 91–142; and Nádia Farage, 'As Muralhas dos Sertões: Os Povos Indígenas do Rio Branco e a Colonização', *Mestrado* Dissertation, Universidade Estadual de Campinas, 1986.

4. For an important statement of the cultural argument, Luís Vianna Filho, 'O Trabalho do Engenho e a Reacção do Índio: Estabelecimento de Escravatura Africana', *Publicações do Congresso do Mundo Português* (Lisbon, 1940), 10:11–29. For an illuminating discussion of Indian slavery as an incomplete process, see Jacob Gorender, *O Escravismo Colonial* (São Paulo, 1978), pp. 468–486.

5. Manuel da Nóbrega to Simão Rodrigues, 9 Aug. 1559, *Monumenta Brasiliae*, 5 vols. (Rome, 1956–60), 1:122.

6. Town meeting of 7 Jan. 1607, *Atas da Câmara Municipal de São Paulo* (São Paulo, 1914–), 2:184–5.

7. Pedro Taques de Almeida Pais Leme, *Nobiliarquia Paulistana Histórica e Genealógica*, 5th ed., 3 vols. (São Paulo and Belo Horizonte, 1980), 1:79.
8. Pedro Rodrigues to Simão Alvares, 15 June 1597, Archivum Romanum Societatis Iesu, Rome, Brasilia 15, f. 424v.
9. 'Devassa tirada sobre a morte de um Índio Principal, Timacaúna, por uns Pombeiros dos Brancos', 5 June 1623, Arquivo Histórico Ultramarino, Lisbon, Catalogados São Paulo, doc. 3.
10. For the dates of the destruction of the missions, see the map in Hemming, *Red Gold*, pp. xx–xxi.
11. It is difficult to estimate with precision the number of Guarani transferred to São Paulo, though Spanish sources repeatedly affirm that 300,000 Indians were enslaved, which was clearly an exaggeration. The best index available for the growth of the Indian slave population remains the concentration of Indians per rural proprietor, which jumped from 13 at the beginning of the century to 22 by the 1620s, peaking at 37 in the 1640s. John Monteiro, 'São Paulo in the Seventeenth Century: Economy and Society', Ph.D. Dissertation, University of Chicago, 1985, p. 92.
12. 'Matrícula da Gente Carijó', 1615, *Registro Geral da Câmara Municipal de São Paulo* (São Paulo, 1917–23), 7:115–57.
13. On the organization of labour on these units of production, see Monteiro, 'Celeiro de Brasil'.
14. Gabriel Soares de Sousa, *Tratado Descritivo do Brasil em 1587*, 2d ed. (São Paulo, 1971), p. 115.
15. Will of José Ortiz de Camargo, 1658, Arquivo do Estado de São Paulo, Inventários não Publicados, caixa 7 (hereafter cited as AESP – Inv.).
16. Monteiro, 'São Paulo in the Seventeenth Century', p. 226.
17. Domingos de Góis v. Antonio da Cunha de Abreu, in inventory of João Furtado, 1653, AESP – Inv. caixa 1; Inventory of Antonio Pedroso de Barros, 1652, *Inventários e Testamentos*, 44 vols. (São Paulo, 1921–78), 20:56–7.
18. Antonio Raposo Barreto to Pedro João Malio, n. d., in inventory of Antonio Raposo Barreto, Taubaté, 1684, Museu de Taubaté, Inventários caixa 1, doc. 10.
19. 'Protesto de Domingos de Góis', Inventory of João Furtado, 1653, AESP – Inv. caixa 1.
20. Joint will of Antonio Domingues and Isabel Fernandes, Parnaíba, 1684, AESP – Inv. caixa 18.
21. Will of Inés Pedroso, 1663, AESP – Inv. caixa 11.
22. Visits of Padre Rodrigues, 15 Jan. 1700, Archivum Romanum Societatis Iesu, Rome, Brasilia 10, f. 2v.
23. Domingos Jorge Velho to Crown, 15 July 1694, in Morse, *The Bandeirantes*, p. 118.
24. Will of Maria do Prado, 1663, AESP – Inv. caixa 7.
25. Monteiro, 'São Paulo in the Seventeenth Century', pp. 282–6.
26. 'Protesto de Domingos de Góis', Inventory of João Furtado, 1653, AESP – Inv. caixa 1.
27. Inventory of Maria Moreira, Taubaté, 1675, Museu de Taubaté, Inventários, caixa 1, doc. 7; Inventory of Caterina Tavares, Parnaíba, 1671, AESP – Inv. caixa 12.
28. Batisados, Santo Amaro, 25 Mar. 1699 and 18 July 1700, Arquivo da Cúria Metropolitana de São Paulo 04–02–23.
29. Batisados, Sorocaba, 21 Jan. 1685, 31 Jan. 1685, and 1 Feb. 1685, Arquivo da Cúria Diocesana de Sorocaba, Livro 1.
30. Batisados, Sorocaba, 20 Feb. 1685.
31. For the purposes of this article, the term 'white' refers to the free population, as distinct from the class of Indian servants. This included, of course, a wide variety of ethnic types, ranging from Europeans to slave holding Indians.
32. Batisados, Sorocaba, 8 Oct. 1690.
33. Inventory of Antonia de Chaves, 1640, *Inventários e Testamentos* 14; Inventory of José Preto, 1653, AESP Inventários de Mogi des Cruzes, caixa 1.
34. Will of Jerônimo de Brito, 1644, AESP – Inv. Estragados caixa 2 doc. 4.
35. For example, sale of Gaspar de Brito Silva to Simão Jorge Velho, 8 May 1690, and Paulo de Proença to [illegible], 18 Oct. 1700, AESP Registros de Notas, Santana de Parnaíba.
36. Will of Isabel de Barcelos, Parnaíba, 1648, *Inventários e Testamentos* 36:223.

37. Inventory of José Ortiz de Camargo, 1663, AESP – Inv. caixa 7; Donation by Capitão-Mor Guilherme Pompeu de Almeida, 11 Feb. 1687, Livro de Tombo de Santana de Parnaíba, f. 31, Arquivo da Cúria Diocesana de Jundiaí, cod. 505.
38. Inventory of Manuel Alves Pimentel, 1626, *Inventários e Testamentos* 31:168; Will of Antonio Vieira Tavares, Itu, 1710, AESP – Inv. caixa 26.
39. Will of Grácia de Abreu, Parnaíba, 1660, AESP – Inv. caixa 5.
40. Francisco Cubas v. Heirs of José Ortiz de Camargo, 1664, AESP Autos Cíveis caixa 6033–1.
41. For a fascinating analysis of slave crime and its relationship to market activities in nineteenth-century São Paulo, see Maria Helena, P. T. Machado, *Crime e Escravidão. Trabalho, Luta e Resistência nas Lavouras Paulistas, 1830–1888* (São Paulo, 1987), especially pp. 100 ff.
42. For example, in Padre Domingos Gomes Albernás v. Frei João Batista Pinto, 1691, a suit over a theft of money by one of Pinto's Indians, the litigant remarked that if one of his Indians were involved in such a case, he would pay damages immediately, 'without contention in justice'. AESP Autos Cíveis caixa 1, doc. 22.
43. Petition of Diogo Mendes, 29 Oct. 1619, in inventory of Isabel Fernandes, 1619, *Inventários e Testamentos* 30: 214–15.
44. Testimony of Manuel Ruivo Bastardo, 12 Sept. 1718, Justice v. Bartolomeu Fernandes de Faria, AESP Autos Cíveis caixa 6.
45. Catarina do Prado v. Bartolomeu Bueno Cacunda, 1682, AESP Autos Civeis caixa 1, doc. 14.
46. See, for example, inventory of Francisco Borges, 1649, *Inventários e Testamentos* 39:97–8; Will of Domingos Dias Félix, Taubaté, 1660, Museu de Taubaté Inventários caixa 1, doc. 2; Inventory of Maria da Cunha, 1670, *Inventários e Testamentos* 17:488.
47. Inventory of Antonio Pedroso de Barros, 1652, *Inventários e Testamentos* 20.
48. Will of Sebastiana Rodrigues, 1669, AESP – Inv. caixa 11.
49. Will of Pedro Vaz de Barros, Parnaíba (São Roque), 1674, AESP – Inv. caixa 22.
50. Salvador Moreira v. Brás Moreira Cabrel, 2 July 1690, in inventory of Salvador Moreira, Parnaíba, 1697, *Inventários e Testamentos* 24.
51. Inventory of Antonia de Chaves, Parnaíba, 1640, *Inventários e Testamentos* 14:1xii.
52. Will of Manuel Rodrigues de Góis, 1662, AESP – Inv. caixa 6.
53. Inventory of Estevão Furquim, 1660, *Inventários e Testamentos* 16:278–9.
54. Will of Ana Machado de Lima, 1684, AESP – Inv. caixa 17.
55. Will of João Missel Gigante, Parnaíba, 1645, *Inventários e Testamentos* 32:122.
56. Will of Pedro Vidal, 1658, AESP – Inv. caixa 4.
57. 'Auto de Sequestro', 18 June 1718, Justice v. Bartolomeu Fernandes de Faria, AESP Autos Cíveis, caixa 6, doc. 98.
58. Testimony of Joana de Siqueira, bastarda, 1718, in Justice v. Bartolomeu Fernandes de Faria, AESP Autos Cíveis caixa 6, doc. 98.
59. On the diffusion of the tipoia, see Alfred Metraux, 'The Guarani', in Julian Steward, ed., *Handbook of South American Indians* (Washington D.C., 1946–50), 3:82.

6

Sexual Demography: The Impact of the Slave Trade on Family Structure

John Thornton

In the past few years, the study of the Atlantic slave trade has shifted emphasis from measuring its volume to judging its effects in Africa. In the recent seminar in African Historical Demography held in Edinburgh, the four contributions dealing with the slave trade assessed its effects on African population size, structure, and density (Diop, Inikori, Manning, Thornton 1981). Emerging from this new concentration on the African side of the slave trade has been the realization that the slave trade had a significant impact on the role and life of women, and researchers are increasingly pointing out that the study of women, both as slaves and as free people in areas where slaving occurred, is a necessary corollary to the study of the slave trade as a whole (Manning 1981a).

The fact that the slave trade carried more men than women to the Americas, about two to three men for every woman according to those statistical series that are available, has long been seen as the cause of the inability of the slave population to grow in America. Low birth rates were largely a product of an extremely unbalanced sex ratio on American plantations, which when coupled with bad nutrition, few incentives to reproduce, and high abortion rates meant that slave populations could not keep ahead of their own mortality except by renewed imports from Africa (Sheridan 1975; H. Klein, this volume).

My own work on the Angolan population of the late eighteenth century suggested what were the effects of the very differently altered sex composition in Africa (Thornton 1980). In Angola, women outnumbered men by nearly two to one in the population left behind after the slave trade. However, unlike in the Americas, the skewed sex ratio did not result in a marked decline in population. Because of the established institution of polygyny, the almost undiminished numbers of women were able to counterbalance some of the losses to the slave trade by continued reproduction. In a study presented at the Edinburgh conference, I charted the probable effects of the slave trade on age and sex distribution in a model population with characteristics similar to those of the population of Angola (Thornton 1981). Then, operating on the assumption that the rest of western Africa had similar population structures, I tried to suggest what would be the effect on such a model population of withdrawing a number of slaves equal to the number known from studies of the volume of the slave trade. Working independently, Patrick Manning created another model, which, while differing in approach and assumptions, nevertheless arrived at similar conclusions (1981a and 1981b). Both models supported the conclusion that the population, although showing no long-term growth, suffered little long-term net loss. However, in both models the population, while not shrinking, did undergo fairly substantial alteration in structure, such that the group of males of working age was substantially reduced as a result of the specific demands of the slave traders and American purchasers for slaves in that age and sex group (Thornton 1980; Manning 1981b). In my own model, in which I tried to establish the minimum population densities necessary to support the known volume of slave exports in the interior behind each of several slave-exporting centers and then compared these densities with probable densities based on modern population size, I found that at the peak period of the slave trade in the late eighteenth century the demand for slaves must have come close to matching the maximum ability of all these regions to supply them. Moreover, in every region, the sex ratio in the age bracket 15–60 would have been only 80 men per 100 women, and in the hardest-hit area, Angola, as low as 40–50 men per 100 women (Thornton 1980).

The older debate on the slave trade had concentrated in one way or another on quantitative assessments of the population changes in Africa caused by the slave trade. Thus in Fage's many papers on the subject he insisted that the total volume of the trade was insufficient to offset natural growth and Africa was not depopulated (Fage 1975). Criticisms of Fage's approach, such as those of J. E. Inikori and L. M. Diop presented at the Edinburgh conference, maintained simply that Fage had underestimated the total number of slaves exported and that depopulation *had* occurred, with its most important negative effect being a less favorable land-to-labor ratio in the remaining population. The approach to the problem suggested by Manning and myself, on the other hand, involves investigation of the quality of the population left behind, and not simply its quantity. This approach supports an argument that the major impact of the trade was not so much the reduction of the total number of people remaining in Africa as fundamental alterations in the ratio of working to dependent populations or of male to female labor. In this reexamination, the position of women is highlighted, since it is they who suffered the most from the trade in Africa.

The alteration in the age and sex ratios affected women in Africa in two ways, both results of the age- and sex-specific nature of the demand for African slaves by the traders. First of all, since they retained their normal fertility, the burden of child care imposed on them was not lessened by the loss in population—all the more so since children younger than age fifteen or so were rarely taken by the slave traders. At the same time their own numbers, and more important the numbers of males who played a vital role in child support if not in child care, were declining. This can be clearly seen if we examine the change in the dependency ratio of a hypo-thetical population in which the working group aged 15–60 has been de-pleted by 10 percent (the effect of having a sex ratio of 80 men per 100 women in this age group). Before the onset of the trade, according to the model life table from which my work was constructed, about 60 percent of the population fell into this age bracket, while the other 40 percent were either younger and required child care, or older and were unable to partic-ipate in productive labor. Thus there were approximately 67 dependents for each 100 working people. After the distortion introduced by the slave trade, however, 54 percent of the population fell into the category of able-bodied workers, while 46 percent were dependent, giving a dependency ratio of 85 dependents for each 100 working people. Thus the burden of work falling on the productive members of society was greatly increased, forcing more and more of their time to be spent in purely subsistence activities and reducing their ability to produce surplus for commerce or to maintain an efficient division of labor.

Women were hit in another way as well, however, and this was due to the alteration of the sex ratios among the producers just at a time when the work load of all producers was increasing. The model suggests that there must have been 20 percent fewer males to perform work allocated to men during the slave trade era, work which would then have had to go undone, or be done by females, or compensated for by purchased items. For ex-ample, in central Africa women did agricultural work, but men did heavy clearing of the fields, chopping down trees and digging up roots. Without this clearing labor, the women would have had to plant less or move their fields less often, both of which would tend to reduce production (Thornton 1983:28–31). Likewise, because hunting, fishing, and the rearing of live-stock were activities which many traditional African societies left to men, the loss of males resulted in a less protein-rich diet for the remaining people.

This model is, of course, an average calculation based on rather crude assumptions. The actual adjustment of particular African societies is much more difficult to determine. The model is a global one applied to all regions of western Africa that supplied slaves, and is based on data obtained from a few rather large areas. How the slave raids affected the population in smaller regions within these larger areas is not considered. For example, a society subjected to raids might lose men and women in equal numbers and the raiding society incorporate the women while selling off the men. Alternatively, slave raiding which matched military forces against each other might result in all the slaves procured by the victor being males of saleable age, since armies select for the same age and sex criteria as plantation managers. My model suggested that the societies that procured slaves selected men ahead of women, and left the societies which gave up slaves with unbalanced sex ratios, while Manning's model assumed that the victims of slave raiding lost men and women in equal numbers, and the unbalanced sex ratios affected the societies that did the raiding. In fact, a variety of different methods were used to procure slaves, from large-scale wars to small-scale kidnapping, including judicial enslavement and raids of organized military forces against disorganized villagers. Each of these methods might have resulted in a different mix of ages and sexes for both the aggressors and the losers, and hence a whole distinct constellation of resulting demographic structures.

In Angola, for example, slaves were procured by major wars between military powers, a method which would probably favor the acquisition of males by the group that sold the slaves (da Silva Corrêa 1782; Birmingham 1966), and smaller-scale kidnapping and raiding against villagers which would have resulted in the acquisition of both men and women (A.P.F. 1705). Moreover, the census data from Angola show unbalanced sex ratios and distorted age structures for both slaves and free people, suggesting that the depletion of males among victims and the incorporation of females by the groups that acquired slaves were going on simultaneously (Thornton 1980). Equally diverse means of slave procurement were probably being used in other regions as well, which future research may do much to clarify.

Although a focus on the age and sex distribution of affected African populations does not tell us as much about the qualitative social effects of the slave trade as we would like, it suggests some lines of research that could reveal more about those effects. For example, one result of the unbalanced sex ratios would be an alteration in the institution of marriage. Since the institution of polygyny was present in Africa at the time that the slave trade began (Fage 1980), the general surplus of women in the marriageable age group would have tended to encourage it and allow it to become much more widespread, driving down the bridewealth that women's families could demand and weakening the stability of the marriages in existence. It might also have favored men building up large households of wives through the purchase of female slaves; these slaves and their children, unprotected by their kin, would have been subject to abuses. This in turn might have had a detrimental effect on the status of marriage even for free women. These effects might vary according to whether the surplus of women was caused by an influx of female slaves, as in a society that was capturing slaves of both sexes but only selling the males to the Atlantic trade; or by a shortage of men, as in a society in which men were being drained off by warfare to the trade, leaving the women behind.

We can examine such qualitative changes in more detail by looking at one region, that of modern Guinea-Bissau (the Upper Guinea coast), for which descriptive data are available. By the early seventeenth century the region had become one of the foci of slave exporting from the western end of West Africa. Witnesses of the time commented on this fact, as for example the memorial submitted by the Jesuit priest Baltasar Barreira in 1606 (Brásio 1958-79, 4:190-98), or the group of Spanish Capuchins who submitted an open letter to the Pope and several other European rulers in 1686 (Labat 1728, 5:215-20; Texeira da Mota 1974:121-33). Extensive slave trade activity is confirmed as well by surveys of the ethnic origins of slaves landing in the New World, such as those compiled from notorial records in Peru by Frederick Bowser (1974:40-43). A fairly large percentage of the slaves leaving Guinea-Bissau were from the numerous small political units in the area (Texeira da Mota 1974:124-28). From the written observations of many visitors to Guinea-Bissau, we can form some idea of the social ramifications of the slave trade there. It was the wealth of written evidence, much of it from residents hostile to the slave trade, that enabled Walter Rodney to write so poignantly and effectively about the distortion of life and justice caused by the slave trade in the region (1970:112-51). These hostile witnesses were mostly missionaries to the coast, which possessed a substantial settlement of Portuguese and Afro-Portuguese residents and was in need of clerical ministrations, and, as a non-Moslem zone, was open to attempts to missionize the African population. The Jesuits worked in the country from the start of the seventeenth century, and were joined by the Capuchins in mid-century (Brásio 1958-80; Carrocera 1957). Unlike lay residents, whose writing is also quite extensive, the missionaries took pains to describe daily life and customs, and were not indisposed to denounce the slave trade since it interfered with their successful proselytization as well as offending their sense of justice.

This corpus of writing allows us to see some of the ways in which women were affected by the Atlantic slave trade. Writing in 1684 in an enlarged recension of a manuscript he originally composed in 1669, Francisco de Lemos Coelho, a Portuguese resident of the area, made some interesting notes on the Bissagos Islands. Although he does not mention unbalanced sex ratios as such, Lemos Coelho noted that polygyny was so widespread there that "there are blacks there who have twenty or thirty wives, and no one has only one," and moreover, "the children in their villages are [as numerous as] a beehive" (Lemos Coelho 1953:178). Given the heavy slave trade in the area, the disproportionate number of women and children remarked by Lemos Coelho is not surprising. This unbalanced age and sex structure may also account for the very large share of work done by women on the islands, which astonished Lemos Coelho. After describing their complicated work in making cloth for clothes, he goes on to say: "They [the women] are the ones who work the fields, and plant the crops, and the houses in which they live, even though small, are clean and bright, and despite all this work they still go down to the sea each day to catch shellfish . . ." (Lemos Coelho 1953:178). Lemos Coelho was not the only observer to comment on the burden of work falling on the women of the Bissagos Islands. Over half a century earlier, André Álvares d'Almada made almost identical observations, noting, "they [the women] do more work than men do in other places" (Brásio 1968–79, 3:317). The men, it seems, were absorbed largely in war, which in this case meant slave raiding, while the women had to engage in production and perform more than the normal share of work. In the case of the Bissagos Islanders it seems probable that the real burden fell upon the extra women, those who had arrived as slaves, although Lemos Coelho's report does not distinguish between slaves and free women.

Elsewhere in the area, other witnesses explicitly drew a connection between slavery, an influx of women, and the peculiar status of slave wives. The Spanish Capuchins, who complained of the state of affairs in the region around Bissau in 1686, believed that the plenitude of female slaves encouraged concubinage (Texeira da Mota 1974:125, 131–32). Manuel Alvares, a Jesuit who wrote of conditions in the same area in 1616, observed, "All have many wives," again suggesting the generality of concubinage. Alvares also noted the special vulnerability of slave women: "If a noble takes his own slave for a wife, and she gives him some displeasure, he will sell her along with her child, even if the child is small, without any regard for the child being his own" (Texeira da Mota 1974:59–60). Others who had lived in Guinea noticed the ease with which subordinate family members might be sold for petty violations of custom (Texeira da Mota 1974:125), although Alvares added that upper-class women were protected from such dire measures. Much of this testimony was used years ago by Rodney to support his thesis that the slave trade had led to substantial legal distortion, and certainly this particular social custom would allow members of the upper classes to hold or sell subordinates at will and according to other needs or the demands of the trade (1970:106–10). Thus slaves held in marriage arrangements such as those described by Alvares could be mobilized for sale without costly wars or risk of retribution. Of course, most witnesses agree that warfare was still the major source of slaves (Texeira da Mota 1974:124–26), and one cannot help but suspect that the marriage customs were reported more for their shock value (and perhaps from isolated cases) than for the importance of their incidence.

Nevertheless, the slave trade brought many surplus women into coastal society in Guinea, and the Spanish Capuchins even noted that housing was inadequate, forcing male and female slaves to share quarters during peak periods of the trade (Texeira da Mota 1974:131). Inquisition authorities were aware that large numbers of slave women were affecting the Portuguese residents as well; in 1589, one Nuno Francisco da Costa was denounced to the Inquisition for having many *mulheres* (an ambiguous word in this case, meaning either women or wives) and reputedly saying that he cared more "for the fingernail of [a particular] slave woman than all the masses and confessions" (Baião 1906:251; Texeira da Mota 1976:15–16). Slavery and surplus women might even have altered the marriage patterns of theoretically monogamous Christians.

These scattered observations on female roles and marriage customs might be taken for no more than passing remarks of writers who were somewhat unsympathetic to African culture, were it not for their close agreement with our expectations based on demographic trends in the area. Just as Rodney's generalizations about the effects of the slave trade on class structure and the institution of slavery have been criticized as being atypical of West Africa (Fage 1980:289–91), so too might these remarks on women's roles and the status of marriage. The data are not quantifiable, and were obtained from observers who were antagonistic toward the slave trade and hence anxious to highlight its ill effects. But they do fit some predictions based on a knowledge of the demography of the slave trade, and as such must be taken with new seriousness.

Scholars interested in understanding the slave trade must undertake an investigation, covering as many areas and time periods as possible, of the status of women (both slave and free) and the institution of marriage in the context of our understanding of the population structure of societies participating in the slave trade. Similarly, it is an urgent task of those interested in the social history of Africa to investigate the nature and dimensions of the internal slave trade, and the strategy of its agents. To what extent did this internal trade involve the transfer of women from interior districts to the regions of the slave-trading states? Can we guess at the volume of this trade in females, which was fairly extensive in some regions? To what extent did the displacements of women within Africa and the siphoning off of men to the trans-Atlantic slave trade affect the precolonial population distribution, and what is the legacy of those effects today? We also need further exploration of how male and female roles were affected by the change in sex ratios.

46   JOHN THORNTON

In addition, more study of slave trades not involving shipment to the
Americas might yield interesting results. For example, Olifert Dapper noted
in the mid-seventeenth century that in every village along the Gold Coast
from Allada to the Ivory Coast there were "three or four whores," recruited from female slaves, whose earnings went to the ruler of the village. To what extent was this widespread prostitution (prevalent in spite
of the polygyny which Dapper also noted) a product of the trade in female
slaves between Benin and the Gold Coast? (Dapper 1670:471). Was it due
to the region's role as an importer of slaves (from the interior and other
points of the coast), its growing role as an exporter of slaves (just beginning as Dapper wrote) (Rodney 1969), or the general concentration of
strangers in the area brought about the area's position as a marketplace
between the zone controlled by interior merchants and that controlled by
European traders? (Vasconcellos 1639:85).

We must accept that the full story of the effect of the slave trade on
women in western Africa is well beyond the range of the sources available
to us. Travelers' accounts, local chronicles, and even reports of residents
often neglect descriptions of women's work and women's status, or present these in categories that are either an "ideal average" or a series of
horror stories like those of the missionaries in Guinea-Bissau. Statistical
evidence for any period save the very end of the precolonial era is likely
to elude us. But we can learn considerably more about this aspect of Africa than we know now by reading over the sources available to us with a
critical eye, informed by a knowledge of probable and possible effects of
the slave trade. We can also try to develop models with greater predictive
power than is possessed by the ones now in existence, models which,
though perhaps not testable statistically, can be effectively tested by the
documentation we do have.

References

Unpublished Sources

A.P.F.: Archivio de Propaganda Fide (Rome). Bernardo da Firenze to Propaganda
    Fide, June 22, 1705. Scritture originali riferitenella Congregazione Generale,
    vol. 552, fols. 64v–65v.

Published Sources

Baião, A. 1906. *A Inquisção em Portugal e no Brazil. Subsídios para a sua
    história*. Lisbon.
Birmingham, D. 1966. *Trade and Conflict in Angola*. London.
Bowser, F. 1974. *The African Slave in Colonial Peru*. Stanford.

Slave Trade and Family Structure 47

Brásio, A. 1958–79. *Monumenta Missionaria Africana*. 2nd series. 5 vols. Lisbon.

Carrocera, B. de. 1957. *Missiones Capuchinas en Africa. II. Missiones al Reino de la Zinga, Benin, Ardra, Guinea y Sierra Leone*. Madrid.

Dapper, O. 1670/1967. *Umbeständliche und Eigentliche Beschreibung von Africa*. Amsterdam.

Da Silva Corrêa, Elias Alexandre. 1782 (1937). *História de Angola*. 2 vols. Lisbon.

Diop, L. M. 1981. Méthode et calculs approximatifs pour la constitution d'une courbe representatif de l'évolution de la population de l'Afrique noire." In *African Historical Demography*, ed. C. Fyfe and D. M:~Master. Edinburgh.

Fage, J. D. 1975. "The Effect of the Export Slave Trade on African Populations." In *The Population Factor in African Studies*, ed. R. P. Moss and R. J. A. Rathbone. London.

Fage, J. D. 1980. "Slaves and Society in Western Africa, c. 1455–c. 1700." *Journal of African History* 21:289–310.

Fyfe, C., and D. McMaster, eds. 1981. *African Historical Demography*. Vol. 2. Edinburgh.

Inikori, J. E. 1981. "Underpopulation in 19th Century West Africa: The Role of the Export Slave Trade." In *African Historical Demography*, vol. 2, ed. C. Fyfe and D. McMaster. Edinburgh.

Labat, J. B. 1728. *Nouvelle relation de l'afrique Occidentale*. 5 vols. Paris.

Lemos Coelho, F. de. 1953. *Duas descrições seiscentistas da Guiné*. Edited by Damião Peres. Lisbon.

Manning, P. 1981a. "A Demographic Model of Slavery." In *African History Demography*, ed. C. Fyfe and D. McMaster. Edinburgh.

Manning, P. 1981b. "The Enslavement of Africans: A Demographic Model." *Canadian Journal of African Studies* 15:499–526.

Rodney, W. 1969. "Gold and Slaves on the Gold Coast." *Transactions of the Historical Society of Ghana* 10:13–28.

Rodney, W. 1970. *A History of the Upper Guinea Coast, 1545–1800*. Oxford.

Sheridan, R. 1975. "Mortality and Medical Treatment of Slaves in the British West Indies." In *Race and Slavery in the Western Hemisphere: Quantitative Studies*, ed. S. L. Engerman and E. D. Genovese. Princeton.

Texeira da Mota, A. 1974. *As Viagens de Bispo d. Frei Vitoriano Portuense a Guiné e a cristianização dos reis de Bissau*. Lisbon.

Texeira da Mota, A. 1976. "Alguns aspectos da colonização e do commércio marítime dos Portugueses na África ocidental nos séculos XV e XVI. *Centro de Estudos de Cartográfia Antiga. Series Separata* 97:15–16.

Thornton, J. 1980. "The Slave Trade in Eighteenth-Century Angola: Effects on Demographic Structures." *Canadian Journal of African Studies* 14:417–27.

Thornton, J. 1981. "The Demographic Effect of the Slave Trade on Western Africa, 1500–1850." In *African Historical Demography*, ed. Christopher Fyfe and David McMaster. Edinburgh.

Thornton, J. 1983. *The Kingdom of Kongo: Civil War and Transition, 1641–1718*. Madison.

Vasconcellos, Agustin Manuel y. 1639. *Vida y acciones del Rey Don Juan el Segundo*. Madrid.

Vogt, J. 1973. "The Early São Thomé–Principe Slave Trade with Mina, 1500–1540." *International Journal of African Historical Studies* 6:453–67.

7

The African Presence in Portuguese India

Ann M. Pescatello

Historians concerned with the Portuguese presence in India generally
have focused on political or military events to the neglect of social or
cultural forces. Due to this predeliction followers of Clio have overlooked a curious character: The African slave in India.** This ubiquitous stranger is more than discernible in archival stores of Portuguese
India as well as in travel accounts of early European imperial interests.
There is not yet sufficient evidence uncovered to write a definitive
monograph on the long history of the African in India. But because his
appearance forms an intriguing chapter in any recounting of South
Asian history, I present here—based on circumscribed materials—a
limited discussion on the functions of the African in early Portuguese
Indian history and his place in the colonial structure. Before proceeding, however, two major dimensions contributing to the story
should be delineated. The first concerns the pre-Portuguese involvement of Africans in Indian societies, including the extent of a slave
trade, its location in India, and the relationship of that trade with the
general Indian population. The second aspect concerns the structure of
sixteenth and seventeenth century Portuguese India into which the
African was thrust.

* The author wishes to thank the University of California, Los Angeles, and
the Ford Foundation Grant in International and Comparative studies for funds
to conduct the research on this paper. Materials for this paper were gathered
during January and February, 1969, in Panaji, Goa, India. For their help in
locating documents, I wish to thank the Director of the Arquivo Nacional, Mr.
Gune, and his assistant.

The travel accounts and some of the documents consulted are published but
for the most part the information in archival sources exists only in MS form in
the Goan archives.

** The term *African* is used in this article to mean anyone from, or whose
ancestors were from, the continent of Africa.

Long before the arrival of da Gama, Albuquerque, and other Lusitanian adventurers, Islamized African communities, called *Habshi*,[1]
existed in India, their ancestors either slaves purchased by Arabs from
the African Horn or military slave troops from neighboring Muslim
countries. The majority of Africans probably were Abyssinian; the
name *Habshi* means Abyssinian but eventually became applied to all
blacks.[2] Later, during Portuguese involvement in India, many so-
called *Habshi* actually were either Bantu or Sudanic Negro.

Our knowledge of the numbers, status, and functions of *Habshis*
prior to the arrival of the Portuguese in South Asia is severely circumscribed and necessarily gleaned from scattered court and travel records.
One of our earliest references is Ibn Battūta who, during his travels in
India (1333—1342), discovered that *Habshis* were distributed throughout the subcontinent from North India to Ceylon, and were employed
primarily as guards or men-at-arms in land and sea contingents.[3] Other
sources indicate that under the Tughluk dynasty in North India,
especially in the late fourteenth century, several African slaves or
descendants of African slaves either became governors of provinces or
were prominent eunuchs in sultanate courts.[4]

African influence, after an initial appearance in the Delhi area,
shifted East. Records indicate that from 1459 to 1481, the Bengali
Ilyās Shāhī sultan Rukn al-Din Bārbak Shāh maintained some eight
thousand African slaves for military service, a few of whom later
acquired powers, usurped the throne, and provided a succession of
Habshi rulers from 1486 to 1493. In 1493 a successful popular revolt
against the last Habshi ruler resulted in the expulsion of these Africans
from Bengal, most of whom dispersed to the Deccan, and later to
Gujrat, the central and western sections of the subcontinent. They were
welcome, for in the Deccan the practice of employing foreigners in state
service had begun in the latter half of the fourteenth century and by

---

[1] Habshi means people of Habash, i.e., Abyssinia.

[2] See, e.g., G. Yazdani, *Bīdar; its history and monuments*, (Oxford, 1947),
pp. 82 ff. for information on and gathered from tombs of Abyssinian nobles and
soldiers scattered throughout this region.

[3] Ibn Battuta, *Travels*, trans. H. A. R. Gibb, (Cambridge, 1929), pp. 224,
229, 236, 260.

[4] For presence of the Habshi as generals, administrators, kingmakers, and in
positions of power and prestige, see R. C. Majumdar, H. C. Raychaudri, and
K. Datta, *An Advanced History of India*, (London, 1948); and R. Pankhurst, *An
introduction to the economic history of Ethiopia*, (London, 1961) Appendix E.

28   ANN M. PESCATELLO

1422 Habshi bodyguards were an important factor in determining succession to the throne. Their successes were short-lived, however, for by the end of the fifteenth century they had come into conflict with other foreign mercenaries in the kingdom. Although they were Sunni Muslims, as was the local populace, and although they were also supported by *Muwallads*,[5] Habshis were not accepted by the lighter-skinned Turks, Persians, and Arabs on the basis of race and color[6] and ultimately lost their positions of power.

In addition to their influence in land posts, Habshis were apparently prominent in Indian navies, first in the Deccan and later, especially, in Gujrat where their power as naval commanders endured until the Marathas rose to supremacy in eighteenth-century western India. Gujrat, however, appears to have received a continuous supply of Habshis not only as exiles from Bengal and the Deccan but also as cargo shipments through several western Indian ports. We are informed that the government of Gujrat in 1376—1377 paid a tribute of four hundred slaves who were "children of Hindu chiefs and Abyssinians," a not uncommon occurrence,[7] while nearly two hundred years later, in 1537, such cities as Ahmadabad, supposedly still counted as many as five thousand Habshis working in government service.[8]

Any discussion of the quantity, the functions, or the status of pre-Portuguese African elements in India is based largely on suppositions drawn from isolated references. Numbers of Habshis prominent in Indian court life and service may have been exaggerated and certainly it is only reasonable to suppose that of the thousands of Africans who entered the subcontinent in servile capacities, only a few attained prominence as governors of Bengal, Bihar, and the Deccan.[9] Those who acquired power did so because of the unique avenue of mobility offered by the Janissary-type arm of Muslim militias and not by the

---

[5] *Muwallads* are mixed bloods: African fathers and Indian mothers.

[6] Henry H. Dodwell (ed.) *The Cambridge History of India*, I—V, (Cambridge, 1928), III, pp. 403—404.

[7] K. K. Basu, *The Tarikh-i-Mubarak Shadi*, (1932).

[8] *Hādjdji al Dabīr, Zafar al-walih* (n.d.) pp. i., 97, 407, 447. (An official court record assumed to be written by an unnamed court official. The copy is in the Institute Vasco da Gama, Panaji, Goa.)

[9] See the *Ma'athir al-umarā'*, the register of Mughal nobility, for biographies of prominent Habshis. Unfortunately, due to the nature of Muslim genealogical historical writing we know practically nothing about the ordinary citizen's daily affairs.

structure of Indian society itself. Supposedly, Ethiopian slaves continued to flow into India as late as the eighteenth-century and some
scholars believe that this influx may have exerted not only a biological
but also a social effect on Indian culture.[10] Since our knowledge of the
numerical composition and geographic location of Africans in Islamic
India is limited and since our awareness of the daily existence and social
circumstances of the ordinary African is severely circumscribed, I shall
leave the problem untouched.

Changes in functions of Africans in India possibly occured with
changes in their ethnic composition. Earlier stocks of Africans, primarily of Hamitic and Nilotic peoples, were from markedly different
cultural milieux than were Africans carried to India after the fifteenth-
century by both Arabs and Iberians. This may be attested to linguis-
tically by the decline in usage of the term *Habshi* as descriptive of all
blacks in India.

Because of vicissitudes of war, weather, and worms, documentation
concerning the African slave trade to Asia is subject to restricted
manuscript collections and extensive speculation. We know that the
Arabic trade in African slaves had been a durable and brisk one during
the centuries preceding Portuguese occupation in India, for the Arabs
had established both commercial and connubial relations with the
Bantu in East African coastal settlements from Sofala to Somalia, thus
fathering a Swahili "civilization."[11] The Africanized Muslims traded
with the Bantu in the interior, exchanging Indian beads and cottons
for African gold, ivory, or slaves. Indian residents on the East African
coast were closely associated with Arab traders and although they were
neither Muslim nor aristocratic much of the ocean-going shipping was
owned, manned, and financed by Indians. A bulk of the actual trading
also was in Indian hands and direct business relations were maintained
between East Africa and the western coast of India.[12]

---

[10] See, e.g., C. F. Beckingham, "*Amba Gesen* and *Asirgarh*," *Journal of
Semitic Studies*, II, (1957), 182—188.

[11] See Robert I. Rotberg, *A Political History of Tropical Africa*, (New York,
1965), pp. 152—153 for speculation on sources and quantities involved in the
African slave trade to Asia.

[12] See S. D. Goitein, "From the Mediterranean to India: Documents on the
Trade to India, South Arabia, and East Africa, from the Eleventh and Twelfth
Centuries," *Speculum*, XXIX, 2, (1954), pp. 181—197 for the composition of the
trade and traders.

30   ANN M. PESCATELLO

The Portuguese arrived in East Africa attempting to usurp the role of the Swahili, their viceroy having been enjoined to enslave all Muslim merchants but to leave the local Negroes unharmed.[13] Initially it proved difficult for the Iberians to establish relations with the Bantu but eventually there developed a cordial commerce, the perquisites of which were gold and slaves. It proved a complementary enterprise to Portugal's fairly lucrative Guinea coast trade in Africans, conducted expressly for a chronically underpopulated Portugal and Spain which needed and relied upon "slave" labor for its farms and homes.

Early records are insufficient in supplying more information concerning arrivals of Africans but we can determine that their presence along the western Indian coast was a well-established fact by the end of the sixteenth century. A European traveler, commenting on Abyssinians (and Arabians), noted that "there are many of them in India that are slaves and captives, both men and women which are brought [thither] out of Aetheopia, and sold like other Oriental nations . . ."[14] He further observed that

> From Mosambique great numbers of these Caffares are carried into India, and many times they sell a man or woman that is growne to their full [strength] for two or three Ducats . . . the cause why so many slaves and captives of all nations are brought to sell in India, is, because everie ten or twelve miles, or rather in every Village and towne, there is a severall King, one of them not like another . . . are in warres, and those that on both sides are taken they keep for slaves . . .[15]

Other sixteenth century references mention figures from which we can determine the character of the trade of African slaves in the early decades of Portuguese rule in India.[16] Albuquerque's letters mentioned one Garcia de Sousa and his "mulatto man" who fought alongside him in his attack on Aden.[17] Later, on leaving the port of Aden, Albuquer-

---

[13] *Cartas de Affonso de Albuquerque*, I—VII, (Lisboa, 1884—1935), II, p. 282. See also Alexandre Lobato, *A Expansão Portuguesa em Moçambique de 1488 a 1530*, I—III, (Lisboa, 1954—1960), I, pp. 75, 81.

[14] Jan Linschoten, *Voyage*, I—II, (London, Hakluyt Series 1, 1885), I, pp. 70—71, 264—265.

[15] *ibid.*, I, pp. 275.

[16] *Provisões, alvaras e regimentos*, unpublished documents, bound in two volumes (Evora, 1515—1598), I, fls. 17 vs, 2 March 1520. For a published account on the Portuguese slave trade see K. G. Jayne, *Vasco da Gama and his Successors*, (London, 1910), pp. 22 ff.

[17] *Commentaries of the Great Affonso de Albuquerque*, I—IV, (London, 1774), IV, p. 21.

que encountered a Moorish boat with "some Abyssinian women and youths whom the Moors were carrying to sell" and whom, after overcoming the Moors, Albuquerque would not allow to be captives "as they were from the land of Prester John."[18]

Additional sixteenth century references in Goa's historical archives indicate other Africans along the more northerly strip of coast, while there existed yet another group, apparently neither part of recent dispersals from Bengal or the Deccan, nor of new shipments from southern or western Africa.[19] Through oral tradition we know of the African's appearance in other guises all along the western Indian trading coast: the Black Jews of Cochin and Kerala. Descendants of African slaves transfered to Malabar in the seventeenth and eighteenth centuries by so-called White Jews,[20] these Africans were primarily domestic laborers who through the centuries have maintained their position in the Malabar communities despite intermarriage with the local population, including White Jews.

Since the African in India seems to appear most often in the role of "slave," some agreement should be reached as to the actual connotation of "slave" in the societies concerned. As far as I am able to discern, "slavery" as a chattel concept did not exist in sixteenth century India. Those locals who occupied positions of menial responsibilities were socially circumscribed within the context of a complex and elaborate system consisting of four *varna* and thousands of *jatis*, but western or African notions of a person as "chattel" seem to have had no basis in Indian social thought.[20a] Also, European definitions had not yet developed from Enlightenment theory. According to Iberian philosophical enquiries and international legal dictates of the time, the concept of "slave" implied a social and economic position rather than a racial subjugation.[21] Thus it would appear that the Africans who lived and

---

[18] *ibid.*, IV, p. 28.

[19] *Livro das Monções do Reino*, MS in bound volumes, (Panaji, 1585—1593), V, fl. 34v (in the old numbering it is volume 3 B).

[20] The White Jews are supposedly refugees from Spanish and Portuguese persecutions against the "new Christians" or non-convertible Jews of the sixteenth and seventeenth centuries.

[20a] The Indic terms *varna* and *jati* have no precise English equivalents. The term *varna* has been translated as "class," and the term *jati* as "caste," both designations unknown until the arrival of the Europeans. In the Indic sense *varna* and *jati* do not imply the same meanings as class and caste.

[21] According to Basham there was no caste of slaves; the *Arthaśāstra* claims

labored in India, both during Muslim rule and later in areas specifically subject to Portuguese suzerainty, were a type of "slave" not related in status to the type of chattel laborer we associate with plantation workers on European, African, and American plantations after the seventeenth century.

Having discussed the pre-Portuguese period of African influence in India, the Arabic and later Portuguese-managed slave trade from East Africa to the subcontinent, and definitions of what a "slave" was not, prior to sixteenth century Iberian intrusions, I want to examine briefly the origins of a Portuguese society in an India in which Africans and black slaves were an important presence. Already by the fifteenth century Portuguese seamen were systematically plying the oceans, their ultimate goal to reach sources of spices for European markets. The Iberians arrived at a propitious time, for not only were the numerous kingdoms that they encountered—from Arab trading states to Javanese Majapahit and its neighboring spice islands—politically splintered, but also the great empires of Egypt, Persia and Vijayanagar (South India) possessed no armed shipping and even the Chinese had been confined by imperial decree to navigating their own coastline. Within a few years of their appearance in the Indian Ocean the Portuguese had begun to regulate maritime commerce between Malacca and Moçambique. To order administratively their growing mercantile interests the Portuguese established the *Estado da India* (State of India) at Goa, to supervise their discoveries, conquests, and markets from the Cape of Good Hope in Africa to Japan in the Far East.

---

that an individual of any caste might become a slave, while for the Āryan the term *śūdra* (or lowest of the four *varṇa*) is explicitly included for slave. The *dāsa*, or member of the peoples conquered by the Aryans, was used to indicate slave and Basham says that the word implies bondsman or serf rather than a chattel slave. A. L. Basham, *The Wonder that was India*, (New York, 1954), pp. 151—153. Davis points out for the western and Mediterranean-Middle eastern worlds (as well as Asia) that slaves have generally been defined as chattels personal, unqualified for legal marriage, property ownership, or judicial testimony; but, he also points out, no slave system in history was quite like that of the West Indies and of the southern states of the United States. The various terms to describe "slave" and the contrary nature of other servile institutions is discussed in detail in David Brion Davis, *The Problem of Slavery in Western Culture*, (Ithaca, Cornell University Press, 1966). For Africa, see Basil Davidson, "Slaves or Captives? Some Notes on Fantasy and Fact," in Nathan I. Huggins, Martin Kilson, and Daniel M. Fox, eds., *Key issues in the Afro-American Experience*, I—II, (New York, Harcourt Brace Jovanovich, 1971), I, pp. 54—73.

Perusal of Portuguese chronicles or early European accounts of Lusitanian expansion in Asia leave the impression that life in the Iberian colonies was one of constant bloodletting and rapacious greed, but this is not a realistic assessment. Recent archival investigations have destroyed some of the myths regarding Iberian actions, derived initially from pietistic Portuguese accounts, and have dusted off the canvas to give us a clearer picture of an active, bustling metropolis. "Golden Goa" had been selected as the *Estado's* capital shortly after its conquest by Albuquerque in 1510 and by 1516 its citizens were exchanging petitions with Lisbon, determining privileges of economic and social consequence. Since the Portuguese crown was eager to promote economic development and political stability as quickly as possible, it granted her married citizens free trading privileges that they requested for themselves, "their business associates, their slaves, and their factors," in all European or Asian provisions or goods, but reserved for itself a monopoly of spices and other special products.[22] The colony prospered and many Portuguese who ventured to India acquired riches and licenses to wealth so that by mid-sixteenth century Goa was a showplace of exquisite homes, retinues of servants, elegant churches, and bustling, flower-bedecked *praças*—a city of beauty!

Throughout the sixteenth century Goa continued its commercial successes and, contrary to previous assessments, was at its apex. In a session of her municipal council on 7 September 1605, pride in the growth and opulence of "this city of Goa, which can nowadays be reckoned as one of the greatest belonging to the Portuguese Crown," was written into the record.[23] All of it was made possible not only by her wealthy citizenry but also by a very large sector of the economy which was organized into workers' guilds. Supposed Portuguese contempt for manual labor also required that other work be relegated to a "vast number" of African, Indian, or foreign-born slaves and servants.

To oversee administrative and political matters shortly after Albuquerque's conquest, a municipal council was established consisting of ten individuals, all with voting rights and probably selected (or elected) from among Portuguese who had taken Albuquerque's advice, married Indian women, and committed themselves to settling in Goa for life.

---

[22] Charles R. Boxer, *Portuguese Society in the Tropics. The Municipal Councils of Goa, Macao, Bahia, and Luanda, 1510—1800*, (Madison, The University of Wisconsin Press, 1965), p. 13.

[23] *ibid.*, p. 37.

The charter and privileges were closely modeled on those of Lisbon and were jealously guarded; no administrative or judicial official, not even the viceroy, could interfere in daily administrative matters of the council and the rights and privileges of Goa's Portuguese citizens were scrupulously respected.[24] A modern assayor of Imperial Portugal has noted that the council was "one of the principal forces which held the ramshackle State of India ... together," that it successfully maintained its privileges and was valued by the Crown, for at least three centuries as a check on both viceroys and archbishops.[25]

Economy and polity were not the only areas of imperial interest, for the Crown was concerned with the education, health, and welfare of its citizenry and quickly transplanted to its overseas territories the *Santa Casa da Misericordia*, a charitable order founded in 1498 in Portugal and which was extremely effective in attending to the needs of the poor, sick, widows, and orphans. The *Misericordia* maintained a hospital and other agencies for the spiritual and corporal welfare of Portuguese Indian society, although its later vulnerability to "borrowing" by Goanese gentlemen aided its decline from the eighteenth century.[26]

The *Estado's* military establishment depended on African slaves as soldiers in all its territories; this was the case in Goa as well as Ceylon where Negro slaves were utilized as auxiliary troops. Not surprisingly, the Sinhalese epic *Parangi Hatane* numbers "Kaffirs" among their important opponents.[27] Other evidence suggests a rather numerous contingent of black militia for there were frequent requests from other parts of the empire for blacks, such as that from the governor of Macao in 1651 for a squad of African slaves as part of additional military for the Macaense garrisons; Goa complied.[28]

Portuguese India appears to have been a complex and profitable state whose social structure was a looser version than that of the mother country and was based on the fact that the original Portuguese settlers were almost exclusively male and predominantly military or

---

[24] *ibid.*, p. 13.

[25] *ibid.*, p. 40.

[26] José Frederico Ferreira Martins, *História da Misericordia de Goa, 1520— 1910*, I—III, (Nova Goa, 1910—1914).

[27] Charles R. Boxer, *The Portuguese Seaborne Empire*, (New York, Alfred A. Knopf, Inc., 1969), p. 302.

[28] *ibid.*, p. 302.

missionary types. Many married and remained in India, forming a class of *casados* rewarded with profitable perquisites, from offices to trading voyages. Clergy (especially Brothers of the *Misericordia*) and municipal councillors were eminently ranked on the social scale and they and other influential citizens profited from bribery and corruption. Most of the lower classes were composed of Indians with some unfortunate whites and Eurasians joined by Africans.[29] Colonial society remained primarily military, mercantile, and maritime. The *casado* class, which earlier had earned their position and wealth from interport Asian trade, later acquired greater income from lands in the so-called "Provinces of the North," ultimately lost to the Marāthās in the War of 1737—1740. Thereafter the social and economic situation in India declined. A growing population, an increasingly unhealthy climate, economic decline, and loss of imperial territories forced the removal of the capital to Pangim (Panaji) in 1760, and from there the derelict state of India lethargically merged into the local landscape. Such then was the once-flourishing, gaudy jewel in the Portuguese imperial crown into which the alien African was thrust and to whose functions in the sixteenth and seventeenth century religious, legal, social, and economic life of the *Estado da India* I shall now turn.

Most references for the sixteenth and seventeenth century African presence in the socio-economic structure of Portuguese India are found in archival collections and travel accounts, most of which are housed in India. Because information on sixteenth century South Asia, in general, and Portuguese India, in particular, is so fragmented, the following discussion might appear somewhat anecdotal. I have tried, in the light of the available evidence, to tie the aspects of the functions of Africans into the general structure of Portuguese Indian society.

Most specific notices refer to Africans in India in servile roles. Religious men provide a substantive amount of information on this aspect. Their records indicate that these African slaves were Christianized, then sold to other Christians to serve primarily as domestics.[30] That practice apparently became *de rigueur* in the following century.[31]

---

[29] This information can be studied in the various collections of documents of the Câmaras. A partial inventory is listed in Boxer, *Portuguese Society*, Appendixes, pp. 153—218.

[30] *Provisões a favor da Cristandade* (15: 3—1840), I, fl. 42 v. Evora, 14 March 1533 (date of the testimonial card: 11 April 1551); fl. 40 v., Lisboa, 24 March 1559.

[31] *ibid.*, fls. 98v., Goa, 5 November 1593.

36   ANN M. PESCATELLO

But "accepting" Christianity did not necessarily reward the slaves
with benevolent treatment. This is especially evident from correspondence, primarily of secular clergy, who were ordained non-Europeans.
(Early in the colonial presence, the regular clergy had erected a color
bar against non-Europeans.) Their petitions afford insight not only
into the conditions of servitude but also into the attitudes of Church
and Crown. Here, as elsewhere in the Empire, for economic reasons
the Portuguese Church (and Court) placed itself in opposition to the
colonists. The incidents were not so isolated, at least during the
sixteenth century. The petitions were applicable both to the African
and the indigenous slaves of coastal western India and the petitions
indicate that the slavery situation was subject to review by the Portuguese monarch, whose aid was enlisted to alleviate grievances. Priests
entreated "His Majesty" to investigate "persons who are cruel to their
slaves" and to allow those "who are cruelly treated" to be "sold away
from them."[32] Priests claimed that the slaves' "sufferings and tor-
ments" were so abominable that "many die" and are interred "em
cazas e quintaes," and demanded firmer treatment of offenders.[33]
Throughout the seventeenth century the situation scarcely changed
if we are to believe other petitions to the Crown to "help the desperate
slaves" who are "evidently in danger of dying."[34]

The Catholic clergy also found itself at odds with commercial con-
stituents of the Empire. Due both to sincere ideological controversy
over the legal and natural order of slavery (See n. 21) and to conflicting
economic interests, the slave became a bandying point. Merchants and
colonists sought a source of labor both cheap and tractable; so did the
clergy, but they were interested also in the spiritual nature of the
slave. Archival accounts in metropolitan Portugal attest to the clergy's
duplicity at isolating the servile elements for their own economic ag-
grandizement while propagandizing to establish their own protective
postures with the King. The merchants engaged in similar haggling.

Despite the selfish conflict of Crown, clergy, colonists, and merchantmen over the spiritual and material value of the slaves, there was legal

---

[32] *ibid.*, fls. 113, Madrid, 26 January 1599. The latter was noted from Madrid
because during the years 1580—1640 the Portuguese Crown came under the
control of Spain. See also, for the sufferings of the slaves, *Livro das Monções do
Reino*, I, (1560—1601), 26 January 1599, fl. 95.

[33] *ibid.*, fls. 113.

[34] *ibid.*, fls. 109, Goa, 19 September 1658.

commitment to bettering the conditions of the servile population. There is asserted, in Portuguese documents, an attitude, often reasonable for its time, of great concern about the treatment and material condition of slaves. And, there are annual notices of numbers of slaves freed each year in Portuguese India, although it is difficult to determine whether this was a result of clerical agitation or an annual gesture on the part of the Crown.[35]

Archival records allow us to review the legal policies and established attitudes regarding African slavery in India, but usually it is travellers' accounts that provide insights into local practices. Necessary to a functioning servile labor force is the merchandising of the labor commodity. This was a dimension of slavery frequently commented upon. An early traveler, Linschoten, observed that in the markets "were many sorts of [captives and] slaves, both men and women, young and old, which are daily sold there, as beads are sold with us where everyone may choose which liketh him best, every one at a certain price."[36]

Pietro della Valle also commented on this process. In his descriptions of Goa, della Valle noted of one of the central squares that "in this plaza are sold all sorts of merchandise; and among other things, quantities of slaves."[37] The sellers first performed a thorough examination of the merchandise, then bantered "all their endowments, skills, strength, and health; and the buyers . . . question and examine them, with curiosity, from head to foot, the same with the men as with the women."[38] While, for their own purposes, the slaves "hoping for better treatment with a change of owner, showed their best disposition and are boastful of themselves in order to stimulate the desire of the buyer."[39]

---

[35] *Provisões e Regimentos*, I—II, (1539—1614), I, fls. 107v. Goa, 3 September 1609. On November 3, 1592, Viceroy Mathias de Albuquerque proclaimed that slaves of infidels who converted themselves to Christianity would be freed. See Cunha Rivare, ed., *Arquivo Português Oriental*, (1865), Fasc. V, pt. iii, Doc. 983, p. 1300.

[36] Linschoten, *Voyage*, I, 185.

[37] *Viagem de Francisco Pyrard de Laval*, I—II, (Porto, 1944), p. 50. I have used the Portuguese version of this account by the intelligent and knowledgeable Italian scholar who travelled in India in the early seventeenth century. There is an English version entitled *The Travels of Pietro della Valle in India*, edited by E. Grey, in two volumes by the Hakluyt Society, (London, 1892).

[38] *ibid.*, p. 50.

[39] *ibid.*, p. 50.

ANN M. PESCATELLO

Those in bondage apparently were of a wide range in source and age, and comprised both males and females. Della Valle noted that blacks from both East and West Africa composed slave cargoes to Portugal's possessions (and other mercantile points of interest) in India. The apparent persistence in Portuguese India of both Moçambicans and Guineans indicates not only the transfer of blacks from both major slave areas of Africa, but also presupposes a relatively long existence for barter operations.

Slaves were not solely African but also included Indians and others who had been captured in pirate raids. Della Valle noted some "very beautiful and lovely young girls and women from all lands in India," while included "among these young women . . . very beautiful whites, and lovely, are others swarthy, dark-skinned, and of all colors."[40] But he also observed that "of all those females [the] most pleasing are the servant girls—*Cafres de Moçambique* and [those] from other parts of Africa, who are of black color, very dark and have curly hair, and who are called negresses of Guine."[41]

The diet of the slaves was similar to the everyday foods of the common people and both commoners and slaves were great consumers of Portuguese wines. Of the many wines brought from Portugal was "a white [one] called *Orraca*, worth not more than ten basarucos, and ordinarily used by people of the lowest status and by the slaves, who, from it, are frequently intoxicated . . ."[42]

Sexual license, a common characteristic of colonization, was a common ingredient in relationships between masters and slaves in Portuguese India. Clerical revulsion of the practice is responsible for our

---

[40] *ibid.*, p. 51.

[41] *ibid.*, p. 51. The term Negro or Negress from *Guine* designated one who was from the western coast of Africa. *Cafre, cafra,* or *Kafir* usually refered to blacks from the East Coast of Africa. The word *kafir* is a term applied by the Arabs to pagan Negroes and means an infidel, or a nonbeliever in Islam. It was adopted by the Portuguese and later by other Europeans. These designations are minuscule segments of the complex linguistic formulae involved in the sixteenth century philosophical enquiries over the legal and natural condition of pagan and Christian or Muslim man. An interesting singular insight into this situation as it occured in the India trade is the issuance of a *cartaz* (the pass bought from the Portuguese and a prerequisite for trade and travel in Portuguese-controlled waters) on a 1613 voyage from Dabhol to Jiddah: The ship could not transport slaves unless they were from Bijapur and *not* Christian! See J. F. J. Biker, *Colleção de Tratadôs*, (Lisboa, 1921), iv., pp. 181—2.

[42] *Pyrard de Laval*, pp. 56—7.

information regarding the practice of Portuguese who "to satiate their passions . . . buy droves of girls and sleep with all of them, and subsequently sell them."[43] Primacy of the male and leniency to mistresses were practices that della Valle observed in relationships of slaves to their masters. According to the Portuguese practice in India, if any man "fathered" a son by his Negress slave, the boy was legitimized and the slave given her freedom.[44]

Abbé Carre also painted a picture of female slaves in their more intimate relationships to the Portuguese gentry. One Dom Pedro de Castro was particularly singled out as a man who "amused himself only with scoundrels and debauchers, and with a troop of womenslaves whom he kept for his sensual pleasures" and, furthermore, that type of living was "one commonly led by all the Portuguese in India."[45] In the Abbé's opinion the other *fidalgos* (gentry) were alike in that they were always "dragging about an appalling number of slaves."[46] And another enclave visit confirmed his opinion of the desolute lives the Portuguese were now leading after two centuries in India, wining, well-dressed, and "followed by a fine troop of slaves."[47]

Next to domestic servants, the largest percentage of slaves either were resold by their owners or were manual laborers who worked at such odd jobs as "conserving fruits and other things; others earned money as carriers and loaders of wares."[48] There were also the young servant girls who were forced into prostitution. They "were called to the houses" and "were made amorous propositions."[49] Some succumbed to the attentions involved in this type of occupation, although many undoubtedly had little choice in the matter. Servant girls and others who labored at menial tasks actually were hired out by their masters and expected to comply with orders issued by temporary

---

[43] A letter from the Jesuit Nicolas Lancilotta to Ignatius Loyola, quoted in A. da Silva Rego, ed., *Documentação para a historia das missões do padroado portugues do Oriente India*, I—XII, (Lisboa, 1947), VII, pp. 32 ff. See also the report of Padre Valignano in XII, pp. 577—81.

[44] *Pyrard de Laval*, II, 52.

[45] *The Travels of the Abbé Carré in India and the Near East 1672—1674*, I—III, Series II of the Hakluyt Society, XCX—XCVII, (London, 1947), I, p. 242.

[46] *ibid.*, p. 245. *Fidalgo* (or in Spanish *hidalgo*) is derived from the combination of *fil (ho) d'algo*, i.e. the son of someone.

[47] *ibid.*, II, p. 342.

[48] *Pyrard de Laval*, II, p. 52.

[49] *ibid.*, 000.

ANN M. PESCATELLO

employers. This was a common labor policy of the Iberian powers in their American possessions. Any monetary gains acquired by slaves, by whatever means available to them, they "hand it over to their *senhor* (master) or *senhora* (mistress)."[50]

Labor conditions fluctuated with the whims of the *senhors*. Linschoten noted that slaves carried on Portuguese and Dutch ships from Moçambique to India included both men and women . . . "to do their filthiest and hardest labor, wherein they only use them."[51] One of the most common slave tasks was to supply water throughout the various cities or hamlets occupied by the Portuguese. It was noted by della Valle that they "carried it to all the sections in earthenware jugs each of which contained two jars, and sold the jugs at five *basarucos*."[52]

Bondsmen of particular households frequently appeared in public as escorts and bearers to their ladies and gentlemen. Whenever the men ventured out they "never left without taking a slave who carried a large umbrella to guard against the sun," or to carry "veils or hats over them in the rain."[53] Ladies, meanwhile, were borne inside a palanquine "carried by four negro slaves attired in silks . . . and accompained by many negress slaves . . . all dressed in silks."[54] This lifestyle was not restricted to Europeans; the sultan who "had a Black-guard of some a Dozen slaves," was a not infrequent personage in Portuguese India.[55]

By far the greatest number of African slaves were employed in

---

[50] This supplements evidence from Brazilian sources of the domineering position that the Portuguese wife assumed in the direction of household affairs. In fact, a probable consistency of practice in various Portuguese colonies was that the Negress as slave suffered an uncomfortable existence at the whims of her Portuguese mistress.

[51] Linschoten, *Voyages*, I, p. 32.

[52] *Pyrard de Laval*, II, 55. Five *basarucos* were calculated to equal nearly six *dinheiros* of the day, accurate value unknown. Twenty-five *basarucos* equalled six *brancos*, value also unknown. The editors of the edition I have used indicate that the six *brancos* possibly equal two *escudos* in the equivalent rate of the Portuguese currency of the time of the edition of about one Indian rupee or 13.5 United States cents.

[53] Linschoten, *Voyages*, I, pp. 193—4. See also, II, p. 257.

[54] *Pyrard de Laval*, II, pp. 58—9. The Palanquine was a type of litter, for one or two persons, and common throughout the interior provinces of India and parts of Asia.

[55] John Fryer, *A New Account of East India and Persia*, I—III, (London, 1909), I, p. 62.

domestic tasks, and it is about the African's function in this capacity that we have the most information. Both Linschoten and della Valle discerned that the riches of the Goan gentry derived from the great number of slaves that each house possessed and that the Goanese commonly held "five, six, ten, twenty, and some more, some less slaves, both men and women, in their houses . . ."[56] Accounts depict an affluent gentry, accustomed to service by slaves, and confident in their own position vis à vis their servile population.

On a visit to Daman,[56a] the Frenchman Thevenot commented that "the Portuguese have Slaves there of both Sexes, which work and procreate only for their Masters, to whom the Children belong, to be disposed of at their pleasure."[57] He further observed the style of living afforded the Portuguese by their African slaves in Daman: "The Portuguese live very great in India, both as to their tables, clothing, and number of Cafres, or Slaves, to serve them; having some of these to carry them in Palanchines on their Shoulders and other great Umbrelloes of Palm-Tree Leaves."[58] The charges for hiring non-slaves to carry the Palanquines was a perfunctory sum, so "they that have no Slaves, pay four Indians but twelve Coslines of Naples a Month for carrying them."[59] The implication is, of course, that there was an abundance of slaves.

Another traveler, Careri, told the story of a son of a neighboring king who came to visit and had two slaves to accompany him. At the place of the visit there were no chairs available so the princeling "caus'd his two Slaves to squat down and sate upon them."[60]

Abbé Carré's observations concur with these social conditions at the end of the seventeenth century. In Daman "most of the houses are

---

[56] Linschoten, *Voyages*, I, p. 193.

[56a] Portuguese India, other than the occasional territories, consisted of the enclaves of Goa, Daman, and Diu. They lost the so-called Northern Territories in the 1737—1740 war with the Marathas.

[57] S. N. Sen, ed., *Indian Travels of Careri and Thevenot*, (Delhi, National Archives of India, 1949), Chapter XLVIII, p. 116. Jean Thevenot (1633—1667), was a Frenchman and a student of geography and ethnology who travelled in the western areas of India.

[58] *ibid.*, p. 116.

[59] *ibid.*, p. 160. "Coslines of Naples" is from the Italian "cosa-llino," meaning a thing of trifling value and designating the smallest coin in use in Naples at the time.

[60] *ibid.*, p. 189.

filled with women who make dainties and sweets, with troops of slaves, who have hardly any food but rice and fish."[61] Carré left an elaborate account of the slaves of landholders:

> On Tuesday, 22 November, I had prepared all my equipage to leave at day-break, but received a message from a P. fidalgo, Dom Francisco Gonsalve de St. Paye, one of the richest citizens of Daman, asking me to wait an hour for him, as he wished to accompany me to Tarapur, where, he was going to visit his farms and tenancies. I waited till seven o'clock, when I saw my Portuguese arriving with an escort of slaves armed with matchlocks, javelins, and some sort of blunderbuss . . . I was amazed at the weight of the arms which these Caffres are obliged to carry . . .[62]

In Goa proper the Abbé considered that practically everyone must have been outfitted with some Negroes and other "large suites of slaves . . . [Everyone], Bakers, fruiterers, and party-cooks, were in clover; and above all those who dealt in human flesh, with which this town is full, made wonderful profits."[63] He even extended his observations on the master-slave relationship to the Portuguese colony at Madras where the Portuguese men "Day and night . . . cannot rest themselves without a dozen mosses, i.e. female slaves to massage and knead their bodies."[64]

It appears that black, African slaves were, at various periods, considered a luxury and prestige element, and the Abbé recorded an incident to which others allude as fairly common practice. On the arrival of any gentleman, or nobleman, or person of major rank, the "Noble ladies sent their kafir slaves to escort him."[65] A similar situation was described by Fryer who noted their special role and observed that although cafirs initially arrived as slaves, "they have become as endeared to their Master, who, as they merit, have the first places of Honor and trust imposed upon them . . ."[66]

---

[61] *Travels of the Abbé Carré*, I, p. 168.

[62] *ibid.*, I, p. 172.

[63] *ibid.*, II, p. 398.

[64] *ibid.*, II, p. 522. The word "mosses" appears to be a Portuguese or French corruption of the French *macer* or *masser*, meaning "to massage" and so designated by another traveler Le Gentil (*Voyage des mers de l'Inde*, I, 128) in 1770. It assumed that the word was used by French colonists in India. It is also conjectured that it is from the Arabic *mass*, to rub or touch, and as a possessive derivative from the Arabic *masis*, one who rubs or touches. The editor of the Carré volume points out that if the last is the case then it is "an incorrect active participle for *mass*."

[65] *ibid.*, III, p. 740.

[66] Fryer, *A New Account . . .*, II, p. 52.

There were, however, definite distinctions between the races in legal matters. For example, orphanages and the care of illegitimate and unfortunate children occupied a certain amount of interest among the religious orders and some secular organizations. The reasons were essentially those of acquisition of labor and salvation of souls. Records on the famous Convent of Santa Monica reveal the nuns' complaints that the 120 slaves alloted them was insufficient and pointed out that even European, Eurasian, or mulatto artisans could have "15 or 20 female slaves," or "26 women and girls," while a *juiz ordinaria* (judge) or a *desembargador* (lawyer) held "85 female slaves . . . and some rich ladies had over 300."[67] These documents indicate vast numbers of slaves in Goa and also are supportive of the Portuguese colonial ideal that maintenance of large slave households lends social status and personal prestige to a person.

Another aspect of slavery seems to have been that particular members of various religious communities were assigned legal responsibilities of guardianship. This practice, in Portuguese communities in India, defined differences in the ethnic composition of the children. For each orphanage, two persons were appointed under an *ouvidor* (i.e. one who would hear cases and oversee affairs): One man was designated for the whites and another was assigned to the blacks,[68] a practice continued by the British when Cooke assumed control of Bombay from the Portuguese in 1665 (Bombay was part of the dowry of Catherine of Braganza to Charles II of England). Again, we are not certain if this implied *all* non-Portuguese occupying these pockets of western India but it probably does include any African orphans, illegitimate offspring of a relationship which the Master refused to sanction.

The synonymous usage of the term *Cafir* for slave indicates the apparently widespread utilization of Africans as bondsmen in western India's coastal sectors, at least in those areas frequented by the Portuguese. However, the seemingly pittance fees paid to free men to undertake tasks for which there was insufficient slave labor available indicates a rather low economic and social position for workers in general

---

[67] Agostinho de Santa Maria, *Historia do Real Convento de Santa Monica*, (Lisboa, 1699), pp. 263, 358—9, and Francisco de Sousa, S. J., *Oriente Conquistado a Jesu Christo pelos Padres da Companhia de Jesus da Provincia de Goa*, I—II, (Lisboa, 1710), I, pp. 739—40.

[68] *Travels of the Abbé Carré*, I, p. 168, N. 1.

in Portuguese colonial society. Documents and time have supported the Fleming Cleynaerts's assessment of the Iberian contempt for manual labor, that for the *fidalgo* it was less shameful to beg than to work with one's hands, a station in life best filled by foreigners, natives, and slaves.[69]

This contempt for manual labor by the *fidalgo* stratum of society necessitated a goodly supply of servile labor. To this end, in the sixteenth and seventeenth centuries a constant trade in slaves was carried on within India and between India and Africa. The Italian Careri, traveling in the seventeenth century, had himself purchased a slave at a sum low enough to indicate either a sudden decline in the esteem of blacks or, even more likely, an oversupply for the demand. "My Armenian Servant, refusing to go to China, on Wednesday 11th, I bought a Cafre, or Black Slave for eighteen Pieces of Eight."[71] Although the slave was available and willing to accompany Careri, the Italian was forced to obtain a license to ship the slave because the carrier was touching at Malacca [where the Dutch were]. He "went on Thursday 12th, to the Inquisitors to have it Pass'd. They made a great difficulty of granting it . . . alledging that some Cafres, who had been Shipp'd at other times, being taken, had turn'd Mahometans."[72]

Careri, who travelled at the end of the seventeenth century, supports the contention that African slaves were numerous throughout Portuguese India:

> There are also abundance of *Cafres* and Blacks; for there are Portuguese that keep thirty, or fourty, and the "least six or twelve; to carry their umbrella, and Andora, and other mean Employments; nor are they at any other charge to keep them, but a Dish of Rice at Noon, and another at Night; for they have no other Garments but what they brought out of their Mothers Wombs.[73]

The Italian also described the carriage of slave cargoes to India's West Coast: "The Slaves are carry'd to sell at Goa, and all along the Portuguese Towns, by the Company's Ships belonging to Lisborn and

---

[69] From Cleynaerts' *desamor ao trabalho*, cited in M. Gonçalves Cerejeira, *Clenardo e a sociedado portuguesa do seu tempo*, (Coimbra, 1949), pp. 159—89, 203—21.

[71] Sen, *Indian Travels* . . ., p. 272. Giovanni Gemelli-Careri, a Neapolitan noble and lawyer, travelled along the western coast during the last years of the seventeenth century.

[72] *ibid.*, p. 272.

[73] *ibid.*, p. 188.

India, who buy them at Monbaza, Mozambique, Zofala, and other Ports along the Coast of Africa."[74]

Careri attributed the superfluity of blacks available in Africa, as did most of his contemporaries, to the constant warfare among African tribal groups. He claimed that the "nations" at war captured slaves and sold them; that children were sold into slavery by their parents; and that many adults, in desperation, often sold themselves as slaves. All of those factors are undoubtedly true. There were problems of survival related to population pressure, food deficiencies, and political turmoil. However, Careri and his contemporaries failed to note that the increase in turmoil and the possible increment in tribal conflicts were due in part to the increased awareness by Africans of European and Arabic interest in human cargo. Hence, the more modern view of the availability of African slaves due to tribal conflict correctly places part of the responsibility on the traders themselves. Nonetheless, there was an abundance of slaves for the trade and "They being very cheap, that is, 15 or 20 Crowns of Naples a Head, it is no wonder there should be such numbers of them, and that the very Vintners keep them to sell their Wine . . ."[75]

Other travelers, in later journeys to Portuguese possessions, left testimonies agreeing with earlier visitors on persisting patterns of slave sale and functions in the Portuguese enclaves.[76] The pervasiveness of the black in his new environs is noticeable in the later archival records. "I declare that all the mosses who are vulgarly called negresses, whom I have in my house, and who have served me for many years are free in becoming New Christians . . ."[77]

In a process of liquidation of losses and other claims filed in the court at Goa city by a family, mention was made of the common practice

---

[74] *ibid.*

[75] *ibid.*, pp. 188—9.

[76] Other travellers' accounts of value include *The Travels of Sebastian Manrique* 1629—43, I—II, in the Hakluyt Series II, (London, 1926—1927); J. S. Hoyland and S. N. Banerji, eds., and trans., *The Commentary of Father Monserrate*, (London: Oxford University Press, 1922); a book concerned solely with the sixteenth century. Others include Jean B. Tavernier, *Travels in India*, I—II, and the various collections compiled by such men as John Pinkerton, Richard Hakluyt, John C. Locke, Samuel Purchas, et al.

[77] *Feitoria Mandados de prisão e supersedencia*, in one volume (1804—1832). The testament is dated 27 May 1706 in proc. 3, fls. 15, *Arquivo Historico*, Goa. Also see *Livro das Monções* . . ., vol. 117, doc. from 1690.

46   ANN M. PESCATELLO

among the Portuguese in India of the "assistence" of cafre servant boys.[78]

The carrying of slaves on ships plying between the coasts of eastern African and western India continued into the nineteenth century. Evidence of this appears in records on the rather steady increase of piracy along the route. In documents devoted to the problem of pirating of slave cargoes between Daman and Mozambique, Portuguese captains lamented that excessive numbers of cafres died in such expeditions and that many of the cargoes (remaining) were sold to the French who were resident in Daman for that purpose![79]

After several centuries of Christian domination the concept of the slave as a piece of merchandise had changed little, despite Pombaline edicts against slavery and prohibition of slave transport "from America, Asia, and Africa to the Kingdom."[80] In 1783—1784 there are records of "black men" sold in Lisbon and other apparently illegal situations according to the cases of formal court charges against such practice.[81] A few decades later such records as sales of "goods available" included a "Negress called Maria with her two sons"[82] and in another area, in Chimbel, additional notices of goods available included a "Negress with her two sons,"[83] while in court processes of liquidations, etc. a "Negress called Rita" was identified as part of the estate of one Sebastiao Joaquim Monteiro.[84]

One of many court records of the above type listed the proceedings about the death of twenty-six cafres belonging to one Joao Rebelo de Albuquerque, who "were part of the overload of the ship Santo Antonio Triunfo de Africa."[85] The fact that so many slaves were part of a single shipload, and that so many died or were killed for expediency's

---

[78] *Feitoria. Esbulbos; liquidação de perdas, danos, e interesses*, (1723—1834), I, fls. 127 (1723), proc., 1.

[79] *Feitoria. Tomadias*, I—IV, (1772—1834), I, proc. 2, fls. 72 (1776) and fls. 81.

[80] *Livro das Monções do Reino*, CXXXV, fls. 303 (12 October 1761). Pombal was the Chief Minister of Portugal who, from 1750—1777 ruled that empire in the tradition of an enlightened despot.

[81] *Feitoria. Causas de libelo*, I—II (1784—1831), I, proc. 1, fls. 25 (1784) and proc. 2, fls. 25 (1783).

[82] *Feitoria. Inventarios*, I—VII, (1730—1833), III, proc. 2, fls. 109, (1807), fls. 6v.

[83] *ibid.*, proc. 25, fls. 220 (1808).

[84] *ibid. Penhoras e execuções* I—LXIII, (1735—1834), XXVI, proc. 1, (1809).

[85] *ibid. Justificações*, I—VII, (1717—1833), IV, proc. 2, fls. 52 (1813).

sake, indicates that the traffic to India in African labor was still an
active concern in the early nineteenth century. Ten years later the
advertisements of marketplace buying and selling included such items
as:

> gold and silver
> . . . .
> four cafres by the names of Ventura, Joze,
> Passarinho, and Furtuno
> one Negress named Junevita
> four pigs with ten sucklings
> . . . .[86]

There are notices of purchases of freedom by slaves as well as the
fairly common practice of slaves being given their freedom by their
masters, but the notices are relatively few compared to the instances of
court actions and confiscations or selling of Negroes as household
merchandise or livestock. Nonetheless, an example of the ability of
slaves to purchase and to petition for their freedom is found in requests of slave girls in the royal cloth factory at Polvora, Goa. His
Majesty, in his compassion, would free the girls given the price, on
their account or anothers to "the said Natalia, Dulcine, Genoviva,
Anna, Maria, Josefa, Rital, and Maria Chimbel."[87] There are also, in
the *assentas baptismo* and *Registos baptismos*, records of the births of
many of the Cafirs' children in Daman as well as their marriages and
baptisms. There seem to have been rare instances of marriages of
Cafirs with Goans except in Salcete and among the very lower classes.

Such is some evidence available in archival records and travellers'
accounts of the transfer, presence, and treatment of the African in
Portuguese India. The materials offer a number of observations. The
first is that Africans not only from the east but also from the west
coasts of that continent were utilized as slave labor. It might also be
possible to assume, as in instances of the Black Jews in Kerala, that
Africans were purchased and utilized, earlier than the Portuguese
presence, as slave labor by the Indians themselves through some
trading mechanisms exclusive of Arabic or Portuguese involvement.
There is reason to believe that wealthy Indians, who had a practice of
slavery as a system of labor among their own peoples and within the

---

[86] *ibid. Inventarios*, I—VII, (1730—1833), V, proc. 4, fls. 125 (1825).

[87] *ibid. Arrematações*, I, (1736—1834), I, proc. 16, fls. 45, on the auction of
these slave girls.

48   ANN M. PESCATELLO

strictures of their own caste system, would not ignore the availability
of an external labor supply. This would seem quite plausible in view
of the flourishing trade in tribal peoples and other groups, as mentioned by Manrique and other travellers, along the eastern coast of
India. It can also be assumed from available evidence pertinent to
Hindu and Muslim societies that slaves would be held by families of
both religious groups.

A second point of observation is that the African was a valued item
in trade because he fulfilled a number of tasks which Indians either
could not (because of caste restrictions) or would not perform, or for
which the Portuguese deemed themselves and the Indians to be un-
suited. There are indications also that the African slave enjoyed a
rather unusual position, at varying times, as a prestige servant or in
the case of females, as suited for amorous duties in a household. The
Portuguese treatment of the African in India follows much the same
pattern as his actions in Brazil and other territories of empire. Cruelties
and inhumane treatment were generally a part of the slave milieu but,
as has been seen, in the African's role as a domestic he was often well
treated and also highly regarded in relation to the indigenous populations of the places to which he was imported.

A thorough and exhaustive investigation of the socio-racial policy
of the Portuguese Crown must be undertaken before postulating a
definitive analysis or judgment regarding the position of the African
as well as other enthralled peoples in the Portuguese imperial scheme.
There are paradoxes in the policy as it was fashioned at the time by
Iberian legal codes and Catholic philosophic enquiries. There also are
gaps in our knowledge about the existing patterns of conduct, legal and
social, by many of the inhabitants of territories visited by the Portuguese. All of these investigations must be undertaken before we can
affect modern judgments on centuries-old social and economic relations
among the races. Meanwhile, it is hoped that this initial overview of
records and accounts will contribute new insights into and add impetus
to study a hitherto neglected chapter in South Asian history: the
presence of the African in India.

8

Black Slaves and Free Blacks in Ottoman Cyprus, 1590–1640

Ronald C. Jennings

Black slaves from Africa south of the Sahara were much in demand in the Ottoman empire in the 16th and 17th centuries, but scant attention has been given to their places of origin, the routes by which they entered the empire, the prices for which they were bought and

*) The three oldest Lefkoşa sicils are housed in the Etnografya Müzesi and most of the remainder in the Evkaf Dairesi, all in Lefkoşa (Nicosia), Cyprus Turkish Federated State. I wish to thank the museum director Bay Cevdet Çağdaş, now retired, and the museum staff for their hospitality on both my visits to Cyprus. I am very grateful to the National Endowment for the Humanities for a Fellowship and the Joint Committee on the Near and Middle East of the American Council of Learned Societies and the Social Science Research Council for a Research Grant which supported visits to Cyprus. I wish to thank Prof. A. Tietze, R. S. O'Fahey, C. C. Stewart, and J. E. K. Walker for reading an earlier version of the text and making helpful suggestions.

Four sicils in various states of preservation survive from Lefkoşa in the period between the Ottoman conquest in 1571 and 1640, and only the fourth approximates its original form.

no.	hicri	
1A	988, 1002-1003	1580 (fragment), 1593-1595
2	1016-1018	1607-1609
3	1018-1019	1609-1611
4.	1043-1046	1633-1637

abbreviations: bn = son of (with Muslims); v./veled = son of (with Zimmis [non-Muslims]); bint = daughter of.

forms of suits: ik/it = ikrar ve iᶜtiraf

td = takrir-i daᶜva

tk = takrir-i kelam

The first form is an acknowledgment or confession; the others occur in contested cases.

BLACK SLAVES AND FREE BLACKS IN OTTOMAN CYPRUS   287

sold, or the process of their distribution to places like Cyprus[1]). Even A. Raymond's important studies of Cairo provide surprisingly sparse information to illuminate the issues raised above, a void which helped inspire T. Walz's study of trade between Egypt and the Sudan. The late C. Orhonlu, who recently completed a major archival study of the Ottoman province of Habeş (Ethiopia), found little in Ottoman archives about slaves and the slave trade there; those materials that he presented about black slavery and the slave trade in the province of Habeş come from western "travellers" or current historians of that region, and almost none concerns the 16th and 17th centuries.

Little may be said about the places of origin or dates of arrival of black slaves or free blacks in Ottoman Cyprus, except that their presence can be documented by the 1590's in judicial registers (şer ʿi mahkeme sicilleri) from Lefkoşa (Nicosia), Cyprus[2]).

---

1) Much has been done to illuminate the large trade in white slaves from north and east of the Black sea, particularly very recently by A. Fisher, but also by A. Bennigsen, Ch. Verlinden, C. Lemercier-Quelquejay, and G. Veinstein. See, for example: A. Bennigsen and C. Lemercier-Quelquejay: "Les marchands de la Cour ottomane..., *Cahiers du Monde Russe et Soviétique* 11.1970.303-390. Mihnea Berindei & Gilles Veinstein: "La présence ottomane au sud de la Crimée et en mer d'Azov dans la première moitié du XVIe siècle", Cahiers du Monde Russe et Soviétique 20.1979.348-465. "La Tana-Azaq de la presence italienne à l'emprise ottomane (fin XVIIe-milieu XVIe siècle)", *Turcica* 8.2.1976.110-201. Alan Fisher: "Chattel Slavery in the Ottoman Empire", *Slavery and Abolition* 1.1980.25-45. "The Sale of Slaves in the Ottoman Empire: Markets and State Taxes on Slave Sales, Some Preliminary Considerations", *Boğaziçi Üniversitesi Dergisi* 6.1978.149-171. Ch. Verlinden: "Esclavage et ethnographie sur les bords de la mer Noire (XIIIe-XIVe s.)", *Miscellanea Van der Essen*, I, Bruxelles-Paris, 1947, 287-298. "La colonie vénitienne de Tana, centre de la traite des esclaves au XIVe et au début du XVe siècle", in *Studi in onore di Gino Luzzatto*. v. 2.Milan, 1950. "Le recrutment des esclaves à Venise aux XIVe et XVe siècles", *Bulletin de l'Institut historique belge de Rome* 39.1968.83f., 185-202.

2) Their presence in Cyprus in the 19th century is noted by the careful historian of Cyprus, Sir George Hill, who reported that by then "many" blacks lived there, mostly as servants to Turkish families. *A History of Cyprus*, (v.4, p. 254n.). The wife of a British colonial officer, Mrs. Scott-Stevenson, wrote in *Our Home in Cyprus*: "No doubt to all purposes they are slaves, for they never dream of leaving their masters, and go in service from father to son. But they invariably seemed well fed and clothed, and looked the most contented part of the population." (p. 20) Of course Hill and Mrs. Scott-Stevenson can tell us nothing of the 16th century even if

Terminology

Black slaves in Cyprus are identified four ways in the judicial records (*sicil*) of Lefkoşa: 1) *zenci*, or *zengi*[3]); 2) *siyah*[4]); 3) *ʿarab*, or *ʿarap*[5]); and 4) *habeşi*[6]). The kadis may not fully have grasped the

they are reliable for the 19th century. Even today a few blacks may be found in the Cyprus Turkish Federated State. In his description of Cairo in 1599 Mustafa ʿAli tells his feelings of repugnance at the widespread miscegenation between local males and black women. Children produced by such shameful unions were unattractive, although Ethiopian women in particular were preferred by the merchants of Cairo. Elsewhere he vituperates "black Arabs", "vile Arabs", who run around "naked" and are like herds of stud horses. *Description...*, pp. 51/128f., 43/117.

Abyssinian women were "weak and flabby", according to A. Mez, and Nubians the most cheerful and adaptable. Black slave women were ugly and had bad odours. *Renaissance...*, p. 161f. Mez further points out Koranic injunctions to treat slaves kindly and to feed slaves the same as oneself. Koran 4:36. p. 168.

3) *The New Redhouse* defines "zenc" as the Ethiopians and "zenci" as an Ethiopian or a Negro. F. Meninski's definitions are more restrictive, namely a region in Africa, and one from that region, which presumably excludes other black Africans. According to Lane's dictionary, "zandj" and "zandji" apply to black Africans south of the equator and beyond Abyssinia, that is, the whole country of the blacks (Negroes), while "Habaşi" refers only to Abyssinians.

4) *The New Redhouse* defines "siyah" as the color black; dark; Negro. Meninski gave "black" as his first meaning and "Arabs or Ethiopians" as his fourth; whether or not that pair are to be considered equivalent is unclear. Mustafa ʿAli tells of black Arabs ("siyeh ʿArablarun..."), and in a Persian verse ridicules the interest of Cairo merchants in "black-faced" ("siyah cahre") Ethiopian slave girls. *Description of Cairo...*, pp. 43, 117; 51, 129.

5) *The New Redhouse* gives Arab as the first meaning for "Arap" and Negro for the second meaning. Mustafa ʿAli refers to "black Arabs" ("siyeh ʿArablarun...") in Cairo in 1599, but that is not exactly parallel to this case. pp. 43, 117. Meninski did not note that usage, although his fourth definition for "siyah" (blacks) is Arabs or Ethiopians, an indication of how the word Arab was associated with black. Cf. B. Lewis, who says the term applies to Negroes and Ethiopians. *Race and Color...*, pp. 64f. and n. The term "ʿabd", as it occurs in the context of the Cyprus judicial registers, certainly has no implication of black slave.

6) "Habeşi" can mean an Abyssinian (or Ethiopian) but it also can mean a slave. *The New Redhouse* defines the word as Abyssinian, but notes that in history it means especially an Abyssinian slave. For a first definition Meninski (1680) uses only Ethiopian, but the 1780 ed. adds slave, servant (*mancipium, servus*); presumably the latter includes all slaves, not just Ethiopian ones. J. S. Trimingham has pointed out that classical Muslim geographers distinguished between Ethiopians (*Habash*) and *Bantu* (*Zanj*). *Islam in East Africa*. p.xin. E. W. Lane showed that people in Cairo in the early 19th century made that distinction, strongly preferring to possess the

precise meanings of those terms, or perhaps there was some ambiguity in the way they were used. Although lexically those four terms do not have precisely the same meaning, the court of Lefkoşa used them, sometimes interchangably, to mean black people. All four terms apparently were interchangable within the context of the court records in which they appeared.

Other words for slave like *'abd*[7]), *memluk*[8]), and *gulam* could apply alike to whites and blacks, and *cariye* applied to all females. Instances occurred of a black female slave identified as *memluk*, of a male black

---

former. *Manners and Customs...*, pp. 136, 190f. In his dictionary a careful distinction is made between "Habashi" (Abyssinians) and "Zandji" (blacks living anywhere from west Africa almost to Abyssinia). B. Lewis presents much evidence regarding that distinction. *Race and Color...*, pp. 29ff., 82ff. Nevertheless, the Lefkoşa judicial registers do not make it clear that court officials in Cyprus distinguished Ethiopians from other blacks, although there *Habeşi* were not always identified as black. T. Walz has noted that *Habeşi* is used as a nickname for dark-complexioned people in Egypt. He suggests that some light colored slaves may have preferred to identify themselves as Ethiopian because they would be more highly esteemed. *Trade...*, pp. 175f.

7) *The New Redhouse* and Meninski agree exactly on "'abd". The former, for "abit", gives servant; slave, in law; and worshipper, human being; the latter gives servant (*servus*); slave (*mancipium*); and men, whether slave or free. In the Arab world, however, the term connotes a black slave. Already in the 11th and 12th centuries, according to Goitein, "'abd" meant a black slave. *A Mediterranean Society*, v.1, p. 131. Raymond and Walz also give that meaning. *Artisans...*, p. 395. *Trade...*, p. 175. In his dictionary Lane defined "'abd" as a male slave but noted that for a long time that term had generally applied to black male slaves (in contrast with "mamluk"). In his book on early 19th century Egyptian society, Lane used black as exactly equivalent to "'abd". *Manners and Customs...*, p. 159. Lewis, who gives some of that information, notes that eventually all blacks, even free ones, became "abd". *Race and Color...*, p. 64.

8) *The New Redhouse* and Meninski define "memluk" in virtually the same way: possessed, owned personal property, and a servant or slave (*servus, mancipum*). Raymond still distinguishes between "mamluks" and white slaves in 17th and 18th century Cairo, the former of which presumably need not have been exclusively white. *Artisans...*, pp. 678, 765. According to Lane and Lewis the term "mamluk" was normally applied to white male slaves. Lewis, *Race and Color...*, pp. 63f. In the Ottoman empire the term "memluk" continued to be applied to male slaves purchased or otherwise recruited exclusively for military service, and also in particular to the system of military slaves in 17th and 18th century Ottoman Egypt; such slaves may have been predominantly white but never exclusively so. Anyway the Cyprus judicial registers show an example of a black "memluk". Walz found such cases in Cairo courts, concerning those "trained in military arts". *Trade...*, p. 175.

slave called *'abd-i memluk*[9]), and of a male black slave called *gulam*, although otherwise those terms may have been restricted to white slaves.

1. The mother of the late el-hac 'Abdul-Kadir disputed the ownership of a black (*zenciye*) female slave (*cariye*) named Fatma bint 'Abdullah with his widow. (4 29-2; II Rebi I 1044) A black (*zengi*) slave named Bilal bn 'Abdullah was accused of striking a villager with a rock. (4 50-1; III Muharrem 1044) A black (*zengiye*) slave (*memlugi*) named Fatma bint 'Abdullah proved that her late owner had emancipated her. (4 56-2; I Sefer 1044) A black slave (*zengi*) named Bilal bn 'Abdullah likewise had been emancipated by his late owner. (4 71-2; I Receb 1044) El-hac Ca' fer beg sold his black slave (*zengi gulamum*) for 4000 akce. (4 179-1; III Cumadi II 1046)

2. Two Muslims disputed the ownership of a black (*siyah 'arab*) slave named Suleyman and two white (*beyaz*) ones named Ridvan and Piyale. (3 56-4; III Cumadi II 1019) A black female slave (*siyah cariye*) named Bahit (?) bint 'Abdullah was freed. (3 145-1; III Cumadi II 1019) A black female slave (*siyah cariye*) named Mercan became pregnant after she was raped by a beardless youth (*emred*) named Ibrahim bn Isma'il. (3 174-4; III Şaban 1019) The estate of the late Mehmed çavuş of Lefkoşa castle (*kal'e*) included a black female slave (*siyah cariye*) of za'im Mehmed çelebi bn Haydar of Aya Kuşano (?) quarter in Lefkoşa, drowned accidentally in a well. (2 29-1; 3 Rebi II 1017)

3. For 9200 akce janissary es-seyyid Hasan bn el-Hac bought a black female slave (*'arab cariye*) and young boy (*'arab oglan*), as well as some other things. (1 309-1; 1 Muharrem 1003. Cf. 311-6; Muharrem 1003) Halil çelebi bn Hizir su başi, racil, freed Mercane bint

---

9) The term "'abd-i memluk" seems identical to "memluk". It occurs only in Meninski, who defines it as a slave or servant (*mancipium* or *servus*), and purchased armor (*aere emptus, proprius*). As Raymond has also noted, prices of slaves vary a great deal, perhaps an evidence of human diversity. Mamluks, for example, ranged between 2000 and 4000 paras early in the 17th century, between 5000 and 10,000 paras at the end of that century. *Artisans...*, p. 395. Walz, too, points to the "infinite variety" of slave prices. *Trade...*, p. 207.

ʿAbdullah, the black female slave (ʿarab cariyesi) he inherited from his late father. (2 27-2; 14 Şevval 1016) Black slave (siyah ʿarab) Suleyman was claimed by two rival claimants. (3 56-4; III Cumadi II 1019) A black female slave (ʿarab cariye) was returned to her owner when she was found defective. (3 73-4; II Receb 1019)

4. (?), an Ethiopian (Abyssinian), or black (Habeşi l-asl) slave, and a Muslim, was freed. (1 234-1; I Şevval 1002) Black, or Ethiopian, (Habeşi l-asl) slave (ʿabd-i memluk) Turmuş bn ʿAbdullah was freed. (1 327-2: 15 Muharrem 1003) A black (Habeşi l-asl) slave (memluk) of medium stature named Faide bint ʿAbdullah was freed (4 43-11; II Muharrem 1044); so was a black (Habeşi l-asl) slave of medium stature named Huseyn bn ʿAbdullah. (4 59-1; I Sefer 1044).

With the possible exception of habeşi, there is no good explanation that can be given for the variations in the terminology used at the court of Lefkoşa. Again, with the possible exception of habeşi, any term could have been used in place of any other one. It was not the practice to use more than one term for "black" in the recording of a particular case, except in the few cases already indicated. Scribal preference may have been the only factor which determined the terminology actually used.

Origins of Black Slaves

In the Lefkoşa judicial registers five black slaves in Cyprus were identified with regions in Black Africa. Of those regions, two can be identified with certainty and a third with some degree of certainty. All three of those regions are located in the Sudan, near the confluence of the White Nile and the Blue Nile in the provinces of Dar Fur and Sinnar. Typically, such slaves were purchased by Arab Muslim merchants who worked out of Cairo and who traveled in caravans along the Nile, particularly to its west. T. Walz has recently documented the importance of the slave trade from that region for the period after 1700. R. S. O'Fahey has demonstrated use being made of those routes beginning at least with the late 16th or early 17th century, a time when Dar Fur was being islamized, partly from Sinnar.

At that time slave raiders from the region of Dar Fur and especially Sinnar occasionally penetrated as far south as Ethiopia, particularly by the route between Gondar and Sinnar, but more commonly Ethiopian slaves were shipped north along the Red sea from Beylul and Zeyla, and smaller ports as well, to Suez and then Cairo. The Red sea port of Massawa, further north, also exported numerous slaves. At least by the 18th century most Ethiopian slaves came from the Galla province in the south. In the 16th and 17th centuries ships carrying slaves criss-crossed the Red sea[10]).

Although the most likely origin of black slaves in Cyprus would have been the Sudan and Ethiopia, important trans-Saharan slave routes connected Wadai, Bornu, Chad, and Kano to Bengazi and Tripoli on the Mediterranean, or even ultimately to Cairo by routes north of the Sahara. Other slaves must have entered the Ottoman world via Tunis and Algiers[11]).

1. On 14 Şevval 1016 Halil çelebi, son of the late Hizir su başi and himself an imperial officer (*yaya başi*), emancipated the female black slave (*ʿarab cariyesi*) Mercane bint ʿAbdullah, of medium height, whom he had inherited from his late father. Mercane was of Tacu origin (Tācuviyy l-asl) (2 27-2). at-Tāguwi was a *nisba* (indicating the slave's geographical place of origin), which T. Walz found in use in Cairo among black slaves in the 18th century[12]). Presumably that must be the same as a people called Tājūwa by R. S. O'Fahey, whom medieval Arab geographers located between Kano (Kanem) and Nubia; that people seem to be connected with a kingdom called Daju which was located in the southern Jabal Marra region in the heart of

---

10) C. Orhonlu, *Habeş...*, pp. 3, 43f., & n., 73f., 100ff. T. Walz, *Trade...*, p. 32. Most of the black slaves in the imperial Ottoman harem also came from Sudan and Ethiopia. Slaves from Dar Fur were "considered honest and hardworking", while those from Sinnar were considered "more handsome", according to Walz. Ethiopian women were deemed to possess "secret sexual powers". *Trade...*, p. 179.

11) T. Walz, *Trade...*, pp. 5 (map), 16-22. R. S. O'Fahey, *Kingdoms...*, p. 160. R. S. O'Fahey, "Slavery...", *passim*. A. G. B. Fisher and H. J. Fisher, *Slavery...*, pp. 72f.

12) T. Walz, *Trade...*, pp. 177f.

Dar Fur region. Peoples speaking the Daju languages today inhabit the area between Chad on the west and Kordofan province east of Dar Fur[13]).

2. Fatma bint Hamze, widow (*zevce' -i metruka*) and executrix of the late el-hac ʿAbdul-Kadir of Aya Sofya quarter of Lefkoşa, was able to prevent a suit by Huri bint ʿAbdur-Rahman, mother (*validesi*) of the deceased, for a black (*zenciye*) female slave (*cariye*) named Fatma bint ʿAbdullah, of Tūnçiriye origin (Tūnçiriye l-asl), whom the widow claimed to have bought six years earlier for 6800 akce. (4 29-2; after II Rebi II 1044) at-Tungurawi is a *nisba* which Walz discovered in use among black slaves in Cairo in the 18th century, with some documents dating earlier found[14]). Around 1800 an "...area (nahiya) of Tangarawa, a province of Dar Sulayh (Wadai)......" is mentioned, where the people were Muslims[15]).

The Tunjur state, according to O'Fahey a much more sophisticated one than that of Daju, had its main center north of the Jabal Marra, and "peacefully replaced" them. "Today people calling themselves Tunjur are to be found scattered from Northern Nigeria to Dar Fur, speaking either Arabic or Kaniere..." They had a brief "but grandiose" empire covering the provinces of Dar Fur and Wadai immediately to the west of Dar Fur which disappeared sometime between 1580 and 1660, perhaps overthrown by Muslim zealots to the east. Later O'Fahey asserts, the break up of Tunjur state c.1580 led local groups to link themselves with foreigners. A contemporary Venetian source attributed that overthrow to a certain person "...who is allied to the Turks" and "supplied with arms by merchants from Cairo"[16]). "A few contemporary records appear...to suggest the cause or motive, the maintenance of the long-distance trade with Egypt and the riverain Sudan across the desert that had

---

13) R. O'Fahey, *Kingdoms...*, pp. 108ff.
14) T. Walz, *Trade...*, pp. 177f.
15) T. Walz, *Trade...*, p. 226 and n.
16) R. O'Fahey, *Kingdoms...*, pp. 108-116.

probably been initiated by Tunjur. By the end of the seventeenth century that trade was well established''[17]).

3. On III Cumadi II 1019 Veli çelebi bn Minnet of Lefkoşa emancipated his very black female slave (*pur siyah cariye*) named Bahit bint ʿAbdullah, who was from Barki (Bārkiyi l-asl) and of medium height (*orta boylu*). (3 145-1) According to Walz, Barqawi slaves sold at the Sudanese slave market of Şandi (Shandi) on the east bank of the Nile were especially esteemed, although slave dealers in Cairo did not have such esteem for them. Possibly the Barqaqi/Barki may be identified with the town of Bara in Kordofan east of Dar Fur and west of Sinnar (although Walz's map places it in Dar Fur.) At least in the 18th century Bara was a commercial center[18]).

Frequency of Black Slaves (See Table I)

Black slaves were common in Cyprus during the period 1590 to 1640. Of 44 slaves from that period whose original homelands were identified, like Russian (*Rus, Rusi l-asl*) and Hungarian (*Macar, Macari l-asl*), half were black[19]). (Blacks were mentioned in other cases as well.) The court records give few hints about the routes by which they reached the island or of how they were used. While the slave markets of Cairo provided the primary source of black slaves introduced into the eastern Mediterranean world in the 17th century, there is no indication whether Lefkoşa had important slave markets of its own or slaves simply reached there sporadically in small numbers in the company of itinerant merchants from Anatolian, Syrian, or Egyptian ports[20]). As the table indicates, neither Greek Orthodox

---

17) R. O'Fahey, *Kingdoms...*, pp. 109-123.

18) R. O'Fahey, *Kingdoms...*, p. 136, and maps pp. 2, 26.

19) An important transit trade in slaves existed in the 16th century between Cairo and Damascus via Palestine, black slaves traveling north and white slaves traveling south. A. Cohen and B. Lewis, *Population...*, pp. 58f. U. Heyd also mentioned the passage of black slaves over that route. *Ottoman Documents...*, pp. 123f., # 73. That could be one way that black slaves reached Cyprus from Cairo.

20) The judicial registers of 18th century Cairo always indicated the color of black slaves, but only infrequently regions of their origin, and then that often was

TABLE I

Cyprus Slaves

origin	male	female	total
Rus (Russian)	5	4	9
black	10	12	22
Eflaki (Wallachian)	1	1	2
Çerkez/Çerkes (Circassian)	3	1	4
Macar (Hungarian)	3	1	4
Gurci (Georgian)	1		1
Rum (Greek)	1		1
Hirvad (Croatian)	1		1
	25	19	44

Prices

Cypriots nor Latins from that island, the archipelago, or Venice provided major sources of slaves; all such slaves would have been white, of course, but the implication is that white slaves too came from beyond the confines of the Ottoman empire *and* the Mediterranean world just as black slaves did.

Male black slaves were only a little less numerous than female black slaves (10 to 12), although some have argued that the norm was a high proportion of females. That was not the case with white females either. In fact, male white slaves were more than twice as

confounded with the region where he had been purchased. T. Walz, *Trade...*, pp. 175f. Y. F. Hasan likewise notes that Arabic sources tell little of the places of origin of black slaves. *The Arabs...*, p. 46. In any case, according to Walz, most black slaves in Cairo apparently came from Dar Fur and Sinnar, especially the former. *Trade...*, pp. 32ff. There some African slaves were designated red, yellow, and green. *Trade...*, p. 176.

common as female white ones (15 to 7). If female white slaves were supposedly more desirable as concubines, they also were scarcer than black ones[21]). Of course, Cyprus was not the only potential market, so there is no way to know to what extent the supply met the local demand. Presumably the female black slaves served as household servants, and to some extent as concubines since their market value was high. It is generally presumed—on the basis of scant evidence—that female white slaves were used almost exclusively as concubines. Male white slaves were sometimes used in urban crafts and businesses, as probably were some of the male black slaves. Some of the males, too, especially the blacks, may have served in household tasks.

The market values (mostly sales prices, but also including the assessed values from some estates) of black slaves in Cyprus do not seem disproportionately below the values of comparable white slaves[22]). If a white slave sold for 3500 akce in 1002, the asking price

---

21) According to Walz, throughout the 18th century female slaves outnumbered males by an average of 3 to 1, although in different years that ratio ranged between 4 to 1 and 7 to 4. *Trade...*, pp. 32, 56. For Ethiopia, according to Orhonlu, 80% of the slaves in the 18th century were females between the ages of 6 and 30. *Habeş...*, p. 101.

22) There seems to be a conscensus of scholars that white slaves were more valuable than black ones in the market place. Cf. R. Brunschvig, "Abd", EI². B. Lewis, *Race and Color...*, pp. 64, 83. A. Mez, *Renaissance...*, p. 158. E. Ashtor asserted that white slaves were much more expensive in Mamluk Egypt and Syria, although his evidence is sparse. *Histoire des Prix...*, pp. 361, 438. Interestingly, Goitein makes no such claim. According to A. Raymond, Mamluk slaves were worth double the value of black slaves in 17th and 18th century Cairo, but in that instance he spoke only of those slaves purchased for and capable of performing as soldiers ("mamelouk"), excluding the other white slaves ("esclaves blancs"), whose value presumably would have been less. *Artisans...*, p. 395. Walz asserts that in 18th century Cairo the selling price of white female slaves was 4 to 6 times greater than black females, while white males sold for 3 to 5 times more than black males, and Ethiopians sold for 20% to 70% more than other blacks. *Trade...*, pp. 207f. Lane's figures for early 19th c. Cairo seem somewhat out of proportion, although sources of white slaves were much restricted in the interval. According to Lane the price of a white slave girl was three to ten times that of an Abyssinian one, while black slave girls might sell for only half to two-thirds the value of Abyssi-

for a black one (*Habeşi*) in 1003 was 7500 akce. (1 31-1; Receb 1002. 184-1; 23 Cumadi I 1003) At about that time a black female slave and her infant (*oglan*) sold for 9200 akce. (1 309-1; 1 Muharrem 1003. 311-6; Muharrem 1003.) In 1016 a black female slave in the estate of a deceased military officer was valued at 5000 akce. (2 89-1; III Receb 1016) Two years later white female slaves sold for 100 guruş, (x 78 = 7800 akce), 11,000 akce, 3 guruş, (x 78 = 234 akce), 26 guruş, (x 78 = 2028 akce), 4600 akce, 3600 akce, and 8000 akce. (3 19-4; 1 Zil-Kade 1018. 21-5; 1 Zil-Kade 1018. 52-7; II Cumadi II 1019. 109-3,4; II Ramazan 1019. 122-22; II Şevval 1019. 129-4; 28 Rebi II 1019. 145-5; III Cumadi II 1019) In 1044 a white female slave sold for 120 riyal guruş, (x 120 = 14,400 akce), and in 1045 a white male slave sold for 6000 akce; a woman purchased a black female slave for 6800 akce in 1038, in 1043 a black female slave in the estate of another woman was estimated to be worth 7000 akce, and in 1046 another black male was sold for 4000 akce. (4 87-2; I Şaban 1044. 127-1; II Receb 1045. 179-1; III Cumadi II 1046. 29-2; II Rebi I 1044. 231-11; III Şaban 1043)

One certainly cannot say that white slaves were more esteemed than black ones on the basis of that evidence from the court of Lefkoşa. Contrary to normal market mentioned elsewhere, the market values of black slaves do not seem to have been lower than those of white slaves in Cyprus.

---

nians. *Manners and Customs...*, pp. 233f. Lewis, *Race and Color...*, p. 83. A smaller body of evidence asserts that female slaves were more valuable than males. B. Lewis, *Race and Color...*, p. 64. Based on a survey of scattered sources, E. Ashtor concluded that between the 12th and 14th centuries male slaves were worth about half the value of females. *Histoire des Prix...*, pp. 499f. Walz says that black females were worth 68% to 74% more than black males. *Trade...*, p. 208. According to Lane, in early 19th century Cairo all women slaves were somewhat more expensive than comparable males. *Manners and Customs...*, p. 192. As Raymond has also noted, prices of slaves vary a great deal, perhaps an evidence of human diversity. Mamluks, for example, ranged between 2000 and 4000 paras early in the 17th century, between 5000 and 10,000 paras at the end of that century. *Artisans...*, p. 395. Walz, too, points to the ''infinite variety'' of slave prices. *Trade...*, p. 207.

298   RONALD C. JENNINGS

Emancipation of Black Slaves

The Koran extols the emancipation of slaves as "an act of piety"[23]. Emancipating black slaves was a normal practice, just like emancipating white ones. All those emancipated seem to have been Muslims, as in fact were all of the other black slaves named.

Kadin Paşa bint Mehmed, wife of the late merchant (*tacir*) Musli of Lefkoşa, freed the 18 year old black (habeşi l-asl) slave of the deceased, who was to be free like all Muslims. (1 234-1, 2; I Şevval 1002) Za'im 'Ali çelebi bn Musa freed his black (*habeşi l-asl*) slave (*'abd-i memluk*) Turmuş bn 'Abdullah. (1 327-2; 15 Muharrem 1003) Racil Halil çelebi bn Hizir su başi freed Mercane bint 'Abdullah, the black female slave (*'arab cariyesi*) whom he had inherited from his late father. (2 27-2; 14 Şevval 1016) Veli çelebi bn Minnet of Lefkoşa freed his black female slave (*siyah cariye*) Bahit (?) bint 'Abdullah. (3 145-1; III Cumadi II 1019) Rahime bint Isma'il of 'Arab Ahmed Paşa quarter freed her black (*habeşi l-asl*) slave (*memluk*) of medium stature named Faide bint 'Abdullah. (4 43-1; II Muharrem 1044) Beyt ul-mal 'amme ve hassa emin Kumari zade Ibrahim beg bn Nasuh declared that the late Nisa hatun of Lefkoşa had one year earlier emancipated her tall black (*zengiye*) female slave Fatma bint 'Abdullah. (4 56-2; I Sefer 1044) Mustafa aga of the notables (*'ayan*), who collects cizye (*jizya*) in Cyprus, freed his black (*habeşi l-asl*) slave Huseyn bn 'Abdullah. (4 59-1; I Sefer 1044)

Legal Procedure and Status

Ottoman legal procedure and the Sharia divided people into two categories, Muslims and non-Muslims (*zimmis/dhimmis*, mostly Greek Orthodox in the case of Cyprus).

---

23) Emancipating slaves was praiseworthy according to the Koran and the Sharia. The Koran counts setting slaves free as an act of righteousness. 2:177; 24:33. Also 58:3 and 19:13 (Pickthall translation). For the Sharia see, for example, d'Ohsson, v. 6, pp. 25f. See also Brunschvig, "Abd"; A. Mez, pp. 168f.; S. D. Goitein, v. 1, pp. 135f., 144f. D'Ohsson also identifies a special kind of emancipation made by the owner in return for the payment of a specified sum of money. P. 26f.

Muslim personal names, which usually had some religious significance, were distinguished in the court records (*sicil*) by the use of "bn" or "ibn", "son of". So Mustafa, the son of Mehmed, was written Mustafa bn Mehmed, a Muslim (by implication), [except occasionally when poor scribesmanship resulted in only the litigant's name being used (e.g., Mustafa)]. Scribes distinguished non-Muslims by using "veled" to express "son of". Then the personal names were neither Arabic nor Turkish. The Lefkoşa judicial register of 1633-1637 is extremely formal in style. In that register, Mustafa bn Mehmed was virtually always "Mustafa bn Mehmed nam kimesne", a person (i.e., a Muslim) named Mustafa bn Mehmed. Ergiro v. Hiristofori was "Ergiro v. Hiristofori nam zimmi", a non-Muslim named Ergiro v. Hiristofori.

In the aforementioned judicial register several exceptions to that pattern occur involving free Muslim blacks at court. Instead of being called "nam kimesne", they were called "nam zenci" ("a black named..."), a designation that has no justification in the Sharia or in Ottoman practice. Indeed, it seems contrary to one of the essential points of orthodox Islam, that all believers are equal[24]).

> Mehmed beşe bn Hasan is legal agent (*vekil*) for his wife (*zevci*) 'Ayni bint Aydin, grown daughter (*kebire kiz*) of the late Rukaye bint Aydin of Lefkoşa, who acknowledges (*ik/it*) before a black (*zengi*) named Bilal bn 'Abdullah, slave of the deceased: Two years ago the deceased Rukaye freed him. (4 71-2; I Receb 1044).
>
> Raziye bint Murid (?) of (?) village of Lefkoşa makes a claim (*da'va/tk*) against a black named (*nam zengi*) Rukan bn 'Abdullah: Rukan has taken possession of (*tasarruf*) of 25 olive trees (*zeytun eşcar*) on the edge of

---

24) Cf. R. Brunschvig, on the equal status before God of free and slave Muslims. "Abd", EI². Of course, the use of that terminology does not necessarily imply that blacks were discriminated against; the court procedure continued as it did with other Muslims. Cf. A. G. B. Fisher and J. J. Fisher, *Slavery...*, p. 100. One can hardly consider that register anomalous. The quality of scribal work far surpasses that of the other Lefkoşa registers read. The style is consistent, with hardly any irregularities. Every case is summarized explicitly, with virtually none of the obscurities and cryptic references which often plague contemporary judicial registers. There can be no doubt that this form was used on purpose.

the village which I inherited from my father. I want justice done (*ihkak-i hakk*). Rukan replies: I bought them from Sunbul aga 8 years ago. When Raziye has no proof, Rukan is invited to take an oath, which he does. (4 95-2; I Ramazan 1044)

A black woman (*zengiye*) named Fatma bint Belal, grown daughter of the late Belal kethuda of Boya (?) hane quarter in Lefkoşa, has her husband (*zevci*) Kara Veli bn ʿAbdullah as legal agent (*vekil*) for making a claim (*daʿva/tk*) against a woman (*hatun*) named Mercan bint ʿAbdullah, wife of the deceased, who has her son ʿOmer halife bn Mustafa as her legal agent: They dispute ownership of a house (*menzil*) in the quarter... (4 128-1; 3 Cumadi I 1045)

Meryem bint Ramazan of Nobet hane quarter of Lefkoşa acknowledges (*ik/tk*) before black (*zengi*) Sunbul bn ʿAbdullah: I was Sunbul's wife (*zevcesi*). Hasan beg, who was Sunbul's owner (*melvasi*), married me to him, giving certain things as dowry at that time. I renounced them in exchange for a divorce which I wished (*hulʿ*). (4 194-1; III Receb 1046. Sunbul apparently was free by that time.) Maro bint Yakimo makes a claim (*daʿva*) against a black named (*nam zengi*) Bereket: He divorced me. (4 240-3; 1044. Unlike most cases in that *sicil*, that entry was hastily and cryptically entered.)

In cases involving other litigants references are made to particular slaves in that form. A black female slave named Fatma bint ʿAbdullah (*cariye* Fatma bint ʿAbdullah *nam zenciye*) was part of the estate of the late Fatma bint Hamze. (4 29-2; II Rebi I 1044) Mehmed beşe bn ʿOmer of Kuri koy village had a black slave named (*nam zengi*) Bilal bn ʿAbdullah who blocked the path of a non-Muslim and struck him. (4 50-1; III Muharrem 1044)

Marriage Between Blacks and Whites

One case refers to a divorce agreed upon by Meryem bint Ramazan of Nobet Hane quarter of Lefkoşa and a black (*zengi*) named Sunbul bn ʿAbdullah whose master (*mevlasi*) Hasan beg had married her to him. (4 194-1; III Receb 1046) In another case Ahmed çavuş bn el-hac Mustafa of Kayik Evran village of Anamur accused a mulatto (*hilasi*) slave of actually being an emancipated slave (*muʿtak*) who had robbed him in Ote Yaka in the company of other brigands (*eşkiya*). (3 46-6; I Cumadi II 1019)

BLACK SLAVES AND FREE BLACKS IN OTTOMAN CYPRUS   301

A black young man (*habeş muşekkel emredd oglan*) named Ramazan, a su başi and legitimate son (*sulbi olgi*) of the late Rustem çavuş, of Larnaka village of Tuzla kaza, makes a claim (*td*) against el-hac Sinan bn ʿAbdullah, who asserts that he had bought Ramazan: My father was Rustem su başi, my mother was Mercan, a black female slave from whom I was born. I have witnesses. Let them be heard in court. Sinan says that he bought Ramazan from zaʿim Perviz beg bn ʿAbdul-Muʿin for 7500 ʿosmani akce. Let him prove that he is of black (*Habeşi*) origin. From ʿudul-i muslimin ʿOsman kethuda bn Rustem, Hasan çavuş bn Mehmed, and ʿAli bn Mahmud confirm Rustem, saying: The late Rustem su başi acknowledged: Ramazan is my slave (*memlugum*), born from my black female slave (*siyah cariyem*) Mercan. He is my legitimate son (*sulbi obli*). (1 184-1; 23 Cumadi I 1003)

BIBLIOGRAPHY

Mustafa ʿAli, *Description of Cairo of 1599*. ed. & tr. Andreas Tietze. Wien, 1975.

E. Ashtor, *Histoire des Prix et des Salaires dans l'Orient Médiéval*. Paris, 1969.

A. Baldacci, "Habeş-eyaleti", *İslam Ansiklopedisi*.

R. Brunschvig, "Abd", EI².

Amnon Cohen and Bernard Lewis, *Population and Revenue in the Towns of Palestine in the Sixteenth Century*. Princeton, 1978.

Allan G. B. Fisher and Humphrey J. Fisher, *Slavery and Muslim Society in Africa. The Institution in Saharan and Sudanic Africa and the Trans-Saharan Trade*. London, 1970.

S. D. Goitein, *A Mediterranean Society*. 3 v. Berkeley and Los Angeles, 1967, 1971, 1978. Esp. "Slaves and Slave Girls", v. 1, pp. 130-147.

I. Gurdi, "Habeşistan", *İA*.

Yusuf F. Hasan, *The Arabs and the Sudan. From the Seventh to the Early Sixteenth Century*. Edinburgh, 1967.

Uriel Heyd, *Ottoman Documents on Palestine 1552-1615*. Oxford, 1960.

Sir George Hill, *A History of Cyprus*. v. 4. Cambridge, 1952.

E. W. Lane, *An Arabic-English Lexicon*. London and Edinburgh, 1865. *Manners and Customs of the Modern Egyptians*. London and N.Y., 1908 (London, 1966).

B. Lewis, *Race and Color in Islam*. New York, [1971].

F. Meninski, *Lexico Arabico-Persico-Turcicum*. 4v. Vienna, 1780. *Thesaurus linguarum orientalium, turcicae, arabicae, persicae*. 3v. Vienna, 1680.

A. Mez, *The Renaissance of Islam*. Tr. S. Khuda Buksh and D. S. Margoliouth. London, 1937 (N.Y., 1975). Esp. "The Slaves", pp. 156-170.

R. S. O'Fahey, "Slavery and the Slave Trade in Dar Fur", *Journal of African History* 14.1973.29-43.

302   RONALD C. JENNINGS

R. S. O'Fahey and J. L. Spaulding, *Kingdoms of the Sudan*. London, 1974.

Mouradgea d'Ohsson, *Tableau Général de l'Empire Othoman*. v. 6. Paris, 1824.

Cengiz Orhonlu, *Osmanlı İmparatorluğu'nun Güney Siyaseti. Habeş Eyaleti*. Istanbul, 1974.

A. Raymond, *Artisans et Commerçants au Caire au XVIIIe siècle*. Damas, 1973.

The New Redhouse Turkish-English Dictionary. Istanbul, 1968.

Mrs. Scott-Stevenson, *Our Home in Cyprus*. 2nd ed. London, 1880.

S. J. Shaw, *The Financial and Administrative Organization and Development of Ottoman Egypt 1517-1798*. Princeton, 1958.

D. Sourdel, C. E. Bosworth, P. Hardy, and H. Inalcik, "Ghulam", *EI²*.

J. S. Trimingham, *Islam in East Africa*. Oxford, 1964.

           Islam in Ethiopia. Oxford, 1953.

           Islam in the Sudan. London, 1965.

Terence Walz, *Trade between Egypt and Bilad as-Sudan 1700-1820*. Cairo, 1978.

9

Resistance to Enslavement in West Africa

Richard Rathbone

Despite the obvious importance of integrating scholarship on pre-19th century African societies with research on black societies in the New World, the Atlantic appears to have remained a formidable barrier to such exchange. Few Africanists can read the Caribbean and American material without wincing when it adverts to the «African background». For the most part such allusions are generalised, often based on rather ancient scholarship and shy of both the complexity and the dynamism of the history of Africa. This remark points no finger of blame but rather seeks to emphasise that historical studies of Africa are now so numerous, detailed and sophisticated that a researcher whose commitment is to understanding the diaspora scarcely has time to master both bodies of data. Students of African history are no more sucessful in their understanding of the American material. Certainly North American and Caribbean scholarship has had a profound impact upon methodology [1] but the rich material on black life on the other side of the Atlantic has never been seriously combed for what it might tell us about the continent from which its subjects had been so recently and rudely forced. An ultimate and obviously desirable synthesis seems remote and it is a matter of regret that a more thorough understanding of the African elements in the world the slaves made is still denied us.

This paper does very little to redress this situation. Its proposition is fundamentally very simple indeed. In the analysis of slave resistance in the Americas there is frequent reference to the significance of the activists' African past. For some authors, the propensity to revolt is in part conditioned by whether slaves were African born or «creole». Others have tangentially suggested that leaders and followers may well have been people traditionally attuned to «jungle war-

(1) This has a long history ; for example all Africanists would happily acknowledge their debt to the pioneering work of scholars on Amerindian language, society and history in the period before the Second World War. More recently there has been a more obvious relationship between the growth of both African and Afro-American historical studies, especially in the United States of America, which is perhaps most obviously seen in the work of and composition of the history group at Johns Hopkins University at Baltimore, Maryland. More generally the work of scholars like Eugene Genovese, Herb Gutman and Nate Huggins has had an inspirational impact upon the growth of a lively school of «revisionist» historians working on the history of Southern Africa, a debt directly acknowledged by some of its most notable figures like Charles van Onselen and Martin Legassick. Recognition of the need to work together and across the canvas is implicit in the career of the late Walter Rodney and is explicitly evoked in recently published conference proceedings such as David W Cohen and Jack Green's *Neither Slave nor free*. Baltimore. 1972 and Shula Marks and Richard Rathbone's introduction to the special number of the *Journal of African History* (Vol. 24, n⁰ 2, 1983) devoted to the history of the family in Africa.

RESISTANCE TO ENSLAVEMENT IN WEST AFRICA

fare», a position betraying a profound ignorance of West African geography but no less attractive for that. Similarly «African» patterns of social and political organisation from chieftaincy, through secret societies, to religious structures have been invoked to explain how rebellion could be mounted in the most disadvantageous circumstances [2]. All such thinking might be true, partly true or even wrong ; what is missing is perhaps a more thorough understanding of a culture of resistance that is discernible through the records and which is rooted very firmly on African soil. By culture of resistance I mean no generalised notion of opposition of the spirit but actual evidence of physical attempts to prevent the forcible removal of people from their home environment. By the time of the high-tide of the Atlantic slave those acts of forcible removal appear to have been more commonly initiated by abuduction, kidnapping and social and economic methods than by outright war and its repercussions. Thus I am not talking about «national» mass resistance, which doubtless was part of the story, but individual acts and especially the actions of those enslaved but awaiting shipment to the Americas. The evidence of resistance at the point of enslavement is thin ; a partial explanation of this is undoubtedly that flight was the preferred method of avoiding the raiders' intentions. The abandonment of villages and fields for the bush whilst slaving parties were in the vicinity was undoubtedly a frequently repeated episode in many peoples, lives but its lack of drama has tended to play it down so far as the record is concerned.

Nonetheless there is clear evidence of the use of main force to prevent capture from the early period when, of course, it was more common for European crews to come into direct contact with their putative victims. The record of Hawkins, third voyage recalls that at Cape Verde» our Generall landed certaine of our men, to the number of 160... to take some Negroes. And they going up into the Countrey for the space of sixe miles, were encountered with a great number of Negroes : who with their invenomed arrowes did hurt a great number of our men...» [3]. By the end of the period such resistance appears to have been as strong. The Commissioner for Sierra Leone reporting to Canning on May 15th, 1824 said that : «In the course of the last year some boats from Bissao... sacked some of the villages there and carried off... to be sold... as many of their inhabitants as they could take. Besides the barbarity of this practise, its

(2) These ideas, crudely caricatured for reasons of brevity, can be found in a large number of works such as Orlando Patterson's *Sociology of Slavery*. London 1967 Roger Bastide's *African Civilisations in the New World*. Eugene Genovese's from *Rebellion to Revolution*. Baton Rouge 1979 and Herbert Aptheker's *American Negro Slave Revolts*. New York 1978 and have found their ways into much of the more general reading.

(3) From Hakluyt's *Principall Navigations*, Glasgow 1903-5, pp. 398-445. Hawkins had in fact encountered no less resistance on the 2nd voyage (1564) where *Principall Navigations* (pp. 9-63) records, *inter alia*, that they, were landing boat after boat, and divers of our men scattering themselves, contrary to the Capitaine's wishes... in the mean time the Negros came upon them and hurt many thus scattered...

Richard RATHBONE

consequence is that the natives within the reach of such kidnapping expeditions are rendered savage and intractable, so much so that they are always disposed to deal harshly with such Europeans as may fall into their hands. He went to relate the story of some islanders seizure of a Portuguese boat's crew who were ultimately released with great difficulty after the payment of a ransom by the Governor of Bissau [4].

Once captured there is no doubt that attempts at escape were frequent. On the long march to the coastal assembly points, captives were frequently manacled as well as harnessed to one another by neck irons. Pinioning was resorted to in some cases as slaves might «strike or stab» their captors [5]. Wadstrom's report goes further in relaying his informant's insight that manacling also prevented captives from suicide attempts. Escape at any point along the extended trails from point of capture to eventual embarkation was clearly perceived as a major risk by the purveyors, and the harsh circumstances of such journeys attest to the vigour and frequency of such attempts.

Despite the forbidding architecture of the coastal forts of West Africa it is clear that captives once ensconced on the coast were no more secure than they had been on the march. The long periods spent awaiting transhipment, periods on occasion in excess of a calendar year, provided the factors with the equally costly alternatives of the risk of escape or more systematic supervision and confinement. If the labour of the awaiting captives was to be used then risks had to be taken. But those risks could result in flight. The strong documentation for the 1680s for the Royal African Company allows us to get some idea of its scale. Conduitt, the chief factor for the Company in Accra reported in June 1681 that flight from the barracoons was common ; he complained that he received insufficient assistance from loc al African political authorities, and in an attempt to force their hands threatened to close down the trade. This threat apparently elicited a guarantee of recompense by the local rulers [6]. Although escape and failure to recapture was clearly being used here as a bargaining counter in local politics, there is less equivocal evidence of escape later in the same year from Accra. The new chief factor, Massell, complained of the lack of legirons in October and other requests from him and his successors for restraining devices are notable aspects of the exchanges between the RAC and its local agents [7]. Visi-

(4) Commissioner to Canning, May 15th 1824, in Correspondance, class A, *Parliamentary Papers* (IUP reprint) vol. XXVII. This and other comments from this useful source suggest on this, and on other occasions, that the anti-slavery squadrons were far from being the only local opponents of the outlawed trade.

(5) From Wadstrom's *An essay on colonisation*, London, 1794. Part 2, p. 14. (the David and Charles reprint of 1968).

(6) This and the following example come from the collection of letters from the *Outfactors of the Royal African Company to the Chief Agents of Cape Coast Castle* which are to be found in the Bodleian library, Oxford.

(7) *Vide supra*.

ON RESISTANCE TO ENSLAVEMENT IN WEST AFRICA

tors to the castles and trade forts today from Gorée southwards are struck not merely by the menacing gloom of the dungeons which let out on to the Atlantic surf, but also by the proliferation of ring-bolts in their walls. It is clear that at no point in the long misery of the march out of Africa were captives safe in the eyes of their captors.

Commodore Collier's second annual report on the settlements on the coast of Africa of the 11th September, 1820 recalls a recent visit to the disused barracoons of Bance Island : During the period of the slave trade... the walls of the slave-yards still prove the whole to have been so contrived as to prevent the chance of escape to the most resolute and infatuated of the miserable victims they inclosed, yet with all these precautions, insurrections, as on board the slave ships, were not uncommon and on one occasion the white managers were threatened ; in the very moment they had dedicated to revelry and licentiousness ; for which the unhappy slaves were all held responsible and condemned to an atonement, by undergoing indiscriminate butchery or suffering dreadful scarification... Armed only with the irons and chains of those who were so confined the slaves audaciously attacked the lock-up keeper, at the moment he made his entré to return them to their dungeons after a few hours of basking in the sun ; but thus bringing upon themselves the close fire of musketry... which they probably neither saw nor contemplated... many obtained their only wish, a relief from their misery by the hand of death, for it can be scarcely be supposed that much value was attached to the life of these beings when a few rusty muskets or three or four bars of iron was the cost per head [8]. Although we cannot often trace the insurrectionary careers of such remarkable rebels, an earlier reference suggests that there was more continuity to resistance than is often supposed. Atkins, the Royal Navy surgeon's *Voyage to Guinea*... of 1735 recalls looking over the slave holdings of a dealer rather aptly called Cracker. «I could not help taking notice of one Fellow among the rest of a tall, strong make and bold stern aspect... He seemed to disdain his fellow slaves for their readiness to be examined... scorned looking at us, refuses to rise or stretch his limbs as his master commanded ;.which got him an unmerciful whipping... ; this same fellow, called Captain Tomba, was a leader of some country villages that opposed them and their trade at the River Nunes ; killing our friends there, and firing their cottages... by the help of my men [says Cracker] surprised and bound him in the night... and made my property». Captain Tomba clearly remained intractable and his subsequent career leads one to suspect that he was not so isolated amongst his fellow captives as Atkins suggested, for he

---

(8) From «Further papers relating to the suppression of the slave trade» in the *Parliamentary Papers* 1821. Vol. XXIII. Collier's writing is unusually sensitive and observant and although this worthy baronet's political heart is worn clearly on his uniform sleeve he seems not to be an elaborator.

Richard RATHBONE

was to lead a mutiny on the Bristol ship *Robert* under Captain Harding's command, a mutiny which Atkins tells us nearly succeeded. What happened to Tomba is unclear although imaginable [9].

Unsurprisingly some of the most dramatic testimony arises out of the circumstances of the Middle Passage. Resistance seems to have taken a wide variety of forms. The Commissioner for Sierra Leone reporting to Canning in April 1825 speaks of something rather like modern industrial action : «A slave vessel entered this river (the Nunes) last November, the residents however refused to load her and she was eventually supplied by the Portuguese from Bissao...» [10] Thomas Phillips' account of the voyage of the *Hannibal* at the end of the 17th century presents us with evidence of suicide which is slightly less equivocal than the log entry of the *James* on April 17th, 1675 which records that» ... a stout man slave leaped overboard and drowned himself». Phillips writes : «... the negroes are so wilful and loth to leave their own country that they have often leap'd out of the canoes, boat and ship into the sea and kept under water till they were drowned to avoid being taken up and saved by our boats... We had about 12 negroes did wilfully drown themselves, and others starved themselves to death for» this their belied that when they die they return home to their own countries and friends again. I have been inform'd that some commanders have cut off the legs and arms of the most wilful, to terrify the rest...» [12].

Phillip's information helps us to understand the circumstances in which insurrection took place, and perhaps to marvel at the clear evidence of the frequency of revolt. Phillips, by no means an inhumane moster [13] tells us that : «When our slaves aboard we shackle the men two and two, while we lie in port and in sight of their own country, for' tis then they attempt to make their

(9) From John Atkins, Surgeon, R.N. *A voyage to Guinea...* London, 1735 cited and quoted in *Documents illustrative of the slave trade* edited, by E. Donnan, Vol II, pp. 265-6, Washington 1930. Other than Atkins' second hand provenance for Captain Tomba his origins remain obscure. It is however a remarkable portrait.

(10) From the Correspondance (Class A) *Parliamentary Papers* Vol. XXIX, 1826. See my comment in footnote 4, supra.

(11) In Donnan *Op. cit.*, vol. 1. p. 199.

(12) *The voyage of the Hannibal, 1693-4...* by Thomas Phillips to be found in Churchill's *Collection of voyages and travels...* London 1732, vol. IV. pp. 218-19.

(13) This comment is based on remarks of Phillips which chime in oddly with his actual role in the trade. Writing of Africans he says, for example, «nor can I imagine why they should be despised for their colour being what they cannot help and the effect of the climate it has pleased God to appoint them. I can't think there is any intrinsick value in one colour more than another, nor that white is better than black». Phillips *Ibidem*. Such comment is less obviously apologetic than for example Atkin's (*Op. cit.* pp. 168-73) whose «it is advisable at all times to have a diligent watch on their actions, yet (abating their fetters) to treat them with all gentleness and civility...».

RESISTANCE TO ENSLAVEMENT IN WEST AFRICA

escapte and mutiny ; to prevent which we always keep centinels (sic) upon the hatchway and have a chest of small arms ready loaden and prim'd constantly lying at hand upon the quarter deck together with some granada shells (grenades) ; and two of our quarter deck guns pointing on the deck thence ; and two more out of the steerage, the door of which is always kept shut and well barr'd ; they are fed twice a day, at 10 in the morning, and 4 in the evening, which is the time they are aptest to mutiny, being all on deck ; therefore all that time, what of our men are not employed in distributing their victuals... stand to their arms ; and some with lighted matches at the great guns that yawn upon them, loaden with partridge (another word for langrage or case-shot)...» [14]. Phillips additionally tells us about how intelligence might prevent mutiny : «we have some 30 or 40 gold coast negroes make guardians and overseers of Whidaw (Whydah) negroes and sleep among them... in order... to give us notice, if they can discover any caballing or plotting among them, which trust they will discharge with great diligence...»[15]. This evidence of the extremely careful policing of slave ships in the relatively early stages of the trade must be seen alongside the frequency of reports of slave revolt aboard ship.

Snelgrave's *New Account of some parts of Guinea and the slave trade...* of 1734 itemises those revolts known to him and they are worth quoting in *extenso*. «Mutinies» he writes «are generally occasioned by the sailors' ill-usage of these poor people... In 1704... on board the *Eagle* galley... commanded by my father (with only 10 crew, and 400 slaves from old Calabar on board)... these circumstances put the Negroes on consulting how to mutiny, which they did at four in the afternoon just as they went to supper (adding weight to Phillips' nomination of the «danger time»)... the Mate fired his pistol and shot the Negroe that had struck my father... at the sight of this the mutiny ended... I went in 1721 in the *Henry*... we were obliged to secure them very well in irons... yet they nevertheless mutinied... «what had induced them to mutiny ?» (the crew enquired). They answered that I was a great rogue to buy them in order to carry them away from their own country and that they were resolved to regain their liberty if possible... A few days after this we discovered that they were plotting again and preparing to mutiny... I knew several voyages had proved unsuccessful by mutinies ; as they occasioned either the total loss of the ship and the White men's lives ; or at least by rendering it absolutely necessary to kill or wound a great number of Slaves... I knew many of these Cormantine negroes despised punishment and even death itself... a month after this... I met.... the *Elisabeth* (upon which a mutiny had taken place)... above one hundred of the Negroes then on board... did not understand a word of the Gold coast language and so had not been in the plot. But this mutiny was continued by a few Cormantee

(14) Phillips. *Op. Cit.* p. 229. Such elaborate precautions were not of course the result of a history of fatalistic Africans who had no option but to play the role of victims in this repulsive commerce.

(15) *Ibidem*. Whether the Gold Coasters were free or slave is not indicated. P. 407.

Richard RATHBONE

negroes who had been purchased about two or three days before... (the Captain of the Ferrers) had on board so many negroes of one town and language it required the utmost care and management to keep them from mutinying...» Snelgrave learnt later that Captain Messervy's «utmost care and management» had failed to prevent a mutiny ten days out from Africa in which Messervy was killed and the mutiny was in the event only put down after the slaughter of 80 of the *Ferrer's* slaves [16]. John Newton, active in the mid 18th century stressed the significance and frequency of such challenges to his and others' commercial success. He believed that insurrection was always' meditated ; for the men slaves are not easily reconciled to their confinement and treatment... they are seldom suppressed without considerable loss ; and sometimes they succeed... Seldom a year passes but we hear of one or more such catastrophes» [17]. The reference to frequency of uprisings seems not to be the «hard-sell» of a merchant group eager to exaggerate the rigours of their business and thus justify the high prices they charged. William Bosman, a man rightly credited with an alert mind and a good eye, wrote in 1705 : «I have twice met with this misfortune ; and the first time proved very lucky to me, I not in the least suspecting it ; but the up-roar was timely quashed by the master of the ship and myself by causing the abettor to be shot throught the head... But the second time... the male slaves... possessed themselves of a hammer... with which... they broke all their fetters in pieces... they came above deck and fell upon our men... and would certainly have mastered the ship, if a French and English ship had not happened to lye by us...

(16) W. Snelgrave. *A New Account of Some Parts of Guinea and the Slave Trade.* London 1734, pp. 162-5.

(17) *Ibidem.* The reference to language homogeneity or heterogeneity in the case of Messervy's ship the *Ferrers* is an important one which I touch on below. The whole question of communication between captives is, to my knowledge, largely untouched. Snelgrave suggests that a large group of mutually intelligible slaves demanded especial care which, to stretch this slight evidence further, suggests that slavers would have taken steps to avoid such a situation. It is interesting to note the drift of the interrogation of John Jackson, a factor for the African Company for 16 years in Africa in the Minutes of Evidence on the settlements of Sierra Leone and Fernando Po on 5th July 1830 in the *Parliamentary Papers* (Cmnd. 661), p. 91. He is asked : Are you aware that the liberated Africans generally speaking speak different languages, and are unable to form a society among themselves from the want of a common tongue ?
Jackson replies : «I have understood so ; but we have some natives at Cape Coast who, I believe belong to the same nations from which the slaves come and have learnt the language of the place ; they continue to speak also the languages of the countries from which they have come». The contemporary evidence of very widespred multi-lingualism in coastal West Africa and the large scale of many of the risings looked at here seem to suggest dynamic processus at work both in the coastal factory area and on ship-board through which usable *lingage francae* emerged. The evidence of the non-participation of some slaves in the revolt on the *Elizabeth* does, of course, suggest a contrary picture and it is, above all, clear that the composition of every slave consignment had its own character and that generalisation is probably dangerous.

RESISTANCE TO ENSLAVEMENT IN WEST AFRICA

(and)... came to our assistance... before all was appeased about twenty of them were killed. The Portuguese have been more unlucky in this particular than we for in four years time they lost four ships in this manner [18].

Newton's own ship the *Duke of Argyle* was subjected to what he argued was a wide conspiracy which was detected but hours before the rising. In 1752 Captain Belson's snow was lost to slaves who later decamped on the Sierra Leone coast [20]. Owen in his *Journal of a slave dealer on the coast of Africa and America* tells of the successful takeover of a French vessel by its captive cargo who managed to kill all the crew. In command, the slaves, or rather ex-slaves, were apparently seeking a safe anchorage when Owen's ship encountered them and attempted to capture both them and their prize vessel. So formidable was their defence that Owen was forced to retire from the exchange and although he tells us little more it seems fair to conclude that the slaves made good their escape. Owen blamed his officers for this reverse ; in another of his accounts he blames his own ill-health for his loss of an entire cargo who rose and decamped to a man off Sherbro Island in 1750 [21].

These are only a few examples of a very large tally of successful and unsuccessful slave risings on ship-board. While there is little direct evidence of a continuum of resistance from capture through the long process of trans-shipment to arrival in the Americas we can at least ask some questions and provide fewer answers about such evidence. Firstly they, and other sorts of incidents, were frequent enough to merit quite prominent mention in the available contemporary sources. There are good reasons to treat these with care. Some of the literature is manifestly «abolitionist» and hence eager to draw attention to examples of barbarism. How generalisable some of the material is can only be a question. Clearly it would be wrong to presume a rebellion in every barracoon, a mutiny on every ship. But through the route of the anti-slavery material *and* importantly through that of the slaving interest itself, I think we do get a picture of geographically and temporally widespread incidence of insurrection. This was equally clearly part of the widespread trader's information about the coast of west Africa. It is notable just how international the examples of insurrection are. Dutch traders, say, knew all about what happened to American or French ships. Africans involved in the trade in a variety of roles were presumably no less aware

(18) William Bosman : *A new and accurate description of the coast of Guinea...* London, 1705, pp. 363-5.

(19) B Martin and M. Spurrel (eds) *The Journal of a slave trader (John Newton) 1750-54* London, 1962, pp. 54-5.

(20) In Donnan, *Op. Cit.* Vol. III. p. 315. A «snow» is described by the *O.E.D.* as : «a small sailing vessel resembling a brig, crrying a main and a foremast and a supplementary trysail mast close behind the mainmast ; formerly as warship».

(21) E. Martin (ed) N. Owen's *Journal of a slave dealer on the coast of Africa and America from the year 1746 to the year 1757.* London 1930, p. 24.

Richard RATHBONE

than their white trading partners whose knowledge of the interior was so light. Wadstrom, for example, uses African informants extensively in his reasoning. Thus I think it fair to assume that these epics, and the smaller and possibly more frequent incidents, were part of the «trading climate» and part of popular knowledge. Given that most slaves destined for the Americas spent long periods within the general confines of the trading establishments it is by no means outrageous to suggest that many of them were well acquainted with the possibly embellished accounts of past events.

Some of the evidence points to the existence of just such an awareness and the prevalence of a «lore» amongst slaves. Phillips writes of Africans whilst still on their native shores «having a more dreadful apprehension of Barbadoes than we can have of hell» [22]. Bosman furnishes us with his ideas of the kinds of fear that gave rise to resistance». We are sometimes sufficiently plagued with a parcel of slaves which come from a far in-land country who very innocently persuade one another that we buy them only to fatten and afterwards eat them... they resolve... to run away from the ship, kill the Europeans and set the vessel ashore [23]. Bosman's implication was, presumably, that such an outrageous idea could only emerge trom a «far in-land» and hence provincial, sensibility, though as with most imputations of anthropophagy a closer examination of the terms being used in the several languages might have yielded him a rather more rational but no less horrific set of apprehensions. But not all captives were from «far in-land». In a very suggestive passage the Commissioner for Sierra Leone writing again to Canning in April 1825 tells of the fate of a French slaver, the *Deux Sœurs*. «The crew» he says «were overpowered by the slaves who killed eight of their (French) number leaving only three persons to navigate the vessel and that under a promise they should land them on some part of the coast near to the Plantain Islands ... *The catastrophe on board may be attributed to several of the slaves who had been employed as labourers and boatman* (in Sierra Leone)... *these men were aware of the consequences of being taken to the coast which no doubt induced them to have recourse to force to effect their liberation* [24].

All institutions have traditions ; and prisons and even concentration camps are and were replete with their own customs and folklore every bit as much as regiments, colleges and public schools. Although we know far too little about the social history of the growing coastal towns in which many slaves spent their last months in Africa, they were indubitably hot-beds of rumour both false and

(22) Phillips. pp. 218-219 *Op. Cit.* The specificity of this comment seems to cast real doubt upon notions of the unawareness or naivety of slaves as to the real natures of what they were enduring.

(23) William Bosman. *Op. Cit.* pp. 363-5. I suggest the linguistic problems with this quotation in the text. Those acquainted with, for example, the ambiguity of the word «chop» in contemporary West African creole and pidgins will be able to imagine some of the difficulties involved in interpreting Bosman's «throw away» lines.

(24) Commissioner Sierra Leone to Secretary Cannings, Apris 10th, 1825. Class A Correspondance, *Parliamentary Papers* Vol. XXIX 1826. My italics. This late but fascinating comment contributes to a wider appreciation of the heterogeneity of slave consi-

RESISTANCE TO ENSLAVEMENT IN WEST AFRICA

true. Against this notion of something akin to «working class consciousness» must be put the plurality of languages spoken within those outposts. The cultural heterogeneity of these forts must be acknowledged and because of the enormous inaccuracy of «ethnic» description it is unlikely that we will ever know what that «cultural mix» was at any point in time [25]. Given the nature of capture and the ways in which trading posts acted as collection points it is highly unlikely that slave «consignments» were often homogenous, however much the traders wished to satisfy the stereotyped preferences of the putative purchasers. But communications clearly did exist, as many of the bigger escape attempts and ship-board mutinies are on a relatively large scale. Moreover it is equally clear that informal leadership emerged within the barracoons. Some will be tempted to see such people as African chiefs, but it would only be the most unlucky chief who found himself enslaved. It would be my suggestion that leadership in the forts, and on ship-board depended less upon traditional status, (a status that would have meant little to strangers to that particular polity), than upon the sorts of factors that throw up group leadership in adverse circumstances. While the world we are dealing with is light-years from the *Colditz Story* it is not ridiculous to suggest that leaders were *inter alia,* the most knowing and those who consistently defied restriction. Francis Moore's description of an attempted break-out of the particularly gloomy confines of Cape Coast Castle in November 1730 (by sawing through the bars at the windows) tells us that the leader had led several such bids for freedom ; his prominence and courage were rewarded by one hundred lashes [26].

gnments as well as to the generation of coastal communities in which, I would argue, slaves played an important and not always brief part. Although the French crew do not succeed, on this occasion, in the impressing of labourers there must have been many cases where such men were carried off. Although it is dangerous to build on single examples, this case raises important questions about the nature of consciousness with which this paper is concerned. The men the Commissioner writes about were manifestly not rural producers nor were they necessarily people clinging in adverse circumstances to older traditional cosmologies.

(25) The inaccuracy either accidental or intended of trader descriptions of slaves are clear to anyone with a working knowledge of the social and political geography of pre-colonial west Africa. There are no fewer problems with ethnic attributions of slave-owners on the other side of the Atlantic, or for that matter, with the ethnic self-identifications of slaves themselves for names, customs and even languages can be acquired. Ethnic categories in pre-colonial west Africa were only rarely the watertight and unvarying identities that a later scholarship infected with 19th century and later nationalisms tended to stress. Most African social systems were absorbtive rather than exclusive and given the area's vivid history of inter-regional trade, human movement and inter-action there is an enormous risk in the over-stretching of trader's taxonomies some of which are clearly casual and ignorant in any case.

(26) Francis Moore : *Travels into the inland parts of Africa* in T. Astley *A new and general collection of voyages* London 1745. Vol. II, p. 49.

Richard RATHBONE

Part of that «knowing» must have included the formidable problem of
what to do with liberty once attained. The coastal belt -and indeed the areas
under the control of the great forest states - were hardly comfortable safe-house
for the self-liberated. Treaty relationships, as we have seen, operated in areas
polluted by the trade and the capture of a runaway- often a fairly obvious
figure in an area dominated by kinship ideology and reality - was often a commercial act. A runaway could be sold or returned for a reward. It is safe to
assume that escape routes and safe territories were part of the essential knowledge of the captive group contemplating escape. Thè fascinating pre-figuring of
maroon societies in the America is visible here, in and just off the the African
mainland. There are many accounts of liberated slave societies in the 18th
century. The Upper Guinea coast has innumerable clusters of islands from Sherbro island northwards. Some of these certainly became favoured sites for the
protection of hard-won independance from servitude. John Matthews in his
Voyage to the River Sierra Leone of 1788 speaks of the Iles de Los just off
modern Conakry as just such a haven [27]. But such free socities also took root
on the mainland. The escape following successful mutiny aboard a Danish
vessel in 1788 lying in the Rokel estuary led to establishment of a free settlement which was called the Deserters' Town a few miles out of Freetown in the
hills [28]. The fact that the narratives of a great many of the initially successful mass escapes end with mass re-captures, sometimes months or even years
laters, suggests that groups stayed together and forged some kind of new society
rather than scattering and attempting to return to their motherlands.

The frequency of escapes, rebellions both successful and unsuccessful
and the intelligence about places of safety for the fugitive, suggests a mounting challenge against not only the Atlantic trade but also against indigenous
institutions of slavery. The 19th century was indubitably the period in which
slavery became a particularly significant economic and social institution within
Africa but it was also a period of extensive self-liberation which threatened
domestic and export economies as well as political control. If was, after all,
the rapid recognition of this that led both British and French to abandon their
opposition to slavery in general and to maintain hostility to the trade in humanity only, whilst smiling upon what they now dignified as «domestic slavery», a
position which was held until the mid - 1920s in some areas of west Africa.
Slavery was a state which few passively accepted or became resigned to. Fear
of captivity haunted all who had any knowledge of this processes and by the
18th century it was only people fortunate enough to live beyond its compass
who could have been innocent of it. There are innumerable accounts of men and
women, like the «free native mariner on board our ship Providence... who once

(27) London 1788, p. 16.

(28) See C.B. Wadstrom. *Op. Cit.* part II, p. 79. The information comes from Wadstrom's
edited version of the *Report of the Directors of the Sierra Leone Compagny* of 1791.

(29) Wadstrom Op. Cit. part II, p. 82.

RESISTANCE TO ENSLAVEMENT IN WEST AFRICA

in irons lost his spirits irrecoverably» and died «by the sulks» [30]. The counterblast to this sense of despair was of course the hope of salvation. Throughout the course of the slave trade, west Africa had become a place in with one could trust few people and, still less, luck to provide such salvation. That much is «fact». What is more elusive is the sense of a growing resistance in thought and action that gave rise to instances where «slaves rose to a man, knocked off each others fetters and... attacked the barricade» [31] as well as the «sulks». As Wadstrom reported, a captain «who surpasses most others in effrontery and hardness of disposition» informed him how best to restrain a cargo : «I put them all in leg-irons ; and if these be enough, why then I handcuff them ; if hand cuffs be too little, I put a collar round their neck, with a chain locked to a ring-bolt on the deck ; if one chain won't do, I put two, and if two won't do I put three ; you may trust me for that... these are not cruelties ; they are matters of course ; there's no carrying on the trade without them» [32]. It would seem as a matter of commonsense, for it is not something that we are likely to be able to prove, that such resistance was part of the cultural baggage the unwilling emigrants took with them to the Americas. It is not a collection of experiences and feelings that will fall easily within the notion of «Africanisms» but it seems likely that they were vital elements in the making of the black diaspora.

(30) *Ibidem*, p. 83.

(31) *Ibidem*, p. 87.

(32) *Ibidem*, p. 85.

10

'By Farr the Most Profitable Trade': Slave Trading in British Colonial North America

Steven Deyle

Much work has been done lately on the nature of slave-trading in British North America. We now have a far more realistic picture of the number of blacks imported into the various colonies, where they came from, and who brought them. Yet most of these studies have focused on individual colonies rather than looking at the overall effect this process had on the entire region. While limited investigations are of course necessary to obtain reasonably accurate results, it is also important to place these findings in a larger context. How did the slave trade affect the various mainland colonies? In what ways were they similar and how did they differ? What function did the slave trade serve in the formation of colonial society? Finally, what constituted the slave trade? Was it only the importation of Africans and West Indian blacks? How important was the selling of slaves between colonists? At what point and why did domestic slave-trading develop? Only by addressing questions such as these can we better understand the influential role the slave trade played in British North America.[1]

I

It is hard to overemphasize the prevalence of slave-trading in colonial American society. It was a normal part of life and conducted in every section of the country. Although much more important in the eighteenth century, slave-trading had also been present from the beginning of settlement. The 'twenty and odd Negroes' who arrived in 1619 may or may not have been the first blacks in British North America, or even actually slaves, but lifetime chattel slavery based on race soon became an established feature in American society. And the

The author would like to thank Doron Ben-Atar, Randy Bergstrom, Betty Dessants, Eric Foner, David Mattern, and Alden Vaughan for commenting on earlier versions of this paper.

ability to buy and sell the labour of individuals and their future offspring was an essential component of the system.[2]

While blacks were present in early Virginia, and their services bought and sold, a full-scale commitment to slave labour did not occur immediately. Initially the colonists favoured indentured servants and not until the 1680s and 1690s did Virginia convert from a labour system of predominantly white servitude to one of predominantly black slavery. A number of factors influenced this decision, including the increasing cost of servants and the decreasing price of slaves, The result was a sharp rise in the number of blacks entering the region. During the 1680s, the Chesapeake imported over 7,000 slaves as opposed to less than 2,000 in each of the three previous decades.[3]

In the eighteenth century the number of slaves imported into the British North American colonies soared. Imports became so heavy that the Virginian William Byrd even feared 'this Colony will some time or other be confirmed by the Name of New Guinea'. Philip Curtin has estimated that from 1700 to 1720 slaves entered British North America at the rate of almost 1,000 per year. This figure rose to over 2,500 in the next two decades and reached a peak of over 5,000 per year in the 1740s and 1750s, only to drop slightly in the period preceding the American Revolution. According to a recent calculation by James Rawley, between 1620 and 1870 traders brought nearly 600,000 slaves into territory that would eventually become the United States, and the vast majority of them came here during the eighteenth century.[4] Simultaneously, the origin of these slaves changed. Initially most blacks entering the colonies came from the West Indies, but by the eighteenth century Virginia was importing most of its slaves directly from Africa. Between 1700 and 1740 over 54,000 blacks entered the Chesapeake, and all but 5,000 of them came from Africa.[5]

The northern colonies also increased their slave imports during the eighteenth century. When New Jersey became a royal colony in 1702 its governor received instructions from the crown to encourage the slave trade, because settlers needed 'a constant and sufficient supply of merchantable negroes, at moderate rates'.[6] Pennsylvania first imported slaves in the late seventeenth century; initially these shipments contained only a handful of individuals, but by the 1730s increased demand stimulated larger cargoes.[7]

New England's commitment to slavery came about through its carrying trade. The first known American-built vessel to bring slaves into the colonies was from Salem, Massachusetts. In 1638 the *Desire* brought back a small parcel of slaves from a trading voyage to the West Indies. New England also sent the first colonial ship to bring slaves back directly from Africa – yet it appears the Puritans did not fully comprehend the nature of that market. In 1645 the *Rainbow* returned to Boston with a small cargo of African slaves, only to have the General Court charge the captain of the vessel with 'kiling, stealing, and wronging of the negers, etc.' To make matters worse this 'haynos and crying sinn of man stealing' took place 'upon a sabboth day'. Since the crime occurred outside its jurisdiction, the Massachusetts Court acquitted the captain, but it returned the cargo to Africa at the colony's expense.[8] By the 1670s Puritan merchants carried slaves from Africa to the West Indies. During the seventeenth century few Africans went directly to New England, although small numbers of West Indian slaves arrived on the vessels' return trips home. By 1700, Boston merchants supplied the entire New England region with West Indian slaves. Rhode Island soon surpassed Massachusetts as the leading slave-trading colony, and New England came to dominate the colonial slave-carrying trade.[9]

In the early seventeenth century New Amsterdam was the principal slave-trading centre in North America. The Dutch West India Company made a decision 'to supply the colonists with as many blacks as it possibly can' and imported slaves as early as 1626. There were few arrivals at first but by mid-century the Dutch had imported enough slaves to give New Netherland the highest black population of all the mainland North American colonies. Officials also encouraged the colonists' commitment to slave labour. Slave-owners could exchange unsatisfactory blacks for company slaves free of charge, and restrictions prevented owners from taking their chattels out of the colony. When one man petitioned to send an insane slave to Virginia the council permitted it only if he imported another as a replacement.[10]

Official commitment to slave labour continued after England gained control of the colony in 1664. The crown ordered government officials to promote the importation of blacks and enacted various policies to accomplish this, including the Board of Trade's 1709 instructions to Governor Hunter to provide a steady and reasonably priced supply of slaves for the colony. As a result, the number of slaves in New York grew from around 2,100 in 1698 to almost 20,000 by 1771, making it the largest slave population north of Maryland.[11]

The northern colonies obtained most of their slaves from the West Indies, and large numbers of Africans did not arrive until mid-century. One reason was the closing of Spanish ports to English ships in 1750, which flooded the market with discounted slaves. Within six years the price of Africans in New York City dropped by 50 per cent. African slaves became so plentiful they had to be quartered in makeshift barracks and sent to neighbouring communities such as Perth Amboy, New Jersey.[12] Also the northern colonies increased their demand for labour, caused in part by the decrease in white servants during the French and Indian War. By the early 1760s Philadelphia merchants began importing blacks directly from Africa, and in 1761 24 firms petitioned the governor to reject an upcoming duty on slaves. They argued for 'the Introduction of Slaves' as the best way to overcome 'the many inconveniencys the Inhabitants have suffer'd for the want of Labourers ... by numbers being inlisted for His Majesty's Service'.[13] The northern colonies always remained on the periphery of the overall trade. Still, they imported their greatest number of blacks during the two decades preceding 1770 and for the first time got the majority of their slaves directly from Africa.[14]

Despite Virginia's earlier establishment, South Carolina became the largest importer of slaves in colonial North America. Englishmen from Barbados began settling there in the 1670s and most blacks brought into the colony during the first few decades came in small shipments from the West Indies. Not until after 1700 did the colony's economy grow large enough to absorb cargoes of from 100 to 300 slaves which the ships in the African trade contained. By the 1720s, South Carolina imported nearly 1,000 slaves each year and more than double that amount in the next decade.[15] The lower south soon surpassed the Chesapeake as the largest importer of slaves. During the mid-1730s, both Virginia and South Carolina imported roughly 2,500 slaves per year. In the Chesapeake this figure dropped somewhat in the next decade due to natural increase among native blacks and sunk to around 800 per year by the early 1770s. However, while Virginia's importation rate declined during mid-century, South Carolina's increased. By the 1760s three times as many slaves entered Charleston as entered Virginia.[16] In the mid-1760s Georgia began direct importation from Africa and soon brought in over 1,000 slaves per year. By the time of the American Revolution three-fourths of all slaves imported into British North America went to the lower south.[17]

Almost every colony attempted to regulate the trade and most enacted some form of import duty. Primarily passed to raise revenue, these levies served a variety of other purposes as well, such as to control debt, increase property values, and prevent insurrection by limiting the number of blacks. Never did the colonies enact duties for humanitarian reasons. However, tariffs proved difficult to collect, due to frequent exemptions, relatively easy smuggling, and the landing of slaves in neighbouring colonies with lower import fees. Officials had little power to enforce laws against slave importations, and Parliament often rejected them. When Virginia passed a high import duty in 1769 the crown vetoed it, claiming it would 'have the Effect to prejudice and obstruct as well the Commerce of this Kingdom as the Cultivation and

Improvement of the said Colony'.[18] South Carolina passed the only effective duty in 1740, following the colonial period's largest slave revolt at Stono. During the 1740s Charleston slave imports dropped to one-tenth the amount of the previous decade. Before 1750 importation returned to its earlier level, but never again did the number of newly imported Africans in South Carolina reach so high a proportion of the slave population as they had in the 1730s.[19]

The main reason for the colonial governments' inability to control the slave trade was the Americans' insatiable demand for labour and the large profits the slave trade provided. By the eighteenth century southern planters invested almost all spare capital in slaves.[20] The Yorktown merchant Francis Jerdone maintained that 'there is not the least fear of selling here, for there is in general as many Purchasers as there is slaves imported', and the Charleston slave-trader Henry Laurens noted there were so many buyers in town 'that a thousand Slaves would not have supply'd their wants'.[21] This seller's market led to high profits for those who could meet the demand. According to Jerdone 'the pay is always better than for any other commodity', and another Virginia merchant claimed it 'by farr the most profitable trade that we have in this part of the world'.[22] Potential large losses from insurrection or death always posed a risk, but the high profit margin made the slave trade a lucrative business. In New York the retail mark-up averaged about 100 per cent of cost, and commission merchants elsewhere charged 10 per cent as opposed to their normal fee of 5 per cent for other merchandise.[23]

The direct importation of Africans dominated the colonial slave trade. Susan Westbury has found that over 90 per cent of the slaves entering Virginia came in this manner, largely in ships designed for the purpose that carried nothing but slaves. English capital controlled it. According to Herbert Klein, English merchants owned 86 per cent of the ships coming into Virginia directly from Africa and carried 89 per cent of the slaves.[24]

The crown did not exclude American traders from the profitable African trade; rather, they usually lacked the capital, resources, and expertise to compete with larger English firms. Even so, West African agents considered Newport merchants important enough to keep them informed of local trading conditions, and most other cities had a few individuals engaged in the trade. In fact, almost all prominent American merchants participated in the African trade at least once. Moreover, the majority of slaves brought by the English passed through colonial factors and commission merchants upon their arrival.[25]

For most colonists the slave trade remained simply another part of their diverse commercial activity. Unlike English merchants, American traders carried a wide variety of goods and usually handled only small parcels of slaves. Sometimes they purchased blacks on consignment, but more often local market conditions determined their cargo decisions.[26] The small handful of merchants specializing in the colonial slave trade indicate its varied nature. And of those few, all traded in other goods as well.[27] Of the 405 firms which imported slaves into Charleston between 1735 and 1775, only three brought in more than 20 vessels and almost 90 per cent had five shipments or less. Of the 1,113 cargoes, one-half had ten or fewer slaves.[28] Similar figures for Virginia indicate that over three-fourths of the boats importing slaves made only one trip.[29] Thus, while the English dominated the African trade, the colonists controlled the local market, bringing in two-thirds of the West Indian and almost all of the small intercolonial trade. Most blacks who came to North America arrived on a small number of English ships, but the majority of boats bringing slaves originated from American ports and had small numbers of blacks on board.[30]

The slave trade became a vital part of the colonial economy. Two-thirds of Rhode Island's ships and sailors directly participated, and an extensive service network developed to support them. Vessels had to be built and mechanics and tradesmen were necessary for repairs. Most important, to supply the ships with goods an enormous distilling industry emerged, making rum New England's largest manufacturing business before the Revolution. And in cities like New York and Charleston, a vast number of legal, financial, and clerical workers handled the voluminous paper work involved in the slave trade: and of course the trade provided the southern colonies with their labour force. As a result, slave-trading became an essential aspect of New England's economy and stimulated economic activity elsewhere.[31]

Like most other mercantile activity in the colonial period, economic and seasonal demands governed the slave trade. Slave imports fluctuated with the various trade cycles, resulting in huge influxes of new arrivals every few years.[32] Two-thirds of the imports came between the months of June and August while almost none entered between December and February. Most planters cited health concerns as the reason for this – newly imported slaves needed to be seasoned before the harsh winter months – but economic factors appear to have been more important. Slaves arriving during the spring and summer could tend that year's crop while those coming at the end of the year performed little work until the next spring.[33]

Slaves, like other cargo, were sold in a variety of ways, with buyers paying in cash, credit, or goods.[34] In Charleston, sales generally occurred at the wharves, although commission merchants sometimes distributed smaller shipments through their stores. Auctions held near the Exchange disposed of those who did not sell quickly.[35] In the northern colonies, some large traders like Robert Ellis of Philadelphia owned their own wharves, and in New York after 1750 only unsaleable slaves went to commission merchants, all others being sold right at the docks. However, most slaves imported into that region either came on consignment or in small parcels on commission. Convenience determined where they would be sold – from ships, warehouses, shops, taverns, or homes. Occasionally, during slow periods merchants such as Thomas Riche of Philadelphia had to 'move them about the Country for Sales'.[36]

Because the Chesapeake lacked major ports, large planters acting as agents for the ship owners sold most of the slaves in that area. For a 5 to 10 per cent fee, they evaluated a buyer's credit, maintained unsaleable slaves, obtained return cargoes, and sometimes leased blacks out on trial. Since the planter had to assume all bad debts, determining a buyer's credit proved most important. Each afternoon the planter waited on board the ship for purchasers to arrive and normally sold a small number of slaves each day. It took anywhere from a few weeks to a couple of months to sell a shipload, depending upon the size of the cargo. Healthy males sold first, followed by women and children, then the elderly and ill. Occasionally middlemen bought slaves to take into the interior for sale. By the late colonial period slave-trading had developed in some Virginia towns such as Yorktown, but most still resembled Williamsburg, where sales were usually local and no regular slave market developed until the nineteenth century.[37]

Colonists frequently complained about the quality of the slaves imported and often refused to buy 'undesirable' individuals. As early as 1679, after receiving a truly 'sad parcell', agents from the Royal African Company warned the central office not to send any more slaves of that sort because 'now good Negroes are soe plenty that few will buy bad though at Low Prizes'.[38] However, judging from the statements of colonial merchants, the poor quality of slaves remained a problem. In 1737 the son of one of Virginia's largest planters and slave traders, Robert 'King' Carter, complained to his agent in Liverpool that 'if it had not been for the long Credit that was given, such a Number of Children as there was in that Cargo, must been given away'. Nineteen years later in Charleston, Henry Laurens explained to his agent in Barbados why his latest shipment had not sold: 'Our People thought them a very indifferent parcell, that they were much too small a People for the business of this Country & on this Account many went away empty handed that would otherways have purchas'd'.[39]

The slaves most preferred by the colonists were young healthy men between the ages of 15 and 25. One Massachusetts captain about to purchase slaves for the South Carolina market had instructions to 'buy no girls, and few women; but buy prime boys and young men'. A Charleston merchant informed his agent in the West Indies to send 'expecially Boys & Girls of about 15 or 16 years of Age of which 2/3 Boys & 1/3 Girls'. Because of this demand men arrived at a rate of two to one over women – with an enormous effect on black demographics and social life. The sexual imbalance delayed the development of black families, a problem especially troublesome in areas experiencing high slave importation such as South Carolina, which did not have a natural increase among blacks until the 1750s.[40]

The origins of slaves also influenced sales. Occasionally buyers ordered West Indian blacks on consignment, but colonists almost always preferred African slaves. They believed cargoes from the West Indies were 'refuse' and often paid much less for them than they would for African slaves. One Maryland slave trader explained that most people are 'fearful of them being Rogues & will not give ye price of new Negroes for them', and a Virginia merchant even claimed that a small African boy, if new, 'will sell considerably better than the best West India Negroes, for it is generally supposed that they are ship'd off for great crimes'.[41] In South Carolina and Georgia, buyers also had strong ethnic prejudices based on stereotyped perceptions of labour capabilities and disposition. They generally preferred Africans from the Senegambia and Gold Coast and shunned those from the Bight of Biafra. In addition, buyers in the lower south favoured tall slaves over short.[42]

Since most slaves sent to the northern colonies worked on small farms or as house servants, buyers wanted their slaves young and seasoned. They valued such traits as honesty, sobriety, and diligence, and numerous advertisements stressed these qualities which greatly added to a slave's worth. The ability to speak the native language also improved an individual's value. Slaves that 'hath ye English Speech' sold for more money everywhere except in some parts of New York. In 1735, Philip Livingston of Albany had to sell a valuable slave solely because the man was 'unable to Learn to speak Dutch'.[43]

However, due to the small number of slaves the northern colonies imported, the blacks brought there normally included only those who could not be sold elsewhere. In 1708, Governor Dudley of Massachusetts complained to the Board of Trade that the slaves sent from the West Indies were 'usually the worst servants they have'.[44] Northern traders frequently had trouble selling the 'refuse' or 'waste slaves' who formed the bottom end of the labour market and often remained on hand for long periods of time. They were usually sickly and 'unlikely', and some even came unclothed. In 1702, Philadelphia merchant Isaac

Norris informed his West Indian agent that he had to dress a woman he received, 'it not being a Custom here for ym to go Naked – people will not buy ym So'. Two years later Norris temporarily quit the business, wanting nothing more to do with 'those kind of Creatures'.[45]

II

While blacks imported from Africa or the West Indies constituted the majority of slaves sold in the colonies, by the eighteenth century a small domestic trade had also developed. The intercolonial sale of slaves never fully materialized into a substantial trade, but occasionally merchants who carried goods between colonies included slaves with their other commerce. In contrast to the nineteenth-century interstate trade in which most slaves went south after sale, in the colonial period the opposite normally occurred. Some northern owners shipped excess or 'undesirable' slaves south, but far more often northern traders brought blacks back on their return trips home from Virginia or South Carolina. One explanation for this was the large number of slaves the southern colonies received from Africa and the West Indies. They had an abundant supply and could easily part with the small parcels the nothern colonies demanded. This proved especially true for South Carolina, where over 40 per cent of all blacks who entered the mainland colonies arrived. Charleston merchants routinely supplied Georgia and North Carolina planters and sometimes sent slaves to Virginia and the northern colonies as well.[46]

Even so, imports from other colonies always remained small, averaging less than 5 per cent of the overall colonial trade.[47] The main reason stemmed from the same concerns buyers had about purchasing slaves from the West Indies: they feared only sickly and 'unruly' blacks would be sent. According to one Virginian 'it is known they are always sent for some bad quality', and in many cases this was true. Several colonies passed higher import duties on slaves imported from New World ports to discourage this practice. In 1721 the South Carolina Assembly placed a tariff three times greater on slaves not imported directly from Africa, claiming 'it has proved to the detriment of some of the inhabitants of this Province who have purchased negroes imported here from the Colonies in America, that they were either transported thence by justice or sent off by private persons for their ill behavior or misdemeanours'. The New York legislature was even more emphatic when it justified a similar act, explaining 'we are supplied with the Refuse of their *Negroes* and such Malefactors, as would have suffered Death in the Places from whence they came, had not the Avarice of

their Owners, saved them from the publick justice by an early Transportation into these Parts'.[48]

The domestic slave trade assumed its greatest impact not on the
intercolonial level but with the increased importance of local trading.
The rise of a native-born black population had the biggest effect
on this change. Slaves had always been sold at estate sales and privately
between owners, but with the growth of a native-born black population in the mid-eighteenth century the significance of such sales
increased. Colonists came to consider Africans 'outlandish' and paid
much less for them than American-born blacks, who were already
acculturated and often had developed some skills. In Virginia, only
small planters who could not afford the more desirable creole slaves
bought Africans. Therefore, while buyers chose Africans over blacks
from other colonies, they preferred blacks native to the area, and
sale notices always mentioned when slaves were born in the colony.[49]

By the end of the colonial period, slaves on the auction block had
become a regular feature in American life. Throughout the country
sheriff's sales always attracted buyers and slave auctions occurred in all
colonial cities. In New York they took place weekly, sometimes even
daily, and most commission houses dealt in this trade. By the 1750s a
public auction block had been established on Charleston Neck to
handle large parcels of slaves. Although indiviuals sold at auction
usually brought less money than those sold privately, it became a quick
and easy way of transferring property.[50]

A major boost in the development of the domestic slave trade
came with the establishment of colonial newspapers, which provided
a wider and more readily available market for the traders' wares.
Newspapers contributed additional services in helping to bring buyer
and seller together. Frequently ads concluded with 'enquire of the
printer', which gave the public an easy place to obtain information
about a sale. Some historians, such as Frederic Bancroft, have argued
that this device helped to conceal the seller's identity due to shame
in having to part with his slaves. While this might have been the
case for some, it does not seem to be the main reason; this instruction to
the buyer often appeared with other forms of merchandise as well,
and indicates that newspapers primarily wanted to help customers
complete a sale.[51]

Editors offered this service because slave sales provided their newspapers with much-needed advertising revenue. The first American
weekly (*Boston News-Letter*) appeared in 1704, and almost from the
beginning it contained advertisements of slaves for sale. From this
initial publication until the legal abolition of slavery, most local papers
listed slave sales. Not only did newspapers come to play a crucial role in

the development of domestic slave-trading but the relationship proved reciprocal and beneficial to both.[52]

House servants and skilled labour constituted the biggest demand in the domestic market. Consequently, native-born slaves prevailed in this group and were sold either alone or in small lots. Sometimes owners offered them with white or Indian servants. Slaves tended to be between the ages of 14 and 20; rarely did those over 40 appear, although one New Yorker tried to sell a 70-year-old man. As previously mentioned, slaves of this nature predominated in the northern colonies, but even in the south the domestic trade flourished by the end of the colonial period, especially in Charleston with its urban demands. Although most slave advertisements in Virginia featured parcels of ten or more (usually for estate sales), those sold individually were normally domestics or skilled labourers. It is not surprising that buyers in the southern colonies valued the same personal qualities in their house servants that northerners did and often mentioned traits such as 'neither a Thief, Whore, nor Drunkard' in their advertisements.[53]

Slaves appeared in the domestic trade for a variety of reasons: an owner's death or need for money, lack of work, foreclosure on a lien, even for speculative purposes. Of course, incompatibility was a common motive. Explanations for sale included everything from 'having too great a spirit for a mistress to manage' to 'too long a tongue'. One South Carolinian sold a family of slaves 'for no other reason, than that they don't like to live with the subscriber'.[54] A frequent explanation for sale was 'given to drink' . While this problem occurred everywhere it proved especially troublesome in Charleston. Numerous sellers complained of slaves who 'cannot be kept from the Dram shops, of which there are too many in this Town'. One owner recommended that since his slave 'cannot be kept from Liquor in Town, she will best suit a Person living in the Country'.[55]

A slave woman's ability to reproduce could also cause her sale and illustrates one of the most striking differences between the colonial slave trade and that of the antebellum period. In the plantation south, owners appraised women for their labour potential, not their child-bearing capabilities. Nevertheless, planters usually welcomed small children because they could do some work and would be of value later. In urban areas and the small-farm north where blacks did more specialized work and lived in closer proximity to their masters, owners considered slave infants a greater nuisance than their worth as increases in capital.[56] Therefore, in contrast to rural planters, and unlike in the nineteenth century when a slave woman's ability to produce children became a valuable asset, in the colonial period urban owners often cited this as a reason for sale, especially in the north. In

New York, one master offered a woman because 'she breeds too fast for her Owner to put up with such Inconvenience', and another sold a husband and wife 'for no Fault, save getting of Children'.[57] In Philadelphia, one woman had 'no other Fault but that she breeds fast'; another owner did not want 'to have a breeding Wench in the Family'.[58] Some buyers in Charleston also preferred their house servants to be 'without a Child'. Sterility became so valued that the advertisement 'has been married several years without having a child' proved a positive selling point. One New Yorker offered to exchange a healthy 17-year-old girl for a middle-aged woman that 'gets no children'.[59]

When buying and selling slaves owners throughout the colonies gave little consideration to familial relationships, although most blacks lived in family arrangements by the end of the colonial period. Sellers sometimes cited slave affections as a reason for sale. One Connecticut master sold a man for his 'too great fondness for a particular Negro wench in his old neighborhood', and a Philadelphian offered a woman because 'she wants to be married, which does not suit the family she is in'. Occasionally, owners showed respect for slave domestic ties, but this was always the exception rather than the rule and usually done more for practical reasons than genuine concern.[60]

Because of their undesirability, children were frequently sold. Mothers and their suckling infants normally stayed together, but this was not always so. One Boston owner offered a nineteen-year-old woman with her six-month-old baby to be sold either 'together or apart'. In New York a master advertised his slave 'with or without her female daughter', and in Charleston a woman's mulatto child 'may be sold with her' if the buyer so desired. Small infants were often sold on their own, and advertisements for children past weaning were common. Sometimes whole parcels appeared, such as the thirty 'Boys and Girls from 14 or 15 down to the ages of two or three years' who were sold at auction in Virginia.[61] Occasionally buyers advertised for small children, such as the New Yorker who 'wanted, a Negro Girl, Between 4 and 8 Years old', but most owners in the north considered slave offspring such a nuisance that many offered to give them away, and one Bostonian actually volunteered to pay anyone who would take his.[62]

Some owners honestly reported the faults of their available slaves, but many others were less scrupulous in their descriptions. Cases of fraudulent slave sales filled the courts. Such practices as darkening the hair of elderly slaves, selling mortgaged slaves as good-titled, and palming off unhealthy slaves as sound frequently occurred. Some owners transacted private sales on a conditional basis, but the courts usually considered most purchases final. The problem became so severe that in 1767 the Massachusetts General Court tried to pass a bill 'to prevent Frauds in the sale of Negroes'. For unknown reasons, after two readings the Court tabled it.[63]

Except for some minor opposition to the African trade from Quakers and individuals such as Samuel Sewall, slave-trading received widespread social acceptance during the colonial period.[64] No social stigma prevailed against individuals selling slaves, whether privately or through a slave trader, and no distinction existed between sales for necessity and those for speculation. No one questioned the moral right of an owner to sell his property. Colonists treated a slave sale as simply another business transaction, a perception true for small owners and large merchants alike.

The high social position of the leading American slave-traders provides the main explanation for this situation. These men had impeccable status and included many of the most honourable names in colonial society. Slave-traders served as judges, councilmen, mayors, assemblymen, governors, and later congressmen and senators. The philathropist Peter Faneuil, who donated Faneuil Hall (the 'Cradle of Liberty') to the city of Boston, amassed part of his fortune through the slave trade, and two Massachusetts slave-traders, William Pepperell and Charles Hobby, were among the few Americans to be knighted by the king. Many of the leading Revolutionary patriots, including John Hancock and Robert Morris, imported slaves. The largest slave-trader in North America was Henry Laurens, who later served as president of the Continental Congress and a negotiator for the United States at the Paris Peace Conference in 1782. The prominent stature of the leading slave-traders helped to legitimatize the selling of slaves and illustrates the widespread acceptance and importance that slavery and the slave trade had in colonial life.[65]

In short, slave-trading was an important part of colonial American society. Although not fully developed until the eighteenth century, slave-trading had been present from the beginning of settlement, and all regions of the country actively participated in it. It was an essential component in the colonial economy, supplying both service employment and a labour force. Most slaves traded in the colonial period were blacks imported from Africa and the West Indies, but a small domestic trade also appeared, supported in part by the emergence of a native-born black population and local newspapers. Slave-trading carried no social stigma because slavery was widely accepted and because the leading slave-traders in America were men of high social and political stature. During the colonial period, slave-trading was anything but a 'peculiar' aspect of American society.

NOTES

1. Jay Coughtry, *The Notorious Triangle: Rhode Island and the African Slave Trade, 1700–1807* (Philadelphia, 1981); James G. Lydon, 'New York and the Slave Trade, 1700 to 1774', *William and Mary Quarterly*, 3d ser., 35 (1978), 375–94; Darold D. Wax, 'Negro Imports into Pennsylvania, 1720–1766', *Pennsylvania History*, 32 (1965), 254–87; Darold D. Wax, 'Black Immigrants: The Slave Trade in Colonial Maryland', *Maryland Historical Magazine*, 73 (1978), 30–45; Herbert S. Klein, 'Slaves and Shipping in Eighteenth-Century Virginia', *Journal of Interdisciplinary History*, 5 (1975), 383–412; Herbert S. Klein, 'New Evidence on the Virginia Slave Trade', *Journal of Interdisciplinary History*, 17 (1987), 871–7; Walter Minchinton, et al., *Virginia Slave Trade Statistics, 1698–1775* (Richmond, 1984); Susan Westbury, 'Slaves of Colonial Virginia: Where They Came From', *William and Mary Quarterly*, 3d ser., 42 (1985), 228–37; Susan Westbury, 'Analysing a Regional Slave Trade: The West Indies and Virginia, 1698–1775', *Slavery and Abolition*, 7 (1986), 241–56; Allan Kulikoff, *Tobacco and Slaves: The Development of Southern Cultures in the Chesapeake, 1680–1800* (Chapel Hill, 1986); Daniel C. Littlefield, *Rice and Slaves: Ethnicity and the Slave Trade in Colonial South Carolina* (Baton Rouge, 1981).

2. For a discussion of the first blacks in Virginia see Winthrop D. Jordan, *White Over Black: American Attitudes Toward the Negro, 1550–1812* (Chapel Hill, 1968), pp.73–5; Alden T. Vaughan, 'Blacks in Virginia: A Note on the First Decade', *William and Mary Quarterly*, 3d ser., 29 (1972), 469–78; and Robert McColley, 'Slavery in Virginia, 1619–1660: A Reexamination', in Robert H. Abzug and Stephen E. Maizlish, eds., *New Perspectives on Race and Slavery in America* (Lexington, KY, 1986), pp.11–24.

3. Our knowledge of the initial status of blacks in Virginia remains inconclusive, but by the mid-1620s they were being sold as commodities and by the 1640s treated as slaves for life. For varied interpretations of the transformation of the Virginia labour force in the 17th century see Jordan, *White Over Black*, pp.74–82; Edmund S. Morgan, *American Slavery, American Freedom: The Ordeal of Colonial Virginia* (New York, 1975), pp.296–308; Russell Menard, 'From Servants to Slaves: The Transformation of the Chesapeake Labor System', *Southern Studies*, 16 (1977), 355–90; Ira Berlin, 'Time, Space, and the Evolution of Afro-American Society on British Mainland North America', *American Historical Review*, 85 (1980), pp.68–71; T.H. Breen and Stephen Innes, *'Myne Owne Ground': Race and Freedom on Virginia's Eastern Shore, 1640–1676* (New York, 1980), pp.19–32, 107–9; Kulikoff, *Tobacco and Slaves*, pp.37–41; and David W. Galenson, *Traders, Planters, and Slaves: Market Behavior in Early English America* (New York, 1986), p.68.

4. Byrd to the Earl of Egmont, 12 July 1736, Elizabeth Donnan, ed., *Documents Illustrative of the History of the Slave Trade to America*, 4 vols. (Washington, 1930–35), 4: 131. Rawley's actual estimate of the number of Africans entering British North America and the United States (including Louisiana) is 596,751 – or approximately 6% of the total number of Africans transported to the new world. Philip D. Curtin, *The Atlantic Slave Trade: A Census* (Madison, 1969), p.216; Randall M. Miller and John David Smith, eds. *Dictionary of Afro-American Slavery* (New York, 1988), pp.677–8. Since the publication of Curtin's book a number of revisional works have appeared. However, except for some minor adjustments most of Curtin's original estimates have held up well. For a good summary of these revisional works see Paul E. Lovejoy, 'The Volume of the Atlantic Slave Trade: A Synthesis', *Journal of African History*, 23 (1982), pp.473–501.

5. While Herbert Klein claims that Virginia did not import a majority of its slaves directly from Africa until the 1720s, Allan Kulikoff places this shift closer to the turn of the century. Susan Westbury also agrees with the 1700 date and argues it could have occurred even as early as the 1670s. The estimates of Kulikoff and Westbury appear the most plausible and it seems safe to assume that most slaves came directly from Africa by 1700. Klein, 'Slaves and Shipping in Virginia', 384–86; Kulikoff,

Tobacco and Slaves, pp.64–5, 320–1; Westbury, 'Slaves of Colonial Virginia', 228–37.

6. Queen Anne to Lord Cornbury, 16 Nov. 1702, Aaron Leaming and Jacob Spicer, eds., *The Grants, Concessions, and Original Constitutions of the Province of New Jersey* (Somerville, NJ, 1881), p.640. For accounts of the growth of slavery in New Jersey see Henry S. Cooley, *A Study of Slavery in New Jersey* (Baltimore, 1896, pp.9–18, 30–1; and Edgar J. McManus, *Black Bondage in the North* (Syracuse, 1973), pp.4, 13.

7. *Ibid.*, pp.4–5, 13–14; Wax, 'Negro Imports into Pennsylvania', 254–87; Gary B. Nash, 'Slaves and Slaveowners in Colonial Philadelphia', *William and Mary Quarterly*, 3d ser., 30 (1973), 225–8. The earliest attack on the slave trade came in the late 17th century from Pennsylvania Quakers, and by 1715 Philadelphia Friends had determined that all members who participated in this business would be 'dealt with and advised, to avoid that practice'. Still, Quakers actively engaged in the slave trade to Pennsylvania, especially before the 1730s, and most did not drop out until the 1760s. Minutes of the Yearly Meeting, quoted from Darold D. Wax, 'Quaker Merchants and the Slave Trade in Colonial Pennsylvania', *Pennsylvania Magazine of History and Biography*, 86 (1962), 156–57. See also Jean R. Soderlund, *Quakers & Slavery: A Divided Spirit* (Princeton, 1985); Sharon V. Salinger, *"To Serve Well and Faithfully": Labor and Indentured Servants in Pennsylvania, 1682–1800* (New York, 1987); and Gary B. Nash, *Forging Freedom: The Formation of Philadelphia's Black Community, 1720–1840* (Cambridge, MA, 1988), ch. 1.

8. An excellent source for material on all aspects of the slave trade in colonial America is Donnan, *Documents of the Slave Trade*, esp. vols. 3–4. For accounts of the *Rainbow* incident see *ibid.*, 3: 6–9; Jordan, *White over Black*, pp.69–70; and Lorenzo J. Greene, *The Negro in Colonial New England, 1620–1776* (New York, 1942), pp.67–8. For New England slave-trading in the 17th century see *ibid.*, pp.18–22.

9. *Ibid.*, pp.22–8, 34–6; James A. Rawley, *The Transatlantic Slave Trade: A History* (New York, 1981), pp.341–84; Coughtry, *The Notorious Triangle*.

10. Not until 1660 did Maryland or Virginia have a larger black population than New Netherland. Charter of Freedoms and Exemptions (7 June 1629), quoted from Vivienne L. Kruger, 'Born to Run: The Slave Family in Early New York, 1626 to 1827', Ph.D. diss. (Columbia University, 1985), p.34. *Ibid.*, pp.11–12, 34–67; McManus, *Black Bondage*, pp.2–5, 8–9; Thomas J. Davis, 'Slavery in Colonial New York City', Ph.D. diss. (Columbia University, 1974), pp.22–6. Valuable information on the early slave trade in New York can also be found in E.B. O'Callaghan, ed., *Voyages of the Slavers St. John and Arms of Amsterdam* (Albany, 1867), esp. pp.99–232. For reference to the petition of Samuel Edsal, 20 Jan. 1661, see *ibid.*, pp.182–3.

11. Board of Trade to Hunter, 27 Dec. 1709, E.B. O'Callaghan and B. Fernow, eds., *Documents Relative to the Colonial History of the State of New York*, 15 vols. (Albany, 1853–87), 5: 136; Evarts B. Greene and Virginia D. Harrington, *American Population before the Federal Census of 1790* (1932; rep. ed., Gloucester, MA, 1966), pp.92, 102; Edgar J. McManus, *A History of Negro Slavery in New York* (Syracuse, 1966), pp.23–5, 172; Davis, 'Slavery in New York', 63–95; Rawley, *Transatlantic Slave Trade*, pp.385–96; Kruger, 'Born to Run', 68–85.

12. McManus, *Black Bondage*, pp.20–3; Lydon, 'New York Slave Trade', 376–86; Kruger, 'Born to Run', 83–4.

13. The Petition of Divers Merchants of the City of Philadelphia, 1 Mar. 1761, proved unsuccessful. See Samuel Hazard, ed., *Colonial Records of Pennsylvania*, 16 vols. (Philadelphia, 1852–53), 8: 576. Nash, 'Slaves and Slaveowners', 229–31; Darold D. Wax, 'Negro Import Duties in Colonial Pennsylvania', *Pennsylvania Magazine of History and Biography*, 97 (1973), 35–7; Darold D. Wax, 'Africans on the Delaware: The Pennsylvania Slave Trade, 1759–1765', *Pennsylvania History*, 50 (1983), 38–49.

14. Wax, 'Negro Imports into Pennsylvania', 254–87; Lydon, 'New York Slave Trade', 378–81; Berlin, 'Time, Space, and Evolution', 51–2.

15. John D. Duncan, 'Servitude and Slavery in Colonial South Carolina, 1670–1776', Ph.D. diss. (Emory University, 1971), ch. 3; Peter H. Wood, *Black Majority: Negroes in South Carolina from 1670 through the Stono Rebellion* (New York, 1974), pp.43–7, 131, 151; Berlin, 'Time, Space, and Evolution', 54–9.

16. Klein, 'Slaves and Shipping in Virginia', 385, 409–10; Westbury, 'Slaves of Colonial Virginia', 228–37; Kulikoff, *Tobacco and Slaves*, pp.64–5, 70–3.

17. Georgia officially legalized slavery on 1 Jan. 1751; however, not until the mid-1760s did its economy grow large enough to absorb direct importation from Africa. See Thomas R. Statom, Jr., 'Negro Slavery in Eighteenth-Century Georgia', Ph.D. diss. (University of Alabama, 1982), pp.156–9; and Betty Wood, *Slavery in Colonial Georgia, 1730–1775* (Athens, GA, 1984), pp.98–9. Klein, 'Slaves and Shipping in Virginia', 409–10.

18. Every colony except New Hampshire, Connecticut, Delaware, and North Carolina passed an import duty on slaves. Maryland enacted the first in 1695 followed by Virginia in 1699. George III to Lt. Gov. Nelson, 10 Dec. 1770, Colonial Slave Document, Manuscripts Department, University of Virginia Library, Charlottesville (UVA); Greene, *Negro in New England*, pp.50–7; McManus, *Black Bondage*, pp.30–5; Wax, 'Negro Import Duties in Pennsylvania', 22–44; Darold D. Wax, 'Negro Import Duties in Colonial Virginia: A Study of British Commercial Policy and Local Public Policy', *Virginia Magazine of History and Biography*, 79 (1971), 29–44; Donald M. Sweig, 'The Importation of African Slaves to the Potomac River, 1732–1772', *William and Mary Quarterly*, 3d ser., 42 (1985), 514–24; Duncan, 'Servitude in South Carolina', 163–77; Rawley, *Transatlantic Slave Trade*, pp.316–19.

19. Duncan, 'Servitude in South Carolina', 169–72; Wood, *Black Majority*, p.325.

20. *Ibid.*, pp.150–3; Kulikoff, *Tobacco and Slaves*, pp.82–5.

21. Francis Jerdone to William Buchanan, 26 May 1750, Donnan, *Documents of the Slave Trade*, 4: 140; Laurens to Devonsheir, Reeve, & Lloyd, 31 July 1755, Philip Hamer, ed., *The Papers of Henry Laurens*, 10 vols. (Columbia, SC, 1968–), 1: 304.

22. Francis Jerdone to William Buchanan, 26 May 1750, Donnan, *Documents of the Slave Trade*, 4: 140; William Allason to Crosbies and Traffords, 4 Aug. 1761, quoted from Wax, 'Negro Import Duties in Virginia', 43.

23. David D. Wallace, *The Life of Henry Laurens* (1915; rep. ed., New York, 1967), pp.47, 75; McManus, *Black Bondage*, pp.12–13; Coughtry, *Notorious Triangle*, pp.19–20.

24. Klein's original estimate of the number of slaves entering Virginia directly from Africa is slightly less than Westbury's (82%). However, in a recent review essay Klein has updated his data and found that while most of his initial observations remain the same, he has raised this figure to 85%. Still, because of her method of tabulation Westbury's estimate of 90% seems more convincing. Westbury, 'Slaves of Colonial Virginia', 234–6; Klein, 'Slaves and Shipping in Virginia', 392, 404–5; Klein, 'New Evidence on the Trade', 871–7.

25. Coughtry, *Notorious Triangle*, esp. pp.5–55; Susan Westbury, 'Colonial Virginia and the Atlantic Slave Trade', Ph.D. diss. (University of Illinois at Urbana-Champaign, 1981), ch. 6. For accounts of colonial Americans engaged in the African trade see Darold D. Wax, 'Thomas Rogers and the Rhode Island Slave Trade', *American Neptune*, 35 (1975), 289–301; Darold D. Wax, 'The Browns of Providence and the Slaving Voyage of the Brig *Sally*, 1764–1765', *American Neptune*, 32 (1972), 171–9; and Virginia B. Platt, '"And Don't Forget the Guinea Voyage": The Slave Trade of Aaron Lopez of Newport', *William and Mary Quarterly*, 3d Ser., 32 (1975), 601–18.

26. Wax, 'Negro Imports into Pennsylvania', 255–60; Lydon, 'New York Slave Trade', 388–90; Rawley, *Transatlantic Slave Trade*, pp.338–51; Westbury, 'Analysing a Regional Trade', 241–56.

27. For an example of the wide variety of goods sold by a major Rhode Island trader see Stanley F. Chyet, *Lopez of Newport: Colonial American Merchant Prince* (Detroit,

1970). One of Philadelphia's most active slave importers was Robert Ellis. See Darold D. Wax, 'Robert Ellis, Philadelphia Merchant and Slave Trader', *Pennsylvania Magazine of History and Biography*, 88 (1964), 52–69. Stephen Loyde was an early slave dealer in Virginia. See his journal and ledger (1708–11) in the Tayloe Family Papers, UVA. For South Carolina traders see *Papers of Henry Laurens*, 1: xiv–xv, and *passim*; Walter B. Edgar, ed., *The Letterbook of Robert Pringle* [1737–45], 2 vols. (Columbia, SC, 1972); and Paul Cross Papers, Caroliniana Library, University of South Carolina, Columbia.

28. W. Robert Higgins, 'Charles Town Merchants and Factors Dealing in the External Negro Trade, 1735–1775', *South Carolina Historical Magazine*, 65 (1964), 205–17.

29. Klein, 'Slaves and Shipping in Virginia', 407–8.

30. *Ibid.*, 383–412; Klein, 'New Evidence on the Trade', 872–3; Westbury, 'Analysing a Regional Trade', 241–3.

31. One demonstration of the size of New England's liquor industry is the fact that in 1774 Massachusetts alone had 63 distilleries which produced 2,700,000 gallons of rum. Greene, *Negro in New England*, pp.24–6, 68–71; McManus, *Black Bondage*, pp.9–10, 12–13, 19; Coughtry, *Notorious Triangle*, pp.8–21.

32. Kulikoff, *Tobacco and Slaves*, pp.320–1.

33. Gerald W. Mullin, *Flight and Rebellion: Slave Resistance in Eighteenth-Century Virginia* (New York, 1972), p.15; Klein, 'New Evidence on the Trade', 874–5; Wax, 'Black Immigrants', 38; Kulikoff, *Tobacco and Slaves*, p.325.

34. Greene, *Negro in New England*, pp.45–7; McManus, *Black Bondage*, pp.26–7; Wax, 'Black Immigrants', 39–40; Duncan, 'Servitude in South Carolina', 156–8; Wood, *Slavery in Georgia*, 99.

35. The many newspaper advertisements in the *South-Carolina Gazette* (1732–75) and *South-Carolina Gazette, and Country Journal* (1765–75) usually mentioned the ship and captain's name, origin of slaves, and at which wharf they were located. See also Ulrich B. Phillips, *American Negro Slavery* (1918; rep. ed., Baton Rouge, 1966), p.41; and Duncan, 'Servitude in South Carolina', 141–8.

36. Riche to Gampirt, Heyman, Hill, and Jacob Miller, 21 Oct. 1763, quoted from Wax, 'Africans on the Delaware', 43. *Ibid.*, 38–49; Greene, *Negro in New England*, 42–3; Wax, 'Robert Ellis', 55; Wax, 'Negro Imports into Pennsylvania', 255–60; McManus, *Black Bondage*, pp.13–14, 22–3; Lydon, 'New York Slave Trade', 392.

37. For accounts of Virginia slave trading see the diary of Robert 'King' Carter (1722–27) in the Robert 'King' Carter Papers; and the letterbook of his sons in the John, Charles, and Landon Carter Letterbook (hereafter Carter Letterbook), both UVA. Good secondary descriptions of this process include Thad W. Tate, *The Negro in Eighteenth-Century Williamsburg* (Charlottesville, 1965), ch. 6; Mullin, *Flight and Rebellion*, pp.13–15; Westbury, 'Colonial Virginia and the Trade', 122–38; Sweig, 'Importation of Slaves', 514–24; and Kulikoff, *Tobacco and Slaves*, pp.322–3.

38. Nathaniel Bacon and Edward Jones (Virginia) to the Royal African Company, 25 June 1679, Donnan, *Documents of the Slave Trade*, 4: 55.

39. Carter to Foster Cunleffe, 28 May 1737, Carter Letterbook; Laurens to Gidney Clarke, 31 Jan. 1756, *Papers of Henry Laurens*, 2: 83. Carter also once admitted to his agent that 'it is best to have a Mix'd Cargo to hit all humours', then went on to complain of the many 'old Men & old women which must be the same Expence in the passage & must be sold in a Manner as the Buyers please', Carter to Foster Cunleffe and Samuel Powel, 3 Aug. 1738, Carter Letterbook.

40. Instructions to Captain William Ellery, 14 Jan. 1758, Donnan, *Documents of the Slave Trade*, 3: 69; Robert Pringle to Edward Pare, 5 May 1744, *Letterbook of Robert Pringle*, 2: 684. Even in the 1760s South Carolina still had a lowcountry black male/female ratio of 1.33. Kulikoff, *Tobacco and Slaves*, pp.66–7, 321; Wood, *Black Majority*, pp.154–5, 159–66; Philip D. Morgan, 'Black Society in the Lowcountry, 1760–1810', in Ira Berlin and Ronald Hoffman, eds., *Slavery and Freedom in the Age of the American Revolution* (Charlottesville, 1983), pp.85–90.

41. Thomas Ringgold to Samuel Galloway, 30 Aug. 1761, and Charles Stewart to

Anthony Fakie, 13 July 1751, both quoted from Darold D. Wax, 'Preferences for Slaves in Colonial America', *Journal of Negro History*, 58 (1973), 377. *Ibid.*, 374–89.

42. Apparently South Carolina planters desired tall slaves over short for the same stereotyped reasons that they preferred certain ethnic groups. Curtin, *Atlantic Slave Trade*, pp.156–8; Duncan, 'Servitude in South Carolina', 133–8; Wax, 'Preferences for Slaves', 389–99; Littlefield, *Rice and Slaves*, esp. ch. 1; Wood, *Slavery in Georgia*, p.103.

43. Jonathan Dickinson to Isaac Gale, 14 Nov. 1719, quoted from Darold D. Wax, 'The Demand for Slave Labor in Colonial Pennsylvania', *Pennsylvania History*, 34 (1967), 338; Livingston to Henry Rensselaer, 19 Sept. 1735, George Arthur Plimpton Papers, Rare Books and Manuscripts, Butler Library, Columbia University, New York, NY. New York sellers usually mentioned when their slaves could speak both Dutch and English. See *New York Mercury*, 7 June 1756, and 5 July 1756. Greene, *Negro in New England*, pp.36–8; Wax, 'Demand for Labor in Pennsylvania', 331–45; Berlin, 'Time, Space, and Evolution', 46–51; Kruger, 'Born to Run', 93–101.

44. Dudley to Council of Trade and Plantations, 1 Oct. 1708, W. Noel Sainsbury *et al.*, eds., *Calendar of State Papers: Colonial Series, America and West Indies*, 44 vols. (London, 1860–   ), 24: 110; Greene, *Negro in New England*, p.35.

45. Norris to Thomas Swan, 11 Aug. 1702, and 13 Mar. 1704, both quoted from Wax, 'Quaker Merchants', 154, 150. Norris and other Pennsylvania merchants often dropped out of the business due to discontent only to sell slaves again at a later date. Norris sold slaves until 1732, three years before his death. *Ibid.*, 150–6.

46. Donnan, *Documents of the Slave Trade*, 3: 21; Wax, 'Robert Ellis', 52–69; Wax, 'Negro Imports into Pennsylvania', 255–87; Duncan, 'Servitude in South Carolina', 104–7; Berlin, 'Time, Space, and Evolution', 59; Wood, *Slavery in Georgia*, pp.99–100.

47. According to extremely rough data Darold Wax has compiled for Philadelphia, 11% of the blacks imported there between 1720 and 1766 came from South Carolina (no other colonies were listed). James Lydon found that in New York only 4% of the slaves arriving between 1715 and 1764 came from other colonies. In Virginia, Herbert Klein attributed 5% to this source; Susan Westbury's estimate is even lower at less than 1%. Since South Carolina was the major supplier in the intercolonial trade it seems unlikely that it received more than 5% of its slaves from the other mainland colonies. Of course, urban merchants often sold to buyers from neighbouring colonies, such as Philadelphia traders supplying farmers from northern Maryland and southern New Jersey, but this trading was more local in nature than intercolonial (i.e., between regions). Wax, 'Negro Imports into Pennsylvania', 260–87; Lydon, 'New York Slave Trade', 382; Klein, 'Slaves and Shipping in Virginia', 395; Westbury, 'Slaves of Colonial Virginia', 234–5.

48. Benjamin Harrison to William Palfrey, 13 Aug. 1772, quoted from *ibid.*, 234; Thomas Cooper and David J. McCord, eds. *The Statutes at Large of South Carolina*, 10 vols. (Columbia, SC, 1836–41), 3: 159–62; *Journal of the Legislative Council of the Colony of New York, 1691–1743* (Albany, 1861), pp.433–4; Wax, 'Preferences for Slaves', 374–89; Philip J. Schwarz, 'The Transportation of Slaves from Virginia, 1801–1865', *Slavery and Abolition*, 7 (1986), 218–19.

49. Mullin, *Flight and Rebellion*, pp.13–15; Littlefield, *Rice and Slaves*, pp.67–8; Wood, *Slavery in Georgia*, p.96; Kulikoff, *Tobacco and Slaves*, pp.134–6. See also the numerous advertisements in the *Virginia Gazette* (1736–80) which always mentioned whenever a parcel of slaves were born in Virginia.

50. Greene, *Negro in New England*, pp.15, 39–43; Duncan, 'Servitude in South Carolina', ch. 4; McManus, *Black Bondage*, pp.19, 24–30.

51. For this reason there is also no indication that a social stigma existed against slave selling. Frederic Bancroft, *Slave Trading in the Old South* (1931: rep. ed., New York, 1959), p.21; Donnan, *Documents of the Slave Trade*, 3: 21n; Greene, *Negro in New England*, pp.42–3.

52. *Ibid.*, pp.33–4; Duncan, 'Servitude in South Carolina', 185–90.

53. *New-York Gazette* (Weyman's), 3 Mar. 1762; *South-Carolina Gazette*, 27 Dec. 1742; Greene, *Negro in New England*, 41; McManus, *Black Bondage*, pp.36–7. See also the many advertisements in the *Virginia Gazette* (1736–80); *South-Carolina Gazette* (1732–75); and *South-Carolina Gazette, and Country Journal* (1765–75).
54. *South-Carolina Gazette, and Country Journal*, 8 Nov. 1768; *Boston Gazette*, 14 Sept. 1767; *South-Carolina Gazette*, 25 May 1765; Duncan, 'Servitude in South Carolina', 190–3; McManus, *Black Bondage*, pp.27–8; Kruger, 'Born to Run', 202–4.
55. *New-England Weekly Journal* (Boston), 8 Jan. 1728; *South-Carolina Gazette, and Country Journal*, 26 Mar. 1771; *South-Carolina Gazette*, 30 Apr. 1771.
56. Greene, *Negro in New England*, pp.214–16; McManus, *Black Bondage*, pp.37–8; Kruger, 'Born to Run', 203, 263–4, 422–4; Wood, *Slavery in Georgia*, pp.96, 101.
57. *New-York Gazette, or the Weekly Post-Boy*, 17 May 1756, 28 Nov. 1765.
58. *Pennsylvania Gazette*, 21 May 1767, 26 Feb. 1767.
59. *South-Carolina Gazette, and Country Journal*, 23 Apr. 1771; *New-York Gazette and Weekly Mercury*, 8 Apr. 1776; *New-York Gazetteer, and Country Journal*, 26 Oct. 1784.
60. *Connecticut Gazette, and the Universal Intelligencer*, 17 Nov. 1775; *Pennsylvania Chronicle*, 9 Mar. 1767; Greene, *Negro in New England*, pp.211–13; Kruger, 'Born to Run', part 2; Merle G. Brouwer, 'Marriage and Family Life Among Blacks in Colonial Pennsylvania', *Pennsylvania Magazine of History and Biography*, 99 (1975), 368–72; Gary B. Nash, 'Forging Freedom: The Emancipation Experience in the Northern Seaport Cities, 1775–1820', in Berlin and Hoffman, *Slavery and Freedom*, pp.27–31; Mullin, *Flight and Rebellion*, pp.27–8; Kulikoff, *Tobacco and Slaves*, pp.353–71; Jean Butenhoff Lee, 'The Problem of Slave Community in the Eighteenth-Century Chesapeake', *William and Mary Quarterly*, 3d ser., 43 (1986), 354–61; Duncan, 'Servitude in South Carolina', 195–9; Wood, *Slavery in Georgia*, 157–8.
61. *New-England Weekly Journal*, 1 May 1732; *New-York Gazetteer, and Country Journal*, 26 Oct. 1784; *South-Carolina Gazette*, 16 Apr. 1772; *Virginia Gazette*, 2 Nov. 1769.
62. *New-York Mercury*, 7 Mar. 1763; *Independent Chronicle* (Boston), 14 Dec. 1780; Greene, *Negro in New England*, pp.212–13; McManus, *Black Bondage*, pp.37–8; Kruger, 'Born to Run', ch. 6. For ads offering to give slave children away see *New-England Weekly Journal*, 15 Nov. 1731, 21 Feb. 1732, 25 Feb. 1734, 4 Jan. 1737, 19 July 1737, 6 June 1738; *Boston Gazette*, 25 June 1754, 19 Oct. 1767; *Boston News-Letter*, 26 June 1760; *Continental Journal* (Boston), 4 Sept. 1777, and 11 Feb. 1779.
63. The best description of this proposed act and why it failed to pass remains George H. Moore, *Notes on the History of Slavery in Massachusetts* (1866; rep. ed., New York, 1968), p.250. Greene, *Negro in New England*, pp.47–9; McManus, *Black Bondage*, pp.28–9.
64. The Quakers began attacking the slave trade in the late 17th century, but except for a few isolated cases such as Samuel Sewall's *Selling of Joseph* (1700) they remained the only group to do so (see note 7). In the 1760s and 1770s the Quakers' appeal began to find a receptive audience, and for some the natural rights of Africans became associated with those of the colonists. Also, many advocated the closing of the African trade as an economic attack against England since British merchants controlled the trade. Ëen then, no stigma was attached to slave-trading, and only war brought the African trade to a halt. A good collection of early abolitionist writings is Roger Bruns, ed., *Am I Not a Man and a Brother: The Antislavery Crusade of Revolutionary America, 1688–1788* (New York, 1977). See also Arthur Zilversmit, *The First Emancipation: The Abolition of Slavery in the North* (Chicago, 1967), chs. 3–4; and Jordan, *White Over Black*, ch. 7.
65. Greene, *Negro in New England*, pp.28–31, 57–60; McManus, *Black Bondage*, pp.18–19, 29–30; Westbury, 'Colonial Virginia and the Trade', 128–31; Duncan 'Servitude in South Carolina', 138–41; Rawley, *Transatlantic Slave Trade*, pp.336–7.

11

A Marginal Institution on the Margin of the Atlantic System: The Portuguese Southern Atlantic Slave Trade in the Eighteenth Century

Joseph C. Miller

SLAVING's economic contribution to the Atlantic system has proven a slippery beast, simultaneously of sensible significance[1] but difficult to measure.[2] Examination of the economics of slave trading on the scale of an "Atlantic system," often mixed with the function of slavery in America, a closely related but analytically distinct economic sector, has until very recently focused narrowly on its direct contribution to the most dramatic and portentous development in the eighteenth- and nineteenth-century Atlantic economy: Britain's transition to in-

---

[1] Eric Williams, *Capitalism and Slavery* (Chapel Hill, N.C., 1944).

[2] Roger T. Anstey, "*Capitalism and Slavery* – A Critique," and John Hargreaves, "Synopsis of a Critique of Eric Williams' *Capitalism and Slavery*," both in Centre of African Studies (University of Edinburgh), *The Transatlantic Slave Trade from West Africa* (Edinburgh, 1965), pp. 13–29 and 30–2, with discussion, pp. 33–43; also C. Duncan Rice, "Critique of the Eric Williams Thesis: The Anti-Slavery Interest and the Sugar Duties, 1841–1853," in ibid., pp. 44–60; Roger T. Anstey, "Capitalism and Slavery: A Critique," *Economic History Review*, Vol. 21, No. 2 (1968), pp. 307–20; Stanley L. Engerman, "The Slave Trade and British Capital Formation in the Eighteenth Century: A Comment on the Williams Thesis," *Business History Review*, Vol. 46, No. 4 (1972), pp. 430–43; Stanley L. Engerman, "Comments on Richardson and Boulle and the 'Williams Thesis'," *Revue française d'histoire d'outre-mer*, Vol. 62, 1–2, Nos. 226–7 (1975), pp. 331–6; Walter Minchinton, "The Economic Relations between Metropolitan Countries and the Caribbean: Some Problems," in Vera Rubin and Arthur Tuden (eds.), *Comparative Perspectives on Slavery in New World Plantation Societies*, Annals of the New York Academy of Sciences, Vol. 292 (New York, 1977), pp. 567–80. For a recent summary, see Seymour Drescher, "Eric Williams: British Capitalism and British Slavery," *History and Theory*, Vol. 26, No. 2 (1987), pp. 180–96.

Portuguese southern Atlantic slave trade   121

dustrial capitalism.[3] Now, however, Barbara Solow and Stanley Engerman have productively both broadened the range of economic effects relating slavery and slave trading to European growth and expanded the focus beyond the boundaries of separate imperial systems to explore the entire Atlantic system as an integrated economic unit extending from the banks of the Zambezi, Plate, and Mississippi – if not also the Indus – to the Bank of England.[4] A paradoxical leitmotif that emerges from this recent work, if not a dominant theme, is that the economic significance of slavery and the slave trade lies not in their centrality to the course of British or European economic growth,

---

[3] With vigorous debate among British economic historians from internal perspectives; see P. J. Cain and A. G. Hopkins, "The Political Economy of British Expansion Overseas, 1750–1914," *Economic History Review*, Vol. 33, No. 4 (1980), pp. 463–90; and the references in David Richardson, "The Slave Trade, Sugar, and British Economic Growth, 1748–1776," *Journal of Interdisciplinary History*, Vol. 17, No. 4 (1987), pp. 739–70. Also see the recent discussions conceived in terms of the profitability of the British African trade: Joseph E. Inikori, "Market Structure and the Profits of the British African Trade in the Late Eighteenth Century," *Journal of Economic History*, Vol. 41, No. 4 (1981), pp. 745–76; B. L. Anderson and David Richardson, "Market Structure and Profits of the British African Trade in the Late Eighteenth Century: A Comment," *Journal of Economic History*, Vol. 43, No. 3 (1983), pp. 713–21; Joseph E. Inikori, "Market Structure and the Profits of the British African Trade in the Late Eighteenth Century: A Rejoinder," *Journal of Economic History*, Vol. 43, No. 3 (1983), pp. 723–8; B. L. Anderson and David Richardson, "Market Structure and the Profits of the British African Trade in the Late Eighteenth Century: A Rejoinder Rebutted," *Journal of Economic History*, Vol. 45, No. 3 (1985), pp. 705–7; William Darity, Jr., "The Numbers Game and the Profitability of the British Trade in Slaves," *Journal of Economic History*, Vol. 45, No. 3 (1985), pp. 693–703; Joseph E. Inikori, "Market Structure and Profits: A Further Rejoinder," *Journal of Economic History*, Vol. 45, No. 3 (1985), pp. 708–11; in addition to an older debate on the profitability of West Indies sugar. Recent debate on the profitability of Caribbean slavery, mostly in relation to British abolitionism, has derived from Seymour Drescher, *Econocide: British Slavery in the Era of Abolition* (Pittsburgh, 1977); see also Selwyn H. H. Carrington, "'Econocide' – Myth or Reality? – The Question of West Indian Decline, 1783–1806," *Boletín de estudios latinoamericanos y del Caribe*, No. 36 (1986), pp. 13–38, with response by Drescher, pp. 49–65, and Carrington, "Postscriptum," pp. 66–7. Even Pierre Boulle's innovative conceptualizations of the problem as it related to Nantes were conceived primarily in reference to British industrial growth, i.e., why a French slave trade with a volume similar to that of the British had not produced comparable industrialization in France; see "Slave Trade, Commercial Organization and Industrial Growth in Eighteenth-Century Nantes," *Revue française d'histoire d'outre-mer*, Vol. 59, 1, No. 214 (1972), pp. 70–112, and "Marchandises de traite et développement industriel dans la France et l'Angleterre du XVIIIᵉ siècle," *Revue française d'histoire d'outre-mer*, Vol. 62, 1–2, Nos. 226–7 (1975), pp. 309–30.

[4] Barbara L. Solow and Stanley L. Engerman (eds.), *British Capitalism and Caribbean Slavery: The Legacy of Eric Williams* (New York, 1987), with the economic history papers also appearing in "Caribbean Slavery and British Capitalism," special issue of *Journal of Interdisciplinary History*, Vol. 17, No. 4 (1987).

where others have sought it and that they demonstrably lacked,[5] but precisely in their marginality to the main currents of economic growth and development around the Atlantic.

Slaving was marginal to the Atlantic economy in structural terms, in a sense not so much inconsistent with formal analysis of a fully market economy as one highlighting the institutional aspects of a mercantilist system fraught with monopoly, privilege, and other imperfections. As it was an integrated economic market, growth occurred throughout the system, and the groups competing within it each found niches in which they enjoyed comparative advantages. Specialization of economic function increased as the scale expanded and the parts worked out their complementarities, with financial resources – central banking, efficient currencies, and credit, allocated responsively to more productive and profitable sectors – and, eventually, fossil fuel–powered technology and higher productivity becoming concentrated in a northern Atlantic core with the capital to stimulate, direct, and draw monetary profits from the other sectors. As the large economies with their gold and silver reserves concentrated as monetary reserves, rather than, say, on gilded altars, Britain, northern Europe, and the United States became central to the system, and Portugal, Brazil, and Africa became marginal.

Slavery and the slave trade operated at the margins of this growing system in the sense that they exhibited fewer of the economic institutions typical of the core, principally costly technology and hard currency assets – that is, capital – and in fact facilitated its concentration there. Beyond lack of specie, the economic characteristics of the slaving margins of the Atlantic system also included lower productivity, higher risks, lower costs of entry, and slower rates of growth that – in the end – resulted in sharply lower levels of wealth. Profits throughout the system might approximate the same level, but the slavers on the margin took their gains in consumption goods and more slaves rather than in the specie and productive technology that accumulated at the center.

Remote and increasingly backward Portugal and its empire present an opportunity to examine the slave trade as a marginal, but critical, element in the development of the Atlantic system in the eighteenth century. Despite the drama of intrepid Lusitanian exploration in the fifteenth and sixteenth centuries, Portugal had always been at the fringes of European and world economic development. Located on

---

[5] Despite the emphasis placed on export-led economic growth in the nineteenth century in David Eltis, *Economic Growth and the Ending of the Transatlantic Slave Trade* (New York, 1987).

Portuguese southern Atlantic slave trade   123

the southwestern periphery of the Iberian peninsula and facing a vast, empty Atlantic, Lisbon played no significant part in the fourteenth- and fifteenth-century intensification of Mediterranean trading centered in Italy and its spice trade with the Levant and gold trade with Africa.[6] It was precisely because of Portugal's exclusion from these main lines of Mediterranean commerce that its kings sent ships south to brave the hazards of Africa's Atlantic coast and to seek the sub-Saharan sources of Africa's gold and, ultimately, a maritime route to Indian Ocean spice markets that would circumvent the Italians and the Muslims to the east.

By the eighteenth century, Portugal had become one of Europe's great slaving nations, but it had moved no closer to the center of European economic growth, by then displaced northward from the Mediterranean to the English Channel. Booms in sugar and gold from Portugal's richest colony, Brazil, had consumed slaves in massive quantities, more than 40% of the total Atlantic trade in the seventeenth century and still nearly one-third of the much greater numbers carried in the eighteenth.[7] If slavery and the slave trade made a significant direct contribution to economic growth, Portugal surely would not have found itself more marginal than ever to the accelerating pace of development around the Atlantic, economically stagnant, lacking internal transport systems, unable to feed its own population, and becoming more and more dependent on manufactures imported from northern European trading partners, particularly the British. But precisely because the slave trade stands out so prominently in the Portuguese context, its general function in sustaining weak and uncompetitive economic sectors appears clearly there in ways not always visible amid all the other elements of the larger and more complex economy of Britain.

The Portuguese southern Atlantic trade in question drew slaves primarily from the Angolan coast, south of the mouth of the Zaire River as far as the Kunene, and there principally from two embarkation points: the colonial capital of Luanda, larger and dating from the 1570s, and Benguela, founded in the 1610s but growing slowly as a source of slaves to a scale comparable to that of Luanda only late in the eighteenth century.[8] Angolan slaves headed mostly for Brazil's

[6] John Day, "The Great Bullion Famine of the Fifteenth Century," *Past and Present*, Vol. 79 (1978), pp. 3–54.

[7] Philip D. Curtin, *The Atlantic Slave Trade: A Census* (Madison, Wis., 1969), pp. 119, 216, and Paul E. Lovejoy, "The Volume of the Atlantic Slave Trade: A Synthesis," *Journal of African History*, Vol. 23, No. 4 (1982), p. 483.

[8] Joseph C. Miller, *Way of Death: Merchant Capitalism and the Angolan Slave Trade, 1730–1830* (Madison, Wis., 1988).

124   *Joseph C. Miller*

northeastern sugar captaincies of Pernambuco and Bahia in the seventeenth century, but in the eighteenth century they went in greater and greater proportions south to Rio de Janeiro and to the mining districts of Minas Gerais, just inland. The resulting shortage in the supply of slaves for the sugar plantations of Brazil's northeast was filled by substantial numbers of captives from West African shores east of the Volta River and on toward the location of modern Lagos, an area known to the Portuguese as the "Mina Coast" but to the British familiar as the "Slave Coast," beginning about the 1680s.[9] Much smaller numbers of captive Africans embarked from Portugal's two small trading towns on the Upper Guinea coast, Bissau and Cacheu, mostly destined for Brazil's far northern captaincies, Maranhão and Pará, in the middle and later eighteenth century.[10] In addition, from time to time in the eighteenth century and in growing numbers from about 1800 on, Brazilians obtained slaves from Portugal's southeastern African possessions in Mozambique.[11]

LISBON SLAVING INTERESTS ON THE SIDELINES OF THE EMPIRE

If Portuguese mariners generally operated on the fringes of the European economy, the Lisbon interests among them who engaged in trading slaves repeatedly entered slaving from positions marginal even to their own domestic and imperial economies. Their African commerce never approached the value of Portugal's commodity trade with the remainder of Europe, or with its trading posts in the Indian

---

[9] Pierre Verger, *Flux et reflux de la traite des nègres entre le golfe de Bénin et Bahia de Todos os Santos du XVIIe au XIXe siècle* (Paris, 1968), translated (by Evelyn Crawford) as *Trade Relations Between the Bight of Benin and Bahia from the 17th to the 19th Century* (Ibadan, 1976) and (by Tasso Gadzanis) as *Fluxo e refluxo do tráfico de escravos entre o Golfo do Benin e a Bahia de Todos os Santos dos séculos XVII a XIX* (São Paulo, 1987).

[10] Jean Mettas, "La traite portugaise en Haute Guinée, 1758–1797: problèmes et méthodes," *Journal of African History*, Vol. 16, No. 3 (1975), pp. 343–63.

[11] Eltis, pp. 177–9, 250–2, for the volume; what little is known about this trade from the Mozambican end may be found in António Carreira, *O tráfico português de escravos na costa oriental africana nos começos do século XIX (estudo de um caso)* (Lisbon, 1979) (Centro de Estudos de Antropologia Cultural, Estudos de Antropologia Cultural, no. 12). Also see José Capela, "The 'Mujojos' Slave Trade in Moçambique 1830–1902" (unpublished paper, Workshop on the Long-Distance Trade in Slaves Across the Indian Ocean and the Red Sea in the 19th Century, School of Oriental and African Studies, London, December 1987); José Capela and Eduardo Medeiros. *O tráfico de escravos de Moçambique para as ilhas do Índico 1720–1902* (Maputo, Mozambique, 1987), and José Capela, "O tráfico da escravatura na relações Moçambique-Brasil" (unpublished paper, Escravidão – Congresso Internacional, São Paulo, Brazil, 7–11 June 1988).

Portuguese southern Atlantic slave trade   125

Ocean or with the colony of Brazil, the jewel in the imperial crown from the 1570s on. Even within the more limited sphere of slave-dependent Brazil's imports and exports, its trade in African labor probably ran less than 10% of imports at most periods and hardly ever more than 20%.[12] Nonetheless, slaving from the very beginning of Portugal's adventures in the Atlantic repeatedly became a target of opportunity for merchants in Lisbon unable to compete with the leading groups of merchants in the city.

During the sixteenth century, when the crown and Lisbon's grandest overseas merchants thrived on African gold and Asian pepper, the buying, selling, and owning of slaves in Portugal's empire fell to foreign interests and to traders and planters without access to the main sources of wealth of the time: specie and spices. Even Portugal's early center of slave-grown sugar on the island of Madeira was an enterprise not of Lisbon investors but rather of the Genoese.[13] The slave-worked plantations on tiny equatorial São Tomé in the Gulf of Guinea, the world's leading producer of sugar for fifty years or so later in the century, grew from an early colony of impoverished exiles into an island of mulatto planters descended from poor Portuguese settler-traders and noblewomen from the Kongo kingdom on the adjacent mainland.[14] Although Portuguese aristocrats collected taxes on their enterprise and Italians bought their sugars, ownership and supply of the slaves in the Gulf of Guinea remained in the hands of local interests. Slaving off the Upper Guinea coast, serving Madeira, the Cape Verde Islands, and peninsular Portugal itself, remained primarily an occupation of colonial settlers.[15] To the extent that merchants from the metropole involved themselves at all in this early trade in slaves, they tended to come from New Christian circles then coming under heavy pressure from the Inquisition at home and seeking respite from persecution in flight to the remote corners of the

---

[12] Miller, *Way of Death*, pp. 452–6.

[13] Themselves secondary participants in an Italian-Mediterranean commercial sphere dominated by the Venetians. Sidney M. Greenfield, "Plantations, Sugar Cane, and Slavery," *Historical Reflections/Réflexions historiques*, Vol. 6, No. 1 (1979), p. 112; Stuart B. Schwartz, *Sugar Plantations in the Formation of Brazilian Society* (New York, 1985), pp. 9–10.

[14] René Pélissier, *Le naufrage des caravelles: études sur la fin de l'empire portugais (1961–1975)* (Montamets, France, 1979), pp. 215–16; John K. Thornton, "Early Kongo – Portuguese Relations: A New Interpretation," *History in Africa*, Vol. 8 (1981), pp. 191–2; Isabel Castro Henriques, "Ser escravo em S. Tomé no século XVI: uma outra leitura de um mesmo quotidiano," *Revista internacional de estudos africanos*, Vols. 6–7 (1987), pp. 167–78.

[15] A. C. de C. M. Saunders, *A Social History of Black Slaves and Freedmen in Portugal, 1441–1555* (London, 1982).

126   *Joseph C. Miller*

empire or to Protestant northern Europe.[16] Portugal's sixteenth-century slave trade – and the ownership of slaves themselves – thus originated as a refuge for Jews, gypsies, exiles, and others excluded from more attractive currents of its Asian and African commerce.

Established Lisbon merchants participated in slaving primarily indirectly, through an interest in its finance and administration. In Spain's *asiento* contracts, awarding well-heeled investors the right to introduce slaves into its American colonies, they perceived a highly attractive opportunity to reap returns in gold and silver, the primary objectives of the bullionist merchants of the era. Lisbon interests dominated those contracts in the sixteenth century and during the sixty years of the Dual Monarchy from 1580 to 1640, when Hapsburg kings in Madrid ruled Portugal as well as Spain. However, they restricted themselves to the financial and diplomatic aspects of these complex affairs; licensed lesser interests to engage in the dirty and risky business of buying, transporting, and selling slaves; repeatedly failed to promote slaving itself sufficiently to deliver the numbers of *piezas* they had promised; and prospered from smuggling goods and specie aboard the slave ships. Thus, only Spain's dazzlingly lucrative American minerals lured prominent Lisbon interests to associate themselves with the slave trade, and even there they held themselves as aloof as possible from slaving itself.

Even as Portugal's northeastern Brazilian captaincies of Pernambuco and Bahia emerged as prosperous plantation colonies in the 1570s, able to supply slave-grown sugar on a scale far surpassing that of Madeira and São Tomé, Lisbon began to harvest the bitter fruits of its consistent failure to establish a firm financial interest in the primary products of its own Atlantic empire. In part for want of capital sufficient to undertake the expensive, long-term investments required by sugar, they had limited themselves to a short-term search for specie, in Africa and in Spain's New World colonies, and had left sugar on the Atlantic islands to the Genoese and to the colonists of São Tomé. With even greater demand for capital from Brazil's much more extensive plantations, the necessary financial resources came from the Netherlands, in part through commercial contacts established by Portuguese New Christian families with branches in northern Europe as well as in Brazil. Even the largest Lisbon merchants

[16] José Gonçalves Salvador, *Os Cristãos-novos e o comércio no Atlântico meridional (com enfoque nas capitanias do sul 1530–1680)* (São Paulo, 1978); idem, *Os magnatas do tráfico negreiro (séculos XVI e XVII)* (São Paulo, 1981).

Portuguese southern Atlantic slave trade 127

found themselves edged to the periphery of the Brazilian sugar trade that came to form the heart of Portugal's early-seventeenth-century empire.

It was as a second-best alternative to Brazil's booming sugar industry, and after African gold and Asian spices had both failed, early in the seventeenth century, that Angola's slaves finally attracted Lisbon's attention, in part because of firming prices for African labor[17] but also because Dutch control of the shipments of sugar making their way back to Europe left them no real alternative.[18] The details of slaving at Luanda then are too little known to identify the precise Lisbon initiatives taken, but during that period Lisbon excluded the early donatary proprietors from further involvement in the colony's affairs, began to bring the first generation of settlers and missionaries there under administrative control, and attempted to regularize the colony's slave exports.[19] It is unlikely that Lisbon made significant inroads on the colonials' slaving at that time, as metropolitan attention concentrated in the 1620s on resisting the Dutch West India Company's attacks on Portugal's colonies in Brazil and Africa and then in the 1630s on breaking free of Spanish overrule.

Restoration of Portuguese autonomy in 1640 under the new royal house of Bragança brought political independence but in the longer term pushed many Lisbon merchants still farther out to the remote edges of their own southern Atlantic empire. Portugal had long depended on England as an ally and guarantor in the arena of continental European politics, and the weak monarchy restored at Lisbon in the middle and later seventeenth century depended heavily on its English sponsor. A dynastic union between the Portuguese princess Catherine and King Charles II sealed this alliance in 1662 and brought the English substantial commercial privileges in Portugal as part of the bargain. Though Portugal was already sensing not only its diplomatic weakness but also its economic decline relative to the northern

[17] Joseph C. Miller, "Slave Prices in the Portuguese Southern Atlantic, c. 1600–1830," in Paul E. Lovejoy (ed.), *Africans in Bondage: Studies in Slavery and the Slave Trade* (Madison, Wis., 1986), pp. 43–77; ibid., "Quantities and Currencies: Bargaining for Slaves on the Fringes of the World Capitalist Economy" (unpublished paper, Escravidão – Congresso Internacional, São Paulo, Brazil, 7–11 June 1988).

[18] Cornelius Ch. Goslinga, *The Dutch in the Caribbean and on the Wild Coast, 1580–1680* (Gainesville, 1971), and *The Dutch in the Caribbean and in the Guianas 1680–1791* (Dover, N. H., 1985).

[19] See the papers of Governor Fernão de Sousa (1626–30) in Beatrix Heintze, *Fontes para a história de Angola do século XVII*, 2 vols. (Wiesbaden, 1985, 1988).

Europeans, it had no choice but to open its domestic and colonial markets to its powerful champion.[20] The famous Methuen Treaty of 1702 confirmed the failure of a long effort at Lisbon to stimulate domestic industry by conceding the entire Portuguese woolen market to England in return for preferential treatment of wines from Portugal there.

For Portuguese merchants, the English woolen trade was both good news and bad news. Lisbon trading houses contracted to represent English importers in Portugal acquired the backing of the wealthiest exporters in Europe as brokers of a profitable reexport of English goods to their richest colonial market, the slave and colonist populations of Brazil. For other houses not so prosperous or so advantageously affiliated, the Anglo-Portuguese connection meant exclusion from the most lucrative market still open to them among the Atlantic and continental economies increasingly closed by mercantilist restrictions and where they could hardly compete with the English, Dutch, and French. The losers in the contest for economic advantage at Lisbon accordingly turned again to the trade of Angola, almost entirely in slaves, as a consolation prize.

In Angola, Lisbon traders ran up against formidable opposition to their plans from the old colonial settlers, not wealthy rivals like the English and their Portuguese factors but nonetheless successors to the slavers established earlier at São Tomé and acclimated residents almost impossible to dislodge from control of Luanda's shipments of slaves to Bahia and Pernambuco. They slaved in close association with Brazilian governors in the colony. Luanda had fallen to the Dutch West India Company in 1641 but had been restored to Portuguese authority by an expedition from Rio de Janeiro at a moment in 1648 when Lisbon remained too weakened by its struggle to consolidate its break from Spain to take firm steps in the faraway southern Atlantic. For the entire last half of the seventeenth century, these powerful Brazilian governors, many of them linked to planter families in Pernambuco, ruled Angola almost as a personal fiefdom and held a firm grip on its exports of slaves. They exploited the surrounding African populations in a highly militaristic style, raiding widely for slaves in alliance with entrenched Angolan settler interests – here termed "Luso-Africans" for their joint Portuguese and African descent – and intricately intermarried with the African gentry who furnished captives to them and were no less committed than the

---

[20] Carl A. Hanson, *Economy and Society in Baroque Portugal, 1668–1703* (Minneapolis, 1981).

governors to war as a means of securing slaves. Portugal's southern Atlantic slaving in that early phase functioned largely independently of metropolitan interests and thus lay structurally on the edges of an Atlantic system defined in terms of commercial initiatives emanating from the centers of finance and credit in Europe, England, and the Netherlands, through Portugal.

In the late seventeenth century, Lisbon interests losing ground abroad took the first feeble steps in what became a lengthy series of efforts to break up this transatlantic alliance of colonial slave raiders and planters. Brazilian sugar, though the most promising trade left to Portugal, had fallen on hard times in the second half of the seventeenth century. Bahia and Pernambuco planters competed on the European market only with difficulty against the new and more efficient English plantations in Barbados and then in Jamaica. Mercantilist policies excluded their sugars from the major continental European and English markets. Lisbon then issued strict, though futile, instructions to its governors forbidding key elements of their strategy of violence in the 1660s and 1670s, but these efforts at control slackened off in the last two decades of the century for want of resources to enforce them.

The losers at Lisbon intensified their campaign to employ Angola and its slaves as a back door to the wealth of America when the stakes in the larger contest over Brazil's commercial potential increased sharply around 1700. Discovery of gold in the mountains of Minas Gerais in south-central Brazil in 1695 opened up entirely new visions of colonial wealth, and by the turn of the eighteenth century, thousands of Portuguese prospectors were rushing to the mining district and drawing tens of thousands of African slaves after them.[21] Clearly, the preferred economic strategy from the point of view of a merchant in Lisbon was to buy the glittering yield of the mines with provisions – Portuguese food products and alcohol, as well as English woolens – and equipment sent direct to Minas Gerais either through Bahia or through Rio de Janeiro, the seaport nearest the gold fields. Lisbon's Anglo-Portuguese factors, already with established connections in Brazil and capable of mobilizing the capital necessary to supply this vast and rapidly growing new market, quickly secured it for themselves.

The Lisbon interests thus excluded from the mother lode of Por

---

[21] A. J. R. Russell-Wood, "Colonial Brazil: The Gold Cycle, c. 1690–1750," in Leslie Bethell (ed.), *Cambridge History of Latin America* (Cambridge, 1984), Vol. 2, pp. 547–600.

tugal's early-eighteenth-century empire seized on the desperate need for several thousand slaves on the placers and in the pits and shafts of Minas Gerais each year as the core of a strategy of using slaves from Angola to gain access to the American gold for themselves. Lisbon prohibited Angolan governors from engaging in slaving in 1703 and, through a series of other strategies,[22] gradually opened the door to metropolitan merchants by the 1730s. The intended beneficiaries appear to have been the old Asia traders, who had lost the spice trade to the Dutch but who controlled supplies of Indian and Chinese cotton textiles that, in Brazil, competed with English woolens but were utterly basic to the purchase of slaves in west-central Africa.[23] They introduced these Asian goods through Luanda with further government assistance in the form of legal privileges conveyed in a royal tax-farming contract on duties levied on the slaves exported there. They sold these goods on terms of credit so generous by Angolan standards – however modest their resources may have been in relation to those of the great merchants who engrossed the gold trade of Brazil – that they substituted credit for conquest as the key to slaving in Angola, secured a strangehold on the financing of the colony's commerce by the 1730s, and with that gained slaves to sell in Rio de Janeiro for gold. By the 1740s they ruled supreme at Luanda, evidently having found in southern Atlantic slaving the returns needed to salvage a colonial commerce, to Asia as well as America, threatened by Britain's growing prominence in Portugal's empire. Though slaving thus produced a roundabout success in this contest for Brazilian specie, it diverted the slavers' attention from domestic production of manufactures competitive with those of the British to a mercantile strategy that enriched the Asians who wove the cottons and the Africans who sold labor.

The looming presence of British merchants, and the example of accelerating industrial growth in Britain, motivated another, more forward-looking group of threatened metropolitan interests to attempt

---

[22] Miller, *Way of Death*, pp. 546–51.
[23] See Joseph C. Miller, "Capitalism and Slaving: The Financial and Commercial Organization of the Angolan Slave Trade, According to the Accounts of António Coelho Guerreiro (1684–1692)," *International Journal of African Historical Studies*, Vol. 17, No. 1 (1984), pp. 1–56, for a detailed list of imports as of 1684–92, and "Imports at Luanda, Angola: 1785–1823," in Gerhard Liesegang, Helma Pasch, and Adam Jones (eds.), *Figuring African Trade: Proceedings of the Symposium on the Quantification and Structure of the Import and Export and Long Distance Trade of Africa in the 19th Century (c. 1800–1913)* (St. Augustin, January 3–6, 1983) (Berlin, 1986) (Kölner Beiträge zur Afrikanistik, 11), pp. 165–246, in general. See Phyllis M. Martin, *The External Trade of the Loango Coast 1576–1870* (Oxford, 1972), for the coasts north of the Zaire.

Portuguese southern Atlantic slave trade 131

to seize Angolan slaving as a means of revitalizing the faltering Portuguese economy in the 1750s. Would-be textile and munitions manufacturers and others unable to compete against British products or
imported Asian cottons in Brazil sought to open a protected market
in Angola behind the forceful policies of the dynamic and authori-
tarian prime minister of king D. José I, Sebastião José Carvalho de
Mello (at first Count of Oeiras, later Marquis of Pombal). At Luanda,
two strong governors, António de Vasconcelos (1758–64) and Francisco Inocêncio de Sousa Coutinho (1764–72), subjected the colony's
Luso-African suppliers of slaves to stricter repayment of the debts
they had accumulated over the years of metropolitan sales of goods
on credit and tried to exclude the superior imports of British and
French slavers active along adjacent coasts from Angola's commercial
hinterland.

With the ground thus prepared, Pombal's protégés arrived about
1760 with monopoly trading privileges granted to two chartered trading companies, the Companhia Geral de Pernambuco e Paraíba (Pernambuco Company) and the Companhia Geral do Maranhão e Pará
(Maranhão Company). The underlying weakness of the Pernambuco
and Maranhão companies was transparent. In Angola they competed
with the old slave-duty contract holders, who controlled too great a
portion of the colony's commercial assets to expel at once without
destroying the entire slave trade. Their contract was finally terminated
formally only in 1769. The transatlantic geography of the privileges
granted under their charters revealed their economic marginality as
well. Their monopolies over the African end of the trade covered only
the parts of the coast theoretically off-limits to wealthier foreign merchants, and in Brazil they were confined to captaincies from Pernambuco north not dominated by agents of the British. None of Pombal's
Angola initiatives attained much success, and the companies foun-
dered by the 1770s on the perennial problem of uncollectable debts
in both Africa and Brazil. Lisbon interests willing to resort to Angolan
slaving had grown too weak relative to the waxing commercial
strength of the northern Europeans to compete with British and
French products even on the sidelines of the empire.

The 1770s and 1780s saw Lisbon all but acknowledge its inability
to influence commerce in Angola and Brazil. In Brazil, the gold boom
had run its course, but agriculture entered into an end-of-the-century
renaissance that Portugal, in cooperation with colonial interests, attempted to channel through metropolitan intermediaries.[24] In Angola,

---

[24] Dauril Alden, "Late Colonial Brazil, 1750–1808: Demographic, Economic, and Polit-

Joseph C. Miller

the government concentrated its efforts on limiting foreign goods in its intended trading preserve at the coast, both by driving away foreign slavers and by introducing closer customs inspections of illegal – presumably British – merchandise entering Luanda aboard Brazilian slavers, the dominant carriers in the trade by that time, who brought it in from Rio de Janeiro. The only faint Lisbon initiative visible in the 1790s was an attempt to buy slaves for an emerging cotton-exporting sector in Maranhão and Pará, in remote northern Brazil, far from the center of British strength at Rio in the south.

Lisbon reentered Angolan slaving only after 1810, but this time it was the Portuguese merchants allied to the British who had fallen far enough behind that they turned to Angolan slaves as a strategy to avoid the next phase of Britain's steadily increasing dominance of the rich Brazilian sectors of Portugal's colonial trade. Napoleon had invaded Portugal in 1807, and the British, solicitous of the welfare of a monarchy so long allied and so open to the products of a domestic textile industry then on the verge of replacing the Indians as suppliers of cottons to Europe, Africa, and America, removed the Lisbon court and its Anglo-Portuguese merchant supporters to the safety of Rio de Janeiro in 1808. They received generous compensation in an 1810 treaty of commerce and alliance that opened the Brazilian market – and through Brazil, also the trade of Angola – to British goods, free of restrictions.[25] That put British shippers in direct control of southern Brazil's imports and its agricultural exports to Europe and left the old Anglo-Portuguese group to broker distribution within Brazil and to exploit Rio's non-European commerce, that is, with Africa.

The Lisbon merchants in exile at Rio became the dominant slavers at Luanda during the last two decades of the legal trade until 1830. Metropolitan merchants and manufacturers of cotton textiles and gunpowder left behind in Portugal also worked the Angolan market, mostly through Pernambuco, where they encountered few British agents, had old contacts of their own, and could supply African labor to cotton plantations in the Brazilian far north that briefly became important suppliers of fiber to Britain through Lisbon. Lisbon merchants thus retreated to the risky, dirty, and increasingly disreputable business of Angolan slaving in the last years of the legal trade, often with financial support from British importers, after Britain had pro-

ical Aspects," in Bethell, Vol. 2, pp. 601–60; Kenneth R. Maxwell, *Conflicts and Conspiracies: Portugal and Brazil 1750–1808* (New York, 1973).
[25] Alan K. Manchester, *British Preëminence in Brazil: Its Rise and Decline: A Study in European Expansion* (Chapel Hill, N.C., 1933).

hibited its own national traders from further participation in the trade in African labor.

Portugal's southern Atlantic slave trade thus repeatedly served Lisbon interests pushed to the sidelines of the empire to compensate for their weakness relative to the merchants – increasingly British – dominant at each era of Portuguese economic history. In the earliest years, when wealth came from the spices of Asia, the gold of Africa, and the silver of Spain's colonies in America, and when Italian merchants financed Portuguese sugar, New Christians and other peripheral interests did well by making Portugal the leading slaving nation of the sixteenth century. Well enough, in fact, that branches of them displaced to the Low Countries underwrote and brokered the new wealth in Brazilian sugar early in the seventeenth century, to the exclusion of Old Christian traders of Lisbon, thereby relegated to slaving but by no means uncompensated so long as Spanish American markets remained open to them and the price of Brazilian sugar – and slaves – remained high. But the 1640 break with Spain and the growing competition from Caribbean sugar left fewer prospects to Lisbon's traders, who turned to Angolan slaves as competition rose in the Indian Ocean and as English woolens flooded Brazil. They achieved a certain local success by the 1740s, though mostly as tax farmers manipulating currencies and the financial aspects of the trade at the expense of colonials left to engage in the direct handling of the slaves. Lisbon's distaste for owning slaves at this stage expressed their own awareness of the marginality of the business relative to the attractions of Brazilian gold.

The Pombal generation of domestic industrialists and traders turned to the slave trade of the southern Atlantic to escape British and French competition in the 1750s and, with gold production in Minas Gerais dwindling and Brazilian agriculture in a midcentury trough, were willing to buy and sell the slaves they carried to northeastern Brazil. They succeeded only against the holders of the slave-duty contract, and that mostly by dint of massive government intervention on their behalf, not by their economic strength or skills. By the 1770s, Lisbon had turned to the agricultural resources of Brazil, leaving Angola's trade in slaves once again to Brazilians, who traded to Africa with their own sugar cane brandies and, increasingly, with goods smuggled by British interests rather than merchandise from Portugal. Rio-based merchants of metropolitan origin returned to slaving for the last time after 1810, no longer as competitors of the British but rather as their agents. Just as old ships often gained a shabby extension of their useful lives by carrying slaves across the southern Atlantic, An gola's slave trade restored the fortunes of a succession of commercial interests on the defensive in Lisbon. But in no case did this happen more than temporarily – except for the Jewish pioneers of the sixteenth century, whose collaboration with the Dutch gave them advantageous access to Brazilian sugars, but only as foreigners – as Portugal and its empire drifted steadily past the darkened hulks of these once-influential merchantmen into the economic straits of nineteenth-century British industrial capitalism.

The Portuguese had thus become more and more specialized as slavers, while foreign suppliers and financiers and Brazilian planters led the economic growth within their empire. Slaving obviously produced profits, as the long series of marginal groups drawn into it frequently built strong positions out of its returns, if only in Angola. However, it marginalized the slavers by drawing them into extractive, destructive, and commercial sectors that lay increasingly on the fringes of an Atlantic system built on more highly capitalized foundations. The slavers' economic prominence in Angola, but less so in Brazil and hardly at all in Lisbon, provided a clear geographical expression of slaving's structural marginality to an Atlantic economy centered on northern European finance and production.

SLAVE TRADING ON THE PERIPHERIES OF BRAZIL'S COLONIAL ECONOMY

If informal British influence in Portugal pressured Lisbon's waning commercial interests to the southern Atlantic periphery of the empire, the tight constraints of colonial rule in Brazil made Angola's slave trade all the more necessary to independent American merchants there. The relevant economic watershed divided metropolitan creditors and their resident agents, whether Anglo-Portuguese, importers of Asian cottons, or domestic manufacturers, from American debtors, planters, and colonial traders in a large local provisioning network excluded from direct participation in the currency economy of the empire. The substantial borrowing requirements of sugar and mining, enlarged by a capitalized labor force of slaves, high currency prices for imports, prohibitions against import-substitution industries in Brazil, high implicit interest rates for the credit extended, and Brazil's uncompetitiveness in cash-earning world sugar markets, made the colony a persistent debtor to Portugal in the eighteenth century. These factors produced shortages of specie so severe that large portions of the colony remained peripheral to the cash economy of the Atlantic system, and even its commercial sectors operated on the basis of commodity currencies and merchant notes of indebtedness.[26] Brazil's colonial economy, in short, functioned very much according to Portugal's intention of concentrating specie and commodities salable for cash in the metropole, leaving planters perennially owing future harvests for slaves and equipment, and forcing local merchants to trade on working capital borrowed in the form of imports purchased from firms based in Portugal and resentful of competition from direct agents – the infamous *comissários volantes* – the same suppliers then sent out to undercut them.

Colonial merchants and planters thus owing cash debts to Portugal found a partial means of covering these deficits in slaving. They devised African trades that used low-value by-products of their export agriculture to acquire the labor they needed, thus lessening the amount of currency they would otherwise owe to metropolitan slavers willing to sell new Africans only for specie, bills of exchange payable in metropolitan currency, or commodities worth currency in Europe. This strategy of exploiting the noncash sectors of the African and American economies had originated in the militarism of the Pernambucan governors in Angola from the 1650s until the end of the seventeenth century, as they conducted their slave raids with African mercenaries compensated in booty and with the partial support of government arms supplied by Lisbon.[27] These wars thus required very little cash to mount but produced slaves salable in Brazil for currency credits or substituting for labor they would otherwise have had to buy from their metropolitan competitors for cash or its equivalent.

The well-known eighteenth-century Bahian tobacco and slave trade to the Mina Coast of West Africa rested on an exchange involving similarly low cash opportunity costs and comparably lessening the struggling northeastern Brazilian sugar sector's debt to Europe. Bahia exported primarily sugar and tobacco to Portugal.[28] But the process of boiling the cane syrup down to the muscovado sugar shipped to Lisbon left molasses and other residues that could be distilled into cane brandies of very high alcohol content, predecessors of modern Brazil's famed *cachaça* known in the African trade as *gerebitas*. In addition, Bahian tobacco fields could be made to yield a third picking of strong, coarse leaf unacceptable in the refined markets of Europe. The Bahians found insatiable African markets for these low-value by-

[26] Mircea Buescu, *300 anos de inflação* (Rio de Janeiro: APEC, 1973); Schwartz, chap. 8.
[27] John K. Thornton, "The Art of War in Angola, 1575–1680," *Comparative Studies in Society and History*, Vol. 20, No. 2 (1988), pp. 360–78.
[28] Schwartz.

products of their main export crops, soaking rolls of the third-grade tobacco in molasses and selling them for slaves on West Africa's Mina Coast.[29] Their *gerebitas* they employed in Angola to undercut much more expensive Portuguese brandies and less potent metropolitan and Madeiran wines.[30]

These Brazilian *gerebitas*, particularly those of Rio de Janeiro's relatively uncompetitive sugar industry early in the eighteenth century, became staples of Angolan slaving, accounting for almost 20% of imports by value and for nearly the entire incoming cargo aboard the Brazilian ships that carried most of the Angola slaves across the southern Atlantic.[31] Thus, Brazil's southernmost port, at least in its sugar industry's earlier, difficult years, appears to have sold *gerebitas* in Angola to compensate not only for colonial debt and Brazil's general uncompetitiveness in world commodity markets but also for its remoteness, relative to Bahia and Pernambuco, from the limited European markets for Portuguese sugars. Slaves bought with inexpensive *gerebita* thus lessened the cash indebtedness of marginal Brazilian slave owners and merchants, unable to offer British woolens, Asian textiles, or other manufactures on comparably advantageous terms, until the end of the legal trade.

Brazilians, for all their advantage in inexpensive American commodities in high demand in Africa, still remained among the weaker economic and political interests in the Portuguese southern Atlantic as merchant capital from Lisbon shifted the trade's basis toward commercial credit. They therefore retreated to its geographical fringes to preserve even their secondary position in slaving, itself the marginal component of the empire. Bahian merchant interests transferred their slaving from Angola to the Mina Coast in the 1680s partly out of frustration at the power of Pernambucan governors at Luanda, as well as in reaction to their inability to trade peacefully in the midst of their continual violence, consequent epidemics, African flight from the war zones, and incipient depopulation in and around the colonial territories. In doing so, they extended a Dutch and English trading region centered on the Gold Coast to the east, thus avoiding, once again, more established competitors and opening up African regions not yet intensely committed to selling slaves. With the gold rush of the early 1700s, Rio traders, marginalized by the miners' preference for Mina slaves available through Bahia, followed Lisbon's Asia mer-

---

[29] Verger.
[30] For price differentials in the 1680s, see Miller, "Capitalism and Slaving."
[31] Miller, "Imports at Luanda."

chants to Angola in search of slaves, whom they hoped to sell to gain a share of the riches available in Minas Gerais.

At Luanda, however, these Rio slavers ran up against not only the Pernambucan governors but also the metropolitan tax contractors. Those who stayed to trade at the colonial capital sold *gerebita* and accepted subordinate positions in the export market as transporters of slaves belonging to the contract holders and the Angola Luso-Africans. More aggressive Rio traders seeking slaves to buy and sell on their own accounts found them at Benguela, Angola's smaller, remote, mortiferous southern port. There they developed an independent trade to Rio, less dependent on credit and complex financial arrangements, and set off a wave of warfare in the populous highlands to the east in the 1720s and 1730s. After jurisdictional conflicts with the tax contractors were resolved in favor of the Rio traders, they developed Benguela's slave trade to a level nearly equal to that of Luanda by the 1780s and 1790s, decades in which searing drought in west-central Africa provoked wars and created refugees and captives available for purchase without heavy commercial investments in trade goods that poor Brazilians could not afford.[32] Benguela, as a refuge for Rio traders excluded from Luanda by the strong metropolitan governors and Lisbon merchants, contractors, Pombaline chartered companies, and others there, once again illustrated the spread of slaving through retreat by the weak to the geographical margins of the Atlantic economy.

In the 1780s and 1790s, Rio merchants not only brought Benguela to its peak exports of slaves but also moved into the void left at Luanda itself by Portugal's virtual withdrawal from Angolan slaving. Though they thus temporarily commanded southern Angolan slaving, these gains came at a time when Lisbon was excluding them from Brazil's revived trade back to Europe in sugar, cotton, and coffee. Removal of the Portuguese court and metropolitan merchants to Rio in 1808 and the Anglo-Portuguese traders' resurgence in Angolan slaving after the British entered the Brazilian market in 1810 once again drove the colonials away from the sources of slaves they had developed at Luanda. As a consequence, Rio traders sought out riskier and more remote sources of slaves in order to retain any niche at all in an early-nineteenth-century slave trade falling under growing British abolitionist pressure.

[32] For statistics, see Herbert S. Klein, *The Middle Passage: Comparative Studies in the Atlantic Slave Trade* (Princeton, N.J., 1978), esp. pp. 27, 255–6; for the drought, see Joseph C. Miller, "The Significance of Drought, Disease, and Famine in the Agriculturally Marginal Zones of West-Central Africa," *Journal of African History*, Vol. 23, No. 1 (1982), pp. 17–61.

Rio traders thus led the way in diverting Mozambique's slave exports from Indian Ocean markets into the long and deadly passage across the Atlantic. They also, along with Pernambuco merchants, momentarily strengthened by the booming cotton exports of the north, replaced the British and French formerly dominant along the Loango Coast north of the mouth of the Zaire River. Bahians, confined to the Mina Coast by their dependence on tobacco for buying slaves and insufficiently prosperous to compete in the southern hemisphere with other Brazilian slavers, particularly those from the rapidly growing capital of the Portuguese monarchy and of British finance at Rio, stuck it out in the illegal trade north of the equator, even at the risk of seizure by British antislavery naval patrols. The forced retreat of colonial slavers to the riskier, more remote, and even dangerous sources of African labor in the early nineteenth century thus helps to explain their persistent defiance of the British West Africa Squadron when Luanda and other ports remained legally available to them.

Other familiar elements in the structure of Brazilian slaving, Bahia's tobacco trade on the Mina Coast and Rio's prominence as a destination for growing southeastern African exports of slaves after 1800[33] thus combine with the importance of *gerebita* in Angolan slaving, Benguela's growth as a source of slaves, and other aspects of Portugal's African trade in the southern Atlantic to illustrate slaving's function as a retreat for colonial planters and merchants so debilitated by Portuguese mercantilism – and eventually British capitalism – that they could find no other method of supporting their pervasive indebtedness. As Portugal moved toward the periphery of the Atlantic economy through increased specialization in slaving, its Brazilian subjects found themselves driven out to its irregular and dubiously legal fringes by Lisbon merchants themselves in retreat from growing British power and wealth.

AFRICAN SLAVING FROM THE PERIPHERY OF THE ATLANTIC ECONOMY[34]

Africa as a whole, and particularly west-central Africa, stood even further from the commercial and industrial growth at the core of the

---

[33] Klein, pp. 51–72; Joseph C. Miller, "Sources and Knowledge of the Slave Trade in the Southern Atlantic" (unpublished paper presented at the Western Branch meeting of the American Historical Association, La Jolla, California, 1976).

[34] Peripheral in the sense of an integrated network of exchange and investment developed in this chapter, and in Solow and Engerman, "Introduction" to *British Capitalism and Caribbean Slavery;* not the position assigned Africa in Wallerstein's

Atlantic economy than did the Portuguese and Brazilian merchants engaged in slaving. Its economies possessed large, and in west-central Africa comprehensively, nonexchange sectors at the moment Christian merchants appeared with trade goods and commercial credit from the Atlantic. Africa also had a technology based mostly on the strength of the human hand and back and a profound lack of financial resources to expand commerce or to invest in costly material technology. Wealthy Africans held their assets instead in the form of human dependents: subjects, clients, wives, junior kin, pawns, and slaves.[15] Africa thus embodied to an extreme degree slaving's apparent association with economic marginality, in the specific sense of its function of supporting groups lacking the financial strength to establish a viable position in the more capital-intensive, fastest-growing, and most cash-profitable sectors of the Atlantic economy. It therefore comes as no surprise that Africa's less commercialized regions borrowed – as receivers of the trade goods that Lisbon merchants sank, on credit, into the Angolan backlands – in order to develop economic contacts abroad and that they resorted to slaving when they lacked other means of paying off what they owed.

Throughout west-central Africa's growing involvement with Atlantic commerce, established authorities, the men in control of labor and hence of productive power, tended to open trade with Europeans not in slaves but rather in commodities – ivory, raffia textiles, dyewoods, copper, wax, and cattle. They consolidated these early commercial relations at very low initial opportunity costs or investments in production, tending to sell off accumulated surpluses of commodities like ivory, disposing of the by-products of productive activities oriented to the domestic economy, or applying labor time unutilized during slack periods in the agricultural calendar. Those who gained wealth and power from selling commodities produced through these low-investment strategies built commercial networks and political systems with overhead costs requiring greater surpluses to support than they could have drawn from the people under their control by other means. Since they seldom possessed sufficient authority to intensify production for export significantly, increased volumes of exchanges tended to deplete their stocks of these by-products or to absorb the time available to produce them. Faced with declining supplies of commodities for export and unable to invest in increasing production of

world-systems theory [Immanuel Wallerstein, *The Modern World System*, 3 vols. to date (New York, 1974, 1980, 1989)].
[15] A perspective sketched more fully in *Way of Death*, chap. 2.

them, they covered their institutional overhead costs by continuing to import, delaying deliveries on what they owed, and thus living off debt to European traders, who – however modestly financed by North Atlantic standards – disposed of commercial capital on a scale all but unimaginable in the nascent exchange sectors of west-central African economies.

Even without rising volumes of trade, herds of elephants retreated to the interior, imported textiles lowered the scarcity value of domestic palm cloths, European demand for African dyewoods or wax failed to grow, or copper exports threatened to deplete reserves of the continent's principal monetary and prestige metal. Exporters then faced both debt to the foreign merchants and dependence on trade with them to preserve the shaky prominence they had achieved, a structural position not unlike that of the colonials in Brazil. In that circumstance, Africans resorted to slaving – though selling rather than buying – to defend political or economic gains they could not otherwise preserve.[36]

In Angola – an ecologically fragile region with commercial institutions rudimentary even by African standards – the early commodity strategy appeared at the coast only as a feeble stream of ivory, dyewoods, and wax exported amid a rapid and overwhelming resort to slaving. The preference for commodities was clearer in other African regions less marginal to the Atlantic system, with more developed commercial systems and greater productive capacity, and commodity trade lasted longer there.[37] The clearest example comes from eastern

---

[36] See the argument applied to the Lake Chad–Fezzan–Libya trade, concentrated narrowly on slaves, that thrived in the nineteenth century. The central Sudan lacked the gold and grain at the heart of desert-side trade in the western Sudan and the relatively low-cost river transport of the Nilotic Sudan to the east; see, e.g., Ralph Austen, "The Mediterranean Islamic Slave Trade Out of Africa: Towards a Census" (unpublished paper, Workshop on the Long-Distance Trade in Slaves Across the Sahara and the Black Sea in the 19th Century, The Rockefeller Foundation Bellagio Study and Conference Center, Villa Serbelloni, Italy, December 1988), p. 8. For the credit involved, see Abdullahi Mahadi, "The Aftermath of the Jihad in the Central Sudan as a Major Factor in the Volume of the Trans-Saharan Slave Trade in the 19th Century" (unpublished paper, Bellagio Conference, December 1988).

[37] Other examples would include the low proportion of slaves in exports from the intensely commercial desert-side economy of Senegambia [Philip D. Curtin, *Economic Change in Pre-Colonial Africa: Senegambia in the Era of the Slave Trade* (Madison, Wis., 1975)], from the gold-producing Akan area [Richard Bean, "A Note on the Relative Importance of Slaves and Gold in West African Exports," *Journal of African History*, Vol. 15, No. 3 (1974), pp. 351–56], or, in adjacent parts of west-central Africa, from the trading economy of the Zaire river basin [Martin, *External Trade of the Loango Coast*, and Jan Vansina, "The Peoples of the Forest," in David Birmingham and Phyllis Martin (eds.), *History of Central Africa* (London, 1983), Vol. 1, pp. 75–117].

Portuguese southern Atlantic slave trade   141

Africa, where the profits of a hundred years or more of systematic ivory hunting allowed hunters to build specialized, well-equipped ivory hunting systems in the eighteenth century that they could no longer maintain once they had depleted the herds of elephant near the coast. As they pursued vanishing supplies of tusks farther and farther into the interior, and as Indian Ocean demand for slaves grew after about 1750, the hunters found it expedient to cover their rising transport costs and to sustain the polities and economic institutions they had created by converting their hunting capabilities to seizing humans.[38] On the Atlantic side of Africa, the large quantities of goods Europeans were willing to pay for African labor, compared to the low valuation they placed on most commodity exports, critically facilitated the early and profound turn to slaving, but the limited capital, marginal commercial institutions, and restricted productive capacity of the African economies also left Africans unable to compete with Europe on the capitalist terms of the Atlantic system in ways that paralleled the marginality of the Portuguese and Brazilians and thus similarly forced them to make use of slaves to participate in it at all.

Just as economically and politically weak Brazilians found slaving relief from the pressures of Portuguese mercantilism in buying slaves, so also did selling slaves in Africa frequently represent a defensive maneuver by parties threatened on the local scene with eclipse. Bush traders in Portuguese Angola often accepted the trade goods Lisbon offered on credit to recover from previous economic failures in Brazil or Portugal, were gypsies or Jews driven out of Portugal by the criminal courts or by the Inquisition, or had come to Angola as political exiles with no choice but to head for the backlands in search of slaves. Beyond the borders of the colony, marginalized African groups took up slaving when other alternatives failed. The earliest systematic sales of slaves in the 1510s came from monarchs of a Kongo kingdom arguably peripheral to the main lines of political consolidation on the opposite, northern, bank of the lower Zaire River, and they seized the captives they sold to merchants from Portugal in raids on still more marginal borderlands. Kings in name more than in their limited

---

[38] Edward A. Alpers, *Ivory and Slaves in East Central Africa: Changing Patterns of International Trade to the Later Nineteenth Century* (London, 1975), and François Renault, "Structures de la traite des esclaves en Afrique Centrale" (unpublished paper, Workshop on the Long-Distance Trade in Slaves Across the Indian Ocean and the Red Sea in the Nineteenth Century, School of Oriental and African Studies, London, December 1987), translated as "The Structures of the Slave Trade in Central Africa in the 19th Century," *Slavery and Abolition*, Vol. 9, No. 3 (1988), pp. 146–65.

ability to dominate their subjects, they also strengthened their domestic position relative to powerful regional competitors within the polity by resorting to slaving.[39]

The Kwanza River mouth developed as a second – and eventually the major – source of slaves in Angola through a congruence of Eur-African and African interests marginalized by Kongo's sales of slaves to Portuguese merchants. The obscure planters of São Tomé in the mid-sixteenth century found cheaper captives there, sold by an African warlord in the remote interior, the Ngola a Kiluanje, whose title became the name of the colony later Portuguese conquerors carved out of his lands, bent on shoring up his defenses against Kongo border raids into his lands. The wars of the Ngola a Kiluanje, exacerbated by two decades or more of drought in the 1590s and 1600s, drove roaming bandits, the Imbangala or "Jaga," out of settled agricultural villages and into the arms of early Portuguese military governors, who welcomed them as mercenaries in their wars of conquest and pillage during the 1610s and 1620s.[40] With drought and disruption, Luanda's slave exports thus leaped after 1610 to their mature seventeenth-century levels, in the vicinity of 10,000 slaves per year, on the strength of captives sold by the next generation of local people driven to desperation by the wave of dislocations thus set in motion. Successful Imbangala war leaders repeated the pattern of slaving by the dispossessed by establishing new states bordering lands controlled by the Portuguese, at first raiding their marcher territories for captives and then brokering sales of slaves sent west from later, still more remote supply areas in a wave of violence peripheral to the growing Atlantic system that spread inland until the end of the trade in the nineteenth century.

These scattered instances exemplify both the marginality of slave selling – though not of slavery itself – in Africa and the degree to which Africans consolidated political systems and created new commercial institutions, at least in substantial part, by borrowing trade goods from the Atlantic. Commercial credit was critical, as people without followers of the sort forced to resort to slaving in Africa could not have got their start without it, nor would established African

[39] The reference is to the Tio; Jan Vansina, *The Tio Kingdom of the Middle Congo 1880–1892* (London, 1973). On Kongo, I expand on the argument made by Anne Hilton, *The Kingdom of Kongo* (Oxford, 1985), with acknowledgment of the rather different approach in John K. Thornton, *The Kingdom of Kongo: Civil War and Transition, 1641–1718* (Madison, Wis., 1983).

[40] For the Imbangala, see Joseph C. Miller, *Kings and Kinsmen: Early Mbundu States in Angola* (Oxford, 1976), and reinterpreted to stress the ecological factor in "Significance of Drought, Disease, and Famine."

commodity exporters vulnerable to depleting resources have survived in its absence. Their precarious successes brought Africa well within the orbit of the Atlantic system, though at its margins, and made African slaving states and networks, like slavery itself in the New World, assets – albeit very risky ones – in which merchants unable to buy directly into American silver and gold, profitable sugar and other valuable agricultural commodities, tobacco monopolies, or other more secure forms of wealth found export markets, investment opportunities, and the productive slave labor that sustained the more marginal contributors to European economic growth from all around the Atlantic system.

THE FINANCIAL CONTRIBUTIONS OF SLAVING AND THE SLAVE TRADE

The fundamental importance of European credit in financing commercial, and related political, growth on the American and African margins of the Atlantic system highlights the general marginality of slavery and the slave trade to sources of expansion in the seventeenth- and eighteenth-century economy in banking and credit. Slavery and the trade in slaves were consequences, as much as causes, of the rapid economic growth. Expanding abilities to finance growth, to offer trade goods on credit in Africa and to sell slaves in America months and years in advance of payment in Europe, greater monetarization, and larger home and reexport markets for slave-grown commodities opened up an Atlantic-wide shortage of labor that firmed the level of wages on the side of the European cash sector and drew Africans in as slaves on the noncash fringes of the system. The slaves, both traded and put to work, permitted newer and faster-growing economic sectors of the sort continuously created in economies undergoing rapid growth, as well as poorer and obsolescent sectors like the Portuguese empire, to participate in the changes underway. Structural change by definition tends to occur at the fringes of established institutions, and it was precisely there – rather than in older or dominant industries – that overseas trade, including slavery and the slave trade, made a difference.

Slaving and slavery were critical because they allowed groups lacking the efficient monetary forms of wealth central to merchant capitalism – specie, currency, or currency credits – to get a start or, in the case of Portugal, to hold out long after they had ceased to perform efficiently in the center ring. European capitalism had itself taken shape on an earlier margin, as merchants and then bankers expanded the small commercial sectors of the late medieval European economy, in some part then itself a Mediterranean periphery of much wealthier and more sophisticated trading economies in southwestern Asia and the Indian Ocean.[41] Christian and European Jewish merchants, unable to penetrate the ecclesiastical, warrior, and landed aristocracies at home, found little opportunity to reinvest the profits they made in anything but more trade, and especially in opening markets abroad.

Succeeding overseas, they converted their peripheral sector of the Asian commercial system to a new Atlantic capitalist center of their own and set about building up stocks of the precious metals that financed their trade. Growth in such a system depended on enlarging the currency base from which bankers could multiply investment capital through institutions of credit. But trade with Asia's still more monetized markets drained specie, and financing growth itself absorbed another portion of Europe's scarce monetary stocks, so that the critical means of expanding the commercial sector of the European economy became the purchase and production of specie – the gold trade of western Africa, Spanish American silver, Brazilian gold – or other forms of commerce not requiring investments of scarce cash. The trade to Africa fit the latter requirement well, despite its risks, because Africa did not monetize silver or gold and would accept European goods, not cash, for gold dust itself, commodities, or – eventually – labor salable for money. Africans in fact often prized goods of derisory monetary value in Europe and, where necessary, monetized them to lubricate exchanges in the expanding commercial sectors of their own economies. Africa's limited ability to expand production and the Atlantic labor deficit turned the early gold and commodities trade so highly advantageous to specie-hungry Europeans to slaves. The advantage was not only that slaves produced sugar, precious metals, tobacco, and cotton worth cash in Europe but also that they were mobile assets obtainable for goods cheap in terms of Atlantic (and Mediterranean, and Indian Ocean) currencies.

The abstract shortage of financial capital available to the growing commercial sector of an expanding European economy manifested itself, inevitably, at its margins, among traders and producers short of cash but trying to compete nonetheless in the dynamic exchange sphere. The African market's advantage was relatively greater for them than for cash-rich bankers, or for merchants established in staple

---

[41] A parallel developed in other, more formal, ways by Stefano Fenoaltea, "Europe in the African Mirror: The Slave Trade and the Rise of Feudalism" (unpublished paper, 1988).

commodities like salt or herring or grain in Europe, or for spinners and weavers of flax or wool. Hence, fifteenth-century Portuguese and Genoese went to Africa to divert its gold from the Arabs and Venetians, but the marginal traders who followed in their footsteps became the slavers and stayed on into the sixteenth century and later, after wealthier interests had abandoned Africa to seek shares of Spain's American silver. Africa's slaves gave these weaker competitors the means to sell wine, inexpensive woolens, shells, and other goods of little value elsewhere in Europe or Asia for American specie otherwise bought up by manufacturers of metalwares and better textiles. The seventeenth- and eighteenth-century sequence of losers in Lisbon and Brazil, all taking their residual stocks to Africa for distribution by exiles and renegades to African upstarts, continued the pattern evident since the start. Their marginality was economic, in the sense that they worked with little currency in a system based on specie, as well as social in their lack of respectability.

Slavery in America functioned analogously as an investment remunerative in terms of cash but requiring relatively little commercial wealth to commence and finance. A salient characteristic of merchant capitalism – indeed, perhaps its defining feature, if not a tautology – is that traders themselves do not invest in processes of production. Under the conditions of rapid growth and attendant shortages of financial capital present from the beginning in the Atlantic, overseas merchants – almost axiomatically strapped for funds – found it cheaper and more efficient to invest in opening new markets than to commit the much larger sums that would have been necessary to create new systems of production. The first ventures into production, in what would eventually become industrial capitalism, fell to established interests, better able to afford them, of varying specific strengths in Europe. Slaves were inexpensive in cash terms, but they represented a collateralized productive asset that would even support credit as a means of purchasing them. Hence the debt ubiquitous throughout the history of Angola's slave trade and Brazil's slave plantation sectors.

Brazilian slavery as a labor system, as well as in its commercial aspects, presented similar advantages in low cash maintenance costs. To the considerable extent that Brazilian plantations grew their own food or purchased it through direct exchange of services or American commodities with local provisioning sectors where specie did not circulate, they required only modest commitments of cash, within the reach even of men at the edge of bankruptcy, to produce sugar or other commodities worth cash. The greater the leverage thus attained

146   *Joseph C. Miller*

on the cash invested, through credit, self-supporting slave populations, illiquid investments in land and buildings, and livestock, the
more rapidly they could expand. Reproduction among slaves to the
limited extent that it occurred, further lessened their need for cash
to buy additional labor. The Bahians' and Cariocas' extremely low-
cost methods of buying slaves in Africa with otherwise worthless by-
products of sugar and tobacco must have been even more efficient in
these terms than breeding, given the negative demographic growth
rates of the slaves taken to Brazil and the large numbers of slaves
brought to Brazil through these means. Most important of all, slaves
required no costly expenditure of cash paid out as wages on a daily
or weekly basis, months or years in advance of sale of their product
for the currency necessary to fund such payments. From the perspective of the currency definition of the Atlantic system, slavery was
a method of borrowing, or extracting, the costs of production from
the worker, whereas wages were an expensive method of remuner-
ating labor affordable only by the wealthiest and most cash-rich European sectors of the economy. With unpaid slave labor from Africa,
the credit arrangements and commercial notes – bills of exchange –
characteristic of the slave trade turned small, even negligible, original
cash investments in surplus goods for the Africa market in Europe
into American labor systems highly productive of commodities worth
sufficiently near their weight in gold to repay the risks and delays
involved.

In the monetary terms pertinent to explaining how a commercial
capitalist system spread throughout the Atlantic with such extraordinary rapidity from the sixteenth through the eighteenth centuries,
slavery and the slave trade thus functioned as a cash-efficient method
of financing the expanding, productive asset base under European
control. As a sector yielding significant cash returns but requiring low
cash investment and maintenance expenditures, it functioned in
a manner similar to peasant economies on the fringes of Asian or
modern world capitalist systems. The defining feature of a peasant
productive sector is its displacement of housing, food, and other
significant labor costs into a domestic economy not involving exchange or expending cash. Peasants can thereby survive, and even
experience a net gain in cash holdings, while selling their product
into the cash economy at prices that return far less than their full
(imputed) costs of production or even subsistence. Family farm labor
systems, and even the unremunerated contributions of women in
modern households, represent more attenuated manifestations of the
same principle of financing economic growth by drawing labor from

Portuguese southern Atlantic slave trade   147

beyond the limited currency resources of a monetizing economy. All operate by drawing labor, time, and effort in from beyond its margins. So also did slave trading, both for west-central Africans and in Portugal, and slavery in Brazil in the ways sketched.

BROADER IMPLICATIONS

On only a preliminary review of patterns of slaving nearer the monetarized center of the Atlantic system, similar themes of marginality – though subtle ones seldom clamoring for attention because of their very insignificance in relation to the more prominent economic sectors surrounding them – appear to lend general significance to the cash-saving function of Portugal's slaving on the fringes of the Atlantic system and the Brazilians' retreat to the periphery of empire. In the Netherlands, early-seventeenth-century Amsterdam's wealthy merchants enjoyed too strong a position in continental commerce, and then in the advantageous Asian trade they seized through their Dutch East India Company, to bother with the hazards of stealing slaves from the Portuguese (and during the Dual Monarchy, from the Spaniards) in the Atlantic. There it was rather the smaller interests of Zeeland in the south that captured Portugal's fort on the Gold Coast, held Luanda, and eventually occupied the sugar-producing captaincies in Brazil.[42] In England, it was not the dominant agricultural interests, or the woolens merchants and manufacturers with secure markets on the continent and, later, in Spanish and Portuguese colonies, or the London banks leading the financial revolution in Britain that forged the way out to Africa. Rather, outport merchants in Bristol and Liverpool evidently found their prospects in these fast-evolving domestic and European sectors so poor that they found relative advantage in the Atlantic, despite the risks.[43] One need not deny the geographical advantages in Atlantic trade that these ports on England's western coast also enjoyed to fit them as well into the larger

---

[42] Goslinga, *Dutch in the Caribbean and on the Wild Coast*. See also Johannes Menne Postma, *The Dutch in the Atlantic Slave Trade 1600–1815* (New York, 1990), esp. pp. 36, 127, 131ff.

[43] Which is not to deny London's role in the trade, though generally as financier rather than as venturer to Africa; the Portuguese parallel lies in the wealthier Lisbon merchants' preference for the financial aspects of the Spanish *asiento*, brokering the British woolens trade to Brazil and – even in Angola – the function of selling goods rather than buying slaves. For London, see James A. Rawley, *The Transatlantic Slave Trade: A History* (New York, 1981), chap. 10, pp. 219–46; also his "Humphry Morice: Foremost London Slave Merchant of his Time," in Serge Daget (ed.), *De la traite à l'esclavage* (Actes du Colloque international sur la traite des Noirs, Nantes 1985) (Paris/Nantes, 1988), Vol. 1, pp. 269–81.

scheme of slaving initiatives coming from the edges of Europe's economies.

In France, the same tendency would help to explain the similarly minor slaving activities of major ports like Rouen or Bordeaux, respectively centers of trade in the English Channel and to the Antilles, compared to Nantes and a dozen otherwise – and significantly – unremarkable Atlantic and Breton towns with no particular superiority in location.[44] In British North America, Boston, New York, and Philadelphia, the major Middle Atlantic and New England ports, never approached small Rhode Island towns in their commitment to slaving.[45] Rhode Islanders bought West Indian molasses, distilled it into strong rum salable for slaves in Africa, returned to the West Indies with their captives, and sold them there for sterling credits to offset persistent sterling deficits with Britain. Their strategy exactly paralleled that of Bahian and Rio de Janeiro planters, trapped in a similar debtor position relative to Portugal, and also buying slaves with by-products of American agriculture. The uniformly peripheral economic position of the major slaving ports of the European and American participants in the trade suggests that the Portuguese were not the only slavers who went to Africa out of weakness rather than strength.

Recent reinterpretations of British economic growth, export trade, and imperialism bring out the marginality, combined with the critical significance, of domestic interests in slaving and slavery. For Cain and Hopkins, who review the *longue durée* of British imperial expansion, the overseas impulse, from the middle of the eighteenth century until World War I, was repeatedly initiated by groups losing at home.[46] The value-for-money efficiency of slaving and slavery made Africa and the sugar economy of the West Indies merely extreme cases of a general phenomenon long familiar in political, if not economic, terms: Foreign wars have saved many a weakened political leader in domestic trouble throughout world history. Looking at the critical period in British industrial development from 1748 to 1776, David Richardson suggests that a declining woolen industry revived its fortunes by selling to Portuguese and Spaniards, who used British textiles to buy

---

[44] A convenient English-language survey of the French trade is Robert Stein, *The French Slave Trade in the Eighteenth Century: An Old Regime Business* (Madison, Wis., 1979).

[45] Jay Coughtry, *The Notorious Triangle: Rhode Island and the African Slave Trade, 1700–1807* (Philadelphia, 1981); Elaine F. Crane, "'The First Wheel of Commerce': Newport, Rhode Island the Slave Trade, 1760–1776," *Slavery and Abolition*, Vol. 1, No. 2 (1980), pp. 178–98.

[46] Cain and Hopkins.

Portuguese southern Atlantic slave trade   149

slaves in Africa and to clothe them in America, that Britain's own colonies in the West Indies provided protected markets necessary to sustain weak "infant" metals fabricators and weaving factories, and that it was these still-peripheral economic sectors – whose export volume he distinguishes carefully amid aggregate figures dominated by other, larger industries – that made the greatest gains from exporting at the crucial early stage in their development.[47] Pierre Boulle makes essentially the same case for Nantes: One significant contribution of slaving to industrial development there was the African trade's ability to dispose of the crude products of early experiments with mass production and mechanization.[48] Robert Stein hints at a related advantage for French merchants on the brink of trouble in emphasizing their tendency to use Africa as an outlet for excess inventories and to mount ventures with minimal expenditures of cash.[49]

In the British and French centers of Atlantic economic growth, resort to low-cash-investment slaving in Africa, or slave markets in the Americas, sustained marginal new industries through early inefficient phases of technical experimentation, high start-up costs, and political weakness and positioned them, in Britain at least, to grow toward later dominance by moving into the domestic, intra-European, and North American markets that alone possessed sufficient size and wealth to sustain the complex transformations visible in retrospect as an "industrial revolution." In contrast, for Portugal and its empire, as well as elsewhere on the peripheries of the Atlantic economy, declining and threatened economic interests resorted to slavery and the slave trade as means of delaying impending collapse. Slaving there entrenched old inefficiencies and removed Portugal further and further from the growth and structural changes gathering momentum elsewhere. The American colonies engaged in slaving, reliant on European credit and drained of specie, thrived on a noncash labor system that brought local prosperity, but their very success concentrated gold, silver, and credit across the Atlantic and consolidated their positions on the margin of a system centered in Europe. Slaving and slavery thus contributed to functional specialization within a capitalist Atlantic system defined more and more in terms of cash. Africa sim-

---

[47] Richardson, "Slave Trade, Sugar, and British Economic Growth." Joseph E. Inikori, "Slavery and the Revolution in Cotton Textile Production in England," *Social Science History*, Vol. 13, No. 4 (1989), pp. 343–79, gives an institutional history of the cotton industry, providing specific details to the same effect.

[48] Boulle, "Slave Trade".

[49] Stein, pp. 17, 22, 64–6ff, 154ff.

ilarly invested its wealth in slaves and trade goods – from the Europeans' perspective, since many were also currencies in the Africans' view – and thus allowed the complementary concentration of the fundamental assets of capitalism, silver and gold, in Europe, and especially in London. With the financial innovations of the City based on the Brazilian gold in its vaults, capital became available to finance nonslave forms of economic growth in Britain and throughout the northern Atlantic.

Slavery and the slave trade, as cash-conserving methods of underwriting growth, thus contributed to apparently contrary features of the Atlantic system, all of them aspects of regional economic specialization that moved Britain toward wage labor and industrialization but left Portugal, the colonies, and Africa in currency debt to Europe. Slaves coming from Africa and laboring in the colonies were far from the only factors involved in this vast and complex process, of course, but their marginality to it is precisely the point.

12
La traite vers l'Ile de France

Jean-Michel Filliot

Les contraintes maritimes

Introduction

Comme les Hollandais l'avaient fait au XVIIème siècle, les Français, à leur arrivée en 1722 sur l'île qu'ils venaient de baptiser *Ile de France,* amenèrent des esclaves pour "être affectés à la construction des ports, maisons, magasins de la compagnie"[1] comme le dit un texte officiel.

Pendant le temps de leur administration, de 1722 à 1810, tout le développement reposa sur les arrivées serviles.

Je rappelle succintement les grandes occupations des esclaves:

— aménagement, protection des côtes avec notamment création et renforcement du Port Louis.

— agriculture avec le manioc, l'indigo et la canne à sucre.

— petite industrie avec des forges, indigoteries, tanneries.

— participation à l'infrastructure (routes, magasins de l'Administration, demeures privées).

— enfin, manutention liée à la marine.

La belle collection d'estampes du Mauritius Institute montre toute cette multitude d'esclaves en train de travailler...

Je viens d'employer le mot multitude; citons les chiffres pour être plus précis:

— en 1735 :   650 esclaves et   200 (?) "libres".

— en 1766 : 18,000 esclaves et 2,000   "libres".

— en 1788 : 36,000 esclaves et 7,000   "libres".

— en 1797 : 49,000 esclaves et 10,000   "libres".

— en 1809 : 55,000 esclaves et 13,500   "libres".

Les officiels eux-mêmes, au cours de ce siècle français, virent bien l'importance vitale de ces apports continuels. Prenons trois exemples avec des phrases de La Bourdonnais, Dumas et Descroizilles (on pourrait en trouver des dizaines d'autres):

La Bourdonnais, gouverneur de 1735 à 1746, peut-être le plus grand administrateur français de l'Ile de France, écrit à propos des communications: "C'est encore un travail de quinze années à 200 noirs pour avoir tous les chemins qui sont nécessaires à la commodité publique".

Dumas, gouverneur de 1767 à 1769, trente ans après, donc, est encore plus précis: "La traite est dans ce moment le plus important object de mon administration, sans elle point de main d'oeuvre".

Enfin, Descroizilles, en 1803, "négociant et planteur, ancien membre de l'Assemblée coloniale", récapitule crûment l'opinion de tous: "Un objet de la plus haute importance... est l'augmentation du nombre des noirs, sans laquelle il est impossible que l'agriculture fasse aucuns progrès sensibles (sic)... Tous les hommes éclairés des vrais intérêts de l'Etat sont aujourd'hui convaincus que l'existence des colonies si intimement liée avec la prospérité du commerce et de la marine nationale dépend du maintien de la servitude, seul moyen de contraindre au travail une espèce d'hommes indolents par nature..."

Peut-être 80 à 90,000 esclaves furent importés pendant cette période française, mais ce chiffre est sujet à caution naturellement, car il est difficile de faire la séparation entre l'Ile de France et Bourbon. De même je pense que 45% de ces esclaves vinrent de la "côte orientale d'Afrique" (Mozambique, Portugais et comptoirs arabes), 40% de Madagascar, 13% de l'Inde et 2% de l'Afrique de l'Ouest (Gorée et Ouidah).[2]

Il était utile de rappeler ces idées pour marquer toute l'importance de la traite dans la vie de l'Ile de France.

Mon propos aujourd'hui est de vous présenter un élément souvent oublié (parce qu'il n'est pas facilement étudiable, les sources étant disséminées), pourtant il est primordial car sans lui il n'y aurait pas eu d'esclaves, je veux parler du transport et des contraintes maritimes.

Pour être simple, je développerai ce sujet en deux parties:

la mer et le bateau.

les acteurs et le voyage.

Première partie: la mer et le bateau

Le cadre maritime

Pour l'Ile de France du temps des Français, tout commençait sur les côtes françaises. L'Orient (avec L apostrophe) Bordeaux, Saint-Malo et Nantes étaient les ports qui commerçaient le plus avec Port Louis.

Mais que signifiait cette mer orientale? Un marchand de Saint-Malo, Pyrard de Laval, avait donné la réponse à la fin du XVIIème siècle: "C'est la mer où nous connaissons les côtes d'Afrique et de l'Asie, avec toutes les îles et presqu'îles de notre hémisphère qui sont au-delà du cap de Bonne Espérance en allant vers Zanzibar avec l'île Dauphine (l'île du Dauphin du roi de France ou Madagascar), les côtes d'Arabie ou de Perse, celles de l'empire du Mogol avec l'Inde, celles de la Chine, les îles Maldives, de Ceylan, de la Sonde, du Japon, les Philippines et les Moluques".

Des cartographes avaient essayé de bien situer les routes avec les îles, les hauts fonds, les écueils... Pour les Français toujours, il fallut attendre le travail de d'Après de Mannevillette, appelé *Neptune oriental,* qui à partir de 1745 rendit les plus grands services: de la côte de Natal à la Nouvelle Hollande (Australie), de Madagascar à la côte de Perse ou à l'île de Bornéo, l'océan Indien fut très bien connu.

Les routes se divisaient en deux groupes:

1. Celles qui avaient leur origine dans les ports français, qui arrivaient dans l'océan Indien au sud du cap de Bonne Espérance et qui aboutissaient en Inde et en Chine (en passant quelquefois par le canal de Mozambique, et le plus souvent par l'est des Mascareignes), ou qui se terminaient au Port-Louis (la fameuse route des îles, bien étudiée par le Docteur Toussaint).

2. Celles, locales, qui partaient (et qui revenaient) du Port-Louis vers Pondichéry et les autres comptoirs français, vers Madagascar, enfin vers la côte orientale d'Afrique.

Pour la traite, on va retrouver toutes ces routes. Je m'étendrai sur les deux dernières directions: Madagascar et la côte orientale d'Afrique.

Quand aux autres, elles ne furent qu'incidentes, je les note seulement maintenant: pour l'Afrique de l'ouest, seule une trentaine de bateaux entre 1728 et 1756 apporta dans les 2,000 esclaves; on s'arrêtait à Gorée, ou on allait jusqu'à Ouidah dans le fond du golfe de Guinée, et on continuait la route vers l'océan Indien.

Pour l'Inde, on recoupe le trafic qui allait et repartait vers la France. Là encore, peu d'esclaves vinrent de la péninsule; notons aussi que la plupart des Indiens étaient déjà au XVIIIème siècle des "engagés", c'est-à-dire des personnes libres...

Madagascar donc. Entre mars et décembre, les bateaux faisaient une sorte de navette entre la grande île et Port-Louis. La mer était calme, la température était alors moins étouffante, les esclaves étaient amenés des hauts plateaux. Cette conjonction climatique et commerciale a réglé le cabotage pendant toute la période française.

En comptant les arrêts à Foulpointe ou Tamatave, ou dans la baie d'Antongil (pour citer les principaux points), les expéditions duraient en moyenne 3 ou 4 mois.

Rodrigues, à 800 km plus à l'est de l'Ile de France, servait parfois de point de repère et même d'escale de rafraîchissement pour ceux qui ne faisaient pas attention aux vents (qui sont presque toujours contraires pour le retour aux îles). Il fallait effectuer alors un détour de 2,000 km pour ne pas tomber "sous le vent". Rodrigues offrait aux malchanceux des tortues de mer, "dont la graisse verte et la couenne sont fort estimées".

La côte d'Afrique maintenant. Tous les bateaux (dont les itinéraires nous sont parvenus) passaient par le nord de Madagascar. On se servait toujours de l'alizé pour franchir le cap d'Ambre, soit en longeant la côte malgache, soit en pointant sur Agaléga. On touchait les Comores, Anjouan surtout, puis on "atterrissait" à Mozambique; chez les Portugais. Pour aller plus au nord, chez les "Arabes", au-delà du cap Delgado, on profitait des vents du sud-ouest: Pemba, Zanzibar, Quiloa, s'étaient réapprovisionnés en esclaves.

Pour le retour, quelques uns passaient par le sud du canal de Mozambique, mais la grande majorité passait par le nord, à 1,000 ou 1,500 km au large de Madagascar. On frôlait l'équateur, parfois même on avait en vue les Maldives, mais la plupart du temps les Seychelles servaient de repaire. La principale de ce groupe de 90 îles et îlots, Mahé, servit ainsi d'escale de rafraîchissement aux négriers. Reconnue en 1742, habitée vraiment à partir de 1770, Mahé rendit les plus grands services pendant plus de vingt ans. Point idéal entre la côte d'Afrique et les Mascareignes du fait des vents dominants, elle avait "l'air très salubre qui rétablit promptement les esclaves fatigués des navires".

Après tous les bienfaits des Seychelles, on profitait du courant nord équatorial pour rejoindre Port-Louis. Le voyage avait duré ordinairement 5 à 6 mois.

Le bateau et sa cargaison

Des navires, vaisseaux et frégates, qui arrivaient de France servirent pour apporter des esclaves. Ces bateaux jaugeaient de 400 à 600 tonneaux, avaient 60 à 80 hommes d'équipage et à Port-Louis recevaient parfois l'ordre de faire un détour au moment où les cyclones n'étaient pas à craindre, pendant la saison fraîche.

Les correspondants locaux des négociants métropolitains gardaient dans leurs magasins ce qui était superflu à la mission. On faisait quelques modifications dans l'entrepont et le "métropolitain" allait "traiter" pendant quelques semaines.

Cependant le besoin s'était fait sentir d'avoir un groupe de navires de petit tonnage spécialisé dans les communications locales. A partir de 1725, l'Ile de France (et Bourbon) eut une flotille de brigantins, senaus, barques, "petites flûtes"; on les appela les "vaisseaux de côte". Par opposition aux métropolitains qui repartaient pour "France", ils furent dits de la "seconde navigation" et servirent surtout pour la traite servile. Ils avaient un tirant d'eau qui pouvait forcer les passes peu profondes des rives malgaches ou africaines et une voilure maniable, se diminuant ou s'augmentant dans le minimum de temps.

Un conseiller des directeurs de la Compagnie des Indes, Lanux, a bien décrit ces bâtiments qui rapportaient des dizaines d'esclaves: "Le tillac est exhaussé au-dessus de sa flottaison, au moins d'un tiers, voici pourquoi: d'abord pour donner plus de hauteur au parc des noirs, construit sur le faux pont, ensuite pour que l'on puisse arrimer beaucoup d'eau et de vivres; enfin pour assurer au navire la qualité essentielle de ne pas embarquer la vague dans les gros temps, car il n'y a de si nuisible à la santé des noirs que d'être mouillés par l'eau de mer.... Une galerie est contruite sur laquelle on place des factionnaires quand la cargaison commerce à se compléter ou que l'on met la voile.... Le tot est confectionné: c'est une tente goudronnée, divisée en plusieurs compartiments, et destinée à couvrir le pont de l'avant à l'arrière pour le préserver du soleil, de la pluie et des lames..."

Cette description de 1729 resta valable pendant toute la période.

La cargaison, les vivres, les pièces à eau, s'entassaient dans l'entrepont et dans la cale. Arrivés sur les lieux de traites, les bateaux déchargeaient la cargaison. C'est elle qui nous intéresse maintenant.

—Prenons l'exemple de Madagascar, puis nous noterons la spécificité de l'Afrique (côte oriental et Sénégal-Ouidah). Cette démarche nous est imposée par les sources, nous sommes très bien renseignés pour la grande île, assez mal pour l'Afrique; en ce qui concerne l'Inde, aucune description n'a pu être trouvée.

Les chefs malgaches, dès les premières grandes traites, dans les années 1730, eurent des préférences nettement marquées. Habitués par les pirates à recevoir des armes et des munitions, ils en voulurent toujours plus. Les fusils venaient des manufactures françaises de Maubeuge, Charleville et Saint-Etienne. La garniture devait être en "cuivre", le calibre "gros", et le fût de noyer.

En 1741, un hollandais du Cap avait bien remarqué la qualité de ces fusils français, "qui étaient si bien faits et si jolis que le nôtre ne peut supporter la comparaison". Corollaire des fusils, "la poudre de guerre en baril", "les balles de plomb" et "les pierres à fusil" étaient négociées en grande quantité.

Après les armes, les toileries étaient demandées. Certaines venaient de France (Elbeuf, Rouen, Cholet), d'autres arrivaient de Pondichéry (les pièces de "Guingan", de "Karikal", de "Madras", de "Patnas"...).

Venait ensuite l'assortiment hétéroclite, avec les métaux (fer, cuivre et étain), les spiritueux (eau-de-vie ou "arack" fabriquée à l'Ile de France) et la "quincaillerie" (miroirs, couteaux, épingles, marmites, rasoirs, etc...).

La piastre d'Espagne était aussi échangée. Mais en petit nombre, et car les agents royaux interdisaient aux traitants privés d'en fournir.

—Pour la côte orientale d'Afrique, tout ce que nous venons de décrire reste valable, mais les fusils n'ont plus la prédominance. Les Portugais et les Arabes semblent avoir goûté davantage les piastres et les étoffes de l'Inde.

En 1792, selon les papiers Decaen, il est bien marqué: "C'est presque toujours avec des piastres, quelquefois accompagnées de marchandises, que l'on traite les noirs".

—Pour la côte occidentale d'Afrique, la marchandise la plus demandée était l'étoffe sous de multiples variétés, puis venaient les "cauris", ces coquillages qui servaient de monnaie, enfin la quincaillerie paraît plus diverse et de moins bonne qualité.

Le résultat peut encore se lire dans des papiers de traitants ou dans des journaux de négriers. Prenons un exemple dans un extrait du journal de Glemet, "régisseur en chef des traites du Roi" à Foulpointe:

"Une femme de 30-35 ans - 2 fusils de traite, 10 livres de poudre, une bouteille d'eau-de-vie...

Un garçon de 15 à 16 ans - 3 fusils de traite, une brasse de toile, 1 miroir, 2 bouteilles d'eau-de-vie".

Deuxième partie: les acteurs et le voyage

"Traitants" et esclaves

—Sous les ordres du capitaine, qui était souvent un "ex-officier de la marine militaire", et d'un état-major réduit (3 à 4 hommes), la maistrance réunissait souvent un maître-charpentier, un maître-calfat, un maître-tonnelier, avec un maître-voilier et un maitre d'équipage. Un cuisinier et un domestique accomodaient tant bien que mal les provisions de bouche. Enfin l'équipage se composait au moins d'une vingtaine d'homme "blancs et noirs"[3], "gens inconnus, ramassés de toute part, sales, débraillés, couverts de misérables haillons", ils étaient hommes décidés, prêts à tout pour gagner quelque argent.

Il faut s'arrêter sur le dénuement de ces négriers. Quand on étudie les "hardes des morts", c'est-à-dire les listes des biens après décès, avec comme seule fortune "un vieil habit", "deux gilets usés", "un vieux chapeau", "de mauvaises culottes", rarement des mouchoirs, on peut noter que la différence entre le matelot et l'esclave était la liberté.

—Les captifs, "mâles, femelles, négrillons, négrittes ou pièces d'Inde", comme on les appelait, n'avaient qu'à subir. C'est l'histoire atroce d'un silence, d'un vide. Comment étaient-ils devenus esclaves dans leur pays?

Ils avaient été pris, kidnappés, souvent faits prisonniers par la guerre, ou punis pour un crime, ou pour une dette. Les quelques textes que l'on a ne sont pas assez précis et donnent certainement une idée fausse de la mise en esclavage.

Puis, cès Français de l'Ile de France les avaient achetés à des Portugais, à des Malgaches, à des Africains, à des "Arabes". Si la traite interne à l'Afrique ou à Madagascar semble avoir existé depuis très longtemps, la demande européenne à partir du XVIIème siècle paraît avoir multiplié le phénomène.

Des humains avaient enchaîné d'autres humains, des humains avaient "marqué" d'autres humains. "Les nègres pour le compte du Roi étaient marqués d'un R", tandis que les nègres de la traite privée avaient une lettre qui pour la plupart était l'initiale du patronyme de leur futur maître. "Marquer" c'est-à-dire faire souffrir avec un fer chauffé au rouge! pour empêcher la fraude.

La seule trace écrite qui reste est une facture en trois exemplaires qui renferme le signalement des esclaves en désignant leur nom, leur taille, leur sexe, leur âge à peu près. L'historien n'a pas de matériau pour exprimer son dégoût.

Le voyage

La cargaison humaine "mise aux fers" et entassé dans les flancs du navire, le capitaine levait l'ancre. Le charpentier avait construit les cloisonnements nécessaires, le tonnelier avait fait provision d'eau douce, et le cuisinier avait stocké riz, bananes, pois, biscuits, fèves et salaisons. Le voyage vers l'Ile de France allait se dérouler, jamais le même, avec des imprévus. Certains préceptes pour réussir s'étaient cependant dégagés, comme l'écrit un armateur: "Pour la conduite des esclaves, le capitaine sait que la propreté, la gaieté, avec de bons vivres, contribuent plus à leur santé que les remèdes".

Comment se déroulait ce retour? La description d'une journée ordinaire peut servir d'approche.

Garneray, peintre, littérateur et négrier, l'a bien décrite: "Les noirs séjournent sous le faux pont depuis le soleil couchant jusqu'au soleil levant...Quand aux négresses et aux enfants, ils couchent au milieu de la grand-chambre... Les plus âgés, les plus vigoureux, ou ceux dont on redoute l'esprit d'insubordinnation, occupent l'avant du navire... Tous les matins, une demi-heure après le lever du soleil, on fait monter les esclaves quatre par quatre sur le pont et on surveille leur toilette; ils sont tenus de se laver la figure et les mains dans des baquets remplis d'eau de mer, et de se rincer la bouche avec du vinaigre pour prévenir le scorbut".

Puis le repas du matin était servi. "Ils meurent d'inanition, il faut avoir quelque chose d'autre en plus du riz cuit avec de l'eau" disent des instructions en 1736. Le boeuf en salaison de Madagascar était la viande préférée pour toutes les traites; un sieur Dejean nous apprend que "cette viande, quoique salée, donnera une substance au riz... mais il est moralement impossible qu'un corps puisse résister pendant un mois de traversée à cette dernière nourriture".

La longueur vide de la journée s'écoulait. Parfois, on leur faisait faire des cordages... "A quatre heures, on leur sert un nouveau repas semblable en tout point à celui du matin", ensuite, si le temps était beau, les danses commençaient. Selon D'Unienville, les Indiens avaient "un chant lugubre et leur danse pantomime ne peut avoir de charme que pour eux. La musique du Malgache porte un caractère de mélancolie... La musique et la danse du Mozambique annoncent la gaieté et la force des gambades grotesques".

Enfin, "au moment où le soleil va disparaître, on donne le signal de la retraite, seulement on a le soin, avant de réintégrer les nègres dans leurs logements, de les fouiller soigneusement afin de s'assurer qu'ils n'ont, pendant leur séjour sur le pont, dérober aucun objet qui pourrait les aider à briser leurs fers...L'équipage se retranche, ayant ses armes placées à portée".

En dépit de toutes les précautions, des accidents arrivaient, notons les maladies, la mortalité et les révoltes.

Les grandes épidémies qui ravagèrent l'Ile de France eurent leur origine dans les bateaux revenant des lieux de traite, ainsi la "petite vérole" en 1791-92, "introduite par un bâtiment revenant de Mozambique qui jeta le deuil sur toutes les familles".

La variole fut bien la maladie la plus redoutable. Le visage "se prenait", puis "le corps, les cuisses, étaient pleins de boutons plats et de la plus mauvaise qualité"; enfin "même si le visage commençait à se nettoyer", le sujet mourait quelques jours après, d'après de nombreux procès-verbaux de chirurgiens.

Le scorbut aussi était la maladie du retour par excellence. On pensait que "les nègres étant empilés dans l'entrepont, les vaisseaux du corps humain relâchés par un air aussi chaud et aussi humide, perdaient leur action. Les esclaves avaient alors le bas de la figure horriblement gonflé. Leurs lèvres béantes, flétries, laissaient apercevoir des gencives noires..." Devant les ravages du "mal escorbutique", les Seychelles servirent ainsi d'antidote.

D'autres maladies, comme les "coliques", "flux de ventre", plongeaient les esclaves dans le "Marasme". Les fièvres "putrides et sinoches", les "plaies gangréneuses" étaient aussi à craindre. Contre l'ensemble de ces maux, bien peu de remèdes étaient efficaces. En 1777, un "état", de l'*Aimable Victoire* nous apprend que pendant la traversée du Mozambique au Port-Louis furent utilisés des "emplâtres, onguents, pommades mercuriales, rhubarbe, eau de rose, thé, sucre et eau de vie escorbutique". Sachons que ce navire embarqua 422 esclaves et en débarqua 303; 119 étaient morts!

Les maladies étaient donc fréquentes et graves, la "médecine" inopérante. La conséquence dernière en fut une effroyable mortalité. L'âge des esclaves (pour la majorité, ils avaiet entre 18 et 25 ans) est trompeur: amoindris, physiquement et moralement, il était prévisible qu'un certain nombre mourrait en moyenne à chaque voyage.

On connaît surtout les cas où la mortalité a décimé d'une façon spectaculaire. Ainsi sur 620 achetés à Mozambique en 1739, 360 périrent durant le voyage. En 1740, sur 80 embarqués à Pondichéry, 6 furent livrés...

Les "procès-verbaux du jour de la mort" et les journaux de bord, avec leurs petites croix latines dans les marges, donnent une précieuse information, mais elle est trop fragmentaire. Il a fallu attendre les travaux du Docteur Toussaint et de A. Lougnon pour avoir des statistiques valables:

pour Madagascar, entre 1775 et 1807, sur 2,423 esclaves, la mortalité est de 12%.

pour la côte orientale d'Afrique, entre 1777 et 1808, sur 15,109 esclaves, le pourcentage est de 21.

pour la côte occidentale d'Afrique, les estimations donnent entre 25 et 30%.

quant à l'Inde, la mortalité devait y être de 20 à 25% si l'on compare les temps de voyage.

Les révoltes étaient le danger permanent. La peur de l'inconnu, le comportement des traitants, faisaient des esclaves des désespérés.

Un sursaut tout à coup étreignait les captifs... La révolte et sa répression ensanglantaient le navire. Prenons un exemple. En 1780, "le 14 du mois de mai, vers dix heures et demie du matin, tous les gens de l'équipage étant dispersés dans le vaisseau et occupés en différentes manoeuvres, les esclaves de traite se sont révoltés et le signal en a été donné par un nommé Bororo, qui a saisi à la gorge le sieur Le Bel, pilote de quart; qu'alors tous les esclaves se sont armés de tous les instruments qui se trouvaient sur le pont, et sortis en troupe sur l'arrière du vaisseau, où ils commençaient à faire violence et à frapper..." La révolte est jugulée et: "Il fut résolu que pour le salut commun, il fallait sacrifier le chef des révoltés Bororo; le capitaine l'a fait lier et hisser au bout de la vergue où il l'a fait fusiller en présence de toute la traite et ensuite jeter à la mer".

Après bien des tourments, parfois même des tempêtes, le bateau entrait dans la passe. Le Port-louis se dessinait... La traite servile, comme tout commerce, allait voir sa fin au mouillage...

Conclusion

Le bateau était "affourché". Un "chirurgien" montait à bord pour vérifier le bon état sanitaire de la cargaison. Les malades étaient emmenés au "lazaret" ou au dépôt.

Les autres, "sans autre vêtement qu'un lambeau de toile autour des reins, étaient rangés, les hommes d'un côté du débarcadère, et les femmes et les enfants de l'autre, et les planteurs les passent en revue et font leurs achats..."

Ou bien on les emmenait dans les nègreries. La vente était alors annoncée par voie d'affiche; ainsi le 15 février 1775 à Port Louis, un avis indiquait: "une cargaison de noirs Mozambiques, arrivés par le senaut le *Diamant* est à vendre chez le sieur N..."

L'état-major et l'équipage avaient touché leurs soldes et leurs gratifications. "Leur zèle et leur émulation" avaient été récompensés. Les "nègres" connaissaient déjà la trique du "commandeur".

Comme j'ai essayé de le montrer, ce trafic était inhumain, dangereux, mais il continuait car les armateurs, les capitaines, faisaient des bénéfices et ces esclaves débarqués étaient le véritable moteur économique de l'île.

Bientôt un précepte révolutionnaire français allait énoncer que "tous les hommes naissent libres et égaux". Cette idée toute nouvelle allait cependant mettre bien du temps à parvenir jusqu'à l'Ile de France.

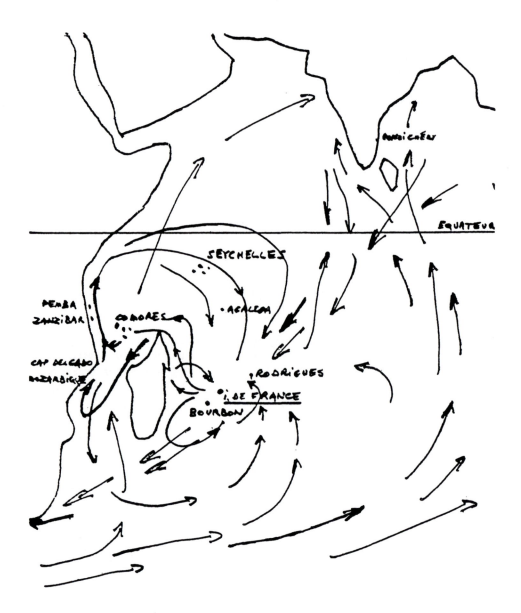

Les routes françaises au XVIIIème siècle.

Notes

1. On suppose connue l'organisation administrative de l'Ile de France... D'abord gérée par la Compagnie des Indes orientales, elle fut reprise en 1766 par la Couronne.

2. Cet essai statistique a été l'objet de mon travail sur les Mascareignes et à 15 ans de distance, peu de choses sont venues modifier mes conclusions: je pencherai maintenant pour un peu plus d'Africains et un peu moins de Malgaches.

3. Ces noirs étaient des Mozambiques (jamais des Malgaches) qui la plupart du temps avaient été affranchis.

Bibliographie succinte

Archives

A L'Ile Maurice

Mauritius Archives.

Séries HB: Madagascar Papers.

Séries OB et OC: Période Royale, journaux de bord, rôles d'équipage....

Séries NA: minutes notariales (quelques sondages seulement).

En France

Archives Nationales (Paris).

Séries C2 : Correspondance générale, Inde.

Séries C4 : Correspondance générale, Ile de France.

Séries C5 A : Madagascar.

Archives du port de Brest.

Séries M : Volume se rapportant aux Mascareignes.

Bibliothèque municipale de Caen.

Papiérs du Général Decaën

Archives du port de Lorient.

Séries IP : Compagnie des Indes.

Imprimés

Ampers, Edward A. *The French slave trade in East Africa 1721-1810.* In Cahiers d'Etudes africaines, vol. X, 1970, 1er cahier, pp. 80-124.

Après de Mannevillette, Jean Baptiste Nicolas Denis d' *Le Neptune Oriental,* dédié par M. d'Après de Mannevillette... Brest, 1775, 201 p.

Supplément au Neptune Oriental Paris, 1781

Benedict, Burton *Indians in a plural society.* A report on Mauritius. Colonial Office. Colonial Research Studies, No. 34, London, 1963 (2ème éd.) 167p.

94

Bissoondoyal, B. *Indians in Mauritius Island.* In Indo-Asian Culture, vol.VII, no. 2, oct. 1958, pp. 193-199.

Chiche, Marie-Claire *Hygiène et santé à bord des navires négriers au XVIIIème siècle.* Thèse de doctorat en medicine. Paris, 1957.

Dazille, Joseph Barthélémy Chirurgien-major à l'Ile de France *Observations sur les maladies des nègres, leurs causes, leurs traitements et les moyens de les prévenir.* Paris, 1786, 1767-1776, 316 p.

Deschamps, Hubert *Histoire de la traite des Noirs de l'antiquité à nos jours.* Paris, 1971, 338 p.

Descroizilles, Frédéric *Essai sur l'agriculture et le commerce des îles de France et de La Réunion.* Rouen, 1803, 114 p.

Filliot, Jean-Michel *La traite des esclaves vers les Mascareignes au XVIIIème siècle.* Paris, 1974, 273 p.

Garneray, Ambroise Louis *Voyages, aventures et combats.* Paris, 1957, 190 p.

Graham, Gerald S. *Great Britain in the Indian Ocean.* A study of maritime enterprise 1810-1850. Oxford, 1967, XIV, 480 p.

Haight, Jackson M.V. *European powers and south east Africa.* A study of international relations on the south-eastern coast of Africa 1796-1856. London, 1967, 368 p.

Hazareesingh, K. *Histoire des Indiens à l'Ile Maurice.* Paris, 1973, 223 p.

Lanux, Jean Baptiste François de *Mémoire sur la traite des esclaves à une partye de la cotte de l'est de l'isle de Madagascar.* In Recueil de documents et travaux inédits pour servir à l'histoire de La Réunion, t.I, 4ème trimestre 1932, p. 79, sept. 1729.

Mahé de La Bourdonnais, Bertrand François *De la coste d'Afrique ou Sophola, adressé à M. de Moras, commissaire du Roi auprès de là Compagnie.* In Recueil de documents et travaux inédits..., t.IV, 1er trimestre 1940, p. 372, 1733.

Noël, Karl *L'esclavage à l'Ile de France pendant l'occupation française, 1715-1810...* (multigr.), Paris, 1953.

Toussaint, Auguste *L'administration de l'Ile Maurice et ses archives (1721-1810).* Port Louis, 1955, 149 p.

Toussaint, Auguste *La route des îles.* Paris, 1967, 540 p.

Toussaint, Auguste *Histoire de l'Ile Maurice.* Paris, 1971, 128 p.

Toussaint, A. et Adolphe, H.*Bibliography of Mauritius* 1502-1954. Port-Louis, 1956, 884 p.

13

Sex Ratio, Age and Ethnicity in the Atlantic Slave Trade: Data from French Shipping and Plantation Records

David Geggus

THE age and sex composition of the Atlantic slave trade has attracted increasing attention in the last decade from scholars who stress its critical significance in shaping black society in both Africa and the Americas.[1] Largely absent from these investigations has been any consideration of the slaves shipped by the French, who constituted close to one-fifth of the Africans exported to the New World at the trade's height during the eighteenth century.[2] Also unexploited in this respect is the rich documentary record provided by plantation inventories from the French colony of Saint Domingue (modern Haiti). Unusually detailed with regard to slaves' origins, they permit a finer focus on the question than do shipping records that offer scant information on ethnic identity.

In this article two samples are analyzed. One is composed of 177,000 slaves transported in French ships during the years 1714–1792, which is taken from the *Répertoire des expéditions négrières* of Jean Mettas and Serge Daget.[3] The other, derived from nearly 400 estate inventories, consists of more than 13,300 Africans who lived on Saint Domingue plantations in the period 1721–97. The results are compared with existing knowledge of the demographic composition of the Atlantic slave trade to show the range of variation that existed through time between different importing and exporting regions and to shed light on the forces of supply and demand that determined the proportions of men, women, and children who were sold as slaves across the ocean.

THE FRENCH TRADE IN COMPARATIVE PERSPECTIVE

Jean Mettas's *Répertoire* provides demographic details for more than 630 of the 3,343 voyages it describes, and shows that, of 176,997 slaves transported, 47·4 per cent were men, 26·0 per cent were women, and 26·6 per cent were children.

* The author wishes to thank Stanley Engerman and Joseph Miller for commenting on an earlier draft of this article.

[1] P. D. Curtin, *Economic Change in Precolonial Africa: Senegambia in the Era of the Slave Trade* (Madison, 1975); H. Klein, *The Middle Passage* (Princeton, 1978); I. Kopytoff and S. Miers (eds), *Slavery in Africa: Historical and Anthropological Perspectives* (Madison, 1977); J. E. Inikori (ed.), *Forced Migration: the Impact of the Slave Trade on African Societies* (New York, 1982); P. Manning, *Slavery, Colonialism and Economic Growth in Dahomey* (Cambridge, 1982); C. Robertson and M. Klein, (eds), *Women and Slavery in Africa* (Madison, 1983); P. Lovejoy, *Transformations in Slavery* (Cambridge, 1983); D. Galenson, *Traders, Planters and Slaves* (Cambridge, 1986); D. Eltis, *Economic Growth and the Ending of the Transatlantic Slave Trade* (New York, 1987).

[2] However, Lovejoy, *Transformations*, 62, incorporates a small sample from Jean Mettas's *Répertoire*, vol. 1.

[3] J. Mettas, *Répertoire des expéditions négrières françaises au xviiie siècle*, edited by Serge Daget, 2 vols. (Paris, 1978, 1984).

24   DAVID GEGGUS

Table 1. *Sex and age composition of captives in selected branches of the Atlantic slave trade*

Carrier, destination, and date	Males per 100 females	Percentage children	No. of slaves
Du., Angola–Brazil 1636–43[a]	105	33	2,064
Du., Guinea–Brazil 1636–45[a]	138	13	3,086
Br., to Barbados, 1663–7[b]	c. 108	9	2,269
Br., to Br. W. Indies, 1673–1725[c]	158	14	73,990
Du., West India Co., 1675–1740[d]	228	13	36,121
Br., to Sp. America, 1715–38[e]	197	34	17,080
Fr., to French colonies, 1714–56[f]	186	27	59,705
Br., to S. Carolina, 1735–40[g]	...	14*	11,562
Du., free trade, 1730–95[d]	144	22	25,051
Pg., Luanda–Brazil, 1734–59[h]	...	7@	239,962
Pg., to Pará/Maranhão, 1756–88[j]	166	20#	20,235
Pg., to Brazil, 1761–86[j]	...	1@	49,344
Fr., to French colonies, 1764–78[f]	171	27	101,533
Br., to Jamaica, 1764–88[k]	165	19*	74,546
Da., 1777–89[m]	175	23	15,203
Br., to Grenada, 1784–8[n]	154	32	13,561
Fr., to French colonies, 1784–92[f]	196	19	13,197
Br., to Br. W. Indies, 1791–8[p]	165	7 < 14*	83,722
Sp., etc., to Havana. 1790–1820[q]	221	43#	101,644
Pg., to Rio de Janeiro, 1795–1811[r]	...	1@	170,651
Sp., etc., to Cuba, 1811–67[s]	229	39	51,577
Pg., to Brazil, 1811–67[s]	188	42	27,365

Br = British; Da = Danish; Du = Dutch; Fr = French; Pg = Portuguese; Sp = Spanish.

Except where noted, the term 'children' apparently designated persons thought to be under fifteen years old.
* Children under 4′4″ in height, probably aged under 13.
@ Children aged approximately under 7.
# Includes adolescents aged under 18.

[a] E. van den Boogaart and P. C. Emmer, 'Dutch Participation in the Atlantic Slave Trade', in H. Gemery, J. Hogendorn (eds), *The Uncommon Market* (New York, 1979), 366.
[b] E. Donnan, *Documents Illustrative of the History of the Slave Trade to America* (Washington, 1930–5), vol. 1, 88, n. 71.
[c] Galenson, *Traders*, 94–6.
[d] J. Postma, 'Mortality in the Dutch slave trade', in Gemery and Hogendorn, *Uncommon Market*, 257. Age data were derived from a sub-sample of the whole.
[e] C. Palmer, *Human Cargoes* (Urbana, 1981), 108, 122. Age data derived from a sample of 970 slaves.
[f] Mettas, *Répertoire*.
[g] P. Wood, '"More like a Negro country"' in S. Engerman and E. Genovese (eds), *Race and Slavery in the Western Hemisphere: Quantitative Studies* (Princeton, 1975), 150.

[h] M. Goulart, *Escravidão africana no Brasil* (São Paulo, 1950), 203.

[j] A. Carreira, *As Companhias Pombalinas de Navegação* (Porto, 1969), 89–95. Children under seven accounted for 0·3 per cent of imports into Pará/Maranhão.

[k] *Two Reports from the Committee of the Assembly of Jamaica to Examine the Slave Trade…* (London, 1789). The percentage of children was estimated from a sub-sample of 7,510 slaves sold in the period 1786–8.

[m] H. Klein in Robertson and Klein, *Women*, 30.

[n] Public Record Office, London, 30/8/348, 246.

[p] H. Klein in Robertson and Klein, *Women*, 31, 33. The lower figure for the percentage of children derives from the whole data-set, in which it seems children were not always distinguished from adults. The higher figure refers to only those shipments where children were counted, and is an average per shipment.

[q] *Ibid.* 31, 33. Children under seven accounted for 20 per cent.

[r] Klein, *Middle Passage*, 37.

[s] Eltis, *Economic Growth*, 256. Mean proportions per cargo.

The overall sex ratio of 179 males per 100 females appears to have been entirely average for the Atlantic slave trade, as Table 1 suggests.[4] The view put forward in Robertson and Klein's *Women and Slavery in Africa* that 'in all trades, between two-thirds and three-quarters' of persons shipped were males is difficult to reconcile with the evidence presently available.[5] Conversely, J. E. Inikori's projection of a sex ratio of about 150 (males per 100 females) for the whole Atlantic trade is certainly too low.[6]

Any generalization will be imperfect, as long as little is known about sex ratio in the eighteenth century trade to Brazil, its more important branch.[7] All in all, Herbert Klein's earlier assessment would seem more accurate – that males constituted between 60 and 70 per cent of captives in almost all slave trades across the Atlantic.[8] Sex ratios fell below this level (of 150 < 233:100) in some minor branches of the trade, such as the French trades to Guadeloupe

[4] As the surviving data somewhat overrepresent the trade of the smaller French colonies, especially in the 1780s, it is useful to assign weights to the trade of each colony for each of the three periods used in Table 1, in order to reflect their true share of total French Caribbean imports. For this purpose the data in P. D. Curtin, *The Atlantic Slave Trade: a Census* (Madison, 1968), 166, 180 were used. The resultant changes are small. The overall sex ratio rises to 184, and the periodic ratios to 183, 172, and 200.

[5] Robertson and Klein, *Women*, 4, 32, 39. In fact, in three of the four data-sets that Herbert Klein presents in this study males made up less than two-thirds.

[6] Inikori, *Forced Migration*, 24.

[7] The Pará/Maranhão statistics cited in Table 1 point to a fairly low sex ratio, but there is every reason to believe that this cotton-growing region supplied primarily from Cacheu and Bissau, and where the male/female price differential was negligible, was quite atypical. Census data indicate that slave sex ratios were much higher in other Brazilian provinces, but themselves are only crude guides to the composition of slave imports. Conversely, some sources mention large numbers of women and youths among Brazilian slave imports. See A. Carreira, *As companhias pombalinas de navegaçao* (Porto, 1969), 92, 161–8; R. Conrad, *World of Sorrow* (Baton Rouge, 1986), 9–12; S. Schwartz, *Sugar Plantations in the Making of Brazil* (Cambridge, 1985), 348–53; J. Miller, 'Slave Prices', in P. Lovejoy (ed.) *Africans in Bondage* (Madison, 1986), 57, 61, 72; J. Miller, *Way of Death: Merchant Capitalism and the Angolan Slave Trade*, forthcoming, 130, 163–4. In the 1983 edition of his study, Carreira states that the data are too unreliable for analysis.

[8] H. Klein, 'Cuban slave trade', in *La traite des noirs par l'Atlantique* (Paris, 1978).

and Cayenne,[9] the late Dutch trade, and the mid-seventeenth century trade to the Caribbean and Brazil (Table 1).[10] However, in no trade from Africa did the known proportion of males exceed, or even equal, 70 per cent.[11] In fact the slave-traders' oft-stated target of two males for every female appears to have been only rarely attained.

If one separates adult slaves from children, the picture changes very little. In five of the trades described in Table 1 sex ratios were actually lower among adults than children;[12] and in the British trade of the 1790s they were identical. Only the nineteenth century trades to Cuba and Brazil exhibited an especially high adult sex ratio, respectively 307 and 211. In the overall French trade it was 183; in the Danish trade, 186; among imports into Grenada, 174, and among those into Pará/Maranhão, 179.

Perhaps a more unusual feature of the French slave trade was the high proportion of children it carried – 26·6 per cent, (or 23·8 per cent, if weighted averages are assigned to the data by colony and time-period).[13] Comparison with slaves supplied to other regions is complicated by differing definitions of child and adult; possibly also by undercounting of the youngest children.[14] Much of the variation perceived therefore may be spurious.[15] Nonetheless, percentages of children appear to have been rather lower in the trade to Brazil, and were clearly much higher in the trade to Cuba. The Dutch, Danish and British carriers more closely resembled the French, but still seem to have

[9] D. Geggus, 'The demographic composition of the French Caribbean slave trade', P. Boucher (ed.), *Proceedings of the 14th Annual Conference of the French Colonial Historical Society, Natchez, 1988* (Washington, 1989), forthcoming.

[10] On the seventeenth century French slave trade see, A. Gautier, *Les soeurs de Solitude : la condition féminine dans l'esclavage aux Antilles du xviie au xixe siècles* (Paris, 1985), 80, which states that around 1660 French slavers carried an equal number of men, women, and children; also J. Petitjean-Roget, *La société des habitations à la Martinique* (Lille, 1980), vol. 2, 1448.

[11] Males amounted to 71·5 per cent of total imports into Havana during the period 1790–1820 only by virtue of local importations of creole slaves from other islands: Robertson and Klein, *Women*, 32–3. A slightly lower proportion is given in Klein, *Middle Passage*, 222.

[12] These were the two later Dutch trades, and the British trades to Barbados, 1663–67, to the British Caribbean, 1673–1723, and to Spanish America, 1715–38.

[13] See above, note 4.

[14] French planters generally classed as adults those seemingly aged fifteen and over, as did British traders of the late seventeenth and early eighteenth centuries: K. G. Davies, *The Royal African Company* (London, 1957), 300. In Dutch practice, the adult classification began at age sixteen: H. Gemery and J. Hogendorn (eds), *The Uncommon Market : Essays in the Economic History of the Atlantic Slave Trade* (New York, 1979), 256. In late eighteenth century trade to Jamaica, a height of 4′4″ was the criterion used. This suggests an age range for children of about 0–11 or –12 years. Cf. G. Friedman, 'The heights of slaves in Trinidad', *Social Science History* vi, 4 (1982). For Latin American practice, see Klein, *Middle Passage*, 223; K. M. de Queiros Mattoso, *Etre esclave au Brésil, xvie–xixe siècle* (Paris, 1979), 97.

[15] Unfortunately, the relative proportions of young children and teenagers were not at all constant. In the Cuban trade children under eleven were much more numerous than those aged eleven to seventeen. However, among imports into Pará/Maranhão the opposite was true, and in the British trade to Spanish America, 1715–35, children under ten were greatly outnumbered by those aged ten to fourteen. This also seems to have been the case in Saint Domingue.

transported fewer children. Even so, Klein's assessment that children generally accounted for less than 10 per cent of most eighteenth century slave trades may need some revision.[16]

REGIONAL VARIATIONS

The range of variation in the demographic composition of slave cargoes was almost as great between exporting regions in Africa as between importing societies in the Americas (Table 2). The Bight of Biafra and the Congo basin exported to the French Caribbean similar proportions of children but radically different proportions of males and females, just as Herbert Klein found in the British trade of the 1790s.[17] The low sex ratio of Biafran exports is also attested to by earlier data from the Jamaican slave trade.[18] The French and British likewise both took a high percentage of children in Sierra Leone and a contrastingly low percentage from Senegambia and the Bight of Benin.

In other respects the regional profiles of the British and French data match up less well, although this seems partly due to different modes of data presentation. The regional sex ratios derived from Klein's raw data, as opposed to the averages per shipment he tabulates, are quite close to those of the French trade, especially for the Windward Coast and Bight of Benin.[19] The comparison is strengthened when Klein's data are combined with those of Inikori on Jamaican slave imports during 1764–88,[20] so as to provide an enlarged British sample.

Some of the observed variations may be attributable to the temporal differences between the studies, but more particularly they may reflect differing national sites of trade within the regions, as in Senegambia and on the Upper Guinea coast,[21] and also differing terminology. The French term 'Côte d'Or' was applied both to the British 'Gold Coast' and to the Bight of Benin, as in Portuguese usage.[22] It would appear, in fact, that its usual meaning was the Bight of Benin. The demographic profile of slaves whose point of shipment was described only as 'Cote d'Or'[23] closely resembled that of the Bight of

[16] Klein in *La traite des noirs*, 85. The extremely low percentages of children reported in Portuguese records prior to 1811 seem scarcely credible in view of the very high percentages obtained for the post-1811 period from more trustworthy sources. Note also the uncertainty surrounding the British trade of the 1790s: above, table 1, n. 13. Cf. above, note 7, and J. Miller's comments in *Actes du Colloque International sur la Traite des Noirs*, Nantes, 1985, 2 vols., forthcoming, vol. 1, 1–33.

[17] Klein, *Middle Passage*, 150; Robertson and Klein, *Women*, 31, 33.

[18] D. Geggus, 'Slaves of British-occupied Saint Domingue: an analysis of the workforces of 197 absentee plantations', *Caribbean Studies*, xviii, 1 (1978), 24n.; Inikori, *Forced Migration*, 23.

[19] Robertson and Klein, *Women*, 31, 33.

[20] Inikori, *Forced Migration*, 23.

[21] It is perhaps relevant that, while Africans described as Congos and Igbos had approximately the same average height in the British as in the French colonies, Mandingoes in Jamaica were three to four inches shorter than in Saint Domingue and Trinidad: D. Geggus, *Saint Domingue Slave Revolt*, forthcoming, ch. 2.

[22] M. L. E. Moreau de Saint-Méry, *Description topographique...de l'isle Saint-Domingue* [1797] (Paris, 1958), vol. 1, 49–50.

[23] Sex ratio: 150; 46 per cent men, 31 per cent women, 24 per cent children; (7,419 slaves).

Table 2. *Sex and age composition of slaves carried by French ships, by region of African provenance, 1715–92*

Region	Sex ratio	Percentage children	Percentage		Number of slaves
			Men	Women	
Senegambia	161	21·2	48·8	30·0	12,545
Sierra Leone	134	35·0	39·6	25·3	2,450
Windward Coast	175	27·8	46·2	26·0	3,205
Gold Coast[a]	163	23·0	47·8	29·2	8,910
Bight of Benin	161	22·4	47·8	29·8	41,121
Bight of Biafra	117	30·9	40·2	28·9	4,685
Congo-Angola	212	30·4	48·1	21·6	63,280
South-eastern Africa	229	25·4	51·0	23·6	1,204
Total French Trade[b]	179	26·6	47·4	26·0	176,997

Note: (a) in French the term was applied more often to the Bight of Benin than to the region designated in English usage. (b) the discrepancy between the regional and overall totals is accounted for by 39,597 slaves of uncertain provenance.

Source: Mettas, *Répertoire*.

Benin sample. In marked distinction, the few slave cargoes sold at Elmina and Anomabu reveal a much higher sex ratio, similarly to those shipped from the Gold Coast by the British.

The rough consonance between the French and British data regarding their major regions of trade makes it clear that the relatively low sex ratio of the British slave trade was due, at least in the later eighteenth century, to its degree of concentration on the Bight of Biafra.[24] Similarly, the greater proportion of males among French slave exports, and their increased prominence after 1783, derived from France's preponderance and increasing concentration on the Loango Coast.[25] The impact of these divergent tendencies was moderated, however, by contrasting regions of secondary concentration – the Bight of Benin for the French, and the Gold Coast, then the Congo, for the British.

Little is known about the sources of supply of Havana's slave imports with their exceptional proportions of children and males. Spanish slavers themselves apparently concentrated on Sierra Leone,[26] from which the British and French indeed took numerous children, but only a portion of Cuban imports was carried by Spaniards. Data from the years 1817–43 suggest that Mozambique and Congo-Angola may have supplied respectively 30 per cent and 25 per cent of imported slaves.[27] This would be consistent with a high sex ratio. However, plantation inventories from before 1820, while showing a similar percentage of Central African Bantu, reveal very few slaves from East

[24] See Curtin, *Census*, 150; P. D. Curtin, 'Measuring the Atlantic slave trade', in S. Engerman and E. Genovese (eds), *Race and Slavery in the Western Hemisphere: Quantitative Studies* (Princeton, 1975), 111–26.

[25] See Curtin, *Census*, 200.

[26] L. Marrero, *Cuba: Economia y Sociedad* (Madrid, 1972), vol. 9, 38–56.

[27] Curtin, *Census*, 247.

Africa.[28] Moreover, they also list one-quarter as 'Carabalí' (from Biafra). A possible solution to this conundrum is the change that took place in the composition of slave exports from the Bight of Biafra early in the nineteenth century. Despite some fluctuations, their sex ratio clearly remained low through the eighteenth century, but some time after 1800 the proportion of women fell sharply, while that of children increased (Table 3). As will be seen below, this would be consistent with an increasing proportion of regional captives being drawn from the Bantu-speaking peoples to the east and southeast of Igbo country.[29]

Other regional trends also show up in the eighteenth century French data. For the Congo-Angola region, which provides the largest sample, the sex ratio remained remarkably consistent, but the percentage of children among captives fell steadily, from 40 per cent prior to mid-century, to 29 per cent in the 1760s and 70s, to 20 per cent in the period 1784–92.[30] This was partly due to the eclipse of the port of Loango in the 1780s, and to the growing prominence of Malimbe, which sold the smallest proportion of children. The trend was nonetheless clearly visible across the several ports of the region, and was perhaps related to the lengthening of trade routes into the interior (see below). Significantly, Portuguese data from Luanda and Benguela also reveal a diminishing proportion of children among eighteenth-century captives.[31] Slaves whose point of departure was listed in the French records simply as 'Angola' included an average percentage of children, but had a somewhat lower sex ratio (194) than those shipped from Loango, Malimbe and Cabinda (214 < 234).

On the Bight of Benin, France's second major area of concentration, the ports with closest ties to the Yoruba, Badagri and Porto Novo, stand out on two counts from those dominated by the Ewe-Fon (Whydah, Jakin, Popo, etc.).[32] The proportion of children among slaves sold there was very low: under 10 per cent, as compared to the regional average of 22 per cent. Their sex ratio (178) was notably higher, too, but especially among the adults, men constituting 58 per cent as opposed to 48 per cent of all captives purchased.[33] The percentages of adult females sold in the eastern and western ports were, even so, quite similar; it was the proportions of men and children that substantially differed. This probably resulted from the differing extent to which

[28] Manuel Moreno Fraginals, 'Africa in Cuba', in V. Rubin and A. Tuden (eds), *Comparative Perspectives on Slavery in New World Plantation Societies* (New York, 1976), 190.

[29] However, the rise in sex ratio may also have been due to increased numbers of Hausa slaves being sent down the Niger to Brass and New Calabar.

[30] Sample sizes were as follows: 1716–53: 10,897; 1764–78: 47,317; 1784–92: 4,851.

[31] Children, apparently aged under seven or eight, dropped from 12·7 per cent of exported slaves in 1733–5, to 7·7 per cent in 1749–52, and for the period 1734–59 made up 7·2 per cent. After 1759, children formed under 1 per cent of those recorded. See M. Goulart, *Escravidão africana no Brasil* (São Paulo, 1950), 203–9. This latter reduction may derive partly from the introduction of a new system of record-keeping, which henceforth took no account of babies. They, however, had represented less than 2 per cent of the 1733–5 and 1749–52 samples.

[32] See W. Peukert, *Der atlantische Sklavenhandel von Dahomey, 1740–1797* (Wiesbaden, 1978), 64–65; R. Law, *The Oyo Empire, c. 1600–c. 1836* (Oxford, 1977), 222–3.

[33] Sample sizes were Porto Novo and Badagri: 4,028; Bight of Benin: 41,121. Slaves exported from Epe in the middle of the coast had a demographic profile midway between those of the eastern and western ports.

30   DAVID GEGGUS

Table 3. *Sex and age composition of slaves exported from the Bight of Biafra*

Carrier and date	Sex ratio	Percentage children*	Percentage		Sample size
			Men	Women	
Br, Du, 1659–1702	126	14	47	40	1,070
Fr, 1714–16	127	25	40	35	814
Br, 1764–74	154				4,065
Fr, 1765–78	103	34	39	28	3,090
Br, 1779–88	129	29			10,772
Fr, 1790–2	146	16	53	31	681
Br, 1791–8	138	14			79 ships
Sp, Pg, Fr, 1821–39	195	39	46	15	24,502

* The children's age range in the first sample and for the French shipments was probably 0–14 years; for the last sample, 0–15 years. In the other British shipments, children were those beneath 4'4" in height, approximately 0–12 years. The British 1779–88 percentage was derived from a sub-sample from the period 1786–8 numbering 2,279 slaves, and the 1791–8 percentage from a sub-sample of 22 ships.

Sources: lines 1, 8: D. Northrup, *Trade Without Rulers* (Oxford, 1978), 78; lines 2, 4, 6: Mettas, *Répertoire*; lines 3, 5: *Two Reports*; line 7: Klein, *Middle Passage*, 150.

supply routes penetrated the far interior. Surprisingly, the proportion of women shipped from the Bight of Benin was very nearly the highest for any African region (Table 2). Though almost entirely unattested in the literature on Africa and the slave trade,[34] the same tendency recurs in the ethnicity data discussed below.

Because of the controversy that surrounds the rise of Dahomey,[35] exports from Whydah were divided into three groups, to see what impact that state's emergence had on the composition of the regional slave trade. During the period of Dahomey's rise to dominance (1720–6) the sex ratio of exports changed little, rising to 188 from a level of 183 during the previous six years. Although this may reflect an influx into the port of prisoners of war, the period also saw a larger proportion of children enter the trade for no obvious reason. Following the annexation of Whydah in 1727, the sex ratio of exports fell considerably in the period down to 1778 to only 126.[36] Exports from Whydah to Jamaica in this period exhibited a similarly low ratio.[37] Insofar as state policy was a factor, this might suggest an attempt not so much to curtail slave exports

[34] Prior to Eltis's recent *Economic Growth*, which finds a comparable pattern for the nineteenth century, only Inikori, *Forced Migration*, 23 recorded a low regional sex ratio – among 4,813 slaves shipped from Whydah to Jamaica in the period 1764–88. Data showing a relatively high sex ratio, but deriving from more restricted samples, appear in Robertson and Klein, *Women*, 33, and Lovejoy, *Transformations*, 62.

[35] Robin Law, 'Dahomey and the slave trade: reflections on the historiography of the rise of Dahomey, *J. Afr. Hist.* XXVII, 2 (1986), 237–67.

[36] Sample sizes for the three periods were 8,583, 7,554, and 13,933. No data were available for the years 1727–34.

[37] Inikori, *Forced Migration*, 22–3.

(as some say) as to restrict the outflow of males. Most probably, however, it reflects the well-known westward shift to the Egun ports of the inland trade routes controlled by the Oyo Yoruba. As will be seen, these carried mostly males.

The last region where the sample size justified the investigation of temporal trends was Senegambia. The data were divided by period into three groups, 1715–52, 1764–78, 1787–92, so as to examine the effect of France's loss of her Senegal trading posts during the 1760s and 70s, when slaving was largely confined to Gorée.[38] The demographic profile of the middle period proved to be quite distinct. The sex ratio of exported slaves was only 146, as opposed to 171 in both the earlier and later periods. And the proportion of children rose from 15 per cent to 32 per cent in the middle decades, before falling back to 20 per cent. Since vessels whose listed point of departure was 'Senegal' dominated the first and last periods but were almost completely absent from the middle one, the explanation for these changes would seem clear. Slaves who came down the River Senegal included more males and far fewer children than those sold at Gorée. Indeed, contemporary traders observed that coastal peoples supplied most slaves sold in these two decades, when the ending of warfare in the Banmana region would anyway have reduced the flow of captives from the interior.[39] This is entirely consistent with previously observed patterns of trade both in Senegambia and West Africa as a whole, where high sex ratios clearly correlated with origins distant from the Atlantic coast.[40]

However, this purely geographic explanation of the Senegambian trends needs to be nuanced somewhat. This is because the percentage of children shipped from Goree was also much lower in the first and last periods than in the 1760s and 70s, while the few shipments from St Louis and 'Sénégal' in the middle period similarly shared its overall characteristics. This suggests a genuinely temporal shift in exports from the whole region. Some have argued that the decline of the Senegambian slave trade that began in the later eighteenth century may have caused a compensatory increase in anarchic local raiding.[41] Since the 1760s and 70s did indeed witness a downturn in the regional slave trade, it may be that the increased exports of women and children in these decades were an expression of such political disruption. Whereas David Eltis found that in the nineteenth century sex ratio varied inversely with the volume of slave exports, this example and that of Whydah during the period 1720–80 show this was not always the case.[42]

An additional and under-utilized source for studying the composition of the slave trade is provided by property inventories of slaveholders in the importing societies. For the colony of Saint Domingue, such slave lists are relatively abundant and more informative as regards captives' origins than those from British America or from other French colonies. Table 4 describes a sample of more than 13,000 African slaves of identifiable origins who lived on some 400

---

[38] The number of slaves in each group was 6,395, 3,983, 2,167.

[39] Curtin, *Senegambia*, vol. 1, 180.

[40] Curtin, *Senegambia*, vol. 1, 176; Geggus, 'Slaves', 23–4. However, the extremely high regional sex ratios Curtin found in the 1680s and 1720s would appear quite unusual.

[41] See P. Curtin, 'Abolition', in J. Walvin and D. Eltis (eds), *The Abolition of the Atlantic Slave Trade* (Madison. 1981), 86.

[42] Eltis, *Economic Growth*, 60. On export volume see Lovejoy, *Transformations*. 50; Manning, *Dahomey*, 35.

DAVID GEGGUS

Table 4. *Sex ratio of selected African ethnic groups in Saint Domingue,*
1721–97

Region and group	Sex ratio[1]	Sample size[1]
Senegambia	214	1,380
Bambara (Banmana and others)	278	718
Sénégal	156	379
Mandingue (Malinke)	167	192
Poulard (Fulbe)	163	71
Sierra Leone	84	206
Sosso/Tini (Susu)	91	128
Timbou (Jalonka)	57	58
Windward Coast	120	253
Mesurade/Canga	110	124
Gold Coast	151	633
Mina	136	441
Caramenty (Akan-Ga)	208	79
Bandia (Guang)	143	73
Slave Coast	99	4,552
Arada (Ewe-Fon)	69	1,694
Nago (Yoruba)	87	1,580
Thiamba/Kiamba (Chamba)	191	297
Aoussa (Hausa)	1,521	227
Gambary (Hausa)	1,900	60
Taqua/Tapa (Nupe)	324	161
Cotocoli (Tem)	116	166
Adia (Ewe-Fon)	89	119
Barba (Bariba)	155	84
Foëda (Hweda)	51	103
Fond (Ewe-Fon)	48	46
Bight of Biafra	103	1,245
Igbo	97	1,129
Bibi (Ibibio)	186	83
Central Africa	166	4,928
Congo	168	4,561
Mondongue	144	283
South-eastern Africa	219	137
Mozambique	231	129
Total	133	13,334

[1] Regional totals include data regarding smaller groups not listed separately in the table.

Sources: Arch. Dept., Arras, 10 J 40, Maulde (1775); Arch. Dept., Le Mans, 1 Mi/16, Beaunay (1755, 1771), and 5F/256, Baudin (1761); Arch. Dept., Poitiers, F 3, Laboube and Chatulès (1785); Arch. Dept., Versailles, E 1748, Breteuil (1779), and J 39, Crepain-Desportes (1787); Arch. Nat., Paris, T 210/1, Bongars, Mte. Noire (1780), T 561, Vaudreui!, Cul de Sac, (1791), and 251 AP 3/5,

FRENCH RECORDS ON THE ATLANTIC SLAVE TRADE   33

Beauharnais (1785); Arch. Nat., Section d'O.M., Aix en Provence, Notariat, Saint-Domingue, reg. 293, (Lamotte, 1788); Baudry d'Asson Papers (courtesy G. Debien), D'Aux (1775); Bermondet de Cromières Papers, château de Cussac, Detroit (1739), Ligurier (1744), Riancourt and Desforges (1788); J. Cauna, 'Une habitation à Saint Domingue', thèse 3me cycle, Poitiers, 1983, (Fleuriau, 1786); A. Gautier, 'Origines ethniques des esclaves de Saint-Domingue d'après les sources notariales', paper presented to 2me Colloque International de Démographie, Paris, 1987, table 3.2, [1,514 Africans in Nippes parish]; G. Debien, et al., 'Les origines des esclaves des Antilles', Bull. Inst. français d'Afrique Noire, ser. B, XXIII (1961) 369, 375, 385, XXIV (1963) 7, 21, 25, XXVII (1965) 360; G. Debien, P. Pluchon, 'Trois sucreries de Léogane', Bull. Centre d'Hist. des Espaces Atlantiques, 2 (1985), 117, 120; G. Debien, Etudes Antillaises (Paris, 1956), 107; G. Debien, 'De l'Afrique a Saint-Domingue', Rev. Soc. Haitienne d'Hist. 135 (1982), 33–38, 41; Geggus, 'Slaves' 5; Geggus, Slave Revolt, forthcoming, ch. 2, [79 North province plantations, 1778–91]; F. Girod, Une fortune coloniale sous l'ancien regime, (Paris, 1970), 125, 132; M. Reible, La sucrerie Lugé à Saint-Domingue, (np, 1976); R. Siguret, 'Esclaves d'indigoteries', Rev. Française d'Hist. d'Outre-Mer, (1968), 200–2; F. Thésée, Négociants bordelais et colons de Saint-Domingue (Paris, 1972), 223, 229, 233, 236.

---

sugar, coffee and indigo plantations in what is now Haiti. Though weighted towards the later eighteenth century, the sample includes data from every decade from the 1720s to the 1790s and from all parts of the colony.[43]

The sex ratio of this group (133) is lower, by one-quarter, than that provided by the shipping records, because male slaves in the New World suffered higher rates of mortality than females. This means that the comparability of the regional data is limited somewhat by the differing age structures of the ethnic samples. As slaves from south-eastern Africa were imported into Saint Domingue in large numbers only after 1785, almost all those in this sample were still young, and their sex ratio had been reduced very little below the level found on slave ships (Table 5). Conversely, the sample from the Bight of Benin, a long-standing source of supply, included many old slaves, and its sex ratio was more than one-third lower than that derived from shipping records. Hence the differing mortality experiences of the two groups exaggerates to some degree their contrasting sexual composition.

In spite of this complication, the plantation records quite strongly confirm the regional pattern revealed in the French shipping data, but with one exception. Africans from Senegambia had a very high sex ratio on the plantations but a fairly low one in the shipping records. Since the plantation sample derived mainly from the 1780s and 90s, this disparity might in part be explained by the temporal shifts discussed above, although it remains enigmatic. Apart from this anomaly, we find in both types of data high sex ratios

[43] Because of the uneven importance of a foreign contraband slave trade in different parts of Saint Domingue, and the contrasting preferences displayed by planters of different crop-types for slaves of certain ethnic groups, the ethnic make-up of the slave population was subject to substantial local variations. Future efforts to reconstruct the ethnic composition of the French slave trade from these sources need to take this into account: Geggus, 'Slaves', 14–23; Geggus, 'Les esclaves de la plaine du Nord à la veille de la Révolution française, IV', Revue de la société haitienne d'histoire, 149 (1985), 23; above, note 9.

Table 5. *Sex ratio of slaves in British and French shipping and colonial records, by region of African provenance*

| Region | Males per hundred females | | | |
	British shipping[1]	Trinidad[2]	French shipping[3]	Saint Domingue[4]
Senegambia	197	187	161	214
Sierra Leone	210	173	134	84
Windward Coast	188	165	175	120
Gold Coast	199	148	163	151
Bight of Benin	130	131	161	99
Bight of Biafra	132	120	117	103
Congo-Angola	191	173	212	166
South-eastern Africa	—	300	229	219
	163	146	179	133
No. of slaves	109,335	13,980	176,997	13,334

Sources: (1) British trade to Jamaica, 1764–88: Inikori, *Forced Migration*, 23 and to the British Caribbean, 1791–8: H. Klein in Robertson and Klein, *Women*, 31.

(2) Trinidad registration returns, 1813: compiled by B. Higman in M. Crahan, F. Knight, eds, *Africa and the Caribbean: The Legacies of a Link* (Baltimore, 1979), 44. The total includes 756 slaves of unknown provenance.

(3) Above, Table 2. The total includes 39,597 slaves of unknown provenance.

(4) Above, Table 4.

among the Bantu of south-eastern and Central Africa, and the lowest ratios among slaves from Sierra Leone and from the Bights of Benin and Biafra.

It is instructive to compare these results both with Klein's and Inikori's figures from the late eighteenth century British slave trade, and with Barry Higman's analysis of the unique 1813 registration returns for Trinidad. This provides two sets of shipping and of plantation data, one British, one French (Table 5). All four sets of data confirm that the Bights of Benin and Biafra exported relatively low proportions of males in marked contrast to Central and south-eastern Africa. They further suggest that the sex ratio of Senegambian captives was generally among the highest, apart from during the 1760s and 70s. The one area for which British and French data on sex ratio are in obvious contradiction is Sierra Leone. This is probably due to the two nations' concentration on different sites within the region, and to the sharply contrasting sex ratios of slaves from its different ethnic groups, which is revealed by the Saint Domingue material.

ETHNIC VARIATIONS

Shipping records are obviously the best guide to the overall age and sex composition of the slave trade, but it is to plantation papers that one must turn to uncover the ethnic mosaic from which the regional patterns outlined above were pieced together. The more than one hundred labels used by French planters to describe their African slaves' origins were of course not those of modern ethnography, but they need not be treated with undue scepticism. Although eighteenth century Europeans knew little of Africa, planters and slave traders paid considerable attention to ethnicity and based business decisions upon the perceived or imagined attributes of different groups. Moreover, the enslaved Africans themselves participated in evolving this Caribbean terminology, which seems to have been applied with some consistency, given its correspondence with such phenomena as average height, occupational patterns, and also sex ratio.[44] Many mysteries remain as regards the ethnic lexicon of Caribbean planters but it is for modern scholars to decipher rather than dismiss it.

The Senegambian region produced the most homogeneous ethnic data (Table 4). All the ethnic groupings had high sex ratios, especially those living furthest from the coast, the vague term 'Sénégal' apparently referring to Wolof and others living along the lower Senegal. A small group labelled 'Mali' contained no females at all. The regions to the south were less homogeneous as regards sex ratio. For Sierra Leone and the Windward Coast we find a contrast between the high ratios (> 200) of the Temne, Kissi, and 'Miserables', and those around or below 100 recorded for the Susu, Timbou (Jalonka?) and 'Mesurades'.[45] Although the small size of some of these samples enjoins caution, it seems that the near absence of Timbou and the much greater presence of Temne and Kissi in the late British slave trade[46] together explain the higher sex ratios exhibited by the British data from these regions.

The most baffling use of ethnic terminology is presented by the labels 'Mina' and 'Caramenty'. Though they doubtless derived originally from the ports of Elmina and Kormantyn situated only some twenty miles apart on the Gold Coast, their 'profiles' curiously contrast, not only with regard to the slaves' sex ratios, as here, but also their morbidity levels, and distribution between different types of plantation.[47] Whatever may be the ethnological basis for these differences, it seems clear that the less numerous 'Caramenty' were introduced by British contraband slavers,[48] and that their higher sex ratio mirrors that of the Gold Coast sample in British shipping records.

Slaves shipped from the Bight of Benin reveal the greatest divergence in

[44] D. Littlefield, *Rice and Slaves: Ethnicity and the Slave Trade in Colonial South Carolina* (Baton Rouge, 1981), 21–34; Geggus, *Slave Revolt*, ch. 2; Geggus, 'Slaves', 14–33.

[45] Both 'Miserables' and 'Mesurades' were as yet unidentified peoples from the area of Cape Mesurado. The latter were also known in the South and West Provinces of Saint Domingue as 'Canga', an Akan term meaning 'barbarous outsider'. It was seemingly bestowed on them by their easterly neighbours, who were more numerous in those parts of the colony, being introduced by British contraband slavers.

[46] See the data in Higman, 'Trinidad', table 2, in Crahan and Knight, *Africa*. Unfortunately, Higman gives only regional but not ethnic sex ratios.

[47] See Geggus, 'Slaves', 17–20, 24, 30.

[48] Akan and Ga speakers were known as 'Coromantees' in the British West Indies, where they were quite numerous and highly prized. 'Caramenty' were rarely found outside those parts of Saint Domingue where the contraband slave trade flourished: D. Geggus, 'On the eve of the Haitian revolution', in G. Heuman (ed.), *Out of the House of Bondage: Runaways, Resistance and Marronage in Africa and the New World* (London, 1986), 122.

sexual composition, ranging from the very low ratios of the coastal Hweda and Ewe-Fon to the exceptional case of the Hausa,[49] very few of whose women entered the Atlantic trade. Groups such as the Chamba, Nupe, Kotokoli, and Bariba, who occupied a geographically intermediate position also did so as regards their relative proportions of males and females. Particularly interesting are the low ratios obtained for the Ewe-Fon and Yoruba, a phenomenon almost entirely ignored in the literature.[50] This low proportion of males casts an interesting light on the nature of slavery in Dahomey and Oyo, where it would seem that the state's extraordinary need for men as agricultural workers, administrators and soldiers kept the sex ratio of exported slaves unusually level. It may also be that the general lack of domestic slavery in the former[51] made for an unusually low local demand for women, notwithstanding the demand of the Dahomean state itself for female slaves. It also follows from these figures that the higher sex ratios found among captives sold through Badagri and Porto Novo probably should not be attributed to Yoruba slaves as much as to Hausa and others from the far interior. It should be repeated here that, because of the different age-structures of the regional samples, some of these figures might have to be increased by about one-half to approximate the sex ratios of captives at time of transportation. Even among Ewe-Fon slaves males presumably predominated, but it must have been by a very small margin.

The Bantu peoples, on the other hand, were characterised by a moderately high proportion of males among their slave exports, whether from Central or south-eastern Africa.[52] In the Bight of Biafra, too, we find a noteworthy contrast between the Igbo and their north-western Bantu neighbours ('Moco', 'Bibi'), who seemingly lost far more males to the Atlantic system than did the Igbo. This fact may help explain the change, noted above (p. 29), in the sexual composition of the Bight of Biafra's slave exports which came about after 1800 or 1810, since non-Igbo were then considerably more prominent.[53]

Why then did the Atlantic slave trade suck in differing proportions of males

[49] Although the French distinguished 'Aoussa' from 'Gambary', I follow Law, *Oyo Empire*, 227n in assuming that the terms were synonyms, 'Gambary' being the Yoruba word for Hausa.

[50] The sole exception would seem a footnote in Gautier, *Soeurs*, 80.

[51] Robertson and Klein, *Women*, 61.

[52] Although numerous peoples were no doubt enveloped in the generic term 'Congo', a majority were probably Kikongo speakers, either native or 'naturalized'. This is suggested by linguistic evidence from colonial and modern Haiti. The chief sub-groups identified in colonial records, apart from Kongo, were Nsundi, Yombe, Mbala and Yaka. While regional trade routes extended far into the interior, there is little evidence even in the nineteenth century that the most distant sources supplied many captives to the coast: Curtin, *Census*, 256, 295–6; L. Degrandpré, *Voyage à la côte occidentale d'Afrique fait dans les années 1786 et 1787* (Paris, 1801), vol. 1, xiv–xxv, vol. 2, 37, 48. For a contrary view see Miller, *Way of Death*. Among the 'Mozambiques' the only peoples identified were Makonde and Makwa.

[53] Igbo constituted 91 per cent of the region's slaves in the French plantation sample; but only 52 per cent in the 1813 Trinidad sample (excluding Hausa); and 68 per cent in a sample of 1,008 slaves sold in 1821–2, 26 per cent being Ibibio: D. Northrup, *Trade Without Rulers* (Oxford, 1978), 231. Although the latter sample, drawn from only two ports, is not strictly representative, it is broadly corroborated by the 1848 Sierra Leone census of freed slaves, which similarly shows a much increased ratio of N. W. Bantu to Igbo: Northrup, *Trade*, 60–1. Eltis, *Economic Growth*, 358–9, however, found that in this period Igbo and Ibibio captives exhibited similar sex ratios.

and females from different African peoples? Various factors may be adduced, but three in particular stand out. We have already seen how in Senegambia and on the Slave Coast the sex ratio of captives broadly correlated with the distance they had been brought from the interior. The groups exhibiting the lowest ratios tended to live within 100 miles of the Atlantic coast, but those with the greatest excess of males over females (Chamba, Banmana, Nupe and Hausa) travelled over 250 miles to their point of embarkation. The principle is difficult to apply in the Bantu regions due to the breadth of the ethnic terms used, but in West Africa it presumably reflects the impact of the trans-Saharan slave trade and its high demand for females to supply the harems of North Africa and the Middle East. The volume of this trade in the eighteenth century was quite small but so, too, was the far inland peoples' share of the transatlantic trade. The paucity of women (and children) sent to the coast from the far interior was surely also a function of the hardships and cost of the journey, which placed a premium on adult males, who could carry more trade goods, and for whom Europeans usually paid the highest prices.[54]

Another major influence on sexual composition was the local demand in societies of matrilineal descent for slave wives. In all types of polygynous society women were easier to integrate than men, but in those of matrilineal descent slave wives were especially sought after, since they provided men with a control over their families they otherwise lacked.[55] Setting apart the furthest inland groups exhibiting very high ratios, we find a general correspondence between matrilinearity and high proportions of males among exported slaves. All groups with a sex ratio below 120 were patrilineal, but most matrilineal peoples exhibited ratios of above 130. Patrilineal societies could absorb fewer females, other things being equal, and hence sold less unbalanced proportions of males and females beyond their boundaries.

The degree of male participation in agricultural tasks also shows up as a significant factor. Where the female role in agriculture was exceptionally prominent, as among the Central Bantu and Ibibio, we indeed find high sex ratios among exported slaves, suggesting a disproportionate retention of females. However, the Igbo were apparently an exception here. For those peoples were men performed an equal or greater share of agricultural work there was an evident tendency towards low sex ratios (notably among the Susu, Jalonka, Ewe and Yoruba), though the pattern is not entirely consistent.[56] Nor perhaps should it be, since the traditional sexual division of labour was not

[54] In West Africa with the exception of Senegambia the coastal price of adult males in the eighteenth century usually exceeded that of adult females by 25 to 40 per cent: J. Atkins, *Voyage to Guinea, Brasil and the West Indies* (London, 1735), 163–6; J. Barbot, *Description of the Coasts of North and South Guinea* (London , 1732), 326; Peukert, *Sklavenhandel*, 112; Curtin, *Senegambia*, vol. 1, 173, 176; below, note 83.

[55] Miers and Kopytoff, *Slavery*, 22, 31; Lovejoy, *Transformations*, 118.

[56] Descriptions of the sexual division of labour were taken from G. P. Murdock, *Ethnographic Atlas* (Pittsburgh, 1967); J. Vansina, *Ethnographie du Congo* (Kinshasa, nd), 14; Manning, *Dahomey*, 70–71. American planters frequently found the women among their Igbo and Congo slaves better fieldworkers than their male counterparts, whereas among Bight of Benin slaves males and females were equally prized: B. Edwards, *History Civil and Commercial of the British West Indies* (Dublin, 1793), vol. 2, 68, 70; Littlefield, *Rice*, 18, 151; Moreau de Saint-Méry, *Description*, vol. 1, 51, 53; C. Malenfant, *Des colonies modernes* (Paris, 1814), 210–11; E. Long, *History of Jamaica* (London, 1774), vol. 2, 403–4; S. Ducoeurjoly, *Manuel des habitants de Saint Domingue* (Paris, 1802), vol. 1, 24. Some also made the same observation of the Akan-speaking 'Coromantee': Long, *Jamaica*, vol. 2, 446, 471–3.

necessarily applied to slaves.[57] Nonetheless, it is significant that the chief exceptions (Banmana, Chamba, Malinke and Hausa) were all probable suppliers of the trans-Saharan trade, among whom the local demand for male slaves would have been counterbalanced by external demand for females. In these partially Islamised societies long associated with slavery, the local demand for concubines, and also for females in textiles production, may in addition have been especially strong.

Two other factors to be considered are the local, large-scale use of slaves outside the household, and the mode of capture. States that employed numerous slaves as soldiers or bureaucrats, or in commercial or state-run agriculture (such as Oyo, Dahomey and the Fulbe-ruled Jalonka of Futa Jallon)[58] appear to have retained more male captives than was usual. This influence, however, is difficult to separate from the patrilineality of these societies, and from the prominent role they assigned to men in field labour. Sexual imbalance could additionally express differences in mode of enslavement. If formal warfare was most likely to produce male captives, kidnapping, pawning and raiding probably fell more heavily on women and children. The prominence of these methods in Igboland and around Whydah[59] may therefore have helped produce the low sex ratios of the Igbo, Hweda and Aja-Fon sold to Europeans. The fact that the Bight of Biafra was the only region to export more girls than boys also points to the prevalence of pawning in Igboland. Conversely, the high sex ratios of slaves from eastern Senegambia and the Gold Coast may reflect the high incidence of warfare in those regions. Indeed, American planters noted among them a high proportion of prisoners of war, and one (Bryan Edwards) observed that, in contrast, captives from the Bight of Benin appeared to have been born slaves.[60]

A final correlation that requires comment is that between low sex ratio and areas of high population density, specifically the immediate hinterland of the Bights of Benin and Biafra. This might suggest that, not only was a high volume of slave exports linked to population pressure,[61] but so, too, was an indigenous willingness to part with females. However, some claim that population density itself was a product rather than stimulus of slave exports, since many acquired outsiders were retained rather than re-exported.[62] Should this be so, then it would appear that these densely-populated regions, by virtue of being so well supplied, were able to dispose of unwanted slaves in a manner less gender-specific than was generally the case.

[57] See J. Goody, 'Slavery in time and space', in J. L. Watson (ed.), *Asian and African Systems of Slavery* (Berkeley 1980), 38–42; J. Thornton, 'The slave trade in eighteenth century Angola', *Canadian Journal of African Studies*, XIV, 3 (1980), 424–5.

[58] Lovejoy, *Transformations*, 114, 116, 119–20; Manning, *Dahomey*, 10, 39; Meillassoux, 'Female slavery', in Robertson and Klein, *Women*, 61.

[59] Northrup, *Trade*, 75–77; S. D. Brown, 'From the tongues of Africa: a partial translation of Oldendorp's interviews', *Plantation Society*, II, 1 (1983), 49.

[60] Of course, the two categories were not necessarily mutually exclusive. See Edwards, *History*, 56–59; Long, *Jamaica*, vol. 2, 473; Moreau de Saint-Méry, *Description*, vol. 1, 48, 50.

[61] Originally advanced by J. D. Fage, this view is espoused in Manning, *Dahomey*, 32, 42, and Northrup, *Trade*, 80–4.

[62] This is argued in Thornton, 'Angola', 426–7; A. van Dantzig, 'Effects of the Atlantic slave trade on some West African societies', in Inikori, *Forced Migration*, 200; Lovejoy, *Transformations*, 64–5.

Whatever was the causal relationship between slave exports and population density, future assessments of population loss will need to take account of these differing ethnic sex ratios. Even if, as Inikori argues, the Atlantic and Saharan slave trades in aggregate drained Africa of an equal number of each sex,[63] certain populations evidently suffered critical changes in sexual composition. Patrick Manning's estimates of the demographic cost of slave exports to the Aja-Fon and Yoruba, for example, would have to have been much more elevated, had he assumed that fertile females made up, not one-fourth of their exported slaves,[64] but between one-third and two-fifths.

AGE COMPOSITION

The plantation sources list an extremely small number of African children (1·2 per cent), and hence offer a very uncertain guide to ethnic variations in the age composition of captives. However, grouped by coastal region, the ethnic data do broadly support the evidence derived from shipping records presented in Table 2. Slaves transported from Sierra Leone, the Windward Coast and Central Africa included above-average proportions of children, whereas Senegambia, the Gold Coast and Bight of Benin exported notably fewer children. Both the Yoruba and Arada (Ewe-Fon) groups contained a below-average percentage of children, but for the latter the proportion was twice that found for the former, thus paralleling the difference observed in the shipping records between the Egun and Ewe-Fon ports. Clearly, very few children from Yorubaland, and not just the regions to the east, were sold to Europeans. The plantation sample from south-eastern Africa consisted primarily of recently-transported slaves, so that its age composition, like its sex ratio, still closely reflected that seen in the shipping records, and was consequently abnormally high. The one true anomaly in this respect was the Bight of Biafra. According to both French and British shipping data, the region exported numerous children,[65] but very few showed up in the plantation sources. As mortality rates were exceptionally high in the trade from Biafra, it could be that few Igbo children survived their transportation.

Insofar as the sale of women must have entailed the sale of children, one might expect the sex ratio and age composition of exported slaves to be linked. However, Tables 1 and 2 show that this was not the case, either at the level of national trades or of exporting regions. The Cuban trade of around 1800 was distinguished by extremely high proportions of both children and males. In the French trade, the two African regions exporting the highest proportions of women (Senegambia and the Bight of Benin) actually exported the lowest proportions of children. Most African children carried across the Atlantic were evidently sold separately from their mothers.

The surprising fact that, despite their very low sex ratios, Sierra Leone and the Bight of Biafra by no means exported the highest proportions of adult women underlines the fact that the sexual composition of slave exports cannot be deduced from adult captives alone and that the sex ratio of children also

[63] Inikori, *Forced Migration*, 25.
[64] Manning, *Dahomey*, 371.
[65] Cf. B. Edwards, *Historical Survey of the Island of Saint Domingo* (London, 1801), 268–71, which contrasts slave shipments from Bonny and Bassam consisting of one-half children with a shipment from the Gold Coast with only one-tenth children.

must be taken into account. As noted above (p. 26), in different branches of the Atlantic slave trade sex ratios were sometimes higher among children than among adults, and sometimes the reverse was true. David Galenson's deduction from the Royal African Company's statistics that Africans were most concerned to prevent the sale of girls rather than of women thus cannot be generalized to the whole trade.[66] In the French shipping records adult sex ratios were higher than those of children only among slaves from the Bight of Benin and south-eastern Africa.

Of the three elements – men, women, children – constituting these human cargoes it was the percentage of children that varied most from one exporting region to another (Table 2). The observed differences may reflect the incidence of certain modes of enslavement, such as kidnapping and debt pawnage, apparently common in Igboland. The distance which slaves had to be brought to the coast was no doubt also relevant in the contrasting cases of Senegambia and the Bight of Benin, on the one hand, and Sierra Leone and the Windward Coast on the other. Lastly, European commercial considerations may also have played a role. The fact that in Senegambia children cost at certain times almost as much as adults[67] must have discouraged their purchase by Europeans. More specifically, however, profit margins on transporting children were probably lower than for adult slaves, and the incentive to purchase them must have partly depended on the general level of regional slave prices. Comprehensive price data are hard to obtain, but it is possibly significant that regions little esteemed by European purchasers (the Congo and Bight of Biafra) sold many more children than did the high-price regions of Senegambia, the Gold Coast and Bight of Benin.[68] By the same token, the incentive to purchase children was greater for traders selling in high-price markets in the Americas. This in itself may explain why fewer children were sold in the British than in the (undersupplied) French Caribbean, and why the premium Spanish American market attracted the highest proportion of all (Table 1).

SUPPLY AND DEMAND

This last point shows how difficult it is to disentangle the forces of supply and demand in shaping the composition of slave cargoes. A similar example is provided by the Bight of Biafra. The relative prominence of females among its slave exports may be attributed to the Igbos' patrilinearity, their proximity to the coast, and their use of enslavement mechanisms other than formal warfare. But it is perhaps also pertinent that American planters often found Igbo

[66] Galenson, *Traders*, 104–10.

[67] Curtin, *Senegambia*, vol. 1, 175. However, this may have been true only in the early eighteenth century, when the Portuguese were seeking children for the Iberian market. Cf. Atkins, *Voyage*, 177.

[68] On ethnic preferences and price levels see Curtin, *Census*, 155–62, 181–3, 189–90, 208–9; Littlefield, *Rice*, 8–21, 45–7, 54; Eltis, *Economic Growth*, 264; M. Craton, J. Walvin and D. Wright, *Slavery, Abolition and Emancipation* (London, 1976), 51–3; Miller 'Slave Prices', in Lovejoy (ed.), *Africans in Bondage*, 66–8; F. Bowser, *African Slavery in Peru* (Stanford, 1974), 80; Donnan, *Documents*, vol. 2, 'Report on the Trade to Africa, 1709', 56; Palmer, *Cargoes*, 15, 62; Geggus, 'Slaves', 14–18, 19n; Geggus, 'Toussaint Louverture and the Slaves of the Bréda plantations', *Journal of Caribbean History* (1985–6), 46; E. P. LeVeen, *British Slave Trade Suppression Policies* (New York, 1977), 114–15, 146.

females better workers than males,[69] and that ships' captains occasionally found them healthier, and in consequence limited their purchases of men.[70]

To a large degree, supply and demand in the Atlantic slave trade appear to have been complementary. As a general rule, American slaveholders wanted adult males for their strength and versatility, while Africans preferred women and children for their ease of assimilation and reproductive as well as productive capacities. However, this is true only as a generalization, whose validity varied through time and space. Scholars who assign primacy either to supply conditions, as does Herbert Klein, or to those of demand, as does Orlando Patterson, both seem to overstate their case.[71] This is particularly true of the latter.

Certainly, the pattern of variation between ethnic groups outlined above is demonstrative of the strength of 'African' factors in influencing the outflow of slaves to the Americas, even if the competing demand from across the Sahara was among the most important of these factors. If Patterson is right that Klein overrated the importance of matrilineality in slave-exporting regions, he is himself in error in entirely dismissing its significance, as seen above. Patterson's claim that in most African societies male slaves were as desired as females would appear without foundation, since the price data currently available suggest precisely the opposite. Female slaves were commonly twice as expensive as males.[72] Nonetheless, such data are not entirely unambiguous,[73] and there is some danger in generalizing about indigenous demand for females from examples that derive mainly from the nineteenth century and from the Sahel, affected as it was by the pull of the trans-Saharan trade. One obviously needs to know more about domestic slave prices in regions such as Yorubaland and Dahomey, and in periods when polygyny was perhaps less common.

As regards American demand, Herbert Klein makes the point that neither labour use nor prices in the New World will account for the large excess of male slaves imported, since planters discriminated little between males and females as field labourers. This seems true up to a point, but it glosses over the fact that American purchasers almost always paid higher prices for newly-arrived males than for females, reflecting the extensive demand for men in artisan, transport, supervisory and manufacturing roles. On the West African coast, Senegambia was the only known region where Europeans paid equal prices for males and females; normally women were about 25 per cent cheaper than men.[74] Using samples of 26 and 29 cases, Richard Bean found that in British American slave markets prices for adult females averaged 82 per cent

---

[69] See above, note 56.

[70] Davies, *Royal African Company*, 78.

[71] Klein in *Traite des Noirs*, 83; Klein, *Middle Passage*, 151, 241–2; Robertson and Klein, *Women*, 34–6; O. Patterson, 'Recent Studies on Caribbean Slavery and the Atlantic Slave Trade', *Latin American Research Review* XVII (1982), 272–3.

[72] See Robertson and Klein, *Women*, 4–5, 10–11, 67–89; Curtin, *Senegambia*, vol. 1, 175–7; Miers and Kopytoff, *Slavery*, 21–2, 53, 62, 125, 297, 320; P. Harries, 'Slavery, social incorporation and surplus extraction', *J. Afr. Hist.* XXII (1981), 322–6; D. Tambo, 'The Sokoto Caliphate slave trade in the nineteenth century', *International Journal of African Historical Studies* IX (1976), 192–202; J. Van Wing, *Etudes Bakongo: Histoire et Sociologie* (Bruxelles, 1921), vol. 1, 136.

[73] See MacCormack, 'Slaves, slave owners, and slave dealers', in Robertson and Klein, *Women*, 288; Miers and Kopytoff, *Slavery*, 108, 161–2.

[74] See above, note 54.

of comparable male prices at point of disembarkation, and 77 per cent on the African coast.[75] The preference for African males in the New World was thus pronounced, although to a lesser degree than was the complementary African preference for slave females. This is only to be expected given the stress on domestic labour, sexuality and reproduction in African slavery, and the centrality of field labour in the American setting, where gender was simply less relevant.

Such generalized data, however, besides being sparse, do not give due weight to temporal and geographic context. Here it may be useful to sketch what appear to have been the main changes in the sexual composition of the Atlantic slave trade during its last two centuries. British, French and Dutch sources, both shipping and plantation records, all suggest that the sex ratio of exported slaves was low during the mid-seventeenth century,[76] but then rose substantially through the early eighteenth century. This trend may have denoted changing conditions of supply. Since the Royal African Company and other middlemen failed to meet their goal of purchasing two men for each woman, it seems that Africa was supplying in these early years, not too few women, but too few men. As slave exports increased, however, presumably so too did the domestic slave market, which caused African societies to absorb more females and produce relatively greater 'surpluses' of males. Rather more certainly, this growing preponderance of males was linked to the spread of sugar cultivation in the Caribbean. Sugar estates both employed numerous male specialists and experienced elevated death rates that were higher among men than women. Sugar also produced higher profits than other crops, which may have encouraged planters to devalue the reproductive capacity of female slaves, inducing the infamous 'buy rather than breed' mentality. Such a change in calculations could also have resulted from the increasing regularity of supply.

The profitability and difficulty of crop-type, and the regularity of visits by slave ships probably did much to determine variations in the sexual composition of slave imports in American societies. Daniel Littlefield has inferred from scattered evidence that British slave traders were more inclined to ship female slaves (and also the generally unpopular Igbos) to the tobacco-growing Tidewater than to the wealthier rice plantations of South Carolina, and still more so than to the sugar colonies, where the male/female price differential was greater.[77] In the French Caribbean, we can demonstrate statistically a similar continuum stretching from the neglected colonies of Cayenne and Guadeloupe to more prosperous Martinique and Saint Domingue. Similarly, Igbo slaves, in large measure females, show up disproportionately in Guadeloupe and the least-developed parts of Saint Domingue.[78] If partly attributable to a genuine demand for females in such regions, this pattern probably also expresses the slave merchants' ability to exploit these neglected markets that were compelled to be less selective and usually to pay higher

[75] R. Bean, *British Transatlantic Slave Trade, 1650–1775* (New York, 1975), 134. Galenson's sophisticated analysis of slave sales in Barbados in the period 1673–1723 also reveals a male:female price ratio of 100:81: *Traders*, 62.

[76] See Table 1; above, note 10; R. Dunn, *Sugar and Slaves: the Rise of the Planter Class in the English West Indies* (London, 1973), 316; French Caribbean censuses in Arch. Nat., Aix en Provence, G1/509.

[77] Littlefield, *Rice*, 56–66, 72.   [78] See above, note 9.

prices. Conversely, the price differentials that obtained between national markets may have helped sustain differing sex ratios among slave imports at the national level; both prices and sex ratio were apparently highest in Spanish America and lowest among the British, with the French in between.[79]

Demand for males and females was additionally influenced by a colony's level of development and, in the later eighteenth century, by a renewed interest in encouraging procreation among slaves. Coinciding with a sharp rise in African slave prices, the growth of humanitarianism, and the levelling off of production in the older colonies, this trend is attested to by numerous sources that show planters increasingly interested in buying female slaves. As early as 1700 a difference was visible in the British Caribbean between the more settled islands and those still in the pioneering phase as to the proportions of men and women that they purchased.[80] In the eighteenth century, a falling sex ratio is clearly visible in the Dutch and most branches of the French slave trade, though in the latter the trend was powerfully reversed after 1780 by the expansion of cultivation in Saint Domingue. The British case is less clear, but in Cuba the trend was evidently downwards after the extreme levels of the early 1790s, if only for the next thirty of forty years.[81]

In the second half of the eighteenth century, therefore, it is difficult to gauge the overall movement in the slave trade's sexual composition. Against the growing concern with procreation, and the end of the mining boom in Minas Gerais, has to be weighed the opening up of Cuba and of the mountains of Saint Domingue, and the growing prominence as suppliers of the Congo basin and Southeast Africa. The importance of these latter trends leads one to doubt that the mid- to late eighteenth century saw a markedly diminished male presence in the Middle Passage, as Klein tentatively suggested.[82] Evidence regarding price differentials on the African coast and in the New World do suggest that slave females were becoming more sought after (either in Africa or the Americas),[83] but this could well have been a function of the general rise in slave prices, not of rising demand for females *per se*.

Developments in the nineteenth century are clearer. Slave prices fell on the African coast; the trade declined in volume and became more concentrated in importing and exporting regions already associated with high sex ratios.[84] These trends suggest that a higher proportion of males was exported than in the late 1700s. A rise in the use of male slave labour in Africa was possibly a

[79] Despite a large urban market for female slaves, Spanish American demand was usually considered by contemporaries strongly pro-male: Littlefield, *Rice*, 59–60. Cf. Table 1. The two French slave cargoes listed by Mettas that were sold in the Spanish Caribbean significantly had a sex ratio of 204:100.

[80] See Galenson, *Traders*, 94–6.

[81] See, Klein, *Middle Passage*, 222–5; Moreno Fraginals, 'Africa', 192–3; Eltis, *Economic Growth*, 257.

[82] Klein, *Middle Passage*, 32–4.

[83] Isolated data suggest that on the Gold Coast the male:female price ratio rose between 1720 and 1770 from about 100:67 to 100:80, then fell back to around 100:77 in the mid-1770s as slave prices declined: see Littlefield, *Rice*, 62n; G. Metcalf, 'Gold, Assortments and the Trade Ounce: Fante Merchants and the Problem of Supply and Demand in the 1770s', *J. Afr. Hist.* XXVIII (1987), 37.

[84] LeVeen, *Suppression*, 117–21; Manning, *Dahomey*, 37. Eltis, *Economic Growth*, passim. The widening gap between African and American slave prices may additionally account for the high percentages of children that also were a feature of the nineteenth century trade.

DAVID GEGGUS

countervailing force, but the available data lead one to believe that males, and also children, were never so strongly represented in the Atlantic slave trade as during its last fifty years.

14

Slaves and Slave Traders in the Persian Gulf, 18th and 19th Centuries: An Assessment

Thomas M. Ricks

For historians of Iran and the Persian Gulf, the subject of slaves and slave traders is a relatively new field of research. Except for a few works that have focused on the issues of piracy, anti-slave patrols and the policies of British imperial rule, little research has appeared on slaves and the slave trade in the Persian Gulf. The extensive research by African and Asian historians has stimulated Middle East historians to re-evaluate the societies and economies of the region in terms of slaves and slave trading as important issues in Middle Eastern social and economic historiography.[1]

Slave trading to the Persian Gulf began well before the eighteenth century. Medieval accounts refer sporadically to slaves as household servants and bodyguards, and as militia men and seamen in Southern Iran and the Persian Gulf. In addition, slaves were both white and black. Prior to the eighteenth and nineteenth centuries, slaves in Iranian and Gulf societies and economies were marginal to the Persian, Arab and Indian population functioning out of the public eye in the homes and workshops of the wealthy merchant, landlord or administrator. Only in the eighteenth and nineteenth centuries did slaves and slave trading assume any significance for Iran and the Persian Gulf. The reasons for the rise in slaves and slave trading, particularly slaves from East Africa and trading through Oman, were threefold:

1. The eighteenth and nineteenth centuries were periods of wide-ranging economic, social and political changes within Southern Iran and the Persian Gulf region due to the collapse of regional imperial rule, the rise of petty lords and the dominance of Britain within the world economy.

2. The Southern Iranian and Persian Gulf import/export trade underwent a mercantile 'renaissance', particularly in the export of pearls, dates, cotton, wool, and opium in exchange for the imports of foodstuffs, dyes, manufactured goods and arms.

3. Labour shortages occurred within the Southern Iranian and Persian Gulf region during the eighteenth and nineteenth centuries resulting in fresh demands for imported labour to work in the Gulf

ports, in the coastal villages and in local militia. The East African slave trade provided the temporary labour force until the First World War.

The first part of the paper focuses on the social and economic changes within the Iranian and Persian Gulf regions during the eighteenth and nineteenth centuries. The second part of the paper will investigate the differences between eighteenth- and nineteenth-century Persian Gulf slaves and slave traders, the shifts in the slave trading 'systems' and the incorporation of slave labour into nineteenth-century Persian Gulf coastal and hinterland economies and societies. There will remain a number of important questions, however. How important was the rise and fall of slave trading to the other changes within the Gulf region? What long-term social and economic impact did the nineteenth-century surge of slave labour have for the region? How did the slave trade overall affect the foreign trade of the Persian Gulf peoples? In what sense did the increase of East African slave trading 'internationalize' the Southern Iranian or Gulf economies and societies?

I

Trade and politics in eighteenth-and nineteenth-century Iran and the Persian Gulf were not dull times. The overall period witnessed a number of significant changes in both the economic and social realms. Indeed, it is important to sketch the major trends in eighteenth- and nineteenth-century Iranian and Gulf social and economic history.

Following the collapse of the Safavid family's central rule in 1722, Iran underwent a period of decentralization, dividing itself into two major regions – Northern Iran and Southern Iran. Both regions witnessed the emergence of independent-minded regional lords (*khans*) backed by local merchants and European trading companies in their rival bids for control over the land, the markets and the trade of each region. Between 1722 and 1782, Northern Iran was dominated first by the Afshars and then the Qajars while Southern Iran was controlled by the Zands.

Administratively based in Tabriz, Mashhad and then in Tehran, the Northern region was tied to the Russian and Ottoman trading zones linked by overland and sea trade routes, by merchant communities and by agricultural, industrial and commercial needs. By 1736, the emergence of Nadir Shah and the Afshar military elite severely challenged the neighbouring regions of Ottoman imperial rule to Iran's west (Eastern Anatolia and the Mesopotamian regions) and the Mughul rule in Afghanistan and India to the east. The military challenges were essentially challenges to Ottoman and Mughul domination over the overland and sea trade routes, over the markets and activities of the merchant communities, and over the domestic agricultural and artisanal products. Merchant capital, long tied to central Iranian imperial demands, now found new life in the post-Safavid period, particularly with the growing importance of the European trading companies. With the revival and expansion of Iran's Northern trade came new demands of increased production, a need for a larger labour (military and agricultural) force and greater demands by the *khans* for luxury goods. The population distribution in Northern Iran was favourable for the 'renaissance' in Iranian products, markets and trade. Labour was abundant on either side of the Iranian–Russian borders and labour migrations accelerated from the last decades of the eighteenth century to the late nineteenth century. Cotton as a valuable cash crop was increasingly introduced into the Northern Iranian economy with considerable financial support and commercial success from Russia.[2]

Iranian merchants began to buy land, introduce new products and industries, and engage in joint trade ventures by the early nineteenth century. The location of the nineteenth-century capital in Tehran greatly facilitated the new directions of Northern Iranian merchant capital 'investments'. Indeed, the very emergence of vigorous capital accumulation as a result of the decentralization of the Safavid political order and Russian commercial 'invasion' soon attracted the attentions of the Qajar rulers in Tehran. From the mid-nineteenth century to the First World War, old landlord and merchant lands were seized by Tehran's Qajar lords and by the local notables in Tabriz and Mashhad while farming surpluses were appropriated through revised tax systems and market restrictions. Foreigners began to lease and even to own lands for cash crop production. The 1872 Reuter Concession is thought to be the watershed between the post-Safavid merchant 'renaissance' and the emergence of the modern state system following the First World War.[3]

Southern Iran experienced a similar transformation. After 1722, Southern Iranian merchants began to seek new ways of utilizing capital without the impositions of empire. From 1752 to 1782, Southern Iran's Zand family created Shiraz as the regional capital and, with the merchants' support, enthusiastically challenged all local hegemony within the Gulf region. The Zands occupied Basra, the major Ottoman port at the headwaters of the Gulf (1776–79), seized the Bahrayn Islands (1763–83) from Northern Arabian chiefs and dominated the lower Gulf zone (1763–85).[4]

The military expeditions followed the trade routes to the major trading centres. Merchants who had once fled Iran in the early eighteenth century, frightened by the political instability of the late Safavid era, were persuaded to return to Iran from their Mesopotamian, Punjabi and Indian exiles. Construction of roadhouses (*manazil*), bridges and covered markets were begun, and irrigation systems (*qanat*) so necessary ᵗfor the semi-arid Southern Iranian agriculture were rebuilt or more rigorously maintained.

The scarcity of labour, however, was a major obstacle to any long-term expansion of cultivation or increase in artisanal production. At the same time, the number of domestic and foreign contenders for control over rural and urban surpluses, greater than in Northern Iran, necessitated the maintenance of larger military forces. Finally, in the wake of the mid-eighteenth-century decline of the Dutch and French trade, England had no further European competition for the shipping, markets or ports of the Persian Gulf. Only the escalating conflicts between the rival powers of Iran, the Ottoman Empire and Oman created major social, economic or political problems in Southern Iran and in the Persian Gulf.

For the region to expand its accumulation of merchant capital, it was necessary to import labour in quantities greater than ever before. The shift in the slave labour practices of previous centuries from marginal imported labour for domestic and agricultural work to slave labour for a wide range of activities was financed by the Gulf brokers and merchants (Indian, Jewish, Persian, Arab and Turkish), organized by the Arab, Persian and Turkish Gulf sea captains (*nakhuda*) and protected by the Gulf Arab, Persian and Turkish rulers. The need for more crew members for trans-Gulf crafts or for the ocean-going dhows, for more military foot soldiers on land, for more porters in the markets and dock labour in the ports, and for more field labour in the irrigated croplands meant cheap imported labour from the Indian Ocean. The East African slave trade was the answer to the growing labour shortages.

The fall of Karim Khan Zand in 1779 and the ensuing demise of Zand family control over Southern Iran during the 1780s allowed the Omanis to assert their hegemony over both Indian and Persian Gulf trade. From the 1780s to 1872, it is possible to maintain that the Omani rulers and merchants shaped the direction, and in the end, the transformation of the Gulf.[5] Nearly all trade tables for the 1870s to the First World War indicate a sharp escalation of trade to the region, new uses of land, and an internationalization of Iran's merchant community.[6] The results of Oman's role with British support in the 'opening up of the Persian Gulf' in the final decades of the nineteenth century are well-documented; the importance of slaves and slave traders to the role has only begun to be researched.[7]

Chief among the various steps that Oman's merchants and rulers took during the 1780s to the 1870s was a vigorous escalation of imported labour into the Iranian, Ottoman and Arabian lands via Oman's major towns and, then, overland and by sea to the Gulf's coastal villages and port-towns. The profits from the importation of slave labour from East Africa to the Persian Gulf via the Omani towns of Masqat and Sur[8] directly benefited the Omani merchants. They had also benefited from the new ties with Persian Gulf merchants and brokers who increasingly became dependent on Oman's commercial interests via loans, debt transfers and credit arrangements. The principal purchasers of the imported Omani slave labourers were the Iranian, Arab, Indian, and Turkish merchants of the Gulf ports and hinterland towns who continued to look for ways of expanding the pearl trade and increasing the production of cotton, Kirmani wool, and opium through expanded labour forces, land and sea fighting units, and improved irrigation systems.

II

During the eighteenth century, slave trading to the Persian Gulf was relatively marginal in scope, but included a wide variety of peoples from East Africa, Ethiopia, Somalia and Baluchistan. The major entrepots of the region were Ras al-Khaymah (Julfa), Bandar 'Abbas, Bandar Lingeh, Bushire and Basra. Slaves were generally used in the following ways:

- As soldiers in Southern Iran (Dashtistan, Tangistan, Dashti and the Abbasi coast), in the Gulf ports (Basra, Bushire, Bandar Rig, Bandar Lingeh and Bandar Abbas, Dubai, and Ras al-Khaymah) and on the islands (Kharg, Qishm and Bahrayn).
- As sailors and dock hands in the major Gulf ports.
- As household servants in port-towns of the Gulf and in the towns of Southern Iran.
- As pearl divers (Bahrayn Island, Bandar Lingeh and Bandar 'Abbas).

In the eighteenth century, therefore, slaves were used in the households of the wealthy, in the pearl beds of the Gulf, and in the local militia and maritime activities. The English East India Company (EIC) agents recorded a lively trafficking in slaves from within the Gulf region. In 1747, the EIC agent at Bandar 'Abbas wrote that a man came to town who had been taken as a slave from Bandar 'Abbas 25 years ago and was still with the Baluchis, saying 'they [Baluchis] have got a very rich booty in slaves, which they brought from the Cold Countries [Shiraz and Kirman], being chiefly of the ancient Persian families their sons & daughters'.[9] In 1751, the EIC agent in Basra reported that Sulaiman Pasha's general punished the headmen or *aghas* of Basra by destroying their ship, the *Menoy*, and by taking the 'old men, women and children sold as slaves'.[10] Slaves used as farm hands in the date plantations of the Bahrayn Islands and Bandar Lingeh, or on Kharg Island, were exceptional cases.[11] While only estimates can be offered, it appears that imported labour between 1722 and 1822 from East Africa to the Persian Gulf averaged no more than 500–600 slaves annually, with the greater portion of slave importations coming in the last two decades of the eighteenth century.[12]

The slave traders, or 'slave peddlers',[13] moved the African slave cargo from port to port in the course of their seasonal shipping obligations. The sea captains (*nakhodah*), usually Arab or Indian, utilized the slaves as shipping crews during the voyage and then sold them at ports known for their slave markets. The buyers frequently were brokers and port authorities (*shahbandar*) who acted both as merchants for themselves and as local administrators for the ruling hinterland family.[14]

The East India Company (EIC) was itself an eighteenth-century participant in the Indian Ocean slave trade. In the 1763 Royal Grant from Karim Khan Zand, Iran's ruler located in the Southern Iranian town of Shiraz, to the EIC 'for trading at Bushire', the Ninth Provision states that 'all soldiers, sailors or slaves of the East India Company must be returned without punishment'.[15] Again, in 1766, the EIC Directors instructed the Bushire resident to take great care in leaving 'any considerable amount' of goods at Masqat 'in the hands of the Black broker' for any length of time, or taking unnecessary risks with interlopers, 'usually private British merchants', and with 'Black merchants or natives'.[16] Finally, in anticipation of a possible EIC attack in 1777 upon Basra to break the Iranian occupation of that town, a British Admiralty communication estimated that 8 ships with 180 guns, 900 Europeans and '600 slaves from Madagascar' would be necessary for a successful operation.[17]

In the nineteenth century, slaves came primarily from East Africa via the Omani ports of Sur and Masqat, or overland to the small Arabian ports of Sharjah, Dubai or Ras al-Khaymah. In addition, direct slave trading between the Persian Gulf ports of Bandar 'Abbas, Lingeh, Ras al-Khaymah and Basra, and East Africa continued according to the eighteenth-century practices. The slave labour was, however, used in a greater variety of ways than in the eighteenth century:

- As soldiers in local or regional forces in Shiraz, Kirman, Basra, Bushire, Bandar 'Abbas, Masqat or Bahrayn Islands.
- As farm labourers in the Bahrayn Islands, Basra and Masqat, or as cash crop workers in Southern Iran and in the Gulf coastal villages.
- As irrigation canal workers in Fars and Kirman (Southern Iran) and in Oman.
- As pearl divers, fishermen, maritime sailors, dock workers and porters.
- As domestic servants in the towns and villages in the Gulf region and the Southern Iranian foothills.

The slave brokers, only incidentally involved in the eighteenth-century trade, became far more important in the nineteenth century, particularly as the anti-slave patrols increased. The nineteenth-century trade altered little the role of the imported female slave labourers, who continued to function within wealthy urban Iranian, Turkish or Arab homes as domestic servants or concubines. It was the male slave whose role in nineteenth-century Southern Iran and the Gulf was so greatly altered. Previously sold to urban and rural lords and administrators as house servants, handymen, pearl divers or bodyguards, in the nineteenth century the functions of the male slave were noticeably expanded to include a variety of farming and fishing tasks including cultivation, irrigation and harvesting activities.

Just as the activities of the imported labour expanded over the two centuries, involving the slave in work usually carried out by the peasantry or urban unskilled labour, so too the slave trader changed in the nineteenth century. Traders or 'slave peddlers' increasingly included sea captains, local port brokers, local merchants and administrators.[18] The nineteenth-century slave trade brought more and more East Africans into the larger labour market of the Gulf both in agriculture and in industry. Traders were more often than not distinguished as 'long-distance' traders and 'short-distance' traders in terms of whether the peddler participated in the oceanic labour peddling or primarily in the movement of slaves from the coast to hinterland regions of the Gulf. In either case, the slave labourer was forced to serve as a crew member, a temporary domestic servant or a caravaneer for the peddler before being 'dropped off' at Omani ports and Gulf towns.

The records for accurate recording of slave importations into the Gulf do not exist. However, a reasonable idea of the volume of the mid-nineteenth-century trade can be drawn from the British reports. Between 1852 and 1858, some accounting of the slave ships entering major Gulf ports was attempted. In July 1852, 8 ships with 435 slaves from Zanzibar were reported at the Gulf port of Ras al-Khaymah with an average of 55 slaves per ship. The ships were owned by the Qawasim chiefs of the coastal region. The report added that 150 of the slaves continued on to the Iranian port of Lingeh, and that ships destined for Sharjah dropped off part of the slave cargo in the Omani ports along the Batinah Coast.[19] While H.J. Disbrowe, Assistant Political Resident for the Persian Gulf, reported the capture of 202 slaves, male and female, at Sharjah, Lingeh, Maghu, Charak, Bushire, Bahrayn and Basra over a seven-year period, he added that the 'slave trade was in its full vigour'.[20]

The 'system' as such did not operate outside the usual trading routes or practices. Like the usual commercial trade routes, the slave trade shifted from town to town or region to region, depending on natural or human obstacles, indirectly creating difficulties for the British patrols.[21] In the eighteenth century, the major port-towns of the Persian Gulf served as entry points and collection centres for the few labourers imported from East Africa. The town of destination for the African slave was rarely the port-town itself, but rather the distant hinterland towns, such as Kirmantown, Shiraz or Baghdad. In the nineteenth century, however, slaves were sent to a variety of locations including relatively small towns along the Gulf littoral and into the villages of the Iranian hinterland.[22]

The table gives an estimate of the numbers of slaves imported into the Persian Gulf region between 1722 and 1902:

	ANNUAL IMPORTS		TOTAL IMPORTS*		% INCREASE
1722–1782	500–600	slaves	30,000–36,000	slaves	0
1782–1842	800–1,000	slaves	48,000–60,000	slaves	60–66
1842–1872	2,000–3,000	slaves	60,000–90,000	slaves	300–400
1872–1902	50–100	slaves	1,500–3,000	slaves	–90–84

* Total imports are equal to the annual imports times the total number of years (e.g., in 1722–1782, 500 slaves × 60 years)

The annual average number of slaves imported into the Gulf region was approximately 920 to 1,240 slaves. If the importations occurred at every one of the Gulf ports (*ca.* 50), each port may have taken approximately 19 to 25 slaves each year, or 1 to 2 slaves per month. Remembering that the estimates of slave importations dramatically increased between 1722 and 1872, annual importations undoubtedly were greater in the nineteenth than in the eighteenth century, with considerably more impact on Southern Iranian and Persian Gulf societies and economies in the later years. Historians have yet to research the social or political impact of a larger population in a traditionally sparse region, such as the Persian Gulf coasts and immediate hinterland. The effect on land and water usage, both of which were scarce in much of the Gulf region, has not been studied, nor has any research investigated the cultural impact of the nineteenth-century slave trade on the small and closed rural societies of the Gulf.

Although the available data is weak, it is possible to estimate that 80–90 per cent of the imported slaves were transshipped from the Gulf into the Ottoman and Iranian hinterlands. Keeping in mind the illnesses and deaths that occur during the 'middle passage', the 10–20 per cent who survived the 'middle passage' and worked a normal lifetime within the societies of the region represent an insignificant number in comparison to the total population. If 20 per cent of the overall importations between 1722 and 1902 brought 28,000–38,000 East Africans into the Gulf region, then 4,667 to 6,333 East Africans were living in the region at any one time, given a 30-year age lifetime average for six generations of slaves over 180 years of slave trading. The total population of the Persian Gulf region, which included Southern Iran in the 1722 to 1902 period, varied between 80,000 and 100,000 so that, in any one decade between 1722 and 1902, the East African slave represented on the average no more than 6.3 per cent of the total population.

A number of important questions still remain unanswered. Although the data is weak, some information does exists in a variety of historical sources. From those sources, it is clear that the nineteenth century witnessed a dramatic rise in slave trading into the Persian Gulf region from East Africa by way of the pilgrimage trade from the Red Sea and by way of Oman. The rise was primarily due to the unfreezing of the Iranian and Omani political and social systems in the eighteenth century, and to the vigorous emergence of Persian, Arab, Indian and Turkish merchant capital, land seizures and cash crop/plantation production. Limitations to merchant capital development already existed within the Southern Iranian and Persian Gulf economies. The integration of the economies into the larger Indian Ocean economy that occurred during the same period further limited the growth of domestic capital. Nonetheless, the increased wealth within Iran and Oman between 1722 and 1872 increased the demand for slave labour for the prosperous merchant, landlord and administrator families in the capital cities and regional towns of Southern Iran and the Persian Gulf. Used in many of the same ways as prior to the nineteenth century, slave labour nonetheless also became involved in new fields of activity, such as agricultural labour in cotton fields and date groves, subterranean irrigation construction, and the port and cabotage trade.

The increase in slave trading was, however, a relatively brief episode in Southern Iranian and Persian Gulf history. Following the First World War, Britain's expanded rule in the Persian Gulf region, the emergence of 'modern states' and the movement of European capital towards oil explorations, mining activities and processing industries redirected the demands for regional labour and the allocation of indigenous capital. Not only did new governmental intervention in the region's economies and societies mean that slaves and slave traders were no longer possible. Because of restrictions on merchant capital, and new priorities for the recently-established national economies, they were no longer needed.

SLAVES AND SLAVE TRADERS IN THE PERSIAN GULF   69

NOTES

1. See Tim Niblock, ed., *Social and Economic Development in the Arab Gulf*, New York, 1980; Daniel Pipes, *Slave Soldiers and Islam*, New Haven, 1981; and Ehud R. Toledano, *The Ottoman Slave Trade and Its Suppression: 1840–1890*, Princeton, 1982.

2. See Marvin Entner, *Russo-Persian Commercial Relations, 1828–1914*, Gainesville, Fla, 1965 and Charles Issawi, ed., *The Economic History of Iran, 1800–1914* (Chicago, 1971), pp.50–2.

3. Vahid Nowshirvani, 'The Beginnings of Commercialized Agriculture in Iran', in *The Islamic Middle East, 700–1900: Studies in Economic and Social History*, edited by A.L. Udovitch (Princeton, 1981), pp.547–91.

4. See John R. Perry, *Karim Khan Zand, 1747–1779*, Chicago, 1979 and Thomas M. Ricks, 'Politics and Trade in Southern Iran and the Gulf, 1745–1765', Unpublished Ph.D. dissertation, Indiana University, Bloomington, IN, 1975.

5. See Calvin H. Allen, Jr., 'The State of Masqat in the Gulf and East Africa, 1785–1829', *IJMES*, XIV, 2 (May, 1982), pp.117–27.

6. See Ahmad Ashraf and Hamid Hekmat, 'Merchants and Artisans and the Development Processes of Nineteenth-Century Iran', *The Islamic Middle East, 700–1900*, edited by A.L. Udovitch (Princeton, 1981), pp.733–4.

7. See Robert G. Landen, *Oman Since 1856*, Princeton, 1967.

8. Arnold Wilson, *The Persian Gulf* (Oxford, 1929), pp.215–16. See Calvin H. Allen, Jr., 'Sayyids, Shets and Sultans: Politics and Trade in Masqat Under the Al Bu Sa'id, 1785–1914', Unpublished Ph.D. dissertation, University of Washington, Seattle, Wa, 1978.

9. India Office, *Factory Records*, 'Gombroon', Vol.VI, 26 Nov. 1747, p.45. In the India Office, *Factory Records*, 'Letters', Vol.XIV, 22 Dec. 1747, p.567, the EIC agent in Bandar 'Abbas recorded that Baluchi 'runaway slaves' reported the movements of Baluchi tribesmen in that region of the Gulf.

10. India Office, *Factory Records*, 'Letters', Vol.XV, 7 March 1751, p.737.

11. India Office, *Factory Records*, 'Letters', Vol.XVI, William Shaw, Basra, 1 April, 1754 reported that the Dutch East India Company (OIC) was 'going to Masqat to purchase Coffree Slaves'. In India Office, *Factory Records*, 'Gombroon', the EIC agent Wood, Bandar Rig, 26 May, 1756 visited Kharg Island and reported seeing 80 families of Chinese farmers while armed 'Coffree slaves' are posted in each pearl-fishing boat to collect all the oyster shells. He further reported that 'above one hundred Coffree slaves' well-armed, well-fed and housed with African female slaves are used to punish the Arabs or 'country people'. See Abdul Amir Amin, *British Interests in the Persian Gulf* (Leiden, 1967), pp.147–8.

12. The European accounts of 18th- and 19th-century Southern Iran and the Persian Gulf must be handled with care when using them for figures of slave imports. See A.H.M. Sheriff, 'The Slave Mode of Production along the East African coast, 1810–1873' (paper presented at the Conference on Islamic Africa: Slavery and Related Institutions, Princeton University, 1977), p.162 where he enumerates 3,000 slaves sent from Mozambique to the Arabian Peninsula and to the Persian Gulf in the 1770s, and 9,000 slaves from Mozambique to the same region in the 1780s, but, in the 1830s, he notes that 1,200 arrived at Oman and in the Persian Gulf from East Africa. See also C. Issawi, ed., *The Economic History of Iran* (Chicago, 1971), p.125 where he compiles figures for the ten-year period between 1832 and 1842; the average imports into the Gulf ports of Basra and Bushire were 300–400 slaves while the figures were much greater for Oman and the Red Sea (10,000–12,000).

13. See Toledano, *The Ottoman Slave Trade*, p.75 where the author speaks of 'transport dealers' who convey slaves from market to market.

14. Mulla Ali Shah of Bandar 'Abbas (1747–1763) is an excellent example of the administrator-merchant active in buying and selling goods, and, on occasion importing slaves (see India Office, *Factory Records*, 'Gombroon', Vols.VI–VIII).

15. India Office, *Factory Records*, 'Letters', Vol.XVI, 2 July, 1763 copy.

16.   India Office, *Persian Gulf Territories*, 'Bushire Letters', R/15, Vol.II, 12 March, 1766, pp.3 and 9–10.

17.   Foreign Office, 'Admiralty – Communications: 1777 to 1805', 83/2, p.15. Estimates for taking Basra by Major McCleod, Major Campbell, 'an Engineer in the East India Companys' Service', and Capt. Waugh.

18.   See the Persian chronicler, Hasan Fasa'i, *History of Persia Under Qajar Rule*, trans. by H. Busse (New York, 1972), p.31 where he states that a female slave worked in the household of Ja'far Khan Zand, the principal ruler in Shiraz in 1789. Again, in 1814, Fasa'i records the story of a 'black slave', the servant of Mir Shams al-Din, who revenged his master's death by killing Mulla Shah Muhammad at the doorway of the 'New Mosque' in Shiraz (p.148); in 1832, the leading notable of Dashtistan and Bushire, Abdul Rasul Khan, the captain (*daryabegi*) of the Iranian fleet at Bushire, was served by a 'black Swahili slave' (p.211), and, in 1834, a black slave named Khosrow was part of the household of Mortaza Quli Khan, the Ilbegi of the Qashqa'i tribe in Fars (p.224).

19.   J.A. Saldanha, *The Persian Gulf Précis: Vol.III, Précis on Slave Trade in the Gulf of Oman and the Persian Gulf, 1873–1905* (London, 1986), p.90.

20.   *Ibid.*, pp.98–100 and 109.

21.   F.O., *Confidential Papers*, 'Persia', No.4337, 23 Nov. 1880 where William Gore Jones states that 'for political reasons, best known to the Indian officials . . . the slave question has been allowed to remain very much in abeyance and our cruizers, acting under the advice of the Political Residents, have refrained from active interference with the Gulf Slave Trade.'

22.   In 1851, the British Consul, Keith E. Abbott, reported that, in the southwestern region of Sistan, 'the cultivators of the soil are, for the most part, slaves both black and white' (quoted in Abbass Amanat, ed., *Cities and Trade: Consul Abbott on the Economy and Society of Iran, 1847–1866*, London, 1983, p.172). In 1907, a Russian consul who had served in Sistan wrote: 'In Sistan, they sell slaves, white and black, delivered openly in Baluchistan and other regions. Almost every village headman in Sistan has a male or female slave' (quoted in C. Issawi, *Economic History of Iran*, p.126). See Ghulamhusayn Sa'idi, *Ahl-i Hava'* (The People of the Wind) (Tehran, 1344/1965), pp.ix, 5–6, 14, 16 and 23 where his research in the villages of Bandar Lingeh, Bandar Kung and Bandar 'Abbas reveals the extensive East African physical and cultural impact on the region.

Survival and Resistance: Slave Women and Coercive Labour Regimes in the British Caribbean, 1750 to 1838

Barbara Bush

Popular stereotypes of slave women have portrayed them as passive and down-trodden work-horses who did little to advance the slave's struggle for freedom. The « peculiar burdens » of their sex allegedly precluded any positive contribution to slave resistance. Many Europeans, howewer, declared that women were more troublesome than men and contemporary accounts frequently refer to « bothersome » domestic servants and « female demons » who thwarted overseer in the field. Through an examination of women in the formal and informal slave economy, this paper will argue that women's non-cooperation at work and tenacity for survival in a deshumanising environment nourished and sustained slave resistance and contributed to the decline of the slave labour regime.

Two major reasons exist for inaccurate assessments of the slave woman's response to the slave labour regime. Firstly, contemporary writings often claimed an alleged preference for male slaves and commented on the marked sexual imbalance which was reputedly as high as five men to one woman on some Jamaican plantations [1]. Secondly, while men were valued solely for their economic contribution, women had additional child-bearing and sexual functions. These factors tended to obscure the true degree of exploitation of slave woman. In reality, if a high ratio of men to women did exist in the earlier period of slavery, plantation lists indicate that by the end of the eighteenth century, this had balanced out. During this later period of slavery, however, abolitionist pressure intensified and the potential ending of the slave trade became a serious threat to planters. It was in the latters' interests, therefore, to continue to exaggerate the disparity of the sexes and the contribution this made to the low rate of natural increase of slaves. Thus they could claim a strong case against the termination of the slave trade as well as conceal the true level of exploitation of women.

Despite planter propaganda, however, evidence indicate that, until very late on in slavery, women were valued primarily as productive labour units and not as child-bearers, although they retained this dual function throughout. This emphasis on the economic value of slave women raises the important question of how planters rationalised the extensive use of female field hands. Slave owners

(1)   Bryan Edwards, *The History, Civil and Commercial of the British Colonies of the West Indies*, London, 1801, 3 vol., 2, pp. 106, 118; Edward Long, *The History of Jamaica*, London, 1774, 3 vol., 2, p. 385; John Stewart, *A View of Jamaica*, London, 1823, p. 309.

had a distorted and ethnocentric image of the women's function in the economy of traditional West African societies. This image was based on contemporary observations of black Africans and a serious misinterpretation of the position of women in a polygynous marriage structure. Travellers to Africa commented on the strength and muscularity of native women and the physical parity between the sexes. It was generally believed that women competed with men « in enduring toil, hardships and privations » and black women were adversely compared to the European middle-class ideal of fragile womanhood [2].

Europeans had little knowledge of economic role division in West African society but none-the-less assumed that, in addition to domestic chores, women were « beasts of burden » who perfomed all heavy agricultural labour, whilst the men remained idle. Planters readily adopted this viewpoint and declared that « polygamy » in addition to allegedly encouraging rampant promiscuity amongst the blacks (another powerful plantocratic myth), reduced women to abject drudges, the « domestic slaves » of men [3]. In emphasising the « workhorse » value of polygynous African wiwes, planters glibly justified the economic exploitation of black women. This justification was facilitated by the fact that many similarities existed between the techniques of hoe cultivation used in West Africa and methods used in sugar monoculture. Field labour on sugar plantations consisted largely of digging holes for canes, hoeing, weeding and harvesting — tasks generally accepted in planter circles as « women's work » in west Africa. In reality, it was the men in West Africa who engaged in heavy tasks while women undertook lighter agricultural work, but planters were either ignorant of or chose to ignore this distinction [4]. In slave society, women thus became the toilers of the fields.

WOMEN IN THE « OFFICIAL » PLANTATION ECONOMY

The Jamaican planter William Beckford wrote :

« A negro man is purchased either for a trade or the cultivation and different processes of the cane — the occupations of women are only two,

(2)   John Adams, *Sketches taken During Ten Voyages to Africa Between the Years 1786-1822*, London, 1822, p. 8. For adverse comparisons between black and white women see Edwards, *op. cit.*, 2, p. 10-11; Thomas Atwood, *The History of Domenica*, London, 1791, pp. 211-212.

(3)   Long, *op. cit.*, 2, p. 303-304; Edwards, *op. cit.*, 2, p. 48, 76; Dr. William Sells, *The Condition of Slaves in the Island of Jamaica*, Shannon, 1972, p. 33.

(4)   For contemporary insight into women's work in Africa see, *Equiano's Travels ; His Autobiography*, ed. Paul Edwards, London, 1967, p. 4-6. The economic status of African women in traditional African societies is also discussed in M.J. Herskovits, *The Myth of the Negro Past*, Boston, 1941, p. 58-65.

the house, with its several departments and supposed indulgences, or the fields with its exaggerated labours. The first situation is the most honourable, the last the most independent. » [5]

Within the complex occupational hierarchy of slaves, the position of the woman slave was far less favourable than that of the male slave. Apart from the midwife, doctoress or chief housekeeper, and, to a lesser extent washerwomen, « housewenches » and cooks, the slave elite consisted almost solely of men. For instance, on Roaring River Estate, Jamaica, in 1756, of the ninety-two women, seventy were field workers. Of the eighty-four men, only twenty-eight were working in the cane fields [6]. Plantation lists for the latter half of the eighteenth century do not reflect any preference for male field hands, and most evidence indicates that there was generally little differentiation made between the sexes, regardless of the nature of the task ; the most important class of slaves was comprised of « the most robust of both sexes » whose work consisted of « preparing and planting... cuting the canes and... aiding the manufacture of sugar and rum » [7].

Women slaves thus became the « backbone » of the plantation labour force. This is reflected in the prices which were paid for slaves. Before the abolition of the slave trade in 1807, a new healthy male slave cost between £ 50 and £ 70, and an equivalent female slave cost £ 56 to £ 60. Creole slaves cost approximately 20 per cent more [8]. After the abolition of the slave trade, planters took more interest in the « healthy propagation » of their slaves and the childbearing role of women slaves became of greater importance, a factor reflected in the new, high price of female slaves with healthy infants. But the demand for prime female field hands remained constant. As late as 1827, « jobbing gangs » of equal numbers of men and women were advertised in Jamaican newspapers [9].

The high economic value planters placed on women as field hands severely restricted social and occupational mobility. Confined to the lower ranks, the favours and privileges accorded male elite slaves were available only to the majority of female slaves through concubinage or the « selling » of sexual favours. A favoured woman slave or the natural daughter of the owner or overseer would perhaps be taken into service in the house. The majority of women remained in the fields, working in harsh conditions and maintained by their owners at bare subsistence level. Although field hands performed the hardest

(5)   William Beckford, *Remarks Upon the Situation of Negroes in Jamaica*, London, 1788, p. 13.

(6)   R.B. Sheridan, *Sugar and Slavery : An Economic History of the British West Indies, 1623-1775*, Barbados, 1974, p. 257-258; M.J. Craton and J. Walvin, *A Jamaica Plantation : The History of Worthy Park, 1610-1970*, London, 1970, p. 138.

(7)   Robert Dallas, *The History of the Maroons*, London 1803, 2 vol., 1, p. vii. A number of relevant plantation lists may be found in *British Sessional Papers, Commons, Report of the Lords of Trade on the Slave Trade*, vol. 26, 1789.

(8)   Edwards, *op. cit.*, p. 132.

(9)   See, for instance, advertisement in *The Royal Gazette*, Kingston, Jamaica, 18 August, 1827.

labour, their living conditions were far inferior to those of élite slaves and, in consequence, they showed a higher death-rate and suffered from greater ill-health than the more privileged slaves [10]. However, although women field hands were more susceptible to coercive physical punishment aimed at extracting the maximum profit from their labour, domestic slaves were not immune from cruelty and punishment. Because of their proximity to whites, they were frequently victims of the sadistic whim and personal caprice of their masters. Moreover, the female domestic could be punished by relegation to field work and their precarious and contradictory position often cancelled out any apparent comforts and privileges.

Pregnancy did not guarantee a lighter work load nor a reduction in physical punishment. Throughout most of the period of slavery women were expected to work in the fields until at least six weeks before delivery and return to work no later than three weeks afterwards [11]. As negro prices began to rise at the end of the eighteenth century as a result of abolitionist pressures, laws were passed which were designed to give better care to pregnant women and mothers and promote a « healthy increase ». In practice, however, profit not procreation remained the primary concern of the planter. Hard work, cruel treatment and the sharp conflict between her economic and childbearing role took a severe toll on the slave woman's health. Gynaecological disorders were common and the conditions under which women laboured undoubtedly contributed to the extremely low rate of natural increase among slaves on West Indian sugar plantations [12].

Work in the fields was hard, monotonous and degrading and slaves gave their labour unwillingly and inefficiently. The productivity rate was low ; labour was extracted only through coercion and women and men alike carried out many daily acts of non-cooperation. Women were subject to the same physical punishment as men ; under the overseer's whip « neither age nor sex found any favour ». Women were, if anything, regarded as more « toublesome » than men and during the later ameliorative period planters in Trinidad opposed legislation forbidding the whipping of black women on the ground that the latter were « notoriously insolent » and only kept in some « tolerable order » through fear of punishment [13]. As Bryan Edwards noted, it was only possible to govern slaves through the enforcement of a punitive legal code [14]. In resisting the system slaves challenged their given legal status and proved they were human beings possessed of free will. Repression tended to be counter-productive — the harsher the system, the greater the insubordination of slaves. The more the

---

(10) Craton and Walvin, op. cit. p. 125. For a description of the daily work regime of field hands, see Beckford, Remarks, p. 44.

(11) Sells, op. cit. p. 17.

(12) For a discussion of such problems, see B. Bush, Lost Daughters of Afrik : Black Women in British West Indian Slave Society, Ormskirk, Hesketh, 1985, ch. 6.

(13) Thomas Cooper, Facts Illustrative of the Condition of Negro Slaves in Jamaica, London, 1824, p. 3, 17-18; Commandant of Chaguanos (Trinidad) to (Governor) Woodford, 20 August 1823, Colonial Office Series, CO 295/66.

(14) Edwards, op. cit. 3, p. 36.

insubordination threatened the legitimacy of the system, the more violent the white response.

The West Indian slave laws sanctioned the punishment of slaves. The fundamental concern of the plantocratic Assemblies which devised the slave codes was the protection of property and the social control of an unwilling workforce. Though « protective » as well as « policing » clauses existed to ensure minimum welfare standards, these were frequently abused in the absence of any effective methods of enforcement. Before 1790, British slave laws, unlike the French *Code Noir*, offered little or no protection for women or for slave family life in general. For most of the slave era, masters had complete control over the lives of their slaves who were legally defined as chattels rather than human beings.

Amendments to the laws were made as socio-economic conditions changed. However, even after ameliorative legislation was introduced in response to abolitionist criticisms, the British slave codes retained their essentially repressive, punitive emphasis. Special clauses were introduced to protect pregnant women and promote family life, but as was stressed above, there is little evidence to suggest that they were adhered to in practice [15]. Though in theory slaves could plead their cases in front of an attorney or magistrate, slave testimonies were non-admissible as evidence against whites. Thus, despite the increasing intervention of the British governements after 1807, the new laws became « specious in words and inoperate in practice ». Under pressure from metropolitan circles, planters had introduced them « grudgingly and of necessity » [16]. They did little to improve the working conditions of women or to reduce the degree of resistance to the system.

Accounts of plantation life from varied sources confirm that women gave their labour unwillingly and were a source of constant frustration for managers and overseers. They habitually shirked work, used verbal abuse, feigned illness and were accused of lying, stealing and inciting unrest. A revealing source of information are plantation journals and punishment lists. Data from the records kept on the estates of the London merchants, Thomas and William King, for the period from the early 1820s to the beginning of the Apprenticeship period, chart the deep level of everyday resistance sustained by female slaves [17].

The Kings owned plantations in Grenada, British Guiana and Dominica. As absentee landowners they left the day to day running of their estates to attorney/managers who were required to keep meticulous records. In plantation journals they entered all punishments meted out to individual slaves, the reasons

(15) Elsa Goveia, *The West Indian Slave Laws of the Eighteenth Century*, Barbados, 1970, pp. 25, 48, 194-196, 244-245. For details of the new legislation, see Edwards, *op. cit.*, 3, p. 181-185.

(16) *Edinburgh Review*, vol. 55, April 1832, p. 148.

(17) These records may be found in the Atkin's Slavery Collection, Wilberforce House, Hull. The main sources used here are Baillies Bacolet Plantation Return (Grenada), 1823-1833, and the Punishment Record Books for Friendhip Sarah and Plantation Good Success (British Guiana), 1823-1833.

why they were carried out, the names of the persons who admnistered and witnessed them and the place and date. If the culprits were female, the manager had to note « the nature and extent of punishment » in a special column. This was obviously to comply with the legislation introduced throughout the British West Indian colonies in the 1820s which forbade the whipping of female slaves. Thus while male offenders received an average of 15 to 20 « strippes » or lashes, the common recorded punishment for women was a varying period of time in the stocks or solitary confinement.

Women were far more often accused of insolence, « excessive laziness », disobedience, quarelling and « disorderly conduct » than were male slaves. Individual women were regularly punished for defiant behaviour. On Friendship Sarah Plantation in British Guiana in 1827, for instance, a female slave named Katherine was punished on 11 and 30 of November for insolence to the overseer and quarelling respectively. Another slave, Henrietta, had to spend a day and a night in the stocks for « continually omitting to comply with her task » [18].

On the King's other plantation in British Guiana, Good Success, where out of 211 slaves, 93 were female, there was a number of consistently troublesome women. From January to June 1830, Quasheba was punished repeatedly for « refusing to go to work when ordered by the doctor ». Another habitual offender, Caroline, was punished on 4 May for « abusing the manager and overseer » and defying the former to « do his worst ». During the same period one particular woman, Clarissa, was reported three times for poor work and malingering. In the first instance she was accused with another women, Lavinia, of leaving work unfinished, « assigning no cause » for so doing. On another instance, she refused to work because of a cut on her finger and when ordered to do so by the doctor, used « abusive language » to the manager. Though her punishments increased in severity from 12 hours solitary confinement to 60 hours in the stocks, her spirit to resist remained undiminished [19].

From the different plantation records an overall pattern emerges of women as persistent offenders. On average, they were punished more frequently than men. For instance, on the Friendship Sarah Plantation in the six months périod from January to June 1827, out of a total of 171 slaves on the plantation, 34 were punished of whom 21 were women [20]. The threat of punishment had little deterrent effect though many methods employed were only marginally more « humane » than the whip. Women still had to suffer the degradation and dis-comfort of the « hand and foot » stocks or solitary confinement, sometimes with the additional debasement of wearing a collar. In contrast to the whip, which was short and sharp, substitute punishments lasted from a few hours up to three days and in very serious cases a longer period was recommended. Sunday, the only free day, when slaves cultivated their own plots, was the favourite date for confinement. All punishment involved public humiliations as it was adminis-

(18) Punishment Record Book, Plantation Friendship Sarah, Nov.-Dec. 1827.
(19) *Ibidem*, Good Success, 1830.
(20) *Ibidem*, Plantation Friendship Sarah, 1827.

tered by slaves, witnessed by white employees and usually took place « before the house » or in the hospital.

Faced with the intransigence of black women which ran to more serious crimes, such as running away, attempts to poison their masters, and « exciting discontent in the gang », hard pressed managers argued that the whip was the only means of keeping females in order. Official records may indeed have conveniently « overlooked » harsher punishments. Even in the 1820s on certain plantations, the whip was still used on women occasionally. For instance, under « general observations » for 1823, the manager of Baillies Bacolet Plantation, Grenada, notes that Eliza had received 20 lashes for « violent behaviour in the field... and for excessive insolence to myself when reprimanding her in presence of the gang ». On the same plantation as late 1833 another woman, Germaine, was given 15 lashes for « wilfully destroying canes in the field » and « general neglect of duty » [21].

Though not so overtly rebellious, domestic servants, the majority of whom were women, also used subtle tactics to frustrate their white masters and mistresses. They may have superficially accomodated to slavery, adopting the habits and dress of the European who they served and lived whith, but in the opinion of contemporary observers they were a constant source of irritation. Arguably, their impact on whites was all the more intense than that of field hands because of their constant and close physical presence. Emma Carmichael was sorely tried by the domestic slaves under the supervision on her husband's Trinidadian estate. Minor thefts were a common occurrence, always denied by the suspects. Her washerwomen never carried out their work properly and « used generally more than twice the quantity of soap, blue and starch » required by washerwomen in England. They also had a tendency to « lose » articles of clothing and, of all the « troublesome » Carmichael establishment, were the most « discontent, unmanageable and idle ». From their arrival in Trinidad, the Carmichaels were harassed by the grumbles, lies and uncooperative nature of female slaves in particular and cited their insubordination as one of the reasons the estate was sold prior to emancipation [22].

Other contemporary observers made similar comments. Long felt that the « propensity of laziness » was chiefly conspicuous in house servants and Lewis complained of their inefficiency and refusal to correct faults. For John Stewart, female domestics were so « refractory, vicious and indolent » that in managing them the white women became a « greater slave than any of them » [23]. Of all slaves, domestics exhibited the greatest duality of behaviour and were in the most contradictory position. Though outwardly they were obliged to conform more than field slaves to European culture and values, they employed convert and

(21) Baillies Bacolet Plantation Returns, 1823, 19 February, 1833.
(22) Emma Carmichael, *Domestic Manners; Five Years in Trinidad and Saint-Vincent*, London, 1833, 2 vol., 1, p. 118-119, 256-258; 2, p. 268, 334.
(23) Long, *op. cit.*, p. 415; Matthew, *Journal of a Residence Among the Negroes of the West Indies*, London, 1845; Stewart, *op. cit.*, p. 172.

subtle means to retain their cultural integrity and to protest their enforced enslavement.

Women were in the vanguard of the cultural resistance to slavery which helped individuals survive the slave experience. Their important contribution to the « private » lives of slaves — the reconstitution of the family and the building of a viable black community life — has been analysed elsewhere [24]. It was this cultural strength, however, which helped women resist the system in their more « public » lives as workers. In the fields, cultural defiance was expressed through language and song. Language in particular was an important element in black identity and cultural unity, a major form of defense against deshumanisation. Women field hands were experts in the use of the rich creole language which, with its double-entendres and satire, was frequently employed as a subtle abuse of whites [25]. Through such channels women helped to generate and sustain the general spirit of resistance.

WOMEN IN THE « UNOFFICIAL » ECONOMY

The importance of the African cultural heritage and the slaves' ability to adapt their culture to survive slavery and resist deshumanisation, is illustrated in the unofficial or « informal » plantation economy, to which women made a significant contribution. In the cultivation of slave provision grounds, marketing and other petty entrepreneurial activities, women exhibited a degree of energy and enterprise which contrasted sharply with their intransigence in the fields.

This informal economy was separate from the externally-orientated plantation economy, which was linked to the international mercantile system, and provides an illustration of the dual response to slavery. In the external or « public » sphere, controlled by and for the benefit of whites, slaves proved « irascible », indolent, dishonest and « artful », the stereotype of the inferior black. This contrasted sharply with the « private » sphere of their lives where « beyond the ken » of their masters, they sought to create a viable family and community life. The informal internal marketing system, created primarily by the slaves themselves, was fundamental to the creation and integration of creole slave society and constituted a positive adaptation to slavery.

The existence of an economy controlled by blacks stemmed from reluctance of West Indian planters to provide slaves with sufficient food. From early times, slaves were encouraged to supply their own food needs. Each adult slave was allocated a plot on marginal estate lands on which to grow provisions. By the late eighteenth century masters were legally bound to appoint a « sufficient

(24) B. Bush, *Lost Daughters*, chap. 5 and 9.
(25) See, for instance, Long, *op. cit.*, 2, p. 278; *Lady Nugent's Jamaica Journal*, ed. P. Wright, Kingston, 1966, p. 153.

quantity » of land for each of their slaves, male and female, and to allow them with enough free time for cultivation of this land [26].

For one and a half days each week, Saturday afternoon and Sundays, the slaves were freed from formal plantation labour to work their provision grounds or « polinks » (as distinct from the tiny plots or yards close to their houses). As the rewards of their labour were their own, not their masters, they expended much effort to produce vegetables, ground provisions, roots and herbs. Any surplus could be exchanged at the Sunday market for money or other necessary articles, thereby offering an additional strong incentive. If owners failed to respect these customary rights or attempted to sell slaves, they met with strong resistance. Slaves became very attached to their cottages and lands and if taken from them often developed « habits of heedlessness and indolence » which rendered them worthless to their owners. This had serious implications in the late period of slavery when estates more frequently changed hand and owners sold off slaves as « stock » with callous disregard for the family bonds or community attachments of individual slaves [27].

The focal point of these « informal » economic activities was the Sunday market which was important from the very beginning of slavery. By 1819 it had become an institution where « several thousands of human beings... principally negroes, were busily employed in all kinds of traffic in the open streets ». The market was so central to creole community life that the stringent laws restricting the mobility of slaves were relaxed to allow them to engage in such activities ; no slave could travel about without a ticket « specially worded and signed » by his or her owner except if going to market [28]. This worked against the plantocracy, as it facilitated communication between the plantation and the co-ordination of slave uprisings.

Women slaves were prominent as marketeers and « higglers » (middlemen), a reflection of their African cultural heritage and successful adaptation to new circumstances in which they found themselves in the New World. In West Africa, women were entitled to sell any surplus from their own farm plots as well as the products of their special skills such as baskets and prepared foods. They were allowed to keep the entire profit from these transactions which gave them a degree of economic independence that was accepted by the community as an integral part of their ascribed role. Though many changes have occurred in both West Indian and West African societies since the slavery era, black women have retained their economic independence and still tend to dominate local markets.

Regardless of the hardship encountered in their formal work-life, slave women were energetic and resourceful in the cultivation of their own provision

---

(26) S.W. Mintz and D. Hall, "The Origins of the Jamaican Internal Marketing System", in S.W. Mintz, ed., *Papers in Caribbean Anthropology*, New Haven, 1970, p. 5-6.

(27) Edwards, *op. cit.*, p. 8. For descriptions of cultivation of plots, see Dallas, *op. cit.*, 1, pp. cviii-cix; Edwards, *op. cit.*, 2, p. 137; Long, *op. cit.*, pp. 410-411.

(28) William Beckford, *A Descriptive Account of the Island of Jamaica*, London, 1790, 2 vol., 2, p. 151-160.

grounds. Whites however had mixed feelings about such activities. Whilst recognising their economic importance, planters were worried by the entrepreneurial independence they fostered. Market women were often described as clever, cunning and untrustworthy. An advertisement for a runaway Kingston woman placed in the *Jamaica Mercury* in 1779 accused her of absconding from her owner with money she had received from the sale of provisions. In the same town in 1827, a similar advertisement appeared for three runaways, an « elderly black woman of the Mundingo (Mandingo) country » and her two daughters. All were described as « well-known higglers » who were « very artful » and likely to pass themselves off as free persons [29]. Participation in the informal economy thus not only offered women independence from black men but a way to freedom from white masters.

After the abolition of slavery, the internal marketing system developed by the former slaves and free coloured became the basis of the West Indian free peasantry and urban *petite-bourgeoisie*. During the slavery period, these economic activities gave meaning and purpose to an otherwise bleak and depressing existence. Whole families were involved in the cultivation of provision grounds and this fostered a sens of communal solidarity essential to survival. Women make a major contribution to this slave « underlife » over which the whites had little control. In addition to contributing to the independence of mind noted by contemporary European observers, the relative freedom of movement allowed to women in their marketing activities enabled them to make an important contribution to organised slave resistance, the collective action which completed the « day to day » individual resistance to the work regime.

SUMMARY

Within the general framework of resistance and survival which ultimately guaranteed emancipation, women were primary agents. Despite the threat of frequent, often harsh punishment which included the whip, women fought fiercely against the system. Through their rebellious and insubordinate behaviour, they not only jeopardised the planters' profits but voiced a strong and effective protest against the harsh conditions of their servitude. This assertion of free will challenged the legal definition of slaves as chattels for it underscored the essential humanity of blacks and presented Europeans with moral dilemmas which ultimately weakened one of the basic arguments for the retention of slaves.

In addition to their contribution to general slave resistance, including organised slave revolts, women were crucial in transmitting the spirit and tradition of resistance to their children through song and oral tradition. Caribbean

---

(29)   Runaway slave advertisements, *The Jamaica Mercury*, 26 June, 1779; *The Royal Gazette*, October 1827.

women have been described by Melville Herskovits as the « primary exponents » of African derived culture. It was this culture which helped to shield the slaves from deshumanisation and give them the strength to survive servitude (30). Strong cultural traditions were evident in the gardening and marketing activities of slave women and their vigorous activities in this informal economy helped to foster a spirit of resilience and independence which prepared slaves for their role as free peasants after abolition.

After emancipation, women essentially retained the economic roles they had been allocated during slavery. Many of the socio-economic problems associated with the plantation system and sugar monoculture persisted, hindering constructive development. Black women remained in low status occupations in the externally orientated cash-crop economy as plantation labourers and seasonal cane-cutters but retained their prominent role in the internal marketing system. They also continued to act as catalysts in the integration of creole society through their continuing contribution to the cultural life of the black community (31). The high degree of economic and social independence of Afro-Caribbean women, which derived from Africa and was reinforced by slavery, has enabled them to play a signifcant role in modern labour struggles and resistance to colonial and neo-colonial domination, as the active participation of women in the recent Grenadian revolution illustrates (32).

Before and after emancipation, women's spirit to resist was heightened by the racism implicit in the Caribbean class system. In an elaborate hierarchy based on the interlinked criteria of colour and economic status, black women were in the lowest position. During slavery, racist stereotypes of black women as passive work-horses or scarlet temptresses sought to degrade them and portray them as inferior species. Such negative stereotypes were used to justify and rationalise the economic and sexual exploitation of slave women and proved extremely durable. A reassessment of existing evidence indicates that, in effect, women did not comply with this stereotyped image. Supported and sustained by their African

---

(30) Melville and Frances Herskovits, *Trinidad Village*, New-York, 1947, p. 8-9.
(31) Of interest here is Wiliam MacMillan's *Warning from the West Indies : A Tract for Africa and the Empire*, London, 1936, p. 76-80; Martha Beckwith, *Blacks Roadways : A Study of Jamaican Folk Life*, New-York, 1969, p. 160, 168-172, and, more recently Frances Henry and Pamela Wilson, "The status of Women in Caribbean Societies : an Overview of their Social, Economic and Sexual Roles", *Social and Economic Studies*, vol. 24, June 1975, p. 165-169.
(32) Modern forms of female resistance are discussed by Rhoda Reddock in "Women's Movements and Organisations in the Process of Revolutionary Transformation : The Case of Grenada", in D. Durham and J.P. Perez-Saintz, ed., *Crisis y Repuesto in America Latina y del Caribe*, Costa-Rica, 1984; "Women Labour and Struggle in 20th Century Trinidad and Tobago", PhD thesis, Institute of Social Studies, The Hague, 1985.

cultural heritage, they resisted European racism and the essentially exploitative system which it sought to rationalise.

The methods of resistance adopted by slave women reflected the ever pervasive influence of their African heritage and the tangible, brutal circumstances of the slave labour regime. At work women showed much courage in refusing to cooperate and in verbal abuse of masters. But they also showed considerable industry and enterprise in the informal economy. As the foremost bearers of Afro-Caribbean culture, women transmitted the « consciousness and practice of resistance » in a system which sought at all times to undermine it. The labour needs of the slave labour regime caused a « crude levelling » of the sexes and ensured that women shared the same experience as black men, but, equally, the harsh conditions of life stimulated rather than squashed resistance and strengthened the resolve and independent stance of women.

16

The Slave Trade, Sugar, and British Economic Growth, 1748–1776

David Richardson

That from the encreasing luxury of our Country [i.e. Britain], the advance of the sugar keeps pace with the advance upon the Slaves.[1]

British overseas trade grew substantially during the eighteenth century. Data derived from customs records indicate that the official value of British exports (excluding re-exports) rose almost sixfold over the century while imports increased over fivefold. The growth of trade was by no means steady and was frequently disrupted by war, but it accelerated distinctly over the course of the century; the annual level of trade rose by 0.8 percent before 1740, by 1.7 percent between 1740 and 1770, and by 2.6 percent thereafter. Overall, overseas trade grew faster than either British population or total output. Per capita imports and exports thus increased significantly during the century, and a rising share of British output, especially industrial output, was exported. It has been estimated that exports' share of output doubled over the century, rising from 7 or 8 percent at the beginning to 16 or 17 percent at the end. Exports' share of industrial production is calculated to have grown from one fifth to one third during the same period.[2]

Although there appears to be widespread agreement about the general contours of British overseas trade and its share of British output, there is little consensus about either the causes of the growth of trade or its relationship to British industrialization. Some historians have regarded the expansion of demand for Brit-

1 Thomas Melvil to the Company of Merchants Trading to Africa, 17 Mar. 1755, Cape Coast Castle, Public Record Office (PRO), C.O. 388/46, Ee 59.
2 Phyllis Deane and William A. Cole, *British Economic Growth, 1688–1959* (Cambridge, 1967), 46; Roderick Floud and Donald McCloskey (eds.), *The Economic History of Britain since 1700,* (Cambridge, 1981), I, 38–39, 89.

ish goods overseas as stemming from essentially autonomous developments abroad, whereas others, notably Deane and Cole, have argued that the growth of British exports, particularly after 1745, was primarily a consequence of the British demand for imports, the resulting expansion of purchasing power abroad filtering back to British exporters by means of a network of colonial trading connections. Similarly, the extent and timing of the expansion of British exports, notably after 1783, has led some scholars to attribute to overseas trade a major role in causing British industrialization, whereas McCloskey and Thomas have recently concluded that "the horsepower of trade as an engine of growth seems [to have been] low" in the century or so before 1860. Historians resident in Western industrialized nations are generally divided in their explanations of the growth of eighteenth-century British exports and in their assessment of exports' impact on the Industrial Revolution.[3]

Caribbean-based historians, by contrast, have generally been much more united in attributing to British overseas trade—particularly the slave trade and related trades in plantation staples— a positive and substantial role in fostering British industrialization. Williams, the major exponent of this view, claimed that profits from the triangular or slave trade "fertilized the entire productive system of the country." Despite recent demonstrations that the slave trade was probably less profitable than Williams alleged and could not carry the weight of responsibility for financing British industrialization that he assumed, his views continue to influence the debate over the origins of British industrial growth during the eighteenth century. In part at least, this influence arises from the fact that Williams presented his argument in broad and sweeping terms, and failed, for instance, to indicate clearly whether he was referring to profits from the slave trade alone or from the combined triangular and bilateral colonial trades. Furthermore, he frequently neglected to locate precisely in time and place the connections that he believed existed between the slave trade, associated plantation trades, and British industrial development.[4]

3 Timothy J. Hatton, John S. Lyons, and Stephen E. Satchell, "Eighteenth Century British Trade: Homespun or Empire Made," *Explorations in Economic History*, XX (1983), 164; Deane and Cole, *Economic Growth*, 83; Cole, "Factors in Demand, 1700–80," in Floud and McCloskey, *Economic History*, I, 42–44; McCloskey and Robert P. Thomas, "Overseas Trade and Empire, 1700–1860," in *ibid.*, 102.
4 Eric Williams, *Capitalism and Slavery* (London, 1964; orig. pub. 1944), 105. See, e.g.,

SLAVES, SUGAR, AND GROWTH | 741

This article investigates these possible connections during the period 1748 to 1776. The investigation ranges outside the question of the relationship of profits from the slave trade and British industrial investment to which several scholars have addressed themselves and seeks instead to explore the impact of Caribbean slave economies and their related trades upon the growth of markets for British industrial output. An examination of market connections among the slave trade, plantation agriculture, and British industry during the third quarter of the eighteenth century is particularly revealing, for available evidence now indicates that there occurred at this time both a substantial rise in the level of British slave trading activity and colonial sugar production on the one hand, and a marked acceleration in the rate of growth of British industrial production on the other. I argue that these developments were not unrelated but that their relationship was more complex than Williams indicated. In particular, the slave trade and slavery should be viewed not as some peculiar promoter of industrial expansion and change in Britain, but rather as integral though subordinate components of a growing north Atlantic economy, the expansion of which was largely dictated by forces from within British society, notably rising consumer demand for colonial staples such as sugar. Rising British sugar imports in turn created enhanced export opportunities for British manufacturers in colonial and African markets and thereby made a significant contribution, as Deane and Cole have argued, to the acceleration in the rate of growth of British industrial output in the middle of the eighteenth century.

During the last fifteen years historians have made major advances in their efforts to ascertain the general volume and temporal distribution of the eighteenth-century British slave trade. Published estimates have suggested that British traders may have carried between 2.5 and 3.7 million slaves from Africa between

---

Roger Anstey, *The Atlantic Slave Trade and British Abolition* (London, 1975), 38–57; Thomas and Richard N. Bean, "The Fishers of Men: The Profits of the Slave Trade," *Journal of Economic History*, XXXIV (1974), 885–914. The debate over profitability still continues however. See Joseph E. Inikori, "Market Structure and the Profits of the British African Trade in the Late Eighteenth Century," *ibid.*, XLI (1981), 745–776, and the comment by Bruce L. Anderson and Richardson, with a rejoinder by Inikori in *ibid.*, XLIII (1983), 713–729. Compare Williams' comment in *Capitalism and Slavery*, 5, with his comments on 52 and 105. See also, *ibid.*, 51–84.

1701 and 1807, with the most recent survey carried out by Lovejoy suggesting a figure of just over 2.8 million. Although there remains much scope for disagreement about the overall size of the British trade after 1701, all estimates indicate that it grew substantially over the course of the century, reaching its peak after 1783. The most widely accepted figures indicate that annual shipments of slaves by the British probably tripled over the eighteenth century, rising from 12,000 to 14,000 before 1720 to around 42,000 during the 1790s.[5]

Currently published estimates of the British trade are invariably constructed on decadal bases and have only limited usefulness for exploring in detail the relationship between the slave trade and economic change in Britain, Africa, and the Americas. For such purposes estimates of the annual levels of the trade are needed. Using new sources of shipping data, I have been able to produce such estimates for the period 1698 to 1807. As yet unpublished, these estimates largely confirm the overall rate of expansion of the trade suggested by most other historians. But they also indicate that expansion was far from smooth. It was largely confined in fact to two main periods: the 1720s and early 1730s and the third quarter of the century. The increase in British slaving during the latter period was especially marked, as annual British shipments of slaves from the African coast in peacetime rose from an estimated 25,800 between 1749 and 1755 to 43,500 between 1763 and 1775. During these last years, British vessels carried more slaves from Africa than in any previous or subsequent period of thirteen consecutive years. The British slave trade may therefore have reached its peak before, not after the American Revolution as most recent scholars have suggested.[6]

Irrespective of whether the British slave trade peaked before 1776 or not, its substantial expansion over the third quarter of the century requires explanation. A detailed investigation of the matter is impossible here, but the evidence suggests that the

5 See Paul E. Lovejoy, "The Volume of the Atlantic Slave Trade: A Synthesis," *Journal of African History*, XXIII (1982), 474–501, for a summary of recent estimates. The annual figures here are based on estimates contained in Philip D. Curtin, *The Atlantic Slave Trade: A Census* (Madison, 1969), 150; Anstey, "The British Slave Trade 1751–1807: A Comment," *Journal of African History*, XVII (1976), 606–607; Seymour Drescher, *Econocide: British Slavery in the Era of Abolition* (Pittsburgh, 1977), 205–213; Lovejoy, "Synthesis."
6 Copies of my tables are available on request. The next highest thirteen-year total in the number of slaves carried was 1783 to 1795.

SLAVES, SUGAR, AND GROWTH | **743**

expansion of the trade owed little to improvements in commercial conditions in West Africa. In comparison with earlier years, the costs of procuring slaves on the coast probably rose significantly after 1750 as dealers in West Africa were unable to accommodate an acceleration in the growth of international demand for slaves within existing cost and price schedules. Data compiled by Bean reveal that the average current price for adult male slaves at the coast increased by some 25 percent between 1748 and 1775 or from £13.9 in 1748 to 1757 to £17.5 in 1768 to 1775. Furthermore, procuring slaves even at these rising prices required British traders to accept mounting shipping costs. My own estimates, based on Bristol and Liverpool shipping data, indicate that the average time spent by British vessels slaving on the coast lengthened considerably during the third quarter of the century and that daily loading rates of slaves at times fell to historically low levels, thereby raising average shipping costs per slave purchased.[7]

Faced with rising expenses in West Africa, British merchants continued in the slave trade because they either anticipated equivalent cost savings on other sections of the slaving voyage or expected proportionately higher prices for slaves in the New World. How much scope there was for achieving economies on mid-eighteenth-century slaving voyages is difficult to assess, but the introduction of new payments mechanisms for slaves in the Caribbean and elsewhere around mid-century and the use of copper sheathing from the 1770s onward to protect the hulls of slave ships from attack by toredo worms—a practice pioneered by the Royal Navy—were both cost-saving innovations. Innovations of this sort, however, took time to introduce and brought uncertain and essentially long-term benefits.[8]

Failing immediate short-term cost-cutting opportunities, merchants had to rely on higher prices for slaves in the New World in order to offset the upward pressure on costs in West Africa after 1748. They were not disappointed. Published data

7 See Ben T. Wattenberg (ed.), *The Statistical History of the United States from Colonial Times to the Present* (New York, 1976), 1174. These estimates are presented in Richardson, "The Efficiency of English Slave Trading in West Africa during the Eighteenth Century: Estimates and Implications," unpub. ms. (1981).

8 Gareth Rees, "Copper Sheathing: An Example of Technological Diffusion in the English Merchant Fleet," *Journal of Transport History*, II (1972), 85–94; Henry A. Gemery and Jan S. Hogendorn, "Technological Change, Slavery and the Slave Trade," in Clive Dewey and Anthony G. Hopkins (eds.), *The Imperial Impact* (London, 1978), 257–258.

indicate that during the first half of the eighteenth century the average current price for adult male slaves in British America varied between £23 and £27, but then rose to £31.9 between 1748 and 1757, to £35.0 between 1758 and 1767, and to £40.7 between 1768 and 1775. A rise of some 27.6 percent between 1748 and 1775, this matched the rise in slave prices in West Africa over the same period and created a rate of mark-up on prices between the coast and the New World after 1748 that was even higher than that prevailing during the previous period of expansion in the trade in the 1720s and early 1730s. Expansion and success in the British slave trade between 1748 and 1776 thus appears to have rested primarily on the buoyancy of markets for slaves in the Caribbean and other parts of British America.[9]

Various factors influenced the demand for slaves in British America; these included the inability of slaves to maintain their numbers through natural reproduction, particularly in the Caribbean, and the regular extension of credit by British merchants to New World planters to assist them in purchasing slaves. However, the main determinant of demand for slaves was the level of income that planters derived from the production and sale of basic staples such as sugar, tobacco, rice, and indigo. Although the number of slaves sold by the British to planters in North American mainland colonies such as Virginia and South Carolina was sometimes considerable, the central markets for British slavers before and after 1776 were in the sugar islands of the Caribbean. Sugar exports constituted the largest single component of British Caribbean planter incomes, and it was revenue from this crop that essentially shaped demand conditions for British slavers between 1748 and 1776.[10]

Detailed evidence about Caribbean planters' incomes is, unfortunately, relatively sparse, but information about the volume and prices of sugar shipped annually to Britain from the islands during the eighteenth century is readily available. From this information it is possible to calculate the gross annual revenues received by planters from sugar exports to Britain. Some sugar

9 Wattenberg (ed.), *Statistical History*, 1174. Mark-ups were 129% and 132% in 1748–1757 and 1768–1775 compared to 94% in 1728–1732 and 101% in 1723–1727. *Ibid.*, 1174.
10 On the role of credit, see Jacob M. Price, *Capital and Credit in British Overseas Trade: the View from the Chesapeake 1700–1776* (Cambridge, Mass., 1980). Curtin, *Census*, 140.

SLAVES, SUGAR, AND GROWTH | 745

was shipped from the islands to markets other than Britain, notably the British North American colonies, but most of the sugar produced in the islands was shipped initially to the mother country; up to 20 percent was re-exported to Ireland and the European Continent. Gross receipts from sugar shipments to Britain offer a clear indication of the total revenues accruing to planters from their sugar exports. Gross receipts provide an imperfect measure of net incomes from sugar sales, but it is reasonable to assume that variations in such receipts over time probably reflect both the short-term fluctuations in planters' fortunes and long-term trends in their net incomes.[11]

Detailed estimates of gross annual receipts accruing to Jamaican planters from sugar shipments to Britain from 1748 to 1775, together with figures on retained annual slave imports into the island, are set out in Table 1. Estimates of the gross revenues received from shipments to Britain by all British Caribbean planters for various periods between 1713 and 1775 are provided in Table 2.

It appears from Table 1 that there existed a direct but lagged relationship between changes in Jamaican planters' gross receipts from sugar shipments to Britain between 1748 and 1775 and the number of imported slaves retained in the island. Excluding war years when trading conditions were uncertain, annual variations in Jamaican revenues from sugar were generally reflected one year later by similar variations in retained slave imports during seventeen of the twenty peacetime years between 1748 and 1775.

11 See John R. Ward, "The Profitability of Sugar Planting in the British West Indies, 1650–1834," *Economic History Review*, XXXI (1978), 197–213, on planter profits. Richard B. Sheridan, *Sugar and Slavery: An Economic History of the British West Indies 1623–1775* (Baltimore, 1974), 22, 32–34, 493–497. The sugar trade statistics provided by Sheridan refer to England and Wales only before 1755 but include Scotland thereafter. Throughout this article I refer to Britain in describing trade figures even when, as in my present discussion of sugar imports or my later discussion of British exports generally, the data relate to England and Wales. As far as sugar imports or British-produced exports are concerned, trade statistics for England and Wales are close approximations to British trade in this period. Available statistics on Scottish trade after 1755 reveal that less than 4% of British sugar imports entered through Scottish ports before 1776 and that less than 5% of total British-produced exports were dispatched from Scotland. Henry Hamilton, *An Economic History of Scotland in the Eighteenth Century* (Oxford, 1963), 414, 419. The omission of Scottish figures from the trade statistics used in this article does not affect the trends suggested by such statistics.

Table 1 Gross Revenues from Sugar Exports to Britain and Retained Slave Imports in Jamaica, 1748–1775

YEAR	SUGAR REVENUES £000	RETAINED SLAVE IMPORTS
1748	688	8004
1749	603	4730
1750	561	2866
1751	569	4127
1752	586	5079
1753	718	6759
1754	702	·7959
1755	836	12125
1756	777	9264
1757	754	6992
1758	922	2994
1759,	1015	4531
1760	1622	5205
1761	1556	5838
1762	1020	6047
1763	994	8497
1764	1104	7574
1765	1001	6945
1766	1070	9536
1767	1234	2873
1768	1278	5465
1769	1210	3155
1770	1350	5988
1771	1294	3512
1772	1264	4355
1773	1501	8876
1774	1856	15937
1775	1618	7663

NOTE: Sugar revenues relate to the gross proceeds from sales in England for the year *prior* to that stated.

SOURCES: Sugar prices: Sheridan, *Sugar and Slavery*, 496–497. Sugar imports from Jamaica: Noel Deerr, *History of Sugar* (London, 1949), I, 193–202. Slave imports: PRO, C.O. 137/38, Hh, 3, 4.

Since the time interval between the dispatch of slaving voyages from British ports and their arrival in the New World was nine to twelve months by the mid-eighteenth century, this twelve-month lag between Jamaican planters' receipts from sugar and their purchase of slaves suggests a high degree of supply responsiveness among British slavers to shifts in Jamaican demand for slaves during the third quarter of the eighteenth century.[12]

An inspection of Table 2 shows that gross annual receipts by Caribbean planters from their total shipments of sugar to Britain rose by some 237 percent between 1713 and 1775, from £959,000 per annum between 1713 and 1716 to £3,235,000 between 1771 to 1775. However, the growth in receipts was by no means steady and was affected by different factors over time. Revenues actually fell after 1716 largely as a result of falling sugar prices, but then rose steadily during the 1720s as shipments of sugar increased markedly and prices stabilized. Declining re-export markets and a collapse in London sugar prices brought about another fall in planter revenues during the early 1730s; they remained below the levels of 1726 to 1730 through the rest of the decade. Sugar prices began to recover in the late 1730s and the 1740s, however, and, despite a doubling in the quantities of sugar shipped to Britain

Table 2   Average Annual Gross Revenues from Sugar Shipments to Britain from the Caribbean, 1713–1775

	AVERAGE GROSS PROCEEDS (£000 PER ANNUM)	SUGAR PRICE INDEX (1713–16 BASE)	CONSUMER PRICE INDEX (1713–16 BASE)
1713–16	959.1	100	100
1721–25	805.6	72	94
1726–30	1049.3	74	98
1731–35	824.8	60	88
1736–40	965.1	75	91
1741–45	1209.5	95	93
1746–50	1479.9	103	93
1751–55	1675.1	105	90
1756–60	2652.1	120	101
1761–65	2617.2	108	98
1766–70	2952.1	110	104
1771–75	3234.8	108	114

SOURCES: Sugar imports: Elizabeth B. Schumpeter, *English Overseas Trade Statistics 1697–1808* (Oxford, 1960), 52–56. Sugar prices: Sheridan, *Sugar and Slavery*, 496–497. Consumer prices: Brian R. Mitchell and Deane, *Abstract of British Historical Statistics* (Cambridge, 1962), 468–469.

12   Richardson, "Efficiency of English Slave Trading." A similar responsiveness of slave supply to changes in planter revenues was apparent in South Carolina after 1748. *Idem*, "The Volume and Pattern of the English Slave Trade to South Carolina before 1776," unpub. ms. (1983).

during the third quarter of the century, these higher sugar prices were sustained through to the American Revolution. During this quarter century, prices of muscovado sugar on the London market only occasionally fell below 33 shillings per cwt., and were usually 40 percent or more higher than they had been in the two decades before 1740. Based in part on a revival in re-exports of sugar after 1748, notably to Ireland, this sustained recovery in sugar prices was due primarily to the buoyancy of the domestic sugar market in Britain. Despite substantially increased imports, the price of muscovado sugar appears to have risen relative to the prices of other consumer goods in Britain during the third quarter of the century. At the same time, the share of British imports coming from the Caribbean rose significantly from 20.9 percent by value between 1748 and 1752 to 28.7 percent between 1773 and 1777. Growing British sugar consumption thus provided the foundation for the silver age of sugar between 1763 and 1775 and the associated rapid expansion in British slaving activity.[13]

Statistics on population and retained sugar imports indicate that sugar consumption per head in Britain rose from 6.5 lbs around 1710 to 23.2 lbs in the early 1770s. By this latter date, per capita sugar consumption in Britain was several times higher than in continental Europe. Explanations for the growth of British sugar consumption and its divergence from continental levels have largely focused upon changes in taste and diet, particularly the growth of tea and coffee drinking in Britain during the eighteenth century. Apparently confined in the seventeenth century to the wealthier strata of British society, tea drinking in particular became widespread in the eighteenth century. Thus contemporary writers often mentioned the growing habit of taking tea with sugar among even the poorest sections of British society.[14]

That increased tea drinking was probably a major factor in extending the market for sugar in eighteenth-century Britain is not to be denied, but available statistics indicate that the increase in sugar consumption in Britain was not steady and may have

---

13 Sheridan, *Sugar and Slavery*, 32; Drescher, *Econocide*, 22. For the use of the phrase "silver age of sugar" to describe the period 1763 to 1775, see Richard Pares, "Merchants and Planters," *Economic History Review*, Suppl. 4 (1960), 40.
14 Sugar consumption figures are based on Sheridan, *Sugar and Slavery*, 493–495; Floud and McCloskey, *Economic History*, I, 21. Sheridan, *Sugar and Slavery*, 18–35.

SLAVES, SUGAR, AND GROWTH | 749

also been influenced by other factors. Close examination of import figures and population estimates shows that per capita sugar consumption increased markedly during the second and third decades of the century and again between 1750 and 1775 but remained relatively static during the intervening period. This leveling out of sugar consumption per head between 1730 and 1750 may have been more apparent than real, reflecting weaknesses in customs records; the period from 1730 to 1750 is thought to have been one in which smuggling, for instance, was particularly rife. However, smuggling was associated more with spirits, tea, and tobacco than muscovado sugar, and it is unlikely that the variations in the rate of growth of British per capita sugar consumption in the half century before 1775 can be attributed to deficiencies in trade statistics.[15]

Available price data suggest that the growth of sugar consumption in Britain during the two decades before 1730 stemmed essentially from improved efficiency in supplying the product. With 1713 to 1716 as a base, the wholesale price of muscovado on the London market fell by over 30 percent between 1713 and 1730 while the fall in price of consumer goods generally was less than 10 percent. From the mid-1730s onward, however, sugar prices rose relative to other prices. Despite substantial increases in sugar imports after 1750, wholesale prices on the London sugar market were some 5 to 20 percent higher than the 1713 to 1716 base throughout most of the third quarter of the century, whereas prices of consumer goods in general, but particularly consumer goods other than cereals, remained below or near to the 1713 to 1716 base until about 1770. In contrast to the period before 1730, the growth of sugar consumption between 1748 and 1776 was essentially the result of rises in incomes or changes in consumer preferences rather than improvements on the supply side.[16]

15 The exact figures of consumption per head are: 1731, 15.7 lbs; 1741, 13.9 lbs; 1751, 15.0 lbs; 1761, 18.0 lbs. Consumption in each year is the average of 5 years centering on the year specified. Cole, "Trends in Eighteenth-Century Smuggling," *Economic History Review*, X (1958), 395–410. On tobacco, see Robert C. Nash, "The English and Scottish Tobacco Trade in the Seventeenth and Eighteenth Centuries: Legal and Illegal Trade," *ibid.*, XXXV (1982), 354–372.

16 Sugar prices based on Sheridan, *Sugar and Slavery*, 496–497; consumer goods on the Schumpeter-Gilboy index as reprinted in Mitchell and Deane, *Abstract of British Historical Statistics*, 468–469. By 1770, the exclusion of cereals from the consumer goods price index lowered the consumer goods index by around 10%.

This last suggestion raises some interesting problems, for most recent studies of eighteenth-century British output and income have indicated that, largely because of changes in the relative growth rates of population and agricultural output and productivity, per capita real incomes in Britain probably rose faster in the half century before 1760 than during the ensuing two decades. In particular, it has been suggested that per capita real incomes may have grown relatively quickly between 1730 and 1750—the era of the so-called "Agricultural Depression"—when unusually low grain prices are alleged to have stimulated consumption of non-agricultural goods, notably manufactures. Recent work has cast doubt on the extent of the depression in British agriculture at this time, however, and its assumed impact on consumer demand and British economic growth may thus have been exaggerated.[17]

Nevertheless, available evidence still points toward a distinct slowing down in the rise of real per capita income nationally around 1760 as the growth rate of agricultural output slackened, grain prices rose both absolutely and relatively, and Britain became periodically a marginal net importer of grain instead of a regular grain exporter. Furthermore, an analysis of data on British wage rates and prices between 1750 and 1792 has led Flinn to conclude that "it would be a brave historian who would assert that real wages were advancing in this period." In view of such evidence, the fact that per capita sugar consumption in Britain appears to have increased by around 50 percent between 1750 and 1775 is especially intriguing.[18]

17 Nicholas F. R. Crafts, "British Economic Growth, 1700–1831: A Review of the Evidence," *Economic History Review*, XXXVI (1983), 177–199; Arthur H. John, "Agricultural Productivity and Economic Growth in England, 1700–1760," *Journal of Economic History*, XXV (1965), 19–35; John V. Beckett, "Regional Variation and the Agricultural Depression, 1730–1750," *Economic History Review*, XXXV (1982), 35–52.

18 On trends in grain exports see John, "English Agricultural Improvement and Grain Exports, 1660–1765," in Donald C. Coleman and John (eds.), *Trade, Government and Economy in Pre-Industrial England* (London, 1972), 45–67; Walter E. Minchinton (ed.), *The Growth of English Overseas Trade in the Seventeenth and Eighteenth Centuries* (London, 1969), 63. See also R. V. Jackson, "Growth and Deceleration in English Agriculture, 1660–1790," *Economic History Review*, XXXVIII (1985), 333–351. Michael W. Flinn, "Trends in Real Wages, 1750–1850," *ibid.*, XXVII (1974), 408. See also Peter H. Lindert and Jeffrey G. Williamson, "English Workers' Living Standards During the Industrial Revolution: A New Look," *ibid.*, XXXVI (1983), 1–25, which includes wage data on the period 1755 to 1781. Their data indicate some squeezing of real adult male earnings between these benchmark dates.

SLAVES, SUGAR, AND GROWTH | 751

Pending further detailed research, any explanation of rising British sugar consumption after 1750 must be regarded as speculative, but two reasons suggest themselves. The first relates to regional variations in income growth and the second to changes in the supply and relative price of beverages, notably beer and tea, after 1750.

Frequent references by early eighteenth-century writers to the growth of new consumption habits among working families and the poor have led historians to exaggerate the extent to which a national market for sugar developed in Britain before the mid-eighteenth century. Despite some transport improvements in the century or so after 1660, Britain continued to exhibit considerable regional diversity in terms of social structure, labor markets, and levels of prosperity and wealth before 1750. As a result the rate at which consumption patterns changed almost certainly varied significantly from one area of the country to another. Comments by eighteenth-century writers about changing habits of consumption should therefore be approached cautiously, for, as Gilboy reminded us, "most of the writers were Londoners, writing either consciously or sub-consciously about London or other growing towns."[19]

Although data on local or regional levels of sugar consumption are presently unavailable, sugar consumption per head probably was higher in London and its surrounding area than in other regions during the first half of the eighteenth century. London was, after all, the center of the British tea and sugar trades and also had a large servant population who were "the chief intermediaries between their masters and the lower classes in spreading standards of conspicuous consumption." Furthermore, available data indicate that, throughout the eighteenth century, money wages of laborers and craftsmen were higher in London than elsewhere, and moreover that the differential was greatest during the first half of the century. Such evidence suggests that general trends in Britain's sugar consumption up to 1750 were determined largely by economic and social conditions in the nation's capital.[20]

However, there are signs that, by the middle of the century, sugar consumption was growing among even the poorest mem-

19 See Sheridan, *Sugar and Slavery*, 18–35; Elizabeth W. Gilboy, *Wages in Eighteenth-Century England* (Cambridge, Mass., 1934), 240.
20 *Ibid.*, 235, 219–227.

bers of society in areas some distance from London. Contemporary writers referred also to the wider use of meat, tea, and sugar in northern working-class diets. Such dietary changes were made possible by relative improvements in real wages after 1750 in industrializing counties such as Lancashire. Recent studies have revealed that, although real wages nationally may not have improved significantly between 1750 and 1790, wages in Lancashire and perhaps other industrializing areas rose markedly, reflecting a growing demand for labor as industrial and urban expansion gathered pace. Thus, between 1750 and 1792, money wages of Lancashire laborers and building craftsmen rose by some 64 percent and 40 percent respectively, whereas Kentish laborers' wages rose by just under 20 percent and London laborers' wages by under 4 percent. Even allowing for price increases, Lancashire workers seem to have made notable gains in real terms after 1750 and, by narrowing the gap in wage levels that existed between themselves and their counterparts in the southeast before 1750, were able to share more fully in the consumption of products that the latter had enjoyed for almost half a century. Increases in per capita sugar consumption after 1750 may thus reflect the emergence of a national market in sugar brought about by dietary changes in industrializing regions experiencing rising prosperity during the third quarter of the eighteenth century.[21]

Rising sugar consumption after 1750 may also have stemmed from shifts in the relative elasticities of supply of tea and more traditional British beverages such as beer and ale. Official statistics on eighteenth-century British tea imports are notoriously unreliable because tea was invariably subject to such high import duties that it was regularly smuggled into Britain on a large scale. Research has suggested, however, that lower duties introduced in 1745 probably reduced levels of tea smuggling during the ensuing

---

21 Jonathan D. Chambers, "The Vale of Trent, 1670–1800," *Economic History Review,* Suppl. 3 (1957), 24; Thomas Percival, "Observations on the State of the Population of Manchester, and other Adjacent Parts, 1773–74," in Bernard Benjamin (ed.), *Population and Disease in Early Industrial England* (Farnborough, Hants., 1973), 43–45; Soame Jenyns, *Thoughts on the Causes and Consequences of the Present High Price of Provisions* (London, 1767), 10–12; G. Nick von Tunzelmann, "Trends in Real Wages, 1750–1850, Revisited," *Economic History Review,* XXXII (1979), 39; Gilboy, *Wages,* 220–221. A sharp deterioration in real wage rates for building craftsmen in London took place in the 1750s and 1760s. See L. D. Schwarz, "The Standard of Living in the Long Run: London, 1700–1860," *Economic History Review,* XXXVIII (1985), 24–41.

SLAVES, SUGAR, AND GROWTH | **753**

quarter century or so. Trends in legal imports may thus reasonably closely reflect patterns of British tea consumption in the twenty years after 1748.[22]

Total legal imports and consumption per head both increased substantially during this period. Recorded tea imports per annum rose by some 123 percent between 1748 and 1767, or from just over 3 million to almost 7 million pounds. As a result per capita tea consumption doubled. During the same period, market prices for tea, including duty, fell by nearly 10 percent while real prices fell by over 15 percent. Even allowing for the possibility of diminishing levels of smuggling between 1748 and 1767, tea supplies in Britain were highly elastic during the third quarter of the eighteenth century.[23]

Any attempt to assess the elasticity of beer and ale supplies over the same period is complicated by two factors. First, retail prices for traditional alcoholic beverages such as beer, ale, and porter were subject to official control during the eighteenth century and often remained fixed for lengthy periods. Information on the price of beer in differing localities is unavailable, but if we extrapolate from information on the price of porter, the staple beer drunk in the London metropolitan area from the 1720s on, retail prices of strong beer and ale may have risen by around 15 percent between 1748 and 1776, or from 3d to 3½d per quart pot, largely as a consequence of an increase in the duty on beer in 1761.[24]

Second, although detailed figures on the annual English output of beer throughout the eighteenth century are readily available, they derive essentially from the excise duties levied on beer sales and as a result almost certainly underestimate actual beer production. The most thorough investigation of the eighteenth-century brewing industry has concluded, nevertheless, that despite the onerous levels of duty on beer, which amounted at times to over 50 percent of all other costs, the excise returns "are more

22   Cole, "Eighteenth-Century Smuggling."
23   Tea imports from Schumpeter, *English Overseas Trade Statistics,* 60–61; population estimates from Floud and McCloskey, *Economic History,* I, 21. Cole, "Eighteenth-Century Smuggling," Table 1.
24   Peter Mathias, *The Brewing Industry in England* (Cambridge, 1959), 109–113, 546. Thomas S. Ashton, *Economic Fluctuations in England 1700–1800* (Oxford, 1959), 65, notes a high level of price elasticity of demand for beer.

reliable as a guide to actual production over a series of years than most other eighteenth-century statistics."[25]

From these returns it appears that, after experiencing either modest growth or, at worst, stability up to the 1740s, per capita beer production in England declined moderately, if somewhat irregularly, during the ensuing thirty years before the American Revolution. Attributable in part to the rising price competitiveness of tea, this decline may also have been caused by the impact of harvest failures and generally rising barley and malt prices on brewers' costs and profits after 1750. Faced with increasing raw material costs and deterred by custom and official restriction from raising retail prices to cover them, many brewers, particularly the smaller victualling brewers, experienced an erosion of profit margins during the third quarter of the century. As a result they were obliged either to adulterate their product by watering it down and using additives to simulate alcoholic strength, which ultimately damaged the reputation of their product, or to cease production altogether, thereby increasing opportunities for alternative beverages. By constraining the growth of beer production, the failure of grain supplies to match increases in British population after 1750 may thus directly have assisted tea and its associate, sugar, in improving their share of the expanding British market for food and drink.[26]

Variations in regional wage movements and shifts in the relative prices of beverages in Britain may have enhanced economic opportunities for Caribbean planters between 1748 and 1776. The 50 percent rise in per capita sugar consumption in Britain in this period is, however, greater than might be predicted by known income or price elasticities of demand for agricultural products at this time; other factors must have contributed to the

---

25 Mathias, *Brewing*, 345.
26 *Ibid.*, 542–543 for beer output statistics. According to Crafts' calculations, beer output fell in the 1760s, whereas output of most major industries experienced accelerated growth compared to 1700–1760. See Crafts, "British Economic Growth," 181. The problems confronting the brewing industry after 1750 may have affected the relative numbers of common and victualling brewers. See Mathias, *Brewing*, 542–543. For trends in Scottish and Yorkshire brewing at this time, see Ian Donnachie, *A History of the Brewing Industry in Scotland* (Edinburgh, 1979), 16–37; Eric Sigsworth, *The Brewing Trade during the Industrial Revolution: the Case of Yorkshire* (York, 1967). The potential of tea as a substitute for alcoholic beverages was noted by Gilbert Blane, writing in the early nineteenth century; see Mary D. George, *London Life in the Eighteenth Century* (London, 1925), 339.

sharp increase in sugar consumption. It is possible, for instance, that greater resort to non-alcoholic beverages reflected public reaction to the excesses associated with the gin age. One should not overlook, either, the contemporary comments about the spread of tea drinking among the laboring population or the more recent evidence produced by historians that the number of families with "middling" incomes of £50 to £400 per annum grew from 15 to 25 percent of the English population between 1750 and 1780.[27]

Why this increase in the number of middle-income families took place at this time, when agricultural prices generally were rising, is still uncertain, but the increase provided a major impetus to the growth of the home market for British industrial products during the third quarter of the eighteenth century. Such families, headed by merchants, wealthy tradesmen, clergymen, members of the legal and other professions, and government servants, were substantial consumers of imported beverages and sugar, being classified, for instance, by Joseph Massie in 1760 among those who "drink Tea or Coffee in the Morning" or even "Tea, Coffee, or Chocolate, Morning and Afternoon." As consumers not only of home-produced manufactures but also of slave-grown products such as sugar, such families, in conjunction with Caribbean planters and slave merchants, played a prominent part in promoting the economic growth and expansion of the north Atlantic world after 1748.[28]

Recent studies of eighteenth-century British output have indicated that, despite an overall deceleration in the growth rate of total

27 Income and price elasticities are discussed in Jackson, "Growth and Deceleration," 333–351; Crafts, "Income Elasticities of Demand and the Release of Labour by Agriculture during the British Industrial Revolution," *Journal of European Economic History*, IX (1980), 153–168. On the spread of tea drinking, see Mathias, *The Transformation of England* (London, 1979), 162; Floud and McCloskey, *Economic History*, I, 58; Jonas Hanway, *A Journal of an Eight Days Journey. . . . with an Essay on Tea* (London, 1755), II, 274–275. Hanway believed that 25,000 hogheads of sugar or some 29 to 35% of British sugar imports a year "are supposed to be expended with tea" (II, 151). Neil McKendrick, John Brewer, and John H. Plumb, *The Birth of a Consumer Society* (London, 1982), 24.
28 David E. C. Eversley, "The Home Market and Economic Growth in England, 1750–80," in Eric L. Jones and Gordon E. Mingay (eds.), *Land, Labour and Population in the Industrial Revolution* (London, 1967), 206–259. Lindert and Williamson, "Revising England's Social Tables 1688–1812," *Explorations in Economic History*, XIX (1982), 349–399; Mathias, "The Social Structure in the Eighteenth Century: A Calculation by Joseph Massie," *Economic History Review*, X (1957–58), 30–45.

output between 1760 and 1780, industrial output increased faster during this period than during the previous sixty years. As a result, growth rates of agriculture and industry, which had largely moved in harmony before 1760, diverged sharply during the following two decades. It is estimated that industrial output rose annually by 0.7 percent before 1760, by 1.5 percent between 1760 and 1780, and by 2.1 percent between 1780 and 1801. Annual growth rates for agriculture were 0.6 percent, 0.1 percent and 0.8 percent respectively.[29]

The flimsiness and unreliability of eighteenth-century statistics and the arbitrary nature of the periods chosen for investigation make one hesitant about accepting these estimates too uncritically, but there is little doubt that the growth rate of British industrial output rose discernibly and diverged perceptibly from that of agriculture during the third quarter of the century. To what extent was this acceleration in industrial growth based on exports and, more specifically, on the purchasing power generated in the Caribbean by rising British sugar imports after 1748?

The debate among historians about the relationship of exports to Britain's industrial expansion during the eighteenth century has to date largely centered on the period after 1783. Despite suggestions by Williams, for instance, that the expansion of eighteenth-century British manufacturing was encouraged substantially by the markets created by the slave trade and Caribbean sugar production, recent work has suggested that British industrial growth before 1780 was largely based on the home market. The importance of the home market has been particularly stressed by Eversley, who pointed not only to the importance of the growth of income of certain middle-income social groups in Britain between 1750 and 1780, but also to the modest rate of growth of British-produced exports and the low ratio of exports to total output in Britain before 1783.[30]

That the home market remained buoyant and British exports in general grew relatively modestly before 1783 is undeniable. The expansion of sugar imports between 1748 and 1776 is itself testimony to rising incomes and changing consumer tastes in Britain at this time. Furthermore, customs statistics indicate that,

29 Crafts, "British Economic Growth," 187.
30 For Williams' views, see his *Capitalism and Slavery*, 65–84. Eversley, "Home Market," 206–259.

in official values, average annual home-produced exports from Britain rose from £7.22 million between 1745 and 1749 to £10.05 million between 1770 and 1774 or by 39.3 percent. This modest increase in exports was no greater than that achieved during the thirty years prior to 1745, particularly when one takes demographic changes into account. Thus, again in official values, exports per capita rose from £0.86 between 1715 and 1719 to £1.11 between 1745 and 1749 and to £1.26 between 1770 and 1774. Overall, the ratio of exports to output in Britain failed to rise sharply after 1750 or to exceed more than 13 percent of total output before 1783.[31]

The recent discovery that trends in industrial and agricultural output diverged sharply around 1760, however, raises some doubts about an explanation of market expansion for Britain's industrial output based almost wholly on home demand. Furthermore, an analysis of export demand which is based primarily on aggregate trade and output figures and neglects to examine the changing composition of British exports after 1748 and their relationship to the shifting regional balance of Britain's manufacturing base is misleading and too pessimistic about the contribution of exports to Britain's industrial performance between 1750 and 1780. Investigation of the connections between exports and growth and structural change in British industry after 1750 requires one to distinguish exports of industrial goods from other goods and, within the group of industrially based exports, to distinguish more traditional exports such as woolens and worsteds, which were already experiencing relative decline by 1750, from new and emerging exports such as cotton and linen textiles.

A division of home-produced exports from Britain between 1745 and 1774 is given in Table 3. Two important characteristics of exports in this period are highlighted by this table. First, exports of non-industrial goods, primarily grain and fish, which together regularly contributed 15 percent of British home-produced exports before 1750, declined both relatively and even absolutely over the third quarter of the century, thereby lowering the overall rate of growth of total domestically produced exports. Whereas total home-produced exports rose by only 39.3 percent

31 Schumpeter, *Trade Statistics*, 15. The ratio of exports to industrial output, however, increased in this period. See Floud and McCloskey, *Economic History*, I, 40.

Table 3 Average Annual Domestically Produced British Exports, 1745–1774, Distinguishing Corn, Fish, and Woolens from All Other Exports

	ALL EXPORTS £000	CORN & FISH £000	WOOLENS £000	OTHER EXPORTS[a] £000
1745–49	7,217	1,132	4,477	1,608
1750–54	8,705	1,370	5,023	2,312
1755–59	8,793	570	5,591	2,632
1760–64	10,448	1,056	5,623	3,769
1765–69	9,639	173	5,267	4,199
1770–74	10,030	93	5,395	4,542

a Other exports consisted overwhelmingly of industrial goods.

SOURCE: Schumpeter, *Overseas Trade Statistics*, 19–22, 25, 37–39; John, "English Agricultural Improvement," 64; Minchinton, *English Overseas Trade*, 63.

between 1745–1749 and 1770–1774, exports of industrial products rose by 63.2 percent, or from £6.09 million annually to £9.94 million.

Second, among exports of industrial goods, woolen and worsted exports grew very slowly between 1750 and 1775, despite the fact that the rising West Riding branch of the industry increased its exports substantially during the third quarter of the century. Official statistics indicate that annual exports of woolens and worsteds rose by less than 21 percent or some £918,000 between 1745–1749 and 1770–1774, with Yorkshire contributing the lion's share of this increase. By comparison, exports of other industrial goods during the same period rose in official values by 182.5 percent or by £2.93 million annually. Notably fast rates of growth were attained by coal, wrought iron, copper and brass, and linen and cotton textiles, all of which achieved increased exports of up to 290 percent by value during the quarter century after 1749, thereby raising their share of domestically produced British exports from 8.5 percent in 1745–1749 to 20.2 percent in 1770–1774.[32]

Symbolic of the changing regional balance of Britain's industrial base in the mid-eighteenth century, each of these growing sectors of British industry, with the exception of coal, exported an increasing share of its output up to 1776 and beyond. Series

32 Richard G. Wilson, *Gentlemen Merchants* (Manchester, 1971), 41–42; Schumpeter, *Trade Statistics*, 21–22, 25.

of production statistics for eighteenth-century British industries are rare and in most cases of doubtful reliability. Estimating the output of particular British industries at any stage during the eighteenth century is thus extremely difficult. Nevertheless, available information indicates that most of the growing export industries had developed significant export markets by 1750 and that their ratio of exports to output rose further between 1750 and 1775. Wilson's study of Leeds' clothiers, for instance, shows that the West Riding's expanding share of British woolen and worsted output during the eighteenth century arose essentially from its successful penetration of export markets, particularly during the 1720s and 1730s and again after 1760. Available data suggest that about 40 percent of the area's output of woolens went abroad around 1700 but, by 1771/72, when a detailed and apparently reliable census of the Yorkshire industry was made, 72.3 percent of the region's estimated output of woolens, valued at £3.5 million, was exported; over 90 percent of the area's staple product, broad cloth, was sold abroad.[33]

Output estimates for other prominent export industries after 1750 are even more sketchy than those for West Riding woolens, but they too suggest an increasing dependence on exports in general after 1750. For example, estimates of British pig-iron output together with imports of bar iron indicate that supplies of raw materials to wrought iron manufacturers may have risen by 70 percent during the third quarter of the century, whereas wrought iron exports increased by 141 percent during the same period. Similar calculations reveal that exports of linen and cotton textiles rose at least twice as fast as the raw materials available to manufacturers in the same period. Only in the case of copper and brass did export markets fail to absorb a rising proportion of the industry's output between 1750 and 1775, but available figures suggest that exports still took as much as 40 percent of British copper and brass production on the eve of the American Revolution.[34]

---

33 Wilson, *Gentlemen Merchants*, 41–42, 51–52.

34 For pig iron output, see Philip Riden, "The Output of the British Iron Industry before 1870," *Economic History Review*, XXX (1977), 442–459. Bar iron imports and wrought iron exports from Schumpeter, *Trade Statistics*. Much bar iron was re-exported; therefore these calculations may understate the importance of export growth after 1750. Estimates of linen and cotton exports are based on data from Schumpeter, *Trade Statistics*. Calcula-

For each of these industries—wrought iron, copper and brass, cotton and linen textiles, and even Yorkshire woolens—export success during the third quarter of the century lay essentially in African and American markets. Detailed information on the proportion of Yorkshire woolens exported to different markets overseas is unavailable, but the most recent work on the industry indicates that its expansion depended heavily on North American markets from about 1760 onward. Fuller information about export markets for the other industries mentioned above shows that dependence on America and Africa as export markets was also pronounced in most instances by 1750; in the case of wrought copper, for instance, over 80 percent of its admittedly small exports in 1750 went to Africa and America. Almost invariably, however, sales to these markets rose both absolutely and proportionally, in some cases markedly, between 1750 and the early 1770s. Excluding Yorkshire woolens, each of the industries dispatched at least 70 percent of its exports to America and Africa by the 1770s, a notable achievement given the considerably enhanced level of exports produced by each of them between 1750 and 1775.[35]

The combined effect of this increased dependence of most leading growth sectors of British exports upon African and American markets was closely reflected in the overall distribution of English exports after 1750. Several historians, most notably Davis, have noted that links with non-European economies exerted a growing influence on the pattern of British overseas trade during the eighteenth century. Africa and America's share of British exports rose from less than 10 percent of total exports at the beginning of the century to almost 40 percent at the end. Closer examination of the trade figures reveals, however, that the shift in this distribution of British exports toward Africa and America largely occurred between 1748 and 1776. Up to 1747 exports to Africa and America fluctuated between 12 and 15

---

tions by Durie suggest that the share of Scottish produced linen that was exported rose from 18% between 1748 and 1752 to around 30% between 1768 and 1777. Alistair J. Durie, "The Markets for Scottish Linen, 1730–1775," *Scottish Historical Review*, LII (1973), 38. A rising proportion of these exports was directed through English ports. On copper and brass, see John R. Harris, *The Copper King* (Liverpool, 1964), 12.

35 Wilson, *Gentlemen Merchants*, 50; Schumpeter, *Trade Statistics*, 63–69; Alfred P. Wadsworth and Julia de L. Mann, *The Cotton Trade and Industrial Lancashire 1600–1780* (Manchester, 1931), 145–169; Durie, "Scottish Linen," 41–42.

SLAVES, SUGAR, AND GROWTH | 761

percent of total exports, including re-exports, but then rose dramatically over the third quarter of the century, reaching 35 percent of the early 1770s.[36]

Underpinned by the changing regional distribution of traditional British industries such as woolens and worsteds and by the displacement of exports of primary goods such as grain and fish by goods from relatively recently established manufacturing industries located in the northwest and midlands of England as well as west-central Scotland, this decisive shift in the general direction of exports was essentially responsible for sustaining the overall growth of British exports between 1748 and 1775. Almost two thirds of the increase in recorded British exports during the third quarter of the century can be accounted for by rising sales in Africa and America, the remaining third being attributable largely to increased sales, notably of re-exported colonial produce, to Ireland. Such changes suggest that, although at the national level home demand may have played a preponderant role in sustaining growth after 1750, exports to Africa and America were at least a capable handmaiden in promoting further expansion in Britain's emerging industrial regions before 1775.

Various factors contributed to the growth of exports from Britain to Africa and the New World between 1748 and 1775. These included the continuing expansion of tobacco and rice exports from the southern mainland colonies and the development of supplementary, subsidized staples such as indigo; the expansion of North American food exports to southern Europe as British grain exports dwindled and cereal prices nudged upward in European markets; and the impact of the Seven Years' War on British government expenditure in the Americas.[37]

The most important single factor, however, was rising Caribbean purchasing power stemming from mounting sugar sales to Britain. As receipts from these sales rose, West Indian purchases of labor, provisions, packing and building materials, and con-

36 Ralph Davis, "English Foreign Trade, 1770–1774," *Economic History Review*, XV (1962), 285–303; Mitchell and Deane, *Abstract*, 309–310. Schumpeter, *Trade Statistics*, 17, Table V, also contains a breakdown of destinations of exports but seems defective for the period 1771–1775. Drescher, *Econocide*, 23, presents data on the shifts in the destinations of exports from England from 1713 onward but fails to comment on the marked change in the destination of exports between 1750 and 1775.

37 For the impact of the Seven Years' War on exports from England to America, see Davis, "Foreign Trade," 296.

sumer goods generally increased substantially after 1748, reinforcing and stimulating in the process trading connections between various sectors of the nascent Atlantic economy. Data on changes in West Indian incomes and expenditure at this time are unfortunately lacking, but Table 2 shows that gross receipts from British West Indian sugar exports to Britain rose from just under £1.5 million annually between 1746 and 1750 to nearly £3.25 annually between 1771 and 1775 or by about 117 percent.

Rising West Indian proceeds from sugar sales had a direct impact on exports from Britain to the Caribbean and, as planters expanded their purchases of slaves from British slave traders, on exports from Britain to Africa also. Customs records reveal that the official value of average annual exports from Britain to the West Indies rose from £732,000 between 1746 and 1750 to £1,353,000 between 1771 and 1775, and that exports to Africa rose over the same period from £180,000 to £775,000 per annum. Annual exports from Britain to the Caribbean and Africa thus rose by just over £1.2 million over the third quarter of the century, a figure equivalent to 27.5 percent of the total increase in annual recorded British exports during the same period. It may be argued that these export data understate the full impact of Caribbean purchases of slaves on exports to Africa. They exclude British goods ultimately bound for Africa which were carried by the small number of British slave ships which first visited continental, notably Dutch, ports in order to complete their cargoes of African trade goods before proceeding to the coast for slaves. Such ships naturally cleared customs from Britain for continental destinations rather than for African ports. At the same time, however, about 5 percent of British vessels clearing for Africa were non-slavers and around 10 percent of British slavers sold their slaves purchased in Africa in non-Caribbean, mainly North American, markets. Overall, available export data provide as accurate a picture of the increases in British exports to the West Indies and Africa after 1748 as eighteenth-century trade statistics permit.[38]

In addition to their direct impact on British exports, rising Caribbean expenditures from 1748 on had more indirect effects on British trade. Two effects in particular are worth stressing.

38 Schumpeter, *Trade Statistics*, 17. Details of the proportion of slaves sold in non-Caribbean markets are to be found in my unpublished ms., "The Volume and Pattern of the English Slave Trade to South Carolina before 1776" (1983), 3.

SLAVES, SUGAR, AND GROWTH | **763**

First, exports from Britain to Africa especially consisted not only of home-produced goods but also of foreign, notably East India, goods. Trade between Britain and the East Indies grew substantially over the third quarter of the eighteenth century, with imports from the East Indies rising from some £960,000 per annum between 1746 and 1750 to £1,750,000 between 1771 and 1775 and annual exports to the area rising from £520,000 to £910,000 during the same period. The expansion of British trade with Africa after 1748 provided an important stimulus to trade with the East, for available data suggest that some 25 percent of exports from Britain to Africa comprised East Indian produce at this time. The growth of Britain's trade with Africa therefore may have boosted East Indian purchasing power by as much as £150,000 per annum between 1748 and 1776. Assuming this increased income was spent wholly on purchasing imports from Britain, such a sum was equivalent to almost one third of the growth of exports from Britain to the East Indies and represented 3.4 percent of the growth of total annual exports from Britain between 1748 and 1776.[39]

Second, Caribbean planters purchased increased quantities of foodstuffs, packaging, and building materials, largely from Ireland and the mainland colonies, and in the words of one contemporary, George Walker, agent for Barbados, "in proportion to their dependence on North America and upon Ireland, they enable North America and Ireland to trade with Great Britain."[40]

Calculating the effect of Irish and North American sales to the West Indies on their own purchases of British goods is more problematical than Walker assumed, however, for detailed information about the level of Irish and North American trade with the Caribbean over any length of time is presently lacking. In the case of Ireland, published trade statistics show that Irish exports generally experienced a significant and largely sustained rise from about £1.25 million in 1740 to almost £3.2 million in 1770. Imports also rose strongly during the same period from £850,000 to

39 Schumpeter, *Trade Statistics*, 17–18; Richardson, "West African Consumption Patterns and their Influence on the Eighteenth-Century English Slave Trade," in Gemery and Hogendorn (eds.), *The Uncommon Market: Essays in the Economic History of the Atlantic Slave Trade* (New York, 1979), 306–307. East India goods comprised up to 85% of foreign goods re-exported from England to Africa.
40 Cited in Sheridan, *Sugar and Slavery*, 475.

over £2.5 million. Founded primarily on expanding sales of linen to Britain, some of which was then re-exported to the American mainland colonies, Irish exports were given a further boost from the 1740s onward by growing sales of provisions, particularly salt beef, pork, and butter. According to one authority, the markets for beef arose mainly from the slave populations of West Indian plantations and the victualling of ships engaged in colonial voyages.[41]

Although recent research has indicated that consumption of beef and other Irish provisions by the slave population of the New World probably was very small, sales of Irish provisions in the British Caribbean rose markedly during the third quarter of the century, reflecting buoyant demand among the white population of the islands. Figures produced by Nash show that exports of provisions from Ireland to the Americas rose from an annual average of £129,000 Irish between 1748 and 1752 to £213,000 Irish between 1773 and 1777, the bulk of these sales taking place in the Caribbean.[42]

Such sales allowed Ireland to create a favorable trade surplus with the Caribbean averaging about £161,000 (Irish) per annum between 1773 and 1777. However, this surplus was more apparent than real, for most of Ireland's export trade to the Caribbean was carried on in British-owned vessels to which Irish shippers were obliged to pay freight and other charges. In any case, exports to the Caribbean constituted less than 10 percent of Ireland's total exports in the early 1770s and the superficial surplus on its dealings with the region between 1773 and 1777 was no more than 12 percent of its recorded exports to Britain in 1771.[43]

By comparison with linens, which constituted some 70 percent of Irish exports to Britain in the period from 1740 to 1770, Irish earnings from sales of provisions to the British West Indies could at best have contributed only marginally to advancing sales of British products in Ireland before 1776. Indeed, in view of the

41 Louis M. Cullen, *An Economic History of Ireland since 1660* (London, 1972), 55.
42 Nash, "Irish Atlantic Trade in the Seventeenth and Eighteenth Centuries," *William and Mary Quarterly*, XLII (1985), 330–341. The £ (sterling) exchanged for between £1.07 and £1.12 (Irish) during the eighteenth century.
43 *Ibid.*, 339. Another calculation which suggests a trade surplus of £142,000 per annum in 1772–1774 can be found in Sheridan, *Sugar and Slavery*, 470. See Cullen, *Anglo-Irish Trade 1660–1800* (Manchester 1968), 45, for Irish exports to England.

SLAVES, SUGAR, AND GROWTH | **765**

fact that re-exported colonial goods constituted over half of Britain's exports to Ireland after 1750, it is probable that Irish linen exports to Britain did more to sustain markets in Ireland for Caribbean goods than sales of Irish provisions to the Caribbean bolstered Britain's exports of home-produced goods to Ireland.

British exporters perhaps derived greater benefits from North American sales of produce to the Caribbean. Hard statistical information about the scale of American mainland dealings with the British sugar islands is largely confined to the years 1768 to 1772. Shepherd and Walton have calculated that the current value of North American exports to the British West Indies averaged £710,000 annually between 1768 and 1772; imports from the islands averaged £684,000 annually during the same period, yielding an average annual surplus on trade of £26,000 in favor of the mainland. This small surplus on commodity trade was supplemented by sales in the islands of slaves purchased by mainland colonists in West Africa and, even more significantly, by mainland earnings from shipping, insurance, and commissions associated with their Caribbean transactions. Mainland exports to Africa which provide one indication of the value of their Caribbean sales of slaves averaged £21,000 a year from 1768 to 1772; earnings from shipping and invisibles associated with Caribbean trade, such as insurance and commissions, have been estimated to have averaged no less than £323,000 and £137,000, respectively, during the same five years.[44]

If these other earnings are added to the small trade surplus, it appears that North Americans achieved an overall balance of payments surplus of some £507,000 annually on their business with the Caribbean between 1768 and 1772. The bulk of this surplus accrued to colonies north of the Delaware, which also accumulated the largest trade deficits with Britain. The official value of annual exports from the thirteen colonies to Britain averaged £1.69 million between 1768 and 1772; their annual imports from Britain averaged £2.83 million. Surpluses on Caribbean trade were thus vital to the mainland colonies, allowing

44 James F. Shepherd and Gary M. Walton, *Shipping, Maritime Trade and the Economic Development of Colonial North America* (Cambridge, 1972), 128, 134, 223–226, 227, 229–230.

them to pay for almost 18 percent of their recorded imports from Britain around 1770.[45]

In the absence of detailed trade and shipping data for earlier periods, it is difficult to assess the contribution of surpluses on Caribbean transactions to mainland purchases of imports from Britain in 1750. However, the level of Caribbean sugar revenues and slave purchases during the 1750s and 1760s, together with the evidence of sharply rising foodstuff exports to the islands from several of the major mainland colonies after 1748, point to a rapid growth in mainland trade and shipping activity with the Caribbean during the third quarter of the century, and therefore to much lower levels of exports from North America to the islands around 1750. Estimates by Shepherd and Walton, based on admittedly flimsy information, suggest that mainland exports to the sugar islands were probably no greater than £200,000 a year in the 1750s, or less than one third of the level reached around .1770. If we apply this tentative figure to the period 1748 to 1752 and also assume that the ratio of mainland commodity exports to their realized surplus on total dealings with the Caribbean was the same in this period as twenty years later, then Caribbean transactions would have yielded a sum of £143,000 annually to North America between 1748 and 1752, a figure equivalent to 11 percent of its average annual imports from Britain in those same years. Comparison of this estimated surplus with that between 1768 and 1772 suggests that, during the intervening twenty years, North American mainland surpluses on exchanges with the West Indies grew by £364,000 per annum. During the same period the official value of average annual mainland imports from Britain rose by £1.53 million to £2.83 million. Surpluses derived from Caribbean trade appear to have paid for almost a quarter of the increased imports that North Americans bought from Britain between 1750 and 1770.[46]

These crude calculations, based essentially on British trade with Africa, the West Indies, and the East Indies, and on North

---

45 Price, "New Times Series for Scotland's and Britain's Trade with the Thirteen Colonies and States, 1740 to 1791," *William and Mary Quarterly*, XXXII (1975), 322–325.
46 On grain exports see, for instance, David Klingaman, "The Significance of Grain in the Development of the Tobacco Colonies," *Journal of Economic History*, XXIX (1969), 268–278; Geoffrey Gilbert, "The Role of Breadstuffs in American Trade, 1770–1790," *Explorations in Economic History*, XIV (1977), 378–388. Shepherd and Walton, *Shipping*, 174; Price, "Time Series," 322–325.

SLAVES, SUGAR, AND GROWTH | 767

American trade with the islands, suggest that the growth of Caribbean purchasing power may, directly and indirectly, have increased total exports from Britain by almost £1.75 million per annum between the late 1740s and the early 1770s. As total annual exports from Britain rose by some £5.0 million over the same period, West Indian demand may have accounted for some 35 percent of the growth in total British exports during these years.

In common with British exports generally, however, exports to the West Indies, Africa, and North America in particular comprised both domestically produced and re-exported goods. Trade statistics indicate that the share of re-exports in total exports from Britain rose from 32 to 36 percent over the third quarter of the century. They also suggest that, although re-exports constituted only a small proportion of Britain's exports to the East Indies, averaging less than 10 percent, their share of Britain's exports to Africa was close to the national figure. Compared to the African trade, re-exports comprised a lower proportion of Britain's exports to the Caribbean and North America, but still provided some 20 percent of exports to these areas in the third quarter of the century. Deducting appropriate proportions from British exports to Africa, the West Indies, and North America to account for re-exports leaves a figure of £1.33 million as the estimated increase in domestically produced exports from Britain arising from Caribbean-generated demands in the quarter century before the American Revolution. As total home-produced exports from Britain increased by no more than £2.8 million annually during the same period, West Indian demands, directly and indirectly, may have been responsible for almost half of the growth of Britain's domestically produced exports between 1748 and 1776.[47]

Impressive though such a figure is, its real significance lies in its relationship to British industrial expansion in the third quarter of the eighteenth century. Available trade statistics suggest that some 95 percent of home-produced exports from Britain to Africa, the East Indies, and the New World consisted of manufactured goods after 1748. Caribbean-related demands, therefore, stimulated the growth of British industrial output by some £1.26 million during the third quarter of the eighteenth century. De-

47 Schumpeter, *Trade Statistics*, 15–16; Davis, "Foreign Trade," 300–303; Shepherd and Walton, *Shipping*, 235; Richardson, "West African Consumption," 306–307.

768 | DAVID RICHARDSON

tailed figures on British industrial production from 1750 to 1775 are unavailable, but according to Cole's estimates, England's annual industrial output rose by some £10.8 million from the late 1740s to the early 1770s, or from £25.9 million to £36.7 million. Using these figures, it appears that Caribbean-based demands may have accounted for 12 percent of the growth of English industrial output in the quarter century before 1776. Furthermore, the indications are that a similar proportion of the increased output between 1750 and 1775 of Scotland's leading industry, linen, was sold in Caribbean markets. Although West Indian and related trades provided a more modest stimulus to the growth of British industrial production than Williams imagined, they nevertheless played a more prominent part in fostering industrial changes and export growth in Britain during the third quarter of the eighteenth century than most historians have assumed.[48]

This article, by examining the relationships between the slave trade, Caribbean sugar, and British economic growth from 1748 to 1776, shows that these relationships were more complex than Williams suggested. Concentrating essentially on eighteenth-century British capital accumulation, Williams perceived of profits from the slave trade and the slave-based plantation regime of the West Indies as providing a powerful exogenous input into British industrial growth. For him British economic growth, to borrow a phrase from a more recent distinguished historian in this field, was "chiefly from without inwards."[49]

It is the contention of this article that an approach which first draws a sharp distinction between external and internal promoters of change and then seeks to give primacy to one, in Williams' case an external one, is particularly artificial in Britain's case. It fails to appreciate the essential interweaving and mutual reinforcement of internal and external forces of change that occurred in eighteenth-century Britain. In the process of linking internal and

---

48   Davis, "Foreign Trade," 300–303. Data on industrial output are provided by Cole in Floud and McCloskey, *Economic History*, I, 40. Cole's figures relate to England and Wales, not just England. In estimating output for the late 1740s I have averaged Cole's figures for 1745 and 1750 and for the early 1770s have averaged his figures for 1770 and 1775. On Scottish linens, see Durie, "Scottish Linen," 30, 38. I assumed that one quarter of Scottish linen exports were sold in the West Indies in this period. *Ibid.*, 41–42.
49   Sheridan, *Sugar and Slavery*, 475.

SLAVES, SUGAR, AND GROWTH | **769**

external stimuli to structural change and industrial expansion, increases in British sugar consumption in the third quarter of the eighteenth century may have played an important role. In their efforts to satisfy these demands, which arose ultimately from changes in British agriculture, incomes, and consumer tastes, Caribbean planters and their slaves created additional opportunities after 1748 for manufacturers and their employees in Britain's emerging industrial regions. In forging more closely than previously a pattern of interdependence between industrial Lancashire, Yorkshire, the English Midlands, and west-central Scotland on the one hand, and American slavery on the other, British sugar imports after 1748 had a substantial long-term influence in shaping social and economic conditions on both sides of the Atlantic over the next century or so.[50]

50 Williams, to be fair, recognized that internal factors may have been important in determining British industrialization, but he failed to discuss them. See Williams, *Capitalism and Slavery,* 105–106.

17

The Slaving Capital of the World: Liverpool and National Opinion in the Age of Abolition

Seymour Drescher

For two decades the Atlantic slave trade has been a subject of intense scholarly interest. The geographical focus of the subject has expanded. Its analysis has become more interdisciplinary and more sophisticated. The economic and demographic aspects of the slave trade have especially profited by the improvement in our methodological tools and have become favourite targets for continuous scrutiny, meticulous conceptual revision and careful synthesis.[1]

Some aspects of the history of the slave trade have remained more elusive. Recent scholarship has strengthened the view that the economic and demographic potential for slavery's expansion was never greater than during the period when maximum political pressure was exerted in order to terminate the slave trade from Africa to the Americas. The historiographical quest to resolve the paradox of abolition against the economic grain has consequently reached a new pitch of intensity.[2] Much of this quest has focused on elaborating the antislavery ideology which flowered toward the end of the eighteenth century, especially in the USA and Great Britain. However, although this ideology has been analysed in greater detail and in a broader conceptual context than ever before, the historical geography of abolitionism's confrontation with the older mentality of toleration remains incomplete, even within the heartland of industrializing England where mass abolitionism first burst forth in 1788.

How did old and new mentalities interact once waves of abolitionist propaganda and petitioning began to sweep across the nation? Did older attitudes collapse overnight and by what process were they defended or abandoned? I would like to trace the change at one of the clearest fault lines between the older slave trade and newer abolitionist mentalities — the city of Liverpool and its national hinterland in the generation between 1787 and the end of the Napoleonic wars.

The data base for this transformation is not a set of systematic arguments but a series of popular documents by which one city, suddenly grown to the status of one of the world's great trading centres, projected its civic identity. These are a set of descriptions and guide books of Liverpool which began to proliferate as the burgeoning city became a centre for visiting businessmen and tourism at the end of the eighteenth century.

By the end of the 1780s Liverpool was the pre-eminent slaving port of the North Atlantic world. More than 90 per cent of the ships carrying slaves to the Americas in British vessels cleared from the Mersey docks. Its slave trade far exceeded that of any Continental slaving port.[3] In the course of the struggle for the trade Liverpool had developed one of the most complex credit and marketing systems in the world, involving exchanges of commodities between four continents and payments schedules extending over years. Although Liverpool supported the national mercantilist framework in which Britain had become the world's foremost trading nation, the port's merchants fought for the principle of equal access to trade for all British subjects in the empire.[4] Liverpool had, in short, played by the eighteenth-century capitalist rules of the game and emerged as one of the winners, growing faster than even Manchester for much of the century.

Suddenly, at the height of its African venture, Liverpool was faced with the problem of adapting to one of the most dramatic changes in the history of British imperial policy since the beginning of its overseas expansion. In 1787 a national abolitionist movement sprang into existence, and by 1808 a substantial portion of Liverpool's capital, captains and craftsmen had to be re-deployed into other channels.[5]

The general outline of the political struggle at the national level is well known. The political dimension of Liverpool's resistance to the change has also been described in scholarly detail. But the battle over the slave trade was not just an economic and political confrontation but a mobilization of national opinion which cut Liverpool off from the mainstream of changing British ideology. The city was faced with a threat not just to its economic base but to its cultural identity.

One must begin to analyse this question by emphasizing the ways in which the national antislavery mobilization did not affect Liverpool's behaviour — at least until the actual implementation of abolition in 1806–8. The mass abolitionist campaign beginning in 1788 did not cause any immediate diminution in the pursuit of the slave trade out of Liverpool. On the contrary, its merchants appear to have again made the most of the new investment opportunities opened up by the decrease in foreign rivals during the French Revolution and the Anglo-French wars which followed it. Liverpool increased its share of both Britain's and the world's slave trade during the two decades after 1787.[6] Slave traders responded to the restrictive legislation on the number of allowed slaves per ton on British vessels (especially after 1799) by increasing both the average tonnage per ship and the total Liverpool tonnage in the African trade. They took the lead in technological innovations such as copper sheathing for their slaving vessels.[7] Liverpool remained so heavily invested in the trade up to the last possible moment that final abolition in 1806–8 caused a short-term drop of about one-eighth in the port's total trade.

Nor did abolition of the British slave trade deter investment in the rest of the Atlantic slave system after 1808. The Liverpool slave ships themselves were largely re-deployed into still expanding areas of British and foreign slave colonies. The evidence of the following decades indicates that the Liverpool merchants re-allocated their capital because of legal constraints, and not because of some deep aversion to the trade in or ownership of persons.[8]

This continuity of priorities in the face of national opinion is equally visible in the collective political behaviour of the elite. For 20 years before 1807 Liverpool merchants and manufacturers unfailingly petitioned against every new abolitionist motion in Parliament, whether partial or total, immediate or gradual, regulatory or prohibitive.[9] Not only the merchants but the corporation of Liverpool, including the legal and clerical professions, sustained a generally anti-abolitionist stance. Craftsmen and seamen in the trade were as ready to mob a Liverpool MP who voted for abolition in 1807 as they had been to pull down the houses of abolitionists in 1792.[10] The only apparent exception demonstrated the rule. In the national elections of 1806, William Roscoe, one of Liverpool's few abolitionists, was elected to represent the city. The slave trade issue was not central to that contest and Roscoe defused potential opposition by pledging himself to support gradual and compensated abolition. When he failed to keep his pledge in Parliament, he was subjected to popular abuse and withdrew from personal campaigning in the following election. Both of his opponents ran on overtly pro-trade platforms and they outpolled Roscoe by margins of three and four to one.[11]

One can also gauge Liverpool's overall political hostility to abolition by looking at the behaviour of its small group of abolitionists. Liverpool abolitionists never considered themselves secure enough to form a local abolitionist society in imitation of Manchester, Birmingham or even Bristol. Their major contribution came in the form of anonymously authored propaganda during the first national campaign of 1787–88. Correspondingly, Liverpool was sent only one-eighth as many annual reports by the London Abolition Committee as Manchester, Birmingham or Bristol. Even anonymous abolitionist activity declined once Liverpool's anti-abolitionist mobilization was in place by mid-1788. Thereafter Liverpool abolitionism went into a general decline. The abolitionist revival in Liverpool, after 1804, was far below the scale of 1787–88.[12] As far as the British world could see, Liverpool's slavers remained unrepentant and unshakeable to the last legal moment. Slave merchants were undeterred even by the legislation of 1799, which required slave ships to advertise the purpose of the voyage in large bright letters on the hull of every vessel.[13]

Was Liverpool therefore immune to the national mobilization against the 'stain' on the honour of British commerce, and to having their city referred to in Parliament as the 'metropolis of slavery'?[14] Liverpudlians found themselves so branded even by visitors within their own precincts. When a famous British actor was hissed for appearing drunk on the stage of Liverpool's theatre he defiantly roared back over the footlights that he had 'not come to be insulted by a pack of men, every brick in whose detestable town was cemented by the blood of a negro'.[15]

There is evidence that despite the continuity in Liverpool's slave trading and in its political opposition, a slow internal transformation of self-identity occurred during the two decades before the trade was abolished from without. Two social trends were at work in this process. The first was Liverpool's evolution into a metropolitan centre and cosmopolitan cross-roads towards the end of the eighteenth century. For the first three quarters of the century Liverpool had been, in the cultural sense, a frontier town. Its elite was characterized by the philistinism of self-made men. Wealth was unabashedly the overwhelming concern and the principal source of self-esteem.[16] Relative to other towns of its size there was a serious dearth of individuals and institutions aspiring to imitate elite culture elsewhere in Britain. Liverpool was correspondingly remote from the early twinges of anti-slavery sentiment produced by individual writers, dissenting academies and legal controversy during the generation before 1788.

Located at the cultural fringe of a world as yet unmobilized against slavery, there is no evidence that the entrepreneurs of Liverpool felt anything but secure in plying their African trade under the sanction of British law. Every act of the government for a century assured them not only that their actions were legitimate but that Liverpudlian capitalists were serving both themselves and their nation by risking their money on, and prospering from, the Afro-Caribbean trade. Even Liverpool Quakers, subject to pressures for divestment long before their neighbours, found it extraordinarily difficult to extricate their capital from the slave trade, not to mention the Atlantic slave system as a whole. Well after the general Quaker prohibition against supplying the African trade in 1763, William Rathbone and his son continued the practice. When they gradually shifted their capital, it was into the West Indian and North American as well as the Baltic trades. The ideological limits of such extrication may be seen in the boast by William Rathbone IV, that his firm was the first to import a consignment of American cotton to Britain, in 1784. However, in the Liverpool context Rathbone was to be among the most notorious of his town's abolitionists and reformers, earning the title of the 'hoary traitor' from his fellow citizens.[17]

The assumption of the 'normality' of the slave trade in Liverpool may also be measured by its role in William Enfield's early history of the city. *An Essay Towards the History of Leverpool* manifested no self-consciousness whatever about the African trade. It appeared full blown in the second table of Enfield's chapter on Commerce and Manufactures, without rhetorical flourish or preface. Each slave ship for the year 1771 was listed, along with the number of slaves carried by each. Another table of total ship clearances showed that those heading for Africa exceeded all long distance destinations except those bound for America, a ranking that remained unchanged in 1805.[18] In short, Enfield had not a word to say either for or against the African branch of the port's activity. His comparisons with other trades were quantitative, not qualitative.

As long as the harbingers of abolitionism remained politically ineffective the Liverpool elite seemed to be indifferent towards it. As early as 1771 William Roscoe's first poem, *Mount Pleasant*, showed abolitionist sympathies, but there is no record of negative reaction to it.[19] Indeed, Liverpudlians were quite used to composing public documents which hailed British freedom, including, of course, freedom of trade to Africa. And Liverpool petitioners certainly identified themselves as members of the freest realm on earth.

Even more revealing of Liverpool's complacency was its relative indifference to the proceedings of the famous Somerset case in 1771–72. At issue was the juridical status of all colonial slaves brought to Britain. As far as I can determine not one writer in Liverpool imitated his counterparts in London by publishing a tract or a letter to the Liverpool newspapers, and rallying around proprietary rights in persons throughout the empire. This was not because the case went unreported. As in other provincial towns, Liverpool newspapers summarized the hearings at some length.[20] Somerset's attorneys were liberally praised for speaking learnedly, ably and eloquently on 'the free air of this realm'. Lord Mansfield, the presiding judge, was even chided for his delay in reaching a decision in which 'humanity must bleed on the one hand, or equity on the other'.[21] Mansfield's decision was published without comment except for the smug observation that 'as blacks are free now in this country, gentlemen will not be so fond of bringing them here as they used to'.[22]

There is no visible evidence that Liverpool's interest was directly involved, as there was to be 15 years later. Indeed, at least one Liverpudlian acted as though the Somerset decision had never been made. In October, 1779 a black youth of 14 was advertised for public auction in Liverpool, apparently the last such notice to appear in the newspapers of Britain.[23]

Well into the 1780s Liverpool appeared to have no doubts about the security of their African trade. In 1783 the first Quaker petition to Parliament against the trade was reported in Liverpool, as everywhere else, without comment. As late as early 1787 a Liverpool editor could benignly sympathize with the sentiment to meliorate the condition of slaves in the colonies.[24] When Clarkson reached Liverpool on his first investigative journey in 1787, the slave merchants were willing to supply details about a trade they believed to be quite lawful. They turned hostile only when Clarkson declared that he regarded their behaviour as criminal and began to request evidence of abuses from the ordinary seamen in the trade.[25]

At the beginning of 1788 abolitionism suddenly broke upon the city like a tidal wave. Liverpudlians were shocked to see the neighboring town of Manchester taking the lead in denouncing Liverpool's ironmongers for displaying chains and shackles for the African trade. Cities and counties sent mass petitions up to Parliament, demanding an end to the shameful traffic in human beings, and renouncing any commonality of economic interest which would tie them to Liverpool's African merchants.[26]

How did Liverpudlians react to this political and ideological onslaught? Counter-petitioning was one way, as we have seen, although it quickly became apparent that no community in Britain was willing to stand beside Liverpool. There were, however, means of reaffirming internal communal solidarity within the city itself. At formal dinners and civic occasions toasts were drunk to the African trade. When the first Abolition Bill was defeated in 1791, church bells were rung for the occasion, and when the Commons reversed itself the following year, Liverpool crowds threatened to pull down the houses of prominent abolitionist sympathizers if the measure actually passed into law.[27]

Despite manifest continuities of economic behaviour and the initial defiance in both elite and popular modes of expression, it is possible to trace a gradual adaptation to the national outlook, and of Liverpool's cultural rehearsal for a re-convergence with those priorities from which the city was so violently alienated in 1788. Especially in documents written by Liverpudlians for an outside audience, one sees a quiet shift of the rationale for slave trade and of a slow withdrawal from the ideological barricades.

Liverpool's first cultural response to political aggression was global counter-attack which affirmed not only the economic motives for the African trade but the whole range of traditional religious and moral justifications for slavery itself. Before the abolitionist mobilization no Liverpudlian ever considered formulating such a wide-ranging defence of the slave trade, and the first anti-abolitionist polemic off the press was written by a native of Spain, trained in traditional apologetics. Early in 1788 a pamphlet entitled *Scriptural Researches on the Licitness of the Slave Trade,* and written by a Reverend Raymond Harris of Liverpool, was widely distributed in London.[28] It was soon known that Reverend Harris was really Don Raymondo Hormaza, a Jesuit expelled from Spain and re-settled in Liverpool. He ran a school, but had been suspended from his priestly functions by the Catholic Bishop of Liverpool. If Harris was in bad odour with his bishop for other reasons, the secular authorities were anxious to bless his pro-slavery efforts. The Liverpool Council awarded him a hundred pounds for having written the pamphlet, and his obituary notice accorded him honours as a respectable citizen of the town.[29]

Scriptural Researches, as David Brion Davis has noted, was a closely reasoned biblical exegesis in favour of the legitimacy of slavery, and a clever demonstration that the abolitionist invocation of the golden rule against slavery undercut all other forms of social subordination as well.[30] A number of abolitionist writers quickly responded, among them an anonymous *Scriptural Refutation* written by William Roscoe.[31] The most obvious first line of attack was to brand Harris's approach as 'alien'. Liverpool's defender of slavery was doubly suspect. His 'subtle' arguments were ipso facto 'totally irreconcilable to the character of an *Englishman* but are perfectly consistent with that of a *Spanish Jesuit*'.[32]

However, although this might have been an effective way to dismiss Harris's pamphlet, it fails to explain why his very cogent biblical defence of slavery was never reissued by the slaving interest over the name of a native Briton. The fact was, as one abolitionist noted shortly after the pamphlet's appearance, that Harris 'had strengthened the cause he meant to injure'.[33] This was less because he was an alien than because the very strength of his argument was its fatal weakness. If the abolitionist application of the golden rule to slavery threatened all forms of social subordination, the scriptural validation of slavery in general threatened the entire libertarian ideology and institutional principles of eighteenth-century England. It forced a choice between the status of the Bible as divine moral authority and the status of 'liberty' as a consensual achievement of British society.[34]

The proof of the flaw was in the ideological pudding. Harris's pamphlet was never republished and had no successors. Never again did the city fathers of Liverpool sponsor a religious defence of slavery in such general terms. Liverpudlians were really no more comfortable than their fellow countrymen in dissociating themselves from a century of libertarian ideology. They were particularly proud of the distance of their local poor law practice from slavery.

> Ne'er let that sordid scheme be practised here,
> The poor to farm, or auction by the year.[35]

Liverpool was much more comfortable with a civic defence of African slavery within the modern Western European tradition. The best example of this second reflexive response to the abolitionist onslaught appeared in the locally authored *Descriptive Poem on the Town and Trade of Liverpool*, a year after Harris's *Scriptural Researches*.[36] The author was John Walker, a shoemaker and native Englishman, whose wife had been nursed back to health in one of Liverpool's public charities. Walker's poem, written over three years, was his public repayment of a debt of gratitude to his fellow citizens. The poet was as proud of his city's mercantile ethic as of its distinctive source.

> With hopes of gain and just ambition led
> In all directions see the vessels speed
> But chief this town it claims the Afric trade
> The merchant's toil this amply has repaid...[37]

Walker alluded to particular religious justifications for the African trade: it saved convicts from death; Africans only 'exchanged' one slavery for another; the trade relocated Africans in a 'civilized soil', bringing knowledge to 'chaotic minds'; it gave some a chance to know Christ and even freedom in Britain, where a servant could (as Adam Smith had noted) enjoy more pleasures than an African King. The entire trade was thus justified by the remnant who passed through the full range of meliorating possibilities and stages to emancipation.[38]

Walker was not impervious to the assault which had swept aside this whole chain of rationalizations. But, if nothing else, what was good for his town was adequate compensation for all else. Even if the trade were proved 'illegal', Liverpool stood 'but half-reproved'. It compensated for ills abroad by good at home, and it was second to none in England in charity and public spirit.[39] In 1789 the proud citizen-shoemaker could still conceive of abolitionism as a flash in the pan of history. What emerged so suddenly might just as quickly disappear:

> Humanity is now the pop'lar cry,
> Some years ago 'twas Wilkes and Liberty,
> Yet so inconstant is the public voice,
> That soon must die − succeeds another choice.[40]

The next 'description' of Liverpool was published in the wake of a second national abolitionist campaign in 1792. This second work was a less strident and more prosaic work, intended for a national rather than just a local audience. The slave trade and Liverpool were still intimately bound together, but *de facto* rather than through extended biblical exegesis or an African pilgrim's progress. James Wallace simply entitled his work *A General and Descriptive History of ... the Town of Liverpool ... together with ... its extensive African trade.*[41] His approach was empirical and historical, not argumentative. Two independent sections of the book, extending over 50 pages, were allotted to the development and magnitude of Liverpool's African trade. The town and the trade were shown as rising together to the eminence of the 1790s.[42] Tables listed the initials of each slave trading house from the Peace of Versailles in 1783 to the renewal of Anglo-French hostilities ten years later. The proportions of Liverpool's African ships and tonnage were tabulated, as in Enfield's less self-conscious *History*.

If Wallace was apologetic it was not for any affiliation with slavery but for the city's one-sided economic development. Liverpool was still 'the only trading town in England' neglecting science and the arts and still without a famous citizen in the Church, at the bar, or in Parliament. Its pride, as well as its livelihood, lay in its ships, its crowded docks, its avid traders and industrious workers.[43] The magnitude of the slave trade, like Liverpool's economy, was therefore its own *raison d'être*. Wallace spent no more than a modest footnote on 'whatever might be advanced in opposition to this trade and in what manner so ever it might be said to be opposite to humanity and religion'. In defence he referred only to one more historical fact – that slavery was ancient and approved by the earliest Christians.[44] The bare factual description of the trade culminated with a series of compelling statistical statements: one quarter of Liverpool's ships were slavers; these accounted for five-eighths of Britain's African trade and three-sevenths of Europe's; Liverpool's total overseas trade amounted to half of London's and one-quarter of Britain's. Such, concluded Wallace, was the 'state of the general commerce of Liverpool in the year MDCCXCV'.[45] The slave trade was to Liverpool what Liverpool was to Britain.

The Liverpool/slaving nexus was human as well as economic. Wallace listed the houses in the trade but also noted that 'almost every order of people' was 'interested in a Guinea cargo'.[46] The material well-being of the traders was diffused to the humblest household in the city. No wonder that many trades had joined the merchants in petitioning against abolition.

Yet Liverpool's trade was not the only aspect of the city developing apace during this period. The city began to take on the trappings of a cultivated town, founding an Athenaeum in 1799 and a botanic garden in 1802.[47] Links between the broader national culture and the trading town were proliferating. One of the signs of this thickening network was an increase in the number of outsiders flocking to the city, as evidenced by the appearance of a new literary genre toward the end of the 1790s – the city guide.

The first to appear was William Moss's *The Liverpool Guide*.[48] Oriented specifically towards visitors, Moss found the slave trade to be a source of difficulty rather than of pride. He entirely avoided all of Wallace's lengthy history of the trade which so obviously tied Liverpool's dynamic growth to its slave trade. Moss began where Wallace ended, with a brief statistical parade of the African trade's significance: one-fourth of Liverpool's ships; five-eighths of Britain's African trade; three-sevenths of Europe's.[49] Indeed, Moss may have deliberately avoided updating the latter two fractions, which would have been even larger in the closing years of the century than in the pre-war period.[50]

Moss then immediately turned to the topic that Wallace had only footnoted – the moral issue. He broached it by ingenuously yielding everything, in principle, at the outset: 'As a strictly moral question considered in the abstract, it can meet with no countenance.' On the other hand, continued the *Liverpool Guide*, 'in a political point of view, everything favours it'.[51] Therefore 'enthusiasms' had to be tempered by reason. In contrast to

Wallace's emphasis on slavery's antiquity among Christians, Moss stressed its ubiquity outside Christianity and especially in Africa. Slavery existed in 'a very considerable portion of the earth', and 'while Africans continue in the same untutored, and consequently defenceless state – they must remain a prey to their more skilful neighbours'.[52] Slavery was barbarous, but the Africans were still barbarians. Was it not futile to expect that 'the government, customs, habits and dispositions of the Africans could be made to undergo a *sudden revolution* at the *command* of a few who occupy but a distand speck, and thus to invert the general order of nature by violent means?' How could one contemplate revolutionary methods with the French experience so clearly in view? Given the existence of slavery in all ages, prudence suggested gradual melioration, not immediate abolition. What was necessary was 'the mean between the extremes of sensibility and apathy of the human mind'. Sensible men were willing to meet abolition half way, to find a balance between the evils of continuation and those of hasty abolition.[53]

To the outsider who wished to understand Liverpool the *Guide* did not defend the morality of its African trade. Nor did it pretend that mere numbers could speak for themselves. John Walker had poetically presented that trade as the distinctive feature of his town. Wallace had empirically intertwined Liverpool's dynamism and its entrepreneurial spirit with the slave trade. Moss, almost incidentally, began to loosen what his predecessors had joined together. The city and the trade were not really one and indivisible. References to Liverpool as the 'metropolis of slavery', wrote Moss, were based upon a misunderstanding. 'Much illiberal and ungenerous reflection has been indiscriminately cast upon this town, on account of this trade, which must have arisen from ignorance, since it is limited to a very few of the merchants.'[54] Suddenly, the centre of gravity had shifted and the slave trade was quietly dispatched to Liverpool's periphery. Indeed, to suggest otherwise was to be 'illiberal'. The trade was not only marginalized. Morally it was now metaphorically dispatched from Liverpool. 'Many of the ships, in that trade, fitted out here, belong to owners and merchants who reside in different parts of the kingdom, and who prefer fitting out here, on account of the superior accommodation; and which did they offer in other ports, would most likely, be as eagerly embraced there.'[55] Liverpool was merely the victim of its own superiority as an overseas trading centre.

This passage was published at the absolute peak of Liverpool's African slave trade, and while the town's governing body stood solidly behind the merchants. It shows that, on one level at least, national opinion was taking its toll too. Respectable boosters of Liverpool were growing weary of having their reputation determined solely by their thriving slave trade.

When the abolitionist campaign was renewed, in 1805, this irritation finally began to be reflected in Liverpool's newspaper press as well.

In 1805 a series of letters challenged the Liverpool African merchants' continued contention that their trade was consistent with humanity.[56] The letters complained that their city was being unjustly vilified because the country imagined that Liverpool's whole commercial interest was dependent upon Africa, and because Liverpool's MP claimed that '*ten thousand of its inhabitants*' supported that trade. The correspondent challenged the MP and the slave merchants to tell when they had ever received 'so respectable a sanction'.[57]

A new Liverpool guide, appearing in 1805, seemed to reflect this greater eagerness for dissociation.[58] Wallace's statistics on the African trade still appeared, as they had in Moss's guide, but now only in a single sentence followed by a lengthy disclaimer. *The Picture of Liverpool* began by repeating Moss's remark about the ungenerous reflection 'indiscriminately' cast upon the inhabitants of Liverpool. Moral distance was now added to economic dissociation: 'It is but too commonly supposed that [the slave trade] had the unqualified sanction of all who take up residence in this town, and it has been hence emphatically called the "metropolis of slavery".' Not only was the latter charge ill-founded, but the new guide further diminished those identified with the trade 'chiefly to three or four houses'. The high proportion of 'outsiders' in the trade was now emphasized as a 'notorious' fact.[59]

This dissociation was not just a qualified clarification, as in Moss's earlier guide. It was 'the duty of those who feel for the honour of the town and disapprove of the traffic to rescue [Liverpool] from this general opprobrium by every means in their power'.[60] One might still praise the public spirit and munificence of the African merchants, but this was now no more than giving 'the devil his due'. How the pursuit of the trade could be reconciled with the slavers' otherwise honourable principles had 'to be left to themselves to explain'.[61] The slave traders were now on their own to justify themelves. Liverpool would no longer allow itself to be made the moral mediator of the slave trade. Instead, it was now emphasized for the first time that Liverpool contained many 'friends of the hapless Africans'. Their anonymous work of 15 years before was now incorporated into the guides as a source of civic redemption. A new poem on Liverpool's progress, which immediately followed the discussion of the African trade in the guide, avoided all mention of the role of slaving either in Liverpool's past growth or present prosperity.

There are indications that this process of moral and social distancing did not end at the pages of the guides to Liverpool. The response to the drunken actor's denunciation of the 'metropolis of slavery' was a general cheer from his audience. And by 1805 at least one member of Liverpool's Council had become impatient enough to speak out against any more public funds being laid out by the Corporation to support pro-trade propaganda against abolition.[62]

On the eve of abolition the process of isolating the slave trade was virtually complete. In the new guidebook of 1807, the rise of Liverpool was tied to 'the rising empire of the United States', Ireland, Northern Europe and, potentially, to South America.[63] Only after this global survey was attention drawn to Africa. The African trade had become inverted from the pride of Liverpool to its shame:

> It is however, a very considerable abatement of the pleasure which arises from the view [of Liverpool's flourishing trade] to reflect that so considerable a part of the opulence of this port is to be ascribed to a trade so degrading to the national character, and so much at variance with sound policy, humanity and religion as the African.

Slaving was a page of tears which the guide would, if possible, have expunged from Liverpool's history. But national legislation would probably soon prohibit slaves from being articles of commerce.[64] News of the passage of the abolition act was celebrated in a pre-publication footnote.

By 1810 the second edition of the 1807 guide quietly realigned Liverpool with the rest of the nation. The African trade had furnished Liverpool with the ships and capital which now enabled it to pursue its interest in common with the other ports of the empire. Slaving was now but a dark shadow of the past which even in its heyday had been confined to only a portion of the mercantile community.[65]

Liverpool might thus have slipped imperceptibly back into its position as one of the leading ports of the empire. But seven years after the passage of British abolition Liverpool had an unexpected opportunity for a massive ritual re-integration into the mainstream of British abolitionism as well. In 1814 the Anglo-French peace treaty allowed France to re-open its slave trade for five years. Abolitionists met the news of the slave trade clause with the greatest petition campaign in British history. Perhaps the most unexpected addition to the abolitionist ranks was a monster petition from Liverpool, signed by 30,000 of its citizens. Liverpool now ranked among the most fully signed-up cities in Britain. Surprise and pleasure was expressed everywhere that Liverpool, weaned from the trade only a few years before, had so explosively joined the abolitionist movement.[66]

Ironically, it was the *slave* interest of Liverpool which provided the bulk of Liverpool's turnout for abolitionism. William Roscoe initiated the petition, but John Gladstone, a major West Indian investor, was instrumental in increasing the signatures from 2,000 to 30,000.[67] The latent clash between capitalist and abolitionist values re-emerged briefly at the public meeting called to decide on the nature of the petition, as Gladstone proposed to add a strong economic argument to the humanitarian appeal. A revived French slave trade would present a competitive threat to British trade interests in Africa, the Americas and Europe. Roscoe successfully carried the day arguing that a policy-based statement would provide the rationale for a retaliatory renewal of the British slave trade as well. Liverpool would therefore disgrace itself by not aligning the grounds of its petition with those of the rest of the nation. The meeting seized the opportunity and voted down Gladstone's motion.[68] Only eight years after he had been attacked by a mob of unemployed seamen for his failure to resist immediate abolition in Parliament, Roscoe was presented with the freedom of the borough.[69]

Of course the fundamental economic interests of many Liverpool capitalists in slavery had not disappeared. But Liverpool was no longer united on the issue. In 1821, it was James Cropper, a Liverpudlian, whose personal 'free trade' crusade against British colonial slavery anticipated and stimulated the abolitionist shift of attention from the slave trade to slavery.[70] The opponents of emancipation in Liverpool were also less isolated from the nation than in their resistance to slave trade abolition. Slave ownership was more broadly spread throughout Britain than slave trading had been and Liverpool had ceased to be identified as the sole metropolitan target of abolitionism.

Liverpool's process of civic re-definition appears to have been unique in the urban history of the Atlantic slave trade. This cannot be attributed merely to the port's domination of Britain's slave trade towards the end of the eighteenth century. In the decades prior to American abolition, Rhode Island's Newport was the dominant slaving port of New England.[71] Nantes was likewise France's foremost slaving port throughout the eighteenth century. Yet neither of these cities had to confront a long-term problem of public opprobrium analogous to that of Liverpool. The difference probably lay less in the relative concentration of the slave trade than in the intensity with which public opinion was mobilized against the trade within Britain. For fifty years before 1787 Liverpool had been fortunate in her location at the edge of the most dynamic industrial region on the face of the earth. For the twenty years after 1787 Liverpool was unfortunate in her location at the edge of the most dynamic abolitionist region on the face of the earth. No other city was so radically altered by both the industrial and abolitionist revolutions than the slaving capital of the world.

NOTES

An earlier version of this essay was presented at the International Conference on the Slave Trade at Nantes, France, in 1985, sponsored by M. Serge Daget.

1. See the following collective studies: Stanley L. Engerman and Eugene D. Genovese (eds.), *Race and Slavery in the Western Hemisphere: Quantitative Studies* (Princeton, 1975); Roger Anstey and P. E. H. Hair (eds.), *Liverpool, the African Slave Trade, and Abolition* (Historic Society of Lancashire and Cheshire, 1976); Henry A. Gemery and Jan

S. Hogendorn (eds.), *The Uncommon Market: Essays on the Economic History of the Transatlantic Slave Trade* (New York, 1979), David Eltis and James Walvin (eds.), *The Abolition of the Atlantic Slave Trade* (Madison, 1981); Barbara Solow and Stanley L. Engerman (eds.), *Caribbean Slavery and British Capitalism* (New York, 1988). On individual studies, see Roger Anstey, *The Atlantic Slave Trade and British Abolition, 1760–1810* (London, 1975); Seymour Drescher, *Econocide: British Slavery in the Era of Abolition* (Pittsburgh, 1977). David Eltis, *Economic Growth and the Ending of the Transatlantic Slave Trade* (New York, 1987) and Robert W. Fogel, *Without Consent or Contract: The Rise and Fall of American Slavery* (forthcoming), contain extensive discussions of the most recent quantitative findings and hypotheses on the slave trade.

2. David Brion Davis, *The Problem of Slavery in the Age of Revolution, 1770–1823* (Ithaca, NY, 1975); S. Drescher, 'Capitalism and Abolition: values and forces in Britain, 1783–1814', in *Liverpool, the African Slave Trade, and Abolition*, pp. 167–95. Howard Temperley, 'Capitalism, Slavery and Ideology', *Past and Present* 75 (1977), 94–118; Christine Bolt and S. Drescher (eds.), *Anti-Slavery, Religion and Reform* (Folkestone, England and Hamden, Conn., 1980); J. Walvin, *Slavery and British Society 1776–1846* (London, 1982); D. B. Davis, *Slavery and Human Progress* (New York, 1984). Thomas Haskell, 'Capitalism and the origins of the Humanitarian Sensibility: Some Analytical Considerations', *American Historical Review* 90:2 and 3 (April and June 1985), 339–61 and 547–66; S. Drescher, *Capitalism and Antislavery: British Mobilization in Comparative Perspective* (London/New York, 1987). See also the 'AHR Forum' on the Haskell essay by D. B. Davis, John Ashworth and T. Haskell, *American Historical Review* 92:4 (Oct. 1987), 797–878, and the works cited in note 1.

3. D. P. Lamb, 'Volume and tonnage of the Liverpool slave trade 1772–1807', Anstey and Hair (eds.), *Liverpool*, pp. 91–112.

4. House of Lords Record Office MSS, 6 May 1806 and 17 July 1806, petitions of merchants, ship owners and manufacturers of Liverpool on trade to Africa and to Latin America. See also Liverpool Public Library Record Office, 900 M D 3 [1804?], Petition of the Corporation of Liverpool to the House of Lords, against abolition.

5. D. M. Williams, 'Abolition and the Re-deployment of the Slave Fleet, 1807–1811', *Journal of Transport History* 2 (1973), 103–15. Liverpool's trade temporarily declined following abolition. Thomas Troughton, *The History of Liverpool* (Liverpool, 1810), p. 257.

6. See Lamb, 'Volume and tonnage', pp. 94–9.

7. G. Rees, 'Copper Sheathing: An example of Technological Diffusion in the English Merchant Fleet', *Journal of Transportation History* I (1971), 87–9.

8. Drescher, *Capitalism and Antislavery*, p. 197, n. 68.

9. Drescher, *Econocide*, pp. 137–8, 252 n. 34; House of Lords Record Office MSS, Liverpool Slave Trade Petitions 1788–1807.

10. F. E. Sanderson, 'The Structure of Politics in Liverpool 1780–1807', *Transactions of the Historic Society of Lancashire and Cheshire*, 127 (1978), 5–89.

11. F. E. Sanderson, 'The Liverpool Abolitionists', Anstey and Hair (eds.), *Liverpool*, pp. 196–238, esp. pp. 226–7.

12. *Ibid.*, pp. 215–21.

13. Lamb, 'Volume and tonnage', p. 94.

14. *Liverpool Chronicle and Commercial Advertiser*, 16 Feb. 1805; *Cowdroy's Manchester Gazette*, 11 Feb. 1807.

15. John Ramsay Muir, *A History of Liverpool* (London, 1907), p. 204.

16. S. G. Checkland, 'Economic Attitudes in Liverpool 1793–1807', *Economic History Review* ser. 2 (1952–53), 58–75.

17. Sanderson, 'Liverpool Abolitionists', pp. 199–200.

18. William Enfield, *An Essay Towards the History of Leverpool*, 2nd ed. (London, 1774), ch. VI, p. 8; John Corry, *The History of Liverpool* (Liverpool, 1801), p. 263.

19. Sanderson, 'Liverpool Abolitionists', p. 202. See also Roscoe's libertarian *Ode on the Institution of a Society in Liverpool for the Encouragement of Designing, Drawing and Painting*, read 13 Dec. 1773 (printed Liverpool, 1774), Liverpool Record Office, 288 LLL.

20. See *The Liverpool General Advertiser*, 22 May–3 July 1772.

21. *Ibid.*, 5 June 1772.

22. *Ibid.*, 26 June 1772.

23. F. O. Shyllon, *Black Slaves in Britain* (London, 1974), p. 168.
24. Frank Sanderson, 'The Liverpool Delegates and Sir William Dolben's Bill,' *Transactions of the Historic Society of Lancashire and Cheshire* v. 12 (1973), 57–84.
25. Sanderson, 'Liverpool Abolitionists', pp. 207–10.
26. *The Leeds Mercury*, 17 Nov. 1787. On dissociations by other trades and industries, see Drescher, *Capitalism*, pp. 266–7.
27. *Gore's General Advertiser*, 17 April 1788; *Sheffield Advertiser*, 29 April 1791; *Williamson's Liverpool Advertiser*, 9 Jan., 20 Feb. 1792.
28. *Scriptural Researches on the Licitness of the Slave Trade, Showing its Conformity with the Principles of Natural and Revealed Relgion, Delineated in the Sacred Writings of the Word of God* (Liverpool, March 1788). On Harris's background, see B L Add MSS 3841 (Liverpool Papers), fols. 29–31, William Walton to Lord Hawkesbury (later Lord Liverpool), 24 Feb. 1788.
29. David Brion Davis, *The Problem of Slavery in the Age of Revolution*, pp. 542–3; Sanderson, 'Liverpool Abolitionists', pp. 213–14; and a description of Harris's well-attended funeral in *Williamson's General Advertiser*, 11 May 1789.
30. Davis, *Problem of Slavery in ... Revolution*, p. 545.
31. *Scriptural Refutation of a Pamphlet, Lately Published by the Rev. Raymund* [sic] *Harris, Entitled 'Scriptural Researches on the Licitness of the Slave-Trade'* (London, 1788).
32. Davis, *Problem*, p. 546.
33. *Ibid.*, p. 543, quoting James Pemberton to James Phillips, 21 Oct. 1788.
34. Harris himself wrote one rebuttal (2nd ed. 1788) virulently attacking his critics. (Sanderson, *Liverpool Abolitionists*, pp. 213–14.)
35. John Walker, *A Descriptive Poem on the Town and Trade of Liverpool* (Liverpool, 1789), p. 51.
36. *Ibid.*, Preface.
37. *Ibid.*, p. 65.
38. *Ibid.*, p. 58.
39. *Ibid.*, p. 59.
40. *Ibid.*, p. 56.
41. Liverpool, 1794.
42. *Ibid.*, pp. 202–55.
43. *Ibid.*, pp. 284–5.
44. *Ibid.*, p. 213n.
45. *Ibid.*, pp. 238–9.
46. *Ibid.*
47. Muir, *History*, p. 194.
48. William Moss, *The Liverpool Guide* 2nd ed. (Liverpool, 1797; 3rd ed., enlarged 1799; 4th ed. 1801).
49. *Ibid.*, 3rd ed., p. 114.
50. Moss's *Guides* eschewed any detailed updating of the African trade data.
51. *Ibid.*, p. 114.
52. *Ibid.*, p. 116. The third edition dropped the earlier explicit comparison of Africans with Northern Europeans, the latter being subject to the inclemency of the weather and the pangs of hunger (*ibid.*, 1st ed., p. 103).
53. *Ibid.*, p. 118. For a similar theme almost 200 years later, see Francis E. Hyde, *Liverpool and the Mersey: An Economic History of a Port 1700–1970* (Newton Abbot, 1971), p. 31.
54. *Liverpool Guide*, p. 118.
55. *Ibid.*
56. *Liverpool Chronicle and commercial Advister*, 27 Feb. 1805.
57. *Ibid.*
58. *The Picture of Liverpool, or the strangers guide*, Liverpool, 1805.
59. *Ibid.*, p. 147.
60. *Ibid.*
61. *Ibid.*, p. 148.
62. *Liverpool Chronicle*, 27 Feb. 1805.
63. *The Stranger in Liverpool; or, an historical and descriptive view of Liverpool and its environs* (Liverpool, 1807), p. 25.

64. *Ibid.*, pp. 25–6 and note.
65. *Ibid.* (2nd edition, 1810), p. 23. See also Henry Smithers, *Liverpool, its Commerce Statistics and Institutions* (Liverpool, 1825), p. 103, for a continuation of the 'dark shadow' metaphor, which has persisted.
66. *Leeds Mercury*, 30 July 1814.
67. See *Cowdroy's Manchester Gazette*, 30 July 1814. On the division of mentalities in Liverpool, see S. G. Checkland, 'Economic attitudes in Liverpool, 1793–1807', *The Economic History Review*, 2nd ser. V (1952–3), pp. 58–75.
68. *Cowdroy's Manchester Gazette*, 30 July 1814, and Liverpool Public Library Record Office, Roscoe Papers, 920 ROS #1807, Roscoe to the Duke of Gloucester, on the Liverpool petition (July 1814). It was Gladstone who first suggested requisitioning a public meeting in favour of the petition. Gloucester presented the Liverpool petition to Parliament. See *Ibid.*, #1790, Gloucester to Roscoe, 26 July 1814.
69. Sanderson, 'Structure of Politics in Liverpool', 85.
70. Davis, *Slavery and Human Progress*, pp. 181–4. The national movement resisted Cropper's plan to emphasize commercial self-interest just as Roscoe had resisted Gladstone's impulse to add an economic rationale to the humanitarian appeal in 1814. Davis attributes the abolitionist reluctance to emphasize commercial arguments to 'traditional habits of political deference', but the abolitionists also had sound political reasons to continue their avoidance of policy rhetoric. See, for example, the letter of Secretary Canning of the British Foreign Office to the Duke of Wellington, on 1 October 1822, explaining hostility to British abolitionist policies by foreign powers (quoted in Robert Conrad, 'The Struggle for the Abolition of the Brazilian Slave Trade: 1808–1853' (Ph. D. thesis, Columbia University, 1967), p. 99. On John Gladstone's opposition to emancipation, see S. G. Checkland, 'John Gladstone as Trader and Planter', *Economic History Review*, 2nd ser. VII (1954–55), pp. 216–29.
71. See Jay Coughtry, *The Notorious Triangle: Rhode Island and the African Slave Trade 1700–1807* (Philadelphia, 1981), ch. 6, epilogue.

Index